D1616382

Political and Economic Interactions
in Economic Policy Reform

IB

Political and Economic Interactions in Economic Policy Reform

Evidence from Eight Countries

Edited by

Robert H. Bates and Anne O. Krueger

BLACKWELL
Oxford UK & Cambridge USA

First published 1993
Reprinted 1994

Blackwell Publishers
238 Main Street
Cambridge, Massachusetts 02142
USA

108 Cowley Road
Oxford OX4 1JF
UK

Library of Congress Cataloging-in-Publication Data

Political and economic interactions in economic policy reform   :
    evidence from eight countries / edited by Robert H. Bates and Anne
    O. Krueger.
        p.   cm.
    Includes index.
    ISBN 1–55786–340–7
        1.   Developing countries – Economic policy – Case studies.
    2.   Developing countries – Politics and government – Case studies.
    I. Bates, Robert H.   II. Krueger, Anne O.
    HC59.7.P576   1993
    338.9′009172′4 – dc20   92–21634   CIP

British Library Cataloguing in Publication Data

A CIP catalogue record for this book is available from the British Library.

Typeset in 10 on 12pt Times
by TecSet Ltd, Wallington, Surrey

Printed in Great Britain by Athenaeum Press Ltd, Newcastle upon Tyne.

This book is printed on acid-free paper

Contents

List of Contributors

Brazil   Deepak Lal, James S. Coleman Professor of International Development Studies, University of California, Los Angeles, and Professor of Political Economy, University College, London
Sylvia Maxfield, Assistant Professor of Political Science, Yale University

Chile   Philip Brock, Assistant Professor of Economics, University of Washington
Barbara Stallings, Professor of Political Science and Director, Global Studies Program, University of Wisconsin

Ecuador   Francisco E. Thoumi, Independent Consultant
Merilee S. Grindle, Research Associate, Harvard Institute for International Development

Egypt   Robert Holt, Professor of Political Science, University of Minnesota
Terry Roe, Professor and Co-director of the Economic Development Center, University of Minnesota

Ghana   J. Clark Leith, Professor of Economics, University of Western Ontario
Michael F. Lofchie, Professor of Political Science, University of California at Los Angeles

Korea   Richard N. Cooper, Maurits C. Boas Professor of International Economics, Center for International Affairs, Harvard University
Stephan Haggard, Professor, School of International Relations and Pacific Studies, University of California at San Diego

Chung-in Moon, Associate Professor of Political Science, University of Kentucky

Turkey   Anne O. Krueger, Arts and Sciences Professor of Economics, Duke University
İlter Turan, Professor and Chair, Department of International Relations, Faculty of Political Science, Istanbul University

Zambia   Paul Collier, Director of the Centre for the Study of African Economics and Reader in Economics, Oxford University
Robert H. Bates, Henry R. Luce Professor of Political Science and Economics, Duke University

Preface

This volume represents the outcome of a truly collaborative effort, in which all of the authors contributed significantly to the intellectual contents of the entire volume. Such a successful collaboration is an occasional phenomenon within academic disciplines, but it is rare between economists and political scientists. We believe that the products of that interaction are visible throughout the volume, and wish to record our appreciation to all of the contributors to the project for their discussions of issues and comments of drafts, as well as their individual contributions.

A project such as this would not have been possible without financial support. We are indebted to the Ford Foundation for providing the bulk of the funding, and for support of the initial proposal. The United States Agency for International Development also provided financial support for the research undertaken on Ghana and Ecuador, which greatly enhanced the total product of the project. Funds from the Duke Endowment are also gratefully acknowledged.

Our major intellectual debt is to the participants in the project. In addition, we would like to thank Seamus O'Cleireacain of the Ford Foundation, and Jerry LaPittus and Alan Batchelder of USAID for their useful comments and suggestions. At a working party of participants when first drafts of papers were presented, Steven Webb, Ronald Archer, Jorge Quiroz, Kathryn Firmin, Stanley Black, Gary Gereffi, Michael Michaely, William Ascher, Robert Conrad, Peter Lange, Malcolm Gillis, and David Orsmond participated and made helpful comments and suggestions.

Last, but by no means least, we have benefited from efficient and dedicated support staff. Doris Cross and then Marlin Smith administered the project in its early phase and we are grateful to both of them. Our largest debt, however, is to Gail McKinnis and Greg Sanders. Gail McKinnis assumed administrative responsibility for the project just as it was entering its final phases; she was invaluable in coordinating all participants' drafts in getting the volume ready for press, and through the editorial process. Greg Sanders and Humphrey Costello checked the manuscript before it went to press, and then at the copy-editing stage, finding numerous items whose correction has vastly improved this volume.

Robert H. Bates and Anne O. Krueger
Durham, North Carolina

1

Introduction
Robert H. Bates and Anne O. Krueger

The 1980s were traumatic for many developing countries. Economic growth slowed abruptly, if it did not altogether cease. Although an initial reaction was to blame adverse external conditions for poor economic performance, it soon became evident that underlying policy weaknesses in the countries had contributed significantly to the difficulties. Some countries were able rapidly to resume economic growth, while others experienced continuing stagnation and even declines in real per capita income. The former group had a markedly different set of economic policies than did the latter. It therefore became evident that the differences in economic policies were closely related to differences in performance.

In an effort to resume growth, governments announced and implemented policy reform programs. In some instances, reforms began with strong reversals of past policies, while in other cases they began timidly. Some programs were introduced as quickly as was feasible, while others were far more gradual. Some started with considerable publicity and fanfare, while others "just happened": without major public statements of policy change. Some were sustained and some abandoned. Some met with fairly rapid success, as judged by the evolution of the economic aggregates of interest, while others took far longer before the hoped-for benefits were realized.

As evidence of both the importance and the difficultuies of reform mounted, economists analyzed the reform programs and their outcomes as they affected economic structure and growth. Simultaneously, political scientists turned their attention to the politics of reform efforts. There was often a dissonance between these analyses. On one hand, the political scientists considered the sources of opposition to reforms and the political difficulties that economic policy reforms created, bemoaning economists' apparent *naiveté* regarding the politically possible.[1] They focused much of their analysis on identification of the political prerequisites for successful reform efforts. On the other hand, economists focused on the policy weaknesses that had previously existed, and lamented the partial nature of reform efforts, mystified as to why policies that clearly yielded inferior economic outcomes were adopted.[2] In a nutshell, what was good politics did not seem to be good economics, and what was good economics was not seen as good politics.

By the late 1980s, "structural adjustment programs" and other policy reform efforts had been studied and analyzed from a number of perspectives. But the puzzle underlying "good economics – bad politics" remained. While the puzzle was and is intellectually important, it is crucial for policy and therefore for the future of the developing countries: it is very often political factors which inhibit or prevent the authorities from adopting programs which, on economic grounds, appear to offer the soundest prospect for resumption of growth and increasing living standards.

From that puzzle emerged a plan for a research project, the Duke Project on Political Economy of Policy Reform in Developing Countries, in which political scientists and economists could bring the insights of both their disciplines to bear on analysis of reform episodes and their outcomes. It was hoped that considerable headway might be made with disciplinary "cross-fertilization." The plan was to seek analysis of reform episodes (or their absence) in individual countries in which an economist and a political scientist would jointly address the economic and political issues associated with the need for reform, the reform measures undertaken, and the outcome of the reform process.

We were fortunate to obtain the financial support of the Ford Foundation to support six teams of researchers, and the US Agency for International Development for the support of two additional teams.[3] Each team had at least one political scientist and one economist. The countries whose reform it was decided to cover included: Brazil, Chile, Ecuador, Egypt, Ghana, Korea, Turkey, and Zambia. The experience in these countries is briefly discussed in section 3 of this chapter. After an initial meeting of all project participants, in which an "issues" paper was prepared by Bates and Krueger and discussed by participants, each team undertook its analysis of the reform process in its country.

The remaining chapters of this volume contain eight political–economic analyses of policy reform episodes and their aftermath, and a final chapter analyzing the findings for the insights they bring to the generic reform process.

In this chapter, we set the stage for the country analyses by doing three things. First, we describe the policy reform process, and the questions that arise about it in general. Second, we indicate the issues that authors were asked to address in their individual analyses. Finally, we discuss each of the papers briefly, indicating how the experience and situation of each individual country sheds light on the overall nature of the reform process. An analysis of commonalities among countries and insights emerging from the analysis is deferred, however, to chapter 10.

1 THE POLICY REFORM PROCESS

There are few economic phenomena whose discussion has aroused as much intense and heated debate as the economic policies pursued by the developing countries. In the 1950s and 1960s, almost all of them adopted a set of very similar economic policies. These policies were vastly different from those of the industrialized countries. They were undertaken in part because it was widely believed that developing countries were "different" in their economic structure. There was also a strong belief that industrialization would bring about economic growth and that government controls and leadership in the economy were essential to bring about industrialization.[4]

Although policies differed from country to country, there were strong elements of commonality. In almost all countries, policies designed to encourage industrialization through "import substitution" were effected. These usually entailed high tariff barriers and/or restrictive import licensing, if not outright prohibitions on imports of goods competing with domestic production. They also involved suppression of domestic interest rates to levels below the rate of inflation, and direct bureaucratic allocation of credit to activities that would produce import-competing goods. Often, too, government budgets were greatly in deficit, with consequent strong inflationary pressures within the economy.

There were some instances of far-reaching policy reversals in the 1950s and 1960s, most notably in Korea and Taiwan. These reforms entailed major changes in the incentives for production for export, sharp reduction in levels of protection for industries producing for the home market, stabilization policies which significantly reduced the government deficit and rate of inflation in the domestic economy, and greater reliance on private economic activity to serve as an "engine of growth."

Despite the spectacular economic successes of these countries after sharp policy reversals, most developing countries continued to maintain the economic policies entailing heavy governmental intervention and regulation throughout the 1960s and 1970s. Indeed, for a variety of reasons, the restrictiveness of the foreign trade regime, the rate of inflation, and other indicators of policy tended to become even more extreme over time.

During the 1960s and 1970s, many countries encountered periods of economic "crisis," followed by changes in policy. Sometimes these changes were addressed only at the symptoms of crisis, as, for example, in Argentina when the rate of inflation accelerated rapidly and reached triple-digit levels. Then, short-term measures would be undertaken to reduce the rate of inflation, but the underlying policies governing foreign trade and industrialization incentives were largely unchanged. In some cases, however, policy reforms were of a longer-term nature, as was the case in Sri Lanka in 1977, for example, when a newly-elected government dismantled many of the controls that had formerly regulated economic activity.

Most developing countries, however, continued their "inner-oriented" policies until the late 1970s. It was not until the early 1980s, with the second oil price increase and the worldwide recession, that it began to be evident that these policies were not compatible with continuing economic growth. The urgent need for policy reform was widely recognized in developing countries and by those concerned with the development process. Many governments announced – often reluctantly and under pressure because of debt-servicing difficulties or other problems – policy reform programs. Sometimes these programs were little more than pious statements of intention made in order to secure support from international creditors.[5] In other cases, governments undertook reforms, and sought the support of international creditors only after major policy changes had been effected.

Thus, although earlier economic policies were similar, and the need for reform was almost equally compelling in a large number of countries, experience with reform programs differed widely. Many announced reform programs failed to meet the objectives that leaders set forth when announcing them. Others were sustained over considerable periods of time and in some instances were followed by resumption of rapid economic growth. It became evident that both economic and political factors had a profound influence on the situation resulting in the need for reform, the nature of the reform effort, and its outcome, and that the interaction of these factors was little understood.

Questions abounded. Why were the Mexican, Turkish, and Chilean authorities able to carry out a sustained program of reforms over periods of several years while Brazilian, Argentine, and Zambian authorities made repeated efforts with little result? There were any number of hypotheses. Among economists, there was a tendency to pinpoint the "too little, too late" aspects of many reform packages as being responsible for many failures. Even then, it had to be recognized that some reforms which began apparently half-heartedly nonetheless gained momentum over time and were sustained, which itself raised questions as to the distinguishing characteristics of those reforms contrasted with those that were followed by resumption of the earlier policies. A considerable economics literature emerged concerning the appropriate "timing and sequencing" of reforms, focusing heavily on the question of whether the pace of reform should be gradual or rapid.[6] There were also debates concerning the appropriate role of the international institutions, the relationship of trade and exchange rate regime changes to efforts to reduce inflation rates and to stabilize the economy, the role of external and internal factors in bringing about the need for reform, and the impact of reform efforts on the poorer members of society. Among political scientists, attention focused far more on the groups gaining from the earlier policy regime and the role of interest groups in supporting and opposing policy reform, and the latitude the government had for maneuver. Issues were also raised about the relative abilities of authoritarian and democratic regimes to undertake and sustain reform programs, the ability of the multilateral institutions to influence policy, and the role of external factors in affecting the reform process.

These discussions were couched in terms of stylized facts which participants in the discussion took as a basis for their analysis. In light of the complexity of the reform process, however, even these facts were in dispute. It therefore seemed appropriate to start with empirical analysis of the situation in individual countries, asking the country teams to examine the extent to which the various competing theories and hypotheses were empirically correct and relevant for their country's experience.[7]

In this chapter, we attempt to set forth the issues, much as they were presented to the country analysts. In chapter 10, we attempt to use the results reported in chapters 2 through 9 to examine the relevance of the various hypotheses and questions on which the analysis of the individual countries' experiences sheds light.

A starting point must be to define what we mean by reform. In common parlance, "reforms" are undertaken all the time. "Tax reforms" can range all the way from small adjustments in marginal tax rates to major overhauls in the types of taxes imposed and the manner of their collection. "Agricultural pricing policy reform" can consist of a once-and-for-all adjustment in administered prices to basic changes in the ways in which markets function. Indeed, as we shall argue below, constant tinkering with administrative procedures, frequent changes in regulations, reorganization of ministries and bureaus, and other minor "reforms" are one of the hallmarks of a "prereform" period, during which it is evident to policy-makers that things are not going well.

These partial, piecemeal, ad hoc efforts to patch up the functioning of economic policies are not what is meant by policy reform in developing countries in the 1980s, nor is it what the project was concerned with. Rather, the term is used to describe significant changes in a sizable number of economic policies as part of a package of policy changes. As will become evident as we proceed, the package of policy changes can vary significantly between countries, but usually involves a major adjustment of the extent to which the state interferes with market forces, which in turn entails institutional and administrative change, stabilization efforts, and removal or relaxation of controls and greater relianace on market mechanisms for allocation of resources.

Policy reform packages vary among countries for a variety of reasons: economic structures differ; the initial circumstances confronting the political authorities vary significantly; and the decisions regarding the relative importance of reforming different aspects of economic policy may also differ. In addition, political reactions can vary significantly and thus permit greater or lesser scope for maneuver on the part of the leadership.

An understanding of the policy reform process may be more readily gained, however, if illustrated by a "typical" case. Frequently, although not always, serious consideration of a policy reform package begins when there are serious economic difficulties. These might be of a crisis nature, such as when a country is unable voluntarily to continue servicing its debts, or when a large fraction of the industrial production capacity of a country is operating at severely reduced capacity because of an inability to obtain imports because the authorities have no foreign exchange and hence issue no import licenses. The difficulties impelling the reform package might, however, be more chronic in nature, as, for example, if real per capita incomes have been stagnant or declining for some time, if export earnings through official channels have been declining (possibly, however, with increased extralegal exports through smuggling or underinvoicing), or if other symptoms of chronic economic difficulty are noted.

Ingredients of the policy reform package   For some reason or reasons, then, the decision is reached to change economic policies.[8] Key questions confronting policy makers include both the policies to be altered and the magnitudes of the adjustments to be made. Again, there is no such thing as a "typical" package. There are, however, a number of major policy instruments which are often altered. These include, but are not limited to (1) the rate of government spending; (2) the financing of government expenditures; (3) the foreign trade and payments regime, (4) policies affecting conditions of operation of private firms, including regulations in the financial system, regulations of conditions of employment in the private sector, and regulations of prices and other controls over private sector economic activity; and (5) policies regarding state economic enterprises.

The first two are interrelated. High rates of inflation in many developing countries have been a major, if not the single most important, difficulty leading to the perceived need for reform. In many instances, large fiscal deficits are a major contributor to these high rates of inflation, and measures to increase tax revenues and/or lower government expenditures are a necessary economic condition for a reduction in the rate of inflation. That raising tax revenues and lowering government expenditures is politically difficult is too well known to require comment here.

Alteration of foreign trade and exchange rate policies is usually a necessary part of policy reform. It is often high inflation, and the authorities' earlier efforts to contain it, that result in a highly overvalued exchange rate, and excess demand for foreign exchange which is contained through quantitative restrictions on imports. When there has been excess demand within the domestic economy generated by an excess of government expenditures over government receipts or by other economic phenomena, the resulting inflationary pressure is to a degree accommodated by additional imports. Simultaneously, the authorities are often unwilling to alter the nominal exchange rate (in an effort to keep down the recorded rate of inflation) and then restrict imports to match foreign exchange receipts (which are often declining). In these circumstances an adjustment is needed in order to permit the exchange rate to reflect the excess of domestic over foreign inflation.

Far-reaching policy reform, however, requires more than an adjustment of the exchange rate to reflect the accumulated differential in domestic and foreign inflation rates. As already seen, policies of protecting domestic industries from foreign competition were adopted in the 1950s and 1960s. Those policies, designed to foster industrialization through "import substitution" (IS), had a number of unintended effects. While they did encourage the development of new domestic industries, those industries often turned out to be of uneconomically small scale, and high cost. Moreover, because they were protected from foreign competition, they were often in a monopolistic position. The combination of these and other factors resulted in the emergence of a high-cost, inefficient set of domestic industries, which became vested interests supporting IS policies.

The fact that potential exporters had to purchase their inputs from these high-cost firms, together with the tendency of the exchange rate to fail to reflect domestic inflation, resulted in relative unattractiveness of developing new industries or expanding existing ones for export markets. As these high-cost industries became a larger and larger factor in the economy, the rate of economic growth inevitably slowed. Resuming more rapid growth, therefore, often required altering incentives away from IS and high walls of protection of domestic industry toward more "outer-oriented" trade and exchange rate policies, which provided adequate incentives for efficient domestic producers to develop overseas markets and to be able to sell profitably to them.

Alteration of policies affecting private firms' behaviour has often been desirable in order to stimulate private sector economic activity. In many countries, legislation and regulation have mandated wages and other conditions of employment (including worker housing, social insurance benefits, training programs, and job security) that have induced firms to use capital-intensive techniques of production, with consequent reductions in employment and low rates of return on investments. Financial regulations have often resulted in severe credit rationing, with firms with access to the "official credit market" able to borrow at negative real interest rates and invest in highly capital-using activities while other firms are unable to obtain funds for expansion or other investments that might have higher yields than those of the favored firms. Other regulations affecting private economic activity have included price controls, requirements that new investment be licensed, governmental control over access to needed inputs, and numerous detailed interventions.[9] The net impact of these regulations and controls has been to raise costs, to prevent quality improvements, to induce firms to adopt uneconomically capital-using production methods, and to reduce the rate of growth of output. When government officials are attempting to find policy packages to spur economic growth, these measures are natural candidates for change. As with fiscal, monetary, and trade and exchange rate policy, however, political resistance to change originates from those who have perceived themselves to benefit from past policies, including especially those who have based their output plans on the existing incentive structure.

Finally, in many developing countries, a large set of economic activities not traditionally undertaken by governments outside the communist world have been undertaken in the government sector. These "parastatal" activities include state economic enterprises producing manufactured goods, distributing inputs to producers, and distributing outputs, in addition to those undertaking more traditional functions of transportation, provision of electric power, and communications. In many instances, parastatal enterprises have been accorded monopolies over the importation and distribution of inputs, and over the marketing of agricultural commodities both for the domestic market and for export. In many cases, they have incurred large operating deficits, thus contributing to the macroeconomic problems mentioned earlier. Frequently, they have not made timely delivery of inputs and outputs to other firms, with consequent losses in efficiency for the rest of the economy. Also, for political reasons, they are usually grossly overstaffed. The consequences for economic growth are obvious, but so, too, are the reasons why there can be strong political resistance to economic reform programs.

The complexity of changing some or all of these policies is considerable. Some – such as the exchange rate – must be altered quickly and without advance public discussion.[10] Other changes can be implemented rapidly, once decided upon, such as the removal of price ceilings or import licensing requirements. Still others, such as tax reform, usually require parliamentary action.

Policy reform can therefore not be implemented instantaneously and is thus a process. Economic responses to policy reform, likewise, also take time. The time dimension adds further complexity to analysis, as the delays in response can be affected both by political considerations and by the expectations of businessmen and others. Their perceptions of the likelihood that reform will continue to influence their reactions, and those perceptions themselves are functions of past reform efforts, political conditions at the time of reform, and a variety of other factors.

During the period in which reforms are being implemented and economic responses are developing, political forces supporting or opposing reform can also change. In some instances, an initial reform package has been so limited in scope or so small in magnitude that most economists would judge it to have had little prospect for improving economic performance over the longer run. In other instances, initial opposition has been so great that the political authorities have decided to reconsider the initial package, reducing it to a point where the economic gains were likely to be quite limited. In still other cases, initial reforms have met with some opposition but also some support, the authorities have pursued the path of reform, and economic gains have been significant, in turn giving rise to an impetus for still further reform measures.

In all circumstances, however, the process is a complex one, involving political–economic interactions in the conditions prior to reforms, changes in both the economics and politics brought about by the reform process itself, and the multifaceted nature of economic policy changes that may be made. It is against this background that the various economic and political analyses of pieces of the policy reform process have been made.

Hypotheses about policy reform   The reform process is complex, and many of the alleged stylized facts are at least challengeable. Moreover, many of the hypotheses set forth regarding policy reform are mutually inconsistent. They nonetheless formed the background against which country authors were asked to analyze the experience of their countries. For that reason, it is worthwhile to mention those hypotheses briefly here. Analysis of the extent to which these hypotheses are consistent with the evidence of the country studies, however, is deferred until chapter 10.

Most hypotheses about policy reform focus upon the reasons for success or failure of the reform effort. They can be grouped around three broad headings: initial conditions; the nature of the initial reform package; and impact of the reform package.

Turning first to initial conditions, several hypotheses as to determinants of the likely success of reform have been put forth. One is that "strong" or authoritarian governments have more capacity to change economic policy than do democratic ones. Another focuses on the impetus for reform, with the hypothesis that when there has been prior discussion and domestic political support for a change in economic policies, the reforms are more likely to be successful and sustained than when external conditions (such as a foreign exchange crisis) are the impetus for change. A second hypothesis, focusing more on economic variables, is that reforms are less likely to succeed the less credible is the reform program itself, which in turn is a function of how governments have behaved in the past. In particular, it will be more difficult to achieve sustained policy change in circumstances in which earlier reform efforts have been announced, begun, and then aborted. As a corollary, a government with a track record of credibility in economic policy has a better chance of sustaining reforms than one with a poor record.

Yet a third hypothesis regarding initial conditions focuses on external circumstances. Policy reform is more likely to be successful, it is held, if it is undertaken in the context of favorable external and other initial conditions. For example, if the world price of a major export crop is steady or rising when policy reform is undertaken, the reforms are more likely to be sustained than if reforms are undertaken as the terms of trade deteriorate sharply.[11]

Finally, there is the hypothesis that reform is more likely to succeed when the impetus originates from domestic sources than when it lies in external factors. Here, focus has largely been on the role of the multilateral institutions, especially the World Bank and the International Monetary Fund, as actors in the reform process. There has been at least an implicit assertion that these institutions have on occasion "forced" governments to initiate policy reforms, and that their role has itself become a focal point for opposition to those reforms.

Turning then to the initial reform package, there are again a number of hypotheses regarding the likelihood of sustainability and success. First, there is the already-mentioned economic hypothesis that failed reform efforts are of the "too little, too late" variety or are otherwise technically deficient.[12] Variants of this hypothesis focus upon the "suddenness" of the changes or their magnitude: sometimes it is alleged that reforms should have been more gradual, while on other occasions it is asserted that they should have been more sudden. Second, some analysts have focused on the interest groups and institutions that have existed at the time of reform, and noted the support or opposition of those groups to the reform program. The interests of the bureaucracy, and its ability to block a reform program, have frequently been noted. So, too, have been the opposition of businessmen in import-competing industries to trade liberalization. Yet a third factor that has been addressed has been the magnitude of external support (both new credits and suspension of debt-servicing obligations) for the reform program: the hypothesis is that more foreign resources in support of reform may facilitate the transition process and thus ease the political pain surrounding the reform effort.[13]

Finally, there is the group of hypotheses focusing upon the timing of the response to the reform program. First, there has been a widespread belief that policy reforms necessarily entail a period of recession and that the political reaction to that recession stengthens opposition to reforms. Second, there is the previously mentioned issue of credibility: as political opposition to reforms is voiced, businessmen may doubt the prospects of maintenance of altered incentives and thus fail to invest in newly profitable lines of activity, thus short-circuiting the economic gains that might otherwise be attained and providing further fuel for opponents of reforms. Third, it has been asserted that the low-income groups are those most harmed by reform efforts and the impact on them is what gives rise to irresistible political opposition to further reforms, either because those truly losing (such as businessmen in import-competing industries) use the harm to the poor to enhance support for their case or because politicians are genuinely concerned about the fate of the poor.

It should be noted that, given the number of variables, it is quite possible that some of these hypotheses are valid for some countries and not for others, although they may be mutually inconsistent within the same country. At this stage of our knowledge, it is impossible to test these hypotheses: the facts are not yet in evidence. All that can be done is to examine a number of cases, and see whether, to a first approximation, the evidence is consistent or inconsistent with those hypotheses. We turn, then, to the questions put to country authors for their analysis in light of these hypotheses.

2   THE QUESTIONS ASKED OF COUNTRY ANALYSTS

The ways in which economic and political phenomena impinge on each other in the course of a reform program are not well understood. It was the purpose of the case studies to analyze these interactions. Clearly, the individual cases studied were quite different, and it was neither possible nor desirable to provide a rigid framework for analysis.

Nonetheless, a set of questions was identified which each country team was asked to address in its paper. The questions were grouped around the three "phases" of a reform process: (1) the period prior to undertaking reforms; (2) the reforms themselves; and (3) the reactions to reforms.

Period prior to reforms   There are two central issues regarding the period prior to reforms. A first is the political and economic determinants of the economic policies that had been in place; the second is the political and economic factors that led to a decision to change those policies.

Economists were asked to provide a good characterization of the policy stance prevailing prior to reforms, with consideration of each of the four elements cited earlier. One important subsidiary question was the extent to which policies had been stable prior to the period of reform, or whether instead they had evolved over time as economic/political phenomena (such as balance of payments difficulties or inflation) had led to efforts to "patch up" the prevailing policies.

Economists were also asked to consider the alternatives open to policy makers in the run-up to reform: was leaving existing policies in place sustainable? Were more far-reaching measures economically feasible and/ or desirable? Had there been earlier efforts to change policies? To what extent was the force of circumstances (e.g., need for external financing of the current account deficit due to terms of trade changes) a major stimulus to reform? In addition, authors were asked to identify which economic groups gained and lost (in the short run and the longer run) by existing policies and by reforms, and to attempt to assess the authorities' perceptions of the economic problem they confronted.

Political scientists were asked to address the politics of the pre-reform period: the extent to which policies had been adopted for reasons other than a desire to achieve economic growth; the influential groups supporting preexisting policies and those supporting reforms (with attention to the extent to which the actual gainers/losers and those who supported/opposed policies were the same, and the relative strength of support/opposition groups). Important issues to be considered were the contribution of ideas and ideology both to the pre-reform policies and to the alignment of supporters and opponents of reform.   In addition, political scientists were asked to examine two key issues: the organization of interest groups (both winners and losers), and the institutional context in which decisions were made and policies effected.

For interest groups, a first question is the basis on which these groups derived their influence (including the industrial structure of business groups), and the extent to which those supporting the earlier set of economic policies had achieved vested interests in the public domain. In this regard, authors were asked to examine the extent to which the "rents" created by restricting markets had been vested in particular groups in society.

One such important group is the bureaucracy itself and authors were asked to examine the role of various groups within the bureaucracy (e.g., ministries of finance and central bankers relative to ministries of industry and trade) in supporting/opposing the pre-reform policies. Political scientists were also asked to consider the relevance of the "capture" theory and the "iron triangle." Capture theory, propounded by Stigler and Peltzman, suggests that bureaucrats eventually serve the interests of the groups they are seeking to regulate. The iron triangle literature, by contrast, derives from the American political science literature, and suggests that bureaucrats provide services to interest groups who then support those politicians who defend the bureaucrats' budgets.

The next set of questions pertains to the institutional context within which groups operate. Questions include the structure of public institutions and the ways in which structure may affect different groups' influence in the decision-making process; the role of political competition and government selection including the structure of parliament, the role of committees, and the accountability of cabinet (and the informal links between major economic interests and government policy makers in cases where government was not elected); and the role of political parties and their links to major economic interests, including organized labor, agriculture, and large business.

Finally, for each country, authors were asked to consider the historical context in which reform was to be attempted: earlier attempts at reform and what had happened; the extent to which economic policy had earlier been formulated after a political struggle over tariffs or in response to colonial rule; and the role of ideology in the formulation of policy.

Obviously, not all of these factors come into play in every country. Nonetheless, for purposes of insights into political economy of the generic process of policy reform, it was deemed desirable for authors to note the absence of phenomena as well as their presence.

The reform period   The questions enumerated above were obviously also relevant for the reform period. In addition, a number of questions about the reform process needed special attention in each study. A first question was the identification of the process by which the demand for reform was felt, articulated, and disseminated within the policy-making system. For economists, the key question was the unsustainability of earlier economic policies, the extent to which reforms were needed (as contrasted with the magnitude of the reform efforts), and the extent to which there was perception of these economic phenomena on the part of economic technocrats within government, politicians, those influencing public opinion (such as intellectuals and the press), and the public itself.

One important issue in this regard, to be analyzed by both economists and political scientists, was the timing of reform. On one hand, pressures may have preexisted for a period of time; on the other hand, some reforms have been delayed much longer than others, and a key issue is the identification of those pressures that finally bring about the decision to change.

For political scientists, one question is how the earlier consensus regarding economic policies had changed. A key question is the process by which perceptions are altered, expectations are changed, and the societal consensus regarding economic policies is modified or reversed. Authors were asked especially to consider the extent of public discussion of the need for reform, the role of various groups in supporting or opposing reforms, and the ways in which reforms strengthened or weakened various groups. Political scientists were also asked to pay attention to the historical and intellectual traditions of the country, the impact of previous reform efforts on attitudes, the relationship between economic policies and other political issues (such as the relative power of different regions), and the group included in the debate, which at one extreme might be limited to a narrow circle of economic technocrats and at the other might be the subject of extensive discussion during an election campaign. One important task was to identify which domestic actors took the initiative in proposing policy reform, and how they related to other important groups.

One issue that arises frequently in the reform process is the role of the international institutions, especially the International Monetary Fund and the World Bank, but also including donor agencies from bilateral aid programs. Their involvement in part comes about because many "crises" have been triggered by balance of payments difficulties, and additional resources are perceived as vital to the success of the reform effort. Political scientists were asked to consider the political ramifications of these institutions' involvement, while economists were asked to address the economic importance of their role.

Especially in the 1980s, large debt to private and official creditors played a major role in determining economic policy in the 1980s. Authors were asked to evaluate the extent to which considerations pertaining to debt were key either to the decision to undertake a reform effort or in the determination of the program itself. In addition, political scientists were asked to evaluate the impact of the debt problem, when it was a factor, on relative political strength in the pre-reform period.

With that background at hand, authors were asked to analyze the reforms themselves. For economists, that meant indicating what was done, what happened, and what would have happened under important alternatives (including making no policy changes). For political scientists, the central questions focused on analyzing why choices were made, and on identifying supporters and opponents of the reform program and of any alternatives that had significant political support.

An interesting question is the objectives of reform: are they narrowly economic, or do they encompass broader changes in the body politic? Are they seen as a necessary evil (to be abandoned as soon as the crisis is resolved) or as a more fundamental restructuring of economic policy? How was the determination of objectives affected by preexisting conditions and by political realities? Were the relevant authorities constrained from "going further" because of political resistance or did they adopt the measures deemed most appropriate given their objectives?

For economists, of course, a key issue is identification of the components of the initial reform program and later follow-ups. This includes attention to both the short-term macroeconomic aspects of the policy reform package and the changes in the structure of incentives affecting the private sector and the role of the state in the economy.

Although reform packages differ enormously both because of differences in preexisting internal policies and because of different objectives of policy, economists were given a "checklist" of items for at least brief mention. These included whether the reform was publicly announced and whether it was seen as one discrete step or the first step in an ongoing process; whether the reform was economically realistic and could be expected to achieve the objectives of the program; what the economic strengths and weaknesses of the program were; whether the follow-up measures were undertaken as intended; the initial impact of reform (taking into account elements of luck and external conditions and support); and the credibility of the reform package.

The post-reform period   A first important question about the aftermath of reforms centers on the short-term impact. From an economist's viewpoint, attention needs to be paid to the immediate impact of reform, including especially on the level of economic activity, the rate of inflation, urban employment, and the balance of payments. In many circumstances, the initial impact on black markets, smuggling, and other extralegal activities is also important. Economists also needed to identify large losers, including the shutdowns of major factories, individuals previously profiting from receipt of import licenses, bureaucrats, and labor union members.

For the short term, political scientists were asked to consider the political ramifications of the program: whether changes were accomplished without political repression or violence, and whether and how support was built for the new policy regime. One interesting question in this regard is the extent to which reform packages were constructed in ways designed to obtain support from previously opposing groups. There are also important questions to be addressed regarding the behavior of the "losers" and "winners" in the initial period. One hypothesis is that the "losers" in a reform program immediately become politically active opponents, while the "gainers" do not provide support for the program in its initial phases.

The longer-term aftermath of reform depends, of course, crucially on the evolution of the political and economic process in the immediate post-reform period. When the short-run economic impact of reform is highly negative, it is a reasonable conjecture that the political support for the program will be eroded and, with it, the credibility of the program and the ability of the authorities to sustain it.

A key question, and one each country study was to address, was the magnitude and speed of responses to the reform program on the part of the major economic participants. To what extent did export volumes start increasing immediately? How much, if any, reverse capital flight was there? What was the behavior of imports and how did that affect the level of economic activity? When the supply response was sluggish, economists were asked to examine the reasons for it, and political scientists to assess the impact on the political support for the program.

Political scientists were asked to assess those pressures which mounted for a reversal of reforms and those which provided political support. This included the nature of the economic response. In addition, authors were asked to identify which politically influential groups gained and lost in the short run and how those gains/losses affected the political evolution of the reform process.

In this regard, interesting questions for political scientists arise when the rate of inflation slows or a flow of imports resumes after a period of shortage. In particular, does a significant reduction in the rate of inflation result in support for reforms? If so, by whom, and how is it manifested? Equally, if other economic difficulties accounted for part or all of the decision to reform, does the amelioration of those difficulties, such as import shortage, build support?

Another important question is the ways in which reformers attempt to protect themselves from negative reactions during the post-reform period. Although experience is obviously very different in different countries, authors were asked to examine the extent to which reformers attempted to indicate what would have happened in the absence of reform to build support for their policies.

Finally, authors were asked to examine the longer-term aspects of reform. Once the process started, did it achieve a momentum of its own leading to further reforms? Or did political opposition mount and succeed in reversing some of the changes that had been made? To what extent did the economic success of reforms alter the political structure? Did new groups emerge in support of the altered policies? And what were the verdicts of important groups with regard to the role of reforms? Obviously, in some instances, reforms are not sustained, and these questions require virtually no attention. In some countries where reform was sustained, however, the answers to them provide vital insights into the reform process itself.

3   COUNTRIES COVERED IN THE PROJECT

From what has already been said, it is evident that no two countries are alike, and that the economic content, as well as the political context, of each policy reform situation differs. Although statistical examination of major economic aggregates can shed useful light on many aspects of the reform process,[14] it cannot serve as the only tool for analysis, especially of political and economic interaction. Moreover, given the variety of variables that a priori play a part in creating the need for policy reform, and in affecting the reform package and its outcome, there are simply too many variables, relative to the number of reform experiences, to expect that statistical analysis is sufficient for full analysis of many questions.

Moreover, in light of the limited extent of our understanding of the interactions between economic and political variables, and the absence of a body of simple, testable hypotheses, it was deemed desirable to undertake in-depth analyses of individual countries. It was hoped that these analyses might permit the tentative formulation of some hypotheses, with the hope that these would then constitute an agenda for future research.

For these, and other, reasons, there was no attempt to arrange country studies from a "representative" group of countries, since there was little basis to ascertain what "representative" might mean. Instead, the selection of countries was based primarily on three criteria: (1) the availability of sufficient data and prior analysis to permit analysts to make the research agenda feasible; (2) the inherent interest in the country's experience; and (3) the availability of highly qualified researchers who could build on their own previous work in undertaking the task at hand.

Eight countries were selected for detailed analysis. The succeeding chapters contain those analyses. Here, what is needed is a brief description of salient characteristics of each country to provide readers with an introduction and some perspective as to how the experience of the country about which they are reading contrasts with that of other countries included in the project.[15]

Brazil   Brazil is the largest country included in the project, both with respect to land area and with respect to population (150.4 million in 1990). Brazil experienced fairly rapid economic growth over the first eight decades of the twentieth century (see Lal and Maxfield, tables 2.6 and 2.8–2.10). Inflation, however, was rapid relative to that of other countries. Brazil's economic policies in pursuit of economic development were geared toward industrialization primarily through protection of private domestic producers against imports, although the government itself owned parastatal enterprises producing steel and a number of other commodities. In addition, government controls over the allocation of credit and other regulations affecting private economic activity gave the government a major role in resource allocation.

Although overall Brazilian economic growth rates were high until the mid-1980s, two factors led to reform efforts. On one hand, because of inflationary pressures arising from fiscal deficits and monetary creation in support of industrialization and other policies, there were reform efforts aimed at reducing inflation. On the other hand, the build-up of excess demand for foreign exchange resulted in balance of payments difficulties, and these, too, prompted announcements of policy reforms. As a consequence of these last two phenomena, successive Brazilian governments undertook a large number of stabilization attempts, starting as early as 1953. Lal and Maxfield identify major efforts in 1953, 1959, 1962–3, 1964–7, 1979, and 1980 to 1984. Even after the period on which their study focuses (the stabilization efforts of 1979 to 1984), further stabilization programs were undertaken, continuing to the time of writing.

In contrast with other countries included in the project, Lal and Maxfield believe that the Brazilian case is interesting as "the dog that didn't bark," i.e., as a country where opposition to reform was so great that reform programs were always abandoned. Their analysis therefore focuses on why political opposition to reform was so strong even when, as in the late 1980s, real GNP was stagnant and even falling. They focus on the efforts of the 1980–4 period, although they also consider other reform episodes in analyzing the process. Judged by the outcome as of 1990, Brazil's economy is clearly one in major economic difficulties, as double-digit *monthly* inflation continues.

Chile   Until the late 1960s, Chile was a "typical" middle-income developing country. Successive governments since the Great Depression had all pursued heavily interventionist economic policies and followed import substitution policies to encourage rapid industrial growth. Minerals were the predominant exports. By 1973, successive democratically elected governments had dealt with economic "crises" generated by balance of payments pressures and inflation, all within the context of state-led economic activity and import substitution.

The last of these governments, led by President Salvador Allende, was avowedly left-wing socialist, nationalizing scores of industries and redistributing land. The government's policies also entailed massive increases in expenditures. These were initially financed in large part by running down foreign exchange reserves, but as these were depleted, inflation accelerated, and real wages (which had been increased by 25 percent by 1971) fell in half by 1973 (see Brock and Stallings, table 3.1).

There followed a violent coup in which the military, led by General Augusto Pinochet, took over control of government. For the next 16 years, Chile was governed by a military dictatorship. Under that dictatorship, the economy was transformed. A highly restrictive trade regime was greatly liberalized as quantitative restrictions on trade were removed and tariffs lowered to a virtually uniform 10 percent. Many industries were privatized, and the role of government controls was greatly reduced.

This process is the focus of Brock's and Stallings' study of Chile. By the late 1980s, Chile's economy appeared to be far more healthy than that of most Latin American countries. The Chilean experience is interesting not only because of the degree of success, but also because of the problems encountered along the way.

Ecuador   Ecuador is a relatively small country, with a population of about 10 million, half urban and half rural. It is divided geographically, ethnically, and politically between the coastal and highland regions. The coastal region is characterized by export-oriented agriculture and industry, while the highlands produce goods, both agricultural and industrial, primarily for domestic consumption.

Until the late 1970s, growth had been slow in Ecuador, and economic policy was relatively passive because of the weakness of the government. The state had traditionally been very weak in Ecuador, relying for its revenue on the economic elites of the coastal zone. However, with the discovery of oil in the 1970s, the autonomous source of revenue permitted a major expansion of state provision of infrastructure and other governmental services. With this change came greater autonomy for the state in economic policy making. During the boom years of the 1970s, when oil production mushroomed from 1.4 million barrels in 1970 to 76.2 million in 1973 and the price of oil rose sharply, government economic policy was more clearly articulated. Domestic energy prices were kept very low, and many basic consumer goods, including food and electricity, were heavily subsidized. Protection for domestic import-competing industries was high. Real per capita incomes rose sharply, as the oil revenue permitted this burst in public expenditures. When oil earnings stopped increasing and began to decline, policies were sustained by borrowing from abroad. When, in the early 1980s, further borrowing was not possible, Ecuadoran politicians were confronted with the need for major adjustment.

The immediate impetus for economic crisis in the early 1980s was debt-servicing difficulties. Grindle and Thoumi trace the responses of three successive presidential administrations to the economic difficulties which lasted throughout the 1980s. They characterize the Ecuadoran response as one of "muddling through," as each successive administration was able to undertake some reforms but was then unable to carry them through without erosion as opposition to the measures mounted.

Thus, Ecuador had three successive, externally visible "policy reform" efforts. There were significant differences among them, but the end result was that some parts of each adjustment were sustained. Grindle and Thoumi thus characterize the Ecuadoran experience as illustrating how reforms take place over an extended period in fragile and fragmented political contexts.

Egypt   Egypt is a poor and populous country, with 53 million inhabitants in 1990 and a per capita income estimated to be $640 in 1989. During the 1950s and 1960s, economic activity came increasingly to be regulated or managed by the state. State-owned enterprises produced almost two-thirds of manufacturing output; government decrees indicated the amount that peasants would plant of each crop; imports were licensed and allocated with preference for state-owned enterprises; and many commodities, especially essential foodstuffs, were subject to price ceilings and heavily subsidized for urban consumers.

During the 1970s, Egypt's economic growth was reasonably rapid, spurred by rapidly increasing export earnings from oil, by Suez canal remittances, and by foreign aid received after the Camp David Accord. There was one major attempt at policy reform in the late 1970s, which involved reducing the very sizable subsidy consumers received for their foodstuffs, but widespread demonstrations impelled the government quickly to rescind the reform. Stimulated by increases in world oil prices, economic growth continued to be rapid and economic performance satisfactory.

In the early 1980s, however, oil revenues fell and foreign aid did not increase sufficiently to take up the slack. By 1986, export earnings were stagnant and almost half of export earnings were committed to debt-servicing obligations, inflation was high and accelerating, and imports were scarce.

It was in this crisis atmosphere that the Egyptian authorities entered into an agreement with the IMF to undertake a series of major policy reforms, including changes in the exchange rate regime, the government budget, the food subsidies, and the deficits of state-owned enterprises. Within a year, however, these policy changes had been reversed, and the Egyptian economy reverted to a state of crisis.

Holt and Roe analyze the 1986 macroeconomic crisis and reform policies, but they also contrast that response with a series of policy reforms undertaken by the Ministry of Agriculture at the same time regarding controls over agricultural production, which they deem to have been highly successful.

Egypt thus represents a case in which an economic crisis came about once there were no further beneficial external circumstances to permit the perpetuation of existing economic policies, and where macroeconomic policy reform failed while agricultural reforms could nonetheless be implemented.

Ghana   Ghana is a country of about 15 million people, which became independent in the late 1950s. At that time, Ghana was regarded as one of the African countries with great promise for rapid economic development. The level of per capita income was above that of countries such as Korea, making Ghana a "middle-income" country at that time.

With independence, economic policies focusing upon industrialization through import substitution and reliance upon state-owned enterprises were adopted. By the early 1970s, economic difficulties were already manifest, as the currency was highly overvalued (and two partial reform episodes took place), inflation was accelerating, and per capita incomes were failing to rise. Despite these failures, policies persisted into the 1970s and early 1980s. By that time, real per capita incomes were falling, production of cocoa (the major crop) was declining rapidly, and the rate of economic deterioration was accelerating. Leith and Lofchie note that, by 1982, even senior civil servants had difficulty obtaining enough to eat.

In 1982, a new government attempted to rectify the situation by adopting radical "Libyan-style" policies with even heavier state controls over economic transactions than had previously been exercised. That policy reform accomplished little or nothing, as inflation accelerated, reaching triple digits, while the maintenance of the nominal inflation left the exchange rate at less than 10 percent of the black market rate (and the real exchange rate at about 10 percent of what it had been 20 years earlier). Simultaneously, a number of other difficulties – the expulsion of Ghanaian workers from Nigeria and weather-induced crises – intensified the crisis. By 1983, the earlier Ghanaian reforms were entirely reversed, and a new set of policy reforms, moving away from reliance upon inner-oriented import substitution and parastatals and toward a more market-oriented economy with greater rewards to farmers (including cocoa growers) and a more realistic exchange rate and trade regime, was adopted.

Leith and Lofchie analyze these reforms and their effects. By the end of the 1980s, Ghana had experienced six years of sustained real per capita income growth (despite a very high rate of population growth), although real per capita incomes had not yet reattained their levels of a decade earlier. There were, however, a number of factors leading Leith and Lofchie to question the prospects for sustained growth under these reforms.

The Ghanaian experience is interesting in a variety of respects. A first interesting question in the Ghanaian case is why failed policies could persist so long. A second question relates to the politics of reform when it finally occurred, and the reasons why it was politically acceptable. Finally, the reasons why reforms have not met with the same assurance for sustainability are of great interest.

Korea   Korea is a country of 43 million people. Its per capita income was one of the lowest in Asia in the 1950s, and it was a "typical" developing country, with most of its population engaged in agricultural activities, and most of what few exports there were consisting of primary commodities. Imports were financed primarily by foreign aid; domestic saving was low. Korea was an aid-dependent "basket case," with a high rate of inflation, an overvalued currency, and government controls over many economic activities. By the late 1950s, import substitution opportunities had been exhausted, and economic growth was decelerating rapidly. Although a stabilization program was undertaken in 1957–8, there was no intent or effort to alter the underlying policies of import substitution, and growth performance deteriorated still further.

The spectacular economic success of Korea over the three decades starting in 1960 is well known, and the conditions surrounding economic reforms in Korea starting in 1960 are therefore of special interest. In 1961 a military government assumed power and undertook to alter the exchange rate and to root out the corruption of the old regime. Over the next four years, a large number of economic policies were changed. These provided the basis on which Korea experienced more than two decades of rapid sustained growth – the fastest in the world for any country with a population in excess of 3 million.

Korea thus represents a case in which the failure of earlier policies was recognized at an early date, and in which policy reform, once undertaken, was sustained over a very long period of time. Haggard, Cooper, and Moon's analysis is addressed to answering three questions: (1) the basis for support for the earlier, import-substitution policies, and the reasons for change; (2) the critical changes that were made during the period of policy change, and their contribution to the outcome; and (3) reasons why the newly adopted policies were sustained.

Turkey   Turkey is a country of 57 million people. The Turkish Republic was founded in the 1920s, and economic policies geared to import substitution and a large role for the state were already begun during the 1930s. There was severe economic dislocation during World War II, but these earlier policies were reinstated in the 1950s. Turkey then continued to follow import-substituting industrialization policies throughout the 1950s, 1960s, and 1970s. As in Brazil, economic growth was rapid during much of that time, although there were periodic balance-of-payments difficulties, accompanied by accelerating inflation, which led to the adoption of stabilization programs in 1958 and 1970.

In the 1970s, however, inflation accelerated, and economic performance deteriorated badly. By the late 1970s, per capita incomes were falling, there were severe shortages of a number of imported commodities (including oil and therefore gasoline), and there was economic and political turmoil.

In January 1980 an economic reform program was announced. It was emphasized that changes would go far beyond the earlier stabilization programs: indeed, there was no International Monetary Fund program in place at the time. There were to be several components to the program: inflation, which was then at a rate of just over 100 percent, was to be reduced; the earlier import-substitution strategy was to be shifted to an outer-oriented trade regime; and the role of the government in economic activity was to be greatly reduced, with increased reliance on the private sector.

The Turkish economic reform program lasted throughout the 1980s. The trade regime was further liberalized, and the structure of the economy greatly shifted toward exporting. Turkish economic growth resumed, slowly in the early 1980s and more rapidly in later years. Expansionary fiscal policy remained a problem, however. While state-owned enterprises' deficits were substantially reduced, increased expenditures on infrastructure resulted in continuing fiscal deficits, and inflation accelerated once again, after a drop in the early 1980s. In addition, efforts to privatize state economic enterprises (SEEs) met with only small success and, as of 1990, Turkey still had a large sector of SEEs.

Zambia   Zambia is a medium-sized African country of some 8 million people. Richly endowed with mineral deposits, it prospered in the first decade after independence. A fall in the price of copper and a rise in the costs of energy led in the mid-1970s to a dramatic decline in growth rates and to an actual erosion in the real value of per capita incomes. From one of Africa's success cases, Zambia became one of the continent's most dramatic economic failures. The government of Zambia responded to this crisis by attempting to postpone necessary economic adjustments and to stabilize the level and distribution of personal incomes. It borrowed heavily, something made easier by the belief of lenders that mineral exports would recover. It continued to support civil service salaries and consumer subsidies, resulting in deficit spending. And it strengthened an elaborate control regime, rationing subsidized consumer goods, maintaining price controls, maintaining low interest rates, and, above all, rationing access to foreign exchange.

In the mid-1980s, the government sought to change these policies. Bates and Collier argue that economic and political support for existing policies had eroded in Zambia. The control regime no longer appeared economically viable, even to its supporters; and it generated a characteristic pattern of domestic political protest, aimed at specific links in the marketing chain and rationing system. Equally as important, the government faced strong international pressures to modify its policies, as Zambia had become one of the most highly indebted nations by comparison with the value of its exports and its per capita incomes.

In their chapter on Zambia, Bates and Collier focus on the market-oriented changes that were introduced in the mid-1980s. Featured in World Bank publicity and championed by those who saw a positive role for markets in the developing countries of Africa, these reforms were dramatically reversed within months after their introduction. The authors focus in particular on the introduction of an auction for the allocation of foreign exchange and find – in contrast to the claims of some noted critics – that the market system was in fact economically sustainable and that its distributive impact was in many respects favorable. Politically, however, the system proved unsustainable, and the authors examine the reasons why this economically positive reform should prove so difficult to implement politically. In doing so, they emphasize the relationship between the government and the major economic interests: trade unions, private businessmen, state industries, farmers, consumers, and so forth. They also focus on the electoral system and the way in which political incentives linked the choices of policy-makers to the interests of the urban consuming population.

NOTES

1   See, for example, Nelson (1990) and the studies contained therein.
2   See, among others, Michaely et al. (1991) for an analysis of trade liberalization episodes and Krueger et al. (1988) for an analysis of agricultural pricing policy. Earlier studies of policy included Little et al. (1970), Bhagwati (1978), and Krueger (1978).
3   The Ford Foundation also provided support for an analysis of policy reform in Poland. Pressures of other commitments prevented the Polish team from completing their research.

4   For retrospective analyses of these views, see the essays in Meier and Seers
    (1984). For further economic analysis of these policies and why they failed, see
    Krueger (1991).
5   Such statements were not new in the 1980s. In the early 1960s, for example,
    Egypt undertook an IMF stabilization program which in fact changed almost
    no economic policies. See Hansen (1975) for an analysis.
6   For an analysis of this issue, see Mussa (1986).
7   Although there have been many studies of various aspects of individual
    countries' experiences, those have been undertaken individually, and usually
    from a particular economics or political science perspective. Those comparat-
    ive studies that were disseminated by the time this project began usually
    focused on a particular type of policy reform, such as the Little et al. (1970)
    focus on industrialization policies, and the Bhagwati (1978), Krueger (1978)
    and Michaely et al. (1991) emphasis on trade policies.
8   In the course of discussions among the participants in the project, it was
    observed that an alternative question might equally be a fruitful focal point for
    research: when it is evident that economic performance is highly unsatisfac-
    tory, what factors are there that support the continuation of failed policies for
    such a long period of time? And why do some political–economic cir-
    cumstances lead to a fairly quick recognition of the need for policy change,
    while others perpetuate the existing policies?
9   For example, in Brazil it has been illegal for a firm to move any item of
    electronic equipment, even within its factory or offices, without government
    permission. In many countries, regulation of the transportation system has
    resulted in significant cost increases for individual firms. Quality standards,
    regulations over the number of shifts, restrictions on movement of commodi-
    ties across the state or provincial lines, and other measures have similar
    effects.
10 If there were public discussion about the desirability of devaluation, the result
    would be an intensified speculative capital outflow from the country in
    question. Exporters would withhold their shipments, anticipating a greater
    return from future than present exporting, while importers would increase
    their desired current shipments in order to pay lower prices in domestic
    currency. Since the need for exchange rate adjustment originates in an
    unsatisfactory foreign exchange position, such a further deterioration is not
    possible: the authorities would be forced to act.
11 The reasoning underlying this hypothesis is that a worsening external situation
    implies economic hardship, which in turn is likely to be blamed upon the
    reform effort. Unpopularity of the reform effort strengthens the political
    opposition to reform, thus increasing the likelihood that the authorities will
    have to respond to that opposition.
12 An example of this may illustrate. In 1966, the Government of India
    announced a major devaluation of the rupee, and accompanied the announce-
    ment by significant alterations of the trade and exchange rate regime,
    removing export subsidies and liberalizing imports. Recorded exports failed to
    rise, and the reforms failed. On careful examination, it turned out that
    exporters had no more incentive to export at the new exchange rate than they
    had at the old one without export subsidies. In this case, there was simply no

change in the incentive for exporting and there should not have been an expectation that export earnings would increase. See Bhagwati and Srinivasan (1975) for an analysis.
13 This is clearly the hypothesis of Jeffrey Sachs (1989) as to why the Turkish reform effort in the early 1980s was more successful than later efforts by other developing countries.
14 See, for example, the summary statistics on adjustment presented by the World Bank (1990).
15 In chapter 10, we summarize the major conclusions arising in each of the countries.

REFERENCES

Bhagwati, Jagdish N. 1978: *Foreign Trade Regimes and Economic Development: Anatomy and Consequences of Exchange Control Regimes*, Lexington, MA: Ballinger Press for the National Bureau of Economic Research.
Bhagwati, Jagdish N., and Srinivasan, T. N. 1975: *Foreign Trade Regimes and Economic Development: India*, New York: Columbia University Press for the National Bureau of Economic Research.
Hansen, Bent 1975: *Foreign Trade Regimes and Economic Development: Egypt*, New York: Columbia University Press for the National Bureau of Economic Research.
Krueger, Anne O. 1978: *Foreign Trade Regimes and Economic Development: Liberalization Attempts and Consequences*, Lexington, MA: Ballinger Press for the National Bureau of Economic Research.
Krueger, Anne O. 1991: *Economic Policy Reforms in Developing Countries*, Oxford: Blackwell.
Krueger, Anne O., Schiff, Maurice, and Valdes, Alberto 1988: "Agricultural Incentives in Developing Countries: Measuring the Effect of Sectoral and Economywide Policies," *World Bank Economic Review*, 2 (3), September.
Little, I. M. D., Scitovsky, Tibor, and Scott, Maurice 1970: *Industry and Trade in Some Developing Countries*, London: Oxford University Press for the OECD.
Meier, Gerald M., and Seers, Dudley (eds.) 1984: *Pioneers in Development*, London: Oxford University Press for the World Bank.
Michaely, Michael, Papageorgiou, Demetris, and Choksi, Armeane M. (eds.) 1991: *Lessons of Experience in the Developing World*, Vol. 7 of Demetris Papageorgiou, Michael Michaely and Armeane M. Choksi (eds.) *Liberalizing Foreign Trade*, Cambridge, MA: Blackwell.
Mussa, Michael 1986: "The Adjustment Process and the Timing of Trade Liberalization," in Armeane M. Choksi and Demetris Papageorgiou (eds.) *Economic Liberalization in Developing Countries*, Oxford: Blackwell.
Nelson, Joan (ed.) 1990: *Economic Crisis and Policy Choice*, Princeton: Princeton University Press.

Sachs, Jeffrey D. 1989: "Introduction," in Jeffrey D. Sachs (ed.) *Developing Country Debt and the World Economy*, Chicago: University of Chicago Press, Chapter 1.

World Bank 1990: *Adjustment Lending Policies for Sustainable Growth*, Washington, DC: The World Bank Country Economics Department.

2

The Political Economy of Stabilization in Brazil
Deepak Lal and Sylvia Maxfield

INTRODUCTION

Brazil's GDP grew faster than most developing countries' during the first three decades after World War II, although it has suffered a serious growth collapse since then, as table 2.1 indicates. Throughout the period, inflation has been endemic. As table 2.3 outlines, there have been numerous attempts to end it, but as of this writing only two periods of sustained commitment to stabilization policy. Of the rest, none lasted more than a year and none succeeded in curbing demand or inflation over the medium or long run. The success of the latest effort, Collor's 1990 stabilization plan, is also in doubt. The Brazilian case, in comparison with others in this project, is like Sherlock Holmes' "dog that didn't bark."

Two things are key in explaining the failure of post-World War II stabilization efforts. First, interest groups opposed to stabilization, specifically industry, labor and to some extent coffee growers, were able to exploit politicians' fears of losing their jobs, either to the military or to other politicians, if they continued the policies. Both prior to the 1964 military coup and as gradual political opening occurred after 1975, government leaders aborted stabilization when it generated or threatened to generate considerable support by antistabilization interest groups for heightened military intervention, or for opposition parties as scheduled times for presidential succession approached.

Industry's opposition to stabilization and its sometimes alliance with labor in a progrowth coalition reflects how Brazil's factor endowment shaped industrialists' interests. As a land-abundant, labor- and capital-scarce economy, Brazil enjoyed a comparative advantage in capital-intensive manufacturing. Both labor and capital had an interest in high growth driven by capital-intensive manufacture or heavily protected labor-intensive production, even at the cost of inflation. The international return to capital for capital-intensive manufacture was high. The return to labor

Table 2.1 Comparative performance indicators 1929–87 (annual average compound growth rates)

	1929–50	1950–80	1980–87	1950–87	1929–87
GDP					
Argentina	2.5	3.4	−0.6	2.6	2.6
Brazil	4.6	6.8	2.4	5.9	5.4
Chile	2.6	3.5	0.6	3.0	2.9
Colombia	3.6	5.2	2.8	4.7	4.3
Mexico	4.0	6.4	1.0	5.3	4.8
Peru	1.8	4.9	1.9	4.3	3.4
India	0.7	3.7	4.4	3.8	2.7
Japan	1.1	8.0	3.7	7.1	4.9
Korea	0.7	7.4	8.7	7.6	5.1
Taiwan	1.8	9.1	7.4	8.8	6.2
GDP Per Capita					
Argentina	0.6	1.7	−2.1	1.0	0.8
Brazil	2.4	3.9	−0.1	3.1	2.9
Chile	0.9	1.5	−1.0	1.0	1.0
Colombia	1.7	2.4	0.9	2.1	2.0
Mexico	1.6	3.1	−1.2	2.3	2.1
Peru	2.0	2.1	−0.7	1.5	2.0
India	−0.5	1.6	2.2	1.7	0.9
Japan	−0.2	6.8	3.0	6.0	3.7
Korea	−1.4	5.2	7.0	5.5	3.0
Taiwan	−0.9	6.2	5.9	6.1	3.5

Source: Appendix 2.1 and Maddison and Associates (1989).

was also high for capital-intensive manufacture because of labor's relative scarcity. In this way factor endowments laid the basis for an industry–labor alliance in favor of rapid growth of capital-intensive manufacturing or internationally protected labor-intensive manufacture.

A second political factor plays a role in explaining the failure of stabilization in Brazil. The financial control institutions of the state, the central bank and finance ministry, were too weak relative to spending authorities to enforce stabilization. Spending/investment-oriented government institutions such as the BNDE (Banco National de Desenvolvimentó Econõmico; the name was later changed to BNDES), the Banco do Brasil, and state-owned enterprises frequently opposed mandates to curb spending. These spending/investment-oriented institutions were often successful in their opposition to spending restraints thanks to specific institutional and legal arrangements which left central monetary authorities weak. Furthermore, the BNDE had powerful pro-spending supporters among its employees, industrialists borrowing from the BNDE, and even military personnel.

The first part of this chapter presents a broad statistical picture of the Brazilian economy since 1950. It sketches the two "big pushes" followed by busts which characterize Brazilian postwar economic history. The second part of the paper outlines the various stabilization failures in more detail, and introduces possible political explanations for them. The third part looks closely at the politics of the failed reform efforts between 1979 and 1984, highlighting the role of industrial opposition to stabilization and the weakness of financial control institutions. The final part uses a Krueger/Leamer three-factor, multicommodity model of an open economy in tying the political explanations to the deeper economic currents flowing from Brazil's changing factor endowments.

1   BRAZILIAN GROWTH AND INFLATION SINCE 1950

Figures 2.1 through 2.5 chart Brazilian GDP growth rates, increases in capital stock, real wages, current account deficits (as a percentage of GDP) and inflation rates from 1950 to 1989. Table 2.2 lists the Presidents of Brazil between 1919 and 1989 and the percentage of the population who voted for them. Table 2.3 lists the various stabilization plans undertaken in the post- war period.

Brazil's postwar economic history can be usefully divided into four phases. The first phase lasted until the military takeover in 1964. It was a period of state-induced industrialization, including the big push in investment under Kubitschek, financed by the forced savings from inflation and rising capital inflows, mainly in the form of direct foreign investment. (Note the big increase in the capital stock between 1956 and 1960 in figure 2.2.) This led to acute inflation by 1963 and a debt crisis (see figure 2.5).

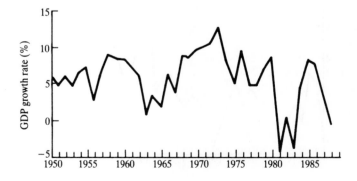

Figure 2.1   Annual growth rates of GDP

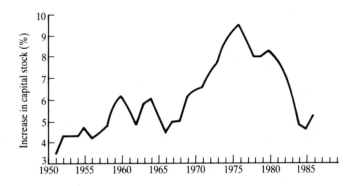

Figure 2.2   Percentage increase in capital stock

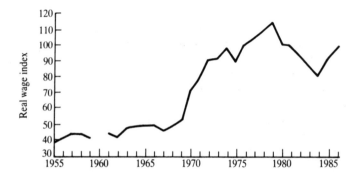

Figure 2.3   Real wage index

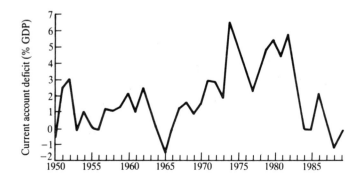

Figure 2.4   Current account deficit as percentage of GDP

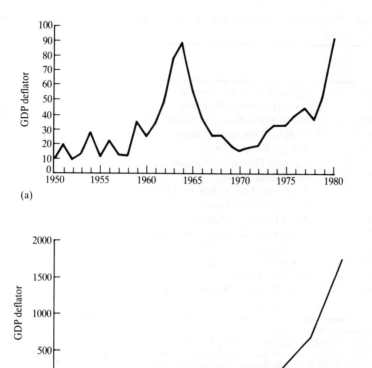

Figure 2.5   Percentage change in GDP deflator

Inflation yields revenue to the government as long as the rate of inflation is less than the rate of growth of money balances. If real money balances start declining, that means people are escaping the inflation tax, whose yield falls progressively. Table 2.4 provides the series on real money balances. It shows that in 1963 and 1964 there was a concomitant decrease in the yield of the inflation tax. The first sustained postwar stabilization program was launched in 1964.

The second phase of postwar Brazilian economic history is the period of stabilization and liberalization under Bulhões-Campos lasting from 1964 until 1967, which is described in slightly more detail below. The third phase, from 1967 to about 1980, included Brazil's miracle years, as well as another big push under Delfim Netto in the late 1970s. This too, like the Kubitschek big push, was financed at first by cheap foreign loans (this time syndicated bank credit frequently offered at negative real interest rates) and later in the 1970s by inflationary financing.

Table 2.2 Presidents of Brazil 1919–89 and percentage of the population who voted for them

Year		Vote (%)
1919–22	Epitacio da Silva Pessoa	1.1
1922–6	Arthur da Silva Bernades	1.6
1926–30	Washington Luis Pereira de Souza	2.2
1930–45	Getulio Dornelles Vargas	0.0
1946–51	Enrico Gaspar Dutra	6.9
1951–4	Getulio Dornelles Vargas	7.2
1954–5	João Café Filho	0.0[a]
1956–61	Juscelino Kubitschek de Oliveira	5.0
1961	Janio da Silva Quadros	7.9[b]
1961–4	João Belchior Marques Goulart	0.0[c]
1964–7	Humberto de Alencar Castelo Branco	0.0
1967–9	Arthur da Costa e Silva	0.0
1969–74	Emilio Garrastazu Medici	0.0
1974–9	Ernesto Geisel	0.0
1979–85	João Baptista de Oliveira Figueiredo	0.0
1985	Jose Sarney	0.0

[a]4.7 percent as vice-president.
[b]In the last "popular" election in 1961, Brazilian registered votes were 22.3 percent of the population and 18.0 percent of the population voted. This compares with the US presidential election of 1960 when registered voters were 59.3 percent of the population and 37.9 percent of the population voted.
[c]6.3 percent as vice-president.
Source: IBGE(1985).

Table 2.3 Brazilian stabilization episodes, 1945–91

Period	President	Common name of plan or key author
Oct. 1953–May 1954	Vargas	Lafer/Aranha
Aug. 1954–Apr. 1955	Café Filho	Gudin
June 1958–June 1959	Kubitschek	Alkim/Lopes
Mar. 1961–Aug. 1961	Quadros	
Jan. 1963–May 1963	Goulart	Furtado–Dantas Plan
1964–1967	Castello Branco (military government after 1964 coup)	Campos/Bulhões
1974	Geisel	Simonsen
Feb. 1979–Aug. 1979	Figueiredo	Simonsen
1980–1984	Figueiredo/Sarney	Delfim Netto
Feb. 1986–Nov. 1986	Sarney	Cruzado I
Nov. 1986–Feb. 1987	Sarney	Cruzado II
Mid-1987	Sarney	Bresser Plan
Jan. 1989	Sarney	Summer Plan
1990–?	Collor	Collor Plan

Table 2.4 Changes in real money balances (1950–89)[a]

Year	Real money
1950	25.80000
1951	−2.400000
1952	5.700000
1953	5.200000
1954	−2.100000
1955	0.200000
1956	−0.600000
1957	19.30000
1958	8.600000
1959	7.099999
1960	12.60000
1961	16.30000
1962	12.90000
1963	−13.40000
1964	−4.900002
1965	17.80000
1966	120.1000
1967	16.50000
1968	16.30000
1969	8.900000
1970	10.70000
1971	12.70000
1972	18.10000
1973	17.40000
1974	−0.500000
1975	9.000000
1976	−4.400002
1977	−7.500000
1978	3.799999
1979	19.60000
1980	−20.30000
1981	−35.10000
1982	−35.60000
1983	−41.39999
1984	−10.00000
1985	111.6000
1986	177.2000
1987	−81.30000
1988	−112.6000
1989	−359.9000

[a]Derived as the change in M1 divided by the GDP deflator.
Source: Appendix 2.1.

This big push also ended with a debt crisis and high inflation – the cure for which was sought in a series of failed heterodox stabilization plans. Once again as in 1963–4, it was not until acute inflation had led to a shrinking of real money balances in 1980–4 that a sustained stabilization effort commenced. Its failure, the lurch to hyperinflation in 1988 and 1989, and a large decrease in real money balances, evident in table 2.4, led to Collor's 1990 stabilization plan.

The timing of the only two sustained stabilization plans in post-World War II Brazil, Bulhões and Campos (1964–7), and Delfim Netto (1980–4), lends credence to a political explanation of stabilization based on state revenue maximization which is implicit in the economic analysis of Lal and Myint.[1] It appears that the state tolerates inflation, if not encouraging it, until the revenues from the inflation tax start declining. While this is a possible explanation of the initiation of stabilization efforts that the government was committed to sustaining, initiation of the numerous failed stabilization efforts corresponds to balance of payments pressure. The failure of stabilization *implementation* in Brazil requires yet a different political explanation. To this we now turn.

2   STABILIZATION FAILURES AND POSSIBLE POLITICAL EXPLANATIONS

Brief history of stabilization episodes

As table 2.3 outlines, Brazil's first post-World War II stabilization effort came under President Getúlio Vargas and lasted from October 1953 to May 1954. It occurred in the context of a $1 billion balance of payments deficit, 21 percent inflation for 1952 (considered a large jump over 1951's 11 percent) and a slowdown in industrial production in early 1953. In June 1953 Vargas's first finance minister, Horacio Lafer, resigned in frustration over the obstacles to formulating and implementing a coherent stabilization plan. The new finance minister, Oswaldo Aranha, had more success. The "Aranha Plan" of October 1953 promised credit restrictions and new multiple exchange controls involving a de facto devaluation. The effort fell apart when Vargas was unable/unwilling to resist pressure for wage increases from civil servants and the military.[2]

Vargas bequeathed a major financial crisis to his successor in 1954, Café Filho. The first of Café Filho's three finance ministers, Eugênio Gudin, previously an Executive Director of the IMF and proponent of orthodox stabilization, pledged in August 1954 to carry out the Aranha Plan. Consulting the IMF and working closely with the head of Brazil's supervisory monetary board (Superintendância da Moeda e Crédito, SUMOC), Octávio Gouvêa de Bulhões, Gudin successfully tightened the money supply. This induced several bank failures and considerable political opposition. Gudin resigned in April 1955 sensing the president's unwilling-ness to support stabilization. This unwillingness was signaled in part by his negotiations with Jânio Quadros, governor of São Paulo, over easing credit controls hurting São Paulo industrialists. The new finance minister, José Maria Whitaker, whose appointment Quadros had recommended, imme-diately eased monetary policy.

The next stabilization effort came on the heels of Kubitschek's ambitious big push and the balance of payments trouble and inflationary pressure associated with it. In June 1958 Finance Minister José Maria Alkim resigned amid complaints that he had failed to secure international financing for Brazil or to control inflation. His replacement, Lucas Lopes, and director of the BNDE, Roberto Campos, drafted a two-stage stabiliza-tion program announced after the October 1958 congressional elections. There were simultaneous negotiations with the IMF over a standby agreement.[3] The IMF pushed for shock treatment to rapidly reduce inflation and for elimination of multiple exchange controls. The Brazilians preferred a more gradual approach and continuation of exchange controls. Controversy over stabilization widened into a debate over development strategy in general. In June 1959 Kubitschek became the first Latin American president to break off relations with the IMF.[4]

Despite Quadros' earlier lobbying for loose credit on behalf of São Paulo industrialists, during his presidential campaign to succeed Kubitschek in 1960 Quadros made the large federal deficit and need for financial retrenchment a key issue. In March 1961, three months after his inaugura-tion, Quadros announced a new stabilization program, drastically cutting subsidies on consumer imports (wheat and oil), simplifying the multiple exchange rate system, devaluing the cruzeiro de facto, and promising to cut the public sector deficit. Before long, however, Quadros resigned.

The Dantas–Furtado Plan, named after unofficial minister for economic planning, Celso Furtado, and minister of finance, San Tiago Dantas, was a three-year plan with a short-term inflation-fighting component announced in January 1963 by President João Goulart. The plan contained proposals to fight inflation through credit, exchange, federal budget, and wage policies. The IMF nevertheless decided to release new funds only in response to detailed stabilization steps specified after an IMF mission to Brazil. Even before this mission could arrive, salary increases for civil servants and the military became a critical test for the stabilization portion of the Dantas–Furtado Plan. Its failure as an antiinflation program began in May 1963 when Goulart was not willing to resist the military's request for a 70 percent wage hike.

The most sustained stabilization and reform effort in Brazil's post-World War II experience to date came after the military coup of 1964 and lasted until a change in military leadership in 1967. The military government headed by General Castelo Branco brought former SUMOC director Bulhões into government as minister of planning and former BNDE chief under Kubitschek, Roberto Campos, into government as minister of finance. Both had experience in previous Brazilian stabilization attempts. These two designed and implemented a heterodox program of gradual stabilization that relied heavily on fiscal, rather than monetary, measures. It encompassed a program of trade liberalization, introduction of a value-added tax, a gradual reduction of the public sector deficit involving cuts in current but not capital expenditure, creation (at least in principle) of an independent central bank and a policy of indexation in financial markets to boost savings.[5] Foreign exchange rates were simplified, ending subsidies on imported goods such as oil, wheat and newspaper which had been ended and reinstated several times before. A crawling peg was also introduced. Interest rate controls were lifted and policies were implemented to promote capital market growth. After an initial large increase in wages, wage growth was restricted. Inflation was brought under control. In terms of reducing inflation this was a case of successful stabilization, yet even in this case orthodox monetary control measures were avoided.

The next stabilization effort came as inflation began to pick up slightly in the early 1970s, although it remained low by Brazilian standards. The then finance minster, Mário Henrique Simonsen, contracted the money supply in 1974 during the administration of General Geisel. But this modest stabilization effort ended by October in anticipation of November elections.[6] In 1979 Simonsen – who was by then minister of planning for the administration of General Figueiredo – designed a stabilization program including the promise of explicit fiscal transfers to cover subsidized credit, greater government control of state-owned enterprise (SOE) expenditure and gradual reduction of export subsidies. In August 1979 Simonsen was replaced by Antônio Delfim Netto, who immediately embarked on an expansionary path. Balance of payments problems forced Delfim Netto into a stop–go cycle of stabilization beginning in December 1980 and lasting through 1984.

The first civilian administration since 1964, headed by President Sarney, attempted four heterodox stabilizations between 1986 and 1989: the well-known Cruzado Plan I (February–November 1986), Cruzado II (November 1986–February 1987), the mid-1987 Bresser Plan, and the January 1989 Summer Plan. The Cruzado I involved a temporary wage and price freeze after an initial 33 percent wage hike. The Plan included no tax increases or spending cuts and allowed the annual money supply to expand without limits. Cruzado II included more flexible wage and price controls involving price hikes for many state-provided consumer goods such as electricity and for some private consumer goods such as autos. In both Cruzado Plans wage and price freezes ended under industry and labor pressure. When wage and price controls were lifted, inflation returned to its high and growing rate.[7] The Bresser Plan might be considered more orthodox than either of the Cruzado Plans because it allowed prices and the exchange rate to adjust dramatically and called for cooperation with international creditors. Nevertheless one government official involved claims that the plan was rushed out because demand collapsed, "which illustrates how the intention was to expand, not just to stabilize."[8] In any case, Bresser quickly gave up on the plan.

Political explanations

There are five general types of political explanations for macroeconomic policy which might provide insight into the impressive history of failed stabilization in Brazil. These rest on ideology, international pressure, domestic sociopolitical coalitions or interest groups, state institutions, and electoral pressure. In Brazil's case, the first two are partly related to geography. The argument based on ideology suggests that, in part because it is a continental economy, Brazil has developed a strong nationalist and development/growth-oriented ideology prevalent among the elite and state actors. Fishlow cites his failure to take ideology into account as one of two reasons why he underestimated Brazil's future economic problems in his early writing. "I underestimated," he says, "how dominating the *grandeza* theme would prove."[9] In Sikkink's case this argument is associated with a view of the Brazilian state as very strong relative to others in Latin America such as Argentina.[10] Leff cites ideology but connects it with a third category of explanations, those based on the strength of different social and political coalitions. Unlike some less-developed countries, Leff writes, "Brazil's monetary tradition is not one of unquestioned orthodoxy and inexorable opposition to inflation. Rather the prevailing doctrine has been that inflation promotes economic growth; and literally no important actor in Brazilian politics has actually opposed inflation."[11]

The argument about the role of international forces in explaining Brazilian economic policy is also usually made in connection with explanations based on the strength of different domestic social coalitions and their policy preferences. Kaufman notes that much pressure for orthodoxy comes from international financiers and their domestic allies. In Brazil, both public and private sector bankers, frequently natural constituents for international creditors, were politically weak. Domestic opponents of stabilization, in this case industry and labor, were much stronger. Fishlow combines the international and domestic constituency arguments in referring to the 1964–7 stabilization episode. He writes that "by closing down the internal political process and giving virtual carte blanche to Campos and Bulhões, the military government also opted for magnifying the external influence upon domestic economic policy."[12]

Frieden makes one version of the social coalition or domestic constituency argument for the Brazilian case. He argues that Brazil was a case of low class conflict and a strong coalition of "fixed asset holders" – with industrialists at the center – opposed to orthodox economic policy. To the extent that the Brazilian government did turn to orthodox policy this was due to the growing power of the financial sector, "liquid asset holders," and the threat of rising class conflict.[13] Fishlow also mentions his underestimation of the power of industrialists opposed to orthodoxy as one of two reasons explaining his earlier mispredictions about Brazil. The strength of the antirecession constituency, Fishlow suggests, is a corollary to the weakness of the Brazilian state.[14] In the absence of a strong state, policy follows the interests of the strongest domestic constituencies.[15]

Although labor fared relatively poorly under Brazil's inflationary growth policies, until the 1970s at least, it was usually opposed to stabilization, fearing lower nominal and possibly real wages. That industry also opposed stabilization is puzzling to some observers. *Institutional Investor*, a journal of the international financial industry, remarked with apparent incredulity in the early 1980s that "the imperative of continued growth – even at the expense of inflation – is accepted by a surprising number of Brazilian businessmen...."[16] A leading private banker also stressed the extent to which Brazilian industrialists are "biased against tight monetary policy" and recalls a discussion with World Bank economists who remarked on this quizzically after a meeting with leaders of the Federation of Industries of the State of São Paulo (FIESP) in the early 1980s.[17]

Industrialists, including owners and managers of SOEs, private national enterprises, and multinational corporations (MNCs) in basic, consumer durables, and capital goods industries supported Brazil's "inflation-be-damned" economic policy because it benefited them.[18] The key to Brazilian industrialists' interest in growth even at the cost of inflation lies in two important economic conditions, both stemming from the supply side of industrial activity. First, following a three-factor multicommodity model of economic growth, Brazil is a relatively land-rich country with a comparative advantage in capital-intensive industry. The relatively low labor-intensity of production lessened industrialists' concern over inflation-driven rising nominal wages.

Second, Brazilian industry through the 1970s and 1980s was very dependent on bank credit, and to some extent on state subsidized credit, as opposed to internal or equity financing.[19] This made industry highly sensitive to cuts in state or private bank credit and/or rising interest rates. Particularly during periods of tight industrial credit, private bankers were targets of industry criticism. The government often chimed in. One observer writes of Antônio Delfim Netto, agriculture minister and later minister of finance in the General Costa e Silva and Médici governments (1967–74) and minister of planning from 1979 to 1985, "if [he] seemed to have a favorite target for attack, then it was the nation's bankers...."[20]

Although large-scale agricultural exporters, in general, were squeezed by the pre–1964 civilian regime's multiple exchange rate system, coffee exporters were supported and protected by the state to varying extents and through diverse mechanisms from 1906 onward. On several occasions, such as during Kubitschek's stabilization program and after the 1964 reforms, they formed a vocal part of the antistabilization coalition along with labor and industry. This was because stabilization limited the government's freedom to print money to fund surplus coffee purchases under its price guarantee program.[21]

A fourth category of explanations for the failure of stabilization rests on state institutions and the weakness of those necessary for imposing austerity. These explanations focus on the institutional context of economic decision making and policy implementation. In the Brazilian context the argument is that the lack of a central bank able to effectively control the money supply and/or a central monetary authority with control over public sector expenditure are institutional shortcomings which made orthodoxy impossible to implement. For example, until 1986 the Banco do Brazil (the nation's largest commercial bank) had an open-ended rediscounting facility at the Central Bank with a symbolic 1 percent annual interest rate. Furthermore, in the 1970s, roughly 50 percent of all credit came from sources such as the BNDES, the Banco do Brasil and the housing finance system, and was outside the reach of Central Bank policy instruments.[22] State financial control institutions were relatively weak because spending bodies had strong supporting constituencies – among their workers, sometimes the military, and/or other business associates – which the Ministry of Finance and the Central Bank lacked.

In combination with an argument about the strength of domestic constituencies for and against orthodoxy, the state institutions approach amounts to saying that the state and social forces in favor of orthodoxy were relatively weak in Brazil, while those opposed were relatively strong. Elsewhere one of us refers to this situation as one of a relatively weak "bankers' alliance," defined as a loose interest coalition including both public and private sector financiers and their allies.[23] This type of argument, focusing on cleavages which cut across state and society in a manner consistent with an "iron triangles" approach, has the potential to resolve the apparent contradiction between those arguments focused on domestic social forces, which paint the Brazilian state as weak, and those focused on ideology, which depict the Brazilian state as strong. Where there is a weak "bankers' alliance" those state institutions generally in favor of orthodoxy and their potential social constituents, such as bankers, are relatively weak while other coalitions of state and social actors are strong. This argument, combining an emphasis on social constituencies and state institutions and focusing on how they interact, responds neatly to Grindle's call for attention to "what occurs within the state and at the intersection of state and society."[24]

A final set of arguments about the politics of economic policy potentially applicable to the unsuccessful record of orthodoxy in Brazil refers to the often cyclical impact of electoral pressure. According to political business cycle-type arguments, politicians choose economic policies expected to maximize their political power.[25] The more secure their tenure, the more likely politicians will impose orthodoxy that is likely to anger popular sectors whose numbers give them political clout. In authoritarian and semiauthoritarian Brazil we would expect orthodoxy to be undermined whenever the specter of elections arose, or vice versa. Skidmore, for example, suggests that the military government of Castelo Branco could carry out stabilization relying heavily on wage cuts in the 1964 through 1967 period because electoral pressure had been removed.[26] While this may be partially true, cross-national evidence does not clearly support a positive correlation between authoritarian government and successful stabilization.[27] Grindle suggests that even the subtler form of the argument, positing a relationship between insecurity of tenure and adoption of power maximizing policies by government leaders, should be couched in terms of a domestic constituency approach. Government leaders, Grindle writes, "are not undiscriminating in terms of maximizing their capacity [to be reelected]. They have historically and ideologically determined coalition partners and support groups, as well as clearly defined opponents whose support they will not seek, even in the interests of staying in power."[28]

In the next section we turn to evidence from an in-depth examination of Brazil's attempted stabilization between 1979 and 1984 based on interviews and periodical searches, and to a brief comparison of this case with the others outlined above. This evidence lends support to an explanation of Brazil's stabilization failures based primarily on the relative weakness of state monetary institutions involved in initiating and implementing orthodoxy and the strength of social actors opposed to orthodoxy. Political, particularly electoral, and international pressures influence the ability of domestic coalitions for and against orthodoxy to affect policy. There is little evidence in support of the role of ideology as a primary, independent explanation.

3   ECONOMIC REFORM EFFORTS 1979–84

The first stabilization initiative in this period began when Mário Henrique Simonsen was appointed minister of planning by General Figueiredo in 1979 (having been minister of finance for the previous military government) and immediately tried to centralize economic control in that ministry. He aimed to curb federal spending by bringing SOEs under central control, limit money supply growth, and begin to shift the Brazilian economy from import substitution to export-led growth by prioritizing agriculture and energy over industry and modestly liberalizing import restrictions.[29]

For reasons discussed below, Delfim Netto replaced Simonsen after only six months and embarked on an expansionary path. This brought Delfim

Netto into conflict with Finance Minister Rischbieter who objected to Delfim Netto's further centralization of power and proposal to create a state commodity trading agency. Rischbieter also disagreed publicly with Delfim's optimistic balance of payments projections.[30] Rischbieter resigned; Delfim Netto named Central Bank director Ernane Galvêas to the finance ministry and brought Carlos Langoni into government to replace Galvêas at the Central Bank.

From August 1979 to November 1980 Delfim followed an "antiadjustment" heterodox approach of increasing deficit spending, lowering nominal interest rates, lifting price controls, preannouncing the rate of exchange rate devaluation after a December 1979 maxidevaluation, preannouncing indexation adjustments, introducing a larger indexation increase for the lowest wage levels and replacing annual wage adjustment with biannual adjustments. Real interest rates quickly turned negative and the cruzeiro became overvalued, leading to a decline in savings and strong incentive to import; reserves dwindled and Delfim began to scramble for foreign loans. Meanwhile in public he held to his Messianic optimism. "...[T]his revolution that is taking place in the real Brazil often goes unnoticed in the big cities," he intoned in early 1980, "where you find these apocalypse predictors, these crises and abysms that exist only in their own minds, minds dominated by uncertainty, by lack of faith and by their inability to understand the country as it really is."[31]

The hint of change in this expansionary policy first came in March 1980 when Delfim raised the IOF (imposto de operações financeiras) tax imposed on all financial transactions to slow imports and curb credit expansion. In mid–1980 Delfim announced moderate cuts in public expenditure and imposed limits on state and federal development bank credit allocation; rumors of overall credit tightening spread. By September 1980 it was clear that Rischbieter's $4 billion balance of payment deficit projections from January 1980 had been accurate, if not low. By November 1980 it was evident that inflation for the year would be a century-long record-breaking 110 percent. Foreign exchange reserves had dwindled from $8.3 billion in November 1979 to $4 billion by November 1980.[32]

November 1980 marks the beginning of a period of attempted "voluntary" – as opposed to IMF-related – stabilization brought on by balance of payments pressure. The new monetary supervision board, the Concelho Monetàmo Nacional (CMN), which replaced the SUMOC in 1964, met on November 12, 1980 and decided to free interest rates and end preannouncement of the cruzeiro devaluation and indexation levels.[33] New restrictions on money supply growth, bank loans, SOE capital expenditure and subsidies were announced. During the months following November 1980, Bacha observes that "Delfim Netto implemented the tightest monetary policy that the country has experienced since...the turn of the century."[34] In March 1981 the BNDE announced it would make no new industrial loans and might have to cancel existing ones due to government funding cutbacks. In July 1981 President Figueiredo announced the formation of a commission to report on selling SOEs. It was immediately apparent that tight monetary policy and fiscal restraint were not sustainable. The public sector deficit rose and internal debt grew, counteracting monetary restriction.[35]

Desperate for foreign financing to cover the balance of payments shortfall, in October 1981 the Brazilian government presented foreign creditors a plan blending short-term stabilization with long-term structural adjustment. This plan helped Brazil secure a patchwork of foreign loans in late 1981 and early 1982. But reserves were dwindling and international funds dried up completely with the Mexican moratorium of September 1982. In October 1982 the Brazilian government began covert negotiations with the IMF, marking the start of the phase of IMF-linked stabilization. A secret deal with the United States for fresh loans took immediate pressure off and allowed the Brazilian government to appear solvent until the November 1982 elections. Immediately following the November elections an IMF mission arrived in Brazil. An agreement was reached in mid-December including reduction of the current account deficit from 5 percent of GNP in 1982 to 2 percent in 1993, a 50 percent cut in the public sector borrowing requirement as a percentage of GDP, strict targets for credit expansion, and the promise of large-scale devaluation. Sealing the deal, the first of seven letters of intent signed by the Brazilians in 1983 and 1984 was ratified on January 6, 1983; a second was signed on February 24, 1983.

Although wage indexation was trimmed by executive decree in January 1983 and a maxidevaluation was announced in February, Brazil failed its first quarterly IMF review with a higher than promised public sector deficit and greater domestic credit expansion. The IMF suspended disbursements and six months of negotiations ensued. A third letter of intent was signed September 15, 1983 and amended on November 14 because of congressional refusal to ratify administration-proposed wage cuts. Again the Brazilians failed to meet targets; target failures and renegotiations led to signing of new letters of intent on March 3, September 28, and December 20, 1984. The Neves/Sarney government, elected in 1985, ended this cycle by switching to a policy of heterodox shock.

Balance of payments deficit

International pressure is crucial to understanding why Delfim first chose, and later stuck to, the stabilization course in light of considerable domestic political pressure against it. Delfim's move away from antirecession policy in November 1980 was forced upon him by "pressure emanating from the international financial system..." write two Brazilian analysts.[36] Economist Bacha suggests that Delfim overestimated the international banking community's willingness to bankroll his unorthodox policies. "This finally forced him into a complete policy reversal."[37] "Delfim," *Veja* hypothesizes, "was able to finesse his [domestic] critics with the support of international bankers."[38] A stream of foreign bankers did pass through Brazil in 1981: Citibank's Walter Wriston, David Rockefeller of Chase Manhattan, the Chairman of Chase Manhattan, and a Morgan Stanley banker, to list a few. Volcker visited in mid–1981 for the opening of the new Central Bank headquarters and minced no words about the need for tight fiscal policy as a condition of international financial support. International pressure was also highly visible in 1983 as Figueiredo tried to get Congress to pass his wage legislation. In the midst of congressional debate in October 1983 Volcker is quoted as saying, "I don't want to make predictions nor interfere in Brazil's internal affairs, but I think it would be best for all concerned if the decree was approved."[39] US Treasury Secretary Regan was even blunter: "If Congress does not want loans from the IMF, the banks and the US, it can reject the [IMF] program."[40] In November 1983, with the wage legislation still not approved, IMF managing director de Larosiere announced he would not allow talks about standby credits to resume until the wage law had been approved.[41]

Industry and labor pressure and political instability

All who had benefited from growth-oriented policies opposed stabilization. The only clear winners from the reforms were bankers who in late 1981 admitted that credit controls had allowed them to increase the spread between deposit and loan rates and increase profits.[42] There was a clear split within the business community between financiers and industrialists. In addition to financiers, exporters may have benefited from stabilization but there is little evidence of their active support for it in contemporary accounts. Labor was also vehemently opposed to stabilization. The economic context is one of recession in which labor and industrialists in consumer durables and capital goods sectors were hurt.

Labor and industry pressure was exercised through direct and indirect channels. It had added weight in the context of the gradual political opening (*distensão* or *abertura*) which began in 1974 and was well underway by 1979 as maneuvering for position in the 1982 direct elections began. To fully understand the weight of labor and industry pressure on political leaders we need to briefly review the history of the Brazilian party system.

The military government which took power in a 1964 coup reformed the Brazilian party system by decree in 1965. The Second Institutional Act abolished all existing political parties and the Supplementary Act No. 4 laid the basis for a weak two-party system which lasted until 1979. ARENA (Aliança Nacional Renovadora – National Renovation Alliance) was the progovernment party controlled by the military; the opposition was grouped in the MDB (Movimento Democrático Brasileiro – Brazilian Democratic Movement). Presidential succession, every five years unless interrupted by illness, was determined by intramilitary debate where the main division was between "castelistas" (moderates associated with Castelo Branco, president from 1964 to 1968) and "linha duristas" (hardliners). ARENA gave a rubber stamp nomination to the chosen candidate, and congress, in which ARENA maintained a majority until 1982, voted the candidate to office. National congressional elections were direct but the governing party tried to control them through intimidation and harassment of the opposition. Although virtually excluded from presidential and state-level politics, the opposition MDB enjoyed some freedom and electoral success at the local level.

Distensão began in 1974 when general Geisel allowed all political candidates access to television. The opposition MDB came close to winning a majority in the national congress, increased the number of seats held in the senate and won control of several state legislatures. In these elections the governing party lost the two-thirds majority in congress needed to approve constitutional changes. ARENA dominance was beginning to slowly give way to coalition government. A party reform bill was passed in 1979 which led to name changes for the two existing parties [ARENA became the PDS (Partido Democrático Social) and the MDB became the PMDB] and opened electoral competition to any other party that met certain minimal requirements. Competition between the parties for seats in the 1982 national congressional elections began immediately.

In this electoral context, the governing party's goal of creating a democracy in which it held unquestioned sway made it sensitive to major interest group opposition to government economic policies. Figueiredo, elected president in 1979, had two main political problems. He had to hold the military "linha duristas," who were opposed to political opening, at bay and he had to maintain as much PDS popularity as possible in order to guarantee the PDS's victory in the upcoming elections. Labor support was important to electoral victory; industry support was needed for electoral success and, perhaps more importantly, to bolster the government against hardline military pressure.[43] Although labor and business were organized in semicorporatist fashion, business had a closer more influential relationship with government actors exercised through noncorporatist channels.[44] Cardoso writes of "bureaucratic rings" or "spheres" which were "circles of information and pressure linking private entrepreneurs in those particular sectors of capital favored by the Brazilian economic model to the occupants of bureaucratic posts." Through them the business community dug itself "into defensive positions in the state system from which it could defend its economic interests."[45] Lafer provides a description of the "bureaucratic ring" around the foreign trade office of the Banco do Brasil,

CACEX, linking it to representatives of major private associations for machine tools, electrical and heavy industry.[46]

Dye and de Souza e Silva conclude that the "dominant pattern" was "close sectoral integration of the most strategic segments of capital with the state, in a technocratic mode that insures the former's active participation and influence over policy."[47] Extensive interviews conducted for two PhD dissertations substantiate the view that industrialists used social ties and personal contacts to influence government both within and outside the context of bureaucratic rings.[48] An example of these ties and how they jeopardized stabilization efforts is found in the relationship between Luis Vidigal, president of FIESP in the 1980s, and Planning Minister Delfim Netto. "Often I would publicly pretend I had lost to him on a specific issue," Vidigal said, "but he would concede in private (for example, on sustaining BNDE spending).[49]

Industry opposition to stabilization in the 1979 to 1984 period was great. Industrialists blamed Simonsen and the private bankers for high interest rates, which in industrialists' minds were the result of tight monetary policy and private bank gouging. According to one prominent private banker, Simonsen was ousted by industrialists, by a business community biased against tight monetary policy.[50] Bankers, he suggested, supported Simonsen but kept a lower political profile than industrialists. A prominent Brazilian economist notes that "except for the financial sector, everyone that counted in the country was quite happy to see Simonsen's policies knocked out by Delfim."[51] Hundreds of São Paulo industrialists travelled to Brasília for Delfim's inauguration. Certainly his popularity among industrialists and willingness to reverse Simonsen's policies helped him win the job as the Figueiredo administration's second planning minister.[52]

Ironically, as soon as he began to even hint at adopting moderately orthodox stabilization measures in mid–1980, Delfim – although he had a large reservoir of industry support – began to face the same criticisms Simonsen had confronted. When Delfim reduced the subsidy implicit in BNDE loans, the influential São Paulo industrialists association, FIESP, criticized him. They argued that his new stabilization policy ran contrary to his frequent statement while "campaigning" for the ministership of planning in 1979 that "growth is the remedy for all Brazil's ills." The campaign for the presidency of FIESP in summer 1980 reflected business's growing concern that Delfim would return to Simonsen's tight monetary policy. Luis de Bueno Vidigal, who won the elections, was one of two challengers to the 14–year incumbent running on a platform stating that FIESP should take a more active role in promoting the interests of São Paulo industrialists before the government.[53]

At the same time as FIESP was becoming more active in opposing the government, leading industrialists began meeting with opposition political figures. In October 1980 industrialists supported the Figueiredo government's policy of political opening against hardline military opposition but still expressed public criticism of Delfim's nascent anti-inflation policy. Shortly thereafter Delfim began inviting key business people to Brasília for discussion about economic policy. Nevertheless, after the November stabilization measures were announced, leaders of the National Industrial Confederation, Brazilian Export Association and National Chambers of Commerce Federation issued a thinly veiled demand for more business influence, a guaranteed veto at least, over economic policy.[54] In January 1981 several generals and businessmen signed a manifesto criticizing the government's economic policy and calling for defense of national industries. In March 1981 FIESP issued a harsh press statement criticizing the government and the banking community for high interest rates which were pushing many industrialists toward bankruptcy.[55] One business periodical survey in mid–1981 found that 41 percent of business people interviewed considered Delfim a "very bad" minister of planning. Another survey found 83 percent believed the IMF should relax its conditionality.[56] In 1980 business opposition to stabilization policies had come largely from isolated industrial sectors hurt by government cutbacks. By 1981 tight monetary policy led to generalized industry opposition to the government and to the banks, once again perceived as benefiting from credit restrictions.[57]

Slight loosening in 1982 as elections approached appears to have lessened industry complaints. However, once the first IMF letter of intent was signed after the November elections, opposition became vocal again. In August 1983 Delfim postponed his return from a Paris meeting to avoid attending the annual business forum sponsored by *Gazeta Mercantil* at which industrialists rejected recession, arguing that tight monetary policy hurts consumers and producers.[58] Industrialists demanded that the government cut interest rates, not wages, arguing that the latter would shrink the already severely restricted domestic market.[59] After the government signed a third IMF letter of intent in September, industry leaders ridiculed it, awarding the letter a "Nobel prize for alchemy."[60]

Tight monetary policy and fiscal stringency were jeopardized by industry opposition and the importance of industry support for the government's political opening and the electoral success of the PDS. Labor opposition also imperiled monetary restriction and government spending because strikes for higher wages, even if forcefully repressed, helped galvanize support for opposition political parties throughout the 1979 to 1984 stabilization attempts. Between January and October 1979 Simonsen faced more than 400 strikes, including a long confrontation with the politically powerful metalworkers union.[61] In September 1980, as the balance of payments situation worsened, Delfim proposed abolishing the biannual wage adjustment for those earning more than seven times the minimum wage, only to back down in the face of strong opposition from labor and industry and from within the governing party, the PDS. Thousands of strikes in São Paulo and other cities against stabilization and the IMF dot news reports from 1982 through 1984.[62] For example, employees of SOEs marched in June 1982 to protest austerity and public sector budget cuts carrying placards saying "Down with Delfim!"[63] São Paulo metalworkers rallied against IMF-imposed policies in March 1983.[64] One of the largest strikes was a university employees strike in July 1984.[65] Due to these high levels of labor mobilization, efforts to cut wages, a *sine qua non* of the IMF agreements, were repeatedly befouled by Congress in 1983 and 1984. In May 1983 Figueiredo was forced to backtrack on a cut in wage indexation promised in the January agreement with the IMF because Congress would not ratify it. Under strong IMF pressure in July 1983 Figueiredo announced cuts similar to those decreed earlier in the year. The move was highly unpopular and the government had "to declare a state of emergency in Brasília during the congressional debate over the bill in order to prevent massive demonstrations...."[66]

The government's economic and political strategies were clearly at odds. Stabilization engendered labor and industry opposition which translated into political vulnerability for the ruling party. Many who were government officials during the stabilization efforts cite political pressures on the PDS as policy constraints. Ernane Galvêas, who replaced Rischbieter as Minister of Finance under Delfim in early 1980, says that political pressure emanating from the return of exiled left leaders and the risk that they could ride economically induced social problems to power mitigated against resorting to orthodox stabilization policies in 1980.[67] A former high-level Central Bank official claims he was able to pursue a tight monetary policy until July 1981 when spending for the November 1982 elections began.[68] Tight monetary and fiscal policy were jeopardized as the governing party began its campaign spending. When the CMN announced a loosening of credit in May 1982, Delfim proclaimed, "It is time to grant the consumer some relief." FIESP issued an approving statement.[69]

Although covert negotiations with the IMF began in October 1982, marking the beginning of the IMF-directed phase of the 1979 to 1984 efforts at stabilization, Delfim says that he felt that he could not publicly negotiate with the IMF until after the November 15, 1982 congressional elections. The PDS feared that the commitment to stabilization implied by negotiations with the IMF would jeopardize their congressional candidates' electoral chances. Delfim is quoted on November 17 as saying, "I needed to get Brazil to the 15th of November solvent, and we arrived."[70] "My major problem," he said in retrospect, "was to hold on until the November elections."[71] After that, in 1983 and 1984, Congress and the imminent presidential elections hindered policy making.

In the November 1982 elections, the governing party, the PDS, lost its majority in the federal congress. After this the reelection concerns of congresspeople obstructed passage of executive branch wage decrees. For example, the IMF and other foreign creditors accepted Brazil's third letter of intent without knowing whether Congress would approve the wage legislation involved. Delfim threatened there would have to be gas rationing if the bill did not pass. It did not. In retrospect, Delfim says Congress failed to understand the need for austerity policy.[72] Another former official who joined the government in 1983 echoed this feeling. "Congress was the central obstacle," he said.[73] Commenting on Delfim's 1983 and 1984 failures, the same former government official noted that the basic "problem was the weak legitimacy of a lame-duck authoritarian regime."[74]

Summing up this explanation for the failure of orthodoxy in this period, former Central Bank director Carlos Langoni points to the resistance of organized social groups such as labor and FIESP, especially in the context of political opening.[75]

Weak central monetary and fiscal control

The powerlessness of national financial and monetary control institutions is the explanation for failure of the 1979–84 stabilization efforts most cited by government officials involved. Coherent stabilization policies were hard to formulate and extremely difficult to implement for several institutional reasons. The government lacked a monetary authority capable of regulating the money supply, and did not have centralized data on public finances and monetary expansion nor a centralized fiscal authority with control over all public spending.

The details of the institutional lacunae are numerous. Law GB–588 mandated that the nation's largest commercial bank, the Banco do Brasil, cover the foreign debts of SOEs. The Banco do Brasil, a majority publicly-owned leviathan with its own ties to the military and militant employees, had an automatic overdraft account with the Central Bank known as the *conta de movimento*. "As Banco do Brasil president," Rischbieter said, "I had to resist dictatorial temptations."[76] Another problem was that at least four budgets existed, a monetary budget, a social security budget, a budget for the states, and the so-called *união* federal budget. Even after an agency was created in 1979 to bring SOE expenditure under central control – the Secretaria de Controle das Empresas Estatais (SEST) – little progress was made because individual SOE presidents had independent political ties to economic and bureaucratic interest groups, and employees and suppliers adept at lobbying SEST. SEST could barely keep track of SOE spending, much less control it. *Veja* wrote in 1982, that the "sacred monsters of state-entrepreneurship, the parastatals, never complied with any budget."[77] For example, in 1984 Petrobras, the state oil company, gave its 50,000 employees a one-time wage increase in direct violation of wage legislation.[78]

Beyond the Banco do Brasil and the SOEs other institutions had political and institutional independence which afforded them financial autonomy. The BNDES had independent control of industrial policy instruments and was powerful enough that in 1982 the head of Internal Revenue was forced to apologize for a ruling cutting BNDES credit; Dornelles stated publicly, "it is not my job to give orders to BNDES."[79] Even departments within the Banco do Brasil had certain independence. Rischbieter reports with frustration that even though directors of the Banco do Brasil and its foreign trade office, CACEX, were appointed directly by the president, CACEX "made policy on its own; this added up to complete lack of organization within the government."[80]

State governments were also fiscally autonomous thanks to existence of state banks with virtually automatic funding from the central government. Finally the CMN, which was designed to be a single overarching monetary authority, was largely a "ministerial assembly with elements of corporative representation."[81] It was too politicized to function well as a central monetary authority.[82]

Former government officials interviewed about stabilization failures between 1979 and 1984 frequently cited decentralized monetary and fiscal control as a problem. Former Central Bank official José Júlio Senna stressed the lack of centralized fiscal control, insufficient Central Bank autonomy, and recalls the impression made by Sargent's 1980 seminar in Rio which highlighted how creating an independent central bank was central to ending all hyperinflations of the twentieth century.[83] Central Bank director Langoni resigned in September 1983 citing institutional problems, namely, lack of Central Bank monetary control and authority. It was virtually impossible he claimed, despite being the first to publish the previously secret monetary budget in 1982, to calculate the government deficit.[84] Simonsen spoke of the need for a central bank not committed primarily "to covering [financial] holes."[85] Delfim noted that having an independent Central Bank would have helped implement stabilization.[86] Central Bank official Claudio Haddad says that the autonomous role of the Banco do Brasil was a problem, as was the independent spending authority of the CMN and BNDES.[87]

Generalizing from the 1979–84 stabilization failure

Detailed study of the 1979–84 reform period suggests the primary importance of two variables: state institutions and the governing party's political vulnerability to domestic antistabilization constituencies. Because international creditors' potential domestic allies were limited by relatively weak financial control institutions, general international conditions put stabilization on the agenda but could not ensure implementation.[88] Weak financial control institutions and the political vulnerability of government leaders to antistabilization interest groups appear to play a role in virtually every case of failed implementation of stabilization in Brazilian economic history both before and after the 1979 to 1984 period.

A brief review of the causes of failure in the stabilization attempts outlined in section 2 supports this claim. In June 1953 Vargas's first finance minister, Horacio Lafer, abandoned his stabilization effort and resigned because he could not gain the cooperation of the president of the Banco do Brasil.[89] His replacement, Oswaldo Aranha, attempted stabilization, hoping to include a reorganization of the finance ministry "in order to increase central direction" in his efforts. This was in keeping with the Joint US–Brazilian Commission which had concluded that Brazil's ability to control inflation "was weakened by the lack of an effective, independent and nonpolitical body entrusted with the supervision of the banking system and the coordination of monetary and credit policy."[90] Unfortunately such institutional change would have taken more time than Finance Minister Aranha or President Vargas had before the political and economic situation became unmanageable.

To understand the roots of this political time pressure we must briefly review the history of the Vargas government. Vargas, who had ruled Brazil under a dictatorship from 1937 to 1945, won the presidency in free elections in 1950 and was determined to prove himself a successful democratic leader. Most importantly this meant trying to avoid giving the military a temptation to intervene. The Brazilian party system was still very weak. Vargas was elected in 1950 for a normal five-year term with a 49 percent plurality and help from an extremely diverse coalition including the rural elite-based PDS; the labor party, PTB (Patido Trabalhista Brasilieiro); PSP (Partido Social Progressista; personal machine of populist politician Adhemar); and even a minority group within the Uniãs Democrática Naçional (UDN), a party linked to one army faction and united largely around opposition to Vargas' dictatorial populism. The UDN tried to block Vargas' inauguration on a constitutional technicality, but a military tribunal rejected the appeal. No party had a majority in congress and most were represented in Vargas' cabinet. The military was a neutral force, at best. Vargas pursued a strategy of reconciliation trying to win full UDN support. This merely succeeded in alienating the PTB and other left-leaning allies. He tried to combine nationalism and orthodoxy in his economic policy in order to maintain the support of as many classes or sectors as possible. But this strategy could not control rising inflation. To buy political cover for a stabilization program Vargas appointed Goulart, a politician with a reputation for collaborating with communists and militant labor leaders, as his labor minister in June 1953. By January 1954 rising prices led workers to the streets to demand an increase in the minimum wage. Goulart recommended a 100 percent increase and did little to restrain militant labor activity. This engendered a rebellion from junior army officers protesting their low wages and articulating widespread middle class resentment of the working class. This emboldened the UDN. Vargas dismissed Goulart but eventually decided on the wage increase anyway, hoping that labor support would pull him out of this political tailspin. The military, supported by the UDN, demanded Vargas' resignation and he responded with suicide.

Turning from the first of Brazil's failed post-World War II stabilization efforts to the second, led by Eugênio Gudin during the administration of Vargas' vice-president and successor, Café Filho, we also see the role of weak state financial control and politicians' tenure insecurity. Skidmore notes that "the Finance Ministry simply did not have under its control total government expenditure (there were semi-autonomous government agencies whose budgets could not be cut back by the Finance Ministry at short notice)."[91] Skidmore also suggested that Café Filho's 1954–5 stabilization effort failed in part because he perceived himself as a caretaker president with too little time or authority to carry out large-scale policy changes.[92]

Under Kubitschek in 1959, during Brazil's third post-World War II stabilization episode, the president of the Banco do Brasil refused to cut industrial credit, severely jeopardizing the finance minister's ability to implement his stabilization plans. Furthermore, credit restrictions met with protest from São Paulo businessmen and coffee growers.[93] Kubitschek had been elected in 1955 with only a 36 percent plurality and support from a PDS-PTB alliance. The UDN tried to block his inauguration as they had Vargas', but failed. The military staged a "preventive" coup to ensure Kubitschek could take office. Like Vargas, Kubitschek tried to campaign and govern without relying on any single party or movement. He endeavored to please as many as possible in order to preserve his reputation and possibly attain reelection in 1965 after a constitutionally mandated term out of office. He began stabilization a little over halfway through his term, calculating that he had established his popularity and could complete the stabilization effort with sufficient time to repair any political damage caused by it before leaving office.[94] But opposition from labor and industry was greater than he anticipated. Kubitschek felt forced to break off negotiations with the IMF in order to preserve his popularity and maximize his reelection potential.

Again under Quadros, government agencies and the "quasi-official" Banco do Brasil would not cooperate with stabilization and exceeded monetary targets set by the minister of finance. Again in 1961 there "were the inevitable complaints from businessmen, workers and consumers," Skidmore writes, "all of whom, although they did not disapprove of stabilization in principle, thought the particular sacrifices imposed on *them* were unfair."[95] Insecurity in his position as president, as he faced mounting opposition due – among other things – to his stabilization policies, led Quadros to abandon them and resign in 1961. Quadros had run in the 1960 elections with a UDN endorsement but tried to distance himself from the party as much as possible both during the campaign and in office. Like his predecessors he pursued a political strategy of trying to please all and alienate none. He ran as an outsider with an "antipolitician", anticorruption, anti-inefficiency stance. This left him without an organized political base when he came to power. Having included the need to curb inflation and the balance of payments deficit in order to preserve national economic autonomy in his campaign platform, Quadros felt he could politically afford quick introduction of a stabilization program.[96] Furthermore, his foreign policy, closely aligned with Cuba, provided him political cover for the stabilization program even if it raised concern among right-wing anticommunists. Nonetheless, traditional politicians were uneasy about his threats to investigate political corruption, government workers were leery of his plans to increase bureaucratic efficiency, and labor and industry opposed his stabilization plan. Before all this opposition could crystalize, Quadros resigned.

Industry, nationalist intellectuals, and trade unions also immediately mobilized against Goulart's stabilization in 1963. The National Confederation of Industry argued that credit restraint was catastrophic for industry. Automobile manufacturers were especially vocal critics of the Dantas–Furtado Plan.[97] Labor disputes rose from 741 in 1962 to over 1,000 in 1963.[98] Goulart's succession after Quadros' surprising resignation, although clearly specified in the constitution, generated a political crisis. He was installed after a ten-day interregnum during which pro- and anti-Goulart military factions debated heatedly. The pro-Goulart forces only barely won out. Goulart's position with the military made it difficult for him to refuse military wage demands. He also had to continually prove his popularity; this also made it difficult to stick to a stabilization policy which engendered labor and industry opposition.

The 1964 reforms also met with business and labor opposition. Opposition was expressed in newspapers including *Útima Hora*, *Tribuna de Imprensa*, *Correio de Manha*, *Desenvolvimento e Conjuntura*, and the journal of the National Industry Confederation. For example, right-wing journalist Carlos Lacerda started to criticize the regime's economic policy in his daily newspaper column in 1965 and in 1966 he joined with two former enemies, populist politicians Kubitschek and Goulart, in an organization pursuing both higher wages to increase internal demand and freedom from IMF restrictions. Coffee-growers were also opposed to aspects of the reform program. In particular, Campos froze the government-guaranteed coffee purchase price (cutting the real price in half in 1965) because he felt it was a great drain on government funds. But domestic opposition to stabilization in 1964–7 had less impact on politicians'/policy makers' actions because they were relatively invulnerable to political pressures which could turn them or their party out of office. Shortly after the 1964 coup, the UDN-controlled Congress approved a constitutional amendment postponing presidential elections for one year in order to give president Castelo Branco's economic team more time to make the unpopular stabilization measures work. When opposition to the regime's economic policy translated into the election of populist politicians in the October 1965 gubernatorial races, the military responded with the Second Institutional Act which made those and presidential elections indirect.

Nevertheless contenders for political office under the military regime were still vulnerable to interest group pressure. The military regime was committed to maintaining the veneer of democratic legitimacy. They chose presidential candidates partly on the basis of how convincing their claims of popular appeal were. Even though the opposition boycotted the 1966 elections, for example, Costa e Silva campaigned throughout the country. According to some analysts, the switch away from austerity by new military leadership in 1967 and 1968 reflected growing conflict between the military and industry, and thus also within the military, over orthodox economic policy.[99] The policy change also no doubt reflected diminished inflation.

Skipping to the post–1984 era, Lourdes de Sola argues that the Cruzado I stabilization took a heterodox form in order to "harmonize austerity with the demands of social sectors making up the anti-inflationary pact."[100] The governing PDS continued to be vulnerable to industrialist opposition as it tried to maintain its popularity and electoral position after the 1985 elections. Olavo Setubal, a prominent private banker, recounted a revealing story. He had been promised the position of minister of finance in the Tancredo/Sarney administration but had to settle for minister of foreign affairs because the administration feared industrialists would oppose the appointment of a banker whose natural sympathies would lie with tight money.[101]

Two former government officials engaged in the Sarney administration's stabilization efforts cited lack of presidential commitment to fighting inflation, at least partially motivated by concern over the popularity of the PDS, as a reason for stabilization failures. Former minister of planning for Sarney, José Sayad, said the Cruzado I, Cruzadinho and Cruzado II "were not undone by Congress, but we were lacking presidential support." He recounts that Sarney was unwilling to raise excise taxes, which Sayad considered crucial.[102] Daniel Dantas, who advised the government after the Cruzado I Plan was first implemented, also cited lack of presidential will, arguing that "Sarney never made cutting inflation his top priority."[103]

Another former government official argues that the Bresser Plan failed due to opposition to fiscal adjustment from Sarney, FIESP, and all ministers other than the minister of finance, who was simply too weak to prevail.[104] Economist Bacha, for example, cited the semiofficial monetary function of the Banco do Brasil as a major problem for proponents of stabilization during the Sarney administration.[105] Sayad recited a long history of lack of central bank independence and noted that he made efforts to close the *conta de movimento*.[106] Andrea Calabi, another public sector financier for Sarney, stressed budget decentralization and the independent spending authority of the CACEX and BNDES. "The principal public federal financial institutions," he writes of post–1984 heterodox stabilization efforts, "found themselves completely unprepared

for a process of fiscal and monetary austerity."[107] Roberto Fendt, who ran
CACEX during Sarney's administration, also spoke of the strength of the
institutional constraints. "CACEX was inherently illiberal," he said, "even
a liberal like me running CACEX could find himself inventing diabolical
new market restrictions."[108] Francisco "Chico" Lopes, one of the architects of the Cruzado Plan, cites the central bank's automatic fiscal bailout
function in the form of the *conta de movimento* as one of the major
obstacles to stabilization. He notes that several finance ministers, beginning with Simonsen, tried and failed to close the facility.[109] His coauthor in
formulating the Cruzado Plan, Andre Lara Resende, pushed for institutional reform, particularly closure of the *conta de movimento*, to be part of
the Cruzado Plan.[110] Later, as part of the Bresser Plan, Francisco Lopes
included transferring the federal government's budget office from the
planning ministry to the finance ministry in order to facilitate financial
control.[111]

A former government official who held various offices from 1964
through 1979 suggested, broadly speaking, that Brazil's policy making
institutions were designed for growth and that institutional change was too
slow to allow for successful economic reform.[112]

4   THE POLITICAL ECONOMY OF THE BRAZILIAN DEVELOPMENT PATH

The political explanation for the repeated failure of Brazilian stabilization
plans in terms of institutional weaknesses and interest-based opposition to
economic orthodoxy itself raises further questions. The major question
which we are finally led to is: What are the deeper economic mainsprings
of the interest-based opposition to orthodoxy?

A brief comparison of the polities and economies of Brazil with
Argentina and Peru, as they have evolved since the nineteenth century, is
instructive. Like Peru (with its large Indian population), Brazil has had a
substantial nonwhite population (the descendants of African slaves) which
has not been part of the polity. This partly explains why various social
indicators relating to health, education and social services in Brazil look
very similar to those of Peru. The poorest in both countries are nonwhite
and with no "voice" in the political process. Little has been done by the
state for their social and economic advancement.[113]

Unlike Peru, however, Brazil is a more resource- and land-abundant
country, closer in its factor endowments to Argentina.[114] Like Argentina,
Brazil too had a large influx of European immigrants at the turn of the
century. This was to meet the rising demand for labor on the booming
coffee estates. "Immigration to Sao Paulo alone rose from 13,000 in the
1870s to 609,000 in the 1890s."[115]

However, the patterns of Argentine and Brazilian economic development and growth until the Great Depression were different. This was largely due to differences in geography and climate, which led to specialization in different types of agricultural products. Argentina specialized in temperate-zone agricultural products, Brazil in tropical products, particularly coffee. As Lewis has emphasized, the product wage in producing temperate-zone agricultural products was higher than that for producing tropical products. "The price of tropical products, per man-hour of labor time, was lower than the price of wheat or wool. Tropical farmers produced less food per head than temperate farmers, and therefore received less per head for the alternative commodities which they supplied in international trade."[116] This meant that even with similar factor endowments real wages would have been expected to be higher in Argentina than Brazil. Moreover, Argentina's temperate-zone agricultural exports were increasingly diversified, which reduced "Argentina's exposure to price fluctuations for any one product."[117] This led to sustained growth in Argentina at one of the highest per capita growth rates in the world, until World War I. Brazil, by contrast, specialized in the tropical crop coffee. It rode the coffee cycle, which led to periods of high growth followed by periods of negative growth. The differing estimates surveyed in Reynolds suggest at best a very low average growth of under 1 percent per year in per capita income for Brazil over the 1863–1913 period.

The polities in Argentina and Brazil were similar and evolved along parallel lines. Both countries were under the oligarchic rule of a small elite. As a result of the growth of the export economy and the increasing size of the domestic market, industrialization began by the turn of the century in both countries and led to the slow evolution of an industrial labor force. This process continued more rapidly when both countries eventually "turned inwards" after the collapse of their primary product exports during the Great Depression.

The ensuing expansion in the urban labor force, which increasingly sought a "voice" in the polity, provided an opportunity to political entrepreneurs – Peron in Argentina, Vargas in Brazil – to challenge the old oligarchy by forging a new political coalition including the urban working class. But whereas Peron polarized the Argentine polity with his form of populism, setting rural landed interests against urban labor, Vargas in his populist attack on the old oligarchy stopped short of fomenting class war in Brazil. There was little polarization between the bourgeoisie and labor in Brazil. Thus when the coffee interests diversified into industry, the sharp distributional conflict that Peron fomented in Argentina did not occur in Brazil.[118]

By 1920 there had been very rapid urbanization in Brazil and in the industrial labor force (see tables 2.5 and 2.6). "The volume of industrial production doubled during World War I, and tripled by 1923... Two

Table 2.5   Population growth of the capitals of the major states, 1890 and 1920

State	1890	1920
Salvador	174,412	283,422
Belo Horizonte	—	55,563
Recife	111,556	238,843
Niteroi	34,269	86,238
Porto Alegre	52,421	179,263
São Paulo	64,935	579,033
Rio de Janeiro (federal capital)	552,651	1,157,873

Source: Burns (1980, p. 313).

Table 2.6   Indicators of industrialization, 1909–40

Year	Number of industrial establishments	Capital invested (1,000 contos)	Value of production (1,000 contos)	Number of employees
1907	2,988	665	669	136,000
1920	13,336	1,815	3,200	276,000
1940	70,026	12,000	25,000	1,412,000

Source: Burns (1980, p. 357).

industries, foodstuffs and textiles, accounted for nearly three-quarters of total factory production. By 1920 industrial production [had increased] nearly five-fold since 1907."[119] It was Vargas's political genius to weld these new and growing urban interests into a political multiclass coalition which challenged the political hegemony of the old "landed" oligarchy. "Concentrated in the sensitive and restive urban areas, the proletariat and middle class wielded influence and power disproportionately to their size," writes Burns. "Numerically they never constituted a majority; most Brazilians continued to live in the country side. Except for the small but powerful rural oligarchy, however, they were politically inarticulate."[120]

With the Great Depression, Brazil introduced import controls, with imports falling by about 25 percent between 1929 and 1932. The resulting import substitution that was induced was financed largely from the profits of the "coffee interests" who were politically disenfranchised during the Vargas years.[121] In the postwar period this coalition of essentially urban interest groups was incorporated into a corporatist populist state, which began with the establishment of the *Estado Novo* after Vargas's coup in 1937. This had two major objectives – to deal with the so-called "social question" concerning the urban proletariat and ensuring that industrial profits remained high.

Beginning with the various forms of social legislation developed by Vargas' minister of labor, Lindolfo Collor, in the 1930s, an important objective of the Brazilian state thereafter was "the process of the incorporation or 'cooptation' (cooptação) of the urban, and later rural, working class into a system where conflict was carefully damped down."[122] An essential element in this incorporation of the "dangerous classes" would seem to have been the desire to prevent any decline in real wages which might occur if the demand for labor was not rising rapidly enough to meet the increased supply flowing from population growth which had accelerated from about 2.3 percent in the 1930s and 1940s to 2.8 percent per annum in the 1960s. This can become a fairly acute problem in a land-abundant economy. It is to avoid this politically dangerous outcome that the basic impetus for Brazil's distinctive postwar growth path (outlined in section 1) – with an inflationary cum foreign-financed "big push" followed by a macroeconomic and debt crisis, which once controlled is followed by another "big push" – can be found.

The analytical framework which best brings out these deeper economic impulses is a Krueger–Leamer three-factor multicommodity open economy model. Thus, consider the simple model of a free-trade world depicted by the Leamer endowment triangle in figure 2.6. The three vertices of the Leamer triangle are the origins for the three factors of production – capital, labor, and land. Along the horizontal edge the capital–labor ratio rises as one moves rightward. On the left edge, the land–labor ratio rises as we move towards the land vertex. On any line emanating from one corner of the triangle, the ratio of the other two factors is the same.

Assume all goods are traded and produced with fixed coefficients. There are five manufactured goods produced by labor and capital, of increasing capital intensity whose input vectors are shown as $M_1, \ldots, M_5$ along the "labor-capital" edge of the triangle. There are two agricultural goods: A_1 which is produced only with labor and land and hence lies on the labor–land edge of the triangle, and A_2 which is more land-intensive than A_1 and also uses all three factors of production. For a given set of commodity prices, the endowment triangle can then be divided into seven "regions of diversification" (by connecting the seven input vector points and the three axis coordinates). Countries with factor endowments in the same region of diversification will have the same factor prices and produce the same commodities with vector inputs given by the relevant vertices. Given commodity prices, relative factor intensities determine factor prices in each region.

Now consider two illustrative development paths in this model. The first is that of a typical land- and capital-scarce but labor-abundant country whose endowment point E_A is on, or close to, the "labor–capital" axis. With capital accumulating faster than the growth of the labor force, assume that the country which we label *"labor-abundant"* moves up the ladder of comparative advantage with respect to manufactured goods, with rising capital intensity. Hence on this development path the wage rises and the rentals on capital and land fall.

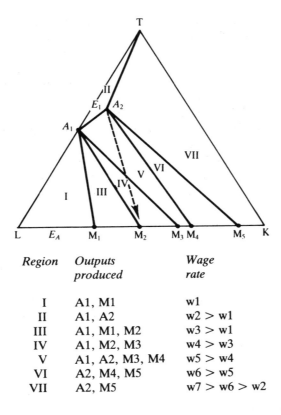

Region	Outputs produced	Wage rate
I	A1, M1	w1
II	A1, A2	w2 > w1
III	A1, M1, M2	w3 > w1
IV	A1, M2, M3	w4 > w3
V	A1, A2, M3, M4	w5 > w4
VI	A2, M4, M5	w6 > w5
VII	A2, M5	w7 > w6 > w2

Figure 2.6   Leamer endowment triangle

The second path is for a *land-abundant*, but labor- and capital-scarce country whose endowment point E_1 lies in the region of diversification II, where it produces both the relatively labor-intensive agricultural good A_1 and the land-cum-capital-intensive good A_2. Consider one possible path of development with both capital and labor growing. Suppose the path of the economy's changing factor endowment is given by the dashed line from E_1. The economy will then move from region I to VII to VI to IV. In this process it will begin to industrialize as soon as it moves into region VI, *but in the most capital-intensive* manufacture. Over time it will move into regions which require *specialization in increasingly more labor-intensive* goods. The factor price consequence of this development path will be a falling wage rate, and from the time the economy moves into region VII, rising rental rates on capital and land. The functional distributional (and *ipso facto* political) implications of the required path of wages on this stylized land-abundant open economy's development path (with a falling wage) would be very different from those of the stylized labor-abundant case (with rising wages) which are also predicted by the standard two-factor models. But note that, even though the wage might be falling in the course of the land-abundant country's development path (for some time), it will still be higher than for the labor-intensive country, until both wage paths converge on the region of *specialization* in region IV.[123]

Some indication of these differences in relative wage levels is provided by average regional wage differentials summarized in Squire (table 16).[124] The manufacturing wage relative to the sample mean of 45 developing countries (1964–72) was: South America 1.27; Central America and Caribbean 1.52; Mediterranean 0.96; Asia 0.44; Africa 0.65.[125] Though these regional categories are by no means coterminous with categories in terms of factor endowments, the gross differences in the relative wage in Latin America and Asia, for example, would reflect the difference between countries in these regions which are closer to the land- and labor-abundant categories, respectively in the Leamer triangle.

Figure 2.7 shows our estimates of the time path of Brazil's changing factor endowments between 1940 and 1987 within the Leamer triangle. The effects on factor endowments of the two big pushes is clear. In the 1940s there is a fall in the land–man ratio and a modest rise in the capital–labor ratio so the endowment point is pushed southward, into the potentially politically dangerous regions where real wages might decline. The first big push of the 1950s leads to a rise in both the land–labor and capital–labor ratios, which will have most likely moved the endowment point into high-wage regions. After a pause in the 1960s, there is another big push in the 1970s with the land–labor ratio roughly unchanged but with a doubling of the capital–labor ratio. The endowment point moves towards the capital vertex, which should have led to rising real wages. The 1980s see the "bust" and a decline in both the capital and land–labor ratios, with their ominous implications for real wages as the endowment path moves southward.

We do not have the requisite information to divide up the triangle into areas of specialization as in figure 2.6, to determine whether the motive behind the two big pushes (in the "deeper" sense of the logic underlying the evolution of the functional distribution of income in the three-factor open economy model) was to avert an otherwise declining wage path (along a counterfactual path of capital–labor ratios). However, if there was such a tendency, the argument underlying figure 2.6 suggests that the polity, besides trying to shift the path toward the capital vertex in the Leamer triangle, would also attempt to enlarge the high-wage areas of specialization artificially through protection.

This last point suggests a way of indirectly inferring whether or not a desire to avoid a potentially politically explosive falling real wage path might underlie the long-run Brazilian cycle of a "big push" with its accompanying dirigiste policies, resulting in macroeconomic instability, which after a hyperinflationary crisis necessitates the standard orthodox cure for past excesses, followed by another big push....

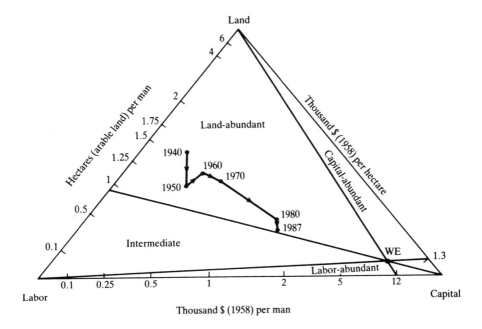

Figure 2.7 Leamer triangle for Brazil; factor endowment path (1940–87). WE = world endowment

Data:

Year	Capital/man	Land/man
1940	0.42	1.53
1950	0.51	1.21
1960	0.63	1.41
1970	1.04	1.24
1980	2.04	1.23
1987	2.02	1.03
WE	12	0.9

If we aggregate the three-factor multicommodity model into the standard two-factor–two-good model (assuming that land requires capital to be made effective) with a composite traded good (which in Brazil would be capital intensive) and a labor-intensive nontraded good, we can derive a relationship between real wage changes and those in the real exchange rate (relative price of nontraded to traded goods) and the capital–labor ratio, within an extended version of the Ricardo–Viner model of trade theory. This relationship is derived formally (including the necessary restrictions on the production function parameters to remove the so-called neoclassical ambiguity in real wage movements) in previous work.[126] It leads to a reduced-form equation which shows the time path of percentage changes in real wages (w) being determined by the percentage change in the real exchange rate (e), and the percentage change in the capital–labor ratio (k). Data on these variables which we have estimated for Brazil is charted in figure 2.8. If the lags between the impact and equilibrium effects of any exogenous change in relative commodity prices and factor supplies are z and q, respectively, and if the constant a represents a time term, and u is a random error term, we have:

$$w_t = a + \sum_{i=t}^{t-z} b_i e_i + \sum_{j=t}^{t-q} c_j k_j + u_t$$

We estimated this model for our admittedly imperfect series for w, e, and k. Using a distributed polynomial lag of 4 on both the independent variables, and with a third-degree polynomial on e, and a first-degree polynomial on k, yielded statistically significant results.[127] The estimated and actual percentage changes in real wages over the sample period 1966–84 are shown in figure 2.8. This provides some confirmation for our hypothesis that Brazil's "big push" cycle is part of the land-abundant country syndrome of avoiding possible real wage declines along its efficient development path.

Further confirmation is provided by the pattern of postwar Brazilian industrialization and its relative efficiency. Bergsman reports that, in the first phase noted above, labor-intensive industries such as textiles (set up initially after the import controls following the Great Depression, and which were further helped during the period of natural protection offered by World War II) had much higher rates of effective protection than intermediate and capital goods industries (see table 2.7).[128] Moreover, he

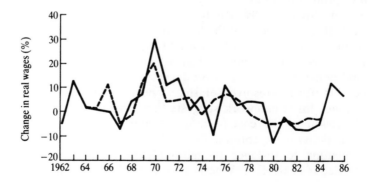

Figure 2.8 Actual (solid line) and fitted (dotted line) percentage change in real wages

Table 2.7   Distortions by industrial sector

Sectors	Protection	Subsidies and other promotion	Import substitutiion
Daddies: consumer nondurables	Very high	Little or none	Had already happened
Infants: consumer durable	Very high	Strong	Virtually complete
Intermediate goods	Low to moderate	Strong	Great
Capital goods	Low	Little	Great

Source: Bergsman (1970, p. 109).

estimates that the production of many of these relatively capital-intensive industries was socially profitable. Secondly, unlike a more labor-abundant country such as India, which followed a very similar industrial strategy, the realized rate of return on investment in Brazil over the 1950–85 period was 21 percent compared with India's 13 percent.[129] This, it would seem, was because within the three-factor framework, Brazil's development (unlike India's) was not, by and large, against its comparative advantage.

As Bergsman concluded, "What are we to make of an LDC which has efficient producers of steel, automobiles and capital goods, but many extremely inefficient textile manufacturers?"[130] The puzzle becomes less acute if we note that a land-abundant country's comparative advantage is likely to lie in capital-intensive industries. Given the difficulties in absorbing the relevant technology and the development of appropriate skills, it will be impossible to realize this comparative advantage "de novo." The development of the "easier" industries like textiles which are labor-intensive would require protection. Once the necessary industrial skills are developed, industrialization could proceed into the capital-intensive sectors in which the country has a comparative advantage. But the earlier "easier" industries would still require heavy protection to survive. The pattern of protection in table 2.7 would thus be in industrialists' interests. They would also naturally benefit from any pump-priming "big push," particularly if the real costs of the foreign financing involved were reduced by what in effect has amounted to debt repudiation! However, without further evidence, on the timing of growth in exports of capital-intensive goods and policy preferences of producers of capital-intensive goods, for example, this effort to resolve Bergsman's puzzle must remain speculative.

If accurate, this framework suggests that Brazil's policy makers have pursued growth at the cost of inflation and eschewed stabilization to prevent the polity being continually at odds with the economy (something which Argentina, for instance, though similar in resource endowments, has not succeeded in achieving). Whether this novel Brazilian tightrope act can continue in the future, unfortunately only time will tell. But if our argument is correct, even if the Collor Plan succeeds, it is more than likely that Brazil will revert to its "bad old ways." Even though the dog may have appeared to bark with the Collor Plan, in this case appearances may be deceptive!

APPENDIX 2.1

Statistical Appendix

Table 2.8 Growth, money and inflation

Year	GDPGRT[a]	M1CHG[b]	GDPDEF[c]	RLMONY[d]
1950	6.100000	35.00000	9.20000	25.800000
1951	4.700000	16.00000	18.40000	−2.400000
1952	6.000000	15.00000	9.30000	5.700000
1953	4.800000	19.00000	13.80000	5.200000
1954	6.600000	25.00000	27.10000	−2.100000
1955	7.400000	12.00000	11.80000	0.200000
1956	2.900000	22.00000	22.60000	−0.600000
1957	6.800000	32.00000	12.70000	19.300000
1958	9.100000	21.00000	12.40000	8.600000
1959	8.400000	43.00000	35.90000	7.099999
1960	8.300000	38.00000	25.40000	12.600000
1961	7.500000	51.00000	34.70000	16.300000
1962	6.100000	63.00000	50.10000	12.900000
1963	1.000000	65.00000	78.40000	−13.400000
1964	3.400000	85.00000	89.90000	−4.900002
1965	2.000000	76.00000	58.20000	17.800000
1966	6.300000	158.00000	37.90000	120.100000
1967	4.000000	43.00000	26.50000	16.500000
1968	8.900000	43.00000	26.70000	16.300000
1969	8.700000	29.00000	20.10000	8.900000
1970	9.800000	27.00000	16.30000	10.700000
1971	10.100000	32.00000	19.30000	12.700000
1972	10.800000	38.00000	19.90000	18.100000
1973	12.500000	47.00000	29.60000	17.400000
1974	7.800000	34.00000	34.50000	−0.500000
1975	5.200000	43.00000	34.00000	9.000000
1976	9.400000	37.00000	41.40000	−4.400002
1977	4.700000	38.00000	45.50000	−7.500000
1978	5.000000	42.00000	38.20000	3.799999
1979	7.100000	74.00000	54.40000	19.600000
1980	8.800000	70.00000	90.30000	−20.300000
1981	−4.400000	73.00000	108.10000	−35.100000
1982	0.600000	70.00000	105.60000	−35.600000

Table 2.8   Continued

Year	GDPGRT*a*	M1CHG*b*	GDPDEF*c*	RLMONY*d*
1983	−3.500000	100.0000	141.4000	−41.39999
1984	5.100000	205.0000	215.0000	−10.00000
1985	8.300000	343.0000	231.4000	111.60000
1986	7.600000	321.0000	143.8000	177.20000
1987	3.600000	128.0000	209.3000	−81.30000
1988	−0.300000	572.0000	684.6000	−112.60000
1989	NA	1423.0000	1782.9000	−359.90000

[a]GDPGRT, Annual percentage change in GDP at factor cost; from Maddison and
Associates (1989, Table B2).
[b]M1CHG, Percentage change in M1 was obtained up to 1953 from Kahil (1973, p. 275);
1978–86 from IMF; 1986–9 from World Bank and IFS.
[c]GDPDEF, Percentage change in GDP deflation; from Maddison and Associates (1989,
Table B2).
[d]RLMONY, M1CHG −GDPDEF

Table 2.9   Balance of payments, wages, real exchange rates and capital labor
ratios

Year	FRKGDP*a*	WAGE*b*	REXCHG*c*	CAPLAB*d*
1950	−0.700000	NA	NA	NA
1951	2.500000	NA	NA	100.6000
1952	3.100000	NA	NA	102.0000
1953	−0.100000	NA	NA	103.4000
1954	1.000000	NA	NA	104.9000
1955	0.100000	37.80000	NA	106.8000
1956	−0.100000	40.70000	NA	108.2000
1957	1.200000	43.50000	NA	109.8000
1958	1.100000	44.00000	NA	111.8000
1959	1.400000	41.10000	NA	114.9000
1960	2.100000	NA	111.1000	115.5000
1961	1.100000	43.40000	99.90000	115.0000
1962	2.600000	41.50000	103.6000	114.1000
1963	1.000000	47.40000	121.9000	115.2000
1964	−0.400000	48.40000	102.4000	119.1000
1965	−1.500000	49.00000	100.0000	122.1000
1966	0.100000	49.10000	114.5000	121.2000
1967	1.200000	46.00000	119.2000	124.0000
1968	1.600000	48.30000	115.7000	126.9000
1969	0.900000	52.00000	111.4000	128.2000
1970	1.500000	70.00000	110.6000	132.9000
1971	3.000000	78.10000	105.8000	136.5000
1972	2.900000	89.60000	100.6000	141.0000
1973	2.000000	91.10000	103.6000	146.4000
1974	6.500000	97.40000	113.3000	153.3000
1975	5.200000	89.10000	113.7000	161.4000

1976	3.900000	100.0000	123.2000	170.4000
1977	2.300000	103.6000	123.3000	178.8000
1978	3.500000	108.5000	118.7000	186.1000
1979	4.900000	113.2000	113.5000	193.8000
1980	5.400000	100.0000	102.9000	202.3000
1981	4.400000	98.5000	117.7000	213.8000
1982	5.700000	91.7000	121.8000	224.5000
1983	3.300000	85.0000	92.8000	233.5000
1984	0.000000	80.4000	90.1000	239.3000
1985	−0.100000	90.5000	NA	244.8000
1986	2.000000	97.0000	NA	251.9000
1987	0.500000	NA	NA	NA
1988	−1.200000	NA	NA	NA
1989	−0.300000	NA	NA	NA

[a]FRKGDP, Current account deficit as a percentage of GDP: 1947–60, Kahil (1973, p. 130); 1960–73, World Bank *World Tables* 1976; 1974–89, (World Bank, 1990).
[b]WAGE, Real wages in manufacturing. Index numbers derived from: 1955–65, Carvalho and Haddad (1981, p. 39); 1966–83, World Bank data (Lal and Myint, 1991); 1984–87, World Bank (1990).
[c]REXCHG, Real exchange rate. Index numbers from Wood (1988).
[d]CAPLAB, derived as shown in notes to Table 2.11.

Table 2.10 Change in capital stock

Year	KSTINC[a]	Year	KSTINC[a]
1950	NA	1970	6.400000
1951	3.500000	1971	6.600000
1952	4.300000	1972	7.200000
1953	4.300000	1973	7.700000
1954	4.300000	1974	8.600000
1955	4.700000	1975	9.200000
1956	4.200000	1976	9.500000
1957	4.400000	1977	8.800000
1958	4.700000	1978	8.000000
1959	5.700000	1979	8.000000
1960	6.200000	1980	8.300000
1961	5.600000	1981	8.000000
1962	4.800000	1982	7.300000
1963	5.800000	1983	6.300000
1964	6.000000	1984	4.800000
1965	5.200000	1985	4.600000
1966	4.500000	1986	5.200000
1967	5.000000	1987	NA
1968	5.000000	1988	NA
1969	6.100000	1989	NA

[a]KSTINC, Percentage increase in capital stock derived from data in table 2.11.

Table 2.11 Derivation of capital–labor ratio

Year	(1) Capital stock (index nos.)	(2) Gross investment	(3) Net investment	(4) KSTINC (%)	(5) LABINC (%)	(6) CAPLAB (index nos)
1950	260.00	12.80	9.20	NA		100.00
1951	269.00	16.20	11.66	3.50	2.90	100.60
1952	281.00	16.70	12.02	4.30		102.00
1953	293.00	17.30	12.46	4.30		103.40
1954	306.00	20.10	14.47	4.30		104.90
1955	321.00	18.70	13.46	4.70		106.80
1956	335.00	20.60	14.83	4.20		108.20
1957	350.00	23.00	16.56	4.40		109.80
1958	367.00	28.80	20.73	4.70		111.80
1959	388.00	33.60	24.19	5.70		114.90
1960	412.00	32.00	23.04	6.20	2.90	115.50
1961	435.00	29.00	20.88	5.60	2.70	115.00
1962	456.00	36.60	26.35	4.80		114.10
1963	482.00	40.40	29.09	5.80		115.20
1964	511.00	36.80	26.50	6.00		119.10
1965	538.00	37.00	26.64	5.20		122.10
1966	615.00	42.60	30.67	4.50		121.20
1967	646.00	45.30	32.62	5.00		124.00
1968	679.00	57.40	41.33	5.00		126.90
1969	720.00	64.20	46.22	6.10		128.20
1970	766.00	69.80	50.26	6.40	2.70	132.90
1971	816.00	81.40	58.61	6.60	3.90	136.50
1972	875.00	93.50	67.32	7.20		141.00
1973	942.00	112.90	81.29	7.70		146.40
1974	1,023.00	131.20	94.46	8.60		153.30
1975	1,117.00	147.70	106.34	9.20		161.40
1976	1,223.00	149.50	107.64	9.50		170.40
1977	1,331.00	148.10	106.60	8.80		178.80
1978	1,438.00	158.80	114.30	8.00		186.10
1979	1,552.00	178.00	128.20	8.00		193.80
1980	1,680.00	187.40	134.90	8.30	3.90	202.30
1981	1,815.00	182.90	131.70	8.00	2.30	213.80
1982	1,947.00	171.30	123.30	7.30		224.50
1983	2,070.00	138.70	99.90	6.30		233.50
1984	2,190.00	141.50	101.90	4.80		239.30
1985	2,272.00	167.10	120.30	4.60		244.80
1986	2,392.00	NA	NA	5.20	2.30	251.90

Notes
The values in this table have been derived as follows:
Maddison (1987, table 6) reports figures supplied by FIBGE (Feb. 1987) for gross increment to capital stock as percentage of 1950 GDP given in column (2), "Gross investment."

Langoni (1974) provides a benchmark estimate of the 1950 ratio of net fixed capital stock to net domestic product (at 1953 market prices) of 2.6. If the index number for real (constant price) GDP in 1950 is 100, this would yield a net fixed capital stock index number of 260 for the 1950 capital stock. This is the first entry in column (1) "Capital stock." The column (2) figures then give us the index numbers for gross capital formation, normalized as is the figure in column (1) on a 1950 GDP index base of 100.

In column (3) we have made a crude adjustment to the figures in column (2) to obtain the relevant index numbers (normalized on a 1950 GDP base of 100) for depreciation. As no figures for depreciation were available for Brazil, we have used the figure for "annual consumption of fixed capital" in India for 1970–82, of 28 percent of gross domestic capital formation, as also applicable to Brazil, as both are large countries with similar industrial structures. This yields the net investment index numbers in column (3).

The post-1950 capital stock series (index numbers normalized on a 1950 GDP base of 100) is then built up by adding each year's net investment figure from column (3) to the previous year's capital stock figure in column (1), on the perpetual inventory method.

In column (4) KSTINC (percentage increase in the capital stock) is obtained as the percentage change between the figures for two years in column (1). Column (6) is derived from columns (4) and (5).

The figures of the annual increase in labor force (LABINC) in column (5) are based on the decadal growth rates implicit in table 11.2(a) of Maddison and Associates (1989).

Table 2.12   Endowment ratios 1940–87

| (I) Years | Percentage increase | | | Percentage change | |
	capital (K) (1)	Labor (L) (2)	Land (N) (3)	K/L (4)	N/L (5)
1940–50	41.00	22.00	1.00	19.00	−21.00
1950–60	57.00	33.00	50.00	24.00	17.00
1960–70	95.00	30.00	18.00	65.00	−12.00
1970–80	142.00	46.00	45.00	96.00	−1.00
1980–87	16.00	17.00	1.00	−1.00	−16.00
(II)				K/L	N/L
1940				0.42	1.53
1950				0.51	1.21
1960				0.63	1.41
1970				1.04	1.24
1980				2.04	1.23
1987				2.02	1.03

Notes
(I) The figures in columns (1) to (3) are derived up to 1980 from table 11.2(a) in Maddison and Associates (1989). The figure in column (1) for 1980–7 is based on the estimate by D. V. Coes and M. Bianconi, cited in World Bank (1990, p. 66). Note that the figures in column (1) differ from those implicit in table 2.11. The decadal figures in this table are more reliable than the crude annual series we have derived in table 2.11. The figure in column (2) for 1980–7 is from the World Bank's *World Development Reports* and in column (3) is assumed to be the same as for 1940–50 base on the judgements contained in the World Bank report cited earlier.

Figures in column (4) are derived from column (1) −column (2); and in column (5) from column (3) − column (2).

(II) We have from Lal and Myint (1991) based on data in Leamer (1984) for the values of the capital–labor and land–labor ratios for 1960. The ratios for the remaining years are derived from columns (4) and (5) in Part (I).

NOTES

Maxfield is indebted to Daniel V. Friedheim for superb and extensive research assistance and to Barry Ames, Thomas Skidmore and the editors of this volume for comments. Lal is grateful to Messrs Roberto Campos and Bresser Pereira in particular for extensive discussions on the themes of this paper. The usual caveats apply.

1   This kind of explanation, developed in the context of economic policies such as taxation, has not been explored in the political science literature on stabilization. On state revenue maximization and tax policy, see Margaret Levi (1989). The economic analysis cited is in Lal (1987) and Lal and Myint (1991).
2   The classic political history of economic policy in Brazil is Skidmore (1967). The more recently published sequel (Skidmore, 1988) is also bound to become a classic.
3   On IMF conditionality in Brazil see Marshall et al. (1983).
4   This set a precedent for Brazil. In the decades of debt renegotiation after the Mexican moratorium of 1982 the Brazilians have more frequently broken off talks with foreign creditors than have other Latin American countries.
5   Indexation later had unintended consequences when it subsequently spread to most of the economy, including to wages. But during this first period of stabilization wage indexation demands by labor leaders were fought off.
6   Fishlow (1989, pp. 88–9).
7   Kaufman (1988) provides a good introduction to the Cruzado Plan history.
8   Interview, Yoshiaki Nakano, August 16, 1990, São Paulo.
9   Fishlow (1989, p. 86).
10 Sikkink (1991).
11 Leff (1968, p. 160).
12 Fishlow (1973).
13 Frieden (1991).
14 Fishlow (1989, pp. 86, 113).
15 The constituent base of government is one of three variables through which politics influences macroeconomic policy choice according to Haggard and Kaufman's broad study of middle-income countries. The other two are state institutions and the tenure security of politicians. The results of the Brazilian case study presented here support their findings (Haggard and Kaufman, 1990).
16 Asheshov and Reich (1980, p. 177).
17 Interview, Olavo Setubal, August 17, 1990, São Paulo.
18 From 1947 to 1962 SOEs and basic capital-intensive industry in general were the main beneficiaries of government economic policy. Kubitschek's Plano de Metas industrialization drive targeted steel, oil, and autos. The majority of lending from the state development bank, the BNDE, between 1952 and 1962, flowed to the steel and electricity sectors. From 1955 to 1961 the government channeled foreign loans to electricity, steel, auto, railroad and

airline, oil, chemical, and metallurgy industries. (Leff, 1968, pp. 40–3). Prior to the mid–1950s, promotion of these basic industries came at the expense of multinationals. However, from 1955 to 1962 MNC investment in basic industries was promoted through favorable exchange regulations, and after the mid–1960s, government policy facilitated MNC domination of consumer durables production.

Domestic capital goods production began to be favored in the late 1960s. In the first capital goods promotion phase both capital and consumer durables producers were winners. The Second National Development Plan, approved in December 1974, made it apparent that continued emphasis on capital goods production was going to cost the consumer durables sector some government support. This fueled the antistate campaign of 1975 led by entrepreneurs from the consumer durables industries and a handful of technocrats. Capital goods producers continued to support the government until the late 1970s when it became apparent that the government could not carry out the pro-capital goods sector policies of the Second National Development Plan. The pathbreaking June 1978 manifesto of business opposition was signed by entrepreneurs from the capital goods sector.

19   There is some debate over the extent of the state credit subsidy. It was at least 2–3 percent below the hypothetical equilibrium market rate.

20   Campbell (1972).

21   The impacts of inflation and stabilization on domestic financiers, and therefore their policy preferences, are less clear than those of labor, industry, or coffee growers. Despite a few periods of high profitability, private financiers' activities and income were restricted, relative to other countries and to their full potential, by the extent of government dominance of credit markets. Before 1964 usury laws severely restricted private financiers' profits. However, they benefited from the 1964 financial reforms, from financial indexing introduced in the mid–1960s, from speculation and arbitrage between subsidized and free portions of the financial market in the 1970s, and, ironically, from credit restrictions in the early 1980s. Whatever their interests, compared with domestic bankers in some other Latin American countries, Brazilian private-sector financiers' economic base and political influence were limited.

Roughly speaking, peasants and traditional small-scale agricultural enterprises and low-technology, small-scale manufacturers have always been losers in Brazil's economic development.

22   Wells (1979).

23   Maxfield (1990).

24   Grindle (1989, p. 46).

25   An excellent example of this type of argument applied to Latin America is Ames (1987).

26   Skidmore (1988, p. 59).

27   Stephan Haggard (1990). Ironically in the Brazilian case, Delfim Netto correlated authoritarian leadership with inflation. "The military is trained to spend," he said. Interview, August 14, 1990, Rio de Janeiro.

28   Grindle (1989, p. 29).

29   Good summaries of policy from 1979 through the mid–1980s include: Lamounier and Moura (1986); Fishlow (1989); and Bacha (1983).

30   In mid-January 1980 Rischbieter predicted a $4 billion balance of payments deficit when Delfim Netto claimed there would be no deficit. Rischbieter also sent a letter directly to Figueiredo expressing concern about the country's untenable balance of payments situation.
31   Quoted in Asheshov and Reich (1980, p. 176).
32   Bacha (1983, p. 329).
33   Real interest rates rose from −22 per cent in the second quarter of 1980 to 47 per cent a year later. Ames (1987, p. 207).
34   Bacha (1983, p. 330).
35   1981 was the first year since 1942 that Brazilian GDP did not grow.
36   Lamounier and Moura (1986, p. 174).
37   Bacha (1983, p. 328). Delfim and Galvêas suggested that at least one international pressure in 1979 and 1980 worked in the opposite direction. They claimed that they were ready to begin privatizing but the 1979 oil shock forced them to continue an interventionist strategy. Interviews, August 6, 1990, Rio de Janeiro and August 14, 1990, São Paulo.
38   *Veja*, December 12, 1981, p. 129. Delfim's Minister of Finance Ernane Galvêas and Delfim himself said that international bankers' support was of no help in the internal debate. "They convinced no one." Interviews, August 6, 1990, Rio de Janeiro and August 14, 1990, São Paulo.
39   *Veja*, October 5, 1983, p. 100.
40   *Veja*, September 28, 1983, p. 26.
41   *Veja*, November 2, 1983, p. 99.
42   *Latin America Regional Report,* August 7, 1981, p. 4; and *Veja*, June 17, 1981, p. 114. In 1983 Banco Itau reported its earnings in 1983 were up 350 per cent over the previous year (see *Veja*, March 28, 1983, p. 104.) The stock market boomed because compulsory investment rules for pension plans gave it a guaranteed source of funds.
43   Although supportive of the military government, industrialists had been at the forefront of popular demands for political opening in part because they hoped to gain more control over economic policy making. See Maxfield (1989) and Cardoso (1986).
44   The definitive book on Brazilian corporatism is Schmitter (1971). Research conducted in the 1960s led Schmitter to conclude that corporatism was breaking down and that consultation between government technocrats and new industry associations and individual entrepreneurs was growing. Skidmore and Dreifuss provide evidence that several noncorporatist business associations played an important role in organizing opposition to the Goulart government in the early 1960s and influenced economic policy making during the Castelo Branco regime (Skidmore, 1988, p. 23; Dreifuss, 1986).
45   Cardoso (1986, p. 140) and Dye and de Souza e Silva (1978, p. 89).
46   Carlos Lafer (1975).
47   Dye and de Souza e Silva (1978, p. 91).
48   Payne (1990) and Boschi (1978).
49   Interview, Luis Eulalio de Bueno Vidigal Filho, August 15, 1990, São Paulo.
50   Interview, Olavo Setubal, August 17, 1990, São Paulo.
51   Bacha (1983, p. 336).
52   Of course in a general sense Delfim's popularity was due to his association with the 1968–73 industrial boom (Fishlow 1989; Carneiro, 1987).

53 FIESP has over 100 sectoral affiliates, including among the largest, ABDIB for capital goods producers, ABINEE for electronic and electrical goods producers and ABIMAQ for machinery producers.
54 Figueiredo should 'democratize' economic policy, they said. *Veja*, December 17, 1980, p. 108.
55 This statement originated with a particularly radical group within FIESP whom the organization's president, Vidigal, was unwilling/unable to restrain. Vidigal himself had recently been angered by a government decision to import railroad train components at a time when the domestic industry, in which Vidigal had a stake, suffered with 40% idle capacity. Signatories included Antônio Ermirio de Morães (Votorantim Group), Claudio Bardella (Bardella Group), Jose Midlín (Metal Leve) and Luis Carlos Bresser Pereira (director of the Pão de Açucar Group and a well-known economist). *Latin America Weekly Report*, January 16, 1981, p. 7.
56 The first was a survey by *Exame*. The second was a two-stage survey by *Gazeta Mercantil* of 15,000 business people asked to name representative business leaders. The opinion survey was of the 106 leaders most frequently named. *Latin America Regional Report*, May 26, 1981, p. 1.
57 *Veja* June 17, 1981, p. 114. Interview, Luis Vidigal, August 15, 1990, São Paulo.
58 *Veja*, August 31, 1983, pp. 3–6 and 36.
59 Singer (1989).
60 *Veja*, September 28, 1983, p. 102.
61 Skidmore (1988, p. 213).
62 Pang (1989).
63 IMF is abbreviated FMI in Portuguese; the placards changed the spelling of Delfim's name to create a pun. *Veja*, June 22, 1982, pp. 100–3.
64 *Veja*, March 2, 1983, p. 68.
65 *Veja*, July 18, 1984, pp. 20–1.
66 Skidmore (1988, pp. 226–7).
67 Interview, August 6, 1990, Rio de Janeiro.
68 Interview, Carlos Haddad, August 14, 1990, São Paulo.
69 *Veja*, May 5, 1982, pp. 128–9.
70 *Veja*, November 17, 1980, p. 140.
71 *Gazeta Mercantil*, February 28, 1985, p. 3. Bacha and Malan claim that the Brazilian government asked US President Reagan to postpone a trip to Brasilia until after the elections in order to avoid political fallout. (Bacha and Malan, 1989).
72 Interview, August 14, 1990, São Paulo.
73 Interview, Affonso Pastore, August 15, 1990, São Paulo. In fairness to Brazilian legislators, in the context of political opening and public pressure for direct elections in the *direitas já* campaign, Congresspeople were under considerable political pressure which limited their maneuverability if they hoped to remain in office. See the interview with a congressional member in *Veja*, May 2, 1984, pp. 5–8.
74 Ibid.
75 Interview, August 10, 1990, Rio de Janeiro.
76 Interview, August 9, 1990, Curitiba (by telephone).
77 *Veja*, January 13, 1982, p. 79.

78   *Veja*, May 30, 1984, p. 100.
79   *Veja*, April 7, 1982, p. 115. Of course there were limits to the independence of the BNDES and other agencies and ministries. BNDES president, Luis Sande, for example, was fired when he clashed directly with Delfim in 1983. CACEX director Moreira lost a battle with Delfim in 1982 and resigned under pressure. In other cases Delfim was outmaneuvered. When the Central Bank's director of internal debt clashed with Delfim and resigned in January 1983, Delfim tried to impose a successor over Central Bank head Langoni's wishes and Langoni simply abolished the position. (Interview, Carlos Haddad, August 14, 1990, São Paulo.)

Another example of lack of central financial control related to the BNDES concerns the Finsocial program created in July 1982. This was effectively a 0.5 percent tax on business meant to finance BNDES social spending. Reportedly only half of its budget went to earmarked social programs while the other half financed the general government deficit. (*Veja*, October 24, 1984, p. 124.)

BNDES financing comes primarily from mandatory contributions to the PIS-PASEP employee insurance funds.

80   Interview, August 9, 1990, Curitiba (by telephone). In fact, for a long time the head of the Banco do Brasil was "indicated" by agroexporters from the northeast.
81   Interview, Carlos Langoni, August 10, 1990, Rio de Janeiro. Historically the CMN played more of a role in allocating credit and coordinating public investment programs than in controlling monetary expansion (Mendonça de Barros and Graham, 1978). In the 1980s the CMN was headed by the Minister of Finance and made up of four other ministers, eight chairmen of federal financial institutions (including the BNDE, the Banco do Brasil and the Central Bank), and eight private "experts" appointed by the minister of finance. Several observers have claimed that business participation made the CMN a cumbersome, "politicized" institution. Disputes within the CMN have occasionally become public as one or the other business member feels pushed out. Abilio dos Santos Diniz, for example, left the CMN in 1984 in a dispute with Finance Minister Galvêas and Vidigal left in 1987 when he differed with Finance Minister Funaro. (On Diniz leaving see: *Veja*, April 18, 1984, pp. 3 and 6.)
82   Interview, Luis Vidigal, August 15, 1990, São Paulo. Interview, Carlos Haddad, August 14, 1990, São Paulo. Ellis (1969).
83   Interview, August 7, 1990, Rio de Janeiro.
84   Interview, August 10, 1990, Rio de Janeiro. The immediate issue leading to Langoni's resignation was an IMF Letter of Intent which he felt was unrealistic.
85   *Veja*, November 7, 1984, pp. 116–7.
86   Interview, August 14, 1990, São Paulo.
87   Interview, August 14, 1990, São Paulo.
88   Reformers themselves did not see ideology playing a strong role in explaining the failure of orthodoxy. This is consistent with Schneider's in-depth study of economic policy making in Brazil. He notes a "developmentalist mentality" which is goal-oriented, i.e., pragmatic more than ideological. This is the basis, he argues, for the lack of coherence of liberalizing forces. "Cutting any one program or firm pits a broad, diffuse coalition based on principles against

a small group of intense material interests" who tend to win out. (Schneider, 1987). The relative unimportance of ideology is evident in Delfim's offhand statement that all Brazilian economists, himself included, have shared the ideology of Eugenio Gudin who was an outspoken proponent of orthodoxy and executive director of the IMF. Needless to say, Delfim's policies in the 1979–84 period, a mixture of Southern Cone international monetarism, standard IMF fare, and Brazilian interventionism, were considerably more heterodox than Gudin would have liked (Skidmore, 1967, pp. 88, 159; Furtado, 1984). The role of ideology in explaining the policies described above is at best ambiguous. Further cross-national and cross-temporal research would be necessary in order to make a definitive statement.

89 Skidmore (1967) cites Lafer's resignation speech in *O Estado de São Paulo*, June 19, 1953.
90 Joint Brazil–US Economic Development Commission (1954).
91 Skidmore (1967, p. 161).
92 Skidmore (1967, p. 161).
93 Marshall et al. (1983, p. 299).
94 Skidmore (1967. p. 175).
95 Skidmore (1967, p. 195).
96 Quadros' talk of controlling inflation and the balance of payments deficit was part of his "anti-establishment" rhetoric. He ran a "throw-the-bastards-out" campaign that was ideologically opaque and appealed to no identifiable interest groups other than political outsiders. There was no obvious "anti-inflation" constituency to appeal to, in part because the most likely center of a stabilization coalition, private bankers, were politically and economically weak.
97 Skidmore (1967, p. 242).
98 Lara Resende (1982). That both industry and labor resisted stabilization policies in 1963 casts doubt on O'Donnell's thesis that Brazil's 1964 turn to bureaucratic authoritarianism responded in part to the threat that rising wages posed to industry.
99 Faria (1988).
100 Sola (1988).
101 Interview, Olavo Setubal, August 17, 1990, São Paulo.
102 Interview, August 16, 1990, São Paulo.
103 Interview, August 8, 1990, Rio de Janeiro.
104 Interview, Yoshiaki Nakano, August 16, 1990, São Paulo.
105 Interview, August 8, 1990, Rio de Janeiro.
106 Interview, August 6, 1990, Rio de Janeiro.
107 Calabi and Pullen (1990).
108 Interview, August 9, 1990, Rio de Janeiro.
109 Interview, August 7, 1990, Rio de Janeiro.
110 Interview, August 16, 1990, São Paulo.
111 Interview, August 7, 1990, Rio de Janeiro.
112 Interview, João Paulo dos Reis Velloso, August 9, 1990, Rio de Janeiro. He also noted that in 1964 the military ignored a congressional mandate to make the Central Bank president's term a guaranteed eight years.
113 In Brazil even though transfer payments have "risen between 1949 and 1973 from 3.1 percent to 8.9 percent of GDP, reflecting the emergence of a

modern social insurance system," and the social security system expanded very rapidly in the 1970s, covering 93 percent of the population in 1975 as compared with 27 percent in 1970, Maddison's recent study concluded "overall, it would seem that the tax-transfer system has had a regressive impact" (Reynolds, 1985, p. 98; Mesa-Lago, 1981; Maddison and Associates, 1989).

114   Lal and Myint (1991).
115   Reynolds (1985, p. 93).
116   Lewis (1970).
117   Reynolds (1985, p. 86).
118   This point was made forcefully by Roberto Campos in a personal interview.
119   E. Bradford Burns (1980, p. 356).
120   Burns (1980, p. 414).
121   Burns(1980,p. 423).
122   P. Flynn (1978).
123   It might seem paradoxical that, whilst the *economy's* capital–labor ratio is rising, it is falling in manufacturing. But remember that the rate of growth of labor for the *economy* is not the same as in *manufacturing*. Then, it is possible for the agricultural labor force to grow more slowly (because of fixed land) than for the economy as a whole, thereby allowing and requiring the labor force in the manufacturing sector to grow more rapidly than for the economy as a whole. Thus a rising capital–labor ratio for the economy as a whole can be associated with a falling capital–labor ratio in manufacturing. Of course, there will be some rate of capital growth at which the capital–labor ratio for manufacturing will also be rising along with that for the economy as a whole, and this paradoxical development path would not occur.
124   Squire (1987).
125   The countries included were: Chile, Peru, Brazil, Argentina, Guyana, Ecuador, Trinidad, Nicaragua, Jamaica, Barbados, Panama, Puerto Rico, Dominican Republic, Honduras, Venezuela, El Salvador, Guatemala, Mexico, Columbia, Turkey, Algeria, Cyprus, Egypt, Korea, Taiwan, Sri Lanka, Burma, Vietnam, India, Thailand, Singapore, Philippines, Pakistan, Kenya, Tanzania, Zambia, Uganda, Rhodesia, Ghana, Malawi, Mauritius, Sierra Leone, and Nigeria.
126   Lal (1986).
127   The relevant statistics for the regression from the 1966–84 period are: $R^2=0.51$, $F=2.06$, DWS$=2.4$.
128   Bergsman (1970).
129   Lal (1990).
130   Bergsman (1970, p. 150).

REFERENCES

Ames, Barry 1987: *Poltical Survival: Politicians and Public Policy in Latin America*, Berkeley: University of California Press.
Asheshov, Nicholas and Reich, Cary 1980: "Has Delfim Worked His Last

Miracle?" *Institutional Investor*, August, 175–93.

Bacha, Edmar L. 1983: "Vicissitudes of Recent Stabilization Attempts in Brazil and the IMF Alternative," in John Williamson (ed.), *IMF Conditionality*, Washington, DC: Institute for International Economics.

Bacha, Edmar L. and Malan, Pedro S. 1989: "Brazil's Debt: From the Miracle to the Fund," in Alfred Stepan (ed.), *Democratizing Brazil: Problems of Transition and Consolidation*, Oxford: Oxford University Press, p. 132.

Bergsman, J. 1970: *Brazil*, Oxford: Oxford University Press for OECD.

Boschi, Renato Raul 1978: "National Industrial Elites and the State in Post-1964 Brazil," PhD dissertation, University of Michigan.

Burns, E. Bradford 1980: *A History of Brazil*, 2nd ed., New York: Columbia University Press.

Calabi, Andrea Sandro and Pullen, Pedro 1990: "Finanças Públicas Federais: Aspectos Institucionais, Evolução Recente e Perspectivas," mimeo, July, p. 4.

Campbell, Gordon 1972: *Brazil Struggles for Development*, London: Charles Knight & Co., pp. 108–9.

Cardoso, Fernando H. 1986: "Entrepreneurs and the Transition Process: The Brazilian Case," in Guillermo O'Donnell, Philippe C. Schmitter, and Laurence Whitehead (eds.), *Transitions from Authoritarian Rule*, Baltimore: Johns Hopkins University Press.

Carneiro, Dionisio Dias 1987: "Long-Run Adjustment, the Debt Crisis and the Changing Role of Stabilization Policies in the Recent Brazilian Experience," in Rosemary Thorp and Laurence Whitehead (eds.), *Latin American Debt and the Adjustment Crisis*, Pittsburgh: University of Pittsburgh Press, p. 36.

Carvalho, J. L. and Haddad, C. L. S. 1981: "Foreign Trade Strategies and Employment in Brazil," in A.O. Krueger et al. (eds.), *Trade and Employment in Developing Countries I – Individual Studies*, Chicago: NBER.

Dreifuss, Rene 1986: *1964: A conquista do estado*, Rio de Janeiro: Vozes.

Dye, David and de Souza e Silva, Carlos Eduardo 1978: "A Perspective on the Brazilian State," *Latin American Research Review*, 14(2).

Ellis, Howard S. 1969: "Corrective Inflation in Brazil, 1964–1966," in Howard S. Ellis and Lincoln Gordon (eds.), *The Economy of Brazil*, Los Angeles: University of California Press.

Faria, Hugo Presgrave de A. 1988: "Macroeconomic Policymaking in a Crisis Environment: Brazil's Cruzado Plan and Beyond," in Julian M. Chacel, Pamela S. Falk and David V. Fleischer (eds.), *Brazil's Economic and Political Future*, Boulder, CO: Westview Press, p. 43.

Fishlow, Albert 1973: "Some Reflections on Post-1964 Brazilian Economic Policy," in Alfred Stepan (ed.), *Authoritarian Brazil*, New Haven: Yale University Press, p. 83.

Fishlow, Albert 1989: "A Tale of Two Presidents: The Political Economy of Crisis Management," in Alfred Stepan (ed.), *Democratizing Brazil: Problems of Transition and Consolidation*, Oxford: Oxford University Press.

Flynn, P. 1978: *Brazil – A Political Analysis*, Boulder, CO: Westview Press, p. 100.

Frieden, Jeffrey A. 1991: *Debt, Development, Democracy: Modern Political Economy and Latin America, 1965–1985*, Princeton: Princeton University Press.

Furtado, Celso 1984: *No to Recession and Unemployment*, London: Third World Foundation.

Grindle, Merilee S. 1989: "The New Political Economy: Positive Economics and Negative Politics," Development Discussion Paper No. 311, Cambridge: Harvard Institute for International Development.

Haggard, Stephan 1990: *Pathways from the Periphery*, Ithaca: Cornell University Press, p. 263.

Haggard, Stephan and Kaufman, Robert 1990: "The Political Economy of Inflation and Stabilization in Middle-Income Countries," PRE Working Paper, WPS 444, Washington, DC: Country Economics Department, The World Bank.

IBGE 1985: *Anuario Estatistico 1984*, Rio de Janeiro: IBGE, p. 374.

Joint Brazil–US Economic Development Commission 1954: *The Development of Brazil*, Washington, DC: Institute of Inter-American Affairs, Foreign Operations Administration, p. 42.

Kahil, R. 1973: *Inflation and Economic Development in Brazil 1946–1963*, Oxford: Clarendon Press.

Kaufman, Robert R. 1988: *The Politics of Debt in Argentina, Brazil and Mexico*, Berkeley: University of California Institute of International Studies.

Lafer, Carlos 1975: *O Sistema Politico Brasileiro*, São Paulo: Editora Perspectiva, pp. 113–14.

Lal, Deepak 1986: "Stolper-Samuelson-Rybczynski in the Pacific," *Journal of Development Economics*, 21 (1), 181–204.

Lal, Deepak 1987: "The Political Economy of Economic Liberalization," *World Bank Economic Review*, 1 (2), 273–299.

Lal, Deepak 1990: "World Savings and Growth in Developing Countries," *Revista di Politica Economia*, 53 (12).

Lal, Deepak and Myint, H. 1991: "The Political Economy of Poverty, Equity and Growth," mimeo, London: University College.

Lamounier, Bolivar and Moura, Alkimar, R. 1986: "Economic Policy and Political Opening in Brazil," in Jonathan Hartlyn and Samuel A. Morley (eds.), *Latin American Political Economy: Financial Crisis and Political Change*, Boulder, CO: Westview Press.

Langoni, C. G. 1974: *As Causas do Crescimento Economico do Brasil*, Rio de Janeiro: APEC.

Lara Resende, Andre 1982: "A política brasileira de estabilização: 1963/1968," *Pesquisa e Planejamento Económico*, 12 (3) (December), 769–70.

Leamer, E. 1984: *Sources of International Comparative Advantage*, Cambridge, Mass.: MIT Press.

Leff, Nathaniel H. 1968: *Economic Policy-Making and Development in Brazil, 1947–1964*, New York: Wiley.

Levi, Margaret 1989: *Of Rule and Revenue*, Berkeley: University of California Press.

Lewis, W. A. 1970: *Tropical Development*, London: Allen and Unwin, p. 42.

Maddison, A. 1987: "Twin Study of Brazil and Mexico – Comparative Graphs and Statistical Tables," mimeo.

Maddison, A. and Associates 1989: *The Political Economy of Poverty, Equity and Growth: Brazil and Mexico*, Oxford: Oxford University Press for the World Bank.

Marshall, Jorge, Mardones S., Mose Luis, and Marshall L., Isabel 1983: "IMF Conditionality: The Experiences of Argentina, Brazil and Chile," in John

Williamson (ed.), *IMF Conditionality*, Washington, DC: Institute for International Economics.

Maxfield, Sylvia 1989: "National Business, Debt-Led Growth, and Political Transition in Latin America," in Barbara Stallings and Robert Kaufman (eds.), *Debt and Democracy in Latin America*, Boulder, CO: Westview Press.

Maxfield, Sylvia 1990: *Governing Capital: International Finance and Mexican Politics*, Ithaca: Cornell University Press.

Mendonça de Barros, José Roberto and Graham, Douglas 1978: "The Brazilian Economic Miracle Revisted," *Latin American Research Review*, 13 (2), 27.

Mesa-Lago, C. 1981: *Employment Policy in Developing Countries*, Oxford: Oxford University Press, p. 86.

Pang, Eul-Soo 1989: "Debt, Adjustment and Democratic Cacophony in Brazil," in Barbara Stallings and Robert Kaufman (eds.), *Debt and Democracy in Latin America*, Boulder CO: Westview Press, p. 130.

Payne, Leigh Ann 1990: "The Political Attitudes and Behavior of Brazilian Industrial Elites," PhD dissertation, Yale University.

Reynolds, L. G. 1985: *Economic Growth in the Third World, 1850–1980*, New Haven: Yale University Press.

Schmitter, Philippe C. 1971: *Interest Conflict and Political Change in Brazil*, Stanford: Stanford University Press.

Schneider, Ben Ross 1987: "Framing the State: Economic Policy and Political Representation in Post-Authoritarian Brazil," in John D. Wirth and Edson de Oliveira Nunes (eds.), *State and Society in Brazil: Continuity and Change*, Boulder, CO: Westview Press, p. 224.

Sikkink, Kathryn 1991: *Ideas and Institutions: Developmentalism in Brazil and Argentina*, Ithaca, NY: Cornell University Press.

Singer, Paul 1989: "Democracy and Inflation, in the Light of the Brazilian Experience," in William Canak (ed.), *Lost Promises: Debt, Austerity and Development in Latin America*, Boulder CO: Westview Press, p. 37.

Skidmore, Thomas E. 1967: *Politics in Brazil 1930–1964*, New York: Oxford University Press.

Skidmore, Thomas E. 1988: *The Politics of Military Rule in Brazil, 1964–1985*, New York: Oxford University Press.

Sola, Lourdes 1988: "The Political Constraints to Heterodox Shock in Brazil: 'Técnicos,' 'Políticos,' and Democracy," paper presented at the American Political Science Association Annual Meeting, Washington, DC, September 1–4, p. 10.

Squire, L. 1987: *Employment Policy in Developing Countries*, Oxford: Oxford University Press.

Wells, John R. 1979: "Brazil and the Post-1973 Crisis in the International Economy," in Rosemary Thorp and Laurence Whitehead (eds.) *Inflation and Stabilization in Latin America*, London: Macmillan, p. 249.

Wood, A. 1988: "Global Trends in Real Exchange Rates 1960 to 1984," *World Bank Discussion Papers*, No. 35, Washington, DC: World Bank.

World Bank 1990: *Economic Stabilisation with Structural Reforms*, Washington, DC: Brazil Department, World Bank.

3

The Political Economy of Economic Adjustment: Chile, 1973–90
Barbara Stallings and Philip Brock

As the last decade of the twentieth century begins, Chile appears to be in a uniquely favorable position within Latin America – and perhaps even the Third World. After completing a profound, but tumultuous, process of economic reforms, the country now enjoys relative stability with respect to its fiscal balance, external accounts, and rate of inflation. During the years between 1985 and 1992, the economy's annual growth rate of gross domestic product averaged a respectable 5–6 percent, and Chile's exports have expanded and diversified. The country's return to democracy in 1990 has given political actors a new flexibility and ability to compromise on social policies. Chile would appear to have many lessons to offer to other nations, and many supporters of the Chilean reforms suggest exactly that.

To others, Chile's lessons appear more problematic. Chile arrived at its current state only after 16 years of a repressive military dictatorship. In the first three years of the government, several thousand people were killed, thousands more were tortured and jailed, and tens of thousands were exiled from the country. In later years, selective use of torture, intimidation, and internal exile to remote villages was employed to stifle opposition to the government. Throughout the period Chile's institutions of political participation were suspended. In addition to concerns regarding the political context of the economic reforms, the favorable quantitative indicators measuring Chile's growth mask social and economic problems that caution against an unquestioning embrace of the new model. Skewed income distribution, relatively low savings and investment rates, and vulnerability of nontraditional exports to swings in the real exchange rate are among the serious obstacles to future economic growth. Focusing on these latter topics leads to a different view about the relevant lessons of the Chilean reforms.

Not surprisingly, then, the Chilean experience remains controversial. Myth and ideology surround accounts of the left-wing government under Salvador Allende (1970–3) and the right-wing government under Augusto

Pinochet (1973–90). Indeed, we ourselves have substantially differing views about the interpretation of Chile's history in the 1970s and 1980s, as a perusal of our previous work and affiliations within Chile indicates.[1] We share, however, a belief that there is value in trying to move beyond the myths to see where the real disagreements lie. Although we have written this chapter with one "voice," we found that writing separate conclusions helped us to emphasize the ambiguous nature of the lessons that one can draw from Chile's economic reforms.

The principal focus of the chapter is the economic reforms of the military government, in particular trade liberalization and privatization. Although far from the only areas of reform in Chile, they are arguably the most important. In addition, these are two of the major areas of reform being tried in other Third World countries in the 1990s. Before looking at the liberalization and privatization processes, however, several other topics are treated: the Allende period, which provided the essential background for the military policies; the new political setting and key actors in place during the military period itself; and an overview of the "Chilean model" to see how liberalization and privatization were related to other policies. After these introductory sections, the liberalization and privatization experiences will be examined. The chapter concludes by discussing our differing interpretations of the lessons from the Chilean experience and implications for the future.

1 BACKGROUND: THE ALLENDE GOVERNMENT (1970–3)

In the 1950s, it became clear that Chile faced a series of political and economic choices. The left–center alliance that had governed the country since the 1930s, and its favored strategy of import-substituting industrialization, had both lost their dynamism. There was no agreement on an alternative, and three possible options were tried in turn during the 1958–73 period.

First was a rightist coalition under Jorge Alessandri (1958–64), which followed traditional orthodox policies oriented towards business. Nevertheless, the state maintained an important role in support of the private sector and protection was significant. Alessandri was succeeded by a centrist government under Eduardo Frei and the Christian Democrats (1964–70). The Frei administration increased the role of the state in an attempt to modernize the economy and society and undertook an agrarian reform and partial nationalization of the copper industry. The political effect of this middle-of-the-road approach was to increase polarization, as some groups thought change was going too rapidly and others criticized its slow pace. Accordingly, the strength of the center eroded, and the left won the 1970 presidential election by a small plurality. Allende and his Popular

Unity alliance of Socialist, Communist, and other leftist parties took office in late 1970.[2]

The Popular Unity had two types of economic goals. One was to redistribute income toward labor and poorer groups in general. This aim was to be achieved through increased government expenditure, wages, and taxes. The second goal was to make major structural changes in the economy to prepare the country for a future transition to socialism. Hundreds of industrial firms were taken over and added to existing state firms to create the Social Property Area. The main copper mines were expropriated from the US-based Kennecott and Anaconda corporations. Virtually all private banks were bought through purchase of shares from individual owners. Agricultural holdings larger than 80 hectares were expropriated, using the agrarian reform law passed by the predecessor Christian Democratic government.[3]

The result of these processes was enormous political polarization as well as economic dislocation. Growth was initially stimulated by increasing demand through large wage hikes as well as increases in government spending. By 1973 private consumption had risen 19 percent, government consumption had grown 37 percent, and total government expenditure (including higher wage and transfer payments) had gone up 119 percent over 1968 levels. Some of the higher demand was met by drawing on idle capacity and some was met by increased imports, which rose by 22 percent over 1968 levels. Legal battles over the ownership of shipments of Chilean copper, together with a 40 percent decline in the world price of copper between 1970 and 1973, reduced the government's copper revenue from $268 million (about 25 percent of fiscal revenue) in 1970 to $39 million in 1971, $26 million in 1972, and $19 million in 1973.[4]

The combination of increased government expenditure and decreased revenue caused the fiscal deficit to rise from 2.7 percent of GDP in 1970 to 10.7 percent in 1971, 13.0 percent in 1972, and 24.7 percent in 1973. Despite the increased size of the fiscal deficits, inflation was initially avoided by drawing down on international reserves and increasing production through use of idle capacity; later it was suppressed by price and exchange controls. By 1973, however, inflation had reached the three-digit level and an active black market for foreign exchange had sprung up. Output, which grew 2.1 percent and 9.0 percent in 1970 and 1971, began a slow but accelerating decline in 1972, falling by 1.2 percent before dropping another 5.6 percent in 1973.[5] The typical pattern of a populist crisis was played out.[6]

The economic problems of the Allende government were partly the result of the government's own policies, partly the result of domestic and international attempts to undermine the Popular Unity, and partly the result of an unfavorable external economic environment. As some Popular Unity officials admitted later, the lack of attention to macroeconomic variables and the lack of coordination between economics and politics undermined their ability to control the economy.[7] Christian Democratic economists (who became the leading opposition economists during the military period) blamed the fundamentals of the Popular Unity strategy itself. They criticized not only the macroeconomic policies but also the structural changes that undermined private property relations.[8] As will be discussed later, the military's economic team was even more fiercely opposed than the Christian Democratic economists to "socialist" economic policies.

2 THE NEW POLITICAL SETTING

In September 1973, the armed forces overthrew the Popular Unity government and Allende was replaced by a military junta, which soon came to be dominated by army commander Augusto Pinochet. In comparison with the 1891 Chilean civil war or with two military coups in the 1920s and 1930s, the 1973 coup was a particularly brutal one. Several thousand people were killed, and a much larger number jailed and exiled. And whereas previous military interventions had almost always left Chile's congress intact and retained civil liberties, following the 1973 intervention the military closed congress, outlawed political parties, and stripped labor unions of their bargaining rights as well as their organizational base. Freedom of speech, press, and assembly were tightly restricted. It was this process and context that set the stage for the reform process over the next 16 years.[9]

Although many of the civilian supporters of the coup thought it would be a short-lived affair, the military quickly made it clear that they intended to stay in power for a long time and that their goal was to completely remake the political, economic, and social systems in the country ("to reverse 50 years of Chilean history," as the Air Force commander put it in early declarations). Nonetheless, the new government had little idea about the particular economic policies it wanted to follow and could not draw on much expertise within the military itself. For such expertise, it had to look to civilian society; the question was to which groups. Perhaps the most logical reaction would have been to bring back the traditional business interests that dominated the anti-Allende movement and governed Chile in 1958–64 under businessman Jorge Alessandri. The main competition was the group of economists who came to be known as the "Chicago Boys." Based at the Catholic University in Santiago but with close ties to the University of Chicago through a US-financed exchange program, they had been preparing an alternative economic project since the late 1960s.[10]

Initially, the business representatives did play the dominant role in economic policy-making, but within a year and a half they had been largely displaced by the Chicago Boys. Starting in middle-level positions, the latter gradually came to dominate through their more clearly formulated ideas and arguments. Moreover, once the economic team was in place by mid-1975, it was given an extraordinary amount of autonomy by the military government. Although Pinochet maintained the ultimate decision-making power, and formed a parallel advisory group within the Office of the Presidency, he intervened only when disputes could not be resolved at a technical level.[11] Thus, in order to understand the basis of economic policy, it becomes crucial to understand the beliefs and theories of the economists.

The ideology of the economic team

On at least four previous instances in Chilean history, periods of civil and economic unrest had led to the adoption of "technocratic" solutions to economic problems.[12] Thus, the elevation of the Chicago Boys to a prominent position in economic policy-making fitted into an observable historical pattern in Chile of actions taken by "law-and-order" governments. Although economic technocrats in Chile generally have not had an independent political base, their beliefs have occasionally come to exert a profound influence on the nature of economic policy-making within Chile.[13]

During the 1970s, the technocratic beliefs of the Chicago Boys can be summarized by two phrases: "rules rather than discretion" and "the subsidiary role of the state." With regard to "rules" in economic policy-making, the adoption of a fixed exchange rate between 1979 and 1982 had much in common with similar fixed exchange rate episodes during 1895–98, 1926–32, and 1959–62. In all four cases, a fixed exchange rate "rule" was to achieve the nondiscretionary use of monetary policy via the automatic adjustment mechanism of the balance of payments. In Chile during the latter half of the 1970s, the belief in "rules" rather than "discretion" was also the driving force behind new foreign investment legislation, the redesign of the social security system, the reduction of tariffs to a uniform ten-percent level, the simplification of the tax system, the 1978 labor law, and the 1986 banking law.

Although the policies of the economic team have been described as "monetarist," the ideology of the Chicago Boys embodied more than just the principles of classical economy as taught at the University of Chicago. The phrase "the subsidiary role of the state," which came to dominate policy-making in Chile by the late 1970s, referred to a much-diminished role for government in national production and economic planning. The economic team may have originally embarked on what one opposition economist labeled as "offensive against the economic state" without an explicitly stated ideology.[14] By the end of the 1970s, however, Friedrich Hayek's work, especially *The Road to Serfdom*, had become the equivalent of the principles of classical political economy in its influence on Chilean economic reforms. *The Road to Serfdom* contained a warning against socialism and totalitarianism based on Hayek's personal observation of Germany and Russia in the 1930s. To a number of members of the economic team who had just lived through the Allende period, Hayek's writing voiced many of their feelings with an emotional intensity that was missing in books such as Milton Friedman's *Free to Choose*. Hayek's ideas greatly influenced reforms in the social area of the economy, especially the labor law and social security law.[15] The combination of a fervent commitment to economic rules and a deep distrust of the state's involvement in the economy produced a peculiar intensity to the reform process through 1981 that is difficult to convey accurately in words. But the following passage by former Labor Minister Jose Piñera is illustrative:

> Chilean democracy was not interrupted so that some Manchesterian economists could realize their dream of having the price of bread determined by supply and demand, but rather to prevent Chile from turning into another Cuba. Possibly no Western country had advanced so far on a *road to serfdom* as Chile had in 1973. A little bit farther and perhaps there would have been no return. Nevertheless, the country got out of the trap. Whoever fails to understand this point of departure of the entire post-1973 experience will not be able to understand the experience itself and, even less, the lessons from that experience.[16]

A somewhat more muted statement by Finance Minister Sergio de Castro, in his January 1979 Report on the State of Public Finance, contains a similar hint of the intensity with which the principles of "rules rather than discretion" and the "subsidiary role of the state" were being applied to economic policy-making by the economic team:

> An analysis of the history of our country and the experience and results obtained during this Government, have strengthened the conviction that a *subsidiary normative State* which permits ample freedom of action and that does not act contrary to the common good, is the central axis of all policy. In the [Chilean] economic order, in-depth studies of the functions and attributes of State organs have permitted the conclusion and the application of an impersonal, *non-discretionary economic system* based on the market, the success of which is by now unquestionable.[17]

In the post-1981 period, economic policies were forced, by circumstance, to become more flexible and less "pure." But even for that period, it continued to be the case that one could not understand economic policy-making in Chile without an awareness of the importance to policy-makers of economic rules and the subsidiary role of the state.

Other actors

Beyond the economists, at least four other sets of actors need to be discussed in order to understand the political process under the military government. The most important interest group was business, both at the level of the individual firm and of the employer associations (sectoral and national). Business was divided in Chile between a few large firms and a large number of small ones. There were also important sectoral distinctions, especially among industry, agriculture, mining, and commerce. In addition to their own individual contacts, the large firms were represented by sectoral associations and the Confederation of Production and Commerce (CPC) at the national level. Smaller firms had their own parallel organizations, which tended to be more militant since they lacked other means of getting their views across.

Although the business groups had traditionally worked in fairly informal ways, and hesitated to confront the government, this pattern had changed during the Allende period. Beginning in 1972, business groups joined with opposition political parties to form the National Front of the Private Sector (FRENAP), a coordinating group to fight against the Popular Unity. In the process, the relative strength of the different business groups was altered, and new types of leaders emerged within the traditional groups themselves. For example, the organizations of truck owners and small commercial establishments came to occupy key positions in FRENAP and led the two opposition strikes against the Allende government in 1972 and 1973. Likewise, Orlando Sáenz, an outspoken industrialist of nontraditional background, became both president of the National Manufacturers Association (SOFOFA) and a leading figure in FRENAP.[18]

These groups worked closely with the military in 1973 to encourage a coup. Once it occurred, the business associations tended to fade into the background, assuming that the military would adequately represent their interests. In fact, those who had been most active in the anti-Popular Unity struggle were generally not favored by military policies, and some of their leaders (most notably Orlando Sáenz) eventually became outspoken opponents of the military policies. Most of the business groups went along, however, until the economic crisis broke out in the early 1980s. Their fear of a return by the Popular Unity was such that they were willing to tolerate not only the loss of political freedom but also substantial economic sacrifice.[19]

If business generally expected the military to favor its interests, labor was in the opposite position. Although there was never completely unified labor support for the Allende government, and the Christian Democrats had some measure of success (especially within the crucial copper sector) in their attempts to divide labor, the bulk of union members were seen as Popular Unity militants. Consequently, the unions were outlawed after the coup, and prominent labor leaders were high on the military list of targets for jail, exile or even assassination. Labor expected to bear the brunt of the military wrath, as indeed happened, and feared that repression would merely increase if open opposition occurred.

Chilean unions had traditionally had a more political than "bread-and-butter" orientation and were closely affiliated with the Communist and Socialist parties. According to the labor code, collective bargaining took place at the plant level, and unions were divided into white- and blue-collar unions. For political purposes, however, there were regional and national federations, topped by the Central Unica de Trabajadores (CUT), which was a pillar of support for the Popular Unity.[20]

During the Popular Unity period, 29 percent of the work force was affiliated with a union, up from 11 percent in the early 1960s and 18 percent during the Frei years. This figure fell back to 12 percent during the 1980–5 period. Even more dramatic were statistics for participation in strikes: 4 percent of the work force participated in strikes in the early 1960s, 16 percent in 1971–3, but only 0.4 percent in 1980–5.[21] This fall in union activity was perhaps the most obvious indicator of the decline in labor's position under the military. Not surprisingly, labor was forced to absorb a large part of the costs of the new policies through falling wages as well as through high rates of unemployment. Even at the end of the 1980s, real wages were still below their 1970 level and unemployment remained in double digits.

Coordinating the political interests of business, labor, and other groups in Chile had traditionally been the role of the political parties. Chilean parties were not only strong but had a definite class-based character, more similar to the European party systems than those elsewhere in Latin America or the United States. By the early 1970s, there were four major parties. The National Party represented the interests of traditional business groups, while receiving the majority of its votes from an upper middle-class clientele. The Christian Democrats tried to be a multiclass party. Their business constituency came from the more modern sectors, while their votes mainly derived from white-collar workers and professionals. An attempt was made to attract labor, with more success in the countryside than the cities. Most blue-collar workers were affiliated with the Communists and Socialists.[22]

After the military intervention, the leftist parties were outlawed and the others recessed. The Socialists, Communists, and Christian Democrats continued to operate underground, but the National Party was inactive until the early 1980s. The military discouraged organization by its partisans, and the latter seemed to see no need to do so until the economic crisis erupted in 1981–2. At that point, two rightist parties emerged. One was the traditional right with a base in the old National Party, the other a new group oriented more toward the military. It was not until the approach of the 1988 plebiscite, called by Pinochet (under the terms of the 1980 Constitution) to legitimate another eight years of military rule, that the parties again became the main actors. The two rightist parties formed an uneasy alliance, while the Christian Democrats and most of the old left united into the so-called Concertation. The latter won, leading the way for a return to democracy in March 1990.[23]

The final group – always important in Chilean politics – was composed of external actors. They included foreign corporations, governments, and international agencies; among them, the United States traditionally played the key role. Until the late 1960s, US companies owned the main mineral resources in Chile and controlled other large businesses as well. Under Frei, copper was "chileanized," but other important investments remained. The US government had also played a crucial role in helping to finance the 1964 Frei campaign against Allende and in providing large amounts of economic aid to build up the government as a showcase to counter the appeal of Castro's Cuba. Ironically, less US money went into the 1970 election since it was expected that Alessandri would win.[24]

With the Popular Unity triumph, Henry Kissinger's three-pronged strategy was put into place. First, loans from the United States were cut off, and pressure was exerted on the multilateral agencies to limit credit to Chile. Second, the CIA was authorized to spend up to $8 million to "destabilize" the Allende government. Third, ties were strengthened with Chilean opposition groups, especially the military. Military aid was increased and training programs continued, as economic aid was eliminated. Although the US support was certainly helpful to the domestic opposition, it was the opposition's own activities, rather than US financial aid, that was the key factor in the overthrow of the government.[25]

Nonetheless, much of the leadership of the United States was happy to see the end of the Popular Unity, even if the end resulted from a military coup. The US government and private banks provided economic assistance to the new government – although it was treated as a pariah by govern- in Europe and elsewhere. Eventually, however, the poor human rights record of the government became an embarrassment even to the leadership of the United States, although the economic policies were seen in a favorable light. As the US government began to pull back, its place was taken by the multilateral agencies (the IMF and World Bank), which provided large structural adjustment loans after the 1982 crisis.[26]

3   OVERVIEW OF THE REFORM MODEL

What has come to be known as the Chilean economic model was an extensive set of policies, of which trade liberalization and privatization were only the best known. The set of policies can be divided into three categories. First were stabilization policies: typical orthodox measures on fiscal, monetary, and wage policies but applied in a particularly rigid way. Second was a set of structural reform policies oriented toward the economic sector. Most important were trade liberalization, financial liberalization, development of a domestic capital market, deregulation of public transportation, privatization of state-owned enterprises, and promotion of exports. Finally there was a group of social policies, dubbed the "seven modernizations." The seven included reforms of the labor code, social security, education, health services, agriculture, justice system, and administrative and regional decentralization. The general thrust of the modernizations was to extend the use of market mechanisms into the social sector. All three were complemented by the authoritarian political structure, which the government had intended to replace by a "protected democracy."[27]

Although the new military government quickly made clear that it wanted to make major changes in the Chilean economy, it was less clear about the precise type of economic policies that would be followed and who would be in charge. The policies and economists in charge of policy evolved over time, becoming markedly "Hayekian" by the time of the introduction of the social reform legislation in the early 1980s. With the benefit of hindsight, it is now possible to sketch out the general chronology of economic reform and the changes that took place.

A first period of about a year and a half (October 1973–April 1975) was dominated by struggles over power and policy measures. The general orthodox direction was clear, but the speed and extent of the changes was not. The first civilian finance minister, Fernando Léniz, came from a business background. He proposed a gradual stabilization program and some timid structural reforms. In late 1974, Léniz was replaced as finance minister by Jorge Cauas, who had some Chicago connections but was not at the center of the group of Chicago-trained economists. Following a 50 percent drop in the world price of copper in later 1974, an accelerating rate of inflation, and a deepening domestic recession, Cauas was placed in charge of a stabilization program. The stabilization program became known as the "shock treatment," following the use of those words by Milton Friedman during a visit to Chile in March 1975. The "shock treatment" – which involved large cuts in fiscal expenditure – was implemented in April 1975 and succeeded in bringing down inflation to double-digit levels, but it was also partially responsible for the 14 percent decline in gross domestic product in 1975.

With the implementation of the stabilization program, the second period began; it lasted from April 1975 until June 1982. During these seven years, structural changes to liberalize the domestic financial system and lower tariffs went forward with much more vigor, especially after Sergio de Castro took over the Finance Ministry in 1976 and became the virtual economic czar. Tariffs were lowered to ten percent, the exchange rate was fixed to the dollar, capital controls were significantly relaxed, and legislation affecting unions and social security was enacted. The privatization program also picked up speed.

The third phase was marked by the major crisis suffered by the Chilean economy and its aftermath. It began with the devaluation of the peso in June 1982 and lasted through a series of ad hoc policy experiments until early 1985. During this period, a number of the reforms already instituted were partially rolled back as a way of dealing with the economic – and eventually political – crisis. Beyond the devaluation, tariffs were increased back to 35 percent and surcharges were added for some goods, especially in agriculture. More importantly, the government took over many of the firms it had privatized earlier as a way of dealing with the crisis. It was also forced to assume responsibility for some of the private sector's foreign debt.

The final phase began in February 1985 with the appointment as finance minister of Hernán Büchi, an engineer with connections to both the business and Chicago groups. It lasted until the military handed over power to the civilian government in early 1990, after having lost the 1988 plebiscite on extending their mandate for another eight years and the subsequent presidential election. The final phase consisted of a more pragmatic version of the Chilean model. The long-term model of a small state and open economy continued but with more interventionalist short-term approach.

4   MACROECONOMIC PERFORMANCE

Before turning to the topics of trade liberalization and privatization, it is useful to try to determine the broad outlines of the macroeconomic performance of the Chilean economy between 1973 and 1990. During a period of rapid structural change, however, it is often very difficult to derive an accurate picture of an economy. For example, tariff reductions, by their nature, change relative prices, thereby affecting the choice of inputs and altering domestic value added in production. As another example, the removal of price controls on basic foodstuffs, together with an opening of the economy, alters the relevant consumption bundle of goods for calculating a consumer price index. A third example is the removal of restrictions on firms' hiring and dismissal of workers, which alters the interpretation of unemployment statistics.

The single greatest difficulty in constructing data that measure the behavior of the Chilean economy over time is the choice of a deflator for converting nominal into real variables. The official consumer price index is used by government publications and international publications such as the IMF's *International Financial Statistics*. But researchers at CIEPLAN (an opposition think tank in Santiago) uncovered and publicized discrepancies in the construction of the consumer price index during the last quarter of 1973 and during 1976–8, which resulted in large underestimates of inflation during those periods.[28]

The underestimates during the last quarter of 1973 were caused by a splicing of price level data that eliminated the rise in prices accompanying the removal of price controls during the first three years of military government. This splicing error, which was eventually recognized in some Central Bank publications,[29] resulted in a reported inflation rate of 508 percent for 1973 rather than a more accurate rate of about 800 percent. The original paper that reported the errors during the 1976–8 period suggested that unannounced changes in the composition of the consumption bundle could have been used to understate the inflation rate during those years.[30] Credible anecdotal evidence obtained after the paper's publication, however, suggests that the figures were deliberately falsified at the highest levels of the Institute of National Statistics.[31] CIEPLAN's corrected consumer price index for the 1970s is now almost universally used by Chilean researchers. The corrected consumer price index and the implicit gross domestic product deflator are very closely correlated during the 1970s, reinforcing researchers' distrust of the official consumer price index.

Examining the relation between the official consumer price index and the implicit GDP inflator in the 1960s leads to a similar discrepancy between the two indices: between 1964 and 1970, the official consumer price index rose by 44 percent less than the implicit GDP deflator. As can be seen in table 3.1, real wages rose by 80 percent during the Frei years (1964–70) if the consumer price index is used to deflate nominal wages, but only by 25 percent if the implicit GDP deflator is employed.[32] Table 3.1 indicates that over the 30-year period between 1960 and 1989, real wages in Chile either rose by 258 percent (if nominal wages are deflated with the official consumer price index), by 58 percent (if nominal wages are deflated with the corrected consumer price indices of Ffrench-Davis, and Cortázar and Marshall[33]), or by 27 percent (if nominal wages are deflated with the implicit GDP deflator). Since the political pressures associated with wage indexing were focused on the consumer price index rather than on the GDP deflator, there is much to be said for the real wage series based on the use of the implicit GDP deflator.

Analyzing the first six years of the military government, the interpretation of the economy's macroeconomic performance differs markedly depending on choice of data. Table 3.2 contains data on the period between 1970 and 1979 that present the official view of the early years of the reforms. According to official statistics, real wages rose by 72 percent between 1970 and 1979 along with a rapid increase in employment. At the same time, unemployment in Chile – whether measured as open unemployment, as in table 3.2, or as open unemployment plus participants in the government's minimum employment program, as in table 3.3 – paradoxically remained at levels of about 15 percent of the work force. Deflating nominal wages with the corrected consumer price index, as in table 3.3, however, suggests that real wages fell by 18 percent between 1970 and 1979 and employment remained essentially stagnant. The difference in the employment series used in tables 3.2 and 3.3 stems largely from an incorrect extrapolation of the growth rate of the labor force of Santiago to that of Chile as a whole.[34] (For a number of reasons, Santiago has historically grown faster than the rest of Chile.) Once the corrected wage series and employment series is used, the paradox of high unemployment during the 1974–9 period goes away.

Table 3.1 Real wages in Chile: 1960–89 (1960 = 100)

Year	Nominal wages Official CPI	Nominal wages Corrected CPI	Nominal wages GDP Deflator
1960	100	100	100
1961	107	107	107
1962	107	107	107
1963	107	105	108
1964	101	98	101
1965	115	112	107
1966	130	126	115
1967	149	143	124
1968	150	143	118
1969	163	153	120
1970	182	167	126
1971	228	206	160
1972	214	158	143
1973	138	78	80
1974	170	98	76
1975	167	95	80
1976	225	120	95
1977	254	121	101
1978	289	129	104
1979	320	141	105
1980	348	153	119
1981	379	167	138
1982	378	166	134
1983	338	149	119
1984	338	149	126
1985	324	142	119
1986	331	145	121
1987	330	145	120
1988	351	153	121
1989	358	158	127

Sources: Banco Central de Chile (1989) for nominal wages, official CPI, nominal, and real GDP series (for construction of the implicit GDP deflator); Ffrench-Davis (1973) for corrected CPI 1960–70; Cortázar and Marshall (1980) for corrected CPI 1971–9; for 1980–9 corrected and official CPIs are identical.

Other differences in data arise with regard to figures for gross domestic product, industrial output, and the government's per capita social spending. According to official statistics, per capita social spending by the government rose by 40 percent during 1970–9, while according to CIEPLAN calculations per capita social spending fell by 18 percent. The

Table 3.2 Chilean economy according to official statistics, 1970–9

	1970	1974	1975	1976	1977	1978	1979
Annual inflation rate (percent)	36	376	341	174	64	30	39
Real wages (1970=100)	100	100	101	108	136	155	172
Gross domestic product (1974=100)	97	100	87	90	99	107	116
Employment (1970=100)	100	112	107	112	123	130	—
Unemployment rate (percent)	4	—	15	13	12	14	14
Per capita social spending (1970=100)	100	116	91	93	116	132	141
Industrial sector output (1974=100)	—	100	75	79	86	94	101
Real price of copper (1970=100)	100	100	55	60	53	51	66
Real exchange rate (1974=100)	56	100	136	121	110	125	124

Sources: Cortázar and Meller (1987) for the annual inflation rate, real wage, employment, per capita social spending, and industrial sector output. Banco Central de Chile (1989) for the unemployment rate, gross domestic product, and the real price of copper. The real exchange rate is the nominal Chilean bank exchange rate times the US producer price index divided by the official Chilean consumer price index.

difference in the two sets of statistics arises out of the government's use of central government social spending, whereas CIEPLAN employs a broader concept of both centralized and decentralized governmental social spending. As a result of methodological differences associated with the splicing of GDP series based on the 1962 Chilean input–output matrix and the 1977 Chilean input–output matrix, the official statistics show output rising by 16 percent between 1974 and 1979, whereas CIEPLAN's statistics show only an 8 percent rise.[35] These same methodological differences give rise to official figures showing a recovery of industrial output in 1979 to its 1974 levels, whereas CIEPLAN's figures indicates a continued depressed level of industrial production in 1979.

Even with respect to measurement of the size of the copper "shock" faced by the military government in the 1970s, there are two alternative interpretations. Table 3.2 shows that the real price of copper fell by 45 percent between 1974 and 1975, and remained at depressed levels between 1975 and 1979. By contrast, table 3.3 shows that the government's revenue from copper recovered substantially during the 1975–9 period and eventually exceeded 1970 levels by 47 percent, largely as the result of increased copper output.

Table 3.3   Chilean economy according to opposition statistics, 1970–9

	1970	1974	1975	1976	1977	1978	1979
Annual inflation rate (percent)	36	369	343	198	84	37	39
Real wages (1970=100)	100	65	63	65	72	76	82
Gross domestic product (1974=100)	92	100	83	87	94	100	108
Employment (1970=100)	100	105	99	95	99	103	—
Unemployment rate (percent)	6	—	18	22	19	18	17
Per capita social spending (1970=100)	100	92	75	71	79	79	83
Industrial sector output (1974=100)	—	100	74	76	81	86	92
Real copper revenue (1970=100)	100	49	42	79	75	65	147
Real exchange rate (1974=100)	89	100	135	112	92	97	95

Sources: Cortázar and Meller (1987) for the inflation rate, real wage, employment, per capita social spending, and industrial sector output. Marcel and Meller (1986) for gross domestic product. Jadresi (1986) for the unemployment rate. Banco Central de Chile (1989) for the government's copper revenue. The real exchange rate is the nominal Chilean bank exchange rate times the US producer price index divided by the corrected Chilean consumer price index.

Thus, depending on one's point of view, Chilean data can be used to argue that the 1970s reform period dramatically improved real wages and governmental social spending, even in the face of extremely negative external conditions. Alternatively, they can be used to make a case that the reform period was accompanied by a large fall in real wages and contraction of governmental social spending, even though the negative external environment facing the economy in 1975 had improved markedly by 1979.

The official Chilean national accounts data, while not beyond question, do not differ dramatically from CIEPLAN's figures over the 1970–89 period. Therefore, the data in tables 3.4 and 3.5 may be regarded as relatively reliable indicators of the aggregate performance of the Chilean economy between 1970 and 1989. Table 3.4 shows that aggregate ouput rose by 66 percent between 1970 and 1989, with two troughs during 1975–7 and 1982–6 that reflected the severe recessions of 1975 and 1982–3. In per capita terms, output rose by only 20 percent between 1970 and 1989, while per capita consumption remained below 1970 levels for all years of military rule except for 1981 and 1989 (and never exceeded the 1971 and 1972 levels reached under the Allende regime). Beginning in 1979, per capita govern-

Table 3.4 Chilean national accounts data: output, inflation, and expenditure

	Real gross domestic product (billions 1977 Chilean pesos)	Percentage change in GDP deflator	Per capita GDP (thousands 1977 pesos)	Per capita consumption (thousands 1977 pesos)	Per capita government (thousands 1977 pesos)	Per capita investment (thousands 1977 pesos)
1970	283	41	30.3	23.4	3.6	6.2
1971	308	18	31.9	25.6	4.0	5.8
1972	305	87	30.9	27.0	4.1	4.6
1973	288	418	28.7	24.8	4.1	4.2
1974	291	694	28.5	19.9	4.4	4.9
1975	253	342	24.4	17.4	3.9	3.8
1976	262	251	24.9	17.2	3.8	3.2
1977	288	103	27.0	19.6	3.9	3.6
1978	311	57	28.8	20.9	4.1	4.2
1979	337	46	30.7	21.9	4.5	4.8
1980	363	29	32.6	23.0	4.0	5.8
1981	384	12	33.9	25.0	3.8	6.6
1982	330	13	29.1	22.0	3.8	4.4
1983	327	28	27.9	20.5	3.6	3.6
1984	348	13	29.2	20.5	3.6	3.9
1985	356	33	29.4	19.9	3.6	4.3
1986	377	19	30.6	20.5	3.4	4.6
1987	398	21	31.8	21.1	3.3	5.2
1988	428	21	33.5	22.8	3.4	5.7
1989	470	14	36.3	24.5	3.4	6.8

Source: Banco Central de Chile (1989). Population figures used to calculate per capita magnitudes from CEPAL, *Anuario Estadístico de América Latina y El Caribe, 1989.*

Table 3.5   Chilean national accounts data: savings and investment, 1970–89 (%)

Year	Gross fixed capital formation	Change in inventories	Trade balance	National savings	Exports plus imports
	GDP	GDP	GDP	GDP	GDP
1970	15.0	1.4	0.7	17.1	29.4
1971	14.6	−0.1	−1.0	13.5	23.7
1972	13.1	−0.9	−3.5	8.7	23.6
1973	12.8	−4.9	−1.9	6.0	29.8
1974	16.9	4.3	0.7	21.9	40.1
1975	17.7	−4.5	−2.0	11.1	52.9
1976	13.3	−0.5	4.3	17.1	45.9
1977	13.3	1.1	−1.8	12.6	43.0
1978	14.7	3.1	−3.3	14.5	44.5
1979	14.9	2.9	−2.8	15.0	49.4
1980	16.6	4.4	−4.2	16.8	49.8
1981	18.6	4.1	−10.3	12.4	43.2
1982	14.6	−3.3	−1.9	9.4	40.6
1983	12.0	−2.2	2.7	12.5	45.4
1984	12.3	1.3	−1.1	12.5	49.6
1985	14.2	−0.5	2.8	16.5	55.4
1986	14.6	0.0	3.8	18.4	57.4
1987	16.0	0.9	4.1	21.0	62.9
1988	16.3	0.7	7.2	24.2	67.5
1989	18.4	1.9	3.2	23.5	71.6

Source: Banco Central de Chile (1989) and *Boletín Mensual* (for 1989 figures).

ment consumption began a long decline from 4500 to 3400 pesos by 1988 (in constant 1977 currency).

Table 3.5 shows that aggregate investment changed less during the 1974–89 period than did national savings, with the rise in the national savings rate in the latter half of the 1980s accompanying a large trade surplus. The last column of table 3.5 indicates that the effective openness of the economy as measured through trade flows (the ratio of the sum of exports plus imports to GDP) lagged the nominal opening of the economy (associated with the 10 percent uniform tariff of 1979) by somewhere between five and ten years.

Tables 3.1 and 3.4 demonstrate an important point regarding the Chilean economic liberalization: without minimizing the importance of external shocks during 1974–89, there was still a long lag between the start of the government's reform and the achievement of an improved standard of living for most Chileans. In particular, not until 1989 did the average Chilean worker's standard of living appear to rise permanently above the standard of living of the late 1960s.

Tables 3.2 and 3.3 demonstrate an equally important point regarding the quality of data generated during a period of economic reforms. Governments engaged in economic reforms have a natural tendency to generate data that build domestic and international support for the continuation of the reforms. Since a government generally enjoys a monopoly in the creation of economic statistics, outright falsification of data may become attractive if the reforms do not produce desired results quickly enough. Even in the absence of direct falsification of data, the rapid structural shifts produced by economic reforms allow government officials to make procedural changes in the collection, compilation, and generation of economic data in order to validate the policy measures taken.

The creation of a misleading statistical picture of the Chilean economy may have had important consequences for the evolution of the economy, as Cortázar and Meller have emphasized.[36] For example, the creation of false consumer price index figures in Chile during 1976–8 not only affected wage indexing but also eroded the real values of pensions and affected those private-sector financial contracts – such as rental contracts, longer-term savings accounts, and loans for the purchase of homes, cars, and consumer durables – that were linked to the consumer price index.

Equally seriously, the Central Bank's exchange rate and capital account policies were affected by the falsified statistics, since the Central Bank appears not to have been informed of the price level tampering.[37] Between 1976 and 1978 the official consumer price index, in conjunction with information on the nominal exchange rate and on foreign prices, indicated that exchange rate and capital account policies had kept Chile's real exchange rate approximately constant, as shown in table 3.2. On the other hand, use of the corrected consumer price index would have alerted officials in the Central Bank to a 15 percent appreciation of the real exchange rate, as shown in table 3.3. Such information could have influenced the rate at which restrictions on capital inflows were lifted and could have altered the decision to fix the nominal exchange rate in June 1979.

5 TRADE LIBERALIZATION

Policy trends

Trade liberalization was a major focus of the government that came to power in 1973. Liberalization was pursued both as an element of the stabilization program (international competition to force domestic firms to lower prices) and as a major plank of the restructuring project (opening the Chilean economy and integrating it with the international economy as a way of increasing efficient growth).

Liberalization went against the grain of economic policy that had been in place in Chile for the previous 40 years. The country was an archetypical example of the import-substitution industrialization (ISI) strategy; protection had been the dominant philosophy since the Popular Front governments began in the late 1930s. Initially, high tariffs were designed to stimulate infant industries, but they remained intact for political as well as economic reasons. During the Allende years, they were increased as the government sought to deal with balance-of-payments crises. By 1973, the average tariff was nearly 100 percent and some reached as high as 700 percent. Tariffs were reinforced by other restrictive policy tools, such as multiple exchange rates, quantitative restrictions on imports (including import prohibitions and prior deposits up to 10,000 percent of the value of imports), and controls on foreign direct investment and capital flows.[38]

Although trade liberalization was on the agenda of the new government from the beginning, the nature and extent of liberalization emerged only gradually. The first measures took place in late 1973 when quantitative restrictions were largely eliminated. The lowering of tariffs began in January 1974, when the government announced a gradual liberalization to take place over three years. No statement about the final level of tariffs was made until May 1974, when the finance minister said:

[I]n 1977, no tariff will be higher than 60 percent. This clearly defines the tariff policy which will be followed in the future so that domestic industries can make whatever adjustments are necessary and prepare themselves so they are in good shape to meet foreign competition.[39]

The 60 percent goal was superseded the following year by the announcement that rates would be fixed between 10 and 35 percent by 1978. Finally in 1977, after withdrawing from the Andean Pact (because of its foreign investment as well as its trade policies), the announcement came that tariffs would be further reduced to a uniform rate of 10 percent.

The initial idea was that exchange rate policy would be handled so as to compensate, at least in part, for the declining protection from tariffs and other trade barriers. According to table 3.2, the real exchange rate between 1976 and 1979 was maintained at a fairly stable level, so the Central Bank authorities could point to a relatively successful application of exchange rate policy. In retrospect, however, it is clear from table 3.3 that the Central Bank had, in fact, permitted a substantial appreciation of the real exchange rate between 1976 and 1979. In June 1979, the exchange rate was pegged to the dollar in an attempt to lower inflation to international levels. Following the pegging of the nominal exchange rate, the real exchange rate continued to appreciate until 1982, severely eroding the ability of Chilean firms to compete internationally.

The politics of trade liberalization

Given this extremely dramatic liberalization, the first questions of interest here are: Who initiated the policy? Who supported it? And who opposed it? The answers are heavily conditioned by the political–economic context described in the introductory section of the chapter.

The initiators of the trade policies, as of virtually all other economic policies, came from within the government economic team. Saying this, however, does not immediately clarify the situation since – as indicated above – there were various factions fighting for hegemony during the first several years after the coup. Their relative influence is mirrored in the different announcements of government policy. The initial economic team, led by Fernando Léniz and composed of individuals who had been active in traditional rightist and even Christian Democratic governments, wanted to eliminate the quantitative restrictions and lower tariffs, but not to levels that would endanger the existence of many firms.[40] By 1975, the constellation had shifted toward the more free-trade group with the replacement of Léniz by Jorge Cauas, but it was only with the appointment of Sergio de Castro as minister of finance that the ultimate decision to push for uniform tariffs at the 10 percent level was reached. Since de Castro had earlier supported a more moderate position, it is unclear whether he changed his mind as time went on or whether he was hiding his true position until he attained sufficient power to implement it.

Beyond the economic team itself, the most important role was played – or not played – by the business community. Business leaders had traditionally been influential in economic policy, sometimes as direct decision-makers, at other times behind the scenes. Under Allende, this influence was not only strictly limited, but business helped to overthrow a government they saw as threatening their very existence. Having been partly responsible for putting the military government in place, businesspeople began as fervent supporters of almost anything the new government proposed – including the elimination of quantitative restrictions on imports and the initial reduction of tariff rates.[41] Even as tariffs continued to fall in 1975–6, there was little outcry except from some individuals (the most conspicuous was Orlando Sáenz, former president of the National Manufacturers Association, who denounced the policy as "suicide") and the Metallurgical Association (ASIMET).[42] More criticism emerged as tariff reductions proceeded to the uniform 10 percent level and the appreciation of the real exchange rate squeezed the profits of import-competing firms. By 1979, however, the protests were too late to reverse the government's trade and exchange rate policies.

Explanations are multiple for the lack of business pressure to protect the profitability of the import-competing sector. Most important was remembrance of the Allende period and the need to support the alternative regime that had "rescued" business. In addition, the private sector was in favor of the general line of government policy, of which trade policy was an important but not the only aspect. Other relevant factors included divisions within the business sector itself, especially between large firms with better access to cheap dollar loans and smaller ones that had to rely on expensive peso credit. The former dominated the business associations with the exception of agriculture. The government strategy – if that is what it was – of gradually tightening policy over time meant that a stand was not taken until it was too late. Finally, when protests were made, the economic officials simply ignored them, so even the potentially powerful business sector felt impotent. The centralization of decision-making did not provide any alternative channels for bringing influence to bear.

Although most business firms eventually came to oppose trade liberalization in its extreme form, some groups – including much of the labor movement and what remained of the leftist political apparatus – were opposed from the beginning. For a variety of reasons, however, these groups had virtually no influence on economic policy during the first decade of the military government. First, their organizational capacity was crushed when the parties and labor federations were outlawed by the military government. Second, divisions within their ranks with respect to relations with the government prevented action. Third, those labor activities that were carried out focused on organizational survival and immediate economic necessities rather than the specifics of the economic model such as trade policy. The exceptions were those sectors especially hurt by liberalization. They also happened to be the sectors most heavily unionized in the past; expanding sectors were not strongly organized.[43]

Perhaps surprisingly, international actors also had little influence on trade policy. The Chilean trade liberalization came a decade before the big push in this direction by the US government and international organizations. Indeed, it is reported that the IMF actually suggested the Chilean government go slower than it had planned with respect to tariff reduction in the mid-1970s, given the severe balance-of-payments problems in that period.[44] Nonetheless, the Fund generally reinforced the direction in which the economic team wanted to move and helped open the doors for external finance. In particular, IMF support was helpful in paving the way for the private bank loans, which were crucial in enabling the trade deficit to continue until 1981. Overall, however, the most significant type of international influence was not international conditionality but ideological influence through US training of Chilean economists. As is well known, many of the principal economic advisors to the government had some connection with the University of Chicago. The economic model, including trade policy, came from this group and represented a concerted attempt to apply the Chicago model of economics in the "real world."[45]

The power of the economists came from the extraordinary degree of autonomy afforded them by the military government from the appointment of Cauas as finance minister in mid-1974 until the dismissal of de

Castro in early 1982. Once the fight for control of the basic lines of economic policy had been won by the Chicago Boys, the military officials running the government not only declined to intervene themselves but also backed the economists in their decision to isolate themselves from the pressures of interest groups, including business. The refusal to accept input from business groups derived from the economists' view that the majority of Chilean firms were not good capitalists and therefore could not be counted on to build a "new" capitalist system in Chile. The businesses were only out to protect their individual interests through access to protection and favors of various types from the state. Apparently the economists managed to convince Pinochet and his generals of the validity of their views.[46]

Initial outcomes/results

Based on the period 1980–1 – the last years before the crisis struck – we can make some comments about the initial economic and political results of the trade policies. Economically, at least three aspects are important: value and composition of imports, value and composition of exports, and trends in the sectoral distribution of GDP and employment. Politically, the issue concerns the possible formation of new coalitions based on winners and losers from trade liberalization.

The evolution of foreign trade between 1970 and 1981 is shown in table 3.6. On the one hand, the table indicates that there was a large increase in imports, especially consumer goods. On the other hand, it also shows an increase in exports and a strong diversification away from copper toward "non-traditional" products. The trade balance became increasingly negative as import rises outpaced exports; by 1981, the trade deficit represented more than 10 percent of GDP.

The main sectoral impact of the new trade policy was on industry, which was gravely weakened by the drastic shifts in tariff/exchange rate policy. Production fell and bankruptcies multiplied, but the effects were not uniform. Industries such as textiles, clothing, footwear, and some of the metallurgical firms were especially hard hit, while food, beverages, and tobacco fared much better. Those who could export did especially well. Overall, however, net industrial employment fell from a peak of 26 percent of the labor force in 1972 to only 16 percent in 1981 (and 14 percent in 1982), as declining industries outpaced growing ones. Likewise, the industrial share of GDP fell from 29.5 percent of GDP in 1974 to 22.3 percent in 1981 (and 18.9 percent in 1982); the fall was compensated by a gain for finance and real estate, which together increased their share from 9.0 to 18.5 (and 20.6 percent) for the same years.[47] The simultaneous operation of other factors – especially the high level of interest rates – makes it difficult to determine the precise role of tariffs and the exchange rate in the industrial decline, but they were clearly important.[48]

Table 3.6   Chilean international trade, 1971–89 (millions of dollars)

Category	1971	1975	1977	1979	1981	1983	1985	1987	1989
Exports	962	1,552	2,190	3,763	3,931	3,831	3,804	5,224	8,080
Mining	813	1,075	1,403	2,254	2,279	2,335	2,121	2,603	4,473
Agriculture	29	86	160	265	365	328	515	796	995
Manufactured	120	391	628	1,245	1,286	1,168	1,168	1,824	2,612
Imports	1,166	1,338	2,414	4,218	6,379	2,845	2,955	3,994	6,502
Consumer goods	245	87	527	852	1,830	1,024	752	900	1,492
Intermediate goods	720	872	1,384	2,487	3,130	1,755	1,867	2,395	3,703
Machinery/equipment	197	378	519	876	1,415	392	650	1,101	1,949
Other	3	—	3	3	4				
Trade balance	(203)	214	(224)	(454)	(2,448)	986	849	1,230	1,578

Source: Banco Central de Chile, *Boletín Mensual* (various issues).

The political question of interest is to what extent new coalitions were formed in Chile, based on the economic winners and losers. Although this is a question that needs more research, our initial impression is that little political organizational activity took place in this period among government supporters. The government itself discouraged such activity, and the military control of all aspects of society made it seem unnecessary. Furthermore, the main winners from trade policy, the exporters, were geographically and sectorally scattered. The growing prosperity of the late 1970s, however, meant that the large Chilean middle class was willing to trade economic well-being (including new access to cheap imported products) for political freedom. And business, still worried by the memory of the Popular Unity period, ceded their traditional policy-making role. As will be seen below, this changed as the crisis emerged.

The losers had much more reason to organize but much less ability. Repression remained strong throughout the 1970s, but divisions within the potential opposition were equally important. Underground party activities pitted Socialists and Communists against the Christian Democrats. Labor unions lost members and also faced their own divisions among government supporters, neutrals, and the old left forces. Although the divisions eventually began to disappear within labor, the unions had no tradition of political leadership. Typically they had relied on the parties for this function and so were not prepared to assume a leading role. As with the winners, however, the crisis would provide a stimulus for the losers to become more active.

Crisis and policy retrenchment

The year 1981 marked the peak of success for the de Castro team. Growth was above 5 percent for the fifth straight year; the budget was in surplus;

inflation fell to a single digit rate for the first time in two decades; even wages and employment were beginning to show improvement. Nonetheless, as opponents pointed out, per capita GDP was still below 1970 levels, and the increasing overvaluation of the exchange rate was threatening the accomplishments achieved.[49]

By 1982, the problems erupted for all to see. Chile's GDP fell by 14 percent that year, the inflation rate doubled, and open unemployment jumped to 22 percent of the labor force. Likewise, a balance-of-payments crisis manifested itself in a large loss of reserves, even though the trade balance moved into a small surplus. In addition, there was a domestic financial crisis of enormous proportions, involving the largest banks in the country as well as industrial firms.[50]

There has been extensive debate about the causes of this multifaceted crisis. Here we will only be concerned with the role of trade policies in precipitating the crisis, on the one hand, and the effect of the crisis on trade policies, on the other hand.

An early victim of the crisis was finance minister Sergio de Castro, who was dismissed in April 1982 as part of a revaluation of policy by the military, who felt they could no longer sit on the sidelines. Allowing the crisis to run its course as de Castro wanted (the "automatic readjustment") would have threatened the government's very survival; rebellion could have been expected from business and the military itself as well as opposition groups.

The most important issue concerned possible devaluation of the exchange rate, which had been pegged to the dollar since 1979. The resulting overvaluation was impeding exports and making it extremely difficult for local industry to compete with imports. At the same time, the fixed exchange rate had been instrumental in bringing down inflation and was keeping debt payments manageable for those who had borrowed abroad. Consequently, a devaluation was controversial for practical as well as theoretical reasons. Those who wanted to maintain the fixed exchange rate system argued that a preferable way to deal with the macroeconomic disequilibria was to lower nominal wages. The latter would require a conflictive process of cutting wages and eliminating the indexation system established through the 1979 labor reform. The alternatives were presented to Pinochet, who felt that the size of wage drop needed to reequilibrate the economy was politically impossible. Thus a devaluation was ordered.[51]

Less dramatic trade measures included raising tariffs in general from 10 to 20 percent and authorizing tariff surcharges for sectors in special difficulty. The tariff increase was officially justified as a temporary revenue measure to help resolve the budget deficit resulting from the crisis. In part, that was probably true. In addition, however, the tariff increases and especially the surcharges resulted from escalating political–economic protests. The best known of the Chilean protests were the 1983–4 street demonstrations, demanding the return to democracy. Much more influential were the protests by business, which began as early as 1981.

The earliest movements were initiated by small businesses to demand a change in economic policy to alleviate the growing bankruptcies. These groups had helped overthrow the Allende government, but had not been favored by the military government's policies. After first limiting themselves to individual public statements about their problems, by 1982 the small businesses moved to broader organizational cohesion and more militant tactics. Large public meetings, demonstrations, and attempts to forcibly prevent banks from taking possession of bankrupt firms all became part of their mobilization.[52]

The larger firms were more cautious in their approach, since they had close ties with the government and had benefited from many of its policies. By mid-1982, however, the severity of the crisis led to new leadership in the umbrella organization, the Confederation of Production and Commerce (CPC). Its new president surprised observers during his inaugural address by saying, "Either we unite and work together or we will all go under together." In July 1983, the CPC presented a document to the government that called for significant changes in the economic policy, such as lowered interest rates on all debts; transformation of dollar debts into pesos; increased government expenditure, including labor-intensive public investment projects; and greater flexibility in dealing with the IMF.[53]

The combination of business discontent and street demonstrations eventually led to a cabinet shuffle and the temporary appearance of a set of ministers who favored not only expansionary aggregate demand policies but also greater protection. But the latter must be understood within the particular Chilean context. The new finance minister wanted to raise tariffs to 35 percent and perhaps extend some of the surcharges. His policies led to new conflicts within the economic apparatus of the government, reminiscent of those in the immediate aftermath of the 1973 coup. The supporters of orthodoxy retained much of their power and persuaded the military to dismiss the new team as soon as the protests were ended (the street demonstrations by repression and the business discontent by cooptation).

Pragmatic liberalization

In February 1985, a new finance minister, Hernán Büchi, was appointed, resolving many of the problems facing the government. His policies combined the earlier laissez-faire model with the more interventionist approach of his predecessor. The almost universal shorthand was that Büchi (an engineer with an MA from Columbia) was a more pragmatic and flexible version of the Chicago Boys. As one observer with close government connections put it: "Büchi favors the business organizations' line but is friends with the Catholic University group. As a consequence he has been able to unite the two factions in the government."[54] Perhaps the most accurate way of expressing the synthesis was a long-term model resting on a small state and open economy but a short-term model that was mildly interventionist. The style of the economic team changed as well. While de Castro refused even to receive Chilean business leaders, Büchi listened to them and tried to obtain their backing for government policies. The combination seemed to regain the support of most of the business class as well as important international actors.[55]

The macroeconomic model in place after February 1985 was aimed at a moderate rate of growth and low inflation through promotion of investment and exports and containment of public and private consumption. Trade policy centered on two main instruments – the exchange rate and tariffs. The peso was gradually depreciated in real terms through a crawling peg combined with occasional larger devaluations in order to maintain an expensive dollar. The latter was considered to be the most important incentive for exports and import substitution. When Büchi became finance minister, tariffs were 35 percent. They were soon returned to a flat 20 percent (and later 15 percent), although the use of surcharges was continued in special cases. Other incentives for nontraditional exports also existed.[56]

Partially as a consequence of the more flexible policies, growth resumed in the export sector (see table 3.6). Nontraditional exports continued to develop, although high copper prices in the late 1980s increased the weight of the traditional metals somewhat. Imports remained depressed since a growing trade surplus was needed to service the foreign debt. Overall, the increase in exports and especially their diversification are praised by most Chileans as positive results of the military period. Criticism centers on the extreme version of trade liberalization in the 1970s which, combined with ill-considered exchange rate and financial policies, led to large deadweight losses associated with the widespread bankruptcies of the 1982–5 period.

6 PRIVATIZATION

Policy trends

In addition to trade liberalization, another main goal of the military government in Chile was decreasing the state role in the economy. The latter had many aspects, but the most obvious was sale of state-owned firms.[57] As was the case with trade protection, a strong state role dated back at least to the Popular Front in the 1930s. A key element was the establishment of the state development corporation (CORFO) in 1939. CORFO had founded many of Chile's most important firms over the years; some had been maintained under its control while others were sold to the private sector once they became profitable.[58]

As of 1970, CORFO had 46 affiliated enterprises, and there were additional state firms under other legal agreements. Together they included producers of key products (steel, coal, oil, paper, refined sugar), utilities (water, electricity, telecommunications), transportation (railroads, airlines), and so on.[59] Under the Allende government, increased state control of the economy was a major aim, so the number of state firms increased through various mechanisms during the 1970–3 period. Some were purchased, some nationalized, others "intervened" (taken over by the government on a temporary basis, according to powers provided by the legal system). By the time of the coup, the number of firms was over 500, of which about half were "intervened." Many of the firms were small, and most were running deficits.[60]

It was clear from the beginning that the government intended to privatize, but which firms, by what means, and over what time period emerged only gradually. Four rounds of privatization ultimately took place – two before the 1982 crisis and two after. Data on the first two are shown in table 3.7.

The first round involved the return of the "intervened" firms. During 1974 alone, 202 of the 259 were restored to their original owners. No monetary transactions were involved, and owners agreed not to initiate legal claims. The remaining 57 were also returned within the next three years as were 3700 farms.[61] The second round involved privatizing most of the other firms under state control. First to go were the banks. Their shares were to be sold in small blocks, whereby an individual could purchase up to 3 percent of a given institution and a firm up to 5 percent. Ways were

Table 3.7   Enterprises and banks controlled by CORFO

	1970	1973[a]	1980	Goal
Nonfinancial enterprises	46	460	23	13
Government control	0	233[c]	0	0
CORFO affiliates[b]	46	277	23	13
Banks	0	19	1[d]	0
Total	46	479	24	13

Source: Vergara (1986, p. 90).
[a]At the time of the September collapse of the Unidad Popular regime.
[b]Includes both enterprises in which CORFO holds stock in the share capital and affiliates of CORFO affiliates.
[c]To avoid double entries, enterprises that figure in more than one category have been excluded. Specifically, 26 enterprises brought under government control or requisitioned, in which CORFO (or its affiliates) already held capital shares, are excluded.
[d]Because of financial and legal problems, this one bank still has not been restored to its owners.

quickly found to get around these limits, and various economic groups gained control of the banks. According to one source, the government was completely aware of what was happening and made no effort to avoid it.[62]

In addition to the banks, at least 180 other firms were auctioned off by 1982, most of them in the 1975–8 period. The government's haste to dispose of the firms led to mechanisms resulting in subsidies to purchasers of around 30 percent of the purchase price.[63] In addition, most were bought with a 10–20 percent down payment, with the rest coming from a CORFO credit. Given the deep recession at the time, few buyers had the resources to bid for the firms, even with the credits and subsidies. Most of the purchasers were the conglomerates ("grupos"), either the traditional ones or fledgling grupos that got their start through the privatizations.[64]

Politics of privatization

In the case of privatization, pressure for action came from the government and the business sector. The economic team announced its intention to return the intervened firms and acted to do so quickly. Justification was on the basis of lowering inflation (by cutting the budget deficit to which the firms were contributing) and efficiency (at which the private sector was considered superior) as well as property rights. With respect to the other state firms, progress was slower and business pushed for action.[65] Once the process began, however, and it became clear that sales were being monopolized by a small group of purchasers with access to government credit, public discontent began to mount. So much resentment arose that the sales process was halted for almost six months in 1976, then quietly resumed.[66] In the case of privatization, as opposed to trade liberalization where the government was acting and business associations accepting with resignation, the government appeared to be acting with the support of a small group of businesses while the rest were marginalized.

Foreign interests were involved insofar as foreign (mainly US) firms had been expropriated. The best known cases were the copper mines, but the military government decided not to return them to their original owners. On the one hand, as will be discussed below, the military were concerned to maintain control of "strategic" industries such as copper. On the other hand, the mines had been expropriated with the unanimous vote of the Chilean congress, which posed a serious obstacle to returning them. Instead, the solution was to compensate the companies. Other foreign firms were also compensated or received their property back.[67] No foreign firms participated in the first round of privatization sales, although they would do so later.

Labor again had no role in the reform process. The most direct way in which labor interests were involved was through workers in firms being sold – or especially being returned – to the private sector. For those firms that had been intervened with the support of the unions, there was great dismay at the prospect of return to the old ownership structure. Nevertheless, the political situation was such in early 1974 that any open resistance would have been suicidal.[68] For workers in other state firms, transfer to the private sector was presumably less threatening.

Ironically, perhaps, the main brake on the privatization process was the military. Much has been written about the anomaly of the military accepting a laissez-faire economic policy, but the limits concerned privatization of firms considered strategic. In addition to the armaments industries controlled by the military itself, these included copper, oil, coal, steel, and infrastructure industries such as transportation and communications. According to one of the leading government technocrats, industries remaining under government control in 1981 accounted for 83 percent of mining output, 12 percent in industry, 75 percent in public utilities, 21 percent in transport, 96 percent in communications and 28 percent in finance.[69] Rather than privatize these firms, the government would later impose new operating requirements that would increase their efficiency and profitability.[70]

Initial results

By the early 1980s, the privatization process seemed to have been successful in the sense that the purchasers of the former state-controlled firms were prospering; the state had eliminated its earlier problems, including the budget deficit to which the firms contributed; and the economy as a whole was expanding. Sectoral changes were occurring, indicating winners and losers in the process. As indicated earlier, the industrial share of GDP fell substantially, while finance, real estate, and other services together increased their share.[71]

The biggest winners, however, were the fast-growing conglomerates, which were fostered by the government as the best type of private actors to spearhead the new economic development model. They managed to concentrate a formidable portion of national assets – much of them through the privatization process. The older conglomerates benefited by recovering their firms that had been intervened. The new ones actually got their start through purchase of state firms, including banks.[72] Economic power translated into what political power was available to civil society during the de Castro period: mainly power to get favors, including information from the government. Communication was facilitated by a good deal of movement back and forth between the government economic posts and the conglomerates. Because the beneficiaries were so concentrated, the privatization process provided little if any possibility for a new support base for the government; indeed the opposite was probably true. Later privatizations would try to remedy this effect.

Crisis and new interventions

Although things seemed to be going well, surface appearances were misleading, as became clear in early 1981. At that point, a major firm failed, calling attention to the impending financial crisis in the conglomerates, which had devoted more attention to financial dealings and speculation than to production. In November 1981, the government had to intervene several small banks to avoid their collapse.

The economic crash, which began in 1981 but reached crisis proportions the next year when GDP fell by 14 percent, further undermined the financial system as did the devaluation of June 1982. Many local businesses had obtained dollar loans, and more pesos would be required to repay the same amount of dollar debt. Many became insolvent and thus unable to service their loans from Chilean banks, which were already in trouble. The two banks in greatest difficulty were the Banco de Chile and the Banco de Santiago, leaders of the two largest conglomerates. In January 1983, the government assumed control of the two banks to stem the financial crisis.

Three options were considered for dealing with the banks: they could have been provided with resources to refinance debtors and remain solvent themselves; they could have been allowed to go bankrupt; or they could have been taken over by the state. As with the devaluation, the question was referred to Pinochet and his advisors, and the decision was made to intervene the banks, i.e., to take them over on a temporary basis.[73] As for the conglomerates themselves, they were dismantled and many of their companies sold off or liquidated. The head of one of the conglomerates served nine months in jail after a lengthy trial; the other decided to cooperate with the government. Even the finance minister who decreed the intervention ended up in jail briefly for his prior role as an official in the largest conglomerate.[74]

For lack of reliable information, interpretations abound as to why a right-wing government would move against the business groups that were its strongest supporters. One possibility is that the conglomerates were getting too powerful, and the military did not want so much competition. Another is that the government needed a scapegoat to deflect blame for its economic problems. A third is that the conglomerates were behaving so badly, in their penchant for speculation and short-term profits, that they were seriously undermining the government's economic policies. Whatever the reason(s), the process of intervention threatened to create yet more problems, since some of the losers in the transaction were foreign banks that had lent money to several smaller banks scheduled for liquidation. Through various types of leverage, the foreign banks eventually forced the government to take responsibility for the debt of the private financial sector.[75]

The decision to intervene the banks left the government officials in a truly anomalous position. Firm proponents of a small state, they found themselves with more control over the economy than even Allende had had. Pundits referred to the process as "the Chicago road to socialism." Although the long-run issue was how to return the firms to the private sector, the immediate problem was how to rescue the ailing private sector. The means chosen involved huge subsidies to the banks and the largest corporations, including the purchase of bad loans by the Central Bank, a preferential exchange rate for holders of dollar debt, the option to turn dollar debt into pesos, and ultimately a government guarantee for a substantial part of the privately contracted foreign debt. It is estimated that these policies cost the government some $3.5 billion between 1982 and 1985, equivalent to 20 percent of GDP in the latter year.[76]

New rounds of privatization

Once Hernán Büchi became finance minister in 1985, the question of reprivatization of the firms came onto the agenda. (For many of them, this was their second privatization. A large number of the firms the government inherited when it intervened the banks had been purchased by the conglomerates in the earlier privatization process.) Methods used included sale through the stock exchange, bidding among prequalified bidders, and "popular capitalism." The last of these methods had been devised, while Büchi was still superintendent of banks, as a way to sell the two large banks. It involved the sale of stock in small blocks to individuals, including workers (and management) in the firm itself. Between 1984 and 1986, the intervened firms were all disposed of, with a subsidy estimated at 50 percent of the value.[77]

The success of this processs and other political considerations led to the fourth round of privatization – the largest by monetary value.[78] It involved sale of the "traditional" large state firms that the military had objected to selling in the 1970s. By 1985, the economic and especially the political conjunctures were different. Privatization had two major political advantages for the government. On the one hand, the shrinking of the public sector would limit the room for maneuver by a successor government. Indeed, once Pinochet lost the 1988 plebiscite, it was announced that privatization would speed up. On the other hand, insofar as "popular capitalism" was involved, it would increase the number of small property owners, who might be expected to become government supporters. The economic benefits were much more dubious. The firms had become a major source of revenue to the government (accounting for approximately 25 percent, including dividends and taxes) and, although their sale would bring in funds in the short run, they would entail losses over time.[79]

The initial goal was to sell a maximum of 30 percent of the stock of some 23 firms. As had happened on other occasions, the list was gradually expanded by the end of 1988 to include 33 firms with an average of 85 percent of the stock transferred.[80] Table 3.8 shows the firms and their situation as of March 1989. This last privatization round was perhaps the most controversial of the four. First, it involved firms that had become legitimated over decades as appropiate for public control. Second, the firms were profitable and well-managed. Third, several were purchased by foreign investors, using discounted debt paper (through the also controversial debt–equity swaps). And, fourth, the political aims of the process were especially obvious, since the privatizations were undertaken just prior to the return of a democratically elected government.

Table 3.8 Goals and results of privatization of public enterprises. 1985–9

Firm (sector)	Goals of privatization (%)					Actual privatization (%)			
	Sep. 1985	Dec. 1986	Dec. 1987	Sep. 1988	Mar. 1989	Dec. 1986	Dec. 1987	Sep. 1988	Mar. 1989
CAP (steel)	49	80	100	100	100	52	100	100	100
COFOMAP (forestry)	30	100	100	100	100	n.d.	n.d.	100	100
COLBUN (electricity)	0	30	30	30	30	0	0	0	0
CTC (telephones)	30	51	100	100	100	11	25	75	86
CHILMETRO (electricity)	30	100	100	100	100	63	100	100	100
CHILGENER (electricity)	30	49	100	100	100	35	65	100	100
CHILQUINTA (electricity)	30	100	100	100	100	63	100	100	100
ECOM (computers)	30	100	100	100	100	100	100	100	100
EMEC (electricity)	30	100	100	100	100	100	100	100	100
EMEL (electricity)	30	100	100	100	100	100	100	100	100
EMELAT (electricity)	30	100	100	100	100	0	100	100	100
ENACAR (coal)	30	49	49	49	49	0	0	1	8
ENAEX (explosives)	30	100	100	100	100	0	100	100	100
ENDESA (electricity)	30	30	49	55	100	0	20	51	90
ENTEL (telecommunications)	30	30	51	75	100	30	33	51	72
IANSA (sugar refinery)	30	49	55	100	100	46	49	58	100
LAB. CHILE (laboratory)	30	49	49	63	100	23	49	63	100
LAC CHILE (airline)	30	33	60	60	100	0	0	16	16
PILMAIQUEN (electricity)	30	100	100	100	100	100	100	100	100
PULLINQUE (electricity)	30	100	100	100	100	0	100	100	100
SOQUIMICH (chemicals)	30	65	100	100	100	55	82	100	100
SCHWAGER (coal)	30	49	100	100	100	0	33	46	95
TELEX (telex)	49	100	100	100	100	100	100	100	100
EDELNOR (electricity)	0	0	49	100	100	0	0	2	4
EDELMAC (electricity)	0	12	49	100	100	12	12	67	100
ISE (insurance)	0	0	33	49	49	0	0	0	2
CHILE FILMS (films)	0	0	0	100	100	0	0	0	100
EMPREMAR (shipping)	0	0	0	35	35	0	0	0	0
PEHUENCHE (electricity)	0	0	0	50	50	0	0	0	2
EMOS (water)	0	0	0	49	49	0	0	0	0
ESVAL (water)	0	0	0	49	49	0	0	0	0
METRO DE STGO. (metro)	0	0	0	35	49	0	0	0	0
EDELAYSEN (electricity)	0	0	0	35	100	0	0	0	0

Source: Marcel (1986, p. 31).

7   CONCLUSIONS

To summarize the preceding sections, the Chilean experience with economic reform was characterized as much by problems as by successes. In fact, if Pinochet had fallen in the early 1980s like most of his fellow Latin American dictators, the Chilean model would be regarded as a colossal failure. The crash in 1982–3 was deeper than in any other major Latin American country, and the disequilibria showed no signs of reversing themselves. The economy was only saved by measures that substantially contradicted the model itself, especially the interventions and subsidies. Ultimately the situation was turned around by Hernán Büchi, the finance minister who changed the style of decision-making as well as the means of implementation, who substituted real-world pragmatism for textbook rigidity. Criticisms clearly remained, but there was also a record of modest success for the new government to build on.

The topic we want to address in these final pages is the lessons that can be learned from the Chilean experience. We will limit ourselves to a fairly narrow subset of problems by accepting (for the purposes of the discussion) the general direction of policy. Stallings will first address what we can say about the relationship between problems that occurred in Chile and the policy-making process, in particular the issue of overkill. Brock will then examine the insurance aspects of the economic reforms.

Overkill in policy-making

Chilean policy-making during the military regime exhibited repeated occurrences of overkill – policies that were carried to extremes. These extremes, in turn, imposed inordinately high costs on the economy and society. In addition to the liberalization and privatization policies discussed above, this section will also draw on a recent analysis of macroeconomic policy to illustrate the issue of overkill. This will be followed by a discussion of how the overkill was related to the policy process.

In examining macroeconomic stabilization in Chile since 1982, Patricio Meller has constructed a model that differentiates between primary and secondary adjustment costs.[81] The former are defined as "the reduction of real absorption necessary to close the existing expenditure–output gap and to generate the required real transfer." The latter are costs "generated by existing structural rigidities (such as price rigidities, capital-sector specificity, market imperfections, and lags) and by adjustment policies that are more stringent than actually required (overkill)." Meller's calculations suggest that secondary costs were as high as primary costs in 1982–3 and about 30 percent of primary costs for the next several years, as tradeable goods took a long time to recover. Furthermore, the costs imposed on society by the particular type of adjustment had future as well as current costs. Total consumption in 1982–3 fell by 24 percent while investment fell by 50 percent. By 1988, investment still had not recovered to its 1981 level, and consumption remained 5 percent below its earlier level.

In trade policy, a similar trend occurred, as documented by Ricardo Ffrench-Davis and Jaime Gatica.[82] The lowering of tariffs to a uniform 10 percent, in combination with inappropriate macroeconomic and exchange rate policies, was another example of overkill. The large overvaluation of the real exchange rate between 1979 and 1982 helped to produce waves of bankruptcies in firms that might otherwise have attained the necessary efficiency increases. This, in turn, helped push the economy further into depression.

The third example of overkill is with respect to privatization. The bankruptcy of the conglomerates in 1981–2 offers prima facie evidence of the failure of the initial privatization policies. The government not only ended up with most of the firms back in its hands but also had to pay enormous amounts to refloat them – in addition to its original subsidies. The idea was that new economic actors with a different "vision" were required to produce a dynamic style of capitalism; once those firms were created, regulatory mechanisms were not only unnecessary but also a hindrance. Evidence shows that privatization and almost total deregulation do not produce a happy mix. Mario Marcel has produced a detailed analysis of the more recent privatizations, which again show the high economic cost that is implicit.[83] Although the government gained money in the short run, it lost in the longer term by selling off firms that contributed some 25 percent of its revenue. Clearly, the usual justifications for privatization (inefficiency and losses) did not exist.

Was there something about the process of policy-making and implementation that encouraged this proclivity toward overkill? The quick and easy response is an authoritarian government, but the answer is more complex. At least four factors seem relevant.

(1) The great rigidity of belief and style that characterized the "Chicago Boys," epitomized by but not limited to Sergio de Castro, was the initial factor. Two Chilean economists, themselves trained at Chicago, point to this same problem. "In Chile, the application of some simplistic and erroneous macroeconomic ideas with religious zeal created a major disequilibrium that not only resulted in the deceleration of growth and eventual disastrous fall in the level of output but also compromised the continuity of the reforms themselves."[84] There was there an unwillingness to listen to criticism, even from people who basically agreed with the policy direction, and a total unwillingness to compromise. In addition, there was the sense of urgency about the reforms that compounded the mistakes, since it was not possible to wait for better timing. The original privatizations in a period of deep recession were an example; few people could bid for firms and therefore ownership was heavily concentrated. Likewise the

combination of large tariff reductions in a period of recession and high interest rates compounded the already difficult adjustment problems.

(2)   The ability to continue their dogmatic style was made possible by the extreme degree of autonomy provided by the economists' military patrons. Once the military government decided to support the de Castro team, the latter was given virtually total control over making economic and later social policy as well. Given the destruction of other institutions of influence (especially the congress) and the centralization within the bureaucracy, there were no alternative channels of influence for critics to use. Some tried to go to high-ranking military acquaintances, but this was unsuccessful even for those few who had such access.

(3)   The autonomy afforded the economists was complemented by their location in a society based on fear, which further prevented challenges to their hegemonic position. The fear was of two main types. On the one hand, there was fear of the government itself on the part of labor and political actors from the left and even the center of the old political spectrum. Their fear was largely based on the government's demonstrated willingness to use repression against its enemies. The coup itself was perhaps the most brutal in Latin American history, and the initial massive repression was followed up by more targeted repression against people who opposed the regime. But economic repression was at least as important. The fear of losing a job, or the limitation on the possibility of getting one, in the context of the high unemployment of the 1970s, was a crucial barrier to challenging government policy at the national or local level.
   On the other hand, business groups and the political right also had a fear that kept them from challenging policy, even when their direct economic interests were threatened. This was the fear of the alternative to the military regime – assumed to be a return of the Popular Unity. Since business saw the Popular Unity and its leftist constituency as a mortal enemy of the capitalist system, its leaders were unwilling to risk actions that might cause waves. The government cleverly encouraged and manipulated this fear so as to increase its own space for maneuver. The vacuum was exacerbated as the rightist political establishment ceded its role to the government. Until the period after the crisis, the right-wing parties were inactive.

(4)   Finally, all of the above factors were exacerbated by the lack of a perceived need by the military for active political support from society. As a consequence, there was little concern for spreading the benefits of their policies or even worrying about the costs. Thus they allowed the economists to follow policies that concentrated resources among a very small number of individuals, and especially the conglomerates, just as they

allowed large numbers of firms to fail. The repression of real wages and benefits was an even more extreme result of the same view. Initially, there was a group within the government with a corporatist approach, but they were eliminated from positions of power in the first few years. Presumably some of the others had a vague "trickle-down" notion about distribution, but they were willing to accept a very long time horizon. Ultimately, this approach contributed to the regime's ouster as a result of the 1988 plebiscite, despite the strong economic performance of the late 1980s.

Fortunately, very few Latin American countries are in a structural position to make this same set of mistakes – although some African countries may well be – since authoritarian governments are generally in recess in the region. In fact, most Latin American countries trying to implement trade liberalization and privatization policies in the 1990s are facing nearly the opposite circumstances: electoral democracies with interest groups of all types free to protest in a wide variety of forums, from the streets to the congress to smoke-filled rooms. Paralysis is often the outcome. If the Chilean experience has anything to offer other Latin American governments in terms of the issues discussed here, it is the need to search for adequate institutional arrangements for carrying out reforms. Despite the excesses observed, it is surely the case that some degree of autonomy and a fair amount of continuity are vital components of success. Eventually, these ingredients paid off even in the Chilean case, when the new set of economic technocrats was installed after the crisis. Thus, a prerequisite for making reforms is the creation of institutions that can permit decisions to be made and implemented. The trade-off between accountability and autonomy, however, will not be an easy one to manage.

Insurance aspects of the economic reforms

A fundamental and continuing problem for the Chilean economic model will be the ability of the government to provide insurance to those affected severely by external shocks to the economy. The dismantling of governmental economic activity in the 1990s left a void for government policies that had previously provided some degree of social insurance, whether by direct government employment or by various forms of rent-seeking.[85] The economic team was aware of this void and gave great importance to the creation of new institutional forms of social security and health care that would eliminate the government's direct role in providing social insurance. Hayekian considerations on social insurance systems heavily influenced the 1980 Social Security Law, one of whose main architects was José Piñera.[86]

From the start of the military regime, social security reform was a high-priority issue, but one of the most complex issues. When the government introduced the new system in 1980, individuals were allowed either to remain in the old, pay-as-you-go indexed system or to move to the new, nonindexed system of competitive, individual-account, social security funds. The tax rate for participating in the new system – 13 percent of income (plus another 4 percent for the new system of privately-administered health care plans, the ISAPREs) – was lower than the tax rates charged by the social security funds of the old system. Those workers who opted to stay in the old system continued to receive their same after-tax salary, but those who switched to the new system received an increase in their after-tax salary of anywhere between 7 and 15 percent, depending on the difference between their old tax rate and the new one.[87]

The difference in after-tax income between the old and new systems was a powerful carrot to get people to leave the old system and to deposit a government-guaranteed "recognition bond" (calculated according to a fixed formula based on salary and years of participation in the old system) to open their account in the new system. The security of the price-indexing mechanism associated with the pensions of the old system was still an advantage that the new system could not offer, however, unless minimum wages were indexed to the price level. Although there is no formal link between the wage indexation provision of the 1979 Labor Law and the incentive structure designed to encourage people to switch to the 1980 Social Security System, a number of well-informed Chileans have stated that such a link was more than a coincidence.[88]

Although the wage-indexation provision of the 1979 Labor Law has been widely criticized as a policy mistake by the government,[89] the legal floor on the real minimum wage in conjunction with the creation of the new social security system provided insurance to workers in two ways. First, the system allowed workers to create an annuity upon retirement based upon the present value of their lifetime contributions, rather than on an arbitrary formula linked to income in the years immediately preceding retirement. Secondly, the system was formally an implicit contract between the government and workers that provided some measure of insurance against external shocks to the economy.

Assuming that the Chilean government has better access to world capital markets than Chilean workers, work by Diamond and Mirrlees, and Merton, suggests that an efficient mechanism for providing social insurance to workers may involve a wage-indexation mechanism in conjunction with individual accounts in the social security funds, since the wage-indexation mechanism creates a put option that provides insurance against negative external shocks.[90] For such insurance to be efficient, one condition is that the workers must "pay" for the wage indexation with a wage that is initially lower than labor's marginal product. Whether intentional or not, the official understatement of inflation during the first five years of the military regime had effectively lowered the real minimum wage prior to the implementation of the official indexation of the wage rate in 1979 and the social security reform in 1980.

A second condition for the efficiency of the government's implicit contract with Chilean workers is the ability of the government to use world capital markets to hedge the put option that it has written.[91] In Chile, the government has not had the ability completely to hedge the risk associated with writing the put option associated with the guaranteed real wage. As mentioned earlier, Chile's successful adjustment to external shocks in the 1980s relied very heavily on assistance from international lending agencies, assistance which is available to governments but not to workers. Such assistance, however, is not equivalent to a perfect hedge for the external risk faced by the Chilean economy. The ultimate abandonment of the wage-indexation policy in Chile in 1982 attests to the incompleteness, although not to the absence, of external insurance mechanisms available to the Chilean government.

To the extent that the Chilean governments in the future cannot provide insurance to the private sector via its access to world capital markets, internal pressures to provide that insurance may lead to demands for policies to redistribute income within the economy. To the extent that the government is too tightly committed to "rules" rather than "discretion" to permit some political accommodation to the competing internal demands for insurance that inevitably accompany an uninsurable external shock, the entire rule-based institutional structure may be destroyed, as happened in Chile during the Great Depression and almost happened again in the early 1980s. The key longer-run challenge to Chile's model, therefore, will be the institutionalization of political processes that permit certain forms of income redistribution to take place, especially in the aftermath of external shocks, without the abandonment of the economy's set of market-oriented institutions and policies.

NOTES

1   See especially Stallings (1978) and Brock (1992).
2   For a historical overview of the three administrations, see Stallings (1978, chapters 4–6).
3   On Chilean economic policy and implementation during the Allende period, see Universidad de Chile, Instituto de Economía (1972, 1973).
4   Data are from Banco Central de Chile (1989).
5   Ibid.
6   On populist cycles, see Sachs (1989); see also Dornbusch and Edwards (1990).
7   Important self-criticisms by former Popular Unity economists include Bitar (1979) and Griffith-Jones (1981a).
8   An example of the Christian Democratic critique of the Popular Unity is Larraín and Meller (1991).
9   On human rights in Chile during the early years of the military, see Amnesty International (1974) and the various reports of the Organization of American States (1974, 1976, 1977). For a more general discussion of the political system, both before and after the military coup, see Garretón (1989).

10   The term "Chicago Boys" is somewhat misleading, since some prominent Chicago economists (such as Ricardo Ffrench-Davis of CIEPLAN) were in the opposition, and many economists not trained at Chicago – such as Jorge Cauas (Columbia) and José Piñera (Harvard) – were considered to be "Chicago Boys."

11   On relations between Pinochet and the economic team, see Aldunate (1987).

12   Following the 1859 revolutionary assault on the regime of Manuel Montt, Chilean disciples of Frenchman Jean Gustave Courcelle-Seneuil – the first foreign advisor to Chile – greatly influenced the establishment of free banking legislation (the 1860 Banking Law) and free trade in Chile during the 1860s and 1870s. Similarly, following the 1891 Civil War, the Chilean congress passed conversion legislation that placed Chile on the gold standard (after 18 years of a paper money regime) during 1895–8. Again, after much civil unrest in the early 1920s, the military took over in 1924 and invited the Kemmerer Commission to create a Central Bank and return Chile to the gold standard (which was maintained during 1926–32). Finally, following the sharp acceleration of inflation and economic stagnation of the middle 1950s, the Ibáñez government brought in the Klein–Saks mission, whose recommendations were important in the Alessandri government's adoption of a fixed exchange rate during 1959–62.

13   With regard to the earliest Chilean technocrats, Albert Hirschman observed that "[Courcelle-Seneuil's] Chilean disciples, several of whom were to reach positions of great influence, were far more royalist than the king and lost all sense of reality and of national interest in their desire to remain faithful to the 'postulates of classical political economy.' " See Hirschman (1965).

14   This phrase was used by Pinto (1987).

15   Hayek was the guest of honor at a large conference held in April 1981 in Viña del Mar to celebrate the apparent success of the Chilean economic model and continued to serve as honorary president of the Centro de Estudios Públicos, a conservative Chilean think tank, until his death in 1992.

16   These were the opening remarks of a talk that Piñera was to have given at a conference at UC Davis; emphasis in the original.

17   The text is included in Méndez (1979); emphasis added.

18   Campero (1984). An update of this important book is Campero (1992).

19   Campero (1984); see also Eduardo Silva, "Capitalist Coalitions and Economic Policymaking in Authoritarian Chile, 1973–1988," PhD dissertation, University of California–San Diego, 1991.

20   On the history of unions in Chile, see Angell (1972) and Barrera (1979).

21   Campero and Cortázar (1988).

22   On the party constituencies, see Stallings (1978, chapter 3).

23   On organization of the right in Chile, see Silva, "Capitalist Coalitions" and Patrick Barrett, "The Political Right in Chile," PhD dissertation, University of Wisconsin–Madison (forthcoming).

24   Petras and Morley (1975).

25   For different views on the role of the United States in the overthrow of Allende, see Petras and Morley (1975) and Sigmund (1977). The best documentary evidence of US activities is contained in the series of congressional hearings on the subject. See *The United States and Chile during the Allende Years, 1970–73* (hearings before the Subcommittee on Inter-American

Affairs of the Foreign Affairs Committee, US House of Representatives, 93d Congress, 2d session, 1974); *Covert Action, 1963–73* (Staff Report of the Select Committee to Study Governmental Operations with Respect to Intelligence Activities, 94th Congress, 1st session, 1975); and *Alleged Assassination Plots involving Foreign Leaders* (Interim Report of Select Committee to Study Governmental Operations with Respect to Intelligence Activities, 94th Congress, 1st session, 1975).

26 On US–Chilean relations under the military, see Muñoz and Portales (1987).
27 For different views of the Chilean model, see Foxley (1983); Edwards and Edwards (1987); and Valenzuela and Valenzuela (1986).
28 Ramos (1975) and Cortázar and Marshall (1980).
29 See Banco Central de Chile (1989, p. 215), for a real wage series that relies on a corrected price index for 1971–2.
30 Cortázar and Marshall (1980).
31 Interview with former Chilean finance minister, Santiago, September 1990.
32 Ffrench-Davis noted that the official consumer price index severely underestimated increases in rents (between 1958 and 1969 the CPI rose by 1,136 percent, but the rental component, which had about a 10 percent weight in the index, only rose by 640 percent). Ffrench-Davis's corrected CPI for the period between 1960 and 1970 drops the rental component of the official consumer price index. See Ffrench-Davis (1973).
33 Ffrench-Davis (1973) and Cortázar and Marshall (1980).
34 Cortázar and Meller (1987).
35 Marcel and Meller (1986).
36 Cortázar and Meller (1987).
37 Ibid., p. 19.
38 On the background of Chilean protection, see Ricardo Ffrench-Davis (1986).
39 Dirección de Presupuestos (1978); this source is a reprinting of the statements of the ministers of finance.
40 Campero (1984); see also Moulián and Vergara (1979).
41 Campero (1984).
42 Moulián and Vergara (1979).
43 On labor under the military, see Campero and Cortázar (1985); see also Barrera and Valenzuela (1986).
44 Griffith-Jones (1981b, p. 30). The IMF was also critical of other aspects of Chilean policy; see pp. 42–3.
45 Valdez (1989).
46 Aldunate (1987).
47 Data are calculated from Banco Central de Chile, *Indicadores económicos y sociales* and *Boletín Mensual*.
48 For an attempt to separate out the various types of influence on the decline of industry in Chile, see Gatica (1989). Other discussions of the impact of trade policy in industry include Vergara (1980) and Edwards and Edwards (1987).
49 Foxley (1983).
50 On the crisis, see Arellano (1983); see also Arellano and Marfán (1986).
51 Interviews with former Chilean government officials, Santiago, 1987.
52 Campero (1984).
53 Ibid. Also interview with former staff member of CPC, Santiago, 1987.
54 Interview with Chilean economist, Santiago, 1987.

55 Interviews with former Chilean government officials, Santiago, 1987.

56 Edwards and Edwards (1987).

57 Privatization of land-reform holdings taken during the Allende government is an important area of privatization that we do not cover. For a good account of the privatization and subsequent changes in the distribution of land, see Jarvis (1985).

58 Marcelo Cavarozzi, "The Government and the Industrial Bourgeoisie in Chile, 1938–64," PhD dissertation, University of California–Berkeley, 1975.

59 Universidad de Chile, Instituto de Economía (1972).

60 Vergara (1986); Edwards and Edwards (1987).

61 Vergara (1986).

62 Edwards and Edwards (1987, p. 96).

63 Foxley (1983); for other estimates, see Vergara (1986).

64 Sanfuentes (1984); Edwards and Edwards (1987).

65 Moulián and Vergara (1979).

66 Ibid.

67 Muñoz and Portales (1987).

68 Interview with Professor Peter Winn, expert on labor in Chile, August, 1989.

69 Larroulet (1984).

70 Marcel (1989).

71 Banco Central de Chile, *Boletín Mensual* (various).

72 Sanfuentes (1984). See also Constable and Valenzuela (1991).

73 Interview with former Chilean finance minister, Santiago, 1987.

74 Constable and Valenzuela (1991).

75 Interview with former Chilean finance minister, Santiago, 1987.

76 *El Mercurio*, November 27, 1985 (citing a confidential World Bank study).

77 Errázuriz and Weinstein (1986).

78 For the three privatization rounds that involved sales, the amounts involved were $543 million, $1.1 billion, and $3.6 billion. See Meller (1990).

79 Marcel (1989).

80 Ibid.

81 Meller (1990).

82 Ffrench-Davis (1986) and Gatica (1989).

83 Marcel (1989).

84 Edwards and Edwards (1987, p. 207).

85 Valenzuela provides the following short description of rent-seeking in Chile in the 1960s: "Whether it was a particular business seeking tax relief, a union organization seeking the establishment of a pension fund, a professional association after legal recognition, or a municipality after a new dam, political leaders and officials were continuously beseiged by an overwhelming number of petitions." See Valenzuela (1978).

86 Hayek's writing in *The Road to Serfdom* expresses well the economic team's beliefs with regard to state insurance policies:

Where, as in the case of sickness and accident, neither the desire to avoid such calamities nor the efforts to overcome their consequences are as a rule weakened by the provision of assistance – where, in short, we deal with genuinely insurable risks – the case for the state's helping to organize a comprehensive system of social insurance is very strong . . . To the same category belongs also the increase of security through the state's rendering assistance to the victims of such "acts of God" as earthquakes and floods. Wherever communal action can mitigate disasters against which the individual can neither attempt to guard himself nor make provision for the consequences, such communal action should undoubtedly be taken.

87 Baeza and Manubens (1988).
88 Interview with former Chilean government officials, Santiago, October 1990.
89 See, for example, Corbo (1985) and Edwards and Edwards (1987).
90 Diamond and Mirrlees, and Merton characterize optimal private wage contracts and pension policies in a world where firms have full access to well-functioning capital markets and workers own only their own human capital (for which there is assumed to be no market). In the model used by Diamond and Mirrlees, and Merton, workers work for two periods and live off a pension in the third period. In this setting, it can be shown that the optimal contract is one in which workers receive a guaranteed wage floor in the second period. This wage floor results in the creation of a put option, or insurance policy, on the worker's second period marginal product, since the worker is guaranteed the wage floor regardless of how low the worker's actual marginal product may turn out to be in the second period. In this model, the worker "pays" for the insurance offered by the put option written by the firm by receiving a first-period wage that is less than the worker's marginal product. See Diamond and Mirrlees (1985) and Merton (1985).
91 In the model of Diamond–Mirrlees and Merton, the firm is able to write the put option to its workers because it has access to well-functioning capital markets that allow the firm perfectly to hedge the put option.

REFERENCES

Aldunate, Arturo Fontaine 1987: *Los economistas y el Presidente Pinochet*, Santiago: Zig-Zag.
Amnesty Inetrnational 1974: *Chile: An Amnesty International Report*, London: Amnesty International.
Angell, Alan 1972: *Politics and the Labor Movement in Chile*, London: Oxford University Press.
Arellano, José Pablo 1983: "De la liberalización a la intervención: el mercado de capitales en Chile, 1974–83," *Colección Estudios CIEPLAN*, 11, December.
Arellano, José Pablo and Marfán, Manuel 1986: "Ahorro-inversión y relaciones financieras en la actual crisis económica chilena," *Colección Estudios CIEPLAN*, 20, December.
Baeza, Sergio and Manubens, Rodrigo (eds.) 1988: *Sistema Privado de Pensiones en Chile*, Santiago: Talleres de Alfabeta Impresores (for El Centro de Estudios Públicos).
Banco Central de Chile 1989: *Indicadores económicos y sociales 1960–1988*, Santiago: Banco Central.
Barrera, Manuel 1979: *Desarrollo económico y sindicalismo en Chile, 1938–70*, Santiago: Vector.

Barrera, Manuel and Valenzuela, J. Samuel 1986: "The Development of Labor Movement Opposition to the Military Regime," in J. Samuel Valenzuela and Arturo Valenzuela (eds.), *Military Rule in Chile: Dictatorship and Oppositions*, Baltimore: Johns Hopkins Press.

Bitar, Sergio 1979: *Transición, socialismo, y democracia: la experiencia chilena*, Mexico: Siglo XXI.

Brock, Philip (ed.) 1992: *If Texas Were Chile: A Primer on Banking Reform*, San Francisco: ICS Press.

Campero, Guillermo 1984: *Los gremios empresariales en el período 1970–1983*, Santiago: ILET.

Campero, Guillermo 1992: "Entrepreneurs Under the Military Regime," in Paul W. Drake and Ivan Jaksic (eds.). *The Struggle for Democracy in Chile, 1982–1990*, Lincoln: University of Nebraska Press.

Campero, Guillermo and Cortázar, René 1985: "Lógicas de acción sindical en Chile," *Colección Estudios CIEPLAN*, 18, December.

Campero, Guillermo and Cortázar, René 1988: "Actores Sociales y la transicion a la democracia en Chile," *Colección Estudios CIEPLAN*, 25, December.

Constable, Pamela and Valenzuela, Arturo 1991: *Chile Under Pinochet: A Nation of Enemies*, New York: W. W. Norton and Company, chapter 8.

Corbo, Vittorio 1985: "Reforms and Macroeconomic Adjustment in Chile During 1974–1983," *World Development*, 13, August.

Cortázar, René and Marshall, Jorge 1980: "Indice de precios al consumidor en Chile: 1970–1978," *Colección Estudios CIEPLAN*, 4.

Cortázar, René and Meller, Patricio 1987: "Los dos Chiles, o la importancia de revisar las estadísticas oficiales," *Colección Estudios CIEPLAN*, 21, June.

Diamond, Peter and Mirrlees, James 1985: "Insurance Aspects of Pensions," in David A, Wise (ed.), *Pensions, Labor and Individual Choice*, Chicago: University of Chicago Press.

Dirección de Presupuestos 1978: *Somas realmente independientes gracias al esfuerzo de todos los chilemos*, Santiago: Ministerio de Hacienda.

Dornbusch, Rudiger and Edwards, Sebastian 1990: "The Macroeconomics of Populism in Latin America," *Journal of Development Economics*, 32.

Edwards, Sabastian and Edwards, Alejandra Cox 1987: *Monetarism and Liberalization: The Chilean Experiment*, Cambridge: Ballinger.

Errázuriz, Enrique and Weinstein, Jacqueline 1986: "Capitalismo popular y privatización de las empresas," Working Paper, Programa de Empleo del Trabajo, Santiago.

Ffrench-Davis, Ricardo 1973: *Políticas económicas en Chile, 1952–1970*, Santiago: CIEPLAN, p. 245.

Ffrench-Davis, Ricardo 1986: "Import Liberalization: The Chilean Experience, 1973–1982," in J. Samuel Valenzuela and Arturo Valenzuela (eds.), *Military Rule in Chile: Dictatorship and Oppositions*, Baltimore: Johns Hopkins Press.

Foxley, Alejandro 1983: *Latin American Experiments in Neoconservative Economics*, Berkeley: University of California Press.

Garretón, Manuel Antonio 1989: *The Chilean Political Process*, Boston: Unwin Hyman.

Gatica, Jaime 1989: *Deindustrialization in Chile*, Boulder, CO: Westview, chapter 3.

Griffith-Jones, Stephany 1981a: *The Role of Finance in the Transition to Socialism,* London: Francis Pinter.

Griffith-Jones, Stephany 1981b: *The Evolution of External Finance, Economic Policy, and Development in Chile, 1973–78,* Discussion Paper No. 160, Sussex: Institute for Development Studies.

Hirschman, Albert O. 1965: *Journeys Toward Progress: Studies in Economic Policy-Making in Latin America,* New York: Anchor Books, p. 222.

Jadresi, Esteban 1986: "Evolucion de empleo y desempleo en Chile, 1970–85," *Colección Estudios CIEPLAN,* 20.

Jarvis, Lovell S. 1985: *Chilean Agriculture under Military Rule: From Reform to Reaction, 1973–1980,* Berkeley: Institute of International Studies, University of California.

Larrain, Felipe and Meller, Patricio 1991: "The Socialist–Populist Chilean Experience, 1970–1973," in Rudiger Dornbusch and Sebastian Edwards (eds.), *The Macroeconomics of Populism in Latin America,* Chicago: University of Chicago Press.

Larroulet, Cristian 1984: "Reflexiones en torno al estado empresario en Chile," *Estudios Públicos,* 14.

Marcel, Mario 1989: "Privatización y finanzas públicas: el caso de Chile, 1985–88," *Colección Estudios CIEPLAN,* 26, June.

Marcel, Mario and Meller, Patricio 1986: "Empalme de las cuentas nacionales de Chile 1960–1985: métodos alternativos y resultados," *Colección Estudios CIEPLAN,* 20, December.

Meller, Patricio 1990: "Chile," in John Williamson (ed.) *Latin American Reform: How Much Has Happened?* Washington, DC: Institute of International Economics.

Méndez, Juan Carlos 1979: *Chilean Economic Policy,* Santiago: Matte and Méndez.

Merton, Robert 1985: "Comment on Diamond and Mirrlees," in David A. Wise (ed.), *Pensions, Labor, and Individual Choice,* Chicago: University of Chicago Press.

Moulián, Tomás and Vergara, Pilar 1979: "Políticas de estabilización y comportamientos sociales: la experiencia chilena, 1974–1979," *Apuntes CIEPLAN,* 22, November.

Muñoz, Heraldo and Portales, Carlos 1987: *Una amistad esquiva: las relaciones de Estados Unidos y Chile,* Santiago: Puehuén.

Organization of American States 1974: *Report of the Status of Human Rights in Chile.*

Organization of American States 1976: *Second Report on the Situation of Human Rights in Chile.*

Organization of American States 1977: *Third Report on the Situation of Human Rights in Chile.*

Petras, James and Morley, Morris 1975: *The United States and Chile,* New York: Monthly Review Press.

Pinto Aníbal 1987: "La ofensiva contra el estado-económico," *Colección Estudios CIEPLAN,* 21, June.

Ramos, Joseph 1975: "El costo social: hechos e interpretaciones," *Estudios de Economía,* 6.

Sachs, Jeffrey 1989: "Social Conflict and Populist Policies in Latin America," *NBER Working Papers*, No. 2897.

Sanfuentes, Andrés 1984: "Los grupos económicos: control y políticas," *Colección Estudios CIEPLAN*, 15, December.

Sigmund, Paul E. 1977: *The Overthrow of Allende and the Politics of Chile*, Pittsburgh: University of Pittsburgh Press.

Stallings, Barbara 1978: *Class Conflict and Economic Development in Chile, 1958–73*, Stanford: Stanford University Press.

Universidad de Chile, Instituto de Economía 1972: *La economía chilena en 1971*, Santiago: Instituto de Economia.

Universidad de Chile, Instituto de Economía 1973: *La economía chilena en 1972*, Santiago: Instituto de Economia.

Valdez, Juan Gabriel 1989: *La escuela de Chicago: operación Chile*, Buenos Aires: Grupo Zeta.

Valenzuela, Arturo 1978: *The Breakdown of Democratic Regimes: Chile*, Baltimore: Johns Hopkins Press, p. 9.

Valenzuela, J. Samuel and Valenzuela, Arturo (eds.) 1986: *Military Rule in Chile: Dictatorship and Oppositions*, Baltimore: Johns Hopkins Press.

Vergara, Pilar 1980: "Apertura externa y desarrollo industrial en Chile: 1973–1978," *Colección Estudios CIEPLAN*, 4, November.

Vergara, Pilar 1986: "Changes in the Economic Functions of the Chilean State under the Military Regime," in J. Samuel Valenzuela and Arturo Valenzuela (eds.), *Military Rule in Chile: Dictatorship and Oppositions*, Baltimore: Johns Hopkins Press.

4

Muddling Toward Adjustment: The Political Economy of Economic Policy Change in Ecuador
Merilee S. Grindle and Francisco E. Thoumi

INTRODUCTION[1]

Ecuador was not one of the stars of structural adjustment in the 1980s. Overall, it is difficult to rate its policy reform record as either "good" or "bad" in terms of the extent of the changes introduced or their impact on the economy.[2] In fact, the country muddled through a decade of adjustment. Its record of stop-and-go economic policies meant that some economic problems were at least controlled and others were avoided. Importantly, the country's fledgling democratic institutions survived – sometimes just barely – in the midst of repeated and severe economic and political crises. These are not spectacular accomplishments, but, taken together, they provide some lessons about adjustment over "the long haul" in contentious political environments.[3]

A decade of muddling toward adjustment did bring change to the country, if not sustained relief from economic and political problems. Economically, Ecuador avoided the hyperinflation that plagued other Latin American countries, and its citizens and policy makers abandoned many of the policy myths that prevailed during the oil boom of the 1970s. Public opinion and policy makers accepted that the nominal exchange, interest, and utility rates could not remain fixed in the face of high inflation and that tax reform, increased tax collection, and labor code reform were necessary for more effective economic development.[4] Politically and institutionally, important changes set conditions for subsequent efforts to adjust. Economic policy became central to political debate during the decade, and the government acquired a more centralized system for economic policy management as well as greater technical capacity to assess policy options. Ecuador's population became accustomed to the need for economic adjustment and more familiar with the nature of such changes. Political parties and interest groups began to develop the technical infrastructure to participate more effectively in discussions of macroeconomic policy.

These and other changes, as well as the introduction of numerous economic reform measures, were not easily accomplished. Throughout the decade, economic policy was debated, decided upon, introduced, and reacted to within a context of extensive contestation over the nature and legitimacy of institutions for resolving conflict. The simultaneous struggle to define economic policy and political and institutional power relationships did not defeat efforts to adjust, but slowed them considerably and limited their success. As for Ecuador, adjustment for many countries may be a long-term process marked by a series of efforts to introduce economic policy changes – sometimes successful, sometimes not – with variation in policy approaches over time providing lessons about how the need for economic adjustment is balanced against the need for achieving short-term political stability and longer-term institutional legitimacy. Analysis of Ecuador's experience may thus be relevant for the large numbers of other countries that disappoint economists because they move slowly yet surprise political analysts because they move at all in introducing and sustaining policy changes. These are countries that muddle towards adjustment.

In this chapter, we use the case of Ecuador to explore the political economy of muddling towards adjustment. Here, muddling refers to a pattern of policy reform in which changes are often successfully introduced but then suffer from considerable slippage as they are altered or reversed in response to a variety of political and economic pressures. We are particularly interested in the analysis of policies introduced in 1982–3, 1984–6, and 1988–90. For each of these reformist episodes, we ask a series of interrelated questions: How did issues of economic policy get on the agenda for government action? What factors shaped the content and timing of economic policy measures? What accounts for the ability (or inability) to implement and sustain important policy changes? What were the economic and political ramifications of the introduction of new policy measures?

What need to be explained in the case of Ecuador are the circumstances and institutional environment that encouraged the periodic policy reform initiatives that were undertaken in the 1980s. At the same time, analysis of the Ecuador case must account for the pattern in which a notable amount of slippage occurred after reforms were announced. The political dynamics of adjustment were repeated with regularity in this case, despite distinct leadership and different policies: policy elites initiated changes, and interest groups, parties, and public protest sought to undo them. An explanation of economic policy change in Ecuador must therefore account for the leadership assumed by policy elites in placing reform initiatives on the agenda for government action and in crafting the content and timing of new policies. Once such decisions were taken, however, societal reaction becomes central to explaining the sustainability of policy change.

More generally, the case suggests a model of policy change that begins with a focus on policy elites, their perceptions, and conflicts within government and between government and international organizations. Initially, then, the analysis focuses on the exploration of the dynamics of state-led reform. The model then focuses on how interest groups, parties, and coalitions respond to economic policy change within a particular institutional context. Indeed, considerable research indicates a large number of cases in which political executives are committed to bringing about significant policy changes and select strategies to do so that reflect their understanding of the crisis, the institutional context of the state, and their bases of support.[5] Similarly, other cases indicate that efforts to sustain policy changes are significantly affected by the capacity of societal groups to put countervailing pressure on the government and to pose a threat to its leadership, its stability, or its legitimacy (see especially Nelson, 1990). It is the interplay of state leadership and political response within a particular institutional context that often results in a pattern of muddling.

1 THE CONTEXT OF REFORM: HISTORICAL AND INSTITUTIONAL LEGACIES

That Ecuador muddled toward adjustment is not surprising, given the political environment into which economic policy changes were introduced:

1 A society deeply divided along lines of region, wealth, ethnicity, and economic interest.
2 A highly mobilized but fragmented structure of interests.
3 Weak democratic institutions.
4 Contention over constitutional provisions for conflict resolution.
5 A highly fragmented, unstable and contentious party system.
6 Frequent elections with no majoritarian party emerging victorious.
7 Deep-seated executive-legislative conflict over economic policy formulation and implementation jurisdiction.
8 A populace accustomed to a government that provided many benefits and imposed few burdens, especially on the economic elite.

These socioeconomic, institutional, and policy characteristics meant that the economic adjustments attempted during the decade were introduced into an environment of sharply divergent economic interests that corresponded to differences in regional development, of weakly legitimized and contentious institutions of governance, and of a society well-used to subsidies and special privileges flowing from the state. Considerable conflict could thus be expected over who would bear the costs of adjustment, over the "rules of the game" for resolving policy conflicts, and over the willingness of society to accept measures that imposed austerity and even short-term hardship in the interests of longer-run national development.

The socioeconomic context

Regionalism and sharply bifurcated economic interests characterized the social context of Ecuadoran adjustment (see especially Kasza, 1981). Ecuador is a small country of some ten million inhabitants who are about equally divided between rural and urban areas. More important than this distinction, however, is the difference between the coastal and highland regions. There are, in fact, three separate regions in the country, each of which has distinct natural resource endowments; they have been relatively isolated from each other until very recently (see Thoumi, 1990, p. 49).[6] The two most important regions, the coast and the highlands, each have well-developed agricultural economies, but that of the coast is primarily directed toward export production while that of the highlands is primarily organized around the production of domestically consumed goods. Industrialization followed a similar pattern, with natural resource-based export manufacturing located on the coast and protected import-substituting industries (ISI) located in the highlands.

Along with regional differences, ethnic and class distinctions continue to be sharply drawn in Ecuador. Approximately 40 percent of the population is comprised of indigenous groups for whom Spanish is a second language. This indigenous population, which has been impoverished and exploited by government and local and national economic elites since the time of the Spanish conquest in the sixteenth and seventeenth centuries, is largely rural and has only recently been accorded greater access to political and economic power.

Income inequality is high, even by Latin American standards. Although income and wealth distribution data are weak, they suggest that while the Gini coefficients of income distribution estimates were only somewhat higher than those of other Latin American countries in the late 1960s, the percentage of the population below poverty lines was significantly higher (Luzuriaga and Zuvekas, 1981). During the 1970s, Gini coefficients showed a steady decrease in inequality as the middle class was strengthened and oil wealth fueled economic growth. However, during this period rural income distribution became more unequal as prices of rural products rose much less than those of the urban sector and as agriculture stagnated. The distribution of wealth was a great deal more skewed than that of income, reflecting the extremely high concentration of land and modern sector enterprises.[7] Differences in income and wealth distribution contribute to weak national identity and cohesion and a high potential for social conflict.

The economic history of the country also leads to expectations that conflict will surround efforts to introduce new policies. Because Ecuador had few mineral resources of interest to the Spanish colonizers, it was largely unintegrated into the world economy until well into the nineteenth century, when it became an exporter of agricultural products. Cocoa, coffee, and bananas were the principal exports until the early 1970s, when oil began to be exported. After the mid-nineteenth century, the domestic economy largely reflected the boom and bust cycles of a primary product exporter. These cycles sharpened regional conflicts. Booms resulted in expansion in the coastal economy and an abundance of foreign exchange which in turn encouraged imports of manufactured goods. Busts penalized coastal interests but encouraged modest import substitution in the highlands. Added to these economic differences was the hold of the traditional highland elites over social status, government patronage, and the military. Government revenues, however, came primarily from foreign trade taxes, largely derived from coastal enterprise, which fueled coastal resentment of the political power wielded for long periods by elites in the highlands (see especially Rodríguez, 1985; Kasza, 1981).

Economic and political rivalry between the two regions became institutionalized in the identities and reputations of their dominant urban areas, Quito and Guayaquil (see especially Kasza, 1981). Quito, a center dominated by government services, ISI, finance, and communications, grew up at the center of a hacienda-based economy of quasi-feudal social relationships between landlords and peasants. This social structure was largely intact until agrarian reform legislation in 1964 and 1972 introduced the bases for more modern productive relationships (see Redclift, 1978). Guayaquil emerged as a more modern and dynamic city centered on export and large financial sectors, where labor relations approximated a more capitalist pattern. Both cities grew rapidly after the mid–1960s as a result of rural-to-urban migration and high population growth rates, but the Guayaquil region far outstripped Quito in its rate of growth. In addition, interregional migration accelerated as peasants and others from the highlands sought jobs in the more dynamic coastal economy.

The political context

As can be expected from this socioeconomic context, political conflict in Ecuador also had a regional basis. As the coastal region increased in economic power, it also demanded a greater share of political power. These claims heightened in the 1970s and 1980s because the state, traditionally weak and ineffective, grew rapidly under the dual impact of a centralizing military dictatorship and significant increases in oil revenues from greater exports and higher prices. For the first time in modern history, oil wealth largely freed the government from dependence on the traditional economic elites and the taxes derived from export agriculture. Oil wealth allowed the military to expand radically government investment in infrastructure, services, and the state sector, and to introduce a wide variety of production and consumption subsidies. Contention over control of this large and interventionist state, and the nature of its policies toward the economic elites, became central to politics in the 1970s and 1980s.

In 1978, the reformist military regime engineered a pact with the country's traditional political elites to return the government to civilian rule and democratic institutions. A new constitution was adopted and a presidential-style government with a unicameral legislature was put in place.[8] Electoral and party registration laws encouraged party fragmentation and lack of programmatic commitment. The constitution extended the franchise to illiterates, empowered congress to interpret the constitution, provided the president with emergency powers, and set few limits on the capacity of small parties to broker power relationships.[9] Presidents were barred from succeeding themselves and from ever seeking the presidency again; deputies, elected for two years, were prohibited from seeking successive terms. Conflict between the executive and congress was encouraged by presidential powers to call for national plebiscites and to rule by emergency decree, and by congressional powers to question and impeach ministers, to appoint supreme court judges, and to interpret the constitution. Moreover, the growth in the state sector in the 1970s, an extensive array of newly introduced services and subsidies, and much expanded regulatory power meant that the spoils of victory were large. Not surprisingly, intense political competition reemerged fiercely in the aftermath of the military regime, which had been in power since 1972.

Traditionally, many political parties in Ecuador served as vehicles for the political aspirations of particular individuals, families, or economic groups and frequently had a regional basis. A populist political style, with extravagant promises of benefits to flow from government, characterized electoral campaigns that mobilized support around clientelistic ties to personalistic leaders. After 1978, political parties proliferated, a tendency encouraged by constitutional provisions for party registration and electoral competition (see especially Conaghan, 1989a). Thus, in the congressional election of 1979, 11 parties competed; in those of 1984, 16 parties competed; in 1986 there were 15; and 16 in the congressional elections of 1988. Parties also competed actively for the presidency. In 1978, candidates of six parties or movements ran for president in the first-round elections; in 1984, nine candidates competed for this post, and in 1988, ten ran for president.[10] The electoral strength of parties fluctuated considerably in these electoral battles and parties emerged, disappeared, or merged with great frequency, often in accord with the political fortunes of particular personalities.[11] Also of note are the legislators' and other political leaders' frequent switches of party affiliation. Only a few parties appeared to have the organizational structure, multiclass base, and durability of modern political parties. Most were highly opportunistic and nonprogrammatic; moreover, their clientelistic support was purely instrumental and disintegrated rapidly if leaders could not readily distribute the expected patronage of "works" such as roads, electricity, housing, water, and recreational facilities (Conaghan 1989a, p. 7).

During the 1970s, when political parties were proscribed, interest groups became better organized and more powerful. In part because of the ephemeral character of most political parties, they remained prominent in the political debates of the 1980s and reflected both sectoral and regional economic interests (see Conaghan, 1988). There was considerable coming and going between public sector and private sector positions by the economic elite who were active in such interest groups. There were national chambers of industry, commerce, and agriculture, but their regional counterparts, based in Quito, Guayaquil, and Cuenca, tended to be more powerful, and, reflecting distinct regional patterns of economic development, often conflicted directly over favored policy positions. At the level of sectoral policy, specific associations – the chamber of producers of cotton, the wood products chamber, the chamber of poultry producers – represented particular interests. Small entrepreneurs and independent workers such as truckers, artisans, and street vendors were associated in guild-like organizations. Here again, there were competing interests among these groups and within them.[12]

The labor movement was similarly divided, a factor that weakened its capacity to speak forcefully during the debates of the 1980s. In addition, the unions were segmented by traditional affiliations with particular political parties, often ones with strong ideological commitments and with long histories of doctrinal conflicts among themselves. Added to this fragmented political scene were the normal differences between urban and rural interests. In Ecuador, as in many other countries, urban interests typically favored cheap consumer goods while rural interests lobbied for higher prices for what they produced. Socioeconomic conditions, of course, determined the capacity of various urban and rural groups to take part in policy discussions.[13] Neither the rural nor the urban poor had sustained political presence in national decision making and were frequently not politically relevant in discussions of major public policy issues, although the urban poor had considerable weight in public reactions to new policy measures, as we will see. The military tended to be supportive of the presidential and anticongressional trends in the 1980s, but it was also internally divided.

While the state became more central to economic development during the decade of the 1970s and economic policy-making became more centralized in the presidency in the 1980s, these political conditions created a difficult environment for those who attempted to introduce policy changes. The fragmented and highly competitive party system increased the vulnerability of political leadership to electoral and partisan pressures. At the same time, democratic institutions and frequent elections increased the political presence and visibility of the highly fragmented economic interest groups. Coalition formation was extremely difficult under such conditions, although presidents often sought to meet this challenge by distributing ministerial and high-level government posts among "sympathetic" political parties and sectoral interests and especially among the economic elite. The institutions of the new democratic system themselves were only weakly legitimized and often the topic of political debate. In the 1980s, there was widespread public commitment to the notion of democratic government, but considerable contention over the legitimacy of particular institutions and their role within a democratic system. These conditions meant that political leadership was essential to spearhead policy reform, but taking the initiative meant accepting very high levels of uncertainty and risk about the political consequences of action.

The policy context

Equally, public policy in Ecuador left legacies that governments in the 1980s had to confront. Price distortions at the sectoral level were extensive; industries were highly protected by tariffs while minimum wage rates and labor legislation increased costs and inflexibility in the labor market; interest rates for various sectors were subsidized as part of national development policy, and bank lending was officially apportioned by sector; price controls on many products were complemented by official subsidies on others. Central among subsidized sectors was energy. From the early 1970s, gasoline and electricity rates were among the lowest in the world.[14] Through such mechanisms, the government became the provider of benefits and subsidies in general and to specific interests in particular, a role that it assumed with abandon in the 1970s when oil wealth made expansive public sector investment possible.[15] The population in general benefited in the short run from highly subsidized energy,[16] food, and transportation prices, and specific groups benefited from access to highly subsidized credit. Price distortions at the sectoral level were exacerbated by an increasingly overvalued sucre,[17] maintained at a fixed rate from 1970 to the early 1980s.

The "room to maneuver" within existing policies to confront problems in the economy was constricted, in part because of the structure of subsidies and benefits that came to be considered entitlements by their beneficiaries. In addition, the budget system was characterized by extensive use of earmarking of revenues for particular purposes, much of them going to the military. Earmarking, particularly in the allocation of the revenues of state-owned enterprises, decreased incentives for efficiency because particular agencies and industries lost the gains from profitable performance to other sectors or agencies and this impeded efforts to manage the public budget (see Thoumi, 1990). As with the socioeconomic and political contexts, the legacies of prior sectoral and macroeconomic policies were hardly conducive to an easy adjustment. The need for such changes, however, became clearer in the first years of the decade.

2 THE CONTEXT FOR CHANGE: ECONOMIC PERFORMANCE, 1970–82

In the late 1960s Ecuador had one of the most backward economies of Latin America. The rural sector was characterized by precapitalist institutions, the government had limited scope as a provider of education, health, and other social services, and social indicators were low. The country's economy had an agricultural base, manufacturing was incipient, and most of the population was rural. Whatever economic growth had occurred had been induced by primary product export booms which had been followed by busts. The small, weakly integrated internal market and traditional social structures had resulted in a manufacturing sector proportionally smaller than in the rest of the region. Ecuador was indeed a late-late-industrializer.

In contrast, the 1970s were years of great social and economic changes. In 1967, large oil fields were discovered in the eastern jungle, and Ecuador became an oil exporter just before international oil prices increased fourfold in late 1973. The income generated by this new boom was mostly public, the windfall gains were considerably larger than in the banana, coffee, and cocoa booms of the past, and for the first time, the economic gains from exports were not concentrated in the coast. The oil fields were in the eastern jungle region, and the public sector that benefited from it was located mostly in Quito.

The World Bank (1984) estimates oil output at 1.4 million barrels in 1970, 1.8 million in 1971, 28.6 million in 1972, and 76.2 million in 1973. However, oil output declined to 58.8 million in 1975, peaking again in 1979 at 78.2 million, and remaining slightly lower in the following three years, before increasing to 86.3 million in 1983. Total exports of goods and services excluding nonfactor services, $265 million in 1971, rose to $1,308 million in 1974. During the following four years exports ranged from $1.1 and $1.7 billion, before increasing to about $2.4 and $2.9 billion in the 1979–82 period. While export revenues obviously increased at a fast average rate, they also were not continuous but rather jumped from one plateau to a higher one. Domestic oil consumption grew at an extremely fast rate, from 9.6 million barrels in 1972 to 30.4 million in 1982, and Ecuador's growth during this period was extremely energy-intensive (Gelb and Marshall-Silva, 1988; Thoumi, 1990).[18] Most observers point out that the decade of the 1970s was a period of unprecedented growth, and cite average annual growth rates between 9 and 11.5 percent. GDP in 1981 in constant 1975 sucres was 147 percent higher than in 1970. However, this dramatic income increase blurred a less optimistic reality. While there is no doubt of the very fast pace of growth, it was unstable and unsustainable. National accounts data in constant 1975 sucres show an average annual GDP growth of 4.7 percent from 1966 through 1971. During the next two years, GDP grew 43.4 percent. After this period, growth rates appeared to have remained at higher levels than those that preceded the boom; the 1974–81 average was 6.05 percent. However, this higher growth rate tended to decline, and was obtained only with an unprecedented and unsustainable increase in external financing. In other words, the oil boom produced a once-and-for-all increase in income, but it did not led to higher long-term growth.

External debt growth during this period was remarkable and far outpaced export growth.[19] In 1970 the total external debt of the country was $241.5 million. The externally financed development of the petroleum industry and other loans raised this figure to $512.7 million in 1975 and to $6185.8 million in 1981. External debt service rose from less than 10 percent of exports between 1973 and 1977 to 71.3 percent and 97 percent in 1981 and 1982. The current account deficit, which averaged $60.4 million a year between 1970 and 1974, increased dramatically from 1975 on, reaching $703 million in 1978 and $1,226 million in 1982.[20]

During the 1970s there was a growing policy bias against exports. The official nominal exchange rate had been fixed for periods of approximately 10 years. It was devalued 11.1 percent in 1950, 20 percent in 1961, and 38.9 percent in 1970 (Sandoval, 1987, p. 82). About 70 percent of all transactions took place in the official market during the 1970s. A parallel free market was used mostly for invisibles and some capital transactions. However, the free market rate remained very close to the official one for the whole decade and exceeded it by more than 10 percent only in early 1981. The World Bank (1988b, p. 217) estimates that the trade-weighted exchange rate in 1977–9 was about 25 percent overvalued relative to the 1970 level, although it could be argued that the post-devaluation 1970 level may have been undervalued.

As noted above, the industrialization process in Ecuador began late relative to the rest of Latin America. However, from the mid-1950s, the promotion of the industrialization process was one of the principal goals of all governments. In 1957, following the standard ECLA recommendations of the time, an Industrial Promotion Law was enacted. This law required public sector purchase of domestically produced goods when possible, prohibited some imports, and established import tariff exonerations for capital and intermediate goods. The law also allowed for tax exemptions on new firms and on loans issued by the financial sector, and created export subsidies and subsidized credit facilities for the industrial sector (Abril and Urriola, 1990). The law was modified several times during the 1970s to expand industrialization incentives. Moreover, tariff protection for consumer goods was relatively high.[21] Effective protection rates estimates, available only for 1981,[22] show levels ranging from negative ones for beer and leather products to over 1000 percent for shoes, glass, plastic, and glass products.

Manufacturing exports during the 1970s, while benefiting from subsidized credit and the Export Tax Credit (CAT),[23] were limited to natural resource-based products in which the country had a great comparative advantage and a few products exported to Colombia and Venezuela that enjoyed special preferences granted in the Andean Group framework.[24] In 1977, 22.3 percent of total exports were classified as manufactures; of these, however, 90.4 percent were foodstuffs, tobacco, and wood.[25] Manufacturing value added grew rapidly during the 1970s. The sector, excluding oil refining, grew at an annual average of 6.7 percent during the 1966–71 pre-oil-boom period and at 10.9 percent from 1972 to 1980.[26] However, this growth was dependent on large input imports, particularly the new sectors that were developing under the protectionist umbrella.[27] Manufacturing employment grew slowly. Using census data, the World Bank estimated that total employment grew at only 2.2 percent per year during the 1974–82 intercensal period and that the "lowest growth rates occurred in agriculture, mining and industry" (World Bank, 1988b, p. 95). During the 1970s the main employment generator was the public sector, which by 1982 employed the equivalent of 39.5 percent of those employed in the private sector (excluding the self-employed).[28]

Government expenditure increased faster than government revenues during the 1970s in spite of the extremely large increase in oil revenues. Non-oil tax revenues declined by more than the increase in oil revenues, as tax collections became more lax (Gelb and Marshall-Silva, 1988, p. 181). Gasoline and electricity prices remained fixed in nominal terms at very low levels, generating an extraordinary subsidy to oil consumption. Widespread government revenue earmarking, traditional in the Ecuadoran budget, became more acute. These policies generated relatively high deficits which were financed with external borrowing. A large proportion of the borrowed money was used to finance current expenditures because private banks seem to have been confident of Ecuador's capacity to repay.[29,30]

Capital markets in Ecuador were largely undeveloped. During the 1970s there was no financial deepening, and while the financial system grew, it did not succeed in increasing the amount of savings it captured. Ecuador had fixed interest rates of 6 percent on savings deposits and time deposit rates were limited to 9 percent. Inflation, which had been low during the 1950s and 1960s, accelerated during the 1970s, averaging 13.5 percent during the 1973–80 period.[31] The passive interest rates were then substantially negative in real terms. However, because savings as a percentage of GDP remained stable, the negative relative interest rates were not considered an obstacle to growth (Pachano, 1987, p. 213). "While the financial system found itself increasingly limited in its ability to capture financial resources from Ecuadorans, the same system was expanding credit to Ecuadorans rapidly. The source of this credit expansion became

Ecuador's central bank....By 1983 it was financing more than a third of their stock of credit" (World Bank, 1984, p. 52).

It is not surprising that the growth pattern of the 1970s was unsustainable. It was based on the euphoria generated by the oil boom; however, oil output actually declined somewhat between 1973 and 1978, while domestic oil consumption was growing. While there were expectations of higher production in later years, the expected increases were not very large. Oil revenues could not increase significantly unless oil prices continued to increase. The government received increased revenues, but did not limit expenditure to current revenues, and borrowed heavily against future earnings. Domestic savings were discouraged, external debt increased extremely fast, and the debt service – which had been very minor – became an increasing burden on the balance of payments. Non-oil exports were discouraged by the exchange rate and other incentive policies and the country exported only natural resource-based products, with the exception of a few minor items to the Andean Group. This development path was taking the country to a certain crisis, independently of external conditions. By 1981 the current account deficit had escalated to $1,012 million. The oil consumption subsidy increased sharply in 1979 to 5.6 percent of GDP, when international oil prices increased. In 1980 it reached a remarkable 7.3 percent of GDP, before dropping to 4.5 percent and 4.2 percent in the next two years, when oil prices fell. It should be noted that after oil prices fell from the 1979 peak, the value of oil exports did not fall as oil output increased by about 11 percent in 1983. Other exports also increased during this period, and remarkably, during the first adjustment episode in 1982–3, total exports were only about $250 million (8.8 percent) less than the 1981 peak, while the current account was showing huge deficits. Furthermore, oil and other exports recovered and in 1985 they peaked at a level 36.7 percent and 15 percent higher than those of 1979 and 1980. Therefore, it cannot be argued that the Ecuadorian crisis was caused by a drop in export revenues, but rather by the increased weight of the external debt service due to the country's heavy borrowing and the increase in international interest rates. However, had international interest rates not increased, the onset of the crisis would have been only a question of time as the current account was deteriorating sharply before the interest rate increase.

Unfortunately, the decrease in international oil prices from the 1979 peaks sharply increased international interest rates, and closing of lending sources acted as a catalyst for the crisis, allowing the Ecuadorans to blame the external conditions for their crisis and to mask the needed domestic policy changes.[32]

3 THE FIRST INITIATIVE: STABILIZATION, OCTOBER 1982–MARCH 1983

Ecuador's first efforts to make major changes in existing economic policies were particularly important, not because they were the most radical or the most extensive of those introduced in the 1980s, but because they broke important taboos about reform.[33] We have seen that society and specific groups within it had come to expect government to provide benefits, not impose economic discipline. Moreover, as shown above, the public was not well-used to changes in macroeconomic policies and variables, as these had generally remained stable over a long period. In many ways, then, the initiatives of 1982 and 1983 were made at a time when there was little widespread concern about the economy and the government's technical team had little experience in economic management or in anticipating the outcomes of major changes in macroeconomic policy.[34] In addition, the policy changes invoked extremely strong public reactions that threatened the viability of the administration in power and of the democratic institutions that had only recently been introduced. Moreover, at the outset of the decade, economic policy reforms were not high on the government's agenda.

Under the terms of a civil–military pact negotiated between the military government and Ecuador's economic and political elites, elections for congress and then for president were held in July of 1978; run-off elections were held in April 1979. The victorious presidential candidate, who won an impressive 68.5 percent of the popular vote in the second round elections, was Jaime Roldós, who was backed by a nonprogrammatic populist movement, the CFP (Concentración de Fuerzas Populares). His vice-presidential running mate was Osvaldo Hurtado of the small christian democratic party, Democracia Popular (DP). Roldós entered office in August 1979 with the support of a loose legislative coalition of 30 CFP members (four of whom were members of the DP party) and 15 members of the Izquierda Democrática (ID), a social democratic party.[35]

Despite the evidence of public support and a majority coalition in congress, Roldós did not come into office with a mandate for economic policy change. The elections of 1978 and 1979 were not fought on the battleground of important economic reform issues. Rather, the principal issues of contention were an increasingly public struggle for power between Roldós and his political godfather, Assad Bucaram,[36] the legitimacy of the new institutions of government, the future role of the military, and charges of fraud, disloyalty, and antipatriotism among contenders. Roldós, running as a moderate reformist, spoke of the need for austerity and morality in government and promised an improvement in the lot of the poor, but few of these campaign pledges were backed up by specific programmatic ideas. All parties relied heavily on clientelistic networks and populist appeals to marshall votes rather than taking clear positions on issues of economic importance (see especially Mills, 1984).

In fact, in 1978 and 1979, few in Ecuador were seriously concerned about evidence of mounting economic problems, and while some mention was made of impending problems of budget deficits and international debt, there were few who felt that urgent action had to be taken. To most, the country was still enjoying the flush of a booming oil-based economy. Those who were concerned about economic issues were clearly counting on the potential for further oil export revenues to resolve the country's problems, particularly after international oil prices doubled in 1979.[37] The ruling coalition was firmly committed to the continuation of Ecuador's state-led development strategy that had molded public investment and regulatory activities since the 1960s.[38]

In the absence of any widely perceived crisis in the economy or in the nature of the government's development strategy, Roldós set about his presidency by paying salary arrears to public employees, establishing commissions to study wage increases, removing political restrictions imposed during the military dictatorship, decreeing (largely symbolic) measures to promote austerity and morality in public administration, initiating new public works, and promising to be the "president of the poor" (Martz, 1987; *Latin American Political Report*, June 29, 1979). In October 1979, in part following Roldós' guidelines, congress doubled the salaries of the public school teachers, and in November doubled minimum wages and increased other wages by lower proportions, and froze water, sewerage, electricity, phone, and mail rates, as well as prices of basic consumer products (Hidalgo and Gordillo, 1989).[39] These wage and salary increases were not accompanied by appropriate financing measures and the government was unable to pay the legislated increases. Strikes and labor conflicts ensued. A five-year plan was introduced, calling for greater efforts to bring social justice to the poor and for increased investments in social, energy, and agricultural sectors. Congressional infighting and executive–legislative conflict, however, impeded any efforts to take action on the plan.

In general, the mood of the government in its early days was optimistic about the economy. "Times were good when Roldós came into power; petroleum was at 32–40 dollars a barrel," recalled his minister of finance.[40] Another official recalled that "When Roldós won, there was a period of exuberance (triunfalismo) both politically and economically....Remember, oil was still at 40 dollars a barrel then."[41] In the course of the normal politics of the time, Roldós traveled at home and abroad, dispensed patronage, and promoted and inaugurated "works." Policy-makers' time was largely devoted to managing political squabbles within the CFP, between Roldós and Bucaram, and between the president and congress (see Conaghan, 1989a; Martz, 1987; Mills, 1984). Thus, the first year and a half of the new government was very much politics-as-usual, with little attention given to macroeconomic issues; the micropolitics of inter- and intraparty conflict, personal animosities, executive–legislative clashes, and bureaucratic politics prevailed. Daily commentary focused on political, not economic, crises.

One important exception to this pattern occurred in January of 1981 when Ecuador and Peru became involved in a small border "war." The government took advantage of the conflict to make some necessary policy changes. Gasoline prices were increased 223 percent, although this increase brought them only to $0.60 a gallon at the official exchange rate; the passive interest rate was increased from 6 to 8 percent and the active rate from 12 to 15 percent; electricity rate hikes followed the oil price increase and import tariffs were raised; and transportation fees were increased (see Martz, 1987).[42] These measures were seen as attempts to deal with the current account and budget deficits, but not as part of a needed structural change for the economy. They met with considerable opposition after they were announced, however, and protests culminated in a general strike in May of that year. The government appealed for public support, but was reluctant to move ahead with further economic measures. The border skirmish was also costly to the government. The budget deficit escalated during the year from 4.5 percent in 1980 to 7.9 percent of GDP in 1982.[43] Ecuador borrowed $1 billion in fresh capital, 60 percent of which was supplied by private banks and could be used for the defense effort (Hidalgo and Gordillo, 1989).[44]

In May of 1981, official attention to economic problems increased significantly, not as a result of dramatically altered economic conditions, but as the result of an accident that altered conditions of leadership and policy-making style. On May 24, 1981, Jaime Roldós was killed in an airplane crash and Osvaldo Hurtado became president of Ecuador. His assumption of power did not promise much. As the successor to Roldós, he represented an increasingly unpopular administration, one that had lost its initial impetus through almost constant squabbling among the political parties and through splits within the CFP. Moreover, the christian democrats held only five seats in congress and were dependent on their ability to put together transitory alliances among 13 other parties, none of which held a majority. Described by political colleagues with terms such as sober, dry, studious, rational, aloof, and cold, Hurtado was not cut in the populist image of Ecuadoran leaders. Although he had proved himself an able party leader, he may even have been reluctant to acquire additional political prominence.[45] He was also known to harbor a strong distrust of the country's business elites. In turn, those who wielded economic power in the country had regularly attacked Hurtado as a statist, a leftist, and an enemy of the private sector.[46] He could anticipate a contentious period in office even if he had not chosen to address the increasingly serious imbalances in Ecuador's economy.

But Hurtado brought with him to the presidency a series of concerns that had impressed him while, as vice-president, he had headed the national planning commission, CONADE. He was particularly aware of the need to impose austerity measures to counter increasing budgetary deficits. In his first major address, in June 1981, he announced to the country that "the era of oil prosperity had come to an end, exports had stagnated and because of that, it was necessary to begin an era of austerity" (Hurtado, 1990, p. 126). He proposed reductions in government spending and warned that salary increases would be held down. He also emphasized that the international economy had entered into a major crisis.[47] He then called for a social pact among business, labor, and party groups, and attempted to establish a working coalition with the parties in congress. Hurtado assembled an economic team to help him and gradually shuffled cabinet positions, integrating individuals in whom he had confidence and using official appointments to buy support from a number of center-left and populist parties in the legislature.

In August 1981, the president announced to congress that further budget cuts were necessary and that taxes would be raised. For the first time in many years, Ecuadorans were being told that the country's economic problems would not go away nor be relieved by increased earnings from the oil sector and that difficult times were in store. When petroleum prices fell and primary export earnings proved disappointing in early 1982, the government limited some imports, put a cap on interest rates, and prohibited further accumulation of foreign debts (Martz, 1987, p. 313; Salgado, 1987, p. 135). These measures were too timid to achieve substantial results, and on May 13 Hurtado decreed a 32 percent devaluation, the first such publicly acknowledged move since 1970. This measure was accompanied by sweeteners that regulated prices and tariffs on some goods and others that encouraged exports and foreign investment, but the drift of national economic policies was becoming clear. The promises of the Roldós presidency and the goals of the five-year plan were now replaced by repeated reminders about declining oil revenues, a rising debt burden, and increasing budget deficits.

Few of the government's measures were designed to ensure the new president's popularity. Hurtado was portrayed by the right as a statist dictator, ruling through decrees, and in turn he characterized the economic elites as selfish, greedy, and unpatriotic. Animosity and mutual recrimination led each side publicly and privately to draw back from the president's earlier call to form a social pact. This tense political relationship mirrored increasing popular sector discontent with the impact of inflation. A general strike in September, although not fully successful, set the scene for later confrontations with labor and put the government on notice that the labor unions would not easily accept new austerity measures (see *Latin American Weekly Report*, September 24, 1982). Business associations began openly supporting labor's resistance to the government. The government lost additional support when it used riot police to put an end to some of the protests (*Latin American Weekly Report*, October 1, 1982).

In October 1982, Hurtado and his economic team – composed of the director of the central bank, the finance minister, and the president of the monetary board – developed a major package of reforms to reduce the fiscal deficit. Measures adopted included a doubling of gasoline prices and increased public transportation prices, a particularly courageous measure because the previous oil minister had just been censured and ousted by congress over the 1981 gasoline price increase.[48] The package eliminated some subsidies – particularly the one on wheat – and transfers, conferred only limited wage adjustments, and cut budget expenditures in several sectors (see *Latin American Weekly Report*, October 22, 1982; Salgado, 1987, pp. 135–6). Discussions on rescheduling the debt with the IMF were initiated, although Fund influence on economic policy played little role in the reform initiatives until 1984.

The style of decision making was symptomatic of the increasing political tensions in the country. According to Hurtado:

> The four of us made all the decisions. We didn't discuss issues with anyone else or consult with anyone else...We didn't consult ministers, we didn't consult parties, we didn't consult deputies. We informed them just hours before an announcement in order to maintain secrecy. Why did I do this? Because my initial attempt at consensus building was a complete failure. I decided not to waste time trying to develop a consensus that no one wanted and that carried the risk that information would be abused...The parties didn't want to build consensus; they saw my policies as a termination of their political careers – they wanted nothing to do with them...And I couldn't build consensus with the business associations because...they were waiting for me to fall on my face. Every person who spoke to me, who advised me, told me the government would fall. It was like swimming completely against the tide.[49]

When the measures were announced to the cabinet, Hurtado's minister of social welfare protested that they would lead to political disaster. "All our heads will end up impaled on the posts of Independence Plaza," he announced to the assembled group (quoted in Hurtado, 1990, p. 139).

He was almost right. The decree of the new measures was met with widespread spontaneous protests, work stoppages, and strikes. Ministers were reluctant to leave the government palace for days at a time, for fear of the violence. Opposition parties in congress accused the government of authoritarianism and mismanagement. In reaction to such widespread and focused protest, Hurtado backed off somewhat on the gasoline price increase and declared a state of emergency and a curfew. Further protests and violence ensued. Hurtado raised the minimum wage and lifted the state of emergency at the end of October, but incremental adjustments went on as the economic benefits of the measures did not materialize, GDP growth fell from 3.9 percent in 1981 to 1.2 percent in 1982, and inflation, which had been a high 14.7 percent in 1981, increased somewhat to 16.4 percent in 1982. The current account deficit reached 8.9 percent of GDP in 1982, when the net capital inflow less interest debt service was −$414 million compared to a positive $629 million in the previous year. Net international reserves fell from $562.9 million in 1981 to $210.0 million in 1982.

Major and extended floods in late 1982 and the first semester of 1983 increased the economic problems of the government. Hidalgo and Gordillo (1989) estimate that the floods caused a loss of $200 million of exports and Swett (1988) puts the total loss at $350 million, or 2.5 percent of GDP. According to the national accounts for 1983, when the impact of the floods was fully felt, banana, coffee, and cocoa output fell a combined 35.4 percent, while the rest of the agricultural sector output fell 23.3 percent.

In February and March of 1983, a new package of reforms was announced. A devaluation of 27.3 percent of the official exchange rate was decreed, and a system of minidevaluations for this exchange rate was introduced. Furthermore, a third exchange rate, that of the curiously named "free intervened market,' was created, in effect formalizing a multiple exchange rate system. Increased interest rates and a new law to limit public expenditures were also put in place, the latter increasing the role of the Central Bank over the budget and decreasing that of the congress. Pay raises for public employees were suspended, some fuel prices were increased, the price of milk was raised, tariff surcharges were introduced, and new import restrictions were imposed (Salgado, 1987, p. 136; *Latin American Weekly Report*, October 25, 1983). The country formally requested $170 million in standby credit from the IMF (*Latin American Weekly Report*, October 31, 1983).[50]

Public protests and recriminations resurfaced and congressional reaction from left, right, and populist parties was outspokenly hostile. Hurtado redoubled efforts to emphasize publicly the need for austerity and adjustment measures and the importance of accepting the fact that quick recovery was not likely to occur. His administration was clearly embattled, however. In retrospect, the period between October 1982 and March 1983 was considered by the policy makers as having been a moment of great peril for the survival of democratic institutions.

One of the effects of the devaluations was to increase the sucre value of the external debt of the private sector. The private sector warned that the devaluations would cause massive business failures because the borrowers could not pay their now larger external debt and argued that devaluation was necessitated by misguided government policies, and thus, the government should be responsible for the external debt. In 1983, the government established a "sucretization" program for the private external debt.[51] This was a fairly complex system that had two results. First, it converted the private external debt to sucres, and, even though the central bank charged some fees to cover the exchange rate risk, it transferred a large proportion of it to the government. Second, it extended the government guarantee to the private external debt. At the end of 1983 the total external debt of Ecuador was $6.9 billion, of which $1.6 billion had been "sucretized" private debt.[52]

Despite considerable effort, the results of the stabilization measures were not satisfactory. Total agricultural output in 1983 declined by over 25 percent, GDP fell 2.8 percent, the CPI increased a record 48 percent, international reserves fell 28 percent to $151.5 (excluding trade payment arrears) –less than one month of imports. Private domestic savings, which had reached 14.8 percent of GDP in 1980, had fallen sharply to 7.9 percent of GDP in 1983. However, the budget and current account deficits did improve considerably and reached manageable levels. The budget deficit declined to 1.4 percent of GDP, and the current account deficit to 2.2 percent of GDP.

Nineteen eighty-four was a year of economic recovery largely because agricultural output rebounded from the disaster of 1983. However, the agricultural sector's recovery was not full, as the output of the main agricultural exports and of the rest of the sector reached only 73 percent and 96 percent of the 1982 levels, respectively. Manufacturing, construction, and banking declined, but GDP grew a relatively healthy 4.2 percent on the basis of the agricultural sector recovery and large expansion in the utilities sector. Inflation slowed down substantially to 25.1 percent. However, the recession was taking its toll in terms of increased unemployment, and private savings declined to an all-time low 4.8 percent of GDP.[53] The international reserve position remained very weak.[54]

In part, as Hurtado and his collaborators were later willing to acknowledge, they only gradually became aware of the magnitude of the problems facing the country. Each effort needed to be buoyed with further measures. According to the then central bank manager, economic policy was put together "brick by brick." "We began by addressing symptoms, not causes, because we didn't know much about the process of adjustment. The price of gasoline was raised as a way of covering expenditures, not as part of a full structural adjustment."[55] Similarly, once announced, many of the measures were modified in response to protests from the parties, the unions, or the business associations. Even when sustained, the measures were undercut by new external shocks in the form of rapidly falling petroleum prices and weather patterns that destroyed major sources of foreign exchange earnings. Nevertheless, this period is important because economic problems and policies became the most salient issues of national politics and because well-embedded expectations about the role of the state and of public policy were dampened after the expansive growth of the 1970s.

Political leadership from the president and his economic team appears to have been critical to the timing and content of the policy changes in 1983 and 1984. Pressures to "do something" on three fronts to stabilize the economy – devaluation, the price of gasoline, and control of public spending – were largely generated by the team's analysis and their perception of impending crisis, not by demands from societal groups. Their convictions, however, were not widely shared, even in the aftermath of the summer 1982 announcement by Mexico that it could not meet its foreign debt obligations. The country was not being badgered by the IMF, the World Bank, or external creditors to take immediate action under the threat of a loss of further credits or conditionality. Some societal groups – the unions in particular – were clamoring for wage increases, and the transport sector was asking for fare increases. There was little political incentive to take actions that would impose hardships on broad sectors of the society. Nevertheless, according to the president of the central bank during this period, a clear effort was made to balance economic and political objectives:

> We had alternatives. We could have done nothing. We rejected this path because we thought the economy was in too bad a state. There was nothing to be gained politically by doing nothing. We could have done only the most unavoidable things. But why take on the political problems of doing something when you know it's not going to have any impact on the economy? We could begin a process of adjustment. We opted for this even though we knew there would be fierce reaction. We opted for a gradual approach to get people used to the idea that there were no economic policy taboos. Given the lack of support for any of the measures, and the inability to marshall legislative agreement to them, how was the president able to move ahead with them at all? In the first instance, he did so by assuming emergency powers. The reforms were decreed, not legislated. He also worked to insulate his economic team from political pressures. Hurtado reported that, "We four...exclusively ran economic policy....You can imagine what would happen if I would have subjected economic policy to debates within the party!...I made my appointments to the economic team on the basis of the fact that they were not Christian Democrats. I did not want economic policy in the hands of people who would politicize it." (Quoted in Conaghan, 1989a, pp. 32–3).[56]

In addition, Hurtado, almost an antipolitician, tried to appeal for public support in a way that made him appear to be above politics. Through a series of television programs at regular intervals, he explained, cajoled, and appealed for support in facing up to what he argued was a severe national challenge (see Hurtado, 1990, p. 122). He also based his appeal on the need to maintain support for the new democratic institutions, appeals that were eventually to be important, given the fierce attacks on him from the right.

Less publicly, Hurtado also permitted and even encouraged accommodation with his most vociferous opponents. This was done in three ways. First, his ministers were in frequent contact with the groups that were opposed to the new measures. Ministers of industry, interior, and labor, in particular, had an open door policy and were in frequent contact with important leaders of business and labor groups. The then minister of the interior remembers that,

Between October 1982 and March 1983, we thought the government would fall....But I had good relations with the private sector. I looked for them and they looked for me. So even when things were hottest against the government from [the economic elite], there was another level – one of dialogue – going on. The door was open through me and they were always talking to me.[57]

Second, there was considerable policy accommodation after the initial measures had been announced. Bit by bit, a number of measures were eaten away by adjustments and bargains with specific groups or allowed to erode through inflation. Third, the government took specific measures calculated to benefit those opposed to the stabilization package. Central among these was the private external debt "sucretization." This in no way gained private sector support, but may have been a critical component of allowing the government to finish its constitutionally mandated term of office.

The Hurtado government's stabilization measures were introduced with little or no negotiation of agreement prior to the announcement of measures in 1982 and 1983. There was instead an after-the-fact set of accommodations in response to reaction to the measures and efforts to manage the political hostility they caused. The government did not make the adjustment decisions unmindful of their political consequences; there is significant evidence that it acted in spite of anticipated political opposition. In the end, however, the government appeared much more capable of making the decisions than of sustaining them.

The Hurtado government put economic management issues squarely on the agenda of political debate in Ecuador. The electoral campaign of 1984 was fought over economic issues, with clear alternatives among the major contenders offered to the voters. In contrast to the normal condition of fragmentation and conflict among the economic elite, the reaction to the Hurtado presidency gave very strong impetus to the unification of business interests behind the banner of the right, held increasingly high by León Febres-Cordero, a congressman and prominent businessman from Guayaquil. Business concern about government policy had begun to coalesce during the military regime in the 1970s, when reformism and state expansion threatened the traditional hold of economic elites over economic policy. By 1983, when the electoral campaign entered full swing, Febres-Cordero had marshalled an unusual amount of unity among the economic elite around political commitment to economic liberalism.

Febres-Cordero campaigned on a platform of antistatism, deregulation, and market liberalization, managing to clothe this liberal ideology in the populist rhetoric of "bread, housing, and jobs," and the appeal of a "can do" leader and manager of state policy (see Conaghan, 1989b). His strongest contender, Rodrigo Borja from the center-left social democratic party, was clearly committed to strengthening the role of the state in national economic development, to increasing state investment, and to addressing income and equity concerns in both rural and urban areas (see *Latin American Monitor*, April 1984). The campaign was often vicious and even violent. Febres-Cordero's political coalition, the Frente de Reconstrucción Nacional (FRN), put together in 1984, pursued its electoral goals through broadside attacks on the Hurtado government's policies – including those that, given Febres-Cordero's expressed ideology, he should have supported – accusations of communist influence, calls for the president's impeachment, and mobilization of strikes in conjunction with the labor unions of the left. The center and the left, in contrast, were unable to unify around strong candidates, and as a result, each party put forth its own presidential and vice-presidential candidates.

The reaction to Hurtado's policies was clearly registered in the first-round elections, when the DP candidate won only 2.8 percent of the total vote, but the direction of change preferred by the electorate was not clearly signaled in the second-round election, where the results were close between the alternative of the right and the alternative of the center and left, Rodrigo Borja. In these run-off elections, Febres Cordero won 52 percent of the vote; Borja of the ID party won 48 percent. Thus, although Febres-Cordero assumed the presidency with a clear program and a much sharper basis of support than had been the normal situation for incoming administrations in Ecuador, he could also count on considerable domestic opposition from the center and left. Nevertheless, his coalition was given impetus to its agenda by the IMF, which was now seriously involved in discussions about policy reform with the government, and by an increasingly apparent crisis in the economy.

4   THE SECOND INITIATIVE: A NEOLIBERAL EXPERIMENT, 1984–6

The Febres-Cordero government had a clear agenda when it assumed office in August of 1984: to reduce government intervention in the economy, to stimulate private enterprise, and to open up the country's development to market forces. Within days of his inauguration, a neoliberal experiment was launched with full support from the IMF and the Reagan administration in Washington. For his economic team, Febres-Cordero selected individuals committed to liberalism and with extensive experience in business and with international financial agencies. The government had strong and vocal ideological support from a wide spectrum of the business communities; the right had come into its own politically with Febres-Cordero (see especially Conaghan, 1989b; de Janvry et al., 1990).

In many ways, the contrast to the initial period of the Hurtado presidency was stark. The style of the new administration was set by

Febres-Cordero, a successful businessman and former president of the Guayaquil Chamber of Industry. Widely recognized for the exuberance of his personality, he was noted for his warmth, emotionalism, and confrontational approach to problem solving, a marked difference from the cool and deliberate style of Hurtado. From the outset, in fact, many were concerned about his administration's potential for violence and authoritarianism, fears that were engendered during the campaign when strong-arm methods characterized FRN vote-getting activities.[58] In further contrast to the nonideological style of the Hurtado period, the new administration clearly had a vision of a new development strategy for the country. This commitment was given added strength by the appointment of a cabinet that included a number of prominent entrepreneurs from Guayaquil.

Putting this vision into effect would not be easy, however. The narrow margin of victory and the polarization of the campaign promised little in terms of congressional coalition building beyond the FRN, which captured 29 seats in the 71-member legislature. The parties that had opposed Febres-Cordero in the election campaign quickly formed an uncharacteristically broad coalition to oppose his policies. The new unity of the right appeared to have given birth to unaccustomed collaboration among parties of the center and left. More similar to the Hurtado years was the continuation of efforts to centralize economic decision making in a small technocratic corps within the executive – in the ministry of finance, the monetary board, and the central bank. The team, committed as it was to these changes, nevertheless believed that they needed to be introduced gradually, just as the Hurtado team had argued.

The team's diagnosis of the situation placed substantial emphasis on financial, fiscal, and trade policy reforms (see de Janvry et al., 1990). Francisco Swett, one of the three members of the government's brain trust, acknowledged that the Hurtado policies had succeeded in lowering the fiscal and current account deficits, but then explained:

> The economic management model, however, remained fairly intact with all known rigidities and further distortions brought about by the accelerated depreciation of the currency. Interest rates became highly negative. With a 40 percent pre-announced rate of devaluation and 20 percent interest levels, it became profitable to acquire sucre debt and buy dollars, thus encouraging capital flight. Continuing price controls and political affinity with agrarian reform issues, added to the effects of the 1982 floods, kept agricultural output in check. The structure of protection and tariff distortions continued intact, bringing a brisk business of contraband, illicit imports, overinvoicing of imports as well as underinvoicing of exports. Price subsidies on fuel consumption kept a regressive subsidy in place, representing also a continuing drain of resources to the tune of 5 percent of GDP. The financial system was left in a shambles. And the government's capabilities for fiscal administration remained highly inefficient with a continuing modest performance in tax effort. (Swett, 1986, p. 11).

Despite the early diagnosis of the economy's ills, Febres-Cordero and his team did not enjoy a "honeymoon" period after assuming office. In fact, the first six months of the new administration were marked by violence and confrontation with the congress, including the use of riot police and tear gas within the legislative chamber, repeated general strikes by the labor unions and street protests by students, and executive actions to curtail such activities. Resurgent guerrilla activity emerged in late 1984 and encouraged the government to take a repressive stance toward any evidence of political protest. Violence and confrontation reached such proportions that rumors began to circulate accusing the president of attempting to foment a coup by the armed forces in order to take over full control of the government. Political pundits quickly labeled his government a "Rambocracia" (see Conaghan, 1989b).

The initial actions of the new government indicated its interest in restructuring the environment for economic development and show for the first time a comprehensive economic perspective of the reforms needed to promote economic growth according to a particular school of thought. In August and September of 1984, the administration attempted to create an altered institutional context and greater executive control over policy by challenging the legislature over the power of appointment of supreme court members. The ensuing conflict with congress brought legislative activity to a standstill (see Conaghan, 1989b; *Latin American Monitor*, September 1984). Under the guise of paralyzed executive–legislative relations, Febres-Cordero moved to disarm the congress further through the introduction of an automatic veto and control over its legislative schedule.[59] With the legislature thus weakened, the president began regularly making policy through executive decree.

The first economic measures of the government were to substitute a fixed exchange rate system for the creeping peg that the Hurtado administration had put in place, to limit the minimum wage increase demanded by the unions and the opposition parties in congress, and to refuse a pay increase for public sector workers. The multiple exchange system was not eliminated. The official exchange rate was fixed at 67 sucres to the dollar, about the level it had at that moment, and the "free intervened rate" at about 96 sucres to the dollar. However, all the non-oil export revenues and most imports of goods and services along with capital movements were transferred from the official to the intervened rate, establishing a de facto devaluation. Price controls on a variety of products were eliminated except for salt, sugar, milk, medicines, and cement. A capital market liberalization program was begun in order to promote increased internal savings. The financial system was allowed to issue certificates of deposit at market rates, and the monetary board passed regulations to allow adjustable-rate long-term loans; the interest rate structure was simplified, allowing only four different rates, and all rates were raised to levels higher than the projected inflation.

In early 1985, the government raised the price of different grades of fuel by 60–90 percent. After difficult political maneuvers, the executive passed a decree raising minimum wages 26 percent, two points above the projected inflation rate. In November 1985 the official and "intervened" exchange rates were unified, and in January 1986 the government conti- nued its reform program by devaluing the "intervened" exchange rate from 96 sucres to 110 to the dollar and transferring all foreign trade and debt transactions to this market. These measures were taken to promote non-oil exports and to limit imports. The official rate remained only as an accounting device of the central bank. These changes left only two exchange rates because the free market rate remained in effect for such activities as tourism, contraband, and some private capital transactions.

In 1986, tax collection was improved; a process to lower tariffs was also begun, and in February 1986 a new tariff was put in place that substantially decreased the tariff and effective protection dispersion. Foreign invest- ment regulations were relaxed and the government signed an agreement with the US Overseas Private Investment Corporation to guarantee US investors against nationalization or expropriation, the first such accord since 1971. A comprehensive debt renegotiation process was undertaken with strong IMF support to achieve a "multiyear renegotiation agreement" with the commercial banks and the Paris Club.

> The agreement with the banks refinanced 95 percent of the country's commercial debt; repriced serially the Republic's debt from 2.25 percent over prime to 1.75 percent over libor saving Ecuador some $200 million in debt service charges for the duration of the agreement; and paved the way for a new agreement such as the establishment of an oil acceptance facility which has also been concluded on a voluntary basis. (Swett, 1986, pp. 17–8).

Many of these changes occurred after defections among the opposition parties in congress gave the government a working majority. According to his then minister of finance,

> Using every power resource available within the law, the executive not only controlled the important instruments of the economy (exchange and interest rates, tariffs, and public spending), but promoted legal reforms. A total of 17 laws were reformed including the Law of Hydrocarbons that resulted in seven new exploration contracts, when none had been signed since 1973. Reforms to banking and monetary laws gave monetary authority greater liberty to establish finance and credit policies, discrimination against foreign investment was dismantled....The president vetoed every decision of the congress that ran contrary to the aim of reordering the economy. (Quoted in Conaghan, 1989b, p. 9.)

These actions earned Febres Cordero a warm welcome in Washington in January 1986, where Ronald Reagan hailed him as the model of political leadership needed to introduce new market-oriented strategies in develop- ing countries. His foreign policy – breaking with the Andean Pact countries over the regulation of foreign investment and ending diplomatic relations with Nicaragua – also earned him kudos from the American president.

The trip to Washington marked a high point of the Febres-Cordero administration. The economy appeared to be responding well to the measures that had been introduced. GDP grew 4.3 percent in 1985, a figure similar to that of the previous year; the budget deficit dropped to 0.6 percent of GDP in 1984 and in 1985 there was a 1.9 percent surplus; the external debt was refinanced and the current account showed modest ($149 million) surplus in 1985. Inflation remained high by historical standards, but the CPI's increase in 1985 was 28 percent, close to the projected rate, and the capital market liberalization policies seemed to have begun to produce results. Financial savings rose from the 5–6 percent range during 1980–4 to 10.4 percent in 1985, and private savings began to recover.

Politically, early 1986 was also propitious. The economic team remained clear in its conviction for the direction of government policy; the political opposition was suffering some disarray in the wake of the strategic and repressive measures taken by the government; the international financial institutions were supportive of the goals of the government; and the government enjoyed the political space to hold all prior policies responsible for the country's economic woes. Febres-Cordero also capitalized on legal precedents from the Hurtado administration to use powers and procedures that gave the executive considerable control over the design of economic policy.

Despite these favorable conditions, the honeymoon did not last long. As with the Hurtado administration, the ability to introduce reform was strongly centered in executive leadership and the political space for taking the initiative was quite large. However, once reform decisions were reached, political reactions determined the ability to sustain them. In this, Febres-Cordero and his economic team fared little better than the Hurtado government after mid–1986. From the beginning of the administration, of course, protests from students and popular sector groups had been a hallmark of each policy change as it was introduced. But their lack of access to the government and the administration's confrontational and repressive style weakened the impact of these groups.

More important to the government's plans was rising discontent among its supporters on the right. The political coalition that brought Febres-Cordero to power began to lose its cohesion under the impact of the policy changes. Much of the unusual cohesion of the coalition had been built around antipathy for the Hurtado government and a general ideological commitment against state interference in the market. As far back as the campaign of 1978 and 1979, Febres-Cordero and the right had attacked Hurtado for his statist and 'dangerously leftist' tendencies and had called for a halt to government intervention and regulation. However, few of the coalition partners could be expected to know what this meant in practice.

As we have seen, over the years, economic groups of very distinct interests had become accustomed to receiving privileged protection from government through subsidized credit, highly specific tariff structures, low taxes, and a variety of other measures. The neoliberal experiment meant the reduction and eventual disappearance of such privileges and much greater vulnerability to international economic conditions. The cohesion built around a general ideology dissipated when the economic costs of new measures became apparent to some, and their benefits apparent to others. In particular, many measures were of great benefit to exporters, who formed the core of the business elite in Guayaquil. Regional differences in economic structure and policy interests soon emerged over the content and beneficiaries of particular policies.

In addition, several other factors came together in 1986 to dilute the reform agenda of Febres-Cordero and his team and then to destroy it. Central among these factors was the collapse of the international price for oil, which dropped from an average of $26 a barrel to under $9 in six months time, causing a 50 percent fall in the value of crude oil exports from $1,825 million in 1985 to $912 million in 1986. This resulted in a total export decline of 25 percent. Because oil accounted for about 50 percent of the central government revenues, the fiscal situation deteriorated so that the 1985 surplus of 1.9 percent of GDP became a 5.1 percent deficit in 1986. On August 15 a stand-by loan for SDR 75.4 million ($95 million) was approved and the government was assisted through credit extended by international banks and multilateral agencies. The total external debt increased $832.4 million in 1986, or about 10 percent. GDP grew about 3.1 percent, propelled mostly by the fast growth of the shrimp industry, nonexport agriculture, and the utilities sector. For manufacturing, 1986 was the fifth consecutive recessive year.

Elections in mid–1986 and deteriorating civil–military relations discouraged the government from taking swift corrective action to limit expenditures (see Conaghan, 1989b; *Latin American Monitor*, April 1987).[60] In the face of continued difficulty implementing the economic reform strategy, the president announced a plebiscite that was expected to generate national support for policies and further ammunition in its "war" against the political opposition. He miscalculated badly, however, as the plebiscite served to rally political and popular opposition to his government, and he was defeated by a two-to-one margin (see *Latin American Monitor*, June–July 1986). Voters also returned a majority of opposition party members to congress.

In the face of the rejection of the plebiscite, the loss in congressional elections, and the poor performance of the economy, the government quickly became ineffective. Nevertheless, the economic team continued to attempt reform. On August 11 it announced drastic new policy changes that, in the words of Francisco Swett, promised important results:

The regime now in force has, in one fell swoop, done away with 56 years of monetary and financial legal practice in Ecuador. In essence, under the new system the exchange rate will be determined by the market (that is to say, a full flotation of the sucre has been established). Savings rates have also been untied from administrative restrictions, although the authorities have negotiated with the banks an 'understanding' to set the rate at a predetermined level. Other rates, including the rediscount rate of the Central Bank, have been allowed to float. Finally, a new structure of protection is being prepared, which will further lower the level and dispersion of the tariffs (Swett, 1986, pp. 25–6).[61]

Congress immediately moved to censure the finance minister and demand his resignation. Added to a thoroughgoing cabinet reshuffle in the aftermath of the June elections, the resignation of the minister meant the disintegration of the economic team. A newly appointed team lacked the deep prescriptive consensus that had characterized the technocrats of the first two years. Congress also began passing a series of measures to counteract the administration's austerity measures (see *Latin American Monitor*, November 1986). The float of exchange and interest rates was declared unconstitutional, a decision ignored by the administration. This action only increased the level of conflict between the president and congress, which proceeded with efforts to impeach the president and several of his ministers.

Political conditions for the government then took on comic opera proportions. In January 1987, Febres-Cordero was kidnapped for 11 hours by a group of Air Force paratroopers. His capitulation to their demands was public and humiliating, and whatever popular support the president had managed to maintain until then disappeared. By April 1987, even exporters – who had benefited most from the government's policies – were saying, "With general elections next January, this is a lame duck government. It has lost control of the situation, its best people are gone, and nobody believes in it any more" (quoted in *Latin American Economic Report*, April 30, 1987). Much of the political opposition argued that the economic problems of the country were the result of economic policies that benefited only a few rich Ecuadorans, including the president and his friends.[62] Business interests spoke of a collapse of the economy and attacked the government for pursuing incoherent policies. Even the vice-president began to criticize the president and the economic policies that were being pursued.

Febres-Cordero counterattacked in typically aggressive fashion, railing against business interests and especially bankers for speculating rather than investing in an improved future economy (*Latin American Weekly Report*, March 10, 1988). The balance of payments deteriorated substantially, as the political conflict promoted another run against the sucre, and the free market exchange rate rose to 150 sucres per dollar by February. Late that month Ecuador suspended payments on its external debt (Armijos and

Flores, 1989; Hidalgo and Gordillo, 1989; Schodt, 1989). Then, with a strong earthquake in March of 1987 and the rupture of the country's main oil pipeline, the government ran out of economic resources. Export losses were enormous. Oil output in 1987 was only 58.2 percent of the prior year's, and oil export revenues fell 29.2 percent to a low of $646 million.

Under the impact of renewed opposition to reform, two major external shocks, the loss of the government's vision and prestige, and the quixotic nature of Febres-Cordero's leadership, the reforms of 1984–6 experienced the same leakage as those of the Hurtado government. In early 1987, there was an abrupt, and puzzling change in the government's management of the economy. Briefly, Febres-Cordero went on a spending spree, disregarding the opposition's accusations that his actions were unconstitutional.[63] Among the expenditures were a large number of works such as roads and housing developments that Febres-Cordero promoted personally in the coastal Guayaquil region. In the presence of a growing budget deficit, Febres-Cordero increased government salaries and stopped the monthly adjustments in utility rates. These increased expenditures were financed with Central Bank credit, increasing inflation and the budget deficit dramatically. By March 1988, even the float of the exchange rate, touted as the centerpiece of the government's economic reforms, had been undone by the government and replaced with a three-tier system called a "controlled flotation" (see *Latin American Economic Report*, March 31, 1988). Eventually, in full retreat, the government returned to a fixed exchange rate system and began imposing restrictions on imports in early 1988.

Analysts of this period appear to agree that much of the policy reversal between 1986 and 1988 was a result of Febres-Cordero's personality and leadership style. From a committed advocate of neoliberalism he became a traditional populist, dispensing favors to friends and initiating and inaugurating works for villages, towns, and regions. Apparently, unable constitutionally to succeed himself, he sought to ensure his place in history as a popular figure who had brought tangible evidence of development to his country (Swett, 1988, p. 37). It has also been argued that the president became increasingly concerned that he would be unable to finish his term of office unless he was able to shore up his popularity (see *Latin American Weekly Report*, February 5, 1987; Conaghan, 1989b). Indeed, impeachment proceedings were initiated in congress against him and some of his ministers. Charges of corruption and fraud against important government functionaries and allies of the government occupied front pages of the newspapers for days at a time. Some have also suggested that the spending spree was at least partially motivated by the desire to leave an economic mess in the hands of his successor. Whatever the reason, between 1986 and 1988 the reforms of the prior two years were not only undone, they were replaced by policies that greatly exacerbated the problems of the economy.[64]

The economy performed badly during the last two years of the Febres-Cordero administration. GDP growth in 1986 was 3.1 percent, substantially lower than in the previous two years, and in 1987 it fell 6.0 percent. Inflation remained under control in 1986 at 23 percent, began to accelerate in 1987, and, following the spending spree of the last year and a half of the Febres-Cordero administration, threatened to get out of control by 1988. By the time the new administration took over in August 1988, monthly inflation was running at an annualized rate of about 85 percent.[65] Although data for 1986–8 on balance of payments and the government budget have to be interpreted carefully,[66] the 1985 budget surplus of 1.9 percent of GDP turned into a growing deficit in 1986 (5.1 percent) and 1987 (9.6 percent). By mid–1988 the estimate for 1988 exceeded 10 percent of GDP. The balance of payments deteriorated badly due to the oil export disruption in 1987. In 1988 oil exports recovered somewhat, but other exports declined so that total merchandise exports were only slightly higher than in 1987. In August 1988 the balance of payments was in dire trouble, and the departing government had left large negative external reserves.[67] The sucre lost value rapidly. IMF data show year-end changes of the exchange rate of 53, 51, and 95.3 percent in 1986, 1987, and 1988, respectively. In the presence of high inflation and devaluation rates, price controls, particularly on gasoline and energy, resulted in extremely distorted price ratios by August 1988. At that time, a gallon of gasoline cost about $0.15. Similarly distorted prices prevailed for electricity, telephone, and other utilities.

The presidential campaign for 1988 got underway in early 1987, amidst the widespread perception of both economic and political collapse. Few gave the parties of the right much chance for a successful showing, and most electoral attention focused on the parties of the center and left. The social democrats, under the banner of the ID party, fielded Rodrigo Borja, a candidate who had lost in two previous elections, most recently to Febres-Cordero. Opposing him in the second round run-off elections was Abdalá Bucaram of the populist Partido Roldosista Ecuatoriano (PRE). Borja promised greater attention to social welfare issues, wages that would compensate for inflation, incentives for business to create jobs, greater attention to efficiency in the public sector, greater intervention of the state in economic management, and fixed interest rates. These campaign pledges, however, held few specific details.

The election itself raised again the issue of the political power of regional economic interests. Borja was clearly identified with highland interests and, as a social democrat, was known to be sympathetic to labor's plight during economically difficult times. Branded as a statist by the right, he was considered to be a populist by the international agencies pressing Ecuador for substantial policy reforms during ongoing debt negotiations. Bucaram, acknowledged to be the candidate of Guayaquil, was also vague in his campaign promises.

As with the 1984 election, much of the campaign rhetoric centered on a rejection of the incumbent administration, both politically and economically, and issues of economic management dominated the debates. Unlike the previous election, however, ideology played a lesser role, and the policy commitments of the two front runners were much less clear. When Borja was elected with 47 percent of the vote in the May elections, business, labor, and the international institutions waited anxiously for signs of what he would do. There was only one clear conclusion that could be reached after the elections. Febres-Cordero and the neoliberal experiment of 1984–6 had been firmly rejected. Although few knew quite what to expect from the Borja administration when it entered office in August of 1988, it had fewer options and less room to maneuver than had either Hurtado or Febres-Cordero when they assumed the presidency. The state of the economy and the need for IMF help set a clear agenda of the problems that had to be attacked.

5   THE THIRD INITIATIVE: AUSTERITY AND ADJUSTMENT, 1988–90

Both economic and political problems demanded the new administration's attention immediately. Borja faced a record fiscal deficit, high unemployment rates, a massive foreign debt, an inflation rate increasing towards hyperinflation, and a country that was more than usually wary of political leadership after the tensions of the Febres-Cordero years. The last months of that administration had witnessed waves of labor unrest over inflation and minimum wage agreements. General strikes and states of emergency had become almost commonplace. After the election, when Borja called for a new round of negotiations on a social pact between government, business, and labor, neither business nor labor responded with any enthusiasm (see *Latin American Economic Report*, July 31, 1988). Some strong business sectors argued for a free exchange rate, the relaxation of restrictions on imports, and no wage increases. Labor, on the other hand, was firmly on record against gasoline price rises and any form of devaluation.

Although facing larger budget and external sector deficits than his predecessors and competing voices among business and labor, the Borja government had an initial advantage not available to Hurtado or Febres-Cordero.[68] The ID party gained 29 seats in the legislature and had relatively firm coalitional agreements with the DP (Hurtado's party) and a small leftist party (FADI), cemented through cabinet and other official appointments of members of these parties. Borja thus had an absolute majority in congress. His efforts to calm political discourse in his initial days in office also helped lower the temperature of debate and confrontation in the congress.

Moreover, Borja's political style was to be more open, approachable, and inviting of negotiation than either of his predecessors. He was seen often in public and, while emphasizing the difficult nature of the economic crisis, he continually encouraged his critics to sit down and discuss their differences with him. At the same time, like his predecessors, he sought to insulate his economic team from political pressures and to maintain executive control over economic policy management. In turn, he relied on his economic team to design policy, while he focused his attention more on political issues. He used his cabinet more fully than either Hurtado or Febres-Cordero had done, seeking to gain a broader consensus on the reforms to be introduced.

Borja moved quickly to capitalize on his congressional support to gain control of inflation and the fiscal deficit, both of which were to be the focal point of most of his government's policy efforts. From the beginning, in fact, the administration was aware of these problems. According to the vice president,

We faced an enormous problem when we came into office in terms of the fiscal deficit and the balance of payments. We had to restrict imports, raise prices, and raise bank deposits. Inflation has been the single most important problem and job of this government. People here are not used to inflation the way they are in Argentina and Brazil. They don't know how to act.[69]

On August 30, just after the administration took office, the government announced a devaluation, the central bank resumed control over the allocation of foreign currency, a substantial increase in the minimum wage was announced, gasoline prices were doubled, and electricity rates went up by a third. Selective restrictions on imports were imposed and higher taxes announced. At the end of the year, prices for edible oil, milk, bread, and some beverages were increased substantially and electricity rates were raised again.

Monetary policy was restrictive. Beginning in August 1988 the Central Bank enforced reserve requirements, limited credit to the public and private sectors, and established a requirement for importers to deposit the value of the imports in sucres when they applied for foreign exchange to import. This measure, which increased the cost of imports, was taken mainly to control the money supply.[70] The monetary program assumed a significant increase of the central government's deposits in the central bank to provide credit to the private sector. However, the government did not meet the deposit goals in the first semester and the monetary board changed the program by increasing reserve requirements and taking other minor measures to control liquidity.

Although many of these changes were more significant than measures introduced by either the Hurtado or the Febres-Cordero governments, each was successfully introduced. Opposition in congress was muted, in part because of a more general consensus that 'something had to be done' to improve the economy, especially to slow inflation. Nevertheless, opposition from labor began to mount by the end of 1988 with an increase in strikes and work stoppages. Borja's low-key negotiating style helped undermine the confrontational tactics of the unions, however. Moreover, the strike, used repeatedly during the previous six years, had lost much of its effectiveness as a political resource. It had become part of normal politics, just as congressional infighting and business sector attacks on the government had lost their capacity to alarm the general public.

Although negotiations with the IMF were also undertaken immediately, Borja worked hard to convince the country that the reforms were not a capitulation to the demands of the creditors and that the IMF and the World Bank were not central actors in the design of the new economic measures. In particular, the government's commitment to gradualism, similar to that of Hurtado and Febres-Cordero, remained strong in the face of creditor insistence on harsher measures to control inflation and deal with the public deficit. The head of the monetary board, who had been part of Hurtado's economic team as head of the central bank, was a principal exponent of a gradualist approach that eventually came to be characterized by weekly minidevaluations, gradual increases in public utility tariffs, regular increases in the price of gasoline and other fuels, and a widening tax base (see *Vistazo*, 1990).[71] In an effort to deal with the ongoing problem of the public budget, the economic team sought to move from a widespread system of implicit subsidies to more explicit ones as a way of increasing political pressures to reduce them, and to raise tax collections by increasing the coverage of income subject to tax withholding and improving the accounting systems at the ministry of finance.

Stabilization measures dominated the administration's efforts to manage the economic crisis. In particular, inflation proved a dogged opponent of economic recovery, as the average rate for the 12 months of 1988 was 58.2 percent, doubling that of the previous year. Borja also introduced some measures more attuned to longer-term adjustment. Exchange rate controls were gradually relaxed, the markets for some basic necessities and agricultural products were liberalized in late 1989 and early 1990, a tax reform was introduced in late 1989, and measures to modernize the stock market were legislated. In a letter of intent with the IMF signed in March of 1990, the country pledged itself to a development strategy that would be export-led (*Latin American Economic Report*, March 31, 1990).[72] None of these measures was expected to have an immediate impact on economic performance, but they did indicate the concern of the administration for the long-range problems of the country's development. Like Hurtado, and in contrast to Febres-Cordero, the policy proposals and commitments of the Borja government offered only limited amounts of privatization or deregulation. The state was expected to continue to play a central role in the development of the country.

The style of the Borja administration, and the severity of the economic crisis, eased somewhat the problems of introducing harsh economic policy changes. In fact, Borja used the crisis effectively to argue for negotiation, sharing the burden of economic adjustment, and patience in the face of grave national problems. The crisis itself was widely perceived to require strong action by the government, a consequence not only of the economic problems themselves but also of increased public awareness of and capacity to understand these problems. Six years of debate and experience with economic policy changes made it possible for the government to introduce measures that were stronger than those that could have been attempted by the previous two administrations. Its efforts to appear to be independent of the IMF in debt and adjustment negotiations and in its dealings with foreign oil companies were also helpful in maintaining some popular support. In addition, Borja gained public approval with an initiative to negotiate an agreement with the country's guerillas, whose activities had escalated noticeably under Febres-Cordero, although his action did not gain the approval of the military and of much of the business community.

But Borja's initiatives also suffered from the leakage that had affected the efforts of Hurtado and Febres-Cordero. His economic team was characterized by more rivalry and internal disagreement than those of the two previous presidents.[73] Eventually, a division of labor emerged within the team between control over fiscal policy and control over monetary policy that partially dampened the tendency toward disunity. In a situation similar to that of Hurtado and Febres-Cordero, Borja's policy initiatives lost momentum as the nature and impact of the changes became apparent. Guayaquil business interests made a concerted attack on the economic management of the country in early 1989 and called for relief from taxes and restrictive trade laws and for more incentives for production (*Latin American Weekly Report*, February 23, 1989). In June 1989, a strike by transport workers paralyzed the country and led Borja to invoke a national security law that allowed him to call out the army to deal with the problem. The government's coalition of support in congress, replicated in the cabinet, formally dissolved in late July 1989, when the DP withdrew from the cabinet. However, this party pledged to continue to support the government informally, when agreement could be reached on the direction of policies. By mid–1989, then, the government was confronting increased political opposition to its economic policies, and was finding it increasingly difficult to sustain them. Its problems were summed up effectively by the president of the monetary board, "Remember, you're always dealing with reaction to policies, not pressures in favor of something."[74] Then, in June

1990, the government fared badly in mid-term elections and lost its ability to marshall an effective coalition in the legislature.

Given the magnitude of the crisis faced in August 1988, some economic measures were fairly successful, while others were not. The increase in gasoline and utility prices, and the conservative fiscal policies of the government reduced the fiscal deficit in the second half of 1988 to only 5.1 percent of GDP for the year. It declined to a manageable 2.2 percent in 1989. The current account deficit, aided by a recovery of oil exports and a decline in imports from the high post-earthquake level, declined from 11.9 percent to 7 percent of GDP.[75] However, the current account deficit financing, while smaller, was quite troublesome because lower disbursements by the multilateral lenders and higher amortization payments resulted in almost all the deficit being financed by increases in external debt arrears. International reserves increased and trade arrears were paid, such that by the end of 1989 international reserves had risen to $203 million and there were no trade arrears. GDP increased substantially (11.2 percent) in 1988 as oil output recuperated.[76] However, inflation doubled to 58.2 percent in 1988, as noted above, and increased even more in 1989 to 75.6 percent. However, after March 1989 inflation rates fell, eventually reaching annual rates of 45–50 percent where they have been stuck for some time. Income increased in 1988 mainly because of the recovery in oil production, but tight monetary and fiscal policies and a decline in oil output resulted in GDP growth of only 0.2 percent in 1989. The Borja administration package reduced credit to the private sector. The financial sector declined in that year also. Open unemployment increased to 13 percent in 1988, while real minimum wages, which had fallen 5.5 percent in 1987, fell 12.7 percent and 21.1 percent in the next two years. Overall policy results were perceived as a failure, particularly by the opposition, and this did as much to undermine the efforts of the government as its overt political opposition. Thus, the Borja administration, whose policies generally resembled those of the Hurtado period, also had sufficient political resources to introduce policy changes, but not enough to maintain them in the face of societal reaction. The mounting economic problems of the country gave the government fewer options in selecting policy instruments and in determining the timing of their introduction. Nevertheless, the effort to balance economic and political goals meant a bias in favor of gradualism in the design and introduction of the measures and negotiation and flexibility after they had been introduced. Charges that economic policy was dominated by crisis management and a failure of vision were logical outcomes of the nature of decision making in this context of political and economic uncertainty. The Borja administration muddled towards adjustment, aided and pressured by an economic crisis, but impeded by incomplete acceptance of measures meant to respond to it.

6   CONCLUSIONS

What can be learned about the political economy of adjustment from this decade-long experience in Ecuador? During this period, three presidential administrations addressed fundamental economic problems in the country, developed policy responses to them, put them into practice, and then struggled to maintain them in the face of considerable public reaction. The problems faced were frequently caused by changing external conditions and natural catastrophes, but they were also the result of misguided economic policies during the 1970s oil boom. Indeed, the development path followed during the 1970s was unsustainable, based as it was on increased external borrowing and domestic policies that did not promote export growth and diversification. Even if external sector conditions had not deteriorated in the early 1980s, Ecuador could not have avoided an external sector and debt crisis by 1984 or 1985. The interest rate increase and oil price decline of 1982 precipitated the crisis and blurred its causes, allowing Ecuadorans to blame external causes and masking the need for structural policy changes and increasing difficulties of developing a broad-based consensus about the need for such reforms.

All presidents faced significant and often overwhelming political opposition. Two of them faced direct challenges to their right to remain in office. One administration, which had a more assured base of support as it assumed office, lost that support under the pressure of economic crisis and the failure of policy changes to resolve it. Sometimes opposition was exacerbated or tempered by presidential and managerial styles; always, however, strong protest was a response to the introduction of altered policies and their real or anticipated effects. Much of that opposition was exacerbated by an electoral and institutional context that encouraged dissensus and discouraged the durability of political coalitions. Within the context of a new constitution and incompletely legitimized political institutions, Ecuador's three presidents demonstrated considerable capacity to introduce policy changes, but fared much more poorly in their efforts to sustain them. The closed, technocratic style of decision making of each of the three administrations gave way to intense political reactions to the reform initiatives and often to direct confrontations over the terms of stabilization and adjustment and the legitimacy of the administrations in power. In this case, political leaders were generally able to marshall the political resources needed to place issues on the government's agenda, to design policies in response to their analysis of these issues, and to commit the government to them. Different kinds of resources were required to ensure the durability of the changes and access to these resources proved extremely elusive to policy-makers throughout the decade. Without durability, most policies seemed to fail in spite of having frequently produced some positive results in the short term.

Agenda setting and policy making

In the Hurtado, Febres-Cordero, and Borja administrations, policy initiatives were undertaken even in the absence of strong coalitional support. The space for policy innovation was considerable and much of the content and timing of policy changes can be understood by viewing them from the perspective of leadership by policy elites. Hurtado and Febres-Cordero came into office with particular concerns about the management of the country's economic development. In the case of Febres-Cordero, the commitment to economic liberalism amounted to a new vision, ideological in nature, of the future of the country's development. As we have seen, Borja was under considerably more pressure than the other two presidents in terms of the kinds of policy changes to be adopted, but even he molded particular measures to be more congruent with his own concerns about social equity and the appropriate role of the state. Each president had clear notions of what needed to be altered in order to improve the economic condition of the country. For Hurtado, the principal issues were budget deficits and foreign exchange imbalances; Febres-Cordero clearly believed that institutions needed to be altered to permit much greater freedom to the private sector and market forces; inflation and debt management were the central problems diagnosed by the Borja government. In addition, the commitment of the Hurtado and Borja administrations to heterodox measures that reserved considerable space for state intervention and price controls, and the orthodox approach of Febres-Cordero, were linked to perspectives of the president about how best to manage economic development and economic crises. Similarly, all three presidents determined that the policy changes would be introduced gradually, in response to their concerns about political and economic feasibility.

Political resources to affect the content and timing of adjustment measures were generally available to the presidents. First, each had control over the appointment of his economic team and each used this power to select individuals he knew to be both competent and committed to his perspectives. Hurtado and Febres-Cordero also used these appointments to ensure that their teams would be unified and could work effectively together; Borja managed the greater competition within his team through a careful division of labor among them. Second, efforts to centralize economic decision making in the executive were a common feature of the three administrations. In this regard, they were substantially aided by the severely factionalized and contentious nature of the legislature and the weak and understaffed technical support available to this branch of government. Constitutional provisions for ruling by executive decree were also put to regular use by the executive. The party system and traditional legislative–executive conflict presented many obstacles to Hurtado, Febres-Cordero, and Borja, and made policy consistency difficult to achieve, but they did not fully cripple the decision-making power of the executive.

A third resource that gave political leaders in Ecuador greater scope for policy innovation was their ability to command media attention. Each of them used his access to the public and his (sometimes flagging) legitimacy as the head of government to persuade, explain, and appeal for support. Particularly in the case of Hurtado, public appeals were often couched in terms of the need to support democratic institutions and to avoid military intervention. Febres-Cordero, at least for a time, held popular attention with his flamboyant personality and his use of the media to gain support. Borja rarely missed an opportunity to appear in public and to invite his opponents to engage in discussions of their complaints with him.

Finally, two of the three administrations used their ongoing negotiations with the IMF, the World Bank, and other creditors to enhance their autonomy from domestic political forces in the design of economic policy measures. For Febres-Cordero, the support and approval of the IMF and the Reagan administration provided an opportunity to negotiate attractive agreements with the multilateral agencies and to bolster his support coalition domestically. Borja used the presence of the multilateral agencies to insist on highly unpopular policy measures while also managing to appear to be protecting national interests vis-à-vis the IMF and the World Bank. As with the power of appointment, the capacity to outpace the congress in analysis and decision making, and access to the public, the power to negotiate with the international financial institutions resided in the executive. The use of these political resources required skill and leadership; nevertheless, these were resources readily available to the presidents that increased their capacity to set the agenda and influence the content and timing of economic policy changes.

Implementing and sustaining policy changes

As we have seen, resources needed to implement and sustain economic policy measures were not as consistently available to the three administrations. None of them was able to count on strong and durable coalitions of support, for example. Hurtado was president-by-accident who never had more than a small minority party backing him in congress. Nor, as a nonelected and increasingly unpopular president, did he have much capacity to put together a broader coalition, either in congress or among the country's diverse and fragmented interest groups. Although he used cabinet appointments to forge party and sectoral support, he was never able to claim much success in doing so. Febres-Cordero's coalition, fairly strong at the outset of his administration, fell apart in reaction to his confrontational style and the impact of the policies introduced. Borja had the strongest legislative coalition, but he was unable to maintain it once he began introducing new policies. In Ecuador, presidents are rarely able to count on strong and durable support coalitions, however much they try. There are few incentives to cooperate established by the electoral system or the constitutionally mandated relationship between the executive and the legislature.[77]

All three presidents initially had military support and use of police powers to manage the confrontations and reactions that followed upon the announcement of new policies, but the power to command this support was never certain. In 1982 and 1983, Hurtado did not know the military would support and protect him against fierce public reaction; for a time, his administration feared a military coup and believed that the business community was actively fomenting one. Febres-Cordero was confronted by military revolts on several occasions before being kidnapped and publicly humiliated by factions within the military. Borja had the clearest support from the military, but even he had to continuously negotiate this support. In the context of a transitional democracy, presidents cannot necessarily assume that they can command military and police support to maintain public order when they announce unpopular public policy measures.

It is also clear that Ecuador's policy makers could not count on positive results from the policies they introduced to aid in sustaining them.[78] Relief from inflation, budget deficits, foreign exchange imbalances, and economic stagnation occurred only briefly during the decade, and by the mid 1980s, "adjustment fatigue" was clearly in evidence. Particular measures may have been inappropriate or overly modest in scope to deal with the country's problems effectively, or they were whittled away by after-the-fact accommodation to protesting groups, or they were severely undercut by repeated external shocks, or they simply needed more time to be effective. In the end, policy makers had few opportunities to point to economic improvement in order to bolster tolerance for naturally unpopular measures.

Muddling

The characteristic pattern of policy change in Ecuador – considerable capacity to introduce new measures but much curtailed capacity to sustain them – contributed to a decade of muddling toward adjustment. This pattern helps account for alteration in the content and timing of policy choices and for the undoing of many of them through accommodation and retreat after they were announced. As important, the pattern of policy change attests to efforts of policy makers to balance economic and political objectives within the context of weak democratic institutions. There is little question that each administration was seriously concerned with economic problems confronting the country and that all sought to introduce what were considered to be appropriate policy responses to them. At the same time, political goals such as sustaining democratic institutions, avoiding violence, and serving out terms of office influenced efforts to manage

Table 4.1 Statistical Appendix

Year	GDP Growth[a]	Per capita GDP growth[a]	Manuf-acturing growth[a]	Banana, coffee and cacao growth[a]	Fishing and hunting growth[a]	Other agri-cultural growth[a]	GDP deflator 1975 base[a]	CPI three cities[b]	New CPI[c]
1966	2.4	−0.8	5.9	1.2	−2.6	0.0	6.4	3.7	
1967	6.9	3.5	8.2	8.9	7.7	8.4	4.6	4.8	
1968	4.0	0.8	2.9	14.4	15.2	−2.0	4.4	3	
1969	2.3	−0.9	5.3	−28.5	7.3	15.2	7.4	5.2	
1970	6.5	3.2	12.7	9.6	10.6	6.1	9.2	5.6	
1971	6.3	3.0	5.0	10.1	36.8	0.0	7.5	9.5	
1972	14.4	11.0	9.2	4.7	8.1	−1.2	2.3	7.7	
1973	25.3	21.6	9.2	−4.7	11.1	1.5	5.9	12	
1974	6.4	3.3	10.4	13.0	4.3	10.5	40.1	22.7	
1975	5.6	2.5	15.2	−10.6	10.7	6.9	10.0	14.4	
1976	9.2	6.1	13.2	−4.5	8.7	4.0	12.9	10.1	
1977	6.5	3.5	11.9	22.9	9.4	−12.1	17.5	12.9	
1978	6.6	3.6	8.2	−1.6	6.0	−14.8	7.9	13.1	
1979	5.3	2.3	9.7	1.0	8.4	1.8	16.1	10.1	
1980	4.9	1.9	3.6	−8.3	41.2	9.5	19.5	12.7	
1981	3.9	1.0	8.8	−0.1	10.1	12.9	14.3	14.7	
1982	1.2	−1.7	1.5	4.6	12.7	−7.4	17.8	16.4	16.3
1983	−2.8	−5.6	−1.4	−35.4	−2.5	−23.3	38.7		48.4
1984	4.2	1.3	−1.9	13.0	13.6	23.4	39.2		31.2
1985	4.3	1.4	0.2	28.8	24.8	4.1	30.9		28
1986	3.1	0.2	−1.5	1.1	15.5	22.6	20.9		23
1987	−6.0	−8.6	2.8	−20.4	36.5	3.3	38.0		29.5
1988	11.2	8.2	0.5	12.8	9.0	11.5	55.5		58.2
1989	0.2	−2.6	−10.2	9.0	−7.6	4.4	75.8		75.6

Sources:
[a] Banco Central del Ecuador (1990).
[b] Central Bank data from Luzuriaga and Zuvekas (1981). (1970 = 100; constructed from Cuencia, Guayaquil and Quinto.)
[c] Central Bank data. The index has a 1978–9 base.
[d] International Monetary Fund (1990) and IMF tapes.
[e] Central Bank data in Valencia (1989).
[f] 1973–82: World Bank (1984); 1984–8: IMF unpublished data.
[g] Gelb and Marshall-Silva (1988).

Total exports: goods and non-factor services[d]	Crude oil exports[d]	Total imports: goods and non-factor services[d]	Current account balance[d]	International reserves[e]	Total external debt[e]	Debt-service ratio[e]	Budget balance as percentage of GDP[f]	Oil subsidy as percentage of GDP[g]
	1		−24					
	1		−54					
	1		−91					
	1		−96					
259	1	359	−113	55.2	241.5	10.9		
265	1	401	−156	24.9	260.8	15.1		
365	60	392	−77	127.9	343.9	11.5		
627	250	509	7	226.0	380.4	8.1	3.1	1.1
1,308	613	1,100	37	339.4	410.0	8.8	0.8	3.4
1,110	516	1,295	−220	245.5	512.7	5.8	−2.2	3.0
1,419	565	1,321	−7	434.4	693.1	7.8	−3.3	2.8
1,602	478	1,774	−343	570.3	1,263.7	9.6	−5.5	3.0
1,703	523	2,161	−703	601.0	2,974.6	31.3	−5.0	2.8
2,410	1,032	2,653	−630	630.9	3,554.1	64.5	−0.5	5.6
2,865	1,382	2,925	−670	356.5	4,651.8	47.4	−4.5	7.3
2,911	1,560	3,149	−1,012	562.9	6,185.8	71.3	−5.8	4.5
2,676	1,184	2,912	−1,226	210.0	6,707.1	97.0	−7.9	4.2
2,643	1,484	1,822	−4	151.5	6,932.1	33.8	−1.4	
2,895	1,622	2,040	−148	170.7	7,438.8	35.7	−0.6	
3,294	1,825	2,175	149	195.9	8,328.5	30.0	1.9	
2,589	912	2,237	−613	144.1	9,160.9	40.9	−5.1	
2,449	646	2,664	−1,131				−9.6	
2,632	875	2,195	−597				−5.1	
2,832	1,033	2,357	−441					

economic crisis. Thus, there were repeated occasions when the ability to achieve important political goals meant some retreat in the pursuit of economic policy reforms. Strategies that contribute to muddling responses to economic problems may result in part from ignorance of economic interactions or a failure to perceive the difficult nature of the issues faced, but they are also a result of clear awareness of the need to balance economic and political objectives and of the concern that the political resources to sustain measures that impose hardships on broad sectors of the population do not exist.

Nevertheless, this case also indicates that some of the sources of muddling towards adjustment can be addressed. In some cases, the failure to pursue effective adjustment policies is the result of the impact of simultaneously pursued policies, lack of administrative capacity or compliance with new measures, or new external shocks that require new stronger policies. The first two of these sources of problems can be addressed through better and more politically sensitive policy analysis. They are problems that can, to some degree, be addressed during the design and deliberation about adjustment measures. Greater attention to implementation and sustainability issues can certainly be a part of initial efforts to design more effective policy responses to deep economic problems in a society. The Ecuadoran presidents often chose to ignore such issues until after they had announced new initiatives, suspecting that otherwise they would have not been able to introduce the reforms they wanted. Moreover, they often initiated reform measures with very little prior consultation, investing instead in the political management of opposition after the announcement of policy changes. In apparently disregarding the problems of sustainability, and in choosing not to engage in greater consensus building prior to making decisions, they may have jeopardized some of their initiatives and may have increased the amount of muddling that occurred.[79]

APPENDIX 4.1

Chronology of important events and policy changes

1978

Jan.	Referendum approves new constitution.
July	First round election. Results delayed, many votes nullified.
Dec.	Official election results given.

1979

Apr. 29	Roldós elected in run-off election.
Aug. 10	Roldós inaugurated.

1981

Jan.   First significant policy changes. "War" with Peru used as a reason to change policy variables. Gasoline prices increased 223 percent to $0.60 per gallon; passive interest rates raised from 6 to 8 percent and active rates from 12 to 15 percent; price increases in electricity and transportation; some import tariffs raised. Parallel market exchange rate increases.

May 24   Roldós dies in plane accident, Hurtado president.

1982

Early 82   Hurtado begins reforms. Some imports limited; interest rates capped; further foreign debt accumulation prohibited.

May 13   Official exchange rate devalued from 25 to 33 sucres per dollar. Prices of some goods and services controlled.

Sept.   Congress censures energy minister who is forced out of the cabinet because of January 1981 price increases.

Oct.   Major reform package: gasoline prices and bus fares doubled; wheat prices up 45 percent; wage adjustments limited; some cuts in government expenditures; initiation of debt rescheduling discussions with IMF. Minimum wages raised at month's end.

Late 82–First semester 83   Extended floods due to "El Niño" current destroy large part of agricultural output.

1983

Jan. $1.2 billion external debt renegotiation. Payments on about 25 percent of public debt, due between November 1982 and December 1983 spread through 7 years. Parallel market exchange rate drops from 67 to 60 sucres per dollar.

Feb-Mar.   Official exchange rate devalued from 33 to 42 sucres per dollar; creeping peg and multiple exchange rates system established; parallel rate shoots up to 90 sucres. Some fuel price increases; milk price increase. Tariff surcharges and new import restrictions established. IMF approves debt renegotiation agreement, and standby loan requested.

1984

Apr.   Febres-Cordero wins very close election with 52.2 percent of the vote.

July   External debt payments suspended until new government takes over.

Aug. 10	Febres-Cordero inaugurated.
Sept.	Neoliberal reforms begin. Exchange rate devalued, and fixed rate system substitutes creeping. Import liberalization begun to lower tariff levels and dispersion. Interest rate decontrol begun. Program to strengthen fiscal administration to increase tax collections established. Most price controls eliminated.
Dec. 28	Gasoline and transportation price increases and union protests.

1985

Mar. 1	Government salaries and minimum wages raised by an amount a little above projected inflation.
Mar. 12	IMF standby loan agreement approved.
May 17	Direct foreign investment treatment liberalized. Conflicts with Andean Group Direct Foreign Investment code.
Aug. 28	Multiple exchange rate system simplified as two official rates unified. Parallel market exchange rate only for a few types of transactions.
Dec. 20	External debt "Multiple Year Refinancing Agreement" (MYRA) reached with the commercial banks and the Paris Club. It covered $4,500 million due between 1 January 1985 and 31 December 1989, and included the supply of $200 million fresh credit and $700 million trade financing.

1986

Jan. 28	Official exchange rate devalued 15.2 percent. New tariff structure approved. No import prohibitions and maximum tariff of 125 percent.
Feb.	Febres-Cordero visits Washington to a warm welcome by the Reagan administration.
First semester	Oil prices drop sharply.
July	Opposition captures 43 of 71 congressional seats. Febres-Cordero's coalition receives only 35.5 percent of popular vote. Francisco X. Swett leaves cabinet, Alberto Dahik becomes minister of finance.
Aug. 11	Final important neoliberal measures taken: exchange rate freed completely; savings interest rates also freed, other rates allowed to float; new tariff structure to lower protection in preparation.
Aug. 16	IMF approves stand-by loan of DEG 75.4 million.
Sept. 20	Minimum wages raised 20 percent.

Nov.	Dahik impeached. Febres-Cordero makes truce with opposition.

1987

Jan. 16	Febres-Cordero is kidnapped for a few hours and gives in to captors' requests.
Feb.	External debt payments suspended.
Mar. 5–8	Several strong earthquakes destroy oil pipeline. Oil exports collapse.
Mar.	Fuels price increased 52 percent, transportation fares raised 25 percent, milk, rice and sugar prices frozen, and government moves against speculators. Government spending is not adjusted to lower revenues.
May	Oil exports resume in small amounts.
July	Minimum wages raised 21 percent, well below inflation level.
Aug.	Direct foreign investment rules liberalized further.
Second semester	Inflation accelerates and currency devalues.
Nov.	Government spending plan for the last year of the administration is not modified. Febres-Cordero wants to finish the projects he began.

1988

First Quarter	Run on the sucre and on March 3 free foreign exchange system changed. Three tiered system established.
May	Borja elected president.
June	3 percent monthly electricity rate increases which had been applied for 6 years stopped and rates frozen.
July	Borja wants social pact with business. Little favorable reaction.
Aug. 10	Borja's presidential inauguration.
Aug. 30	Third adjustment episode measures begun. Central Bank resumes control over exchange rate; currency devalued; weekly minidevaluations established; gasoline prices doubled; electricity rates up 1/3; substantial increase in minimum wages; selective import restrictions imposed; and program to raise taxes and tax collections established. Credit to private and public sectors severely restricted and prior import deposits established. Government spending cuts.
Sept.	Negotiations with IMF begun.
Nov.	Prices edible oil, milk, bread and some beverages increased. Electricity rates up again.

Nov.   Tax reform introduced and new legislation to promote
                           stock market approved.

End 1988   Exchange restrictions gradually relaxed and some pri-
–early 1989   ces of some basic necessities and agricultural products
                           liberalized.

1989
Mar.   Letter of agreement with IMF.

NOTES

We are grateful to Robert Bates, Anne O. Krueger, Clarence Zurekas, David
Orsmond and Ronald Archer for help and comments on an earlier draft of this
paper.

1   The reader is encouraged to look up the chronology of events and policy
    changes and the statistical appendix at the back of the text, to facilitate the
    reading of this essay.
2   Efforts to rate reform performance are, in any event, difficult because they are
    time bound and face difficult problems of definition and application. Rankings
    differ markedly between whether the initiatives or the results are being
    assessed; and they assume that policy is the measure of performance, not
    international conditions or domestic structures of production. For recent
    efforts to rate country performance, see World Bank (1988a) and (1989).
3   The idea of adjustment over "the long haul" comes from Nelson and
    Contributors (1989). Conaghan (1989a, p. 14) describes the political problem-
    solving style of Ecuador's democratic institutions as one of "muddling
    through."
4   Labor code reform debates have focused on the issue of allowing temporary
    employment status. Legislation in effect in the 1980s imposed extraordinarily
    high lay-off costs for permanent employees, granted wage payments to the
    workers during legal strikes, and in some cases allowed unions to attach the
    personal property of the plant owners to pay these wages, even after a firm had
    gone bankrupt.
5   For a discussion of a number of such cases, see the concluding essay by Joan
    Nelson in Nelson (1990).
6   The eastern half of the country is a sparsely populated tropical rain forest that
    produces most of the country's oil. The highlands cover approximately a
    quarter of the national territory, but are subdivided into miniregions formed
    by valleys that were traditionally very isolated. The coast, comprising a quarter
    of the country, is well-suited to the production of tropical agricultural
    products. Distinctions among regions and their basis in history and economic
    development are well discussed in Rodríguez (1985).
7   The Centro de Estudios y Difusión Social (1986) estimates that in the
    mid–1980s the 200 largest firms (most of them owned by holding groups),
    controlled about 50 percent of the modern sector assets. Luzuriaga and

Zuvekas (1981) estimate a Gini coefficient for agricultural land of 0.82 for 1976. There is much less data for recent years. However, the national accounts (Banco Central del Ecuador, 1990) show that between 1980 and 1989 wages and salaries dropped from 33 percent to 15 percent of GDP, while the remuneration to capital remained rather stable at about 14 percent. During this period the share of the households increased sharply from 42 percent to 61.6 percent of GDP, reflecting the large growth of the informal economy and the weakening of the formal middle class.

8   Conaghan (1989a) presents a comprehensive discussion of the constitutional and party environment in Ecuador.

9   Interestingly, to prevent the proliferation of small parties, the constitution provided for the elimination of parties that failed to obtain 5 percent of the vote in two consecutive national elections. However, the small parties succeeded in getting Congress to interpret the constitution in a way such that this clause is not applied.

10 Second-round elections are limited to the two top contenders who emerge from the first round.

11 Between 1978 and 1988, twenty parties participated in elections at one time or another. Conaghan (1989a, p. 7) refers to Ecuador's as a "predatory multiparty system."

12 For example, Placencia (1989) shows that competition also existed within competing groups. For example, two laws that regulate and promote artisan activities were implemented by different government agencies that competed for the artisans' loyalty and membership.

13 The urban poor were mobilized cyclically around election campaigns. The rural poor increased their political importance after 1978, when the franchise was extended to illiterates and began organizing at the communal, regional, or ethnic level to make demands on government.

14 In the mid–1970s, domestic gasoline prices were the equivalent of about one dollar a barrel, or about eighteen cents a gallon (see Thoumi, 1990, p. 45).

15 Many have noted the difficulties of initiating reform when prior policies have created strongly vested interests in the status quo (see, for example, Bates, 1981; Haggard, 1985). Mancur Olson has written of the policy impasse that results when political demands come from large numbers of narrowly defined interest groups, each in pursuit of its own self-interest, and when distributive coalitions capture control over government policy (see Olson, 1965; 1982).

16 It must be noted that the energy subsidy was highly regressive as the per capita energy consumption of the upper and middle classes was much greater than that of most of the population (Gelb and Marshall-Silva, 1988).

17 The sucre was overvalued in terms of external competitiveness, but not in terms of external balance, which was achieved with the help of large external borrowings.

18 Part of the increase in energy consumption is fictitious as the extremely low gasoline prices in Ecuador led to contraband exports to Colombia and Perú, however, the increase in energy consumption was so large, that there is no doubt of the energy intensive nature of the country's development process during the 1970s.

19 Valencia (1989) presents an excellent survey of the evolution of the external debt.

20 These data are taken from the IMF (1990) presented in table 4.1. The data from the Ecuadorian Central Bank follow a similar pattern with small differences (see Valencia 1989, p. 165).

21 Curiously, the studies available (Sepúlveda 1983; World Bank 1984; Vos 1987; Villalobos 1987; Abril and Urriola 1990; Hidrobo 1990) do not provide estimates for actual tariff levels, even when the main subject of the work is industrial incentives (Abril and Urriola, 1990). This suggests that in the Ecuadoran context tariff protection is taken for granted, and that what is considered as productive incentives are only those above and beyond tariff protection.

22 Consumer protection rates were estimated as part of a large industrialization study done by a team from the Center of Latin American Studies of Boston University (1985), but never published in book form.

23 This subsidy, the Certificado de Abono Tributario, was given to exports that had more than 35 percent of domestic value added, and ranged from 7 to 15 percent, depending on the value added percentage (Hidrobo, 1990, p. 46).

24 The best-known of these products were the exports of large household appliances assembled in Ecuador.

25 Remarkably, garments and textiles, the main manufacturing exports from many countries similar to Ecuador, accounted only for 3.3 percent of manufacturing exports, a proportion equal that of metallic products, machinery, and equipment (Abril and Urriola, 1990, p. 50, table 10).

26 These are estimates based on the national accounts data at constant 1975 prices (Banco Central del Ecuador, 1990, pp. 31–2).

27 Vos (1987, p. 43) shows that by 1980 about two thirds of all intermediate inputs of the paper and printing, and chemical and plastic products industries were imported. These coefficients were also very high in other industries: 54 percent in the large textile plants, 47 percent in mineral products and 42 percent in machinery and equipment.

28 The data on employment are weak and the available series are frequently revised (Luzuriaga and Zuvekas, 1981). This is why the World Bank (1988b) uses census data. Dávila (1986), using data for 1975 and 1985, shows that the public sector employment increased 116 percent during this period. Most of this increase took place before the 1982 crisis. The increase in the public sector employment took place in all branches of government since the Central Government employment increased 120 percent and the largest increase was 126 percent in the health sector.

29 As late as the fourth quarter of 1979 Lloyds of London lent $200 million to the government of Ecuador to finance current expenditures.

30 Table 4.1 shows estimates of the consolidated nonfinancial public sector surplus and deficits (−) and the implicit subsidy to domestic oil consumption for the 1973–82 period as a percentage of GDP.

31 Luzuriaga and Zuvekas (1981, p. 287) supply the 1950–80 composite consumer price index for Quito, Guayaquil, and Cuenca. During the 1950s and 1960s, the consumer price index increased less than 4 percent during most years, and during the 1955–60 period it actually declined slightly.

32 The unsustainability of the 1970s growth path also appeared to escape foreign analysts who blamed the need for adjustment during the 1980s on the external sector only (see, for example, de Janvry et al., 1990).

33 Interestingly, a recent econometric analysis of the adjustment in Ecuador during the 1980s does not include this episode, and studies only the adjustment attempts that began in 1984 during the Febres-Cordero regime (see de Janvry et al., 1990).

34 It appears that a few middle-level, well-trained economists at the central bank perceived the magnitude of the crisis; however, their superiors argued that the measures needed to solve the external and internal disequilibria were too harsh to take, and they backed down. It is also possible that the technocrats were not believed.

35 The unicameral legislature contained 71 seats.

36 The relationship between Bucaram and Roldós transcended politics as Roldós was married to Burcaram's niece, and became a candidate when the constitutional reform required both parents of any presidential candidate to have been born in Ecuador, blocking Bucaram's bid. Thus the CFP's campaign slogan: "Roldós a la presidencia, Bucaram al poder."

37 According to the government's campaign document, gains from oil wealth were to be spurred by increased investment in exploration, attracting further foreign investment in the sector, and enlarging the role of the state oil company.

38 Ecuadorans did not perceive that this growth pattern would be in danger, a fact that is perhaps best exemplified by Assad Bucaram's introduction in congress, immediately after the Roldós government took over, of a law project to revalue by 20 percent the currency, as a measure to combat inflation (*Latin American Political Report*, August 24, 1979).

39 These are known as "productos vitales de primera necesidad" and are composed mostly of staple foodstuffs, drugs, and transportation fares.

40 Interview with former minister of finance, Quito, Ecuador, May 4, 1990.

41 Interview with former vice-minister and then minister of energy and mines, Guayaquil, Ecuador, May 3, 1990. Another former official indicated that the primary concern of the Roldós government had to do with the viability of democratic institutions. "In the last days of the military government and the first days of Roldós, we were most concerned about whether the military was going to cede power or not; we weren't really concerned about economic problems, although here and there in official documents you'll see mention of them" (Interview with former general secretary of government, Guayaquil, Ecuador, May 3, 1990). Another remarked that "In September of 1980, we had our first concerns that economic difficulties lay ahead. But then the Iran–Iraq war occurred and increased our expectation that the price of oil would increase." (Interview with former minister of education and culture and then minister of interior, Guayaquil, May 3, 1990).

42 An earlier effort to introduce higher fees for public transportation in January 1980 was met with a wave of rioting and put a damper on other such initiatives to impose more realistic prices on goods and services in the country (*Latin American Weekly Report*, 25 January, 1980). The war provided a more conducive environment for trying to raise prices.

43 The actual cost of the military operation cannot be estimated because the military budget is not known in Ecuador. However, Central Bank technocrats suggested informally a figure of $600 million. However, it is not clear what is included in this figure because it is presumed that a large proportion of the

hardware used was already Ecuadoran and because it is not known how much of the lost hardware was replaced, and so on. The armed forces were one of the main beneficiaries of the oil boom as part of the oil revenues were earmarked to the military. Gelb and Marshall-Silva (1988, p. 181) argue that according to Central Bank estimates, 22.8 percent of oil revenues were used in 1974–78 to service the public debt and support the military, although a more precise estimate is not available.

44   The private sector's lack of confidence in the economy seems to have begun before the conflict with Peru as the parallel market exchange rate began to rise in the first quarter of 1981, reflecting capital flight.

45   "I never wanted to be president – never!" he stated in an interview in Quito, April 25, 1990.

46   Some people even maintained that Hurtado was part of a worldwide conspiracy of Christian Democrats who wanted to gradually nationalize private property.

47   It is unclear whether Hurtado understood the complexity and depth of the crisis or thought the main cause was external rather than structural domestic policy causes. Interviews with Central Bank technocrats suggest that Hurtado was aware of the complexity of the situation but thought that he did not have the political support to implement policy changes of the magnitude needed.

48   Interestingly, the movement in congress against energy minister Eduardo Ortega was spearheaded by León Febres-Cordero, in spite of the fact that a gasoline price increase would have been clearly identified with the free-market philosophy supposedly espoused by Febres-Cordero.

49   Interview, Quito, Ecuador, May 25, 1990.

50   This was actually SDR 157.5 million.

51   There are no good studies of this episode and no one has questioned the economic basis of the private sector reasoning. It is not clear how the devaluation affected the private sector. It had borrowed abroad because fixed exchange rates and internal inflation during the 1970s made it extremely profitable to do so. Furthermore, it can be argued that the reason why the private sector was in trouble was the recession that the country was experiencing, not the devaluation because domestic inflation had been at least as high as the devaluation. Thus, the private sector firms in trouble were those that sold products whose prices did not adjust as fast as the inflation rate or those who faced a weakened demand. Certainly, there should have been some firms whose product prices increased at least as fast as the inflation rate.

52   Ecuadoran authors such as Hidalgo and Gordillo (1989) argue that the "sucretization" was required by the foreign banks to the Ecuadoran government as a renegotiation condition. However, since the domestic private borrowers greatly benefitted from it, it is likely that their own political pressure had been very strong.

53   Unemployment data are very weak and probably not consistent through time. However, the available estimates for the period suggest a substantial increase in open unemployment from 1982 on. Bilbaos (1986) estimates 6.15 per cent for 1981 and continuous increases to 7.23, 10.47, 10.91, 11.53, and 12.56 percent in the following five years.

54   The estimates of international reserves merit some comments. The regular methodology used to estimate net international reserves does not include

international trade payment and debt-servicing arrears. According to Swett (1988), trade payments arrears were about $400 million at the end of the Hurtado administration. The official Central Bank data shows $118 million in reserves on July 31, ten days before the transfer of power of less than one month's imports.

55 Interview, Quito, Ecuador, April 27, 1990.

56 According to the then minister of finance, "We analyzed what would happen if we did nothing; what would happen if we used a shock treatment, and what would happen if we moved gradually. We always opted for measures that would cause the least social problems. Hurtado did this. We always thought in economic terms; he applied the social logic." Interview, Quito, Ecuador, May 2, 1990.

57 Interview, Quito, Ecuador, May 3, 1990.

58 Febres Cordero was described by a contemporary in colorful terms. "Febres Cordero was a charmer, a very warm and sympathetic person, very energetic, very socially active, very talkative. But he was also *overwhelmingly* violent. He was also very regional and he brought regional politics to greater public attention during his administration; he made it more of an issue. He always had to be the one who gave the orders, who made the decisions. He was not a team player. He was aggressive...Febres couldn't negotiate. He was too violent, too confrontational. This was his style." Interview, Quito, Ecuador, April 24, 1990.

59 An executive order made congressional acts invalid until published in the official register, whose content the executive could determine. The executive could also determine the legislative schedule and use tactics to tie up action over procedural issues or matters of little national importance (see Conaghan, 1989b).

60 In March 1986, two small military revolts indicated considerable discontent within the armed forces over the conduct of the Febres-Cordero government. Charges of corruption and authoritarianism came from the military and there was considerable popular support for the leaders of the revolt.

61 Two objectives were sought with these measures: to give exporters a clear sign that the government wanted to promote and diversify exports and to promote domestic savings (see Swett 1988, p. 29). They were also taken to control a run against the sucre and growing import overinvoicing and export underinvoicing.

62 The promotion of exports was seen by many Ecuadorans as favoring natural resource-based industries, particularly the shrimp producers of the coast. This industry is natural resource-intensive, generates very little direct employment – according to the national accounts, wages and salaries account for less than 3 percent of the sector's value added – and Febres-Cordero and some of the members of his cabinet had extensive investments in it. De Janvry et al. (1990) argue that the concentration of the benefits of these measures became the undoing of the reform.

63 Another interesting episode in 1987 was Febres-Cordero's attitude toward renegotiating the debt to commercial banks. After sending mixed signals to his economic team about this, he pulled away from a deal that his minister of financed had virtually wrapped up.

64 One striking characteristic of the economic and political debate during this period in Ecuador is the lack of awareness of the inability of the spending spree

to stimulate the economy. The debate in Ecuador was couched in terms of a political confrontation and personality conflicts; however, the simple fact that a foreign-exchange constrained economy cannot be reactivated by increasing domestic government spending was not mentioned.

65 The August 1987–August 1988 rate was 63 percent, and in the month of August of 1988 the CPI increased 7 percent or about 85 percent a year. The 12-month rate peaked at 99 percent in March 1989.

66 It appears that beginning in 1986 the Central Bank began tampering with the data to impress the foreign lenders and the IMF, and to hide information from the mounting political opposition. Later on, in 1987 and 1988, many of the accounts at the Bank were altered to hide the growing budget deficit. In September 1988, while one of the coauthors of this chapter was working in Ecuador, a five-member IMF mission spent at least three weeks untangling Central Bank data to assemble more accurate balance of payments and budget data. When the Borja government took over, it claimed that the budget deficit was about 17 percent of GDP; the IMF mission estimated it at about 10–11 percent. The central bank data tampering was confirmed by long-term staff interviewed in the fall of 1990.

67 The international reserves series is hard to interpret because apparently there was some tampering with it, and because it does not include trade payments arrears. Central Bank series for 1990 shows negative external reserves beginning in mid–1986 and growing to $–330 million by August 1988. Adding the trade, although not the debt-service arrears to this figure a total of about $–600 million is reached. Armijos and Flores (1989) argue that the repayment of $220 million to Venezuela and Nigeria for oil lent the previous year after the earthquake was obviously a factor in the 1988 deterioration of the balance of payments situation.

68 The Borja administration faced less pressure from the multilateral lending agencies than his predecessors as the collapse of the Febres-Cordero policies had undermined the credibility of the Neoliberal reforms advocated by them, who besides, were very much aware of the predicament of the new government and realized that they had to help; thus, they were more willing to support heterodox policies than under other circumstances.

69 Interview, Quito, Ecuador, April 24, 1990.

70 Soon after August 1988, the value of these deposits was about $150 million. This policy was modified in late 1989, lowering the deposit requirement so that by the end of the year they amounted to only about $12 million.

71 Interview, Quito, Ecuador, April 27, 1990.

72 Later, reforms were made to the labor code to facilitate the development of export assembly industries that until then had been opposed by the unions as exploitative of the labor force.

73 The two main parties in the governing coalition had substantially different perceptions of what should be done. Borja wisely named representatives from the left of the coalition to the "social" ministries – health, education, labor, etc. – and those from the right to the central bank and the "economic" ministries – finance, industry, agriculture. However, this distribution of power could not eliminate the conflict between those who wanted to expand expenditures to improve social services and those who had to face the macroeconomic crisis.

74 Interview, Quito, Ecuador, April 27, 1990.
75 These figures are based on data from the IMF. The Central Bank claims a lower deficit of 4.4 percent of GDP.
76 This increase is, frankly, remarkably large since the previous year's decline had been 6 percent and the economy had grown at about 3–4 percent during the three previous years. It would not be surprising if the Central Bank revises down this figure in a few years, when another government is in power.
77 Analyses of a number of country experiences in the 1980s indicate that substantial political support for the chief executive is a critical ingredient of efforts to introduce reform. A majority party in the legislature or a strong and disciplined political party are evidence of this kind of political support (see, for example, Nelson, 1990). Examples of policy change in the 1980s also indicate the importance of strong institutions of government and the ability to establish and maintain coalitions of support that endure, even in the face of popular protest (see, for example, Haggard, 1985; Waterbury, 1989; Callaghy, 1990; Kaufman, 1990).
78 Among lessons of experience in economic adjustment in the 1980s is the importance of a positive short-run economic impact of changed policies if they are to be tolerated by society (Díaz-Alejandro, 1981; Lindenberg, 1989).
79 It is interesting to note that Dahik (1989), one of the main actors during the Febres-Cordero administration, argues that one of the main reasons for the adjustment failure was the lack of national goals or consensus about national goals, basic to the development of a sustainable policy consensus.

REFERENCES

Abril, Galo and Urriola, Rafael 1990: *Incentivos de Fomento Industrial en el Ecuador: 1972–1986*, Quito: Centro de Planificación y Estudios Sociales.

Armijos, Ana L. and Flores, Marco A. 1989: "Las Politícas Económicas Aplicadas en la Décade de los Ochenta: Respuesta a la Crisis," in R. Thorp, et al. (eds.) *Las Crisis en el Ecuador: los Treinta y Ochenta*, Quito: Corporacion Editoro Nacional.

Banco Central del Ecuador 1990: *Cuentas Nacionales del Ecuador 1950–1989*, No. 13, Quito.

Bates, Robert 1981: *Markets and States in Tropical Africa*, Berkeley: University of California Press.

Bilbao, Luis F. 1986: "El Problema de la Crisis y el Empleo en el Ecuador", in Federación Nacional de Economistas del Ecuador (ed.), *El Ecuador en la Encrucijada: Crisis, Empleo y Desarrollo*, Quito: Corporación Editora Nacional.

Callaghy, Thomas 1990: "Lost Between State and Market: The Politics of Economic Adjustment in Ghana, Zambia, and Nigeria," in Joan M. Nelson (ed.), *Economic Crisis and Policy Choice: The Politics of Adjustment in the Third World*, Princeton, NJ: Princeton University Press.

Center of Latin American Studies 1985: "Estructura de Incentivos Industriales del Ecuador en 1981", Boston University, mimeo.

Centro de Estudios y Difusión Social (CEDIS) 1986: *Los Grupos Monopólicos*, Quito: CEDIS.

Conaghan, Catherine 1988: *Restructuring Domination: Industrialists and the State in Ecuador*, Pittsburgh: University of Pittsburgh Press.

Conaghan, Catherine 1989a: "Loose Parties, Floating Politicians, and Institutional Stress: Presidentialism in Ecuador, 1979–1988," paper prepared for a research symposium on "Presidential or Parliamentary Democracy: Does It Make A Difference?" Georgetown University, Washington, DC, May 14–16.

Conaghan, Catherine 1989b: "Dreams of Orthodoxy, Tales of Heterodoxy: Leon Febres Cordero and Economic Policymaking in Ecuador, 1984–1988," paper prepared for the XV International Congress of the Latin American Studies Association, Miami, FL, December 4–6.

Dahik, Alberto 1989: "Los Programas de Ajuste en la Ultima Década," in R. Thorp, et al. (eds.), *Las Crisis en el Ecuador: los Treinta y Ochenta*, Quito: Corporacion Editora Nacional.

Dávila, Oswaldo 1986: "El Sector Público y la Generación de Empleo," in Federación Nacional de Economistas del Ecuador (ed.), *El Ecuador en la Encrucijada*, Quito: Corporación Editora Nacional.

de Janvry, Alain, Sadoulet, Elisabeth and Fargeix, Andre 1990: "Adjustment with Political Stability and Equity: The Ecuadorian Experience and Some Alternative Options," University of California at Berkeley, July.

Díaz-Alejandro, Carlos 1981: "Southern Cone Stabilization Plans," in William R. Cline and Sidney Weintraub (eds.), *Economic Stabilization in Developing Countries*. Washington, DC: Brookings Institution.

Gelb, Alan H. and Marshall-Silva, Jorge 1988: "Ecuador: Windfalls of a New Exporter," in A. Gelb and Associates (eds.), *Oil Windfalls: Blessing or Curse?*, New York: Oxford University Press.

Haggard, Stephan 1985: "The Politics of Adjustment: Lessons from the IMF's Extended Fund Facility," *International Organization*, 39 (3), 505–34.

Hidalgo, Francisco and Gordillo, Eduardo 1989: "Innovaciones de Políticas Económicas y Comportamiento de los Actores Sociales en el Contexto de la Crisis, 1980–1987: el Caso Ecuatoriano," *Economía y Desarrollo*, No. 13, Pontificia Universidad Católica del Ecuador, December.

Hidrobo, Jorge A. 1990: *Industriales, Estado, Industrialización en el Ecuador*, Quito: Universidad de San Francisco de Quito.

Hurtado, Osvaldo 1990: *Política democrática: Los últimos veinticinco años*, Quito: Corporación Editora Nacional.

International Monetary Fund 1989: *Balance of Payments Statistics*, Vol. 40, Yearbook, Part 1, Washington, DC: IMF.

International Monetary Fund 1990: *International Financial Statistics Yearbook*, Washington, DC: IMF.

Jácome, Luis I. 1989: "Reflexiones en Torno a la Flotación de las Tasas de Interés y al Tipo de Cambio en el Ecuador," in Instituto de Investigaciones Económicas, *Neoliberalismo y Neoestructuralismo en América Latina*, Quito: Pontificia Universidad Católica del Ecuador.

Kasza, Gregory J. 1981: "Regional Conflict in Ecuador: Quito and Guayaquil," *Inter-American Economic Affairs*, 35 (2), 3–41.

Kaufman, Robert R. 1990: "Stabilization and Adjustment in Argentina, Brazil, and Mexico," in Joan M. Nelson (ed.), *Economic Crisis and Policy Choice: The*

Politics of Adjustment in the Third World, Princeton, NJ: Princeton University Press.

León Velasco, Juan Bernardo 1989: "Ecuador 1978–1988: Diez años de elecciones. Cambios y constantes electorales," Quito: unpublished paper.

Lindenberg, Marc 1989: "Making Economic Adjustment Work: The Politics of Policy Implementation," *Policy Sciences*, 22, 359–94.

Luzuriaga, Carlos and Zuvekas, Clarence Jr. 1981: *Distribución del Ingreso y Pobreza en las Areas Rurales del Ecuador 1950–1980*, Quito: Banco Central del Ecuador.

Martz, John 1987: *Politics and Petroleum in Ecuador*. New Brunswick, NJ: Transaction Books.

Mills, Nick D. 1984: *Crisis, conflicto y consenso: Ecuador, 1979–1984*. Quito: Corporacion Editora Nacional.

Nelson, Joan M. (ed.) 1990: *Economic Crisis and Policy Choice: The Politics of Adjustment in the Third World*, Princeton, NJ: Princeton University Press.

Nelson, Joan M. and Contributors 1989: *Fragile Coalitions: The Politics of Economic Adjustment*, New Brunswick, NJ: Transaction Books.

Olson, Mancur 1965: *The Logic of Collective Action: Public Goods and the Theory of Groups*, New York: Schocken Books.

Olson, Mancur 1982: *The Rise and Decline of Nations*, New Haven: Yale University Press.

Pachano, Abelardo 1987: "Políticas Económicas Comparadas: Ecuador 1981–1987," in Corporación de Estudios para el Desarrollo (CORDES), *Neoliberalismo y Políticas Económicas Alternativas*, Quito: Imprenta Cotopaxi.

Placencia, Maria Mercedes 1989: "Costos de Legalización de las Empresas Informales en el Ecuador," Santiago, Chile: mimeo.

Redclift, Michael 1978: *Agrarian Reform and Peasant Organization on the Ecuadorian Coast*, London: Athlone Press.

Rodríguez, Linda Alexander 1985: *The Search for Public Policy: Regional Politics and Government Finances in Ecuador, 1830–1940*, Berkeley: University of California Press.

Salgado, Germánico 1987: "Ecuador: Crisis y Políticas de Ajuste. Su efecto en la Agricultura," *Revista de la CEPAL*, 33, 135–51, December.

Sandoval, Carlos 1987: *Política Cambiaria en el Ecuador*. Quito: ILDIS.

Schodt, David M. 1989: "Austerity Policies in Ecuador: Christian Democratic and Social Christian Versions of the Gospel," in H. Handelman and W. Baer (eds.), *Paying the Costs of Austerity in Latin America*, Boulder, CO: Westview, pp. 171–94.

Sepúlveda, Cristián 1983: *El Proceso de Industrialización Ecuatoriano*, Quito: Instituto de Investigaciones Económicas, Pontificia Universidad Católica del Ecuador.

Swett, Francisco X. 1986: "Turnaround: the Political Economy of Development and Liberalizartion in Ecuador 1984–1986," presented at the Americas Society Dinner Seminar Series, September 22.

Swett, Francisco X. 1988: "Vuelta a Medias: los Vaivenes del Liberalismo Económico en el Ecuador: 1984–1988," Guayaquil: mimeo.

Thoumi, Francisco E. 1990: "The Hidden Logic of 'Irrational' Economic Policies in Ecuador," *Journal of Interamerican Studies and World Affairs*, 32 (2), 43–68.

Valencia, Mauricio 1989: "La Dinámica de la Deuda Externa Ecuatoriana,"

Economía y Desarrollo, No. 13, Quito: Pontificia Universidad Católica del Ecuador, December.

Villalobos, Fabio 1987: *La Industrialización Ecuatoriana y la Utilización de los Recursos Productivos 1976–1983*, Quito: Facultad Latinoamericana de Ciencias Sociales.

Vistazo 1990: "Gradualismo de abajo hacia arriba," Quito, April 26, p. 4–8.

Vos, Rob 1987: *Industrialización, Empleo y Necesidades Básicas en el Ecuador*, Quito: Corporación Editora Nacional.

Waterbury, John 1989: "The Political Management of Economic Adjustment and Reform," in Joan M. Nelson and collaborators (eds.), *Fragile Coalitions: The Politics of Economic Adjustment*. New Brunswick, NJ: Transaction Books.

World Bank 1984: *Ecuador: an Agenda for Recovery and Sustained Growth*, Washington, DC: The World Bank.

World Bank, 1988a: *Adjustment Lending: An Evaluation of Ten Years of Experience*, Washington, DC: The World Bank.

World Bank 1988b: *Ecuador: Country Economic Memorandum*, Washington DC: The World Bank.

World Bank 1989: *Africa's Adjustment and Growth in the 1980s*, Washington, DC: The World Bank and the UNDP.

5

The Political Economy of Reform: Egypt in the 1980s
Robert Holt and Terry Roe

In the mid 1980s the Egyptian government was forced to confront a deterioration in its international trade situation that approached crisis proportions. The magnitude of the problem is suggested by a balance of payments deficit of 15 percent of GDP in 1985–6 and debt service obligations of 50 percent of receipts. In 1987 the Egyptian government reached an agreement with the International Monetary Fund (IMF) on a wide ranging reform package which allowed an initial drawing of SDR 116 million to alleviate the immediate crisis.

Within the year, however, the Egyptians were failing to live up to their part of the agreement. New foreign debt was contracted and the arrears in payments increased. Little progress was made on some basic economic reforms. In June of 1987 the IMF canceled its standby arrangement for additional SDRs. The basic economic situation remained largely unchanged.

There was little disagreement over the basic economic features of the proposed reforms. But the Egyptian government had neither the political will nor the decision-making capacity to make the basic reforms in the economy that seemed so necessary.

In 1986 the Egyptian Ministry of Agriculture (MAO) was working with the United States Agency for International Development (USAID) on a plan for major structural reforms in the agricultural sector of the economy. By 1989 the bulk of the plan had been implemented and there was reason to believe that additional reform would soon be underway.

The failure of the economic adjustment reform package and the success of the agricultural reform program seems incongruent. The agricultural sector of the economy is the sector most rooted in tradition, most intertwined with kinship ties and values, and closely linked to politically sensitive issues such as the massive food subsidy program. Reform should be difficult and time consuming. While an effective economic adjustment reform program would involve some wide-sweeping structural changes, it would seem that a highly centralized government, like Egypt's, should be able to set realistic exchange rates (or let the currency float), raise interest rates, remove energy subsidies and make some changes in import/export regulations that could have a major impact on resolving the country's economic crisis.

This chapter will try to explain why the economic readjustment effort failed in 1987 and why the agricultural reform program was adapted and implemented. To set the stage we must provide some background.[1]

1   THE PERIOD OF GAMEL ABDEL NASSER (1952–70)

The history of contemporary Egypt began in July of 1952 when the free officers, with Gamal Abdel Nasser as their leader, overthrew the monarchy, and brought to an end the British military presence and influence in the country. There is no need to repeat the story of the coup and what followed. Several characteristics about the Nasser period should be discussed, however, if we are to understand the political and economic situation of the 1980s.

Economic changes

The most spectacular and widely publicized economic decision made by the Nasser regime was to construct the high dam at Aswan. While the dam and the related hydroelectric and irrigation systems had a significant impact on production and productivity, its relationship to the economic crisis of the mid–1980s is not as significant as that of other economic decisions. Four are worth highlighting: (1) the sweeping program of public ownership, (2) the employment guarantees, (3) the consumer subsidies, and (4) the land reform.

(1)   *Public ownership*. Nasser and his brother officers in the revolutionary council had little ideological commitment to any particular approach to economic organization. They were, however, deeply committed to economic growth, and to the elimination of gross economic inequities. The state, in their opinion, would have a necessarily important role in economic leadership to reach these objectives. While explicit socialists they were not, their views on economic management would have had much in common with those of the British Labourites and their arguments for public ownership of the "commanding heights" of the economy.[2] The decision to nationalize the Suez Canal and use its revenues to finance the high dam is an example of the kind of leadership role that could only be played by the state.

In 1957 further steps were taken by repatriating the ownership of and largely nationalizing all commercial banks, insurance companies, and commercial agencies for foreign trade. The big moves, however, were made with the so-called "socialist laws" beginning in 1961, which put a considerable portion of the nonagricultural sectors of the economy under public ownership or control. By 1964 the list included (1) all banking and insurance, (2) all foreign trade, (3) all heavy and medium industry, all major textile manufacturers, all sugar-refining and food processing plants, (4) all air and most marine transport, (5) all public utilities, including urban mass transit, (6) major department stores and some additional urban retail trade outlets, (7) hotels, cinemas and theaters, (8) all newspapers and publishing houses, (9) all reclaimed land, (10) outlets for basic agricultural inputs, (11) all major construction companies, and (12) large infrastructure assets (the high dam and the Suez Canal).[3]

(2) *Employment guarantees.* In 1964 the government assumed the responsibility for employing all university graduates. In a country where unemployment has long been a major problem, such a guarantee greatly increased the attractions of a university education. Enrollments in universities soared, more than doubling between 1968 and 1976. By 1969 the government was actually employing about 60 percent of the 750,000 graduates the universities had produced.

The civil service also grew, increasing from 900,000 in 1965 to 1,300,000 in 1972. With the growth in numbers matched by an increase of agencies, the number of ministries doubled. Even more significant is the fact that 46 General Organizations were created to oversee approximately 370 public companies.

(3) *Consumer subsidies.* While the beginning of government policies to suppress the prices of food in urban centers predates the Nasser regime, the 1960s witnessed a new commitment to welfare state principles that included a guarantee of inexpensive food. At that time the Ministry of Supply established the fair price shops (known as coops) to market basic necessities at government-subsidized prices. While the portion of the central government budget spent on subsidies remained low during the 1960s, a precedent was established that later drove costs up dramatically.

(4) *Land reform.* One of the first acts taken by the free officers after they came to power was to launch a land reform program. In September of 1952 a new law limited the amount of land that could be individually owned to 200 feddans (1 feddan = 1,038 acres). Another 100 feddans could be owned by wives and children of the prime landowner. Further steps were taken over the next 17 years which reallocated some land for political reasons and finally set the maximum ownership at 50 feddans for individuals and 100 for a family.

In the 1960s the government increasingly imposed price controls, delivery quotas, and acreage allotments that significantly limited the decisions that farmers could make. These will be discussed in detail below.

Essentially, the Nasser regime transformed the fundamental structure of the economy by significantly impeding the role of markets in economic decision making. These changes provided a safety net for the urban population and created a bureaucratic class which managed industrial and commercial operations, but which had little incentive to improve production or productivity. These changes have obvious political implications, but before discussing them we should focus on some decisions that directly affected the political system.

Political changes

The regime that came to power in 1952 was a military autocracy. Any independent source of political power that was a threat to its existence was eliminated. No opposition was tolerated. The institutional infrastructure of political expression and participation was abolished; that of control and direction was taken over by the Revolutionary Command Council. Thus the constitution was superseded, parliament was dissolved, political parties were abolished and the political arm of any interest group was suspended. The army, the police and the state bureaucracy remained, but they were, of course, controlled by the Revolutionary Command Council.

Government by edict and coercion is expensive and unnerving to ruled and rulers alike. It is much better to govern with cooperation, or at least with acquiescence, but that requires political institutions for informing the populace, persuading the reluctant, enlisting the support of the potentially influential. Political parties and parliaments are normal institutions for these activities, even though genuine participation of the populace is beyond the interest of any autocrat.

Nasser made several attempts to establish political parties or reasonable facsimiles thereof. The first was the Liberation Rally (1953–8). Beyond the staging of popular rallies to demonstrate mass support of the regime, its only accomplishment was to capture a part of the trade union movement and enlist its support for Nasser in intraregime struggles.

In 1956 a new constitution was promulgated which established a parliament and a new universal political party, the National Union, to which all citizens were to belong. The people in most villages and urban neighborhoods were organized in a hierarchical structure that had at its top a national conference and an executive committee. Building a widespread base of support for the regime was a major purpose of the National Union, but when local units fell under the influence of established elites, it developed the potential for independent action. The coup in Syria that broke up the United Arab Republic worried Nasser about the vulnerability of his own rule, and he abolished the National Union in 1961 lest it provide the base for an assault on his regime from the right.

The final attempt to create a political party had a more lasting impact. In 1962 the Arab Socialist Union was formed. It had the universal membership feature of the National Union, but there was also explicitly a vanguard elite created by establishing different grades of membership. Local organization was, in theory, based on functional categories as if it reflected a corporatist view of political organization. The practice of some professions was predicated on membership in the ASU, as was any participation in political activity.

The formation of the ASU coincided with the widespread move to public ownership referred to above and the party was to provide some of the ideological justification and organizational support for these activities. But socialism is fundamentally a more controversial topic in the Moslem world than in the West. In its Marxist form socialism is explicitly atheistic and organized religion is an instrument of the capitalist state to distract the masses from their plight – not an easily acceptable proposition for those of a religious persuasion. Even the socialists who were not Marxists were secular, and therefore not acceptable to powerful forces in the Moslem establishment. The extent of the hostility is suggested by the alleged plot of the Moslem brotherhood to dispose of Nasser, and the mass arrests and execution of its venerable leader that followed the exposure of the scheme.

Sectors of the society, other than those organized under the banner of Islam, resisted thrusts of the ASU to co-opt the leadership of potentially autonomous groups. Activists in the labor movement, in the youth organizations and in the bureaucracy were never brought completely under the rubric of the ASU. As with the popular organization that preceded the ASU, it was ineffective in mobilizing support for the Nasser regime, as long as it was perceived to be only a creature of the autocrats. Any hint of autonomy, however, frightened the regime, which could always use the coercion of the police to eliminate opposition. Police, however, cannot win confidence and support.

The repeated but unsuccessful efforts to create a political party to win public support was paralleled in the attempts to use the parliament. The 1956 constitution created a new parliament. Although the executive committee of the National Union screened all candidates that stood for election, there were some independent voices among the victors. In fact, the parliament showed enough independence to refuse to limit access to the universities as demanded by the Ministry of Education. In 1958 the parliament was dissolved and replaced by an appointed body. The 1956 constitution was suspended and a new one for the United Arab Republic was drafted. With the breaking up of the UAR in 1961 the parliament was again dissolved and the constitution abrogated. Under Nasser parliament never again had independent voices that could challenge his policies. It also never provided a base for legitimacy for his regime.

Without political institutions that could either mobilize the citizenry and direct their efforts, or through which the citizenry could express its opinions, the regime was vulnerable to mass demonstrations. In January of 1968 thousands moved into the streets to protest the lenient sentences imposed on officers for bungling the June war (1967). Nasser promised that the demands made on the street would be met in a resentencing of the officers. Again, in November, new demonstrations broke up protesting the incompetence of the response to an Israeli helicopter raid in the heart of upper Egypt. The populace had no way to express their positions except through the mass demonstrations. Nasser had to rule through the power of his will, supported by some former comrades-in-arms and backed by the coercive power of the police and military. The security apparatus of the latter was efficient enough to uncover plots before their perpetration could overthrow the regime, but not ruthless enough to turn machine guns on demonstrators and massacre them in the streets.

Nasser's legacy

In September of 1970 Nasser died. He was a genuine Egyptian hero, and there was a deep sorrow in the hearts of the mourners who turned out in the hundreds of thousands to grieve his passing. He had addressed deep grievances of long standing. His dream of Arab unity was widely shared, but from the point of view of the issues of concern here he was something less than successful.

At his death there was widespread public ownership of the means of production with increased emphasis on an import-substitution industrialization policy. The economy was teeming in inefficiency, because of structural rigidities such as an employment policy that led to increases in public employment. There was a poverty of political institutions, particularly of those that could confer some letitimacy on rulers and their decisions. In their absence the bread-and-circus formula for keeping a populace quiescent that had been invented in the Mediterranean region not too far from Cairo was used by the Nasser regime with a high ratio of bread to circus.

2 THE SADAT PERIOD

Anwar Sadat, vice-president under Nasser, succeeded to the presidency after Nasser's death. He very quickly reversed Nasser's economic policies by making it both legal and profitable for foreign money to be invested in Egypt, and by dismantling part of the structure of public ownership. Both actions strengthened the private sector. Politically, however, he continued Nasser's efforts to create viable political institutions. Sadat needed the kind of institution that could confer legitimacy upon rulers and their decisions even more than his predecessor. He could not lay claim to Nasser's source of legitimacy as the victor over oppressors and the founder of the regime. Let us sketch briefly some of the relevant economic and political decisions of the period 1971–81.

Economic policies

Sadat moved quickly on economic policy. Two years before the term *infitah* (opening or open door) was given official sanction, Law 65 was enacted in 1971. The law opened the economy for foreign investment by establishing a five-year grace period on taxes on income for foreign investors, creating free trade zones and treating joint ventures between public and private firms as autonomous.

In 1974 another statute (Law 43) provided even more favorable terms for foreign investors. It put an end to the public sector monopoly in banking, allowed foreign firms to hold majority interest in Egyptian companies and extended the tax exemption to eight years. More importantly, public companies joining with a foreign firm were relieved of the special requirements of public sector firms – salary ceilings, profit sharing, workers' representation and special labor laws.

In 1977 further legislation made it more attractive for foreign firms to invest in Egypt by modifying some of the onerous foreign exchange requirements.

While the opening of Egypt to foreign capital had the effect of strengthening the private sector at the expense of the public, in 1975 the government took more direct action. It abolished the General Organizations, and this put public sector companies on their own. The weak could be liquidated; the strong could have their shares sold to the public. Public firms were also relieved of some of their social obligations. They did not have to take on workers assigned to them by the Ministry of Labor and Human Resources, and they could fire unneeded labor after paying a terminal fee of 60 percent of the previous six months' wages.

Political institutions

It is unlikely that Sadat was ever a supporter of the Arab Socialist Union, but not until after the October war of 1973 did he have enough personal standing to give consideration to tampering with an institution he inherited from a great hero. In 1974 he began, cautiously, to criticize the ASU and made some suggested changes which he turned over to a "Listening Committee" which was chaired by his brother-in-law.

A wide range of ideas were openly presented to the Committee. Some urged a return to full parliamentary democracy with freedom for parties to organize and compete in honest elections. Others supported a revitalization of the ASU in a single-party system along Nasserite lines. By the end of 1975 the executive committee of the ASU provided for the existence of four factions within the party; the following year this was narrowed to three: a left, a right, and a center. Each was authorized to contest parliamentary elections in October of 1976.

Sadat's group – the center – won a decisive victory (280 out of 352 seats) in the first contested election in Egypt in 25 years. The left won only two seats, the right 12, but 48 unaffiliated independents were victorious. While it was small, the opposition had a legitimate voice in parliament without having the numbers necessary to really threaten Sadat's rule.

In January of 1977 Sadat granted a general authorization to establish political parties and shortly thereafter, in effect, abolished the ASU. There was no remnant of popular support, nor any entrenched special interest that made an effort to preserve it. It began and ended as a creature of an autocrat. It did not – perhaps could not – fulfill the functions for which it had been created.

The freedom to found political parties and an openness in the media that accompanied this decision signaled a new approach to establishing some basis for regime legitimacy. But before the political liberalization proceeded too far, events dictated to Sadat a change in direction. The balance of payments situation was deteriorating and negotiations began with the International Monetary Fund for a standby agreement. The IMF demanded a reduction in government spending which could only be accomplished by reducing the consumer subsidies. Sadat reluctantly agreed and an announcement to that effect was made to the parliament. The next day massive riots broke out, up and down the Nile Valley.

The government withdrew its proposals and shortly thereafter laid down stringent conditions for the formation of political parties. They did not, however, prove adequate to tame an increasingly vigorous opposition. The old Wafd party reconstituted itself and became a true parliamentary opposition. Sadat responded by harassing the members of the party to the point where it was unable to function and it moved to dissolve itself.

Sadat found himself in the same predicament that Nasser had. In the absence of viable political institutions the security forces would have to be used more frequently as instruments of control. Sadat responded as did Nasser: he created a new political party – the National Democratic Party. Unlike Nasser, however, he simultaneously created an opposition party, the Socialist Labor Party, which in the next parliamentary election won 29 seats. It proceeded to act as a genuine opposition, challenging Sadat's economic policy and attacking the Camp David accords. Like the reconstituted Wafd it was harassed to the point of extinction. The price to be paid to gain legitimacy from the institutions of elections and parliaments is to tolerate an opposition. Sadat understood this, but when the opposition had even the slightest opportunity to mobilize support that might force a change in policy, the price became too high.

Sadat tried another technique to build popular support for his policies, the referendum. Whenever he felt frustrated by parliament, annoyed by his opponents, or compelled to demonstrate that the masses were behind him, he called for a national referendum. No issue was too trivial, or too enormous to escape the test. The Wafd was eliminated following a referendum that denied political rights to anyone who had ever been convicted for corruption. The Camp David accords were put to the people for their approval. The results of the referenda were always the same – virtually 100 percent of the electorate was reported to have cast their ballots; 99 percent was reported as having voted to support Sadat's position. The enormity of these victories created not legitimacy, but cynicism.

In the end Sadat, as Nasser before him, had to rely on the police. In September of 1981 he ordered the arrest of more than 1,500 politicians, journalists, and religious leaders. A month later he was assassinated.

Sadat left an economic system that was freer than that left by Nasser, but many restrictive regulations and much government ownership was still in place. The consumer subsidies were a much larger portion of government deficits and the obligation for the government to be an employer of last resort was still in place.

The political system still suffered from a paucity of institutions that could confer legitimacy on the government and its decisions. Indeed, the problem was even more severe. Nasser, and Sadat in his first years, could rally the populace under the banner of challenging the Israeli state and by opposing the Western capitalists. In the end, Sadat could do neither. Peace with Israel inflamed the religious-based opposition, and the consorting with western capitalists and the policy of *infitah* alienated those who genuinely supported a socialist organization of the economy.

3 THE MUBARAK PERIOD

Mubarak, as Sadat had earlier, moved into the presidency from the vice-presidency upon the death of his predecessor. Unlike Sadat, however, he made no dramatic changes in the basic course. Foreign policy remained the same and the economy continued with its mix of some relatively free areas and considerable government control and ownership. Some details on this mix on the eve of the IMF negotiations will be presented below. The struggle between autocratic rule with little legitimacy, and the toleration of some opposition in the hope that some measure of freedom would contribute to generate support for the regime, continued.

There is no need to repeat the details of this conflict here. The central point is the same as made in the previous section. Some illustrations are in order.

The Wafd was allowed to reorganize a new party; the Ummah (Party of the Nation) was authorized even though it was explicitly an Islamic Sectarian Party. The Moslem Brotherhood began participating in coalition politics by supporting the Wafd candidates in the 1984 Parliament elections, which helped it win 15 percent of the vote. Mubarak's National Democratic Party captured 73 percent of the vote. No party that received less than 8 percent of the vote could win any seats and independents could not stand for office.

These restrictions made the election and the Parliament somewhat tainted, particularly after the election law was challenged in the courts.

Mubarak responded by supporting a change in the election law and calling a referendum to dissolve the parliament and order new elections, which were held in April of 1987. Mubarak's Party won 70 percent of the vote and 313 of 448 seats. The opposition held a surprising 31 percent of the seats, led by the Socialist Labor Party, which had the support of the Moslem Brotherhood.

The new parliament quickly nominated Mubarak for another term as president, which was endorsed in a referendum. While this new parliament probably had more legitimacy than its predecessors, the election was held under stern monitoring of the Ministry of Interior and there was some reported intimidation and arrests. A rumbling discontent continued and the police and the army remained the necessary bulwarks of the region.

Thus the economic crises of 1986–9 were faced by a still fragile government with a weak institutional framework. It is doubtful if it commanded a loyalty and possessed a legitimacy that would allow it to gain support for tough economic measures. The need for tough economic decisions can be established if we examine the economic record of the 1970s and 1980s.

4 THE ECONOMIC RECORD 1970–86

While both Sadat and Mubarak had to face a major balance of payments crisis, the basic economic record of the period was not altogether bleak. Indeed, some statistics suggest that there was enough strength in the economy to keep levels of living on the rise, while avoiding the deteriorating foreign trade situation. Let us review the record.

The 1973–9 period

During the last half of the 1970s, the economy grew at unprecedented rates, with per capita GNP growth averaging 6.2 percent and GDP growth averaging 10 percent per annum in real terms (table 5.1). Inflation remained at modest levels of about 10.8 percent per year during the period (table 5.2). Real value added grew in the service and industrial sectors of

Table 5.1 GDP per capita and sectoral growth rates, in real terms; Egyptian pounds, 1973–88

	GNP/ capita	*GDP*	*Agriculture*	*Industry*	*Manufacturing*	*Services*
1974	0.0	2.7	0.3	−3.3		16.2
1975	5.5	9.1	6.1	16.1	6.5	9.3
1976	11.8	15.3	1.4	15.6	7.8	20.5
1977	10.2	13.5	−2.8	22.0	6.7	9.0
1978	1.5	5.9	5.6	15.6	5.7	5.9
1979	2.0	6.2	4.1	9.1	7.8	12.5
1980	6.9	10.3	3.5	14.6	9.2	10.3
1981	0.4	3.8	1.8	3.7	3.9	5.1
1982	7.5	10.1	4.0	2.6	9.2	21.7
1983	5.1	7.6	2.9	6.9	6.4	9.6
1984	3.4	6.2	2.1	9.2	8.1	5.5
1985	0.9	6.7	3.2	8.0	6.5	6.9
1986	−1.3	2.7	2.1	1.5	3.5	3.6
1987	0.4	2.5	2.1	2.2	2.1	2.9
1988	6.0	3.2	2.6	2.4	2.6	2.9
Average						
1975–9	6.2	10.0	2.9	15.7	6.9	11.4
1980–4	4.7	7.6	2.9	7.4	7.4	10.4
1985–8	1.5	3.8	2.5	3.5	3.7	4.1

Source: World Bank Tables, supplemented with data obtained from the Ministry of Finance.

the economy at the rapid rates of 11.4 and 15.7 percent per year, respectively, and far more slowly in manufacturing and agriculture. Average annual growth rates in these sectors were 6.9 percent in manufacturing and only 2.9 percent in agriculture. Basic indicators suggest that growth also translated into higher living standards. Life expectancy increased from 50 to 58 years on the average, per capita caloric intake increased to 128 percent of the minimum daily requirements, infant mortality decreased from 117 per thousand to 93, while school enrollment ratios increased from 72 to 78 percent of the eligible population (World Bank, 1990–91).

The major sources of growth in the mid and late 1970s were largely due to a more efficient allocation of resources attributed to the *infitah* policies, and from an increase in foreign exchange earnings. This increase in earnings induced an increase in demand for final goods and increased the country's capacity to import intermediate factors of production. Petroleum exports grew from 21.9 percent of foreign exchange inflows (including

Table 5.2 Government revenue, expenditures, deficit, inflation, and growth in the money supply, 1973–88

	Revenue current + capital receipt (£Em)	Revenue to GDP (%)	Expenditures: current + capital payment (£Em)	Expenditures to GDP (%)	Budget deficit to GDP (%)	Change in CPI (%)	Growth in money supply (%)
1975	2,235	43.9	3,227	61.8	−18.0	9.8	21.5
1976	2,424	37.6	4,086	60.7	−23.1	10.3	26.0
1977	3,301	41.3	4,562	54.7	−13.4	12.7	34.0
1978	3,778	39.0	5,066	51.7	−12.7	11.1	27.0
1979	4,363	36.9	6,650	52.3	−15.5	9.9	31.3
1980	6,912	41.9	9,486	57.5	−15.6	20.6	51.4
1981	7,893	46.7	9,177	53.0	−6.3	21.2	30.9
1982	9,116	46.8	13,271	63.9	−17.1	11.3	31.2
1983	10,714	45.8	13,441	55.6	−9.8	15.1	22.6
1984	11,951	43.3	15,604	54.7	−11.4	18.1	18.8
1985	13,299	42.0	17,339	52.3	−10.4	14.4	18.3
1986	15,319	41.4	20,537	53.5	−12.1	16.1	21.0
1987	16,737	39.5	20,464	45.2	−5.8	25.2	21.0
1988	19,179	36.9	24,858	45.6	−8.6	17.8	21.5
Average							
1975–9	3,220.2	39.7	4,718.2	56.3	−16.5	10.8	28.0
1980–4	9,317.2	44.9	12,195.5	56.9	−12.0	17.3	31.0
1985	16,133.5	39.9	20,799.5	49.2	−9.2	18.4	20.5

Source: Government revenues and expenditures were obtained from World Bank Tables and supplemented by data obtained from the Ministry of Finance. Changes in the CPI are computed from table 5.7. Money supply estimates were obtained from the World Bank.

worker remittances and official transfers) in 1976 to 38.5 percent in 1978 (table 5.3). Worker remittances were another major source of foreign exchange earnings. Remittances grew from 27.2 percent of total inflows in 1976 to 41.9 percent in 1978 and then declined to 34.9 percent in 1980 as petroleum's share rose to nearly 46 percent of foreign exchange earnings. However, the lack of international competitiveness in manufacturing and nonfuel primary product sectors of the economy is reflected by their stagnant share, averaging about 9.5 percent and 17.8 percent, respectively, during 1975–9.

While real growth was relatively high during the mid and late 1970s, the government's fiscal deficit averaged 16.5 percent of GDP (table 5.2) as foreign aid declined from 21.7 percent of foreign exchange earnings in 1975 to less than 2 percent in 1980 (table 5.3).[4] Budget revenues grew at an annual average rate of about 21 percent while expenditures grew by about

Table 5.3 Major components (percentages) of Egyptian foreign exchange earnings (inflows), 1973–88

	Nonfuel primary products	Petroleum	Manu- factures	Worker remittances	Official[a] transfers	Total
1973	32.5	6.6	13.1	6.2	41.5	100.0
1974	26.9	11.1	16.2	12.4	33.4	100.0
1975	23.4	19.8	11.7	23.3	21.7	100.0
1976	26.3	21.9	13.0	27.2	11.6	100.0
1977	16.7	26.7	11.2	39.0	6.5	100.0
1978	12.0	38.5	6.4	41.9	1.2	100.0
1979	10.3	47.5	5.1	35.7	1.3	100.0
1980	10.9	45.9	4.9	34.9	3.4	100.0
1981	10.9	50.8	6.7	26.3	5.4	100.0
1982	7.1	45.2	6.0	34.4	7.3	100.0
1983	7.5	42.2	6.2	37.0	7.2	100.0
1984	7.5	42.9	6.1	32.5	10.9	100.0
1985	7.4	40.8	6.8	31.5	13.6	100.0
1986	7.5	33.5	10.0	35.8	13.3	100.0
1987	6.9	31.2	13.0	37.9	11.0	100.0
1988	7.3	28.1	12.1	41.4	11.1	100.0
Average						
1975–9	17.8	30.9	9.5	33.4	8.6	100.0
1980–4	8.8	45.4	6.0	33.0	6.8	100.0
1985–8	7.3	33.4	10.6	36.6	12.2	100.0

[a]Includes foreign aid in the form of grants, technical assistance, and food aid.
Source: Computed from World Bank Tables.

27 percent. The resulting budget deficit as a percentage of GDP increased initially until petroleum revenues began to grow in 1976, after which the budget deficit declined and then resumed growth in 1978–9. Government revenues from petroleum grew from less than one percent of total revenue in 1973 to nearly 20 percent in 1979, thus making revenues increasingly dependent on petroleum. Much of the increase in the budget deficit was due to human resource expenditures, food subsidies, and increased salaries to public employees.[5]

The deficit in the country's balance of payments followed the excess demand created in part by the fiscal deficit. During the 1975–9 period, the average annual deficit in goods and nonfactor services was about 19 percent of GDP (table 5.4). Petroleum exports trended strongly upward during 1975–9, growing from 13.7 percent of GDP in 1973 to nearly 32 percent in 1979. Merchandise exports also experienced strong growth during the period (table 5.4). The value of imports exceeded exports in all years. Annual growth in the real value of imports of goods and nonfactor

Table 5.4   Foreign trade as a percentage of GDP, 1973–88

	Exports of goods and services to GDP (%)	Merchandise exports to GDP (%)	Imports of goods and services to GDP (%)	Merchandise imports to GDP (%)	Trade deficit to GDP (%)
1973	13.7	10.5	20.9	15.0	−7.2
1974	22.4	17.4	39.8	34.6	−17.5
1975	20.9	15.2	44.2	37.3	−23.3
1976	25.4	16.2	41.8	34.8	−16.5
1977	24.0	14.1	38.5	30.7	−14.5
1978	21.7	13.1	37.9	30.7	−16.2
1979	31.7	22.1	56.4	43.4	−24.7
1980	31.0	20.5	49.5	37.5	−18.4
1981	36.0	24.6	59.2	45.3	−23.1
1982	31.8	21.8	52.6	39.2	−20.7
1983	32.5	19.2	52.8	35.3	−20.3
1984	36.0	22.3	62.3	42.6	−26.3
1985	39.4	24.5	72.7	46.8	−33.3
1986	33.6	20.0	65.6	40.7	−32.0
1987	31.1	15.6	56.6	32.6	−25.5
1988	34.8	17.2	58.8	41.3	−24.0
Average					
1975–9	24.7	16.1	43.8	35.4	−19.0
1980–4	33.5	21.7	55.3	40.0	−21.8
1985–8	34.7	19.3	63.4	40.3	−28.7

Source: Trade and GDP values were obtained from the World Bank Tables.
GDP was converted to dollars using the weighted average rate of exchange reported in the last column of table 5.6.

services averaged 11.4 percent per year, while export growth averaged only 9.1 percent per year.

Reflecting the country's food policy, agriculture accounted for about 44 percent of average annual import shares. Within agriculture, grain imports tended to dominate, accounting for about 43 percent of annual shares during the period. While export earnings became increasingly dominated by oil exports, agriculture's share in the value of non-fuel primary exports declined from 61 percent in 1974 to about 28 percent in 1979 (USDA). Of the agricultural exports, cotton maintained the largest share of total agricultural export earnings, averaging about 70 percent per year during the period. However, the decline in agriculture's share reflected a transfer of land and other resources out of cotton and into the production of those commodities not directly part of agricultural policy, namely fruits, vegetables, and dairy products.

External borrowing, foreign aid, and expansion of the money supply were used to confront the twin trade and budget imbalances. Medium- and long-term debt grew from 23.4 percent of GDP in 1973 to about 68 percent by 1979 (table 5.5). Debt service payments averaged about 17 percent of GDP and about 37 percent of the exports of goods and services during 1977–9. Meanwhile, money supply expanded at an average annual rate of almost 28 percent (table 5.2). The resulting excess demand pressures led to an average annual increase in the country's CPI of over 11 percent in 1977–8, and to over 20 percent in 1980. In 1976, the government responded to these pressures by devaluing the Egyptian pound.

However, foreign exchange was manipulated in ways that clearly discriminated among users. It was rationed through two "within-bank" exchange pools: the commercial banks and the Central Bank. Another "tolerated market" was the parallel or tolerated market for foreign exchange (see table 5.6). The Central Bank pool handled exports of petroleum, cotton, and rice, canal dues, imports of the five essential foodstuffs (wheat, wheat flour, sugar, tea, and edible oils) and capital transactions of the public sector. These transactions received the lowest rates of exchange and thus served to discourage the mentioned exportable goods and to encourage imports, and notably so for foodstuffs. The commercial bank pool received proceeds from worker remittances, tourism, and exports not going through the Central Bank. This pool also provided foreign exchange for public sector payments not covered by the Central Bank pool. The tolerated market tended to satisfy demand by the private sector for transactions not covered by the other two pools.

In 1976, the nominal value of the pound in the commercial bank pool was devalued from 0.39 £E per dollar to 0.7, while the official rate in the Central Bank pool was maintained at the 0.39 rate until 1979 when it too was adjusted to the 0.7 £E/dollar rate. The nominal rate of exchange in the tolerated banks market (or parallel market) closely tracked rates in the commercial market during 1976–80. These adjustments brought both the

Table 5.5   External debt and debt service to GDP and to exports of goods and services, 1973–88

	Debt: Outstanding plus disbursed medium and long-term (US$m)	Short-term debt (US$m)	Total debt service (US$m)	Medium and long-term debt to GDP (%)	Short-term debt to GDP (%)	Debt service to GDP (%)	Debt service to exports of goods and services (%)
1973	2,224			23.4			
1974	3,076			29.4			
1975	4,850			39.2			
1976	6,246			46.7			
1977	8,261	4,287	1,410	49.6	17.1	16.9	35.2
1978	10,444	3,308	1,786	53.4	12.0	18.2	42.1
1979	12,236	3,476	1,932	67.9	15.6	15.2	33.9
1980	14,101	3,933	2,627	61.7	15.7	15.9	37.1
1981	15,584	3,515	3,610	68.4	14.0	20.8	44.0
1982	15,864	4,904	4,110	60.0	18.5	19.8	48.8
1983	18,585	5,044	3,919	68.1	18.9	16.2	44.2
1984	21,139	5,653	3,980	79.8	22.7	14.0	41.6
1985	23,741	6,103	4,099	95.9	27.4	12.4	42.0
1986	25,400	6,855	4,245	97.6	31.3	11.1	48.5
1987	27,387	6,267	4,903	105.5	31.3	11.2	60.8
1988	30,087	6,522	5,379	115.3	39.1	9.4	59.2
Average							
1975–9	8,407.4	2,214.2	1,025.6	51.3	14.9	16.8	37.1
1980–4	17,054.6	4,609.9	3,649.2	67.6	18.0	17.3	43.1
1985–8	26,653.8	6,436.6	4,656.5	103.6	32.3	11.0	52.6

Source: Estimates of medium- and long-term debt and debt service payments were obtained from USDA. Levels of short-term debt were obtained from the World Bank Tables.

Central and commercial pool rates in 1979 into close alignment with the tolerated banks rate of 0.75 (table 5.6). Of course, the rate of domestic inflation led to only a slight depreciation in the weighted average value of the currency in Egypt's three markets for foreign exchange. The weighted value of the real rate of exchange in all markets depreciated from 0.554 £E/$ in 1978 to 0.807 in 1979 (table 5.7).

Economic distortions at the sectorial level of the economy were also pervasive. Estimates of the average direct rates of protection for the four commodities cotton, wheat, rice, and maize are −48, −64, −27, and −12 percent, respectively.[6] When account was taken of the distortions in the value of the country's currency and protection afforded the nonagricultural sector of the economy, the level of implicit taxation increased. Protection of the industrial sector tended to contribute more to the implicit tax on producers of these commodities than did the effect of the overvaluation of the country's currency.[7] These distortions likely contributed to the ineffi-

Table 5.6 Currency exchange rates, market share, and weighted average rates of Egyptian pounds to the US dollar

	Exchange rate (£E/$)			Market share			Weighted average	
	Central Bank	Comm-ercial banks	Outside banks market	Central Bank	Comm-ercial banks	Outside banks market	All markets	Official markets
1973	0.400		0.650				0.400	0.400
1974	0.390	0.390	0.640	0.650	0.250	0.100	0.415	0.390
1975	0.390	0.390	0.710	0.650	0.250	0.100	0.422	0.390
1976	0.390	0.700	0.740	0.650	0.250	0.100	0.503	0.476
1977	0.390	0.700	0.720	0.650	0.250	0.100	0.501	0.476
1978	0.390	0.700	0.720	0.650	0.250	0.100	0.501	0.476
1979	0.700	0.700	0.750	0.650	0.250	0.100	0.705	0.700
1980	0.700	0.740	0.760	0.570	0.225	0.206	0.722	0.711
1981	0.700	0.830	0.870	0.586	0.266	0.148	0.760	0.741
1982	0.700	0.830	0.950	0.516	0.313	0.173	0.785	0.749
1983	0.700	1.000	1.080	0.445	0.302	0.252	0.886	0.821
1984	0.700	1.300	1.400	0.420	0.305	0.275	1.076	0.952
1985	0.700	1.360	1.800	0.300	0.300	0.400	1.338	1.030
1986	0.700	1.400	2.000	0.280	0.270	0.450	1.474	1.044
1987	0.700	1.700	2.165	0.250	0.250	0.500	1.683	1.200
1988	2.165	2.165	2.250				2.193	2.165

Source: Data through 1985 were obtained from Dethier (1989). Data for remaining years were obtained from the Ministry of Finance.

ciencies in capital investments realized during this period, and they almost surely increased the country's vulnerability to the decline in petroleum revenues during the 1980s.

The 1980–8 period

During the early 1980s growth in the real GDP remained fairly high, averaging about 7.6 percent per year through 1983, and then falling to 2.7 percent in 1986 where it roughly remained through 1988 (table 5.1). The shock to growth rates during 1980–2 and historically high rates of inflation in 1980–1 of over 20 percent (table 5.2) were due partly to falling petroleum revenues (see table 5.3 and table 5.8) and a monetization of the resulting government's budget deficit. Money supply growth averaged 41 percent during 1980–1 (table 5.2). Growth then rebounded slightly as foreign exchange earnings from petroleum and worker remittances increased the value of exports of goods and services from 31.8 percent of GDP in 1982 to 39.4 percent in 1985 (table 5.4). It was also during this period that the trade deficit reached a high of 33.3 percent of GDP. Annual average growth in value added in agriculture remained virtually unchanged from the 1970s while growth in manufacturing generally

Table 5.7 Weighted average real currency exchange rate in official, tolerated, and all markets, Egyptian pounds/dollar

	Egyptian CPI (1981=100)	US WPI (1981=100)	Weighted average real exchange rate[a]		
			Official banks market	Tolerated market	All markets
1973	0.370	0.462	0.400	0.812	0.499
1974	0.410	0.549	0.522	0.857	0.555
1975	0.450	0.564	0.488	0.889	0.528
1976	0.497	0.600	0.575	0.893	0.607
1977	0.560	0.641	0.545	0.825	0.573
1978	0.622	0.688	0.527	0.797	0.554
1979	0.684	0.783	0.801	0.858	0.807
1980	0.825	0.903	0.779	0.832	0.791
1981	1.000	1.000	0.741	0.870	0.760
1982	1.113	1.027	0.691	0.877	0.725
1983	1.282	1.040	0.666	0.876	0.719
1984	1.514	1.065	0.670	0.985	0.757
1985	1.732	1.060	0.630	1.102	0.819
1986	2.010	1.029	0.534	1.024	0.755
1987	1.516	1.056	0.503	0.908	0.706
1988	2.963	1.098	0.813	0.834	0.813

[a]Based on nominal rates reported in table 5.6.

declined (table 5.1). However, during the last three years (1986–8) of the period, growth stagnated and averaged only 2.3, 2.0, 2.7, and 3.1 percent per year in agriculture, industry, manufacturing, and services, respectively.

Much of the growth through 1985 was sustained by the expansionist type of policies pursued in the 1970s. During the 1980–4 period government expenditures averaged 56.9 percent of GDP, and then fell to about 52 percent of GDP in 1986 (table 5.2). The budget deficit remained at a fairly constant average annual level of about 12 percent of GDP during the period.

Pressures to sustain government expenditures increased as revenues from petroleum and canal fees fell. In 1982, petroleum and canal fees accounted for over 24.0 percent of total government revenues, and declined to 15.5 percent in 1985 and to about 12 percent in 1987 (table 5.9). The sharp decline in world petroleum prices in the latter half of 1986 accounted for most of the 1986–7 fall in government revenue.

The lower panel of table 5.9 shows that government total subsidies, as a percentage of revenues, also fell during the mid 1980s, but at a slower rate. Total subsidies as a proportion of total revenues fell from about 35 percent in fiscal 1982 to 21.1 percent and 19.2 percent in fiscal 1983 and 1984,

Table 5.8 Composition of merchandise trade, in millions of US dollars, and in percent of total merchandise trade, 1982–7

	Fiscal year					
	1982	*1983*	*1984*	*1985*	*1986*	*1987*
(a) Millions of US dollars						
Merchandise exports	5,779	5,248	5,924	6,075	5,193	4,040
Petroleum	4,669	4,164	4,532	4,781	3,995	2,679
Cotton	380	314	452	414	356	343
Other agricultural	190	159	211	140	119	123
Textiles	280	199	265	294	288	350
Other manufacturing	260	411	463	446	436	545
Merchandise imports	10,380	9,619	11,328	11,593	10,581	8,453
Wheat and flour	1,130	834	1,056	1,013	983	718
Other agricultural	1,550	1,559	1,877	1,698	1,583	1,293
Intermediate goods	3,425	2,815	3,369	3,532	3.100	2,222
Manufactured consumer						
goods	1,100	1,218	1,667	1,875	1,681	1,808
Capital goods	3,175	3,193	3,359	3,475	3,234	2,412
(b) Percent of exports and imports, respectively						
Merchandise exports						
Petroleum	80.8	79.3	76.5	78.7	76.9	66.3
Cotton	6.6	6.0	7.6	6.8	6.9	8.5
Other agricultural	3.3	3.0	3.6	2.3	2.3	3.0
Textiles	4.8	3.8	4.5	4.8	5.5	8.7
Other manufacturing	4.5	7.8	7.8	7.3	8.4	13.5
Merchandise exports						
Wheat and flour	10.9	8.7	9.3	8.7	9.3	8.5
Other agricultural	14.9	16.2	16.6	14.6	15.0	15.3
Intermediate goods	33.0	29.3	29.7	30.5	29.3	26.3
Manufactured consumer						
goods	10.6	12.7	14.7	16.2	15.9	21.4
Capital goods	30.6	33.2	29.7	30.0	30.6	28.5

Source: World Bank Tables and Ministry of Finance.

respectively. The sharpest decline in total subsidies occurred in 1987 when they fell to only 12.2 percent of total revenues.

Reflecting the importance placed on food, wheat and wheat flour remained the key component of total subsidies through 1984, averaging over 43 percent of total annual subsidies and about 8 percent of total revenues (table 5.9). However, these subsidies fell to only 16.3 and 11.5 percent of annual total subsidies in 1986 and 1987, respectively, thus bringing their proportion of total revenues to only 3.7 and 1.4 percent for

Table 5.9   Estimates of the major sources of government revenue and expenditure, fiscal years 1981–6

	Fiscal year					
	1982	*1983*	*1984*	*1985*	*1986*	*1987*
Revenue[a]						
Petroleum(%)	19.9	16.5	13.7	11.9	11.8	8.3
Canal fees (%)[b]	4.6	5.0	4.3	3.6	3.8	3.9
Other taxes (%)	45.9	44.4	46.8	47.2	46.3	46.8
Expenditures[a]						
Total subsidies						
Percentage of revenue	35.0	21.1	19.2	17.7	22.7	12.2
Wheat and flour						
Percentage of revenue		7.8	8.3	5.4	3.7	1.4
Percentage of subsidy		36.9	43.4	30.6	16.3	11.5

[a] *Source*: Ministry of Finance.
[b] Major components are income and foreign trade taxes.

these years. Hence, starting in about 1985, the government was making efforts to address the deficit, and as the data for 1986 suggest, with modest success.

The continuance in the 1980s of the policies pursued in the 1970s decreased the country's participation in world markets. The exports of goods and nonfactor services reached a high of over 39 percent of GDP in 1985 and then fell to a low of about 31 percent of GDP in 1987 (table 5.4). The rationing of foreign exchange combined with quantitative restrictions and domestic price controls contributed to a system of incentives that discouraged exports. The trade deficit became more difficult to sustain during this period. The need to make debt service payments, and the declines in exports, forced sharper declines in imports. The trade deficit in goods and nonfactor services initially fell from 23 percent of GDP in 1981 to about 20 percent in 1982–3 and then increased to an average of about 27 percent during 1985–8.

The decline in export earnings was broadly based. The high annual growth in the value of petroleum exports, which reached over 50 percent of foreign exchange earnings in 1981, and 80 percent of merchandise exports (table 5.8), stagnated thereafter, and then declined to about 30 percent of earnings in 1987 and 1988 (table 5.3). The share of agriculture in merchandise exports declined from its highs in the mid–1970s to about 9 to 10 percent during the 1980s. Only slight changes in the export shares within agriculture occurred; fiber exports continued to dominate while wheat, wheat flour, and other agricultural products accounted for over 20 percent of merchandise imports (table 5.8). The growth in worker remittances experienced in 1982–3 stagnated in the mid–1980s and then grew modestly through 1987.

The budget imbalances in the early 1980s were sustained largely by money creation and, for the remainder of the period, by increasing reliance on foreign credit and modest increases in official transfers (table 5.3). The growth in the money supply to GDP fell from an average annual high of nearly 31 percent in 1981 to less than 19 percent in 1984–5, and then remained at historically modest levels through 1987 (table 5.2). Medium- and long-term debt grew from about 60 percent of GDP in 1982 to over 100 percent of GDP in 1987 and to 115 percent in 1988 (table 5.5). During the same period, short-term debt grew from about 18.5 percent to nearly 39 percent of GDP.

The growth in debt service placed considerable pressures on the country's ability to finance its growing debt burden. Debt service grew from 41.6 percent of the value of exports of goods and nonfactor services in 1984 to about 48.5 percent in 1986, and then to about 60 percent of goods and services exports in 1987–8. Resulting increased excess demand pressures led to an acceleration in the rate of inflation. Inflation increased from a low of about 11 percent in 1982 to a high of 25 percent in 1987 (table 5.2). Through the 1980–5 period, the Central Bank rate of exchange remained at 0.7 £E/$ (table 5.6). In 1981, the commercial bank rate was increased to 0.83 £E/$. The commercial bank rate was increased from 1.0 £E/$ to 1.3 and 1.36 £E/$ in 1983 to 1985, respectively. However, throughout the 1980s, an increasing percentage of foreign exchange transactions were occurring in the tolerated market, and the wedge between the tolerated banks' rate of exchange and those of the Central and commercial bank continued to diverge.

The proportion of total transactions in the tolerated market grew from about 20.6 percent in 1980 to 45 percent of total transactions in 1986, while the pound depreciated, in nominal terms, from 0.76 £E/$ in 1980 to 1.8 £E/$ in 1985. Throughout the 1980–7 period, the real value of the currency appreciated in the Central and commercial bank markets, while through 1985, it depreciated in the tolerated market (table 5.7). However, the high rates of inflation experienced in 1985–7 caused the pound to appreciate in all markets up to the time of the standby agreement in May of 1987 which led to reform of these markets.

Government interventions in agriculture continued to distort agricultural prices through at least 1985, and then, as discussed in more detail later, some price liberalization in selected crops occurred. Dethier reported average direct rates of protection for cotton, wheat, rice and maize of −30, −39, −33, and −10 percent respectively.[8]

There are both positive and negative aspects of the economic statistics from 1970 to 1986. The positive aspects are, of course, the relatively high rate of real economic growth until the mid–1980s and the improvement in living standards that accompanied the growth. The negative aspects are virtually everything else: high rates of inflation, a large budget deficit in most years, and increasing foreign debt. We wish to emphasize the fact that Egypt was not a country with a stagnating economy that was forced to run up foreign debt just to prevent a deterioration in living standards. Its growth, however, was heavily dependent on earnings from three sources: remittances, Suez Canal fees, and petroleum exports. Declining petroleum prices and/or a decline in the demand for Egyptian labor in the Gulf region could create serious problems. Self-sustaining growth would require the development of more efficient industries and agriculture.

5   AREAS OF REFORM

While the decline in oil prices helped to precipitate the foreign exchange crisis, the fundamental cause of the crisis was much deeper. We have identified three areas where significant reform would be needed to reduce the budget deficit, curtail inflation, and increase exports. These are the consumer subsidies, the inefficient public sector, and the peculiar system of exchange rates. Let us lay out in a bit of detail some of the essential characteristics of each of these areas.

Consumer subsidies

As was pointed out above, the consumer subsidies date from the Nasser period. Essentially, the market for wheat flour and bread was allowed to clear at a fixed uniform price throughout the country. Other commodities, such as sugar, tea, cooking oil, rice, beans, and lentils were rationed and sold at subsidized prices, based on monthly quotas. Meat, poultry, and frozen fish were also subsidized, but in limited quantities.[9] Except for many of the perishable commodities, this complex set of interventions de-linked variation in prices at the producer level from those at the consumer level. This de-linking in some cases resulted in negative marketing margins. For instance, bread prices were below the price of wheat, in bread equivalents. The negative margin induced some farms to sell wheat to the government and then to buy back day-old bread to feed to livestock. Price controls of various sorts also existed on at least 19 other commodities. Examples are cigarettes, sugar, cotton yarn, milk and yogurt, soap, soft drinks, refrigerators, and passenger cars.

Alderman et al. report that food subsidies alone grew from 2.3 percent of GDP in 1973 to 9.4 percent in 1975 and about 8.1 percent in 1979.[10] The General Authority for the Supply of Commodities reported direct subsidies paid that amounted to a high of 10.5 percent of GDP in fiscal 1981 and then averaged about 4.5 percent of GDP through 1986 at the time negotiations with the IMF began. Food subsidies accounted for the major portion of direct subsidies paid from the special fund for subsidies and from the treasury fund. Food subsidies averaged over 60 percent of total subsidies paid from these funds for the entire 1973–86 period. Of the total food subsidies, wheat and wheat flour alone accounted for the largest share, equaling 32 percent of total food subsidies during 1981–6.

Clearly these subsidies had to be reduced if the budget deficit was to be controlled. Any tampering with them, however, could have precipitated urban demonstrations on a large scale.

Public ownership and regulations

While policies pursued in the post-Nasser period have permitted market signals to have a greater influence in the allocation of resources, numerous state enterprises were required to implement policy, and a large number of these enterprises still dominated many sectors of the economy. Through the 1980s, state enterprises accounted for a majority share (averaging 69 percent) of the value of industrial production (table 5.10). The state enterprise shares ranged from about 66 percent in 1983/84 to a high of about 74 percent in 1986/87 in the five industries classified as chemical, engineering and metallurgical, foodstuffs, mining and refractory, and spinning and weaving (table 5.10). These enterprises accounted for over one half of the value of national industrial production and they employed a large share of the labor force. Preliminary data from the 1986 population census indicates that employment in the public sector accounted for over 30 percent of the total labor force of about 13 million in 1986. Moreover, many of the state enterprises in these industries were largely geared to the local market due to their uncompetitiveness in foreign markets and

Table 5.10 Production and distribution of industrial goods by the public and private sector, in millions of current Egyptian pounds

	1983/84	1984/85	1985/86	1986/7	Average 1983–7
Public sector					
Chemicals	681.2	836.0	1010.9	1291.4	954.9
Engineering and metallurgical	1598.0	1795.0	1982.4	2070.5	1861.5
Foodstuffs	1870.8	2371.5	2673.8	3636.9	2638.3
Mining and refractory	89.2	113.2	141.7	155.4	124.9
Spinning and weaving	1411.0	1692.5	2091.2	2216.7	1852.9
Total public share (%)	5650.2	6808.2	7900.0	9370.9	7432.5
	(65.9)	(66.9)	(71.5)	(74.1)	(69.6)
Total private share (%)	2926.8	3375.0	3154.1	3273.0	3182.2
	(34.1)	(33.1)	(28.5)	(25.9)	(30.4)

Source: Data obtained from the Ministry of Industry.

protection from foreign competition. Hence, in the presence of policy reform, they were vulnerable to major restructuring.

A number of other regulations also contributed to the inefficient allocation of resources, among which were those that dealt with energy and credit. Of all intermediate products, energy prices remained among the most in need of reform. Domestic energy prices, in 1986–7, measured as the unweighted average of refined petroleum prices at Egyptian refineries, were only 36 percent of their equivalent product prices at Italian refineries. Since foreign exchange earnings were dominated by petroleum exports and since the government sources of revenue were largely energy based, higher energy prices would likely reduce domestic consumption of petroleum products and increase exports, exchange earnings, and government tax revenues.

Credit policies had been designed and targeted to specific sectors of the economy. Interest rates were kept low and mostly negative in real terms through 1987. Data from the Central Bank show that rates on three-month deposits were 8.5 percent through the mid–1980s, while the annual rate of change in the urban CPI (table 5.2) ranged from 11.3 to 25.2 percent. Negative rates can be expected to discourage domestic savings, induce undesirable capital flows, and encourage inefficient resource use and investment decisions. Negative rates amounted to significant subsidies to many of the state enterprises.

Foreign exchange

The Central Bank accounted for the majority share of foreign exchange transactions through 1984, after which the tolerated market tended to dominate (table 5.6). This switch was partially accounted for by the rationing of foreign exchange in the official markets, which forced some enterprises to obtain needed exchange at the higher prices prevailing in the tolerated markets. Access to the official exchange markets amounted to an implicit subsidy to public enterprises, many of which were in any case not profitable. The subsidy also permitted them to sustain targeted prices for a number of commodities, the most important of which was wheat flour. The higher price of foreign exchange in the tolerated market placed pressures to pass on price increases for some commodities. In other cases, imports of intermediate goods were simply curtailed to assure foreign exchange availability to sustain the importation of food staples. This practice was also noted by Scobie during previous periods of foreign exchange shortages. Since the official markets served the exchange needs of the public sector, the major burdens of exchange rate realignment would fall on this sector and its clients.

6   THE RESPONSE TO A DETERIORATING ECONOMIC SITUATION

In the last months of 1986, in response to the low rates of economic growth, high rising inflation, and the increasing portion of exchange earnings required to service external debt, Egyptian policy makers devised a program of economic reforms that tended to be more comprehensive and far-reaching than previous efforts. The components of this program included a steady annual retrenchment of the fiscal deficit, exchange reform, reductions in cost/price distortions, and some enhanced role for the private sector. For example, energy prices and electricity tariffs were brought closer to world prices, while charges for telephone, water, and railway services were brought more in line with production costs. Consumer subsidies were reduced by increasing prices and reducing the list of subsidized goods. Customs tariffs were introduced to replace a number of quantitative import restrictions, the commercial bank rate of exchange was increased, and selected agricultural policy reforms were also undertaken. However, at the consumer level little reform occurred in the pricing of essential commodities. These commodities included wheat flour, sugar, tea, and edible oils, and at the farm level they included cotton, sugar, and one-half of the rice crop. Only slight adjustments occurred in interest rates, energy prices remained far below world values, and a number of subsidies on other items remained in effect.

In spite of these reforms, in 1987 the CPI increased by over 25 percent while debt to GDP also continued to grow. Debt service grew from over 48 percent of the exports of goods and services in 1986 to over 60 percent in 1987 (table 5.5). To cope with foreign exchange shortages, import controls were used, which further reduced supplies of imported intermediate inputs to the industrial sector. The impending crisis induced the Egyptian authorities to seek consultations and balance of payments support from the IMF.

7   MAJOR COMPONENTS OF RESTRUCTURING

Beginning in April 1987, Egypt engaged in article IV consultations with the IMF and made the first drawing of SDRs in May of 1987. However, in November of 1987, the IMF canceled the agreements owing to the nonobservance of performance criteria, including the accumulation of external debt and the intensification of exchange restrictions. Let us review some of the major elements of the arrangement.

Initial agreements

The general quantitative targets of the reform program advanced by the staff of the IMF and supported by the IBRD for 1987–9 was to attain a growth rate in real GNP of 2 percent, a reduction in inflation to about 20 percent, a containment of the current account deficit of the balance of payments to about 18 percent of GDP ($5 billion) and an increase in net international reserves. Key instruments of the reform included exchange rate realignment, capital market adjustments, reform in commodity and factor prices, and several other adjustments designed to increase government revenues and decrease expenditures. Among the essential components of these reforms were the following.

Exchange rate realignment　A central component of the reform program was a simplification of the exchange system through establishment of a new bank foreign exchange market, and the devaluation of the pound to 2.165 £E/$, the rate prevailing in the "tolerated market." The Central and commercial bank rates were to be unified.

Capital market reforms　Nominal interest rates had been increased by 1–2 percentage points in May 1987, and an agreement on a schedule to bring them to internationally competitive levels by June 1988 was to be reached during the first program review. The government also agreed to eliminate all external arrears by June 1988.

Commodity market reform　As part of the standby agreement with the IMF, the authorities also agreed to increase average petroleum product prices in May 1987 by 66 percent from their levels of about 35 percent of world market prices for energy, and then to eventually bring them to world market levels. Agreement was also reached on increasing electricity tariffs by about 28 percent from their levels of only about 22 percent of long-run marginal costs, and then eventually to bring them to international levels.[11] A plan to bring energy prices to the international levels was to be delayed for later program reviews. Initially, energy prices were to be increased by about 20 percent. Allegedly, the IBRD had suggested an increase in nominal energy prices of about 35 percent per year. Reform in prices of public sector industry was also to be achieved during the phasing-in period ending in mid-1988.

Government revenues were to be enhanced by increasing the consumption duties on a number of commodities, including cigarettes, and by converting a number of firm specific import licenses and duties to an ad-valorem basis. Reform of income taxes and the introduction of a general sales tax was also to be undertaken. Consumer subsidies for the five basic food commodities – wheat, wheat flour, sugar, tea, and edible oil – were also discussed as part of the reform package. However, the Egyptian authorities allegedly maintained that subsidies on these commodities were sensitive social issues and that increases in the ration prices of these commodities as part of the reform program would not be part of the package. Hence, while reform in producer prices of crops other than cotton, sugar, and one-half of the rice crop was agreed to, significant decreases in consumer subsidies for these commodities was not to be part of the reform program.

8 KEY AREAS OF DEPARTURE FROM AND ATTAINMENT OF REFORM COMMITMENTS

Conversations with Egyptian officials indicated that the agreed-to reform quickly stalled in various ways shortly after the standby agreement was reached with the IMF. Despite the number of policy reforms mentioned above, the broad objectives of the 1987/88 program to ease pressures on inflation and the balance of payments were not met. Important slippages in policy implementation occurred with budget expenditures, the exchange and trade system, the pricing of key commodities, and interest rates. At the same time, the weakening of petroleum prices, anticipated capital inflows that did not materialize, and unanticipated payments to the Paris Club creditors exacerbated the country's difficulties in attaining the previously agreed to targets. Agreement could not be reached on the pace of additional reforms in a number of areas, including exchange rate realignment, interest rates, energy prices, government revenue and expenditure adjustments, and agricultural procurement prices. In November of 1987, the arrangements with the IMF lapsed owing to the nonobservance of the previously agreed-to performance criteria.

Exchange rate realignment A new bank market was established in May of 1987 in which the price of foreign exchange was to be set by a chamber of participating banks on the basis of four indicators: supply, demand, working balances of the banks, and assessment of the general market trends. The initial rate was set at the mentioned tolerated bank rate of 2.165 £E/$. Essentially, the Central Bank and commercial bank rates were to adapt the tolerated bank rate. Statutes making transactions in the tolerated market illegal were enforced, thus forcing many private transactions into the new bank market.

The immediate result of the devaluation of the currency in the Central and commercial bank markets was to cause a large real depreciation of the currency in these markets. Since these markets accounted for about half of all foreign exchange transactions, the real depreciation increased the domestic prices paid and received for traded goods. This adjustment fell largely on the public sector since, as mentioned, it accounted for a large majority of transactions in these markets. However, since transactions in the tolerated market were incorporated into the new market at the 2.165 £E/$ rate, in the presence of inflation in 1988 of over 17 percent, in real terms, the rate appreciated for transactions formerly associated with this market by 9 percent. Thus, while the real exchange rate, as the weighted average of all markets, showed a modest depreciation of 15 percent from its 1987 level, the nominal value of the pound in the tolerated market in 1987 would have had to depreciate in 1988 by at least 13 percent to maintain its purchasing power parity at the 1987 level.

Further evidence to support the notion that the pound remained overvalued was reported of a growing excess demand for foreign exchange. Long delays in responding to applications for import letters of credit and other actions to delay meeting foreign exchange demands were reported in late 1987 and 1988. The effects of the modest real depreciation in the weighted average rate of exchange was further diminished by the government's refusal to pass through the higher prices for selected imported commodities that depreciation implied. The government indicated that the depreciated rate of exchange would not be passed through to final consumers for the five basic commodities – wheat, wheat flour, sugar, tea, and edible oils – at this time. Moreover, the government allegedly expressed the view that, for other major consumer commodities, a five-year period would be required before the depreciated value of the pound could be passed through to final consumers without creating social unrest.

Capital market reforms The high rates of inflation in the late 1980s, when interest rates were fixed at low levels, resulted in negative real rates of interest. Still, the government was reluctant to alter these rates, arguing that the rates were adjusted upward by 1 to 2 percent in 1987. Rather than bring rates to international levels, as suggested by the IMF, the government agreed only to consider raising rates by another 1 to 2 points in the near future. The resistance stemmed from the indebtedness and anticipated credit needs of the public sector, and from the country's growing subsidized housing loan program. The government-owned credit bank, Credit Forcier Egyptian, provided 4 percent interest loans to organized professional groups including military officers' groups, lawyers, medical doctors, and others. These groups allegedly lobbied against large increases in interest rates because of the threat higher rates posed to the sustainability of the program.

Commodity market reform The government was reluctant to increase petroleum prices by more than 20 percent per year, even though it was clear that, at rates of inflation in excess of 15 percent, energy price increases on the order of 35 percent per year would be required for domestic energy prices to closely approximate border prices ten years thence. Price controls also remained for a number of industrial enterprises, many of which were below world prices. In the case of public enterprise, the position of the government was allegedly that price reform alone would cause serious disruptions to their financial viability and create financial burdens on the government. Instead, what was needed was an investment program to rehabilitate plant and equipment and to improve management in order to increase productivity and decrease costs.

Efforts to decrease pressures on the government's budget in other areas also tended to stall. For example, several measures of the reform package were submitted to the Egyptian parliament. These included a broadening of consumption taxes, changing to ad-valorem rates, increases in certain government fees, and reductions in subsidy payments through changes in distribution requirements. The latter reform was an effort to target food subsidies to lower-income households. However, these reforms still remained under the consideration of Parliament in 1989. The failure to take effective action in a number of these areas soon manifested itself in the foreign accounts.

Why did government officials who recognized the need for reform fail to follow through on its initial proposals and agreement? Certainly the specter of the massive street demonstrations in 1977 following the announcement that food prices would rise haunted Mubarak and his chief ministers. But could not some of the real economic growth that had occurred from 1978 to 1986 have been used to buffer the change for a more rational economic system in order to make it less threatening to the populace? In addition to the strong expression of concern in street demonstrations, there are probably some partially organized interests that strongly oppose the reforms and are in positions where they can affect the process of change. But before trying to hypothesize about the reasons for the failure to make some needed reforms, let us look at a case in which some significant reforms were successfully put in place. In order to understand the reforms that were initiated, it is necessary to review in some detail the situation in agriculture in the 1980s.

9 THE PATTERN OF GOVERNMENT INTERVENTION BEFORE REFORM

The Nile Valley and Delta have been under intensive cultivation for over 3,000 years. From the beginning of recorded history government intervention in agricultural production and marketing has been pervasive. But the pattern and nature of that intervention that concerns us is a product largely of the policies put into effect during the mid–1960s under the Nasser regime and can be summarized under three topics: (1) the control of prices; (2) the establishment of delivery quotas; and (3) the regulation of cropping patterns.[12] Indirectly, the whole system of food subsidies is related to the creates for implementing an effective reform in agriculture will be discussed below.

Regulating prices

The regulation of crops falls into one of four somewhat overlapping categories. One group consists of those crops which were sold on the free market without direct government intervention. Most fruits and vegetables and berseem would fall into this category. The second group is made up of those grains which are imported in large amounts, as well as produced locally. The Ministry of Supply controlled the price at which imported wheat and maize was sold in Egypt and thus effectively controlled the price of that part of the domestically produced grain crop that was sold on the free market.

In a third group which includes, most significantly, rice, wheat, and for a brief period in 1985, maize, farmers were forced to deliver to pooling centers a specified quantity of grain which would be sold at a fixed price. The Ministry of Supply had a major input into setting the prices for these forced deliveries but the final decision on the price was actually made by the Council of Ministries. These are the food grains, of course, that are most directly affected by the policy of food subsidies. For the fourth category, which includes cotton and sugarcane, farmers were forced to deliver all of their production at set prices. While the price of cotton was officially set by the High Committee for the Economy and Planning of the Council of Ministers, many ministries were actually involved in the decision. Because it supervised the cotton gins, the Ministry of Economy and Finance was directly involved and was typically the first to recommend price changes. But the Ministry of Cotton, because it supervised the publicly owned spinning and weaving companies, had a strong interest in the prices of cotton and generally resisted any proposed increase. The Ministry of Agriculture also made itself felt and usually would support increases that would bring prices closer to shadow prices and increase agricultural incomes.

Sugarcane prices were essentially set by the publicly owned refineries, which were supervised by the Ministry of Industry.

In addition to setting, either directly or indirectly, the price of the important crops, the government also controlled the price of the major inputs to agricultural production. The price of fertilizer at agricultural cooperatives was set by ministerial decree well below the current world price. (It should be noted that Egyptian fertilizer use per acre exceeds that of all developing countries.) Pesticides, 80 percent of which were applied to the cotton crop, were also highly subsidized.

In addition to setting prices to the farmers for these inputs at a level that required a significant subsidy, the government, through the Principal Bank for Development and Agricultural Credit, subsidized the credit that farmers used to purchase these inputs. Interest rates averaged about 2 percent below those prevailing in the rest of the banking system, which as mentioned were themselves artificially low and negative in real terms.

The establishment of delivery quotas

In the above section reference is made to delivery quotas for some crops. A further explication is required in order to appreciate the magnitude of distortions that can be introduced through the use of this technique and the large number of people and agencies that get involved. Cotton, sugarcane, wheat, and rice are the major crops affected, but there are a number of others which also have delivery quotas.

As contradictory as it may seem, delivery quotas stated in terms of a physical quantity per unit of area (e.g., canters/feddan) without regard to variations in yield were established by decree, with the Ministry of Agriculture and the Ministry of Supply being the chief actors. The quotas varied from year to year and were not always applied to all crops authorized by the enabling statute. In 1979–80 quotas were 100 percent for cotton, 66 percent for sugarcane, 52 percent for rice, 17 percent for groundnuts, and 16 percent for beans.[13]

One can imagine that with prices for quota deliveries well below market prices, farmers had considerable incentive to avoid making the forced delivery. Violation was pervasive.[14] This, of course, increased both the cost of attempting to enforce the deliveries and the efforts of farmers to circumvent.

Government regulation of a cropping pattern

When administered prices were too low to provide producers with incentives to produce the targeted crops for which delivery was mandatory, it was clear that the government had also to establish and enforce acreage allotments for the various crops. The process was complex.

The Ministry of Agriculture consulted with the Ministries of Energy, Supply and Irrigation in June of each year to assess domestic needs, export opportunities, and the availability of water, and made a preliminary aggregate projection for the acreage allotments for each of the crops. The Institute of Agricultural Economics, along with the directors of local services, were charged with meeting with local officials to determine local conditions that would affect the required planning. The Institute of Agricultural Economics then drafted a preliminary plan in which the national requirements were translated into specific cropping patterns for specific regions. Areas for fruit and vegetables and sugarcane, mostly in upper Egypt, were specified first. Next came cotton, then wheat and rice, then maize, and finally beans and lentils. The appropriate crop rotation pattern had to be taken into consideration when assignments at the farm level were being made.

The plan proposed for each local area was taken by the supervisor of the local unit of the cooperative to the farmers, and he reported their reactions, along with suggested alternatives back up the chain of command to the Ministry of Agriculture. A penultimate version of the entire detailed plan was developed by the Ministry of Agriculture and sent to the High Committee for Planning and Economy of the Cabinet. Before the beginning of the agricultural year the cropping plan was published as a ministerial decree.

It was remarkable (and an indicator of how distorted the agricultural sector of the economy was) that the planning and assignment of cropping patterns was done almost totally independently of planning for the prices of commodities with the required acreages.[15]

We thus saw a pattern of massive government intervention with dozens of ministries and other government agencies, each with different interests to protect and objectives to be reached, interacting to set prices, delivery quotas, and cropping patterns. Over two decades these kinds of agricultural policies brought inefficiencies to the agricultural sector, misdirected capital investments, and led to a failure to exploit one of the most productive agricultural regions of the world in crops in which Egypt had the comparative advantage. The economic crisis of the 1980s was most obviously reflected in the macroeconomic indicators, but it was obvious why USAID, the World Bank, the IMF, and the Egyptian government realized that major reform in the agricultural sector of the economy was a significant part of the solution to the crisis.

10   THE PLAN FOR REFORM

Following discussions and exchanges of correspondence between officials from USAID and the Ministry of Agriculture, a meeting was held and a plan for reform was agreed upon. This plan, called the Agricultural Production and Credit Project (APCP) was to be implemented in three tranches, with a transfer of USAID funds to the Ministry of Agriculture after the demonstrated completion of each objective:[16] $33 million at the completion of Tranche I targets, $40 million after the completion of Tranche II targets, and $27 million after the completion of Tranche III targets.

Let us review in some detail the general purpose of the APCP and the specific targets in each tranch. The vision was far-reaching. The plan called for the elimination of controls on planning, pricing, and marketing and the phasing out of input subsidies. The overall objective was to expose Egyptian farmers to market signals and thus to enable them to produce and sell freely the crops in which Egypt has a comparative advantage. It was anticipated that the reform would lead to significant increases in production and productivity.

The specific reform goals were (1) to remove government farm controls, (2) to remove government crop area controls, (3) to remove government crop procurement quotas, (4) to remove government constraints on private sector processing and marketing of farm products and inputs, (5) to eliminate subsidies of farm inputs, and (6) to limit state ownership of land.

The Tranche I benchmarks that had to be met before the release of the $33 million were as follows: Ministerial decrees were to be issued to: (1) remove farm price controls on all crops except cotton, sugarcane, and quota rice; (2) remove area controls on all crops except sugarcane and quota rice; (3) remove procurement quotas on all crops except cotton, sugarcane and quota rice; (4) remove processing and market controls on all crops except cotton, sugarcane, and oranges; (5) order an increase in the farm price of cotton from 91.5 £E/kintar to at least 116 £E/kintar before the 1987 plantings; (6) order an increase in the price of cottonseed cake from £E 44/ton to at least £E 82/ton; (7) order a total elimination of important restrictions on livestock feed and feed ingredients (except cottonseed).

Memoranda were to be sent to USAID with the content and dates of all of these decrees. In addition, USAID was to receive memoranda to: (1) request assistance in monitoring the requirements for total decontrol of the agricultural sector and to measure the economic impact of the reforms; (2) indicate that there was no constraint on the import or marketing of red meat; (3) indicate the scheduled elimination of livestock feed subsidies over three years, with public sector prices to meet world price equivalent; (4) indicate the intention not to increase the nominal value of farm input subsidies; (5) indicate the intention to privatize the farm input distribution system of the principal bank for development and agricultural credit; (6) indicate the proportion of nonsubsidized agricultural loans with the intent to achieve market rates on all loans within three years; (7) indicate that state ownership of land be limited to 4 percent to be used for agricultural experiments and crop testing; (8) indicate that new land, feasible for reclamation, would be sold to the private sector.

In May of 1987 the Ministry of Agriculture sent to USAID copies of all the required Ministerial decrees and memoranda. USAID determined that the Tranche I benchmarks had been met and released $33 million to the Ministry of Agriculture. Thus far nothing but paperwork. Each written page must have been worth about $10,000 and no real reform had taken place. Government action to get reform started, however, had occurred.

The benchmarks in Tranches II and III demanded evidence of real accomplishments. For Tranche II the benchmarks were to confirm the following through surveys at the farm level (where appropriate): (1) the elimination of price controls; (2) the elimination of area controls; (3) the elimination of crop quotas; (4) the extent and rate of decontrol of private and public sector farm product processing and marketing entities; (5) the absence of red meat import and marketing constraints; (6) the elimination, in part, of processing and marketing restrictions on livestock feeds; (7) the scheduled elimination of livestock feed subsidies; (8) reduction of the 1986 subsidy level on farm inputs; (9) the elimination of state ownership of land and sale of new land to the private sector.

In addition there were to be studies and analyses of the following: (1) the total agricultural sector decontrol undertaken by the policy and analysis unit; (2) livestock feed and feed ingredient processing and marketing, with the objective of determining the most feasible way of eliminating government restrictions on this industry; (3) the extent of PBDAC farm input supply distortions; (4) the economic impact of the reduction of subsidies.

USAID determined that all Tranche II benchmarks had been met and released $40 million to the Ministry of Agriculture.

The Tranche III benchmarks involved a replication of the surveys specified in Tranche II, the completion of the analyses specified, and the publication of studies. In addition there was to be a confirmation by survey of the reduction in the real value of subsidies on credit for farm inputs and changes in the still regulated prices of cotton, sugarcane, and rice to bring them closer to their shadow prices.

In June of 1988 the Ministry of Agriculture submitted to USAID nine reports based on the specific field studies that verified significant progress towards the achievement of the goals of the Agriculture Production and Credit Project. Producers of wheat, broad beans, sesame, onions, lentils, and groundnuts reported no government controls on the areas planted, their method of marketing, or the prices they received for their crops. Cattle feeders reported that the subsidies on the credit they received to purchase feed had been reduced and the farmers who used fertilizer made a similar report. Citrus exporters and private feed importers reported no direct government controls. More than one-third of the cotton farmers knew about the 1987 cotton price increases before they planted. All land reclaimed in 1986 and 1987 was allocated to private individuals and organizations. Four studies were completed, and a fifth one dealing with the divestiture of the PBDAC's marketing and distribution facilities was initiated.

In October of 1989 USAID concluded that all Tranche III benchmarks had been met. The surveys indicated that the ten crops decontrolled by decree under Tranche I remained free of government controls on area, procurement, and price. The evidence suggested that there had been a substantial impact on production and productivity.

USAID was particularly interested in the progress made in reducing the real value of subsidies on inputs, including credit, and bringing controlled prices on cotton, sugarcane, and rice closer to their shadow prices. On the former, USAID concluded that substantial progress had been made. The subsidy on imported corn used as feed was totally eliminated (it was worth £E 207 million in 1985–6). Fertilizer prices almost doubled in 1988.

Furthermore, progress was made in reducing subsidized credit. The subsidized portion of the PBDAC's portfolio was reduced from 28.4 percent to 25 percent from October 1986 to September 1988. In June of 1989 interest rates on most loans were increased 2 percent, which further reduced the subsidies.

Progress towards the goals of raising prices on controlled crops was not as great. While prices were increased on cotton, they were offset by the appreciation in real terms of the Egyptian pound and the increase of over 20 percent in the world price of long-staple cottons. The Ministry of Industry vigorously opposed any substantial increases in the prices paid by publicly owned processing firms.

There are difficulties is estimating the shadow price of sugarcane, but USAID estimates that by 1989 the difference between the local price and the shadow price was very small and perhaps had been totally eliminated.

In 1986 and 1987 the farm gate price of rice fell from 122 percent to 73 percent of the world price, but action in 1987 brought it back up to 86 percent. USAID concluded that the distorting effects of the difference between the farm gate price and the world price was less distorting in 1989 than it had been before the beginning of the project.

USAID concluded that the willingness of the Ministry of Agriculture to undertake a significant reform program set it apart from the rest of Egyptian government and that the success of the APCP was exceptional. Agriculture had become the model sector in the economic reform effort.

11   SUCCESS AND FAILURE

The agricultural reform program was a success. The objectives that were established at the outset were with few exceptions achieved. Furthermore, there is evidence that it provided the basis for further reforms which presently are underway. The reforms agreed upon by the IMF and the Egyptian government in 1987 were not implemented and the balance of payments crisis became more severe. Why the differences? We must recognize at the outset that the adjustments agreed upon with the IMF were more wide-ranging than those proposed in agriculture and had more severe implications. This observation by itself might contain an important lesson. If the IMF had been more modest in its reform proposals and scheduled the proposed changes over a longer time period, there may have been a better chance of success. But even this approach may not have worked unless some other techniques employed by USAID and the Ministry of Agriculture had been employed; more on this point below. First let us look at some crucial issues on which the IMF reform broke down and which were deliberately bypassed by the agricultural reforms.

It was crucial to improving the foreign trade situation to reduce the larger and growing budget deficit. Reducing government expenditures was necessary to this end. The consumer subsidies, particularly those for food for urban dwellers, made up a significant part of government expenditures and thus were an obvious target for reduction, if not total elimination.

But it was not only the proposal to cut the deficit that had a severe impact on the level of goods subsidy. If the Egyptian pound was devalued, the price of imported food would rise. Unless the government put more money into subsidies, the price of these goods would also increase.

The food subsidy programs, it must be pointed out, also had implications for the agricultural reform program. If the reforms had the effect of increasing the price of wheat and rice this would have the effect either of raising food costs or of increasing government expenditures to keep food at the preexisting prices.

The government, it will be remembered, refused to yield to the pressure from the IMF to lower food subsidies and did not allow the price increases on wheat and rice to be passed through to consumers. There is further evidence of the sensitivity of the government to food prices. Scobie found that in periods of foreign exchange shortages, foreign exchange was rationed to favor food imports. Exchange shortages tended to result in a decline in the impact of intermediate inputs, while food imports were generally unaffected.

If a reduction in food subsidies is such an essential aspect of meaningful economic reform, why is the government so reluctant to take what is widely recognized as a necessary step?

There is one obvious answer. When price increases were proposed in 1977 there were civil disturbances in all major urban centers. The government quickly backed down. That seems to be the kind of pressure it is most vulnerable to and thus it refused to act if it anticipated that the reaction would be massive street demonstrations. We believe, however, that it is a mistake to see these demonstrations as simply the reflex reaction of an enraged urban population that values low food prices above everything else. Households are composites of interest whose welfare is affected by a number of factors. The price of food is certainly one. Others include returns to the factors of production they possess and their social position tied to place of employment or membership in other organizations, which impacts utility either directly or indirectly through real income. In the short run some of these interests may be affected more adversely by policy reform than others.

These affiliations of household members may be manifested in participation in group activity outside the household.

There is some evidence to suggest that private sector capitalists operating nonagricultural enterprises that are either marginally profitable or are protected from foreign competition share some common interests with urban consumers. (They are, of course, likely to be urban consumers themselves.) Since food accounts for such a large weight in the cost of living, real wages are sensitive to the prices of food. At the same time, these private sector capitalists are likely concerned with the nominal level of their wage bill. Lower food prices translate into higher real wages which in turn lessen the pressure to increase nominal wages. Thus private sector capitalists may share the interests of urban consumers in preventing price increases in commodities that dominate the consumption basket, and particularly so if the assets in these enterprises are not easily allocated to alternative activities that became more profitable following reform.

There are other groups that have an even more direct concern. The government-run fair price shops would have no reason for existing if consumer subsidies were removed. Thus those who are on the public payroll to manage these shops could lose their jobs. These public employees must relish the thought of the urban consumers ready to turn out in the hundreds of thousands at first mention of a reduction or elimination of subsidies.

There are many government bureaucrats in a similar position. Clerks and accountants in large numbers (all of whom need managers) are required to run the rationing system, keep the books in balance, and manage the purchasing and distribution of a considerable quantity of goods. Indeed, the bureaucracy is probably one of the most effective groups in shackling reforms that may cost them their jobs and the social position which accompanies them.

Thus, common interests among urban households include those whose real incomes are dependent on the labor market, the bureaucracy, and food expenditures.

There are, of course, sectors of the society that will benefit from the reforms and the number of households involved is very large. As is the case of most countries that implement extensive goods-subsidy programs, Egypt's food policies discriminate against rural households and in favor of urban households. In the case of both household categories, food is an important component of total expenditures. Alderman et al. found that in 1981 the share of the total budget allocated to food by all farm households averaged 59 percent compared to 50 percent for urban households.[17] Not surprisingly, this difference in the cost of food was found to be largely caused by the urban bias in Egypt's food rationing and subsidy system. Their computation of the consumer price index for all items consumed during the period 1973–81 shows that the index was, on an average annual basis, 20.5 percent lower for urban households than it was for rural households. Dethier also finds that Egypt's food and agricultural policies are strongly biased in favor of urban households.[18]

Since price differentials of these magnitudes and the ease of access to ration shops in urban relative to rural areas are surely observable to urban households, they may perceive their real incomes to be threatened from reforms that increase food prices. This threat is heightened for households that do not realize that wages and returns to factors of production, and hence real incomes, will likely increase at some point following reform.

However, urban households may perceive a far greater threat to their real incomes than rural households because the rural household can observe the offsetting effect of an increase in the price of farm-produced food. In contrast to the urban households, the rural household that produced a market surplus of food can be made better off in the short run from price reform.

These rural households that would benefit from a reduction of food subsidies and a relaxation of the regulations that prohibit them from producing and selling more profitable crops also have natural allies. The producer of trade competing goods has an interest in common with the rural household.

Why will those who clearly would benefit from the reform not organize to support the government? There is something incongruous, if not downright preposterous, about the idea of turning out thousands in the rural areas to demonstrate in support of an agreement between the government and the IMF to reduce food subsidies. Moreover, the losers from inflation (e.g., low-income households and wage earners) and the losers from overvaluation (e.g., potential exporters) are unlikely to know each other and, in any case, their estimates of potential gains must be highly subjective and uncertain. Together, these factors likely make the cost of forming a coalition prohibitive. But what else can those supporting the arguments do? As we have pointed out, there are no institutions through which interests can effectively be expressed; no institutions that can effectively organize a coalition among those with interests in common and neutralize the impact of those interested that need to do nothing but demonstrate in the streets. And those demonstrations would not only challenge a policy but throw out a government if it were necessary. Indeed, they would be willing to destroy the very institution of the presidency, for it commanded very little loyalty.

Let us look at the problem from a somewhat broader perspective. There seems to be little doubt that many in top positions in the Egyptian government recognized that significant economic reforms were necessary. The huge deficits in current accounts and the increasing arrears in debt payment threatened Egypt's international trading position. The lack of growth and manufacturing and agriculture foretold stagnant living levels as income from oil remittances and canal revenues seemed unlikely to grow and oil revenues and remittances might well decline. With inflation rates of over 20 percent it was the government deficits that had to be reduced and interest rates had to be deregulated so that they reflected the true cost of money.

The reasons for not acting were largely political. There are two different scenarios that have the same outcome but different remedies. Perhaps the government fears that it cannot survive the reforms and thus will not act; alternatively it may not have the capacity to make the necessary decisions, and thus cannot act. Let us examine briefly the two alternatives.

A government that will not act

One of the consequences of some of the most distorting policies – an overvalued currency, large deficits in current accounts, and large budget deficits – is that the country is living beyond its means. People are enjoying living standards that cannot be maintained. The initial impact of reform is likely to be a decline in living standards. A number of countries that have tried to increase food prices have experienced mass political demonstrations and rioting, or the threat thereof, and have withdrawn or delayed proposed action.

Governments that have a great deal of legitimacy have a chance of surviving these initial reactions to reform and staying in power long enough to benefit politically from the positive economic results of reform. But typically governments in developing countries do not have the kind of legitimacy that enables them to effectively call for sacrifices in the short run for the benefit of the commonwealth in the long run. We do not believe that the Mubarak government has that kind of legitimacy.

This is no place to rewrite the textbook on legitimacy (although some rewriting could be useful). Several points must be made to set the discussion below. We distinguish between a moral basis of legitimacy and a procedural basis, although, of course, they are related. Ultimately, in any authority relationship there is a moral reason why the receiver of instructions has an obligation to obey. Much of this justification comes from a system of religious values, and the closer the link between religious authority and secular authority the greater the significance of religious precepts and religious organizations in providing or withdrawing legitimacy from secular authorities.

The Mubarak government is not blessed with a high degree of legitimacy, either moral or procedural. In the Moslem world the authority of a political regime is more directly based on religiously revealed truth and precepts than is the case in a predominantly Christian culture. The Christian theology acknowledges that there is a domain of Caesar's that is distinct from the domain that is God's, and believers are expected to render unto each his just due. State and Church can legitimately be separate. In the Anglo-Saxon tradition the common law and canon law are separate. On the continent the canon law and civil law are separate.

The Moslem religion provides no such convenience. The Sharia, ideally, is both civil and religious law. There is no recognized domain of sheik or sultan that is separate from the domain of Allah. The religion provides positive legitimacy to a regime when these principles are accepted. Even religious moderates acknowledge the primacy of the Sharia.

The Moslem Brotherhood, hardly a moderate organization, is the most significant organization in Egypt that can use religious authority, either to provide legitimacy for a regime or to deny it legitimacy based on moral authority. While the Brotherhood could support the anti-imperialist position of the Nasser revolution, it could never support what was essentially a secular thrust in the direction of the polity. The conflict between the State and the Brotherhood is identified by the fact that Nasser ordered the execution of a leader of the Brotherhood and that it was a member of the brotherhood that assassinated Sadat.

The situation has actually become more complex in Mubarak's Egypt because in the 1980s the Brotherhood had developed very considerable economic power through the development of a number of successful holding companies. A more thorough analysis of the politics of economic reform in Egypt might well reveal that the reforms that are demanded by the IMF could go against the strong economic interests of the Brotherhood, and thus give it an interest in common with urban consumers.

The moral basis of a legitimacy can also come from secular ideologies and it is important to recognize the significant role that socialist ideologies have had in the anticolonial independent movements in Third World countries. The socialist ideologies directly link the imperialism of the West to the capitalism of the West. Many members of the intelligentsia of the independence movements had their education in England or France – indeed, some in the Soviet Union – and their mentors explained the imperialism under which the colonies were suffering by the same theories by which they explained the depression that plagued western Europe and the United States in the 1930s. Getting rid of capitalism and the system that gave rise both to economic stagnation and to imperialism would disappear. For the British colonies, the British Labour party, which by and large supported the independence of the colonies, also justified significant intervention in the economy through public ownership and many types of economic controls.

Those that fought colonialism also fought capitalism, and it is not surprising that the newly independent regimes pursued economic policies that would have had the endorsement of Sydney and Beatrice Webb.

This creates problems for the political leaders in the next generation, who find that the economic reform measures they would like to put in place can be attacked because they will lead to a return of the repression of the past.

We believe that it is interesting that those Third World countries that have had the most economic success in the post-World War II period are those that had an atypical colonial experience. Korea suffered under Japanese, not Western, military and cultural imperialism until World War II. South Korea's opponent after World War II was communist North Korea. For Taiwan the enemy was not the capitalist West, but communist China. Hong Kong wanted to remain a part of a Western colonial system, not to shed British rule. It feared communist China. In Singapore's political history and mythology, Malaysia and not the colonialist West is the major opponent. In none of these cases does the theory of imperialism that comes from socialism make much sense in interpreting the problems these countries have faced.

Tanzania would probably be the best example on the other side, where the independence ideology was closely linked with a form of socialist ideology and where the economic policies that were pursued after independence were an integral part of the independent ideology and a cornerstone of the moral legitimacy of the regime.

The Mubarak regime was not blessed with much legitimacy that derives from the dominant belief systems in Egypt. While acknowledging the Sharia, it is a secular regime that the Brotherhood cannot really endorse, and it follows the *infitah* of Sadat and thus cannot command the support of the socialistically inclined. Unfortunately, what it lacks in legitimacy based on moral authority, it does not make up in legitimacy based on procedures.

In the twentieth century procedural legitimacy is based on competitive political parties, free elections, a representative parliament, and an independent judiciary, all enshrined in a widely accepted constitution. The government which is elected to power and which proceeds with a reform through statutes passed by the representative parliament has a reasonable chance of surviving the short-term sacrifices that are involved, at least until the next election.

Egypt does not have the political institutions and procedures that confer much legitimacy on the Mubarak government. Parties, elections, and the parliament are of little consequence. The government has little basis for asking for sacrifices from the people because the people put it in power. One can conclude that it will not act on major reforms because it runs a high risk of widespread disobedience, demonstrations, and possibly a revolution or coup d'état.

Government that cannot act

While the concept of legitimacy is written about a great deal in political science, the concept of "capacity," as we will use the term, is almost unknown. We believe, however, that it is an important concept when dealing with such issues as explaining why certain kinds of economic reforms are so difficult to pursue. It is a concept, however, which requires much more work, and here we will just provide some suggestions on how it might be used.

We will use the term "capacity" in a manner which would be comparable to the use of the term in the statement "the market mechanism has the capacity to allocate resources optimally in a classical decision environment." The market mechanism generates the kind of information and presents the economic agents with the kinds of alternatives that allow them to make decisions which will have, in the aggregate, the effect of allocating the resources optimally. Note that no variance in outcome is dependent on individual characteristics of economic agents. There is no attention given to the character of economic agents, how well they are educated, or whether they are honest, or what their leadership capabilities are. There is only a simple assumption about their motivation. Note also that the statement "a market economy has the capacity to allocate resources optimally" refers to economic theory, not the real world, and thus the concept "capacity" is the property of a model of empirical reality and not a property of empirical reality itself. When one studies markets empirically, one studies their performance, not their capacity. But because there is a well-developed model of a market, it is possible to ask the important question of whether or not a market is performing up to its capacity.

Political science theory is not well enough developed to enable us to build a model of the Egyptian government (or any other government for that matter) that would enable us to answer the question of whether it had the capacity to pursue certain reform policies. In the absence, however, of well-developed theories and models, we can provide illustrations of the varying capacities of different political systems. The parliamentary system with disciplined political parties is relatively immune from local constituency-based special interests. The government, particularly in the first three years after a general election, can pass legislation on major economic issues without a significant probability of being stopped by constituency-based special interests, short-term shifts in public opinion against the policy, or even opposition from powerful nationally based interest groups associated with opposition political parties. The economic policies of the Thatcher government in Great Britain in its first term and the decisive actions of the Kohl government in dealing with the German reunification in the 1990s are examples of the decision capacity of certain types of political structures. We would argue that if Great Britain had the exact political institutions in the early 1980s that the United States had, and if the Thatcher government had come to power with exactly the same cast of characters that were present in Britain in the early 1980s, it would have been impossible to have pursued the economic reforms that the Thatcher government, in fact, pursued. We attribute the difference to the different capacities of models of the British parliamentary system and of the American presidential system.

The American presidential system, with undisciplined political parties and a congress that has developed its procedures to maximize the probability that incumbents will be reelected, does not have the capacity to deal effectively with the federal deficit. The authority of the American president, deriving as it does from the constitution, and not as majority control of a popularly elected house, has the capacity to act in a way the British Prime Minister cannot.

How does this apply to Egypt? The Egyptian government is a complex system of a number of powerful ministries, each deeply involved with some part of the economy. The Ministry of Industry supervises many of the publicly owned firms. The Ministry of Agriculture, as you have seen, is deeply involved in managing many aspects of agricultural production. The Ministry of Supply, which one suspects may in one incarnation or another have existed since the days of the pharaohs, is responsible for securing the supplies for the subsidized food system. The bureaucracies in these ministries have strong vested interests and also close ties with interest groups outside the government.

The kinds of reforms called for by the IMF affected the operation of a number of powerful ministries. Each one had reason to oppose the proposed reforms. The modifications in the proposed reforms that might satisfy one ministry would have made them worse for another. There was no general reform package that would not have enough powerful ministries opposed to prevent any action. The government did not have the capacity to decide to implement a general reform package. Its own employees could, when it was in their interest, tie up effective action.

12 CONCLUSIONS

The government's proposed reforms in the industrial and agricultural sectors studiously avoided any major modification of the food subsidy program. Even though it was clearly recognized that it would be difficult to deal effectively with the budget deficit and its economic consequences unless some changes were made, it would not act. The government perceived that it would not survive the mass demonstrations that would follow any significant change. It did not have the legitimacy required to push through a policy that at least in the short run would require sacrifices by the urban population. This is clearly the case of a government that would not act.

But in the other issues the outcome of the reform efforts were different. The government could not deliver an agreement with the IMF to realign the exchange rates, reform the capital market by increasing interest rates, reform the commodity markets, and make changes in taxes and fees that would reduce the budget deficit. It could, however, eliminate acreage quotas and mandatory deliveries at fixed prices on some key crops. It could raise interest rates on agricultural loans and eliminate many subsidies on agricultural inputs. Why is it that the government could act on the agricultural reforms and could not act on the foreign trade- and capital market-related reforms?

As was pointed out above, the realignment of the exchange rates created a significant price increase for the public sector that had received an implicit subsidy of an overvalued Egyptian pound. This could lead to the closing of publicly owned firms and loss of employment. Many ministries were affected and these bureaucrats in the agencies had good reason to coalesce to block effective action. The proposed capital market reforms also hit the public sector hard, as did the removal of price control on producers' goods for public firms. The interests within the government and public sector probably made it impossible even for an autocratic leadership with public and military backing to follow through on the proposed reforms.

Our description of the process by which acreage allotment was made suggests that many people were involved and threatened by the reform of these policies. Nevertheless, significant reforms in these policies were undertaken.

There are two major reasons why the agricultural reforms were successful. First, only a single government ministry was involved. Those who had reason to oppose the reforms could not find allies in other ministries. Indeed the increased production in grains that quickly followed reform had advantages for those in other ministries, such as the Ministry of Supply. Second, and more important, specific payments were made to the ministry following the successful implementation of each tranche of reform. These could be used to deal with the most threatened dislocations and may be looked upon as "political compensatory payments" or "side-payments." Information is not available on how those whose livelihood was threatened by agricultural reforms were prevented from stalling them. The fact that these reforms have not been stalled suggests the hypothesis that compensatory payments were used to alleviate their most negative impacts.

The bureaucracy in any governmental system with extensive public ownership and/or governmental intervention is in a powerful position to resist reform. It is not only responsible for policy implementation; it has, as pointed out above, some interests in common with others, particularly urban residents who may be short-term losers and thus in a position to form political coalitions.

The government bent on reform has, essentially, two options. It can dismiss those made redundant by reform and earn their opposition or it can "buy them off" in one way or another. Egypt, because the government is, in effect, the guarantor of employment for university graduates, would find it difficult to do only the former. But it could use grants to buy off those in the most crucial positions and use some of the product of increased efficiency to modify the impact of further reform on those who are in a position to block actions.

It is interesting to point out that both Japan and England in the early years of their industrialization bought off those who could effectively resist reform – the Daimyo and Suminsas in Japan and holders of sinecure offices in England.[19]

In the absence of external constraints, such as a foreign exchange crisis, we conclude that the Egyptian government will not act on reform measures if it anticipates mass demonstrations and cannot act if crucial interests in the bureaucracy are opposed. In the agricultural reform program, it found a way to neutralize that opposition, but the proposed foreign trade reforms were by a coalition within the government that had much to lose if they were enacted.

The government of Egypt has set its eye on further economic reform. It is unlikely that the Mubarak regime will have the kind of legitimacy that will enable it to take bold action that will trade off short-term dislocations and hardships for long-term stability and economic gain *without* a change in the perspective of urban populations, i.e., of labor surplus–food deficit urban households. A change in perspective of the impact of reform on household welfare may come about in a number of ways. Perspective may change to accept or tolerate reform if a program, supported by foreign assistance, compensates low-income households for the higher cost of food during the adjustment phase, while at the same time, building confidence that the cost of adjustment will eventually be rewarded with higher real incomes. At the other extreme, the government could take cautious steps that over several years would dramatically change the economic structure of the country, making it more productive and efficient. International financial institutions would likely need to help by making loans and grants contingent on measured successful reform. They must also, however, recognize the political obstacles to reform and, even in this case, allow financial resources to be used to help overcome the resistance of those made worse off in the short-term and of those faced with major adjustments as resources are reallocated from the public to the private sector of the economy, and from the production of home goods to the production of traded goods.

NOTES

Paper prepared for Ford Foundation–Duke University Project on the Political Economy of Structural Adjustment.

1   The material on the economic and political changes in Egypt contained in the following sections represents our interpretations of widely reported events. Particularly useful works are Waterbury (1988) and Springburg (1987).
2   Crosland (1956).
3   Waterbury (1988, p. 76).
4   Budget deficits of this magnitude generated surprisingly low rates of inflation. The explanation lies, in part, in foreign aid and grants to offset fiscal deficits.
5   Scobie (1983).
6   Dethier (1989, p. 53).
7   Schiff and Valdes (1992).
8   Dethier (1991, p. 34).
9   Dethier (1991).
10 Alderman et al. (1982).
11 This estimate was obtained in conversations with ministry of industry officials.
12 The following sections draw heavily on Dethier (1989).
13 Ministry of Agriculture and Land Reclamation (1989).
14 See Abdou et al. (1986).
15 Habushy and Fitch (1981).

16   Material on the Agricultural Production and Credit Project was gathered in interviews in USAID, Cairo, and in the Egyptian Ministry of Agriculture in February 1990.
17   Alderman et al. (1982).
18   Dethier (1989, pp. 131–57).
19   Holt and Turner (1966).

REFERENCES

Abdou, D., Gardner, V. D. and Green, R. 1986: "To Violate or not to Violate," *American Journal of Agricultural Economics*, 68 (I) 120–6.

Alderman, Harold, von Braun, Joachim and Sakr, Sakr Ahmed, 1982: *Egypt's Food Subsidy and Rationing System: A Description*, Research Report 34, Washington DC: International Food Policy Research Institute.

Crosland, C. A. R. 1956: *The Future of Socialism*, London: Jonathan Cape.

Dethier, Jean-Jacques 1989: *Trade, Exchange Rate, and Agricultural Pricing Policies in Egypt*, vol. I, World Bank Comparative Studies, Washington, DC: World Bank.

Dethier, Jean-Jacques 1991: "Egypt," in Anne O. Krueger, Maurice Schiff, and Alberto Valdes (eds.), *The Political Economy of Agricultural Pricing Policy*, vol. 3, Baltimore: Johns Hopkins University Press.

Habushy, N. and Fitch, J. 1981: Egypt's Agricultural Patterns, Research Paper No. 4, Cairo: Farm Management Survey Project.

Holt, Robert T. and Turner, John E. 1966: *The Political Basis of Economic Development*, New York: Van Nostrand, pp. 236–7, 242.

Ministry of Agriculture and Land Reclamation 1989: Report to the US Agency for International Development on the Tranche III Benchmarks for the Agricultural Production and Credit Project, July.

Schiff, Maurice and Valdes, Alberto, 1992: *A Comparative Study of the Political Economy of Agricultural Pricing Policies*, vol. 4, Synthesis: The Economics of Agricultural Price Intervention in Developing Countries, Baltimore: Johns Hopkins University Press, table 2.1 wd.

Scobie, Grant 1983: *Food Subsidies in Egypt: Their Impact on Foreign Exchange and Trade*, Research Report 40, Washington, DC: International Food Policy Research Institute.

Springburg, Robert 1987: *Mubarak's Egypt*, Boulder, CO: Westview.

Waterbury, John 1988: *The Egypt of Nasser and Sadat*, Cambridge, MA: Princeton University Press.

World Bank 1990–91: *Stars Data System 1990–91*, Washington, DC: International Economics Department, IBRD.

6

The Political Economy of Structural Adjustment in Ghana
J. Clark Leith and Michael F. Lofchie

INTRODUCTION

Ghana is a paradigmatic case of policy-induced economic atrophy. Following independence in 1957, the government implemented a set of economic policies that ultimately proved to be self-destructive. The policy thrust initially failed to generate sustained economic development.[1] Later the policies led to economic decline. While there were some relatively brief episodes of policy reform, the various civil and military governments which ruled the country for the first twenty-five years after independence continued the same general direction until April 1983. At that time the Provisional National Defense Council (PNDC), as Ghana's present government is called, initiated an Economic Recovery Program (ERP).[2]

By many objective indicators, the ERP has achieved considerable success. Real GDP stopped falling, and has resumed growth, with an average annual growth rate of 4.8 percent from 1983 to 1988. Even in the face of a population growth rate of 3.5 percent, there is modest real growth of per capita incomes. Exports, which in the early 1980s had fallen in terms of dollars, have recovered rapidly. The government deficit has been eliminated, and government consumption expenditures have grown from 6.5 percent of GDP to 10.6 percent (1987 versus 1982). The real level of many government services, especially in education and health, has been restored.

One of the more notable aspects of Ghana's structural adjustment program is its longevity compared with other prominent efforts at structural adjustment in Africa. Ghana's ERP is, at the present time (end of 1990), in its seventh year and the government remains officially committed to furthering the process of economic transformation.

The Ghanaian experience, first with economic atrophy and then with structural adjustment, casts considerable light on important issues of economic policy, and the interaction between economics and politics, in developing countries. To deal systematically with that experience and to be consistent with the intellectual agenda suggested by Professors Anne O. Krueger and Robert H. Bates, we consider the following broad topics:

Policy origination.   Why did the government of Ghana, following independence, implement a set of policies that were so manifestly inappropriate for economic growth?

Policy persistence.   (A) Why was the initial policy framework continued for so long, even after its damaging economic effects had become apparent? (B) The issue of policy persistence has an additional and, perhaps, more fundamental ramification. It is not simply a matter of why the initial policies were continued, but of why they were continued to the point where the entire economy sank to extreme deprivation.

Policy transformation.   Why, after so long a period of policy persistence, were the initial policies changed so abruptly beginning in 1983? This issue involves two subtopics. (A) What factors or circumstances led the government of Ghana to conclude that an economic change was essential? (B) Of the various economic changes possible, why did the government adopt an ERP based on orthodox economics?

What is the ERP?

Sustainability. How sustainable is the process of economic reform?

We will argue, among other things, that the interests created by the initial set of economic policies were an important determinant of the political choice of economic policies which were followed. Further, the extreme to which the Ghanaian policy-induced atrophy took the economy, beyond any kind of political optimum, was the outcome of a set of political institutions which permitted a "tragedy of the commons" to emerge. In the end, the economy and the state hit bottom, and both were rejuvenated by an economic reform program based on orthodox economic principles.

1   BACKGROUND MATERIALS

Political background

Ghana, a small African country with a 1990 population of about 14,000,000, became independent in March 1957. (See table 6.1 for a chronology of regimes and events.) By that time, its governing party, the Convention People's Party (CPP), had already held office since 1951 and its leader, Dr Kwame Nkrumah, had acquired an international reputation for his leadership of the Ghanaian anticolonial movement. At the time of its independence, Ghana was one of the most prosperous and promising of sub-Saharan Africa's new nation-states. With robust exports of cocoa, gold and timber, Ghana had accumulated foreign exchange reserves of over $500 million and Ghanaians then enjoyed a per capita income of about

Table 6.1 Chronology of regimes and events since World War II

1946	African majority in Legislative Council.
1948	Political agitation against 1946 constitution.
1951	New constitution granted internal self government; election won by Nkrumah in landslide.
1954	Further elections won by Nkrumah as prime minister, and again in 1956.
1957	Independence (March 6), Nkrumah as prime minister.
1960	Ghana becomes republic and Nkrumah president.
1964	Single-party (CPP) government.
1966	Military coup replaces Nkrumah and establishes National Liberation Council; Brigadier A. Afrifa initially commissioner of finance and later chairman.
1967	Devaluation of cedi from ¢0.71/US$ to ¢1.02/US$.
1969	Elections (August) and elected government led by K. Busia takes office (October).
1971	Devaluation of cedi from ¢1.02/US$ to ¢1.82/US$ (December).
1972	Military coup overthrows Busia government; establishes National Redemption Council with I. K. Acheampong, Chairman (January); revaluation of cedi to ¢1.28/US$; import and exchange controls tightened (February).
1975	Acheampong replaces NRC with all military Supreme Military Council.
1977	Inflation exceeds 100 percent for first time.
1978	SMC replaces Acheampong with General Akuffo (July); cedi devalued to ¢2.75/US$ (August); urban strikes and unrest (June 1978 to May 1979).
1979	J. J. Rawlings attempts coup (May), put on trial; mutiny of lower ranks replaces SMC with Armed Forces Revolutionary Council (June), headed by Rawlings; scheduled elections held (July), won by Limann who takes office (September); meanwhile campaign against corruption and black marketeering, Acheampong, Akuffo, and Afrifa executed, Makola market razed (June–October).
1981	Rawlings leads new coup (December 31), establishes Provisional National Defence Council government.
1982/3	Series of disastrous events – drought, fires, murders of judges, expulsion of Ghanaians from Nigeria; failed coup attempt (November).
1983	Economic Recovery Program launched (April); exchange rate devalued and unified at ¢30/US$ (October).
1986	Auction of foreign exchange begun (September); import licensing system abandoned.
1988	Foreign exchange bureaus established (February).

$300 per year. This made Ghana a middle-income country with a per capita income approximately equal to that of South Korea.

To understand fully the political and economic trajectory of Ghana following its independence, it is useful to take 1948 as a starting point. During the first two weeks of March, violent anticolonial protests erupted in the capital city of Accra. The causes of the riots lay principally in a reenforcing set of primarily urban discontents. Foremost among these were widespread unemployment among ex-servicemen and primary school leavers, a severe shortage of housing and a sharp rise in the cost of imported consumer goods. The volatility of the political forces unleashed by these factors constituted a powerful object-lesson for future governments: the key to political survival is to minimize the discontents of urban lower classes.

The CPP was founded in the aftermath of the 1948 protests and its early membership consisted largely of the urban social groupings whose grievances had given rise to them, not only the large numbers of unemployed ex-soldiers and school leavers, but low paid African civil servants such as teachers, clerical and hospital workers, custodial and service personnel and manual laborers.[3] The energies of the CPP were largely directed against the traditional elites who governed Ghana's large ethnic kingdoms, especially Ashanti where the bulk of the country's cocoa was grown.

The CPP government remained in power until late February 1966, when it was overthrown by the first of the military coups that have been a part of Ghanaian politics since. The new government, under Colonel A.A. Afrifa, called itself the National Liberation Council (NLC) and offered a series of justifications for its coup. Its indictments of the Nkrumah period began with a list of the CPP's political shortcomings, including the excessive concentration of power in the hands of a single person, the tendency for the government to act more and more oppressively toward its political opponents and critics, and the corrupt practices of high-ranking government officials. But at the basis of the coup was Ghana's serious economic decline since independence.[4]

The NLC thoroughly demolished the parliamentary bases of Ghanaian politics: it dissolved the CPP, suspended the constitution, closed down the national assembly and proscribed all other political parties. Indeed, the NLC went so far as to declare political activity illegal. In so doing, the NLC introduced a second object lesson into Ghanaian politics: the precondition for political reform is the complete dismantling of the previous regime. The NLC coup also revealed a profoundly important underlying dimension of Ghanaian political culture; namely, the tendency to assign the responsibility for poor economic performance on the corruption of the country's political leaders and on their managerial inadequacies, rather than the underlying policy framework.

The NLC returned Ghana to civilian rule in October 1969 after a few years of carefully setting the stage. A general election, held on August 24, was decisively won by a new political organization called the Progress Party (PP), which gained 105 seats in the newly constituted 140-seat National Assembly. Its principal opposition, the National Alliance of Liberals (NAL) won 29 seats and various minor parties won the remaining 6 seats.

The Progress Party coalition was significantly different from the CPP's coalition for independence. Though some oversimplification would be involved, it could be said that the PP's strongest support came from regions and ethnic elements for which cocoa production was of great economic importance. The PP had its support principally among Ghana's Akan peoples who inhabit Ashanti, Central, Western, and Brong-Ahafo regions. In the urban areas, it did not rely on the workers and other lower-income groups who had supported Nkrumah. Rather it drew more heavily on the support of the urban elite. The NAL's support came from regions and ethnic elements for which cocoa was not as central to the economic base, and was drawn predominantly from the country's Ewe peoples who inhabit the country's two southeastern regions, Eastern and Volta.

The PP government had been in power only slightly more than two years when it was overthrown in January 1972 by the second of Ghana's military coups and replaced by a new government that called itself the National Redemption Council (NRC). The NRC government, which renamed itself the Supreme Military Council (SMC) in 1975, governed Ghana for almost seven and a half years, until June 1979. The NRC/SMC period is remembered today for its high levels of official corruption and resort to inflationary finance. By steadfastly refusing to devalue, the NRC/SMC regime ushered in a period of extreme overvaluation of the currency. Indeed, one observer has referred to the Acheampong period in Ghana's political history as a "pinnacle of decadence."[5] Ghana's economic decline continued unabated throughout this period.

The NRC/SMC government made refusal to devalue a political sticking point, treating the exchange rate of the currency as a matter of national pride.[6] Its corruption and policy rigidity helped set the stage for the moral puritanism and intense reformism that inspired the junior officers' revolt of June 4, 1979 which first brought J. J. Rawlings to power and which continue to infuse his revolutionary ethos.[7] To demonstrate the depth of its commitment to an elimination of corruption, the new Rawlings government, which termed itself the Armed Forces Revolutionary Council (AFRC), executed a number of generals, including three former heads of state. The AFRC remained in power for only three months and, having held a previously scheduled general election during its first two weeks in office (June 18), it handed the reigns of government to a civilian administration in late September 1979.

Ghana's Third Republic was inaugurated on September 24, 1979. Political power was held by another new political party, the People's National Party (PNP) whose head was Dr Hilla Limann, an academic and former diplomat. According to Naomi Chazan, the PNP styled itself after the CPP and its leaders claimed to be following a socialist program based on Nkrumah's principles. This may have reflected the fact that their party had a social basis that was reminiscent of the CPP.[8] Its core support consisted of the urban unemployed, students, low-paid white-collar workers in government and business, and people dependent upon government contracts or protection. The Limann party also enjoyed strong support, however, from northern and western Ghanaians, ethnic elements that had been largely marginalized during previous administrations.

The Third Republic lasted for two years and two months and was overthrown by the second Rawlings coup on December 31, 1981. The reasons for its failure are myriad. At one level, the PNP government faced an utterly impossible set of tasks: to rebuild a set of parliamentary and legal institutions that had been officially discredited and cast aside during the period of military rule; to restore confidence in those institutions among a population made cynical and mistrustful by years of corruption but which was, simultaneously, expectant of immediate politicoeconomic improvements; and, perhaps most importantly, to deal with an economy in a state of utter collapse. At another level, it seems clear that the PNP was barely up to any of these objectives. Observers today tend to regard it as, at best, ineffective and, at worst, a mere repetition of the worst incompetence and corruption of the past.

The Limann government chose agricultural reform as its highest economic priority but, according to Gwendolyn Mikell, its efforts in this direction were particularly ineffectual.[9] The PNP, for example, did raise the producer price of cocoa beyond the international market price (at the official exchange rate) but, because of the weakness of other income-generating activity in the economy, in part due to the failure to adjust the exchange rate, this could not be sustained. In addition, the PNP seemed completely unable to do anything about the now decrepit state of the country's physical infrastructure, a fundamental constraint on agricultural recovery.

The new Rawlings government, which termed itself the Provisional National Defense Council (PNDC), has been in power since the 1981 coup. During its first 15 months in office, it sought to rebuild Ghana politically and economically by instituting a Libyan style socialist or "people's" revolution. When this failed to ameliorate the country's economic conditions or to attract external support, the PNDC initiated the present ERP in April 1983.

Economic background

Ghana's post-independence economic performance was dismal. The key economic data are outlined in table 6.2. For the first 17 years, real GDP per capita (figure 6.1) fluctuated around a level modestly above what existed at the time of independence.[10] Then began a period of significant and virtually continuous fall in real GDP per capita until the ERP.

One major source of the problem was the significant government budget deficit and inflation (figure 6.2). The latter, when combined with exchange

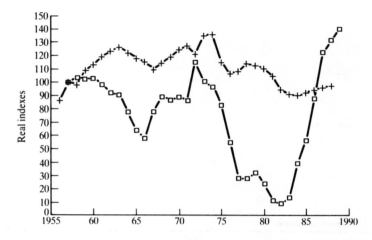

Figure 6.1   Real GDP/capita, 1955–89, (1957=100).□,cedis/SDR;+,GDP/capita

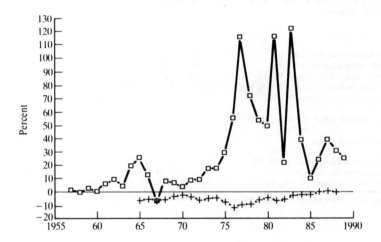

Figure 6.2   Inflation rate (□, %) and government budget/GDP (+, % of GDP)

rates fixed for long periods, generated one of the most severe reductions in the real exchange rate[11] ever recorded (see table 6.2) – to less than 10 percent of the real exchange rate at independence.[12] The currency was revalued by Acheampong immediately following the 1972 coup, and was not devalued again until the end of 1978, when the Akuffo government devalued by barely enough to keep the real exchange rate from falling further the next year. Despite the fact that increases in the money supply continued to spur a high rate of inflation, the nominal exchange rate

Table 6.2 Economic overview

	1960	1965	1970	1975	1976	1977	1978
I. Income and prices							
1. Real GDP (cedis b, 1985 prices)	225	268	313	334	323	33	358
2. Real GDP/capita (cedis, 1985 prices)	33,130	34,606	36,336	33,878	31,290	31,688	33,289
3. Rate of inflation (%)		26	4	33	63	108	74
II. External sector							
1. Merchandise exports (US$,m)	343	321	427	801	779	890	893
2. Merchandise imports (US$,m)	349	439	375	651	690	860	780
3. Current account balance (US$,m)	−48	−223	−68	18	−74	−80	−46
4. Nominal exchange rate (US$/cedi, avg.)	1.4000	1.4000	0.9800	0.8696	0.8696	0.8696	0.6601
5. Real exchange rate indicator (¢/SDR, 1957=100)	104	64	89	83	55	28	29
6. Real producer price of cocoa (1963=100)		66	59	51	35	20	21
III. Government sector							
1. Government expenditure (cedis, b)		0.378	0.487	1.211	1.606	2.228	3.290
2. Government revenue (cedis, b)		0.284	0.437	0.810	0.870	1.232	1.393
3. Deficit (−) or surplus (cedis, b)		−0.094	−0.050	−0.401	−0.736	−1.057	−1.897

Sources: IMF International Financial Statistics, for all but line II.6: Ghana Cocoa Board, for line II.6.

1979	1980	1981	1982	1983	1984	1985	1986	1987	1988	1989	1990
347	347	340	316	318	326	343	361	378	402		
33,065	32,295	30,743	27,535	26,681	26,346	26,969	27,654	28,243	28,430		
55	51	116	22	123	40	10	25	40	31	25	36
1066	1104	711	607	439	566	632	773	827	881	807	
803	908	954	589	500	533	669	713	952	993	999	
122	29	−421	−109	−174	−39	−134	−43	−97	−66	−98	
0.3636	0.3636	0.3636	0.3636	0.2899	0.0283	0.0185	0.0112	0.0068	0.0050	0.0037	0.0031
33	24	11	9	14	40	57	88	123	133	141	138.37
											34
27	27	13	31	· 14	17	23	34	37	49	43	
4.400	4.759	7.986	9.704	15.175	27.485	47.890	73.327	106.987	149.880		
2.600	2.951	3.279	4.856	10.242	22.642	40.311	73.626	111.046	153.791		
−1.800	−1.808	−4.707	4.848	−4.933	−4.843	7.579	0.299	4.059	3.911		

remained fixed until April 1983. It was unchanged, in other words, not only through the remainder of the NRC/SMC government, but for four years following it.

These declines were accompanied by severe deterioration in the quality of the country's educational and medical services which, by the end of 1982 functioned, for all practical purposes, in name only. For the vast majority of Ghanaians, it had become all but impossible to obtain education for one's children, or medical services for one's family. One Ghanaian respondent commented that, by early 1983, even senior civil servants were finding it difficult to obtain food.

Another victim of the economic deterioration was the forest. The extremes of poverty and shortages of imported fertilizers and fuels led to greater reliance on shifting cultivation and fuelwood. It has been estimated that by 1980 the total forest area was one-third of the area at independence.[13] The net result was a collapse of the country's morale and growing sense of political cynicism, brought about by the combined effects of all-pervasive corruption, an inflation psychology, and a ubiquitous desperation about the prospects of physical survival.

At the heart of Ghana's economic collapse was a decline in real foreign exchange earnings generated by the fall in the real exchange rate. In the case of cocoa, the principal export, the low real exchange rate was exacerbated by a bloated state Cocoa Marketing Board which further increased the wedge between the world value of the cocoa and the price paid to domestic producers of cocoa. By the time the ERP was launched, the real domestic producer price of cocoa had fallen to less than one-eighth of the price in the early 1960s, and the volume of cocoa exports had fallen to one-third of the level achieved in the early 1960s (see figure 6.3).

Figure 6.3   Cocoa prices and production (1963 = 100).□, Real producer price; +, total purchases

Ghana's economy, like that of most small predominantly agricultural societies, had always been highly dependent on the foreign exchange generated by exports. Foreign exchange was indispensable to the agricultural sector where virtually every piece of harvesting and transportation machinery as well as chemical inputs must be imported. Hard currency earnings were equally vital in the construction and maintenance of physical infrastructure. Road and railroad construction equipment, rolling stock and the electronic components for telephone, telegraph, and radio communication must all be imported as well.

The import-substitution strategy, however, created a situation where the country's supply of foreign exchange was not only subject to additional economic pressures, but likely to diminish over time. The new manufacturing sector, for example, consisted of industries which had to import practically everything they required from capital goods and replacement parts to the raw materials used to produce finished products. And the policies employed to promote these industries (protectionism, currency overvaluation) were biased against exports to a degree that diminished the country's foreign exchange earning capacity.

In April 1983, the Ghanaian government launched its ERP. The program was designed by a few Ghanaian technocrats, and was supported by the Bretton Woods Institutions (World Bank and IMF), as well as a number of bilateral donors. Ghana initiated a series of policy reforms intended to stimulate an economic recovery. Two of the major components were to eliminate the government budget deficit, and to restore a realistic real exchange rate. The program was effective in both respects (see figures 6.1 and 6.2).

Exports have recovered rapidly, due to both rising cocoa exports and increases in the exports of timber and gold. By the late 1980s, annual cocoa exports had begun to average about 300,000 metric tons, almost double the low figure of 1983/84 and nearly 60 percent higher than the 1981–5 average. Exports of Ghana's two other important exports, gold and timber, also began to rise and there was indication of a growth trajectory for nontraditional exports such as horticultural products.

Net overseas development assistance more than tripled from 1983 to US$375 million in 1987. Debt service payments were resumed and arrears eliminated. Total net long-term capital inflow of all types grew rapidly in the early years (see figure 6.5 below). This helped to finance a significant recovery of gross investment from 3.5 percent of GDP to 11.7 percent (1987 vs 1982).

Agricultural production also rose dramatically with marked increases in the production of both export and food crops. Due largely to increased supply, food prices began to fall and, since food prices account for a large proportion of the average Ghanaian's cost of living, this had a significant effect in producing an initial deceleration of inflation. Growth in manufacturing has averaged 14 percent a year, raising capacity utilization to 50 percent in many industries.

The longevity of Ghana's commitment to structural adjustment contrasts vividly, for example, with Zambia's, whose commitment to economic reform has been of an intermittent nature, with periods of policy reform interrupted, sometimes for long periods, by intervals of return to the earlier policy framework. Ghana also provides a striking contrast to Tanzania which, though officially committed to a process of structural adjustment since mid-1986, has found it difficult to implement fully certain of the most basic policy changes.

Despite all the foregoing positive results, it remains true that Ghana's real GDP per capita has not yet recovered even to the levels of the late 1970s. The ERP appears to be running out of steam. The set of policy reforms initiated in 1983 do not appear to be sufficient to generate a return to the levels of real income which Ghanaians enjoyed at the time of independence.

2   POLICY ORIGINATION

Nature of post-independence policy regime

Just as Ghana pioneered the African movement for independence from colonial rule, stimulating comparable movements in other African countries by force of example, during the late 1950s and early 1960s it also pioneered in the introduction of a set of economic policies that contributed to economic decline. To set the stage for our analysis of the reforms of the 1980s, it is helpful to understand the rationale for those economic policies. The principal thrust was a mixture of nationalism and socialism which associated industrialization with development.

Industrialization Policy   To promote development, modern industries had to be established. This, in turn, was to be accomplished with two instruments: a protectionist trade regime and state-owned enterprises.[14] The trade regime was to be used to promote the establishment of import-substituting industries (ISI).

The Ghanaian trade regime restricted imports through an increasingly cumbersome system of tariffs, quotas, exchange controls, and outright bans. The resulting structural transformation of the economy was rapid. From 1955 to 1969 manufacturing value added grew more than 16 percent per annum faster than GDP, both in nominal terms.[15] The import-substituting industries thus established typically utilized imported inputs and were devoted principally to the last stage processing of consumer goods for the small domestic market.

The strategy also involved the establishment of numerous state-owned enterprises as a vehicle to create modern industry and agriculture. The state enterprise was "seen as a means of reconciling Nkrumah's desire to modernize and develop the economy on the one hand, and to increase the degree of economic independence on the other."[16]

The state enterprise presence in major sectors of the economy was substantial. By the mid–1960s over one-quarter of Ghana's industrial value added (at protected prices) was generated in state or joint state–private enterprises.[17] Further, major state corporations had been established in farming, mining, construction, wholesale and retail trade, hotels, and airlines.

The critical difference between Ghana and many other developing countries did not lie in the strategy of industrialization as a means to achieve economic development but, rather, in the implementation. To illuminate this difference, it is useful to contrast Ghana's approach to industrialization with the theoretical version of how the strategy would work.[18] Several fundamental contrasts emerge, including the following.

(a) *Selection criteria.* Proponents of import substitution stress the need for industries to be carefully selected on the basis of explicit economic criteria such as the capacity to develop regional export markets. In Ghana, however, the number and range of industries chosen for protection were so vast that it is difficult to discern any economic criterion for the selection of industries that were protected.

(b) *Complexity and degree of protection.* The theoretical version of import substitution also calls for protection to be simple in form and limited in scope. Ghana's system of industrial promotion was a chaotic jumble, consisting of a bewildering assortment of cheap credit, state-owned enterprises, tariffs, import quotas, exchange controls, indirect taxes and outright import bans. As a result, it was virtually impossible to discern any economic rationale for the various forms or levels of support.[19]

(c) *Nature of industrial enterprises.* A natural and effective limit on the extent of the cost of import-substitution industries is private ownership. As developed in Ghana, however, import substitution was pursued through a system of state-owned enterprises (SOEs) and, as a result, there was often no limit on the costs of the firms.

Ghana's method of implementing import substitution practically insured that the operating results of the SOEs were dismal from the beginning. Even where state enterprises were granted monopolies, many made substantial losses.[20] The system was structured in such a way that losses were virtually inevitable. Since the SOEs typically enjoyed at least implicit budget guarantees from the central government, they had virtually unlimited borrowing rights from the banking system. There was a further practice of making up any operating deficits by an appropriation from the central treasury. For these reasons, the state enterprises introduced an extreme form of "moral hazard" into the society's fiscal and economic processes. They combined decentralized authority to spend with central responsibility to provide operating revenues.

In sum, the problem with the post-independence economic strategy in Ghana was not so much industrialization per se, but the utter indiscipline with which it was implemented. Industrialization was carried out not with modest protection of import substitutes, disciplined by some exposure to international competition, but by cutting Ghanaian industries off from virtually all international *and* domestic competition. Nor were SOEs disciplined by the hard budget constraint of the market place. The system was so chaotic that the Ghanaian government undoubtedly supported industries it had no intention of supporting and, in some cases, generated a system so extreme that some firms had negative value added even at domestic prices.

Exchange rate policy   Excess demand for foreign exchange emerged in the early 1960s as the result of failure to maintain macroeconomic control while persisting with a fixed nominal exchange rate[21] (see table 6.2). At this early stage, while foreign exchange reserves permitted the excess demand for imports to be met, the low real price of foreign exchange meant a cheapening of the cost of imported capital goods and raw materials for the import-substituting industries, thus encouraging capital- and import-intensity of production rather than the formation of industries that might have utilized the nation's most abundant and inexpensive factors, labor and natural resources.

As the foreign exchange reserves were exhausted, the authorities turned to rationing of foreign exchange to deal with the excess demand for foreign exchange. Those that wished to acquire foreign exchange to import goods were required to obtain an import license and, having done so, a foreign exchange allocation from the Central Bank. Initially the rationing of foreign exchange favored imports of raw materials and equipment for the import-substituting sector, and discriminated against use of foreign exchange to import goods competing with domestic production. The net result, then, was an increase in the degree of protection for the IS industries. However, it must be noted that the process of import license and foreign exchange distribution proved to be so haphazard that, while this general presumption was roughly correct, it was by no means uniform: the degree of protection was largely random. Some IS industries received very substantial protection from the combination of licensing and exchange control while others received very little protection.[22]

The real price of foreign exchange had fallen to about 70 percent of the independence level by the end of the Nkrumah period. While this cheapened the prices of tradable goods, since the IS industries were protected by the discriminatory application of the import licensing and exchange control policies, the major result was discrimination against the producers of exportable commodities. Inasmuch as Ghana's most important exportable item was cocoa, the most obvious economic impact of the depressed real price of foreign exchange was on the cocoa sector. The policy contributed the major portion of the decline in the real producer price of cocoa in the late Nkrumah period (see figure 6.3). Exchange rate policy under Nkrumah, then, provides a substantial part of the explanation for early decline in new planting of cocoa, and the ultimate decline in Ghana's cocoa exports.

The low real price of foreign exchange had comparable, if less spectacular, effects on numerous other exports as well. The real price of foreign exchange rate facing noncocoa exporters fell by over 35 percent from 1960 to 1966, and exports fell by roughly 20 percent in real terms over the same period.[23]

Currency overvaluation also affected the relative attractiveness of saving in local currency. Given a relatively low actual price of foreign currency, together with both a higher rate of return abroad and an expectation that the cedi would continue to decline in purchasing power relative to international currencies, savers naturally did everything possible to move their money abroad. Many succeeded.[24]

Agriculture policy The agricultural root of Ghana's economic stagnation merits particular notice.[25] The policy-framework just described involved transferring resources from the one sector capable of providing them; namely, agriculture and, in particular, export-oriented agriculture. The foreign exchange and tax revenues that for so long sustained Ghana's commitment to import substitution, state-owned enterprises, and currency overvaluation, that paid for the imported inputs required by the import-substituting industries, and that supplied the rents to consolidate the political system were, to a substantial degree, provided by agricultural exports.

For the principal Ghanaian export crop, cocoa, the procurement, transportation, storage, and international marketing were under the direct jurisdiction or control of the Cocoa Marketing Board (CMB). The CMB had been established in the colonial era as a means of stabilizing producer prices in the face of unstable world prices, and to deal with foreign trading firms. Under Nkrumah it was transformed into a state-owned enterprise, extending its activities beyond cocoa to include oil seeds, coffee, groundnuts, and bananas. From the early 1950s the share of cocoa revenue taken by government, both directly in the form of a tax and in the form of CMB costs, grew. The resulting decline in the real return to the producers has already been described. Under Acheampong and Limann even larger portions of the sales proceeds were taken by the CMB.[26]

The mechanism worked as follows. The tax on cocoa exports and producer prices in local currency were determined by the government and administered through the CMB. The cocoa exports generated hard currency, but local producers were paid in domestic currency, usually at substantially less than even the undervalued price of foreign exchange would dictate. There thus emerged three components of the wedge between the real value of the foreign exchange earnings and the local currency payments to the cocoa farmers: (i) the undervaluation of the foreign exchange earned from cocoa exports; (ii) the revenue paid to the government; and (iii) the bloated costs of the CMB.[27]

Why were inappropriate policies first pursued?

At independence, one of Ghana's principal goals was the achievement of sustained economic development. Yet the set of policies pursued following its independence failed to generate sustained economic development. This contrast between declared intention and actual accomplishments aroused Bates' classic conundrum: "Why should reasonable men adopt public policies that have harmful consequences for the societies they govern?"[28] This question has been extensively debated.[29] In the Ghanaian context, three approaches appear to have explanatory relevance. These are (1) urban bias, (2) dominant development ethos, and (3) transaction and agency costs.

Urban bias[30]   The dominant political coalition which decisively influenced Ghana's post-independence economic policies was composed of a number of urban-based social groups. As our discussion of Ghana's political background indicated, the politically active membership of the CPP, especially during its early years, consisted overwhelmingly of highly volatile urban elements, most notably returned servicemen, unemployed school leavers, and low-paid workers. The party's membership was also heavily comprised of a series of urban white collar groups which had particular occasion to unite in the struggle against colonial rule, especially lower-level civil servants such as teachers and clerical workers as well as urbanized professionals such as journalists and lawyers. In addition, the issues that galvanized the movement to political action were also of greatest concern in the urban context. These included unemployment, housing scarcity, the rising cost of consumer goods, and the lack of opportunity for upward career mobility in the civil service.

The urban bias approach suggests that the post-independence policy framework of the CPP government can be explained by its determination to pursue policies that would offer the greatest prospect of maintaining the loyalty of these volatile supporters. A variety of policies were employed to shift society's resources toward these groups and away from rural populations in a weaker bargaining position: (a) overvaluation of the currency; (b) suppression of producer prices of cocoa; (c) labor market policies; and (d) financial sector policies.

Overvaluation of the currency is, as we have noted, a "tax" on the export sector, much of which is rural. Overvaluation lowers the real price, of local currency, received by export producers. Overvaluation was also used in the early stages to provide cheap imported inputs to urban industries. Since no compelling economic criterion for the selection of industries could be discerned, we conclude that the real purpose of the protected industries was not only to generate the employment opportunities demanded by the growing numbers of school leavers and urban immigrants but also to provide high-ranking managerial and administrative posts demanded by the large numbers of educated Ghanaians who appeared otherwise to have limited career opportunity.

The functioning of the CMB provides perhaps the best illustration of the use of economic resources to gain or maintain the loyalty of important political supporters. It absorbed a large proportion of the value of the cocoa crop merely to sustain highly inflated levels of bureaucratic employment and remuneration scales that were utterly disproportionate to the level of development of the country. The CMB was not, as originally intended, a modality for price stabilization but an instrument of patronage, nepotism, and corruption for the country's leading politicians. Time and time again, critics of the CMB pointed out the perverse effects of these practices: the tendency for its costs to rise even as the crop volume it processed declined and the resulting tendency toward higher and higher per unit operating costs.[31]

The labor market policies of the post-independence Ghana government are also plausibly explained by the notion of urban bias. By providing a high degree of protection for the import-substituting sector, it was able to provide workers in those industries not only with a high level of wages (relative to productivity) but with a range of additional benefits including job security, generous termination allowances, and retirement benefits. The costs of Ghana's generous wage and benefit system were, of course, borne partially by both urban and rural consumers, who were forced to pay high prices (relative to international levels) for poor-quality goods, but principally by cocoa farmers whose export earnings provided the major financial basis for the entire system. It is not at all surprising that workers in protected industries have consistently been among the strongest opponents of economic reform.

Financial sector policies, particularly low real interest rates, have also discriminated in favor of the urban sector. Low or negative real interest rates create a transfer to the modern, largely urban, sector[32] (see figure 6.7 below for real interest rates.)

Dominant developmental ethos   A second explanation for Ghana's post-independence economic policies was the dominant developmental ethos of the early 1960s. Much of the economic theory of this era was characterized by a profound pessimism about the extent to which international trade might stimulate growth in the world's developing regions. The intellectual atmosphere of the early 1960s was very much dominated by economists such as Gunnar Myrdal, Raoul Prebisch, Ragnar Nurske, and Hans Singer. These thinkers shared a profound conviction that international trade would not contribute to the development of poorer countries. Hans Singer and Javed Ansari have summarized this position in the following terms:

> ...there are systematic forces at work in world markets which tend to reduce the gains of the poor countries in international trade; consequently, trade may actually widen the gap between the rich and poor countries. Furthermore, the adverse movement in the terms of trade of the poor countries transfers the benefits of technological innovations from the poor to the rich.[33]

During the 1960s, there was a vast outpouring of literature on the terms of trade between poor and developed countries. This literature tended to stress the adverse movement in the terms of trade for primary commodity exporters and, in the view of some, it tended to reinforce the idea that poorer countries would not maximize their prospects of economic growth by emphasizing the production of tradable commodities.

Pessimism about the extent to which trade could lead to economic development for poorer countries was widely shared across the intellectual spectrum and this helped contribute to its influence among the political leaders of developing nations.[34] This set of views, for example, was held by a number of economists who were particularly influential in Ghana. Of this group, none was as influential as W. Arthur Lewis, a personal economic advisor to Nkrumah on several occasions in the 1950s. For Lewis, the principal problem of development had to do with the low marginal productivity of labor in agriculture. Supplies of labor were basically unlimited, hence the central challenge was to find means to move labor from the low marginal productivity agricultural sector into a high marginal productivity sector, namely, industry. To accomplish this, Lewis advocated a government-led developmental strategy of industrialization.[35]

Lewis' emphasis on the need for a public policy of industrialization was powerfully reinforced by another economic viewpoint common during this period; namely, that African countries, Ghana included, lacked an entrepreneurial class of sufficient size and capital resources to promote a Western-style industrial revolution. This view was held and expressed by Barbara Ward who, as Lady Jackson, was the wife of Sir Robert Jackson who had been commissioner of development in Ghana. Her ideas reflected the intellectual climate of the day when she noted that

> [T]hroughout most of Africa today, you can count the number of effective African businessmen on two hands...Clearly an almost nonexistent entrepreneurial class can hardly launch the revolution of sustained growth. The men are quite simply not there to do it. This is the primary reason why we find a much greater emphasis upon government activity in raising the necessary savings today.[36]

The dominant intellectual atmosphere of the 1960s, then, combined two ideas: trade pessimism and a conviction about the weakness of the entrepreneurial class.

This atmosphere contributed greatly to the policy framework adopted by the Ghanaian government. The CPP's commitment to the idea of the state as a necessary generator of industrial growth and hence of expanded employment opportunity arose directly from the view that Africa lacked an entrepreneurial class capable of performing this function. And the withdrawal from world trade implicit in import substitution grows directly out of the trade pessimism of the era. Tony Killick has suggested that these ideas led to Ghana's choice of economic policy:

> ...[E]conomic strategy in Ghana was inspired by a vision of economic modernization similar to, and influenced by, that of many professional economists who were concerning themselves with the problems of underdeveloped countries: a "big push" primarily involving a major investment effort, a strategy...emphasizing import-substitution, and a less open economy, to be achieved largely through the instrumentalities of the state.[37]

According to Killick, a study of the dominant ideas in the development economics of the 1960s explains much of what occurred in Ghana during that period.

The prominence of industrialization via import substitution and state enterprises not only in the development theories of the early 1960s but in the economic practice of a significant number of non-Western countries seeking rapid economic growth, places Africa's commitment to this strategy in a different perspective. It suggests that the strategy did not grow out of urban bias but rather out of an intellectual acceptance of a widely discussed and, at the time, widely respected and practiced set of economic ideas. The industries may then have generated a network of urban constituencies whose political influence contributed to a *continuation* of the strategy. This interpretation, then, changes the order of cause and effect, suggesting that urban bias was the outcome, not the cause of import substitution.

Transaction and agency costs A further explanation of the initial post-independence set of policies is that the choice of taxes and transfers may be viewed as a rational response on the part of the government to transaction and agency costs facing it. Lacking the administrative capacity to impose and collect complex forms of revenue such as taxes on income, property, sales, or value added, or to distribute transfers such as social security, welfare, or in-kind payments, government turned to other instruments which made the collection of revenues and distribution of transfers less costly and more certain.

The new institutional economics sheds important light on this subject. Margaret Levi, for example, in her book *Of Rule and Revenue*, considers the economic basis of various systems of taxation. She defines "transaction costs" in the following terms:

> Transaction costs are the positive costs of bargaining a policy and of implementing a policy once it has been bargained. The most important transaction costs are those of negotiating agreements, measuring revenue sources, monitoring compliance, using agents and other middlemen, punishing the noncompliant, and creating quasi-voluntary compliance. A policy is not viable if the transaction costs are too high.[38]

A specific instance of transaction costs has to do with "agency costs"; that is, the personnel and operating costs of a government's tax-collecting mechanisms. As Levi points out, "agents can shirk and cheat, particularly at the point where they extract revenue and the point where they turn revenue over to rulers."[39]

The transaction and agency costs of collecting taxes and distributing transfers in predominantly peasant societies can be inordinately high. Peasants tend to receive the bulk of their income during a fairly brief period of time, the weeks immediately following a harvest season. But a tax bureaucracy, by its very nature, must be maintained on a year-round basis. Individual peasant incomes are very low relative to the salary levels and other costs of government agents. Peasant farmers, moreover, can easily conceal much of their income from bureaucratic inspection, thereby raising the costs of monitoring and insuring compliance to exorbitant levels.

Given all these characteristics, the factor of transaction and agency costs provides an explanation of why many African governments including that of Ghana chose at an early stage to use particular mechanisms for extracting resources from peasant producers and transferring those resources to other sectors of the economy.

Two major elements of the policy mix are consistent with this explanation. The first is suppression of the real price of foreign exchange. It reduces the price that export producers receive for their products, and transfers the surplus to the recipients of the foreign exchange proceeds. The second is more direct: suppression of producer prices through the use of state monopoly systems of crop procurement, processing, and distribution. Compared to the transaction and agency costs of other forms of taxation, these methods appear to governments to be low cost. The ratio of transaction costs to revenue collected is low and the proportion of resources collected that actually makes its way into the government treasury and other intended destinations is relatively high. Indeed, the fact that some of these methods of extracting revenue do not have to pass through the treasury may be viewed by some in government as a distinct advantage. A tax that can be levied and directly turned over to the intended recipient does not have to be accounted for on either the receipt or the expenditure side, and does not have to be defended within government or in public.

The argument that government is rational in resorting to these taxes is, however, very much a partial equilibrium argument. It fails to take into account the damage the policy set does to the economy as a whole. We will return to this problem below.

3 WHY DID INAPPROPRIATE POLICIES PERSIST?

The economic policies set in place in the late 1950s and early 1960s may have appeared to have some element of validity to the governments of the time. But these policies were maintained in place long after it had become obvious that they had not only failed to help Ghana achieve rapid economic growth, but, indeed, that they had produced a calamitous economic collapse. In view of this experience, it is critical to ask why Ghana's governments remained committed for so long to this policy framework. Several factors help explain this policy persistence.

Persistence of the original reasons

To some degree, policy persistence can be explained by factor persistence. The factors which explained why Ghana initially chose the approach to development through a controlled trade regime – urban bias, the influence of dominant economic ideas, and the low direct transaction and agency costs of particular forms of taxation – all continued to be important throughout the 1960s and 1970s. But persistence of the original reasons is probably not enough to explain policy persistence, for there was growing evidence that those policies were not generating sustained growth.[40] Something more must have been at work to explain why the policy thrust continued.

Outcomes of original policies

Policy persistence was not independent of the initial set of policies, however. Part of the explanation of policy persistence lies in the effects which the original policies had on the structure and strength of political interests in the country. Many of the policies which were initiated in the 1950s and 1960s created larger, better organized interest groups with tangible vested interests in maintaining those policies. These new interests were both larger and far more intense than the interests which led to the adoption of the policies in the first place. Merilee Grindle's analysis aptly sums up the point in the following manner: "Relatively autonomous in their choice of policy at the outset, they [African leaders] soon become captive of the beneficiaries of the policies they have introduced and lose their capacity to alter policy."[41] The winners from inappropriate policy, then, gain sufficient power to demand the perpetuation of policies that benefit them.

Urban interests   The initial policy regime both rewarded urban interests and led to the growth of the urban sector. Urban interests thus became a powerful force for the maintenance of the initial policy thrust. In other words, the urban factor is more helpful in explaining the *persistence* of inappropriate policies than in explaining their origin.

There is an important methodological issue here concerning timing and order of precedence. Do powerful clienteles such as urban interest groups use their leverage to insist upon policy choices that reflect their economic and other interests? Or does a policy choice precede and then bring about the rise of a set of clienteles which then insist upon its continuation? Part of the answer to this question would require the resolution of methodological conflicts that are far beyond the range of this research. A precise answer to the question of timing and precedence would also require a detailed analysis both of the latitude of policy choice available to the Ghanaian government upon attaining independence and of the timing of the emergence of the associational and other clienteles for its chosen policy framework.[42]

The political literature on Ghana does not specifically address itself to this question. But some guidance is available. The most authoritative research on Ghanaian politics during the 1960s is that of Naomi Chazan, whose book, *An Anatomy of Ghanaian Politics*, provides a wealth of detailed information about the whole range of associational and ethnic interest groups that populated the Ghanaian political arena during that period.[43] While Chazan, like other authors on Ghanaian politics, does not specifically deal with the question of urban bias or the order of precedence question, the evidence it includes does provide a partial answer.

Chazan's analysis of the sequence of post-colonial political events in Ghana is that the CPP actively sought out and created clienteles for its economic policies. When the post-colonial CPP government assumed power, it began to initiate a policy framework of trade restrictions and import substitution. This policy gradually built a series of highly protected industries in such areas as textiles, tinned beverages, cigarettes, construction materials, footwear, and other easily manufactured items such as office supplies. As these industries developed over time, their owners, managers, investors, and workers came to constitute a sizable constituency for policies that would benefit them economically.

As Chazan describes Ghana, then, the policy of controlled trade and import substitution preceded the clienteles that quickly came to support it. Her analysis strongly suggests that the Nkrumah government and others that followed it (except, possibly, that of K. Busia, 1969–72) actively encouraged or permitted the formation and organizational development of groups that benefited from, and therefore depended upon, its policies, while discouraging or even banning those that had occasion to be opposed.

One reason why the CPP government sought so hard to establish a relationship to the trade union movement that was partly based on patron–client ties and partly on legalized coercion, had to do with the fact that the most powerful workers' groups in the country were initially opposed to its restrictive trade policies. One brief example may help to illustrate this point. At the time of independence in 1957, Ghana's organized working class was primarily connected to and dependent upon the health of the export sector, cocoa, timber, and manganese. The most powerful and well organized labor union in Ghana was the Sekondi-Takoradi Railway and Harbour Workers Union whose membership consisted almost entirely of the workers who shipped and loaded these commodities. This union, which had been formed prior to World War II, was a product of the country's powerful commitment to an export orientation and its ongoing interests clearly lay in the direction of a continuation of a trade-based economic strategy that would include strong government support for the export sector. In furtherance of that objective, the Railway and Harbour workers aligned themselves with the opposition United Party.[44]

During the early years following independence, the country's manufacturing workers, who later became a powerful constituency for a controlled trade regime and import substitution, were small in number, organizationally weak and lacking in a clearly articulated set of economic interests. The unions in the manufacturing sector arose in tandem with the growth of import-substituting industries.

The tendency to create interest groups which might serve as props for the regime and its policies was further abetted by the organizational character of the CPP. Despite the somewhat monolithic appearance created by its radical ideology and rhetoric, Ghana's governing party was, in fact, a highly fragmented organization whose leadership was heavily individualistic. To gain a position within the elite and to remain in power, ideological solidarity was inadequate. Individual leaders had to have structured relationships with important social constituencies that they could claim to represent, constituencies that could boost their candidacy for high office. This was, in fact, the basis of the well documented patron–client dimension of political power in Ghana. It meant that individual leaders who aspired to higher positions with the party or government or who simply wanted to increase their influence had a strong incentive to stimulate the formation or growth of organizations with which they could ally.

The upshot of these observations is that the emergence of some of the social constituencies that supported the policy framework of industrialization in Ghana followed the initiation of the policy. This perspective partially reverses the order of cause and effect suggested by the concept of urban bias: urban bias may be as much an *outcome* of import substitution as it is a *cause*.

If Ghanaian political leaders were, as Grindle suggests, relatively "autonomous at the outset," a larger burden of explanation for the initial adoption of industrialization via import substitution and state-owned enterprises, as well as of the willingness of the Ghanaian government to continue that policy thrust for a sustained period of time, would have to do with its having been the dominant developmental ethos of the 1960s. To the degree that Ghanaian leaders then lost this autonomy owing to the growth of interest groups, the urban interests constitute a substantial part of the explanation of policy persistence.

New sources of finance for government and politics   It is arguable that until the early 1970s the economic policies of the various Ghanaian regimes were inappropriate to achieve sustained economic growth, but that they were not yet self-destructive. By 1975 something fundamental had changed: persistent and high inflation had appeared, and real per capita income had begun its long decline.

The factors we have thus far identified as explaining policy origination and persistence, however, do not explain why the Acheampong regime moved from policies which redistributed the national pie (albeit at the price of economic stagnation) to policies which *reduced* the national pie. The question remains, therefore, why would political leaders pursue a set of policies that had transparently destructive effects on their country's economic base? In Bates' book, the answer to this question lay in the contradiction between the interests of governing elites (survival, state resources, sustaining coalitions, etc...) and the policy requisites of economic growth.[45] Political leaders were not acting irrationally or unreasonably in imposing the policies they did. While they were arguably implementing a set of economic policies that were not in the collective economic interest, those same policies were generating political support and were thus in the private interests of members of the regime.

Two new dimensions to the economic policy package emerged in the first half of the 1970s: reliance on the "inflation tax" and the generation of significant quota rents. Both had their roots in the earlier policy mix – especially overvaluation of the currency – and both can be explained in terms of the governing regime.

(1) *Inflation tax.*   Inflation had first emerged in the later Nkrumah years, but had been kept under control by both the NLC and Busia governments. However, from the first the Acheampong government was prepared to tolerate significantly higher inflation (see figure 6.2). This generated resources for it in the form of the "inflation tax." The tax arises because holders of money lose the real value of their asset, while the issuer of the money, the Central Bank, collects the tax in the form of reduced real value of its liabilities, in this case the base money stock. The inflation tax emerges when government commandeers resources from the Central Bank in excess of the seigniorage on the issue of new money.

The inflation tax, like currency overvaluation, can also be thought of as a myopically rational response by government to the transaction and agency costs of collecting taxes by other means. It is easily imposed and, because it does not involve the creation and maintenance of an additional bureaucracy, not only has minimal transaction costs but is less susceptible to revenue dilution through side-payments between bureaucrats and their clients than virtually any other form of taxation. An additional attraction of the inflation tax for governments is that it imposes taxation on groups not fully reached by overvaluation and the agricultural parastatal system; namely, urban wage-earners. Like overvaluation and producer price controls, however, the inflation tax also bears heavily on peasant export crop producers because they are captives of a cash system, while urban dwellers can find alternatives to money through barter.

Beginning in 1973 the inflation tax became an important additional source of resources for government. It quickly preempted a substantial share of GDP for government (see figure 6.4). When inflation pierced 100 percent for the first time in 1977, government extracted 7.6 percent of GDP from this source. Even though inflation rates later exceeded the rate of 1977, the response of the holders of money to the tax, naturally, had reduced holdings of money. Hence, the ratio of the base money stock to GDP declined, reducing the share of GDP available to be extracted by the inflation tax.

(2) *Rents.* Until the Acheampong government, reliance on an overvalued currency and suppression of the real producer price of cocoa did not appear to be permanent features of the policy and political landscape. Both the 1967 and the late 1971 devaluations corrected for past inflation, and restored the real exchange rate to roughly its independence level. While the real producer price of cocoa was not restored to its heights of the early

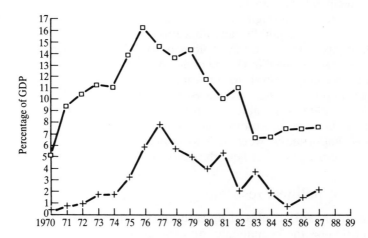

Figure 6.4   Inflation tax.□, Money stock; +, inflation tax; both as percentage of GDP

1960s, the extreme erosion of the real producer price that was to follow was not yet evident.

Perhaps the political support-generating potential of the policy mix may not have been entirely appreciated initially. However, under Acheampong, as the policies which had been initiated by earlier regimes for other purposes started to show their potential as political devices, the resistance to policy reversal stiffened. Policies which gave rise to political resources were retained in spite of the evident negative economic consequences.

Foreign exchange rationing, import licensing, and state-owned enterprises (including the CMB), all created resources for the political system to appropriate. Members of the political elite, first and foremost, were able to enrich themselves personally. In addition, they were able to provide jobs, subcontracts, import licenses, and foreign exchange licenses for political friends, clients, and supporters. It was, in effect, a system capable of generating massive transfers to the members and supporters of the regime.

This is aptly illustrated with the case of the overvalued currency. Excess aggregate demand policies with a fixed nominal exchange rate lead to balance of payments difficulties, represented by excess demand for foreign exchange at the official exchange rate. When reserves were exhausted, some mechanism to ration the scarce foreign exchange was required. Economically, a higher exchange rate or a tariff would have accomplished the end of limiting the demand for foreign exchange, but the use of detailed allocation of foreign exchange offered an important political advantage. Administrative allocation of foreign exchange meant that a scarce item was distributed at a price that was well below its scarcity value to the recipient. The value of the scarce foreign exchange over and above what the recipient formally had to pay for it is the quota rent.[46] The person who distributed the foreign exchange also distributed the complementary quota rents. More generally, any allocation mechanism which distributed valuable rights at less than their true scarcity value also distributed rents.

As the system evolved in Ghana under Acheampong, the distribution of the rents became central to the management of the scarce foreign exchange, import licenses, and state-owned enterprises. The members of the political elite were able to provide jobs for political friends and supporters, lucrative subcontracts for political contributors and associates, and, most importantly, were able to enrich themselves personally. The rents became the glue that held the political system together.

Absence of political resistance

If a straightforward calculus of short-term costs and benefits to incumbent regimes provides the beginning of an explanation of policy persistence, it does not explain why Ghana's economic losers were so passive. Since the socioeconomic conditions of the vast majority of people in Ghanaian society were deteriorating badly, it seems surprising that there was so little political opposition, especially from those who were the objects of the government's most invasive predations, namely, the export-oriented cocoa farmers. Three factors help explain this phenomenon.

Collective action The political quiescence or acquiescence of these farmers arose from that most classic of difficulties, the problem of collective action. Part of the cocoa farmers' difficulty had to do with sheer physical distance from the capital. If urban bias is partly the product of simple proximity to the heart of political power on the part of some groups, it is to be expected that farmers will be at a relative disadvantage because of the difficulty they have in making their presence felt in the capital city. Ghana's cocoa farmers were not only widely dispersed throughout the countryside, being distributed over four of the country's largest regions (Ashanti, Volta, Brong-Ahafo, and Western) but physically distant from Accra, the capital city.

Because of the country's poor infrastructure, which in fact became progressively worse as economic conditions deteriorated, the costs of forming and maintaining a political organization would have been prohibitive. Such costs would have included the need to rent and equip office space in the capital, to employ a fairly permanent staff including paid lobbyists, and to provide for travel back and forth between farmer representatives and their rural constituencies.

Efforts to enable Africa's rural populations to become politically effective have also been hampered by well-documented organizational difficulties such as the "free rider" problem and the problem of "agency." The former has been painfully evident in Ghana. It arises precisely because the costs and difficulties of forming rural organizations are so high relative to the prospective gains for the individual farmer. In this circumstance, individual farmers inevitably have a strong temptation to hold back, hoping to share in the economic gains while allowing others to incur the costs of political mobilization.

African rural organizations have also foundered because of chronic problems of agency. The political efforts of these organizations have been stymied by leaders who compromise the purposes of the organization for personal gain, who engage in corruption or other forms of mismanagement, or otherwise dissipate their organizations' energies and financial resources.

Collective action was further deterred by the great social diversity of the cocoa farmers. As Polly Hill's work has shown, Ghanaian cocoa farmers represent a highly differentiated group ranging from a small number of large estate-scale farmers who derive considerable wealth from cocoa, to the vast majority of cocoa farmers who were basically middle or smallholder farmers.[47] Hill's work goes so far as to suggest that there were very real class differences among cocoa farmers, with some needing to supplement their cocoa income by becoming migratory agricultural laborers while the large cocoa farmers were able to hire migratory labor to tend and cultivate their trees. Social differentiation among cocoa farmers was so great that, according to Hill, the very "concept of the cocoa farmer could be rather elusive."[48] Not only would Ghana's cocoa farmers have experienced the economic downturn very differently, but the considerable socioeconomic differences among them would have made it difficult to establish an agreed upon set of economic interests on which they could unite.

Vast numbers of Ghanaian cocoa farmers also enjoyed secondary or even tertiary sources of income. Some were low-paid agricultural workers on farms belonging to others but many had additional employment as local civil servants, school teachers, or officials in the cocoa organizations. Some of the more successful cocoa farmers had developed secondary business interests in transportation, construction, small-scale manufacturing, hotel-keeping, or in the local mercantile sector as merchants and traders. For some, these businesses had become so large that cocoa farming was, in fact, their secondary occupation. The tendency toward economic diversification complicated the problem of political action not only by insulating cocoa farmers somewhat from the effects of the country's predatory agricultural policy, or diverting their energies and attention, but because it meant that political action would often expose other economic assets, sometimes primary ones, to great risk.

Exit not voice   Perhaps the major explanation for the political acquiescence of the cocoa farmers, however, was the relative ease of "exit" from the officially controlled economic system. In Ghana, exit could assume any one or combination of several different forms. Cocoa farmers relatively close to the country's borders with Ivory Coast or Togo could, because of the corruptibility of the customs and other border services, smuggle their produce fairly easily into these two countries. The neighboring countries, all Francophone, were especially attractive destinations for smuggled cocoa because, due to their participation in the franc zone, their currencies were not as overvalued. In addition, the Ivory Coast imposed far lower taxes on cocoa. As a result of these factors, neighboring countries tended to offer higher real prices for cocoa than Ghana's throughout the 1960s and 1970s.

By its very nature, smuggling eludes official observation and recording and there are, therefore, no precise figures for the amount of cocoa that would have been smuggled out of Ghana during those years. But some observers suggest that as much as 50,000 to 60,000 metric tons per year may have left the country during the mid to late 1970s, a figure that, if correct, would represent 15–20 per cent of the country's production during that period.[49]

Cocoa farmers could also have exited the official economy by shifting their resources from cocoa production to the production of local food crops whose prices were not controlled by the government. This form of exit may well have been far more substantial than slowly declining official production figures for cocoa suggest. As a tree crop, cocoa is far slower to respond to the withdrawal of vital inputs than such annual export crops as tobacco or cotton. As a result, cocoa farmers continued to harvest bearing trees even while devoting the bulk of their energies, inputs, and other resources to the cultivation of maize, cassava, and yams. Indeed, since a cocoa tree begins to bear after five years but continues to do so for another 20, the downturn in cocoa production in the late 1970s reflected, in large part, a withdrawal of farmers' energies that began in response to falling real producer prices as early as the first half of the 1960s.[50]

The most visible form of exit from the Ghanaian economy was out-migration. During the 1970s, more than a million Ghanaians left the country, many of them semi- or unskilled workers from the rural areas, including the cocoa regions. The overwhelming majority of these workers went to Nigeria, where they were relatively easily absorbed into the labor force because of the economic boom generated by rising oil prices. But many went to other West African countries such as Liberia and Sierra Leone. Vast numbers of the Ghanaian intelligentsia, including huge numbers of its doctors, scientists, and academics, became more or less permanent immigrants in Western Europe or North America, some of them forming vocal opposition groups to criticize trends within Ghana. Often, the remittances from Ghanaians abroad helped ease the economic strain on their families at home.

Much of the out-migration from the cocoa sector also assumed the form of internal migration within Ghana, as tens of thousands of Ghanaians responded to the economic incentive to move to the import-substitution sector, and to the country's innumerable parastatals including the Cocoa Board. The availability of these opportunities for economic exodus helped to reduce the pressure in the internal political environment. More importantly, the sheer vastness of this out-migration reflected a political and economic situation in which exit had become an easily available and highly preferable political option to internal opposition against the government.

Political repression and side-payments Internal political opposition was also lowered by the government's ability to repress rural political organizations. Starting with Nkrumah, successive regimes found it comparatively easy to prevent rural protest groups from emerging.[51] Combine these considerations with the fact that various Ghanaian governments have been adept in developing systems of "side-payments" that benefit the larger farmers who might potentially have organized and led political protest (for example, subsidies for spray machines and chemical pesticides, free tree planting through the agricultural extension service) and that they have been prepared to accommodate themselves to important noneconomic values of interest to the cocoa farmers (the preservation of traditional political institutions) and insurrection would be the surprising political phenomenon, not its opposite.[52]

Why persistence beyond an optimum?

So far we have explained why a set of policies which have net negative economic consequences for the nation might nevertheless be pursued by a political regime. As long as the members of the political regime are able to benefit from the rents generated by the economic policies, and the costs of the economic policies to the members of the regime are not large, the regime quite rationally, in terms of its personal interests, accepts the cost to the nation of economically destructive policies.

Indeed, from the personal point of view of the regime's members, there is an optimum degree of intensity of the economic policies which generates the greatest net benefit to the political regime. This is a standard monopolist's profit maximization problem. The optimum degree of policy intensity for the political regime would be the point at which the (rising) marginal costs equaled the (declining) marginal benefits from the policy intensity, where costs and benefits are *as viewed by the members of the regime*.

Yet this optimum appears to have been totally ignored as policies were pushed to a point of such utter economic devastation that there was scarcely anything of value left to distribute. Why were the policies pushed so far beyond any reasonable politicoeconomic optimum (from the point of view of the regime)?

The critical distinction here is between adoption of policies which generate resource transfers or "rents," and pursuit of such policies to the point where the rental yield becomes nil or negative. A metaphor drawn from the real estate industry may help to frame this question in a more exact way. No reasonable landlord would raise rents to the point where the building was emptied or so otherwise ruined that its rental value became nil. Yet this appears to be exactly what occurred, thus denying the regime further benefit from the rental stream. A combination of factors suggests why.

"Tragedy of the commons"   The first reason why the rent disappeared has its parallel in the well-known "tragedy of the commons" problem.[53] A common property resource, such as the village common, is a type of public good to which access is free, but which has finite benefits. If one individual uses more, less is available for others to use. Each individual has the incentive to ignore the effect of his use of the finite resource on others, and use the finite resource to the point where the marginal gain to the individual equals the marginal cost to that individual. For example, as long as a villager's cow can find some food, the villager will graze his beast on the common, even though the additional cattle on the common will reduce

the fodder available to all the other cattle. Since all villagers do this, the result is overgrazing of the common. If the village as a collectivity were to maximize its net return from the common, it would limit the grazing to a point where the net benefit to the collectivity is maximized. Such a point is where the marginal cost to the village as a whole in terms of decreased grazing equals the marginal benefit in terms of an increased cattle population on the commons. This is exactly the same utilization that a profit-maximizing individual private owner of the grazing land would choose.

The parallel of the commons in the case of the Ghanaian economy is the pool of rents attributable to the set of economic policies. The rent pool was finite. The political regime, in turn, appears to have granted all rent-seekers unlimited access to the pool of rents. Rather than limit access to the rents, thereby maximizing the value of the rents which, in turn, would have been worth the most in maintaining its support coalition, the regime appears to have tried to extend its support base by extending access to the rent pool.

If, in addition to the finite size of the rent pool, the individual rent-seekers have rising marginal costs of gaining access to the pool, they will continue to seek the rent to the point that their (rising) marginal costs of seeking the rent equal the (declining) marginal benefits in terms of rent.[54] The result, then, is that in equilibrium the rent will be exhausted. Thus, allowing unlimited access to the rent pool did not simply mean that the average size of the rent to an individual rent-seeker declined; it meant that the greater the number of rent-seekers allowed access, the less the aggregate rent.

Why the regime failed to recognize the fact that unlimited access to the rent pool could ultimately consume much of, or in the extreme, all of the rent remains to be explained. In part, the explanation may lie in the fact that many of the institutions which provided access to the rents were in place from an early stage, long before the extreme form of rent-seeking emerged. Thus, state-owned enterprises emerged from early in the Nkrumah period. In the later Acheampong period these enterprises were a major conduit of access to the rents. Similarly, the Cocoa Board, which had been in place in the colonial period, under Acheampong became a significant conduit for distribution of rents to the supporters of the regime. A third channel was the military itself, again an institution which had been in place long before. It is alleged that senior military officers were given preferential access to foreign exchange, and as the military expanded, the access to the rent pool expanded. Finally, the civil service may also have been a channel through which virtually unlimited access to the rent pool was allowed in the later years of the old regime.

Shrinking of the rent pool A further reason why the policies were pushed to the point where the rent disappeared has to do with the reliance on policies which shrank the rent pool itself. Again, the basic policy thrust was established at an early stage: the maintenance of a fixed exchange rate in the context of rising domestic prices. However, such a policy thrust has different effects on rent, depending on how severe the degree of overvaluation of the currency. It is convenient to think in terms of three phases of overvaluation.

In the initial phase, overvaluation simply means that importers are able to purchase foreign goods cheaply, and exporters are forced to accept a lower price for their exports, both in terms of local currency. At this stage, there are no premiums due to the quantitative restrictions (QRs), and hence no rents from the overvalued currency. Later, in the second phase, as the foreign exchange reserves are exhausted, because the entire excess demand for foreign exchange cannot now be met, rationing of the available foreign exchange has to occur, and QR premiums (i.e., rents) begin to emerge. In this phase, increases in the degree of overvaluation mean that the rents increase. However, as the degree of overvaluation continues to increase, a third phase is entered as the size of the rents eventually begins to decline. (This is the same effect that arises when tariffs are raised beyond the revenue-maximizing tariff.)

Movement through the second phase, where the rent pool initially increased, into the third phase, where the size of the rent pool declines due to the deterioration of foreign exchange earnings, appears to have occurred around 1977. By 1977 the real price of foreign exchange had fallen to less than 25 percent of the real price after Acheampong's revaluation of 1972. As a result foreign exchange earnings began to decline, which in turn left less in the way of foreign exchange to distribute to the rent-seekers. Imports in terms of foreign currency declined from 1977 to 1978 and again from 1978 to 1979. The Limann government, mostly by increasing payments arrears and short-term borrowing, increased imports again, but this strategy could not last: imports in 1982 plunged to two-thirds of their 1981 level.

Depending on what was happening to the scarcity value of the licenses, it is probable that the rents available as political glue were shrinking as imports shrank.

Increased political discount rate   A third explanation of why policies persisted beyond the optimum may lie partly in another concept suggested by Margaret Levi, the idea of the political "discount rate." Levi defines this notion in the following terms:

> Rulers' discount rates – that is, how much present value future returns have for them – are another major factor in the calculation of the costs and benefits of a policy choice. Rulers with high discount rates care little for the future. They will be less concerned with promoting the conditions of economic growth and increased revenue over time than with extracting available revenue even at the risk of discouraging output.[55]

Anyone even faintly familiar with the political economy of African governance will find the relevance of this observation immediately striking. African governments generally have very high discount rates: because of political instability, they strongly discount the future worth of their political assets. As a result, long-term economic growth has less valence in the day-to-day policy decisions of political leaders than the immediate need to build and maintain a viable day-to-day political coalition.

Ghana's discount rate would have been especially high since the mid–1960s because of the tendency toward rapid and unexpected regime changes and the high incidence of military coups. For military coups tend to shorten the time horizon of all governments that follow them since they create an environment in which political leaders can no longer expect to retain custody of their assets so long as they choose to do so. Once an unexpected military coup had terminated the Nkrumah regime, no Ghanaian government could possibly feel secure about its survival prospects. As the discount rate rose – regimes thinking of their political survival as more and more likely to be short-lived – political leaders may well have been inclined to seek even greater levels of rent-extraction as a kind of risk premium for rulership even though this might further accelerate the long-term structural process of economic decline.

The discount rate has a direct bearing on the question of why governments resist policy reform even under the most adverse economic circumstances. A policy reform involves a present cost to the regime for an expected future benefit. If the expected future returns are heavily discounted, then the regime is less likely to be willing to accept those present costs.

One important aspect of structural adjustment in developing countries is the extent to which it has become associated with short-term economic privation, at least for some important groups in the society. Indeed, most students of structural adjustment accept the premise that the pains of economic change become apparent well before the benefits begin to materialize: the losers appear before the winners do. Although economic reforms can be expected eventually to improve the material well being of a society as a whole, most political leaders believe that its immediate impact is to generate increased political opposition.

Since the first losers will tend to be the various clienteles that have been associated with the old regime (workers in protected industries, rent-seeking bureaucrats and politicians, traders with privileged access to foreign exchange, etc.), their deprivations have potentially explosive political consequences. As the Busia government (1969–72) learned to its ultimate discomfiture, the pains of short-term economic reforms such as devaluation can be far more destabilizing than simple continuation of an existing policy framework. The calculus of political costs and benefits is not complex: incumbent administrations incur huge risks from short-term economic change but bear few of the costs of policy persistence.

The concept of aggregate national welfare, therefore, misses the key political question when it looks solely at the net of benefits minus costs of a particular economic policy. Although the prolonged commitment to a controlled trade regime came to impose far more costs on Ghana than benefits, individual governments making rough calculations about their political lifespan undoubtedly considered themselves far better off by continuing it. Moreover, as in the case of any economic framework whose costs are somewhat intergenerational, the benefits are immediate and tangible – the increased possibility of collecting sufficient rent to remain in power for an additional day – whereas the costs are distant and less measurable – diminished economic performance in the future. The costs, in other words, would be borne by someone else and that, in some perverse way, makes the decision to continue an economically inappropriate policy rational.

The political discount rate in Ghana must have risen especially sharply after the Rawlings coup of June 4, 1979. One of the earliest actions of the AFRC was the execution of three former heads of state, Generals Acheampong, Akuffo, and Afrifa, along with a number of other high ranking military officers who had held key positions in their governments. Indeed, because two of the former heads of state were executed after the general election that brought the Limann government to power, the atmosphere of political insecurity under which the Limann government operated must have been excruciating.[56] Rawlings and his key advisors were waiting in the wings, watching every step of the new administration.

4   POLICY CHANGE IN 1983

The later Acheampong/Akuffo period and the Limann government were marked by extremes in the rate of inflation, falling real price of foreign exchange, declining real per capita incomes, erosion of government services, and deterioration of the national infrastructure. Intense shortages of imported inputs and spare parts reduced industrial capacity utilization to well below previously abysmal levels. The real producer price of cocoa in the 1980/81 crop year reached about 12 percent of its 1963 level, and cocoa purchases by the official Cocoa Board continued to slide, hitting about 60 percent of the level of the early 1960s in that same crop year.

On December 31, 1981 Rawlings once again took power. Much of his support came from the left, and much of the rhetoric of the new government had a populist ring to it. His initial policy thrust was focused on rooting out the corruption which had permeated Ghanaian society. The real exchange rate continued to slide. The real producer price of cocoa, after a brief increase under the Limann government, again fell to less than 15 percent of its 1963 level, and purchases of cocoa by the Cocoa Board in 1982/83 were about 40 percent of the 1963 level.

In April 1983 the government launched its "Economic Reform Program" (ERP). Its key features were a major reform of the exchange rate, a reform of the tax system, and a slashing of the government bureaucracy, the government deficit, and state owned enterprise subsidies.[57] It was nothing less than a complete reversal of direction from that which had been taken previously by Rawlings himself as well as by his predecessors.

If, as we have argued, it was narrowly rational for the earlier governments to act the way they did, why would Rawlings now countenance such a radical change of direction? This, in turn, consists of two subquestions: why the change of course, and why the change in the direction of the ERP?

Why change course?

Diminishing political glue   Economic decline can be usefully viewed as a dialectical process which, by its very nature, transforms the economic structure of a society and, in so doing, fundamentally alters its patterns of political and socioeconomic relationships. Most importantly, economic change can undermine the fundamental bases of political stability.

Our analysis of policy persistence under the earlier regimes suggested that one of the principal reasons for the persistence of policies which proved to be economically destructive was the fact that those policies were generating rents which served as the glue to hold together the political support of those regimes. Rents extracted by politicians and bureaucrats were used to construct coalitions of supporters and followers. We also noted that the circumstances created a set of incentives which took the system well beyond the optimum degree of rent generation (as seen from the viewpoint of the members of the regime). Not only were the policies shrinking the rent pool, but the regime permitted rent-seeking to become competitive, thereby dissipating the resources in the pursuit of rents rather than in maintaining political support.

The ranks of rent-seekers had grown, but under conditions of growing political instability, as manifested in the high incidence of political coups and regime turnovers, there was an increasing element of risk to involvement in the politically dominant coalition. In this situation, rent-recipients would require a higher return in exchange for political support to offset the element of risk.

With the cedi fixed for extended periods, and domestic inflation accelerating, the real exchange rate in 1982 dropped to 10 percent of the rate at independence. The consequent erosion of export earnings, and the drying up of credit from both donor and commercial sources, meant that the volume of foreign exchange available to distribute for rent-generating import licenses shrank. In the final year before the economic reform package, imports (in dollar terms) were less than two-thirds of the previous year (see table 6.2). What little foreign exchange was available was allocated in large part to imports of essentials, which did not generate substantial rents.

If the new government were to have persisted in the policies of its predecessors, it would have faced a combination of an increasing number of claimants, requiring a risk premium to support the regime, seeking access to a shrinking pool of rents. The rent available as political glue had been diluted: ultimately, nothing was left to hold a rent-seeking political regime together. Even if Rawlings had wanted to follow in the footsteps of his predecessors, and use the former regimes' economic policies to generate political support, it would not have been possible. Some policy change was necessary to generate support for the regime.

Shock events of 1982/83   A series of seismic economic shocks struck the country in 1982 and early 1983 and these constituted a tripwire for policy change.

(1) *Drought and severe food shortage.*   By early 1982, Ghana was beginning to experience severe food shortages. These were partially the result of a serious drought but principally the outcome of the utter collapse of the country's economic system, including the severe deterioration of infrastructure and extreme shortage of operating transportation equipment. In the countryside, the actual and expected prices for cocoa had finally fallen to the point that it was no longer considered worthwhile even to harvest this perennial tree crop. Instead, the urgency of growing food to survive had become a paramount consideration. But the country's transportation bottlenecks due to the increasing shortage of foreign exchange made it virtually impossible to transport food to the cities. As a result, there was widespread hunger among some urban dwellers, including senior civil servants and academics at the University of Ghana.

(2) *Forest fires in the middle regions of the country.*   These burned approximately one-third of the cocoa-growing areas. Today, many Ghanaians believe that these fires were set by the cocoa farmers out of a sense of frustration and despair over the fact that cocoa prices had fallen to the point where the farmer's return was less than the cost of harvesting the crop. Others believe that the fires were set to flush small game from the bush in a desperate search for food. Whatever the reason, the outcome was traumatic.

(3) *Murder of high court judges.*   In June, 1982, three senior high court judges and the personnel director of the Ghana Industrial Holdings Corporation were kidnapped and murdered. One of the founding members of the PNDC was forced to resign and, later, tried and executed. Another, despite a widespread public belief that he was also responsible, was officially exculpated. Whether the murder of the three judges by PNDC extremists was a result of their opposition to an alternative judicial system

of military and popular tribunals the PNDC was preparing to introduce or to their suspected involvement in the corrupt practices of previous administrations remains unclear. What is clear is that the murders aroused a wave of popular revulsion against the PNDC and its efforts to introduce Libyan-style socialism to Ghana.

(4) *Nigeria's expulsion of between 600,000 and 1,000,000 Ghanaians who had to be reabsorbed into the Ghanaian economy.* The reabsorption of this many returnees to Ghana forced some economic adjustment on the system. Even if one assumes the lower number, the returnees amounted to approximately twice the level of public sector employment in the country and this did much to dispel the myth of government as the necessary employer of last resort. Of at least equal importance was the fact that the culture of the returnees must have conflicted sharply with prevailing economic circumstances. Despite their expulsion, many had become accustomed to the wide-open, wheeler-dealer, devil-take-the-hindmost style of the Nigerian economy and were unprepared to accept the doctrinaire statism and worker populism the PNDC was then attempting to impose on Ghana.

(5) *Failed coup attempts in November 1982 and June 1983.* By September 1982, the PNDC had already created a special committee to investigate the causes of Ghana's economic decline and prepare recommendations for a reform program. The purpose of these coup attempts, especially the November attempt, was to prevent PNDC adoption of a program of economic liberalization. Whatever the intention, the result of the coup attempts was to expose the intellectual bankruptcy of the Ghanaian left.

Reflecting on this series of disasters, one eminent Ghanaian has said "It looked as if the very elements and gods were enraged against us."[58] The point here, quite simply, is that a remarkable conjuncture of political and apparently natural events combined to create an environment in which drastic policy changes that might previously have aroused popular resistance were broadly welcomed as an opportunity to start afresh.

Political space One critical difference between the Ghanaian experience and that of numerous other countries that have attempted economic reform is that the government of Ghana took power in a popularly supported – indeed, almost called for – military coup that overthrew an ineffectual, corrupt, and highly unpopular civilian administration. This sharp break with the past afforded the PNDC government a relatively high degree of freedom to pursue new economic policies.

The PNDC's flexibility can be contrasted with the political situation in Tanzania, for example, where a constitutional succession occurred within an ongoing political system whose dominant party remained officially committed to socialism. In Tanzania, Julius Nyerere, the former, highly popular, virtually adulated head of state remained in a key power position as Chair of the governing party which, at least in constitutional terms, was the supreme organ of government. The government of Ali Mwinyi has been forced to adopt the polite political fiction that Tanzania is still a socialist country and that its policies do not represent a radical break with those of Julius Nyerere.

In Ghana, the form of regime change (military coup versus constitutional succession) represented a sharp break with the past. Limann, the former head of state, remains a virtual political unknown, is relegated to an almost invisible private existence, and has no present political role whatsoever. Unlike Tanzania's governing party, the PNDC was expected to adopt a strikingly different policy stance from its predecessor. It would have been in violation of its revolutionary mandate to have suggested or adopted some sort of policy continuity with the past.

Why adopt the ERP?

The collapse of the old system did not dictate the direction to be taken in the new. Indeed, as the account of the Rawlings government's first year in office illustrates, there was a lengthy period of debate about the appropriate direction for the PNDC to take. The unifying theme in that debate was that the venality of the old regime, in which the profits of the regime went to members of the kleptocracy, must end. The early attempts to do so by force, including beating of the Accra market women, were eventually recognized as unsustainable.

But the question remains: Why choose a market-oriented solution? We suggest that the answer lies in a coming together of a combination of circumstances that, taken as a group, may help explain why Ghana and numerous other countries, in Africa and elsewhere, have adopted orthodox economic solutions to their development problems.

Prior adjustment   Among the many reasons why the Rawlings government might have chosen to proceed with an official policy of structural adjustment in 1983, one would have to be the fact that so many of Ghana's domestic prices, including those paid by government agencies, had already risen to reflect the scarcity price of foreign exchange.[59] Ghana had, therefore, already gone through a de facto process of economic adjustment but had not captured the rewards of this change, including foreign recognition and assistance.

The Ghanaian excess demand pressure under the previous policy regime was bottled up by quantitative restrictions on international trade and payments.[60] As a result the domestic prices of most importables reflected the scarcity price of foreign exchange rather than the official exchange rate. In these circumstances a devaluation would mean that the official local currency price of foreign exchange would rise toward the scarcity value of foreign exchange, but the scarcity value of foreign exchange would be unaffected in the short run. Hence the actual domestic price of most importables would be unaffected by the devaluation. In a few cases, which had received sufficiently large priority allocations of foreign exchange to permit the retail price to reflect the official exchange rate, the devaluation would have a price-raising effect. Overall, however, the short-run impact of devaluations on the domestic price level would scarcely be noticeable.

The de facto price adjustments that preceded official adjustments paved the way for an official change of policy. Devaluation, thus, would not change the price structure of importable goods whose prices had already increased in the market place to reflect the diminished real value of the cedi.

Indeed, the real purchasing power of formal sector wages had already fallen in terms not only of importables, but also of foodstuffs and other necessities.[61] Further, the educational system and health care system had previously ceased to deliver these services to the vast majority of the population. By 1981 Ghana government expenditures on education amounted to less than 1.9 percent of GDP, and on health to less than 0.7 percent of GDP, in contrast with the average for all of sub-Saharan Africa of 4.6 percent and 1.6 percent respectively.[62]

These observations help to shed light on a controversial aspect of structural adjustment; namely, the relationship between adjustment and social hardship. The conventional allegation from many quarters holds that structural adjustment produces social hardship, as when currency devaluation reduces the real value and purchasing power of incomes. The evidence in Ghana in 1982 and early 1983 points in a different direction: the growing hardship that accompanied economic decline had already set in before the structural adjustment program was launched.

The fact of prior adjustment helps explain why various social groups whose opposition might have been anticipated instead accepted adjustment without political resistance. For the urban sector, for example, much of the deprivation associated with economic decline had already taken place. Urban wage-earners were among the principal constituencies for preadjustment policies, yet they had suffered a decline in real income as inflation outpaced their nominal wage increases. Not all had faced a decline in real wage *rates*, but nearly all experienced a decline in real *incomes*, as virtually all modern sector workers suffered from high levels of unemployment due to input scarcities and broken down infrastructure.[63]

Not only had many of the negative consequences of adjustment already taken place, but, in addition, the Ghana government was motivated by the likelihood that economic reform would stimulate a growth of foreign exchange earnings and thereby help improve living standards for all Ghanaians. There was every reason to expect that additional foreign exchange earnings would derive from at least three sources: (a) a real devaluation and its impact on exports; (b) an increase in foreign exchange availability from donors' contributions; and (c) emigrants' remittances.

This improvement, in turn, held out the prospect of a growth of imports (valued in terms of foreign exchange), thereby *reducing* the domestic price of importables below what would otherwise have been the case.

Failed alternatives   It is useful to recall that during its first year or 15 months in office the Rawlings government pursued a radical populist approach to economic recovery. Driven by the premise that the source of Ghana's economic difficulties was the profiteering (rent-seeking) of greedy politicians and their corrupt business clienteles, the PNDC sought to implement a kind of Libyan "peoples' revolution." Working on the principle that if the country's problem is its elite, then empower the mass, the PNDC nurtured a deeply politicized atmosphere of radical activism. People's Defense Committees (PDCs) were created in local communities and at district and regional levels. On the grounds that if politically appointed managers are corrupt then workers should become managers, workers were encouraged to form Workers Defense Committees (WDCs) and to participate in the management and governance of their firms. Comprised of revolutionary cadres, the purpose of these committees was to monitor, report on, and arrest business people, including market traders who were suspected of counterrevolutionary activity. As stated by the PNDC, the purpose of these committees was

> [To] defend the rights of the ordinary people; expose and deal with corruption and other counterrevolutionary activities, ...maintain collective national discipline and supervision of national resources, ...afford everyone the opportunity to participate in the decision-making process in the country.[64]

Military tribunals were established to bypass the existing court system and to try, convict, and sentence civil servants and business people accused of profiteering, corruption, and "antistate" activities.

There seems little doubt that the PNDC's efforts to produce a radical populist state only succeeded in making economic matters worse by creating an atmosphere of social chaos. The conditions that prevailed then have been described by Baffour Agyeman-Duah in the following terms:

> Persons in positions of authority, particularly managers of businesses, heads of commercial (state and private) enterprises, and traditional chiefs, were barred from membership (in the PDCs and WDCs). Without clearly defined operational guidelines and key objectives, with the assumption that effective political power had been transferred to the "common people," and under the guidance of PNDC "radicals," the PDCs/WDCs initiated a reign of terror reminiscent of the Red Guards in China during Mao's cultural revolution.[65]

The conditions that prevailed in Ghana during this period were characterized by extreme lawlessness and economic uncertainty as some soldiers and other supporters of the PNDC regime took advantage of the unsettled situation to engage in terrorism, armed robbery, and economic pillage. The downward spiral of the economy continued.

The PNDC's foreign strategy during this period was equally unsuccessful. The government had energetically courted financial assistance from Libya, the USSR, and various eastern European countries. Though Libya did make modest financial assistance available (some food and a shipment of 500,000 barrels of oil), the opening to the eastern bloc produced no economic assistance whatsoever. Even the diplomatic rapprochement with Libya may well have been a net cost to the PNDC government as it alienated one of Ghana's major financial supporters, Nigeria, which immediately began to insist upon cash payments for its oil shipments.

Not only had the alternatives failed to find a path out of the increasingly desperate economic mess by early 1983, but the prevailing mood among influential members of the Ghanaian elite seemed to be one of profound moral revulsion against *both* economic alternatives: the statist economy that had been installed following independence, and the radical populist state that had been created the previous year. There seems little doubt that one of the most powerful factors leading to Ghana's commitment to structural adjustment was an all-pervasive social disgust with the imperfections of previous economic strategies.

The "statist" economy alternative had come to be explicitly identified, though not in these precise terms, as the rent-seeking state. This was the state, especially, of Acheampong, Akuffo, and Limann. Ghanaians had become profoundly aware that, whatever the economic theory of the statist economy, its real-world outcome had become a ruinous degree of venality, corruption, and economic mismanagement.

The moral indignation against that system has been expressed time and time again. Dr Kwesi Botchwey, the PNDC Secretary for Finance and Economic Planning, said to us "you cannot imagine what it was like...little girls became contractors." This point has been particularly well stated by Richard Jeffries:

> It is important for an understanding of subsequent developments that one appreciates just how seedy and sordid Ghana's "commanding heights of the economy" became during this period as "top officials issued chits to young women who paraded the corridors of power offering themselves for libidinal pleasures in return for favours." ...Ghanaians were under no Weberian illusions as to the steady historical development of rational–legal bureaucracy and authority. There were many of them nevertheless quite genuinely shocked by the blatant disregard of official rules and popular sensitivities displayed by the Acheampong regime in its later years.[66]

The effect, then, was to create a moral barrier against a return to a statist economy, even among many whose personal economic views tended in that direction.

An equally strong moral revulsion at the excesses and turmoil caused by the radical worker-populism of the first Rawlings government, such as the burning of Accra's major Makola market in 1979, and the similar outbursts of populist anarchy during the early PNDC government in 1982, remained vividly in the minds of many Ghanaians. The populism of the early PNDC administration offered no alternative to the corrupt statism of the old regime. It too was despised by Ghanaians.

The moral revulsion at the old regime and the failure of the new experiment opened the way for a market-oriented solution. This solution would deprive the kleptocracy of benefits, and at the same time reward those who contributed to the good of society. This point was well put to us by a high official of the PNDC government. Addressing himself to the issue of winners and losers under structural adjustment, the official noted that "the losers are people who should never have been winners in the first place. The winners are people who should have been winners all along."

In sum, by the end of 1982, conditions of social chaos, the failure of its foreign policy initiatives and the sheer severity of Ghana's continuing downward economic spiral would have compelled the more reasonable members of the PNDC to acknowledge that its populist approach to national recovery was not working and that the country's continuing decline had now produced visible suffering throughout the society. It had also become clear that there was negligible prospect of any future financial support from eastern-bloc donors including the Soviet Union. Moreover, since Ghana's economy was in such desperate condition that commercial borrowing from international financial markets was not an available option, the only sources of significant financial assistance were Western official donors and the Bretton Woods institutions. Neither the Western governmental donors nor the Bretton Woods institutions would provide substantial additional financial aid without major economic reforms.

Influence of now dominant paradigm   In this era of "rational choice" approaches that emphasize interest-driven behavior, both by individuals and institutions, the extent to which political choices are driven by the power of dominant ideas is all too easily overlooked. But in the late 1950s and early 1960s, as we have already noted, Ghana's choice of development strategy was very much influenced by the most powerful economic ideas of the time. In the early 1980s, Ghanaians found that the policy prescription of the economics profession was much less focused on import-substituting industrialization and more outward-oriented. Undergraduate textbooks, mirroring the professional consensus of the times, were repeating the lessons of the now dominant paradigm:

> For small countries .... [T]he choice is either to tie the economy to world prices through outward-looking policies or to accept the costs of inward-looking, protective regimes. For the small country these costs can be very high, severe enough to retard development for long periods....[67]

That conclusion was already extensively shared professionally in the mid- to late-1970s with, for example, the publication of the volumes in the Bhagwati–Krueger series, *Foreign Trade Regimes and Economic Development*, including a volume on Ghana which was widely circulated among economists in Ghana.[68]

Thus, by the early 1980s the weight of professional economists' opinion had reached the conclusion that the sort of inward-oriented restrictive trade regime that Ghana had now pursued in the extreme for over 25 years was not capable of generating rapid economic growth, and indeed was capable of generating economic atrophy of the kind Ghana was experiencing. The prescription was clear: outward-oriented economic policies were a major part of the solution.[69]

In the specific context of Ghana, Jeffries made a probing effort to uncover the reason for policy change. He assigns the greatest importance to the intellectual factor, Rawlings' conversion to a new set of ideas:

> One cannot, I would suggest, ultimately explain this [policy change] except as the product of a genuine intellectual conversion on the part of a highly moralistic young man. This should not really be very surprising in view of the influence recently exerted by Batesian economics on many Africanist social scientists.[70]

Many influences were at work on Rawlings and the PNDC during 1982. One, which in retrospect appears to have been decisive, was the intellectual influence of an articulate former member of the University of Ghana's Economics Department, Joseph Abbey. In the turbulent days of 1982, he took on the task of leading a small group of technocrats in the evaluation of the policy options. He quickly concluded that the heart of the problem was the overvaluation of the currency and the producer price of cocoa. He was then able to explicate the problem to Rawlings and other members of the PNDC in terms that reflected their genuine concern for the impoverished society that they now governed: the overvalued cedi was depriving the farmer of his just reward, and was generating rents for the corrupt.[71]

Availability of material assistance The small cadre of technocrats which had been at work since mid 1982 examining the economic options had outlined some key elements by the time of the annual IMF/World Bank meetings in 1982. Ghana took the opportunity to raise informally the possibility of assistance for a reform program and, we understand, was encouraged by the response from the international lending institutions.

The amount of assistance available from the Fund and the Bank was potentially quite substantial. In 1983 and 1984, the Fund provided stand-by arrangements and credit-tranche drawings. From 1987 it also provided resources under the structural adjustment facility and the extended Fund facility. Beginning in 1983 also, the Bank had committed funds under IDA terms for projects, programs, and technical assistance. Initially, the long-term gross capital inflow from all sources was a large portion of GDP, but by 1987 the net capital inflow had shrunk to roughly 1 percent of GDP (see figure 6.5). Virtually all of the capital inflow has been debt rather than equity, and the bulk of the increase in external debt has been to multilateral agencies, about half of which has been concessional.[72]

By early 1983, then, Ghana's options had narrowed to one: a market-oriented, outward-looking structural adjustment program. Nothing else offered a prospect of reversing what was widely accepted both within and without Ghana as a desperate situation. The solution did not require significant adjustment of either prices or the level of public services. It offered a way to eliminate corruption, both in the public and the private sectors, and offered substantial external assistance. In short, it held out the prospect of being able to make large numbers of Ghanaians better off.

5   NATURE OF THE ERP[73]

The first phase of the ERP concentrated on what had to be done immediately to attack the proximate causes of Ghana's economic atrophy: (1) change the exchange rate to a level which would both restore an incentive to export and remove the rents on foreign exchange; and (2) tackle the government budget deficit. The second phase was more focused on the rehabilitation of the economy. Rather than think of the ERP in terms of this time sequence of reforms, it is informative to think instead of the degree of administrative and political difficulty the Ghana government

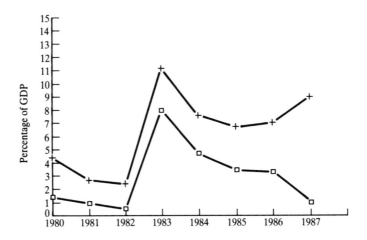

Figure 6.5 Long-term capital inflow. Disbursements as percentage of GDP:□, net; +, gross

faced in tackling the various reforms. In this way we shed some light on the ultimate question of sustainability of the reforms.

Administratively easier reforms

Exchange rate reform   In launching the ERP, the PNDC government was severely constrained both by the complete breakdown of government and by the political mythology that associated devaluation with political suicide. At the same time, the technocrats working on the reform program, and gradually most members of the PNDC, recognized that the incentive to export had to be restored. Hence they designed a system of export bonuses and import surcharges which radically altered the relative returns between export producers and importers. The official exchange rate in April 1983 stood at ₵2.75/US$, the level which had held since August 1978 in spite of inflation averaging over 60 percent per annum since then. The real price of foreign exchange index (1957 = 100) had sunk to less than 15.

The political difficulty of devaluing the cedi may be illustrated by the fact that, as late as April 1983, with the country's economy reduced to shambles, not even Rawlings was able to proceed with a forthright devaluation. Instead, his government introduced a system of exchange rate bonuses for exports and exchange rate surcharges for imports that created a de facto weighted average exchange rate of approximately ₵25/ US$. The system of bonuses and surcharges started from the recognition that, in order to persuade recipients of foreign exchange to turn over their proceeds, a bonus had to be offered. This left the question of how to finance those bonuses. Surcharges were the only way, short of resorting to the now overused inflation tax which would only exacerbate the problem.[74]

The bonus/surcharge scheme was not welcomed by the IMF, for the introduction of multiple exchange rates constitutes one of the cardinal transgressions of the IMF's code. Further, the system of bonuses and surcharges was going to be difficult to administer. Nevertheless the Ghanaians insisted that this was an essential first step and the IMF agreed. It lasted for only six months: the administrative difficulty of running the bonus/surcharge system was formidable, and in October 1983 the exchange rate was formally devalued to a uniform exchange rate of ₵30/US$. In addition, the long since ineffective price control system was abandoned. Once the taboo had been broken, it proved possible to adjust the exchange rate periodically to keep the real price of foreign exchange rising. This was done three times in 1984, with the nominal exchange rate rising by two-thirds over the year to ₵50/US$ in December 1984. However, periodic devaluations, unlike the initial devaluation which had relatively little effect on domestic prices, were starting to affect domestic prices. During 1985 there were three further devaluations, each one relatively small, in total raising the exchange rate only a further 20 percent. At the end of 1985 the real exchange rate stood at 57: clearly there was still a long way to go to restore the incentive to exporters to the situation that had pertained 15 years earlier. The January 1986 budget announced a 50% devaluation, raising the nominal exchange rate to ¢90/US$, an evident attempt to improve the return to exporters.

The task of periodically raising the exchange rate was becoming increasingly difficult politically. Something had to change. The new rate of ¢90/US$ was retained until September 1986 while a new system was worked out. Once again, the pragmatism of the Ghanaians was important in stepping out of the potentially vicious circle of inflation–devaluation and the insistence of the Fund on uniform and realistic exchange rates. An auction system was inaugurated in September 1986. Initially the auction rate applied to only a few items, but its coverage quickly expanded, and before long a unified exchange rate was restored. Most importantly, the auction rate applied to foreign exchange earnings surrendered to the Bank of Ghana.

The auction represented an enormous political improvement over the periodic devaluation system: it removed the burden of acting from the government and, thereby, depoliticized exchange rate policy. Ghana now had, in effect, a managed floating exchange rate for virtually all current account transactions. The rate of increase in the exchange rate was effectively determined by how much foreign exchange the authorities chose to put on the market each week, relative to the demand as revealed in the bids. However, unlike the previous system in which there was a periodic official announcement of a devaluation, the auctions appeared to the public to be the outcome of market forces, and not under the direct control of the government. It had the further advantage to the Ghanaians that the Fund was no longer constantly carping about when and how much the next devaluation should be.

The final innovation in the foreign exchange area came in February 1988 with the introduction of foreign exchange bureaus. Recognizing that there remained a parallel market, particularly at the retail level, fed in part on the supply side by emigrants' remittances sent to relatives at home, and in part on the demand side by those shut out of the formal banking system by virtue of the small size of their transactions, the Ghanaian authorities decided in effect to license the parallel foreign exchange market.

The foreign exchange bureaus buy and sell just about any convertible currency at rates determined by supply and demand. Sometimes a local excess supply or demand for a currency sets up some disorderly cross rates, but for the most part there is a consistent set of bureau rates for the full range of foreign exchange commonly traded. There remains a small parallel market which relies on the margin between the buy and sell rates of the bureaus, but this is relatively small and hence the room for profit is limited.

The bureau rates and the auction rates have been converging (see figure 6.6). As of August 1990, the bureau rates were within 5 percent of the auction rates. The bureaus have become the retail end of the foreign exchange market, with the banks acting as wholesalers. This outcome, a more differentiated financial system, is meeting the needs of the economy for different services.

Perhaps most importantly, the creation of the foreign exchange bureaus, in the view of many Ghanaians, has made the market-determined foreign exchange rate a permanent fixture. Even if a subsequent government attempted to suppress the foreign exchange rate again, there would be considerable political resistance from the constituency which now benefits from the higher real exchange rate and this would be difficult to contain. The approximately 175 foreign exchange bureaus themselves constitute a fairly significant political constituency and their influence would also contribute to keeping an open foreign exchange market throughout the country.

Trade and tax reforms One of the important effects of the exchange rate reforms was to increase the real value of the import duty collections, for the higher exchange rate meant a larger local currency value of the imports on which the duty was collected. These increased from less than 1 percent of GDP in 1983 to 2.8 percent in 1986 before slipping back a little in 1987 and 1988 to 2.4 percent.

Later, a uniform tariff rate for most imports was established, which greatly simplified the collections process. Further, after the foreign

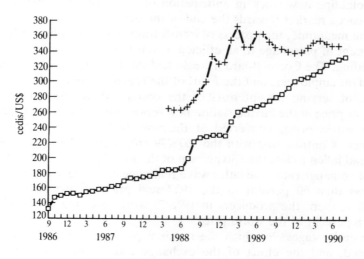

Figure 6.6 Exchange rates (□, auction rates; +, bureau rates); cedis/US$; monthly averages

exchange auction was introduced, the now redundant (in economic terms at least) import licensing system was abandoned.

More generally, a key part of the ERP was a strategy of decreasing the inflationary impact of the government budget deficit. As noted in figure 6.2, the government budget deficit has gradually been eliminated. New credit to the government is no longer fueling inflation, although the remaining inflation is eroding the real value of outstanding government debt.

Central to the elimination of the government deficit was a major effort to improve tax collections. Part of this involved setting up special tax police to check whether or not individuals had paid their taxes. While this may have been reminiscent of the earlier people's revolutionary atmosphere, it did provide rough equity in the administration of taxes, and consequently has relatively widespread acceptance.

The improved government revenue collections permitted government to increase real expenditures, and to focus those expenditures on economically and socially beneficial sectors.

Cocoa price reform   One of the keys to the Ghanaian economic recovery has been the cocoa sector. As traced in figure 6.3, cocoa purchases by the Cocoa Board have responded to the initial increase in the real producer price of cocoa which was part of the ERP. However, in recent years, the declining world price of cocoa has made it difficult to maintain the upward movement of the real producer price. It appears that the present strategy is to avoid putting additional pressure on the world cocoa market at this time, while planting new stock in anticipation of a significant recovery in the world cocoa market towards the end of the decade.

In the meantime, the process of transforming the Cocoa Board from an instrument of patronage to an efficient extension and collection service is proceeding. The Cocoa Board has also had substantial "redeployment" of redundant employees, and the focus of the remaining employees changed to one of serving the interests of the cocoa farmer. As a result, the producer price at the buying station now represents a little over 45 percent of the world price, converted at the now high real price of foreign exchange. Contrast that with the 1978/79 crop year, when the producer price had fallen to less than 30 percent of the world price, converted at the official exchange rate. The latter was a real price of foreign exchange which was less than 60 percent of the 1957 real price of foreign exchange. Together, then, the producers in 1978/79 were receiving effectively less than 18 percent of the world price.

The early stages, in which the nominal producer price of cocoa was increased, and the effect of the exchange rate reform on transferring resources back to the Cocoa Board, thereby permitting it to pass on a greater share of the world value of the product to the producers, were administratively easier to accomplish than the process of institutional change for the Cocoa Board itself. The latter task is proving more difficult and drawn out, but until it is accomplished the cocoa farmer will not receive the full benefits of the reforms, and will not generate the full potential benefits for Ghana.

Administratively and politically difficult reforms

Labor policies One of the most sensitive, yet at the same time complex, areas of any structural adjustment program is the impact of the program on the labor market. Adjustments of employment, wage rates, and earnings follow from many different dimensions of the program: (1) the reallocation of factors across sectors arising from changes in the relative goods prices; (2) the direct reduction of public sector employment as part of the attempt to control the government deficit and excess aggregate demand; (3) the reduction of excess demand in general; (4) changes in particular labor market policy interventions such the minimum wage policy; and (5) changes in relative factor prices, due in part to the foregoing adjustments, but also due to changes in the costs of capital, and imported inputs. Because the issues are so complex and difficult to disentangle, the design of the labor policy part of the structural adjustment program is far from an exact science. This is especially so when the political dimension is also introduced. There are significant redistributions of income that occur as a result of the reform program which leave the losers aggrieved and the winners uncertain about the permanence of their improved situation.

The Ghanaian case is no exception to this general problem. Initially the labor market was not part of the direct policy focus of the ERP. The second phase of the ERP, outlined by the government in 1987, did contain reference to "Human Resource Utilization and Labour Mobility." Its principal focus was on the problem of the civil service, and put the problem starkly:

> An aspect of the long period of economic decline ...[was that] ... the public sector came under increasing pressure to take on additional personnel beyond what they needed to operate efficiently. In the result, ... it is a common sight in public services to find people reading newspapers endlessly and engaging in lotto "arithmetic" throughout the day. This overstaffing also has the effect of making resources unavailable to improve conditions, especially pay for those who do work.[75]

The solution involved two elements: (1) the redeployment of public sector employees; and (2) elimination of distortions in government wages and salaries.

The redeployment of thousands of public sector employees – out of the public sector – would be a daunting task for any government, let alone a government also facing a severe budget constraint. Yet some 12,000 civil servants were removed from the public payroll in 1987, and an equal number targeted in each of 1988 and 1989. While some of these were undoubtedly "ghost" employees, most were genuine cases. This was not accomplished by the stroke of a pen the way the devaluation of the cedi or the increase in the cocoa producer price was introduced. This was a massive operation of dealing with individuals whose lives were changed profoundly as a consequence of the decision.

At the same time, the compensation structure in the civil service was changed to reflect the differential contributions of the higher and lower grades. "It is the government's view that it is better to have a small well-trained and well-paid civil service with a consistently high level of productivity."[76]

The other major element of public sector labor policies concerns the employees of the state-owned enterprises. Substantial numbers of employees in this sector were also overpaid and redundant. The issue is taken up below.

Beyond the public sector, government affects the private labor market sector in a potentially significant manner by setting the minimum wage rate. Since this is set in nominal terms, it is eroded by inflation. Prior to the launching of the ERP the real minimum wage had fallen significantly, reaching 17 percent of the 1970 level in 1983. Since then it has risen, reaching 36 percent in 1986.[77] Despite the populist rhetoric of the PNDC, setting of the minimum wage is evidently not being used in an attempt to redistribute income.

The impact of the entire ERP policy changes on the labor market is extremely difficult to gauge accurately. Some information, however, is available from the Ghana Living Standards Survey (GLSS).[78] A comprehensive sample of the Ghanaian population was taken in 1987–8. While it is a cross-section, it does permit some insights into the effects of the ERP.

First, it is possible to construct a rough comparison of the distribution of employment by sector between the GLSS and the two previous censuses (1970 and 1984).[79] The major change appears as the redistribution of employment from manufacturing and government to agriculture, forestry, and fishing. That redistribution was already under way in 1984, and evidently continued in subsequent years. This suggests that the major portion of the Ghanaians expelled from Nigeria and those who were redundant in the modern sector as a result of the ERP were absorbed in the agriculture, forestry, and fishing sector.

Second, some econometric work using the GLSS data base by P. Beaudry and N.K. Sowa sheds further light on the working of the Ghanaian labor market:

> [H]ourly labour earnings conform relatively well to a combination of human capital theory, the theory of equilibrating migration flows and to the theory of compensating differentials; i.e., returns to human capital are positive, regional differences are not extremely important, and compensating differen-

tials are related mostly to being off the farm, and especially being in the mining industry.[80]

On the basis of this and other evidence, they conclude that

[T]he ERP reliance on market signals as a means of achieving structural adjustment has probably been helped by a labour market sensitive to profitable opportunities.[81]

Together, the foregoing suggests that the effective functioning of a now relatively undistorted labor market will contribute to the Ghanaian economy performing at its production possibility frontier, rather than at a point well to the interior.

Financial sector policies   The second phase of the ERP took aim also at the financial sector. It recognized that: "Indeed the successful implementation of ERP II depends on a well-functioning and broadly based financial system mobilizing and efficiently channelling resources into productive activity."[82] Two major elements were involved in the attempt to get the financial sector to perform this function. First, the efficiency of the system had to be improved, and second, the financial sector itself had to be restructured. To contribute to the former, it was recognized that "the interest rate on savings and time deposits should be at least as high as the rate of inflation..."[83] The means to accomplish the latter, however, were less clearly set out in the official statement.

The Bank of Ghana raised the nominal discount rate in 1984, 1986, 1987, and again in 1988. As the inflation rate came down in 1984, and again in 1989, the real discount rate was able to reach the zero level (see figure 6.7). However, the deposit rate remains negative.[84]

The willingness of the public to use the banking system was severely shaken by the experiences prior to the ERP – the massive inflation of the PNDC's predecessors, and the early PNDC's frontal attack on the symbols of the corruption of the old regime, including demonetization of ¢50 notes, and the freezing of bank accounts in excess of ¢50,000. The ratio of Central Bank reserve money to GDP remains at less than 8 percent of GDP. It is thus far from clear if the public will respond to the marginal new incentives by increasing its use of the formal financial sector. Meanwhile, the Ghanaian monetary authorities are engaged in a major effort to restructure the financial sector, with the assistance of a World Bank/IDA credit. This involves amending the regulatory framework and improving the capabilities of bank supervision, setting risk exposure limits, capital adequacy ratios, and audit requirements. At the same time, in part because of a long history of inadequacies in the areas just enumerated, but also in part because of the fact that the ERP has changed the entire set of profitable and unprofitable enterprises, large numbers of Ghanaian banks face severe problems.

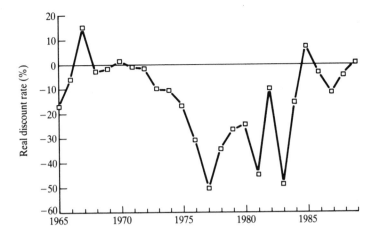

Figure 6.7   Real interest rates (%)

Divestiture of state-owned enterprises[85]   Reform of the SOEs is among the most urgent priorities presently on the agenda of Ghana's reform program. These enterprises had absorbed vast economic resources and used them in an unproductive manner. If Ghana is to continue to sustain a high rate of economic growth, these resources must be freed up. The burden of future economic growth rests heavily on the country's ability to transform its wasteful, inefficient, and loss-producing system of state-owned industries into productive economic activities.

To achieve this objective, Ghana has officially committed itself to the divestiture and privatization of the vast majority of SOEs. This process has been unduly protracted. It did not begin until early 1985 when the government of Ghana commissioned a study, whose purpose was to identify the problems plaguing the SOEs and make a set of recommendations as to what should be done. Among these recommendations was a suggested divestiture list of 32 SOEs. The government of Ghana agreed with this recommendation and, in October 1987, concluded an agreement with the International Development Association (World Bank) to set up a Divestiture Secretariat that would handle the sale of these and other enterprises that the Ghanaian government might wish to sell off. That agreement also provided a development credit agreement for this purpose.

A further two years went by with very little movement on this agreement. During 1989, a few recommendations for divestiture were made, but none was approved by the PNDC.[86]

To speed the process of divestiture, the Ghana government reconstituted the divestment process in January 1990. The divestiture secretariat, which had been located within the State Enterprises Commission, was moved out and reorganized as a separate unit and the government also reconstituted the Divestment Implementation Committee. In 1990, considerably more was accomplished. As of January 1991, a total of 38 enterprises had been divested, of which 23 were liquidations and 15 privatizations of various types – joint ventures, management contracts, leases, sale of shares, and outright sales.

Following its reorganization, the Divestment Secretariat also undertook, for the first time, to create a systematic data base concerning the SOEs. Although the creation of such a data base is the necessary first step in the divestment process, this had not been done by the former divestment secretariat.

Various explanations help to account for the slowness of Ghana's approach to the divestiture of SOEs.

(1) *The ideological factor.* The most obvious and, in certain respects, most compelling explanation for the slowness of divestiture in Ghana is a lingering ideological attachment to state-owned enterprise within the PNDC. Although the PNDC has founded its principal moral claim to political legitimacy on the elimination of corruption on the part of government officials, its revulsion against the blatant rent-seeking behavior of previous regimes is accompanied by an almost equally profound mistrust of the profit-seeking behavior that would be an inevitable accompaniment of a capitalist economic system.

Indeed, numerous segments of Ghanaian society appear to see no significant economic distinction between the rent-seeking behavior of corrupt government officials and the profit-seeking of entrepreneurial classes. Key PNDC members are reflecting and resonating an important theme in Ghanaian political culture in their tendency to view profits not as the rewards for productive entrepreneurship and risk-taking but, rather, as the moral equivalent of rent-seeking. This view is shared, for example, by important segments of Ghana's Trade Union Congress (TUC) and by influential members of Ghana's intelligentsia.

Reinforcing this sentiment is the economic argument that the problem with the strategy of import substitution through state-assisted enterprise was not generic but, rather, lay in the extremes to which this strategy was pushed. The ideas that initially gave rise to a dirigiste trade regime and an industrial strategy based on SOEs continue to appeal to some members of the technocracy who have no obvious personal stake in the survival of the SOEs but who genuinely believe that state industries provide Ghana with its only chance for industrialization and with an opportunity for serious consideration of what should be the appropriate boundary between public and private enterprise.

(2) *Rationalization of political interest.* While ideological conviction alone provides a partial explanation for the deep reluctance of some officials to divest the SOEs and transform them into privately held companies, material interest is also an important factor. Underlying the veneer of

populist anticapitalism there may also be the temptation to use the SOEs for their enormous potential as economic assets for attracting political clienteles and building political coalitions. If the SOEs are retained, but are not constrained to run in a manner that requires them to price outputs and inputs competitively, then they could once again become, as they were in the past, the source of jobs for political cronies, cash and subcontracts for political allies, and popular support from protected labor organizations and subsidized middle-income white-collar workers. This was exactly the reason why SOEs were so attractive to previous Ghanaian regimes and, given Ghana's likely return to a more open and competitive form of politics, it must be a powerful consideration in the government's apparent reluctance to proceed more expeditiously with the divestiture of the SOEs.

To preserve a proportion of the SOEs, some Ghanaian officials have argued that divestiture, while an appropriate goal of economic adjustment, should not be applied indiscriminately to all state enterprises. Instead, they suggest, Ghana should conduct a sort of economic triage, dividing its SOEs into three categories that reflect wholly different claims for governmental clemency. The first category would consist of those SOEs that the Ghanaian government deems vital and indispensable to the operation of its economic system (e.g., Bank of Ghana, Cocoa Marketing Board, Airport Authority), or to the provision of public services to its population (Electricity Board, Water Board, Ghana Airways). These SOEs would be automatically exempt from the divestiture process.

The second category would consist of those state corporations that are potentially profitable. These are corporations that may not have been badly managed in the past but which have been adversely affected by the successive economic shocks of the adjustment process (e.g., the cutoff of subsidized and guaranteed credit, loss of inexpensive productive inputs cheapened by currency overvaluation, or the end of noncompetitive access to domestic markets). According to the notion of economic triage, many SOEs in this category could, with only modest amounts of temporary assistance from the government such as low interest loans or modest tariff protection, weather the impact of structural adjustment. These firms might emerge at the end of the process as viable and productive enterprises, able to compete on their own with international firms.

The principle of divestiture, then, would be presently applied only to those SOEs in a third category, the "fatally wounded." For such SOEs, it is acknowledged, no amount of assistance would provide a prospect of economic recovery. Such SOEs would have to be dealt with through bankruptcy, sale for junk value, or some other form of outright divestiture.

Although the triage approach makes a certain superficial economic sense, its practical effect would undoubtedly be to forestall the divestiture of literally hundreds of economically questionable enterprises that would find some means to avoid being placed in the "fatally wounded" category and, thereby, advance a claim for government support. It is difficult to believe that the operative basis for these decisions would not be the desire of political leaders for control over a resurgent system of rent-conferring assets.

(3) *Technical considerations.* Technical difficulties constitute a third reason for the slowness of the divestiture process. To place a firm for sale requires that there be a full sorting out and valuation of its assets and liabilities. This is a daunting enterprise. The assets of a state-owned corporation would include its real estate (office space, factories, warehouses, farmlands), its capital stock including transportation equipment, inventory of unsold goods, stocks of unused inputs and accounts receivable. The liabilities of an SOE might well represent an equally bewildering assortment including debts to employees (unpaid salaries, end-of-service benefits, unfunded retirement liabilities), debts to suppliers (both domestic and foreign) and outstanding loans at commercial banks.

Merely computing the net worth of an SOE is a formidable task. But it would be irresponsible to the taxpayers of Ghana who have already been taxed heavily to provide assets for the SOEs to sell them off before some appraisal of this worth had been completed.[87]

(4) *Legal considerations.* The legal complexities that surround the sale of an SOE are at least equally formidable. Recall that Ghana is a highly legalistic society, and sorting out the legal issues is, therefore, an important cultural value. Among the legal issues to be sorted through are included: (1) the ownership of the assets of the SOEs that have been pledged as security for loans to banks or other creditors; (2) the ordering of debts to employees; and (3) the ordering of debts to commercial banks, to foreign shareholders, and to the Ghanaian government itself. Further, since these are government-owned corporations, does government have an ultimate financial responsibility for the unfunded liabilities of the SOEs, including termination benefits for workers? How the proceeds from sales of SOEs will be handled and whether the proceeds from these sales will be "netted out" on an SOE-by-SOE basis or across the group as a whole also has to be settled.

(5) *Administrative problems.* The administrative difficulty of actually setting up a system to handle the potential divestiture of 200 corporations is serious.

Ghana appears to be moving toward a resolution of these difficulties with the creation of a new administrative apparatus more amenable to technocratic influence. However the divestiture of SOEs is a long way from completion. As long as it remains unresolved, much of the industrial sector continues in a state of semiparalysis.

6   CONCLUSION: SUSTAINABILITY OF THE ECONOMIC RECOVERY

Is the path Ghana chose in April 1983 one which will yield sustained economic growth? The answer is by no means clear, even after almost eight years. The reasons for the uncertain answer are complex, but largely arise from the combination of circumstance which led Ghana to launch the reform program in the first place.

Economic sustainability

Ghana's economic reformers have done most, but not all, of the things that today's economic orthodoxy would recommend. They have stabilized the macroeconomy by balancing the government budget; allowed the exchange rate to seek its own level; significantly increased the producer price of cocoa; opened the economy to international trade; obtained substantial financing for imports to permit industry to purchase badly needed materials and spare parts; reconstructed the infrastructure; restored a measure of effective government services; and begun to reform the financial sector. Yet, after an initially promising start, the economic recovery is now generating economic growth barely in excess of population growth.

Why is the reform program not generating substantial ongoing economic growth? The explanation lies in several interrelated factors including the motivation behind the ERP, the nature of the remaining bias and the relationship between economic and institutional reform.

Ambivalence toward the new economic system   The principal explanation may lie in the fact that Ghana's policy reforms are partially motivated by a noneconomic consideration, the determination of the Rawlings government to root corruption and rent-seeking out of the political system. The government remains ambivalent in its underlying attitude toward the idea of a market-based economy and this ambivalence continues to engender a certain amount of insecurity and reluctance among would-be Ghanaian entrepreneurs.

The PNDC is committed first of all to a noncorrupt economic system. During its first year in office it attacked directly what it saw as evidence of corruption. This included arbitrary measures such as the demonetization of ¢50 notes, the freezing of bank accounts in excess of ¢50,000, the beating of the market women, and the arbitrary enforcement of tax collection. The structural adjustment reforms of 1983 were adopted as indirect mechanisms to achieve the same objective: to reward the deserving and to deprive the undeserving of their ill-gotten rents. However, it is important to recognize that there is not an ideological commitment to the "free market" per se.

A market-oriented system was seen in 1983 as the best way of establishing a noncorrupt economic system. The experience over the intervening years suggests that a market-oriented solution will continue to be viewed as the most effective protection against corruption.

Government remains ambivalent in its attitude towards private entrepreneurs, however. The distinction between rewards to entrepreneurship and the rents from the control system is not one which is easy to make in practice, and is not fully appreciated by many Ghanaians. Both are treated as suspect, especially when many of the individuals who respond to entrepreneurial opportunities of the reform program are the same individuals who responded to the opportunities to capture rents under the old regime.[88] Hence, private entrepreneurs, both domestic and foreign, remain uncertain about just how favorable the business climate really is, and thus are hesitant to commit substantial long-term investments.

Further, the business community is not certain how long the reform program will be able to sustain itself. The donors are making it clear that they expect Ghana to be weaned from the substantial assistance it has been receiving, and there is a widespread consensus in the business community that by 1992 Ghana will not be able to count on the extraordinary level of assistance it has received as part of the ERP. This means, in turn, that the business community is regarding 1992 as a potential terminal date for the good times, and consequently that if profits are to be made they should be made before then. This shortening of the business time horizon means that few of the longer-term commitments that are necessary for sustained growth are being made by the private sector.

Does a bias persist? If so, what is it? Ghana's ERP has reversed a long-standing bias in favor of the import-substitution sector and tilted the incentive structure back toward relative neutrality between export and import-substitution production. Much of the import-substitution sector was urban based, and hence a facile interpretation would see structural adjustment as reversing the urban bias.

A number of observations qualify that conclusion. First, the old regime, in its extreme form, was biased against any economic activity that relied on the outside world, either to acquire inputs or to sell outputs. That the massively inappropriate real price of foreign exchange was hard on the export sector is well recognized. What is also worth noting is that the decline in export earnings led to extreme shortages of imported inputs, spare parts, and machinery for the import-intensive import-competing producers.[89]

Second, services for the urban sector deteriorated sharply as the old regime crumbled. In the end, the social services of roads, urban transport, electricity, water, garbage collection, education, and health were no longer differentially available to the urban sector – they were in extreme shortage everywhere. Yet the urban sector had become dependent on these services, and hence the urban sector was harder hit by the decay of the old regime. In the end, as both food and transport shortages became serious, urban dwellers were seriously disadvantaged because they had no means to search for what little food was reaching the urban areas. In other words, the old regime was no longer delivering advantages to the urban sector.

The structural adjustment, by allowing the free flow of imports at the scarcity price of foreign exchange, has benefited *both* the export sector and parts of the import-dependent importables sector. The reform program removed the domestic monopoly and allowed competing imports of final goods on payment of moderate import duties. The import duty means that a moderate bias against exportable production relative to import-competing production remains.

The restoration of basic urban services has meant that many urban sector dwellers are now better off than they were under the old regime. Thus, it is clear that the structural adjustment has in fact been beneficial to income generation in the urban sector. This has been offset, in part, by relatively faster inflation in Accra than in the rural areas since mid–1983. On balance, the urban sector is better off than it was before the reform program.

The reform retains a significant potential for public sector bias. The SOEs will likely continue to have a significant role in the economy. The generic potential of SOEs for waste and the freezing of resources in outmoded uses are not motivating a privatization thrust the way the corruption of the old regime motivated the elimination of policies which gave rise to the rents. Many SOEs are seen as actually or potentially efficient and effective providers of goods and services. It appears that the case for privatization of a particular enterprise has to be made on enterprise-specific grounds rather than theoretical grounds.

Among the major winners of the reform program have been the upper-level civil servants and other public sector technocrats, in many cases deservedly so in terms of their contribution to the economic recovery. Yet there remain many in the public service who are there primarily to collect the in-kind components of public sector remuneration, such as subsidized housing and automobiles. This leads to the conclusion that while structural adjustment has not reestablished the significant urban bias of the earlier regimes, the potential for persistence of public sector bias remains.

Does the residue of a public sector bias act as a drag on the reemergence of sustained economic development? That depends critically on what role the public sector plays in the economy – productive or predatory. In the past the public sector's role was overwhelmingly predatory, but this need not be so. To the extent that the public sector uses resources to facilitate the functioning of the economy such as in the establishment of law and order and the provision of infrastructure, the allocation of those resources to the public sector is well spent, for it enhances private output.[90] In many respects the choice of mix is still open, for the future role of the public sector is not settled. Yet the choice which is made will be critical in determining the sustainability of the economic recovery.

Institutional reform   The slow emergence of institutions necessary to support the effective functioning of the economy is constraining the economic recovery. For example, it is well recognized that a smoothly functioning economy requires financial institutions to perform the critical function of financial intermediation. Yet the reform of the Ghanaian financial sector has been slow to emerge because this involves far more than simply changing a set of price signals. It involves establishing a set of behavioral norms for lenders (banks and other financial institutions), for borrowers (businesses, both private and state-owned), and for the regulators, which are known and widely accepted. Since many of the norms required in a modern financial sector are foreign to the control regime, it takes both time and concerted effort to reform the institutions in a way that makes them contribute positively to the efficient functioning of the economy.

A further element concerns the slow eradication of negative externalities. A characteristic feature of "underdevelopment" is a significant amount of economic "friction" in the relationships between economic agents. An individual firm, for example, cannot rely on other firms to supply the necessary inputs or to purchase its output at a predictable price in a timely manner. The individual firms pay for telephones that don't work, contract with suppliers that don't deliver on time, and deliver to purchasers who haven't accumulated sufficient cash to pay for the product as promised. Governments often also form part of the picture, failing to provide such essential inputs as passable roads or reliable police services, and, in the extreme, harassing businesses. These negative externalities are typically exacerbated by an exchange control regime. Both directly and indirectly, an exchange control regime makes interfirm and firm–government relations unreliable. Hence, even where the individual firms are efficient, the system conspires to deprive the economy of the fruits of that efficiency. This effect is the negative of the well known Marshallian (positive) external economies which are external to the firm, but not to the economy, such as the availability of a trained labor force.

One of the major potential benefits of a structural adjustment program is the eradication of some of these negative externalities. The availability of imported inputs and spare parts yields an immediate dividend, for example. However, the old habits of doing business in a shortage economy die hard. The take-it-or-leave-it approach of suppliers, for example, does not disappear overnight. Until the interfirm and firm–government relationships become less encumbered by these frictions, the full potential of the economy cannot be achieved.

This discussion suggests a more general point. The principal focus of an economist's thinking about structural adjustment is usually on restoring an appropriate set of incentives which, given the technology and endowments that a country has at its disposal, should result in restoration of output to its potential. Such an approach misses the key role that institutions play.[91] The new set of price signals changes more than simply the incentive structure. It also changes the optimal set of rules and constraints governing the way economic agents relate to each other. Yet, as the Ghanaian experience with financial sector reform illustrates, the new institutional arrangements, the rules and constraints, do not emerge automatically. They must be formulated, understood, and become accepted practice. The required changes take time. Much of this depends on government, or state institutions such as the central bank, but because government itself is constrained, it is not able to act speedily to remove the institutional development constraint. But the slow emergence of appropriate institutions is constraining the rate of growth of the economy.

The slowness of the reform program to achieve sustained rapid economic growth points to an important lesson. The overall constraint on a country's economic development is not simply a scarce factor such as capital or foreign exchange which might be removed by additional domestic resource mobilization or additional foreign assistance. The constraint consists of an interrelated set of elements which act together to limit an economy's ability to produce goods and services as efficiently as those same resources could be produced elsewhere in the world. This means that if an economic reform program is to achieve the most possible, getting the prices right is simply the first, albeit critical, step. A long process of relaxing many different constraints is involved, rather like peeling back the layers of an onion – after each layer is removed, another one appears.

Political sustainability

Structural adjustment in Ghana is, in some respects, the product of a negative coalition. It is not the sort of policy that elicits an enthusiastic burst of popular support. It is doubtful, for example, that there would ever be a demonstration of university students or urban workers demanding greater implementation of structural adjustment.

Ghana's nascent political parties, if they are allowed to operate openly on a national basis, would in all likelihood campaign for popular support on the basis of their criticism of structural adjustment and their determination to modify the program in essential respects. This is, of course, especially true of the parties on the left. Despite the fact that it has produced a period of sustained economic growth after a generation of economic decline, outside government circles structural adjustment is associated with austerity and sacrifice and hardship, and therefore with the need for continuing political control.

The difficulty of arousing widespread popular enthusiasm for structural adjustment or of mobilizing a coalition of powerful interest groups to sustain it raises a fairly basic question. Is there a political coalition that supports structural adjustment and, if so, how can it possibly be empowered to sustain the process of economic reform? The foregoing observations suggest strongly that structural adjustment would not enjoy the support of the country's most powerful political actors and that, if the process of economic reform is to continue, the PNDC would need to maintain its political control at the national level.

But structural adjustment may enjoy a form of coalition, best termed for want of more felicitous language, a negative coalition. The politics of structural adjustment are closely akin to the politics of the budget deficit reduction package in the United States which is, after all, a form of structural adjustment. No one really wants it but most people seem to realize that it is necessary and beneficial in the long run. In Ghana, there is a strange discrepancy. Even the people who are publicly critical of structural adjustment because of the hardships and austerity they associate with it privately acknowledge that there is no alternative if Ghana is to develop. There is an implication that, if empowered, they could do little to alter the country's present economic course.

How this might play out is entirely hypothetical and unclear. The critical question for Ghana's future is whether political leaders who may come to power on the basis of their criticism of structural adjustment will feel obligated to recreate the old statist coalition.

Does this mean that, to continue structural adjustment, Ghana must eschew participant politics at the national level? This issue, more than any other, may have some explanatory bearing on the Rawlings government's reluctance to see a full restoration of democratic politics at the national level. There is an almost palpable sense on the part of some political leaders, including Rawlings himself, that if full democracy were restored, elements of the old statist coalition (civil servants, manufacturers, trade unionists) would use it to seek to recapture political control. Rawlings is constantly issuing public warnings against those who use the idea of democracy as a means to deceive the masses. For, if the old coalition reestablishes itself, its leaders might well see their interests in terms of a reestablishment of at least portions of the old dirigiste, rent-seeking regime.

The idea of democracy could well provide a legitimizing norm to rebuild an antireformist coalition. In the 1960s, the idea of socialism provided the ideological banner that was used by a statist coalition to manage political power in the interest of certain urban groups. Now, socialism is broadly discredited not only in Africa but elsewhere. As a result, the old coalition of public officials, manufacturers and trade unionists would possibly use the banner of democracy as a vehicle to recreate the policies of the past.

There is an important theme here about democracy and development in Ghana. National politics in Ghana, as in so much of independent Africa, has really meant the politics of the capital city. The major political actors are, for all practical purposes, located within a very small perimeter around the Accra city limits, particularly if one includes the adjacent port city of Tema. As Robert Bates has underscored, rural communities, which is to say agricultural interests, have rarely been effective in translating their economic importance into political influence. The reasons for this are myriad and were touched upon above (see "Absence of Political Opposition"). These have to do principally with the formidable problem of collective action faced by export oriented farmers. Suffice it to say here that a restoration of democratic politics at the national level might do little, if anything, to empower the geographical regions or social groups that contribute a substantial share of Ghana's income; namely, the cocoa and food farmers of Western, Brong-Ahafo, and Ashanti regions.

In this light, it is not at all surprising that the Rawlings government has chosen to emphasize district assemblies as the chosen institutional vehicle for the restoration of participant politics in Ghana. The district assembly system is quintessentially rural in character; it empowers precisely those populations that were politically marginalized from independence until the early 1980s. But the district assembly system represents more than an attempt to marry participant politics with the country's economic winners. Since it also operates in northern Ghana, it is also an attempt to marry the process of participant politics to the social groups that have always been Ghana's most deprived economic losers. Small wonder that some members of Ghana's urban intelligentsia have sought to discredit the district assembly system as cynical and manipulative.

The politically portentous feature of Ghana's ERP is that it has yet to empower its economic winners. The most important winners, the cocoa farmers, benefit from an externality they had no hand in creating and have no voice in sustaining. The major source of the economic changes that benefit them is the PNDC's revulsion against economic corruption and the degree to which this has led to the introduction of policies intended to eliminate rent-seeking from the society. As one of our informants concluded: "Ghana's recovery is fragile; the economic winners do not have power and those who have power are not economic winners."

NOTES

The authors wish to thank the numerous Ghanaian officials and academics, IMF and World Bank officials, and other knowledgeable individuals who gave so generously of their time to enlighten us on the Ghanaian experience. At the risk of singling out individuals, the authors are especially grateful to J. E. K. Amoah, T. P. Jones and K. Sigrist for their comments on an earlier version. Comments of academic colleagues at the University of California, Los Angeles, the University of Western Ontario, and elsewhere are gratefully acknowledged. Other participants in the project, especially the project directors, provided stimulus and valuable feedback on earlier versions. The authors especially wish to thank Mr Jose Campos who provided valuable research assistance in the preparation of the data and graphs. Campos was supported by a Sloan Foundation grant to the University of Western Ontario. Responsibility for the final product, however, rests with the authors.

 1 The initial policy framework, especially those aspects dealing with foreign trade and the exchange rate, has been analyzed in Leith (1974).

 2 The literature on Ghana's economic decline and recovery program is already too voluminous to cite in one footnote. We have especially benefited from Jeffrey Herbst's unpublished paper "How 'Soft' is the State in Africa: The Case of Exchange Rate Reform in Ghana" (Woodrow Wilson School, Princeton University, n.d.) and from his willingness to share reflections that will appear in his forthcoming book on this subject.

 3 Austin (1964).

 4 These events are described in Austin (1976).

 5 Ray (1986).

 6 Jeffries (1989, p. 79).

 7 Rawlings had first attempted a coup unsuccessfully on May 15, 1979. Arrested and placed on trial, the trial proved to be a showcase for his opposition to the SMC government.

 8 Chazan (1983), see esp. pp. 228ff.

 9 Mikell (1989).

10 The data underlying the graphs are contained in an appendix which is available from either author on request. The real GDP data used in this paper are drawn from the IMF, *International Financial Statistics*, and do not correspond to the data found in Leith (1974). In particular, the IFS GDP data for the early 1960s appear to have been revised upward from the data which were available at the time the Leith book was prepared.

11 The real exchange rate index is the nominal cedis per SDR exchange rate divided by the ratio of the Ghana consumer price index to the industrial countries' consumer price index, set as an index with 1957 = 100.

12 Compare, for example, the real exchange rate data reported by Edwards (1989). Table 4.3 reports the maximum and the minimum index for quarterly data, for 33 countries, 1972 to 1985. The highest ratio of maximum to minimum index was for Chile at 7.9, followed by Sri Lanka at 3.85. For the same period, using annual data, the Ghanaian ratio of the highest to the lowest was 12.5.

13 See Gillis (1988).

14 The trade regime is extensively described in Leith (1974). The state-owned enterprises are described in Killick (1978).

15 See Leith (1974, p. 51).

16 Killick (1978, p. 215).

17 Leith (1974, p. 54).

18 For a recent rationale for import substitution, see Bruton (1989).

19 Leith (1974, p. 77) described the system as it had developed by 1970 in the following terms: "The protection of Ghanaian industrial establishments ap-

pears to be largely random. When set against the declared policy of promoting industrialization per se, the rationale for this apparently random dissemination of protection is not at all obvious...we conclude that the variability and randomness of the protection of Ghanaian industrial activities was largely unintended."

20   Killick (1978, p. 219).

21   Terminology concerning exchange rates suffers from different conventions used in different parts of the world. In this chapter, we use the exchange rate to mean the local currency price of foreign exchange. When there is an excess demand for foreign exchange, this means that the price of foreign exchange is below its market clearing price.

22   See Leith (1974, chapter III).

23   See Leith (1974, pp. 42–43). Some extreme examples are worth noting. The labor costs alone of gold production rose to a level where they were greater than the cedi return to the mining industries. Diamond production (through official channels, at least) had virtually disappeared by the early 1960s. (See Leith, ibid., p. 14).

24   See discussion in Leith, ibid., pp. 86–96.

25   A thorough description and analysis of Ghana's agricultural pricing policies is contained in Stryker et al. (1990).

26   See Stryker et al., ibid., table 8.

27   The way in which this extractive system worked, not only in Ghana but throughout much of independent sub-Saharan Africa, forms the core of the analysis by Bates (1981). The producer price of cocoa is at the buying station in the countryside. The bloated costs of the CMB included transportation, which was handled by a CMB subsidiary, the Produce Buying Company. Ghana, however, differs from most African countries described by Bates in that neither the producer nor the retail prices of the country's principal food staples were subjected to effective government control.

28   Bates (1981, p. 3).

29   See, for example, Bienefeld (1986).

30   Michael Lipton is the principal proponent of the urban explanation of policy bias. See Lipton (1976). See also Bates (1981).

31   For an elaboration, see Stryker et al. (1990).

32   See, for example, Roemer (1971). Roemer shows that the wage–rental ratio rose by about 25 percent from 1960 to 1966 (Nkrumah's last year). The 1967 devaluation restored the ratio to about the level of 1960.

33   Singer and Ansari (1977).

34   See for example Hollis Chenery's 1960 *American Economic Review* article which appears as chapter 7, "Comparative Advantage and Development Policy," of Chenery (1979).

35   One of Lewis' books originated as a series of lectures at the University of Ghana (Lewis, 1969).

36   Ward (1961).

37   Killick (1978, pp. 1–2).

38   Levi (1988, p. 23).

39   Levi, ibid., p.31.

40   There remains, however, the puzzling question of why the dominant economic ideas retained such influence in Ghana, let alone in the rest of the world, for so

long after it became evident that the prescription was not generating the hoped for response.

41 Grindle (1989).
42 For an articulate warning against the use of the urban bias concept in an overly deterministic manner, see Barkan (1983).
43 Chazan (1983).
44 For an interesting discussion, see Drake and Lacy (1966).
45 Bates (1981, p. 3).
46 For further discussion see Krueger (1974).
47 Hill (1956).
48 As quoted in Genoud (1969).
49 See Stryker et al. (1990, pp. 265ff). These estimates are partly based on the fact that Ghana's Western Region, directly adjacent to Ivory Coast, has recently emerged as the country's largest cocoa-producing area. This suggests that cocoa production had developed earlier in that area in response to the "pull" of higher prices in Ivory Coast.
50 Leith (1974, p. 133) reports that the real producer price had fallen below the price required for new plantings in 1964, and was not breached again with the producer price adjustment associated with the 1967 devaluation .
51 For a detailed study of the United Ghana Farmers' Council, which was the farmers' wing of the CPP, see Beckman (1976). Beckman argues "The Council was an organization for controlling the surplus of the cocoa economy in the interest of the state and of its own cadres. It was not, as it was made out to be, an organization for increasing the farmers' share in the profits of the cocoa trade." (p. 235).
52 One of the mechanisms of side-payments even involved farmers' participation in the corrupt practices of the licensed buying agents which replaced the UGFC as the buying agency in 1966.
53 The term "tragedy of the commons" refers to the overgrazing of the medieval village commons, and was used by Hardin (1968).
54 See Krueger (1974).
55 Levi (1988, p. 32).
56 A feel of this period is conveyed in a popular press book (Yankah, 1986).
57 More detail on the reform program is provided in section 5.
58 Adu-Boahen (1989).
59 One informant indicated to us that, by 1983, the Ghana government itself was having to procure inputs of goods and services at the unofficial exchange rate, even while calculating other transactions at the official rate.
60 See Leith (1974), esp. pp. 37ff. and 201–2 for a full discussion.
61 Ewusi (1987) reports data for the real average industrial wage. The index (1970=100) for 1978=37, and for 1982=17.
62 See UNDP and World Bank, *African Economic and Financial Data* (Washington, DC 1989). These data, as with most other Ghanaian data for the period, can at best be taken as broadly representative rather than precise measures of the magnitudes involved.
63 This is not to suggest that structural adjustment does not produce some temporary incremental hardship, but the marginal worsening of social conditions after economic reform has proven frustratingly difficult to measure not only in Ghana but in other adjusting countries. For a full discussion, see Squire

(1991). See also our discussion "Reversal of Urban Bias?"

64   PNDC Initial Proclamation; see *Daily Graphic* (Accra), January 12, 1982, as quoted in Agyeman-Duah (1987, p. 619).

65   Agyeman-Duah, ibid., p. 620.

66   Jeffries (1989, p. 78). Jeffries' quote is from Ocquaye (1980).

67   Gillis et al. (1983).

68   *Foreign Trade Regimes and Economic Development*, NBER, directed by J.N. Bhagwati and A.O. Krueger, vols I through IX, country studies, including the Ghana study (vol. II, by Leith) and vols X and XI, syntheses.

69   It is interesting to note that in the more popular press the consensus is also widely shared now: "A reforming government first needs to 'stabilize' its economy — i.e., cut its budget deficit and stop printing money in order to finance whatever deficit remains. After that it needs to open its economy to international trade and, most likely, devalue its currency; this will align domestic prices with prices in world markets and force the economy to use resources more efficiently." *The Economist*, January 5th, 1991, p. 51.

70   Jeffries (1989, p. 96).

71   Abbey (1989) describes some of the experience.

72   Data on capital inflows and the structure of external debt are from UNDP and World Bank, *African Economic and Financial Data* (Washington, DC, 1989). These data do not correspond to the balance of payments on long-term capital account data. The source of the discrepancy may be definitional, as these data are net of interest repayments.

73   For a brief description of the ERP, as told from the IMF viewpoint, see Chand and van Til (1988).

74   On imports, a dual system of surcharges was adopted with ¢23/US$ for essentials such as food and ¢30/US$ for the remainder. The weighted nominal exchange rate implicit in the bonus/surcharge arrangement was ¢25/US$, and the corresponding real price of foreign exchange index rose to approximately 55 (1957 = 100).

75   Republic of Ghana, *National Program for Economic Development*, July 1, 1987, p. 17

76   Ibid., p. 18.

77   Data are from Ewusi (1987).

78   Republic of Ghana Statistical Service, *Ghana Living Standards Survey, First Year Report, Sept. 1987 – Aug. 1988*, Accra, 1989.

79   Available from Leith on request.

80   P. Beaudry and N.K. Sowa, "Labour Markets in an Era of Adjustment: A Case Study of Ghana," Boston University and University of Ghana, manuscript, March 1990.

81   Ibid, p. 43.

82   Republic of Ghana, *National Program for Economic Development*, July 1, 1987, p. 23.

83   Ibid., p. 24.

84   Ghanaian posted interest rates should be treated with considerable caution as there is no information available on rates actually charged.

85   We have benefited from seeing a number of preliminary drafts of papers on the divestiture issue, including E. Gyimah-Boadi, "SOE Divestiture: Recent Ghanaian Experiences" (presented at Johns Hopkins University, April, 1990)

and Roger Tangri, "The Politics of State Divestiture in Ghana" (University of Ghana, January, 1991).

86 Tangri, ibid.

87 Note that the Resolution Trust Corporation in the United States has been subjected to severe political criticism for selling off some of the wounded Savings and Loans in "sweetheart deals" that brought the government far less than their prospective worth.

88 See Baumol (1990) for a discussion of the importance of the relative incentives to entrepreneurs between rent-seeking and productive enterprise.

89 As a result, the balance of incentives favored the non-tradables over the tradables sector. This does not mean that the balance of incentives between exportables and importable production was neutral under the old regime: in fact, it continued to favor import-competing producers relative to export production, for the import-competing producers enjoyed domestic monopoly rights which enabled them to charge consumers high prices for low-quality goods in short supply.

90 This distinction is modeled in Findlay (1990). For a helpful discussion of the role of the state, see Lal and Rajapatirana (1987).

91 For a useful survey of relevance of the new institutional economics to development economics, see Nabli and Nugent (1989), especially Part One.

REFERENCES

Abbey, J. L. S. 1989: "On Promoting Successful Adjustment: Some Lessons from Ghana," *The 1989 Per Jacobson Lecture*, Washington, DC: IMF.

Adu-Boahen, Albert 1989: *The Ghanaian Sphinx: Reflections on the Contemporary History of Ghana 1972–1987*, Accra: Ghana Academy of Arts and Sciences, pp. 44–5.

Agyeman-Duah, Baffour 1987: "Ghana, 1982–6: The Politics of the P.N.D.C.," *Journal of Modern African Studies*, 25(4).

Austin, Dennis 1964: *Politics in Ghana 1948–1960*, London and New York: Oxford University Press, p. 16.

Austin, Dennis 1976: *Ghana Observed*, Manchester: Manchester University Press, chapter VIII.

Barkan, Joel D. 1983: " 'Urban Bias,' Peasants and Rural Politics in Kenya and Tanzania," Department of Political Science, University of Iowa, Report No. 1, September.

Bates, Robert 1981: *Markets and States in Tropical Africa: The Political Bias of Agricultural Policies*, Berkeley and Los Angeles: University of California Press.

Baumol, Wm. J. 1990: "Entrepreneurship: Productive, Unproductive, and Destructive," *Journal of Political Economy*, 98(5), October, 893–921.

Beckman, Bjorn 1976: *Organizing the Farmers: Cocoa Politics and National Development in Ghana*, Uppsala: Scandinavian Institute of African Studies.

Bienefeld, Manfred 1986: "Analyzing the Politics of African State Policy: Some Thoughts on Robert Bates' Work," *IDS Bulletin*, 17(1).

Bruton, Henry 1989: "Import Substitution," in H. Chenery and T. N. Srinivasan (eds.), *Handbook of Development Economics*, volume II, Amsterdam, Elsevier, pp. 1602–3.

Chand, Sheetal K. and van Til, Reinold 1988: "Ghana: Toward Successful Stabilization and Recovery," *Finance and Development*, March, pp. 32–5.

Chazan, Naomi 1983: *An Anatomy of Ghanaian Politics: Managing Political Recession, 1969–1982*, Boulder, CO: Westview Press.

Chenery, Hollis 1979: *Structural Change and Development Policy*, New York and London: Oxford University Press, p. 275.

Drake, St. Clair and Lacy, Leslie Alexander 1966: "Government Versus the Unions: The Sekondi-Takoradi Strike, 1961," in Gwendolen M. Carter (ed.), *Politics in Africa: 7 Cases*, New York and Chicago: Harcourt, Brace & World.

Edwards, S. 1989: *Real Exchange Rates, Devaluation, and Adjustment*, Cambridge, Mass.: MIT Press.

Ewusi, K. 1987: *Structural Adjustment and Stabilization Policies in Developing Countries: A Case Study of Ghana's Experience in 1983–1986*, Tema: Ghana Publishing Corporation, table 26, pp. 56–7.

Findlay, Ronald 1990: "The New Political Economy: Its Explanatory Power for LDCs," *Economis and Politics*, 2(2), July, pp. 193–221.

Genoud, Roger 1969: *Nationalism and Economic Development in Ghana*, New York: Praeger, p. 29.

Gillis, M. 1988: "West Africa: Resource Management Policies and the Tropical Forest," in R. Repetto and M. Gillis (eds.), *Public Policies and the Misuse of Forest Resources*, New York: Cambridge University Press, p. 304.

Gillis, M., Perkins, D. H., Roemer, M., and Snodgrass, D. 1983: *Economics of Development*, New York: W. W. Norton.

Grindle, Merilee S. 1989: "The New Political Economy: Positive Economics and Negative Politics," Harvard Institute for International Development, Development Discussion Paper No. 311, August, p. 38.

Hardin, G. 1968: "The Tragedy of the Commons," *Science*, 162, December, 1343–8.

Hill, Polly 1956: *The Gold Coast Cocoa Farmers*, London: Oxford University Press.

Jeffries, Richard 1989: "Ghana: The Political Economy of Personal Rule," in Donal B. Cruise O'Brien, John Dunn, and Richard Rathbone (eds.), *Contemporary West African States*, Cambridge and New York: Cambridge University Press, p. 79.

Killick, Tony 1978: *Development Economics in Action: A Study of Economic Policies in Ghana*, London: Heinemann.

Krueger, Anne O. 1974: "The Political Economy of the Rent-Seeking Society," *American Economic Review*, 64(3), 291–303.

Lal, Deepak and Rajapatirana, Sarath 1987: "Foreign Trade Regimes and Economic Growth in Developing Countries," *World Bank Research Observer*, 2(2), July, 189–218.

Leith, J. Clark 1974: *Foreign Trade Regimes and Economic Development: Ghana*, New York: National Bureau of Economic Research.

Levi, Margaret 1988: *Of Rule and Revenue*, Berkeley and Los Angeles: University of California Press.

Lewis, W. Arthur 1969: *Some Aspects of Economic Development*, Accra-Tema: University of Ghana.

Lipton, Michael 1976: *Why Poor People Stay Poor: Urban Bias in World Development*, Cambridge, Mass.: Harvard University Press.

Mikell, Gwendolyn 1989: *Cocoa and Chaos in Ghana*, New York: Paragon House, pp. 212–14.

Nabli, M. K. and Nugent, J. B. 1989: *The New Institutional Economics and Development*, Amsterdam: North Holland.

Ocquaye, Mike 1980: *Politics in Ghana, 1972–1979*, Accra: Tornado Publications.

Ray, Donald I. 1986: *Ghana: Politics, Economics and Society*, Boulder, CO: Lynne Rienner Publishers, p. 22.

Roemer, M. 1971: "Relative Factor Prices in Ghana Manufacturing," *Economic Bulletin of Ghana*, Second Series, 1(4).

Singer, Hans W. and Ansari, Javed A. 1977: *Rich and Poor Countries*, London: George Allen & Unwin, p. 65.

Squire, Lyn 1991: "Introduction: Poverty and Adjustment in the 1980s," *The World Bank Economic Review*, 5(2), May.

Stryker, J. Dirk et al. 1990: *Trade, Exchange Rate, and Agricultural Pricing Policies in Ghana*, Washington, DC: World Bank.

Ward, Barbara 1961: *The Rich Nations and the Poor Nations*, Toronto: Canadian Broadcasting Company, pp. 57–8.

Yankah, Kojo 1986: *The Trial of J. J. Rawlings*, Accra: Ghana Publishing Company, p. 31.

7

Policy Reform in Korea
Stephan Haggard, Richard N. Cooper and Chung-in Moon

INTRODUCTION

In the early 1960s, Korea undertook wide-ranging policy reforms, launching the country on the path of export-oriented growth that has been the hallmark of its development ever since. The key components of this transition to export-led growth included stabilization, devaluation, and selective import liberalization, though the government also promoted exports through financial subsidies and a variety of other more targeted interventions.

How are such reforms to be explained? One hypothesis is that the adoption of export-oriented policies is likely to be a response to international economic and political constraints. Persistent balance of payments problems and the prospect of declining American assistance did motivate devaluations in 1960 and 1961 as well as the gradual introduction of export-promotion measures. In 1963, the balance of payments position once again deteriorated, and the United States explicitly used aid leverage to secure the military government's compliance with a stabilization plan. The prospect of declining aid served as a spur to export policy, foreign borrowing, and efforts to increase domestic savings.

A second hypothesis is that reforms can be explained by domestic economic conditions. In the late 1950s, economic growth slowed as a result of efforts to stabilize the economy and the exhaustion of possibilities for continued import substitution. Poor economic performance probably contributed to Syngman Rhee's overthrow in 1960, and was a major motivation for the military's entry into politics in 1961. Inflation also played a role in 1963, serving as the impetus to the initial reform effort, which centered on stabilizing prices. As we will argue, certain economic conditions contributed to the economic success of the policy reform efforts once launched, and thus contributed to their political viability. A substantial pause in real wage growth in the early 1960s contributed to high business profits.

An explanation of the reform process that relies on international constraints and domestic economic conditions leaves important puzzles unsolved, however. The first concerns economic thresholds and the timing of initiatives. All economic policy adjustments are a response to economic conditions; the real question is the sensitivity of the government to those conditions. The answer is likely to reside in the political realm. The American government exerted pressure on the Korean government throughout the 1950s, and though it succeeded in stabilizing prices, it was unable to force the Rhee government to undertake other structural reforms. Nor did declining performance induce Rhee to adjust policy in any but a marginal way. GNP growth rates declined steadily from 8.8 percent in 1957 to 2.3 percent in 1960 (table 7.1) with little coherent government response.

Second, once a decision has been taken to launch policy initiatives, their precise content and the pattern of implementation are likely to reflect political calculations and constraints. In the early 1960s, the military had a strong interest in revitalizing the economy. Yet they sought to do so through an expansionist macroeconomic policy and new forms of intervention designed to address political grievances that accumulated during the Rhee period. Only when this strategy proved politically as well as economically unsustainable did the generals turn toward a more market-oriented approach. When they did, however, the new strategy bore a

Table 7.1 Korea: basic economic indicators, 1955–66

	GNP growth (% per annum)	CPI[a] (% per annum)	GNP deflator (% per annum)	Balance on current account ($m)	Fiscal expenditure (% GNP)	Deficit (% per annum)
1955	6.1		67.4	−266.7	12.9	6.7
1956	1.2	23.0	30.1	−329.3	15.0	7.9
1957	8.8	23.2	20.9	−387.5	20.2	12.7
1958	5.5	−3.6	−0.7	−311.2	23.0	14.1
1959	4.4	3.2	2.3	−227.5	20.9	8.9
1960	2.3	8.1	9.3	−262.3	19.6	7.6
1961	4.2	8.2	16.1	−198.4	22.0	12.4
1962	3.5	6.7	13.9	−290.2	27.3	16.5
1963	9.1	19.7	30.9	−402.8	10.0	8.4
1964	8.3	27.9	34.5	−221.0	13.8	6.6
1965	7.4	13.6	8.3	−198.6	15.2	6.6
1966	13.4	12.1	14.7	−323.0	19.0	8.2

[a]CPI is the Seoul Consumer Price Index; data are unavailable for 1955.
Sources: Bank of Korea, *Economic Statistical Yearbook*, various issues; for fiscal data, Bahl et al. (1986, table 1, pp. 8–10).

number of military imprints, including a nationalized banking sector and extensive use of subsidies and other command instruments.

A final objection to a purely economic argument is that politics can affect economic outcomes not only through the choice process, but through its effect on the confidence of the private sector and the credibility of reforms. Exchange rate policy under the Rhee government was less unfavorable to exports than is frequently thought, but the unpredictability of trade policy constituted a major constraint on export growth. The Chang Myon government had reformist intentions, but an uncertain political environment dampened investor response.

An analysis of policy change can clearly benefit from closer attention to politics. The political economy approach favored by most economists focuses on the interests of organized social groups, which are assumed to pursue their economic interests by attempting to exercise influence in the political realm. This approach is useful in characterizing a given status quo or political equilibrium, but it confronts several difficulties that have to do with the public goods quality of reform efforts. First, the beneficiaries of reform are likely to be poorly organized in comparison to those who benefit from the status quo. Any interest group explanation of reform must confront the substantial collective action problems that arise when any particular agent can benefit by remaining exempt while others are exposed to reform. Second, the beneficiaries of reform may resist policies ex ante that favor them ex post because of uncertainty about their effects. Any policy reform can only be consolidated on the basis of a new coalition of "winners," but the *initiation* of policy reform may succeed precisely because of the government's *independence* from particularistic interests.[1]

Put differently, governments can be 'out ahead' of the beneficiaries of policy reform, and policy changes can create their own constituencies. It is therefore important to focus not only on interest groups, but on the power, ideology, political interests, and coalitional strategies of political elites. We place particular weight on the nature of political institutions, which structured the incentives to political action and thus played an important role in understanding the transition to export-led growth.

Our argument can be outlined briefly. In the 1950s, the financial weakness of the ruling Liberal Party, and its declining political fortunes, made it rational for Syngman Rhee to maximize his dependence on aid, limit the domain of coherent planning and maintain discretionary control over a variety of policy instruments. As the rent-seeking literature would predict, the dense networks that developed between the Liberal Party, the bureaucracy and the private sector acted as an impediment to any reform effort. As import-substituting policies reached their limits and growth slowed, some sectors and firms did seek export opportunities and the government did undertake a devaluation. Yet the private sector's interest in policy reform was ambivalent because of the benefits they secured from the policy status quo. Predictably, their lobbying efforts were aimed at securing particularistic gains rather than broad reforms.

The brief Chang Myon government (1960–1) provides an analytically important point of comparison both with the Rhee government that preceded it and the military regime that followed. Riding strong popular demands for reform, the government sought to reverse Rhee's neglect of the economy and initiated a number of policy changes, including raising state-owned enterprises (SOE) charges, devaluing the exchange rate and initiating new export promotion measures. The economic effect of these measures during the tenure of the Chang Myon government appears to have been mixed, however; in any case the government proved too weak politically and organizationally to sustain them. Indeed, the reforms probably contributed to the government's political difficulties.

Unlike right-wing military coups that seek to curb "unrest" or restore a status quo ante, the military wrapped itself in the banner of reform. Like Rhee, the military under Park Chung Hee used economic instruments for political ends, and its initial policies had a strong populist cast. But the military's reliance on economic development as the main legitimating rationale for its intervention in politics and increasing American pressure made the government more amenable to American advice.

Equally important, however, was that the military under Park Chung Hee had the *institutional capacity* to act decisively and to construct a new political coalition around an alternative development model; in this, the military government differed from is civilian predecessor. With the concentration of decision-making authority in the hands of the executive during the period of military rule, the power of the legislature, political parties, and politicians was eliminated. Nor did the military initially have any ties to the business networks that constituted the political foundations of import-substituting industry (ISI). Though the government was forced to reach compromises with the private sector to achieve its objectives, it did so from a much strengthened position that enhanced the credibility of its initiatives.

The changed political milieu had implications for the relationship between political elites and technocrats, which in turn constituted a second order influence on the reform process. During the 1950s, the economic bureaucracy might be described as "dualistic."[2] Technocrats sought to advance a reform agenda, but they occupied a peripheral role in a policy system dominated by politicians. Particularly in the 1950s, when the economic bureaucracy was weakly developed, planning efforts were organizationally scattered and lacked executive support. The military, by contrast, launched a series of institutional reforms aimed at enhancing the government's ability to plan and implement economic policy: a purge and reform of the civil service, the creation of new policy instruments and the centralization of economic decision-making. These institutional reforms outlasted the military interregnum and contributed to the coherence and credibility of subsequent policy.

1   THE POLITICAL ECONOMY OF IMPORT-SUBSTITUTION UNDER SYNGMAN RHEE, 1954–60

Analysis of Korea's economic policy must begin with the central role of US assistance. Between 1953 and 1960, aid financed nearly 70 percent of total imports, and aid and counterpart funds accounted for 73 percent of the government's borrowing requirement. From South Korea's independence in 1948, the United States consistently sought to link this foreign assistance to economic policy. The components of this conditionality have a familiar ring today: close monitoring of foreign exchange and a realistic exchange rate, sound fiscal and monetary policies, privatization of state-owned properties inherited from the Japanese, and a rationalization of the economic policy-making structure.

There were some limited successes in this effort. After acrimonious debates over the exchange rate following the signing of the armistice in 1954, US policy gradually shifted to emphasize control of macroeconomic policy and inflation. Beginning in fiscal year 1958, the Ministry of Finance worked closely with US advisors in devising annual stabilization programs that sharply reduced government borrowing from the Central Bank. As table 7.1 shows, however, the program did not have the effect of curbing Rhee's propensity to spend. The programs were effective because of monetary restraint and above all because of aid financing of the deficit. The stabilization programs did not succeed in addressing fundamental distortions in the allocation of resources, corruption, or the lack of a rational planning process, however. Stabilization thus contributed to the steady economic deceleration typically associated with the exhaustion of ISI.

Two political factors help explain this policy pattern, one external, the other internal. The first is the reluctance of the Eisenhower administration to place strong pressure on the Rhee government because of strategic concerns. The 1950s were the high tide of the Cold War, and Rhee was masterful in exploiting American interest in maintaining its nominally democratic Asian showcase. Aid did drop after its peak in 1957, particularly in 1958 (table 7.2). But aid in the mid–1950s was unusually high even by past Korean standards, and the drop in assistance in the mid–1950s appears to have reflected the end of basic reconstruction and internal American reassessments of aid commitments. At that point in time, there was no consistent effort to use aid as a lever on the government except with reference to macroeconomic and exchange rate policy, and in both of these areas there was latitude for the Korean government to evade American scrutiny.

Table 7.2 Foreign economic assistance received ($ millions)

		Of which	
	Total	PL480	ICA[a]
1953	194.2		5.6
1954	153.9		82.4
1955	236.7		205.8
1956	326.7	33.0	271.0
1957	382.9	45.5	323.4
1958	321.3	47.9	265.6
1959	222.2	11.4	208.3
1960	245.4	19.9	225.2
1961	199.2	44.9	154.3
1962	239.3	67.3	165.0
1963	216.4	96.8	119.7
1964	149.3	61.0	88.3
1965	131.4	59.5	71.9
1966	103.2	37.9	65.3

[a]International Cooperation Agency and its successor, the Agency for International Development.
Source: Bank of Korea, *Economic Statistical Yearbook*, various issues. Differences between the total and US aid figures are accounted for primarily by multilateral assistance.

The more profound reason for the policy impasse was domestic. Rhee began to face more intense political competition during the late 1950s. Running unopposed in 1956, Rhee managed to capture only 55 percent of the popular vote, down from 72 percent in 1952. There was a shift in Rhee's style of leadership in an even more autocratic and defensive direction following this election.[3] Police intimidation of the opposition increased, and, in December 1958, a harsh National Security Law was passed which provided for prison terms for those "libeling" the President or top government officials or who aided the enemy by spreading "false information."

The very nature of the political institutions imposed on Rhee by the Americans demanded that he play the electoral game, however. One obvious way of mobilizing funds to finance elections and other party activities was to forge a closer alliance with the private sector, particularly the new businessmen who had arisen in the post-World War II period through commerce or the acquisition of state-owned enterprises. As these firms sought to diversify beyond their commercial activities into manufacturing, they sought government support. The grant of various privileges generated rents that could be partly recycled back to government officials, to the party, and to individual legislators.

Since Rhee's preference for an overvalued exchange rate was one of the most contentious issues between Washington and Seoul in the 1950s, and since exchange rate policy was a crucial component of subsequent reforms, it is worth tracing this issue in some detail.[4] Under a settlement reached in February 1953, the United States paid $85.8 million for its wartime *won* drawings, an amount reflecting a highly overvalued rate given high inflation. In return for this settlement, however, the United States demanded that a more realistic rate be set by April 30. An acrimonious negotiation ensued, with the United States arguing for a rate based on a price index and subject to quarterly readjustments. The new agreement on rates made significant concession to the Koreans but was broken almost at once. In part by holding up procurement contracts, the United States got the Korean government to devalue in December 1953 in an agreement that also included a number of other policy reforms, including increased taxation, fiscal restraint, controls on the money supply, and the privatization of the banking sector (see table 7.3).

Rhee visited Washington in July 1954, and again the United States extracted pledges to maintain a realistic rate.[5] Despite the agreement, US aid coordinator E. Tyler Wood was subjected to a tirade from Rhee on his first meeting with the president in September 1954 on the need to maintain a fixed rate in order to avoid inflation and restore confidence.[6] Rhee

Table 7.3   Won-dollar exchange rates, 1953–66

Date[a]	Official rate	Free market rate/US greenbacks	Real effective exchange rate
Aug. 28, 1953	6	26.4	55.6
*Dec. 15, 1953 (200%)	18	38.7	152.5
Aug. 8, 1955	50	80.2	55.7
*Aug. 15, 1955 (177%)	50	80.2	154.8
Average 1956	50	96.6	136.6
Average 1957	50	103.3	117.6
Average 1958	50	118.1	125.3
Average 1959	65	125.5	122.5
*Feb. 23, 1960 (30%)	100	144.9	150.5
*Jan. 1, 1961 (53%)	130	139.8	207.5
*Feb. 2, 1961 (30%)	130	148.3	256.9
Average 1962	130	134.0	232.1
Average 1963	256	174.5	192.6
*May 3, 1964 (100%)	256	285.6	270.0
Mar. 22, 1965[b]	256	316.0	264.5
Average 1966	271	302.7	249.4

*Indicates date of devaluation.
[a] Official won–dollar rate adjusted for relative movement in consumer price indices.
[b] A number of separate rates were unified on March 22, 1965.
Source: Frank et al., tables 3-1 and 3-2, pp. 30–1, 32–3.

threatened that if the United States did not agree, he would revert to an even more overvalued rate. Following an exchange of threats and counterthreats, a new agreement was reached in August 1955 that devalued the official and counterpart rates. The agreement specified that the won–dollar rate could be readjusted, but only if an agreed price index were to increase by 25 percent; not until January 1960 was this adjustment mechanism invoked, apparently because of the very success of the stabilization plans in slowing inflation.

Neither the 1955 nor 1960 devaluations signaled a firm commitment on the part of the Rhee government to expanding exports, however. First, the combination of declining aid, rising budget deficits, and numerous changes in the exchange rate regime under Rhee no doubt served to undermine the confidence in government pronouncements. Perhaps even more telling was the unwillingness of the government to exploit its proximity to Japan, which, given its demand for raw materials and differences in level of development, constituted a natural trading partner for Korea.

Over the 1950s, trade relations between the two countries were dictated by Rhee's almost fanatically anti-Japanese stance. A trade and financial agreement was signed between the two countries in June 1950.[7] Following the agreement, Korean imports from Japan rose sharply, but Korean exports were sluggish, despite the fact that exporters to Japan were granted an exchange rate that was significantly higher than the official rate and frequently approached, or even exceeded, the black market rate in dollars. The result was a bilateral imbalance, which, though not as absolutely or proportionately large as the imbalance with the United States, was nonetheless substantial. In April 1954, the Seoul government introduced a trade-balancing measure under which South Korean traders were authorized to import Japanese goods exclusively with exchange proceeds from exports to Japan.

Under other settings, the combination of a relatively favorable exchange rate and the additional premium resulting from access to quotas might have constituted a powerful incentive to expand exports to Japan. But the Rhee government twice severed trade with Japan altogether for political reasons over the decade: once in August 1955 to protest Japan's opening of trade relations with China and North Korea, and again in June 1959 for Japan's repatriation of some Korean residents in Japan to North Korea. Trade was not resumed with Japan following this last cutoff until just before the student revolution in April 1960 and several months after the January devaluation. Thus, the surge in exports in that year reflects the reopening of trade relations, as well as the lifting of Japanese quotas on rice and fish and the effects of the devaluation.

US criticism of the exchange rate and trade regimes was usually couched in terms of the need to encourage the productive and efficient use of resources. But the battle over exchange rate policy also clearly reflected a concern with the abuses permitted by controls, particularly since the allocation of foreign exchange was lodged at the highest levels of government and influenced by Rhee's chief of staff, Park Chal Il and by Rhee's wife.[8] A GAO report noted that "laxity" by the Bank of Korea in the allocation of aid dollars to importers had encouraged speculation and led to a number of procurement irregularities, including collusion between supplier and importer, shipment of defective merchandise, kickbacks, and overpricing. The auditing efforts of the US aid mission were weak, however, and even those devices intended to limit abuse, such as the auctioning of foreign exchange, were circumvented. By nominating "eligible" bidders, the government circumvented the control that the auction was designed to generate and engineered opportunities for collusion.[9]

Trade policy was naturally closely tied with access to foreign exchange, though in this area US policy advice was far from liberal. In 1957, an amendment to the tariff law lowered tariffs on capital goods and raw materials and higher tariffs were imposed on locally manufactured goods and on finished and semifinished goods, but tariff policy does not appear to have been central to controlling imports. The main opportunities for rent-seeking appear to have been in the distribution of aid goods that were priced at the official exchange rate. Firms in a range of processing industries, including the famous 'three whites' (wheat flour, sugar, and cotton) had liberal access to PL480 shipments of wheat, raw sugar, and yarn. For example, wheat was provided virtually free of duty to millers through PL480. The cost of producing a sack of wheat flour was estimated at 350 won, including a 3 percent margin and processing costs. But domestic manufacturers were able to charge 1,200 won per sack, and shortages sometimes drove prices to 5,000 won.[10]

The sources of rent-seeking extended beyond the trade and exchange rate regime to a variety of domestic policies. One of the most controversial elements of economic management under the Rhee regime was the allocation of bank loans. In the 1950s, capital was scarce and inflation relatively high, but interest rates were kept low, reflecting a policy of financial repression. Government ceilings on loan rates meant windfalls for those firms gaining access to finance. The most notorious preferential loans came prior to the election of March 10, 1960, which ultimately resulted in Rhee's fall. From August 1959 to March 1960, a total of 10.7 billion won were released to 45 selected firms, of which 6.2 billion returned to the Liberal Party in the form of political contributions. Host firms paid "commissions" of 10–15 percent on the loans, but some of the largest loans – one billion won to Daehan Cement, 500 million won to Taichang Textiles – were passed on in their entirety.[11]

Government contracting was another area in which extensive irregularities were later uncovered. The United States was aware of the fact that government contracts were frequently awarded without open bidding, that the bidding pool was limited to those "nominated," and that apparently open bidding frequently involved collusion.[12] Privatization also provided opportunities for corruption. These were most visible in the financial sector. In November 1954, the government initiated a series of public auctions of Japanese financial institutions that had fallen into state hands. Through 1955, six auctions were held, but all proved unsuccessful because of the low bids. Two months prior to the presidential election of May 1956, the seventh open bidding was held. In two cases, the third highest bidders were able to gain controlling interests in major banks. The government justified the irregular decision by claiming that the banks could not be entrusted to financially weak firms, but it was known that the two firms, Samsung and Sam Ho Textiles, provided not only short-term election funds through the sale but a longer-term pipeline for funds.

These examples of the political use of economic instruments suggest how planning efforts were undermined not only by market reactions but by outside political pressures as well. Not only were policy instruments used for political purposes, but the staffing of the bureaucracy itself was an important form of patronage.[13] The aggregate picture demands some modification, however, since portions of the bureaucracy were open to innovation and planning. The bureaucracy might be described as "dualistic": technically-oriented "developmental enclaves"[14] existed, but their functioning was circumscribed by the political interference of the top leadership. Nonetheless, the administrative innovations that did occur provided the bureaucratic raw material from which later institutional developments were forged.

In 1955, Rhee established the Ministry of Reconstruction (MOR). As a counterpart to the US aid mission, the purpose of the MOR was to develop plans that could be used to nail down US aid commitments over a longer time horizon. The first Minister of Reconstruction was Son In-sang, an ex-banker with experience at the World Bank. The MOR was involved in the coordination of annual stabilization plans with the American aid mission through the revived Combined Economic Board, which provided a working link with foreign advisors interested in rationalizing economic management.

It was not until 1958, however, that domestic planning efforts got underway, influenced by the Indian model.[15] An Economic Development Council (EDC) was formed in March 1958 as a consulting and research agency for the Ministry of Reconstruction, financed partly by counterpart funds. In April 1959, the EDC economists drafted a Three-Year Plan which was to be the foundation for later planning efforts. The macroeconomic framework was a relatively sophisticated one that stressed employment objectives and based investment requirements on specified capital–labor ratios by sector. The plan spurred reforms in the government's statistical capabilities and became an important educational device for all those immediately concerned, even if its technical sophistication far outstripped the government's capacity to implement it.

The fate of the Three-Year Plan was decided by politics both within and outside the bureaucracy. The semi-independent status of the EDC created interministerial jealousies, particularly with the Ministry of Finance which resisted MOR's efforts to extend its authority. Additional problems were raised by the relative youth and low rank of the reform group. The nature of the broader political milieu guaranteed that support for the reformers would not be forthcoming. As the discussion of rent-seeking behavior suggests, the economic bureaucracy as a whole had little autonomy from pressures emanating from the Party, the private sector and the executive itself.

Conditions only worsened as the political situation deteriorated over the late 1950s. Preoccupied with political problems, Rhee reviewed the Three-Year Plan only twice during the two year period of its formulation. Besieged by political difficulties in 1959, the Liberal Party shelved the final draft of the plan for a year, approving it only a few days before the student revolution that ended Liberal Party rule. The last years of the Rhee administration were thus a period of some innovation within the economic bureaucracy, but these innovations took place in a larger political context that blocked reform.

2   THE SECOND REPUBLIC, APRIL 1960–MAY 1961

The Second Republic was launched following a series of demonstrations against the Rhee government that culminated in the "student revolution" in April and Rhee's resignation.[16] The opposition Democratic Party came to power in July, replacing an interim government. "Political" demands were central to the student revolt, but many of these were tied to the rent-seeking system outlined above. Not surprisingly, the elimination of corruption was a top political priority of the new administration. It is also undoubtedly significant that rising opposition to Rhee occurred against the backdrop of steadily deteriorating economic performance.

The change of government permitted a change in the bargaining relationship with the United States. The Chang Myon government continued to seek aid, but took the initiative in raising sensitive issues such as the rationalization of public enterprises and in general the move toward a more market-oriented economy. The new government agreed to a devaluation of the won from 650 to the dollar to 1,000 on January 1, 1961, and the unification of the exchange rate at the further devalued rate of 1,300 to the dollar on February 2. This action had long been sought by the United States, which backed it with a $20 million stabilization fund.

High-level support was also given to new planning efforts. In November, 1960, the Ministry of Reconstruction was instructed to draft a new five-year development plan that would improve upon and supersede previous efforts. Written with assistance from American advisor Charles Wolf, the new plan stressed the need for a "leading sectors" approach that would concentrate investment in power, coal, cement, and several other industries, as well as agriculture. Work was also begun on restructuring the economic bureaucracy itself in an effort to link planning efforts more squarely with implementation.

If public statements by Chang Myon and international bureaucratic alignments seemed to be moving toward reform, the larger political context was much less favorable. Part of the problem lay with short-term economic policy reforms themselves. Devaluation and the increase in rates for government-subsidized services may have been appropriate policies, but they reduced popular support for the government at a particularly vulnerable moment. Food shortages in April and May and upward pressure on grain prices were annual events, but strong upward pressure on food prices was visible in January, usually a period when adequate stocks guarantee price stability. Price trends thus probably reflected a high level of uncertainty.

Economic problems were not the only difficulties facing the new regime. The Democratic Party was a loose coalition of anti-Rhee politicians. Many saw the ascent to power as the opportunity to exploit the patronage benefits of office so long denied them. Members of the ruling party quickly moved into positions in public enterprises and administrators with a party affiliation were favored for promotion.[17]

Chang Myon also suffered broader political weaknesses. He had been selected as prime minister only after a factional struggle that ultimately split the party. Reform of the military, purge of corrupt officials, confiscation of illicitly accumulated wealth, and unification with the North gained the attention of intellectuals and students and became highly divisive issues. Labor, including teachers and bank employees, took advantage of the political opening to organize and press their demands, putting additional pressures on the government.[18] The Second Republic represents a classic case of broad political mobilization coupled with weak political institutions. Chang Myon was unable to reconcile the conflicting demands placed on the government from left and right, and lacked autonomy from his own supporters. When the government appeared incapable of maintaining order, the military intervened.

3   MILITARY INTERREGNUM, MAY 1961– DECEMBER 1964: POLITICAL AND INSTITUTIONAL CHANGE

Before we turn to the evolution of economic policy under the military, it is important to outline some of the enduring political and institutional changes in the Korean political system that resulted from the military coup of May 16, 1961. First, the military broke the old political networks centered on the legislature by centralizing power in the executive. Even after the transition to nominal democratic rule in 1964, the new political structure had resulted in a higher degree of executive independence from the legislature and even from the ruling party than had been enjoyed by Rhee. A second major change was the restructuring of business–state relations. A new alliance with the private sector was forged in the early 1960s, but the opportunities for rent-seeking were reduced and the government achieved substantial independence from the demands of what Mancur Olson has called "distributional coalitions."[19] Finally, the centralization of political authority was matched by a centralization of economic decision-making within the government in the Economic Planning Board, with greater control exercised over clientelistic ministries. These institutional reforms increased the power of the reformist technocrats by elevating their stature within the bureaucracy and by expanding the range of policy instruments at their disposal. In sum, the military attacked the three institutional legs of the rent-seeking system: the political parties, the private sector, and the bureaucracy itself. We discuss each of these changes briefly before turning to the dynamics of policy reform.

An important feature of the Korean military was that it had few sociological ties to the dominant political elite, and thus had no reservations about a thorough-going restructuring of politics.[20] The coup leaders were relatively young, in their mid to late thirties, and most of them came from poor rural backgrounds. The coup leaders were not 'above politics' prior to the coup. Park Chung Hee and his followers had been strongly critical of the corrupt and incompetent military leadership, which was closely tied to Rhee's rent-seeking system.[21] These reformist military officers, mostly colonels and lieutenant colonels from the fifth and eighth class of the Military Academy, supported the reformist goals of the student revolution and had called for a purge of corrupt officers. The Chang Myon government proved incapable of launching such a reform, and had simultaneously sought to cut military spending as part of its austerity efforts, thus alienating both younger and older officers alike.

Following the coup on May 16 and the declaration of martial law, all political parties and organizations, including unions, were banned and the press was subjected to censorship. A Revolutionary Court and Prosecution was established in July to try those accused of various crimes, including the "illicit" accumulation of wealth and corruption. In the spring of 1962, 4,369 politicians and government officials were forbidden to participate in politics unless undergoing a screening by the military, a process that failed to clear the top leaders of the Democratic Party. The bureaucracy and military were not immune from the drive for "purification." In July, 2,000 officers were retired, including 40 generals, and 1,863 government employees were found to have been involved in corruption and "antirevolutionary" activities.

The actual consolidation of political authority proved circuitous because of deep splits within the military itself.[22] In August 1961, Park promised a return to civilian government in May 1963. Hoping to capitalize on the opposition's disarray, the junta announced an early election, with Park accepting the nomination of the newly formed Democratic Republican Party (DRP). The decision to return to a democratic system brought the factional splits within the Supreme Council for National Reconstruction (SCNR), the body of coup leaders, into the open. The younger officers wanted an extension of military rule to carry out a wide-ranging transformation of society and economy, with the DRP acting like a vanguard party.[23] When Park sought to heal the split within the military by announcing he would postpone the elections, however, he precipitated a general political crisis and strong protests from Washington. Park relented, but even with a fragmented and politically tainted opposition, Park won only a narrow victory amidst charges of election fraud.

Despite the nominal return to democracy in January 1964, the new constitution greatly strengthened the power of the executive.[24] The legislature proved to be a weak body, having, for example, only feeble control over the budget. Ministerial bills emanating from the executive outnumbered those originating from assemblymen and were formulated without close consultation with assemblymen. A stringent Political Party Law placed various restrictions on political activity, and even served to weaken the DRP. The president had complete say in the appointment of the cabinet, including the prime minister, great influence both formal and informal over the judiciary, and a range of emergency powers. Moreover, Park explicitly drew a link between such a centralized political system and the tasks of economic development. The following is but one example of a theme sounded throughout his political career:

> In order to ensure efforts to improve the living conditions of the people in Asia even undemocratic measures may be necessary...It is also an undeniable fact that the people of Asia today fear starvation and poverty more than the oppressive duties thrust on them by totalitarianism...In other words, the Asian people want to obtain economic equality first and build a more equitable political machinery afterward.[25]

The importance of state power for reform is also visible in the restructuring of business–government relations. After the fall of the Rhee government, the punishment of those who had illicitly accumulated wealth during the 1950s became a major political issue that the military could not ignore. Two weeks after the coup, 13 major businessmen were arrested. Though eight of these were induced to make large "contributions" to the government and were released, the investigation was broadened to include another 120 businessmen. The definition of "illicit" wealth accumulation was inclusive, covering the entire range of rent-seeking and rent-granting activities that had been pervasive, if not unavoidable, under Rhee. Moreover, radical members of the junta were arguing that all illegally accumulated fortunes should be confiscated outright and the profiteers put before a firing squad.

The government did seize all outstanding shares of commercial bank stocks, thus gaining direct control of an important institution. Bargains were ultimately struck with large manufacturing and construction firms, however. The reason is summarized neatly by Kyong-dong Kim: "the only viable economic force happened to be the target group of leading entrepreneurial talents with their singular advantage of organization, personnel, facilities and capital resource."[26]

On their release, the members of the newly formed Korean Business-men's Association submitted a plan to the Supreme Council identifying 14 key industrial plants – cement, steel, fertilizer, cable, etc. – in which they were interested in investing if the appropriate supportive policies were forthcoming. All of these projects were import-substituting in nature; there was no demand from the private sector for the reforms that are generally associated with export-oriented policies. A key issue for the government was access to investment capital, both foreign and domestic, since the penalties imposed for the illicit accumulation of wealth that were to be invested in new plants totaled less than one-sixth of the cost of the Association's plan.[27]

The interpretation of the illegal wealth accumulation episode is the subject of substantial controversy. Some accounts have stressed the continuity with past practice and the structural power of business.[28] Despite its initial populism, the military was forced to make peace with a newly organized private sector. Park was no different from Rhee in favoring certain entrepreneurs who could help him politically, and politicians in the Democratic Republican Party were as dependent on business contributions as Liberal Party politicians had been. The practice of "political taxation" of the private sector was an open secret, as were corrupt practices that were reminiscent of the Rhee era. The question of preferential loans became a major political controversy in 1964 and 1965, when it was discovered that bank lending was heavily concentrated in a small number of large firms, and similar controversies surrounded the granting of foreign loan guarantees.[29]

The thesis of continuity overlooks important changes in the nature of business–government relations that were to persist through the 1970s. Even where discretionary favors were extended to larger firms, they were generally tied to some developmental purpose. Business developed forms of collective organization that had not existed in the past, but the agenda of the business–government dialogue now included developmental as well as purely political considerations; there was an *economic* quid-pro-quo for government support. This change was possible because the government had acquired greater analytic capacity, as well as greater control over the instruments of economic policy, than it had during the 1950s. The seizure of the banking system was particularly important in this regard, since it provided the government a powerful lever over business behavior.

Finally, as we will argue in more detail below, the economic reforms launched by the military reduced the opportunities for the directly unproductive profit-making activities that had existed under the Rhee government. While the government retained a high level of discretion over some policy instruments, others, such as loans to exporters and access to imported inputs, were extended to exporting firms on a nondiscretionary basis.

The third political change undertaken by the military was a restructuring of the bureaucracy and of the economic decision-making structure. The change of government provided an auspicious opening for reformers within the bureaucracy to push forward the ideas concerning administrative restructuring that had already been developed in the Rhee and Chang Myon periods. The reformers' plans for an Economic Planning Board fitted with the centralizing tendencies that accompanied the period of military rule, resulting in a ministry that had an unusual level of intrabureaucratic independence and control over the activities of other ministries. The centralization of decision-making authority outlasted the period of military rule and became a central feature of Korea's system of economic management.

The new ministry consisted of the budget bureau, transferred from the Ministry of Finance, the statistics and research bureau, moved from the Ministry of Home Affairs, and the planning coordination offices from MOR. From its initiation, however, the EPB came to have a powerful say over other ministries, through the budget. EPB's Bureau of Budget prepares the broad guidelines for the annual budget, collects annual proposals from the other ministries and evaluates their feasibility. EPB's power lies in its ability to designate specific projects for which other ministries prepare the budgetary implications, and above all, its power to adjust the budget estimates submitted by the ministries, which generally exceed that called for by the total budget. EPB then passes the budget on to the president for approval, and though the National Assembly is given 60 days to deliberate on the budget, it has little power to alter the budget's structure.

A capital import bureau was also established in 1961, and EPB's power extended to the area of foreign borrowing. In July 1962, the ministry was given the power to grant government guarantees to loans and to audit and oversee the activities of the borrowing firms. When coupled with the power to approve and extend incentives to foreign direct investment and the ability to select those capital goods imports and importers which qualified for government-aided deferred payment privileges, the new ministry effectively gained complete control over Korea's import of foreign capital. These laws naturally gave EPB a strong say over the money supply and industrial policy as well.

In 1963, the special status of the EPB within the cabinet was further enhanced when its minister was also given the title of deputy prime minister. At the same time, an Economic Ministers' Meeting and an Economic Vice-Ministers' Meeting were created, for which EPB served as the support staff. Ministries established special ad hoc committees for the analysis of certain policy issues and private experts might participate in such committees, but these committees generally approve policies proposed by the ministry.

In addition to consolidating the economic planning structure, the military also launched a number of reforms designed to improve bureaucratic performance and implementation. Under the guidance of the minister of cabinet administration, a series of reforms rationalized the system of personnel administration and moved toward a more meritocratic system. As a study conducted by the US aid mission noted, "with the advent of the Military government the door to personnel administration improvements swung open."[30] These included centralizing recruitment and selection; improving examinations; installing a performance-rating system; adapting a new training system; improving pay administration; and installing a position-classification system.

4   MILITARY INTERREGNUM, MAY 1961– DECEMBER 1964: THE SHIFT TOWARD ECONOMIC REFORM

The changes in the Korean political system under the military proved important for the adoption and implementation of a coherent economic strategy. Changes in political institutions enhanced the freedom of maneuver of the executive vis-à-vis the legislature, the ruling party, and interest groups and administrative reforms elevated the technocrats within the bureaucracy and expanded the instruments at their disposal. Yet these institutional changes did not constitute a development strategy; we must therefore analyze the way in which government preferences concerning development were shaped by the political milieu.

The military justified its intervention in politics by reference to the tasks of economic development, but its initial conception of this task was a quasi-populist one in which certain groups that had been relatively neglected under Rhee, particularly farmers and small businessmen, were targeted for special attention. Economic policy was also affected by the need to cement support within the military government itself through payoffs to junta members and civil servants. Only when this strategy proved politically unsustainable did the government move to follow the more orthodox advice of the technocrats and American aid advisers.

Two factors played into this crucial shift. First, the military faced a number of domestic economic problems that were the unintended consequence of their initial policy stance. The most important of these was a sharp increase in inflation, particularly in 1963, which was felt strongly in urban food prices. The most binding economic constraint, however, was a rapidly deteriorating reserve position. Dwindling foreign exchange deprived the government of access to capital-goods imports that were necessary not only for its ambitious development plans, but also for the new political arrangement with business. This external constraint was not simply a result of the economics of the military's initial program, however. More importantly, the United States was willing to exploit the military's short-term economic plight to exercise policy leverage.

Understanding the economic reform thus demands exploring in closer detail the interests of three sets of actors: the military, the United States, and the technocrats. A technocratic team had completed an Economic Development Plan for the Chang Myon government only shortly before the military coup. On coming to power, the junta assigned the newly forming Economic Planning Board the task of drafting a new plan in order to distinguish the incoming government from its predecessor. The junta outlined a series of quantitative objectives, including an annual growth rate of 7.1 percent for 1962–6, that were derived from the previous plan, but artificially inflated.[31] The overall philosophy of the plan was outlined as "a form of 'guided capitalism' in which the principle of free enterprise and respect for the freedom and initiative of private enterprise will be observed, but in which the government will either directly participate in or indirectly render guidance to the basic industries and other important fields."[32]

Beyond the broad goals of industrialization and reviving growth through government activism, the military did not have any clear ideas about how to achieve its economic objectives. The junta thus turned to technocrats from the old Ministry of Reconstruction to draft "The Economic Bluebook for the Korean Military." Completed in July, the Bluebook became the basis for the formulation of a full-fledged plan, which was published in January 1962.

A major goal of the technocrats was to eliminate the range of controls that had permitted the corruption and misallocation of resources of the Rhee period. The plan is replete with references linking state intervention not only to economic inefficiency and distortions, but to corruption. Disequilibrium interest rates allowed bankers to become "not the servants of customers, but arrogant lords meting out special favors." Public enterprises were charged with "rampant nepotism" and the channeling of political funds. Overall:

> the lack of...planning, the abnormal system of interest rates, the corruption and injustice which thrived on the low official exchange rates and the haphazard and inefficient management of state-operated enterprises have caused the waste of even what meager capital was available. As a result, industrial output was disappointingly small in relation to investment.[33]

Interestingly, the plan was extremely cautious with reference to macroeconomic policy; indeed, the language even suggests some skepticism about the targets imposed by the military:

> While the plan implementation calls for procurement and supply of enormous amounts of investment capital, pursuit of policies tending to undermine

financial stability in favor of excessive investment is bound to offset the beneficial effects of the Plan, and might even lead to its complete failure. Therefore, in determining financial and banking policy for the period, it is essential that the volume of investment be maximized only within the framework of financial and monetary stability.[34]

Not surprisingly, this approach did not fully jibe with the immediate political interests of the military, which was in any case divided between conservative and more radical elements. While relying on the technocrats for the drafting of plans, the Supreme Council for National Reconstruction, the body of coup leaders, also set up an advisory board on economic questions that gave several populist economists access to the junta. These economists and their sympathizers among the colonels were critical not only of the corruption of the Rhee period, but of the market system more generally.

A series of policy actions reflected a populist outlook designed to rectify some of the injustices of the Rhee period. The junta decreed the abolition of all "usurious" debts of farmers and fishermen, guaranteed government repayment of those debts that were within legal interest rate limits and moved to guarantee high and stable prices to farmers through subsidies. The trials for illicit wealth accumulation constituted an attack on big business, but efforts were made to assist small and medium firms through the creation of the Medium and Small Industry Bank. These measures, the ambitious investment demands of the plan, and a round of pay increases to public servants contributed to a large jump in government spending and in the budget deficit in 1961 and 1962. In 1961, there was a *fourfold* increase in total bank credit to the public sector, and a 64 percent increase in 1962.

These policies created new economic problems as well as tensions within the cabinet. In May 1962, Yu Ch'ang-sun, the respected Governor of the Central Bank, resigned as a result of differences with the SCNR over macroeconomic policy. A crucial event came shortly thereafter when the government attempted to capture resources for financing planned investments by freezing large bank deposits and currency holdings into long-term time deposits. The action was advertised as part of the attack on illegally accumulated wealth and on curb-market lenders who had flourished because of the system of disequilibrium interest rates. Sequestered funds were to go into an "industrial development corporation," the details of which were poorly formulated. Confidence in the government fell and business slowed to a crawl.

More narrow – and mundane – political considerations drove other elements of the junta's policy, resulting in a series of damaging scandals.[35] All involved the newly formed Korean Central Intelligence Agency and were tied to schemes to finance the new ruling party: a massive manipulation of the stock market in the spring of 1962 with funds extorted from the Central Bank; the duty-free import and resale of cars and pinball machines from Japan; price-rigging schemes in the sugar, flour, and cement industries that harked back to the Rhee period. In January 1963, the infighting within the junta led to public disclosure that the military had opened negotiations with the Japanese as early as October 1961. Public charges followed that the ruling party had received $130 million from the Japanese for the financing of the First Five-Year Plan, as well as $20 million to "finance" the October 1963 elections.

With the military and the technocrats, the US aid and consular machinery was the third protagonist in this drama. The American attitude toward Korea during this period was influenced both by changing events in the country itself and by a broader reassessment of US interests that took place under the Kennedy administration immediately prior to the military coup.[36] This assessment argued that US interests were being undermined by the weakness of the Chang Myon government, the continuation of widespread corruption, and failures in the organization of the US aid program. Initially, the US signaled its displeasure at the intervention of the military. By June, however, a Presidential Task Force on Korea advised for a strategy that included establishing ties with the "moderate" elements of the regime and encouraging the development of a coherent planning effort.[37] Particular attention would be given to the reform of policies that provided the opportunities for corruption. Credit allocation, budgeting, government contracting, taxes, and interest rates were given as examples. The US would also encourage foreign direct investment.

The need to exert pressure to achieve reform was explicitly recognized: "experience has shown the effectiveness of sanctions, based upon withholding of inducements of economic aid, as a means of ensuring Korean performance."[38] By August 1961, cables from Seoul and internal documents showed a grudging admiration of the ability of the military government to get things done, and a willingness to support Korean planning efforts. There were also reasons not to lean on the government too hard. Until Park's announcement of March 1963 that military rule might be extended, the US was constrained by the fear that Kim Jong Pil and the younger colonels would gain in power. In January 1963, the embassy went so far as to argue that the military's, and Park's, complete withdrawal from politics was neither "feasible nor desirable."[39]

If the embassy was cautious, the June 1962 currency conversion plan and freezing of accounts, the revelations of corruption and KCIA malfeasance, and the inflationary consequences of the military's economic policies gradually moved the US aid mission to adopt a tougher position on economic reform.[40] In March 1963, officials overseeing the Far East in Washington noted that it had been almost a year since supporting assistance to Korea had been released. When this was investigated, it was found that, unbeknownst to Washington, the director of the aid mission in Seoul had been withholding portions of US aid, including PL480 assistance, with the purpose of forcing the Korean government to adopt a stabilization plan. American shipments of agricultural commodities typically included grains during years of bad harvest. In 1962 and 1963 there were, however, no exports of wheat or barley despite particularly poor harvests in the fall of 1962 and the spring of 1963. The expectation of devaluation and rumors of a US aid cutoff encouraged hoarding and speculation, pushing grain prices up dramatically and worsening the usual "spring famine."

The desperate need to generate foreign exchange to pay for imports, including grain, and the requirements of the ambitious investment plans pushed the military government to several innovations in support of exporters, including new financing schemes, tax exemptions and a revival of the system that linked the right to import to export proceeds in 1963.[41] These programs appeared to have a dramatic effect. In 1962, total exports grew 34 percent. Manufactured exports, however, increased by 68 percent. In 1963, nominal export growth was 58.4 percent, and manufactured exports grew an astonishing 302.1 percent. Yet surprisingly it does not appear that the promotion of exports received consistent government attention at this point. In particular, macroeconomic policy continued to move in the direction of *discouraging* exports by contributing to real appreciation of the exchange rate. Frank, Kim, and Westphal have calculated a purchasing-power effective real exchange rate on exports that includes the net effect of all subsidies. This rate declined steadily from 319.6 in 1960, to 289.1 in 1961, to 264.0 in 1962, before turning up slightly to 275.8 in 1963.[42]

It appears that Park's main preoccupation at this point in time, driven in part by business interests, was in maintaining his expansive economic policies through foreign borrowing.[43] Though AID was skeptical of the plan targets and the general thrust of policy, foreign banks and firms were willing to grant credit to the regime on the condition that repayment assurances were granted by the government. The government, inexperienced in foreign borrowing, had not foreseen the high interest rates, front-end fees, and short repayment periods that lenders were seeking. Foreign exchange reserves dropped from $193 million in June 1962 to under $100 million in July 1963 as foreign exchange was used to import rice. Import controls, which had been relaxed to speed the recovery and to allow the import of investment goods in line with the plan, were tightened in November 1962 and again in July 1963.[44]

In 1963, the pressures exerted on the economic front by the AID mission came to overlap with growing concern in Washington about the country's political direction. Park's announcement in March that military rule might be extended was met by an extremely tough American response. We still do not have definitive proof because crucial documents remain classified, but United States pressure appeared to be important on both the political and economic fronts. Park agreed to elections in the fall as well as to a stabilization plan that included ceilings on the money supply, budget deficit, and commercial bank credit and a floor on foreign exchange reserves.[43]

5 ECONOMIC POLICY UNDER PARK CHUNG HEE, 1964–6

The election by no means marked the end of opposition to Park's rule, but Park's victory in the 1963 election did put the government in a position to concentrate its efforts more squarely on economic development. Moreover, Park was able to use his considerable powers, including control of the National Assembly through the DRP, the temporary imposition of martial law, and a new round of press controls to override opposition. The years 1964 through 1966 are years of remarkable economic policy reforms: devaluation, tax and interest rate reforms, an opening to foreign capital, and the drive to expand exports.

Two features of these reforms are striking. First, American influence is visible in every one, less through the exercise of short-term aid leverage than through the development of a network of working relationships between the AID mission and strategically important actors within the Korean economic bureaucracy. Second, almost all the reforms centered on the mobilization of resources. This was a crucial selling point, since US aid had shown a steadily declining trend.

A more controversial political motive ran through the government's interest in resource mobilization, however. In each instance of reform – increased tax collection, the expanded role of state-owned banks in financial intermediation brought about through the interest-rate reforms, government control over the allocation of foreign loans – allegations followed that newly mobilized resources were being tapped for political purposes. Unlike in the Rhee period, however, the *nature* of the reforms reduced the tension between corruption and the efficient allocation of resources. Though the government retained discretion in some areas, such as the allocation of foreign credits, its discretionary control was narrowed in others, particularly in trade finance and access to imports.

The first issue the AID mission sought to address was devaluation. Given that this devaluation was a critical component of subsequent export performance, it is worthwhile considering the politics surrounding it in more detail.[44] To estimate a realistic exchange rate, AID hired a consultant to undertake a set of price comparisons. Armed with these calculations, an American delegation met with their Korean counterparts to negotiate the rate. Though some members of the AID team sought a nominal rate of 300 won to the dollar, the US position was that 285 would be appropriate; in 1963, the rate averaged 130 to the dollar. The Korean government returned with representatives from business who said that they could not live with 285. Interestingly, while business was to later benefit from devaluation, and while the Korean Businessman's Association had advanced a number of proposals calling for greater government support for exports in 1963, there was uncertainty about devaluation because of its effect on the cost of imported inputs; this concern appears to have dominated private sector interests in expanding exports. But the United States insisted on a large devaluation, and on May 3, 1964, the official rate was devalued to 255, a fairly revealing ex post indicator of the relative power positions of the two sides. The new regulations called for a floating rate, but it was not until March 1965 that some flexibility was introduced into the exchange rate system.

Viewed comparatively, the quiescence of the urban working class is equally if not more important in understanding the politics of real devaluation. Labor was weak because of its relatively small size, slack conditions in the manufacturing sector prior to the reforms, and a relatively conservative union organization. Unions had been tightly controlled under Rhee, and under military rule their operations were banned altogether. Labor enjoyed greater freedom of maneuver after the transition to nominally democratic rule in 1964. The effect of the 1964 devaluation on the urban working class appears to have been largely mitigated, however, by the fact that the country had already witnessed a bout of speculative inflation and because most imports were intermediate rather than consumer goods. The relatively mild effect of the devaluation on prices had an important political effect, since it contradicted the critics who argued that devaluation would be inflationary.

The weak position of labor may also be important for explaining the success of the devaluations of 1960, 1961, and 1964. A remarkable fact is that real product wages (monthly wages in manufacturing divided by the wholesale price index, a rough measure of wages relevant to business firms) declined 17 percent in 1960–4 and real consumption wages declined by 24 percent. Thereafter, both series started to rise, but they did not attain their 1960 levels until 1967.

Several explanations are possible for the behavior of real wages during this period. One is that the fall in real wages reflected the expansion of a low-wage export sector. This does not appear to be the case, however. The decline in real wages took place in most sectors, whether export-oriented or not, so it did not result mainly from a change in the industry composition of employment. Moreover, wages in the export sectors were not, in general, lower than average (mining and apparel were above average, for instance, but food-processing and textiles were below average).

A second explanation, following the Lewis model, is that low real wage growth reflected a continuing labor surplus, and only reversed when the labor surplus evaporated. Viewed over a longer time period, this explanation has merit, but it does not account for the particularly sharp drop in real wages, particularly in 1962–3.

The most plausible explanation for the fall in real wages combines money illusion with the temporary weakening of labor's ability to negotiate under the military. The real wage slowdown reflected the net effect of a considerable increase in nominal wages (following an exceptionally low increase of 5 percent in 1961, the year of the coup) coupled with an even sharper increase in the rate of inflation, from 7–8 percent a year in 1959–61, to 20 percent in 1962, to 29 percent in 1963. It is likely that wage-earners failed to anticipate the sharp increase in inflation rates, and even if they had, unions were barred from either political or strike activity during the period of military rule.

In any case, the drop in real wages in combination with rising product prices and a growth in real output implied a sharp increase in profits, thus providing internal resources for additional investment, as well as a stronger base for raising tax revenues. Profits as a share of business sales rose several percentage points in the early 1960s, and taxes on business as a share of total tax revenue more than doubled between 1960 and 1964, from 5 to 11 percent.[47]

If labor did not have the power, or interest, in opposing devaluation, neither is it the case that the devaluation was undertaken for the purpose of assisting a rural constituency.[48] It is true, though, that there was also no strong rural–urban cleavage, nor any rural-based agricultural export elite that stood as clear beneficiaries of the shift in course. In this indirect way, land reform may have reduced the sectoral clash which frequently accompanies such policy shifts in other contexts.

Prior to the summer of 1964, the substantive focus of discussions between American aid officials and the Korean government centered largely on devaluation and stabilization. In the summer of 1964, there were important changes in the leadership of both AID and EPB that signaled a new and ultimately more collaborative course.[49] In May, Chang Key Young took over as deputy prime minister and head of EPB, where he was to stay until 1967. Prior to his assumption of the position, EPB had seen six changes of leadership in its short history, and had been implicated in the conflicts with the colonels over the management of economic policy. Chang, while maintaining close contact with Park and the DRP, was granted wide leeway in the development and implementation of economic policy. The new AID chief, Joel Bernstein, met on a regular basis with Chang to outline the details of various reforms AID sought to implement, generally getting the support of Chang, who would mobilize the bureaucracy for action. This influence at the top was matched by close interaction at lower levels of the bureaucracy as well. AID advisors assiduously cultivated connections with a number of American-trained middle-ranking bureaucrats, primarily in the EPB, but also in the Ministry of Finance and the Ministry of Commerce and Industry.

When Joel Bernstein took over at AID, David Cole took the position as chief AID economist. Bernstein and Cole did not openly abandon the money supply targets of the 1964 stabilization program, but they signaled that AID would take a more lenient view of plan targets. Working with his Korean counterparts, David Cole began the formulation of a new stabilization plan in late 1964. Cole took issue with the economic approach that had been followed under previous stabilization plans, arguing that it was counterproductive to push strict monetary targets while simultaneously undertaking difficult reforms of the fiscal and financial system required to increase the level of domestic savings. The issue was not getting the prices right, but getting them "overright": the exchange rate low, credit to productive activities and exports cheap, and perhaps above all interest rates to savers high. The inflationary consequences of such a policy course would be partly offset by the mobilization of new resources through tax increases and through the financial system, but some inflation was seen as tolerable.

Though AID worried about budgetary expansion, they did not get intensively involved in fiscal policy. They urged, however, that the government increase the ratio of revenues to GNP by about one percentage point a year. The improvement in tax collection is probably one of the clearest examples of the link between administrative reform, political change, and the state capacity. Since the early 1950s, the AID mission had financed a succession of advisors on all aspects of the tax system, but tax collection remained poor. Privately, government officials admitted that a barrier to more effective tax collection was the belief that increased revenues would hurt the possibilities of securing aid, but no doubt discretionary control over taxation in the form of audits and petty corruption also played a role.[50] Tax collection improved under Park Chung Hee. Two more advisory teams visited the country in 1964 and 1965, and in 1966 the government turned its attention in a concentrated way to the question of improving tax collection. In March 1966, under the direction of a close military associate of Park Chung Hee's, a sweeping reorganization of the Taxation Bureau was launched, new tax investigative procedures were developed, centralized internal audit and security functions were built up, and a public relations campaign was launched. Due to inflation, real tax collections actually fell in 1964, but they increased 30.9 percent in 1965 and 56.6 percent in 1966, with little change in the tax structure or rates.

A concern with domestic resource mobilization was also behind the crucial interest rate reform of late 1965.[51] Studies commissioned by the U.S. pointed to the decline of organized financial institutions and the negative effects of inflationary policies and low interest rate ceilings on domestic savings. A particular concern to the government was the rapid growth of the financial power of the curb market. The outstanding assets and liabilities in the unorganized market ranged from 56 to 64 percent of total domestic credit at the end of 1964. A major incentive to reform, therefore, would be to move money into the banking system, which was state-owned and over which the government had wide discretionary powers. After reviewing studies by Korean economist Lee Chang-nyol and a set of recommendations by American consultants John G. Gurley, Hugh T. Patrick, and E.S. Shaw, Park pushed a doubling of interest rate ceilings through the National Assembly in September 1965. Cole and Park explain the US role:

> One factor that contributed to this rapid implementation was a provision in the annual stabilization program for 1964, jointly agreed upon by the American and Korean governments as the basis for the annual US aid program to Korea, that a financial reform would be implemented by the end of the third quarter of that year. Thus, the reform met this time schedule and the flow of aid funds was not interrupted.[52]

While the foregoing reforms have attracted wide attention, the defining aspect of the new course was the single-minded emphasis placed on exports. The neoclassical interpretation of the success of this effort was that it hinged largely on incentive reforms, including particularly devaluation and the liberalization, albeit selective, of imports. In addition, preferential credit provided a particularly strong incentive for firms to shift into export activities.

The effects of these policy incentives were well known and documented. Less attention has been given to the institutional innovations that accompanied and supported the export drive, perhaps because it is admittedly more difficult to gauge their precise effects. Nonetheless, it is plausible that institutional change had a number of important consequences, contributing in particular to the coherence and credibility of the reform effort.

First, new structures for supporting exports mirrored the more general centralization of decision-making authority within the government. By engaging the power of the president, support could be mobilized for the export sector across normal bureaucratic lines.

Second, the new institutions linked the public and private sectors in a new way that combined access and the representation of business interests with government control. On the one hand, the new quasi-corporatist channels created by the government provided for the flow of information between the public and private sector. This enhanced the credibility of policy by engaging the private sector in its formulation and allowing the government to respond expeditiously to particular private sector grievances. On the other hand, however, the government developed extensive informational capabilities and expertise within the bureaucracy that allowed it to monitor the private sector and to use discretionary policy instruments to guarantee compliance, in some cases down to the level of the firm. Coupled with tight centralized controls over bureaucratic behavior, the new structure served as a check on previous patterns of rent-seeking.

In late 1964, while AID was absorbed with developing a new stabilization program for 1965, a program for export expansion was being formulated within the Ministry of Commerce and Industry.[53] The key American advisor in this effort was Amicus Most, a businessman who had been hired as an advisor in AID. In March 1965, a Joint (i.e., US–Korean) Export Development Committee was established as a subcommittee of the Economic Cooperation Committee, cochaired by the vice-minister of commerce and industry and the deputy director of AID. Though the Export Promotion Subcommittee (EPSC), as it was called, was not a government agency and only had the power to recommend, it became a central organizational locus for mobilizing support for the policy reforms and assistance required to expand exports. This was in part due to the fact that the EPSC received direct support from Park Chung Hee himself. Equally important, however, was the composition of the committee, which included both the public and private sectors, and around which informal networks evolved. In addition to the co-chairs, the EPSC consisted of the vice-ministers of the economic ministries and relevant agencies, governors and officials of the Bank of Korea and the commercial banks and representatives from private sector associations; the Korean Chambers of Commerce, the Korean Businessman's Association, the Korean Traders Association, and the Small and Medium Business Cooperatives Association. At the working level, the EPSC consisted of a series of private–public task forces assigned to examine problems of finance and taxation, agriculture, fishing, mining, heavy industry, light industry, marketing, information, quality improvements, and technical assistance. Through the task forces, the EPSC made their recommendations concerning export policy and influenced the annual export promotion policy proposals emanating from the Ministry of Commerce and Industry.

Despite the fact that the most important incentives – the exchange rate, export credit, and access to imports – were extended on a nondiscretionary basis, an interesting feature of the export promotion effort was its sectoral emphasis. Through the Ministries of Commerce and Industry and Agriculture and Forestry, 35 "commodity chiefs" were assigned to develop programs for specific commodities and to coordinate with representatives of the appropriate industry. The organization of export interests had been facilitated in September 1961 by the creation at government behest of exporters' associations for all export products.[54] Organized under the Korean Traders Association, these sectoral organizations provided services such as marketing, advertising, inspection, and arbitration assistance, and were provided various special favors, such as the right to allocate import quotas among member firms.

The sectoral focus of the program is clear in the setting of export targets, by region, by industry, and in some cases by individual firm. At the beginning of the export drive, targets were command in nature with implicit and explicit threats used to gain compliance. Gradually, target-

target-setting became a kind of indicative planning exercise in which business and government were jointly involved. The government role included aggregating and processing information supplied through the export associations and keeping track of industry-level and even firm-level progress. But the targets were more than just projections. A survey of firms by Rhee, Ross-Larson, and Pursell reveals that the firms themselves felt that the target-setting process had resulted in a more rapid expansion of production than they would have otherwise undertaken.[55] Half of the firms surveyed for 1974 and 1975 claimed this, and three-fifths of the firms in 1976. Only one-twentieth said the targets made no difference in 1974, and though a quarter said they made no difference in 1975, this was a year in which exports were adversely affected by the world recession.

Second, the surveys reveal that the government maintained mechanisms for guaranteeing compliance, or perhaps more accurately, good faith efforts. Only one firm claimed that it had been penalized for failing to meet an export target. Of 85 firms polled, however, 68 percent mentioned that the rigor of tax collection was linked to export performance while another 45 percent mentioned that export performance was tied to greater facility and speed in their dealings with government. Seventy-two percent ranked "assurance of continued government support for the firm's efforts" as an advantage of good export performance.

The institutional mechanisms through which the public and private sector were brought together extended up to the president himself. In 1965, the first National Export Promotion Meeting was held. Chaired by the president, the meeting included the economic ministers, the chief executives of the export associations, and the presidents of several of the largest enterprises. The moderator of the meeting was usually an economic minister who would begin with a briefing on the general progress on meeting targets before turning to the problems facing specific industries. The main advantage of the meetings stemmed from the centralized political structure described above. The president could act directly on problems that individual industries were facing, often by simply issuing directives on the spot that had the force of law.

A second set of institutions that evolved during the early 1960s were those concerned with disseminating information and the transfer of what might be called "managerial technology." These efforts were addressed to solving a number of practical transaction and information cost problems that frequently posed collective-action dilemmas. For example, prices charged by small producers could be talked down by one-time bargain hunters below the level at which average costs of production could be recovered. One way of managing the problem was to fix prices through cartel arrangements, a practice which the government tolerated because of a concern with predatory pricing. Over time, international prices became the standard by which domestic prices were set. In 1964 and 1965, for example, it was believed that Korean goods would be competitive if prices were approximately 10–15 percent below Japanese prices, a premium required by the country's uncertain reputation and additional transport costs. Such rules of thumb were gradually supplemented by the dissemination of modern cost-accounting practices, at least in the larger firms. AID assisted in these efforts through support for the formation of a national accountants' organization and for business education and research.

Given that Korea did not have an advantage in heavily automated machine production that would act to ensure quality, quality control became a crucial issue in establishing a competitive position, and above all, a longer-term reputation.[56] The improvement of quality poses a collective action dilemma. Any given firm benefits from the efforts of other national firms but has an incentive to sacrifice quality for price in markets that are price sensitive. The government acted in two ways to overcome this dilemma. The first was the effort to prevent the export of items that did not meet certain standards or contract specifications; the second was to disseminate international standards and promote the sampling techniques that would allow rigorous testing without excessive cost.

The government also played a direct role in "making" markets. The most obvious channel for marketing Korea's exports were those large retail chains (in the United States) and trading companies (in Japan) willing to take a developmental approach to their relations with Korean firms by supplying technical assistance, product specification, and samples. The problem, however, was in generating the initial interest, since information is scarce on a potential producer entering world markets for the first time, and reputation, of course, is nonexistent. A key recommendation of the EPSC was that an effort be made to induce the executives of leading US chains to come to Korea at the expense of Korean firms and business associations.[57] Once again, a collective action dilemma is visible. Korean business representatives balked at the idea. Since there was initially no great enthusiasm on the part of the American firms, a more concerted effort was launched with AID support. In October 1965, representatives of ten of the largest American buying chains doing a total of $15 billion of retail business annually were invited to Seoul.

Establishing the market nexus worked both ways. Not only did foreign firms have to discover Korea, it was imperative for Korea to establish permanent presence in foreign capitals.[58] The Korean Trade Promotion Corporation, modeled on Japan's JETRO, was founded as a public entity in 1962. KOTRA was the overseas arm of the Ministry of Commerce and Industry and functioned as commercial attachés of embassies normally do. KOTRA assisted manufacturers in locating markets, advised on market requirements, and served as a conduit for information between Korean producers, traders, and foreign buyers.

The various economic incentives extended to exporters – fiscal incentives, wastage allowance, etc. – have been listed elsewhere, and need not be discussed here in detail. Probably the most important way in which the government enhanced the profitability of exporting was through its control of credit.[59] This policy instrument is worth discussing in some detail, since it reveals how government policies can contribute to forging and widening a coalition of beneficiaries with strong vested interests in export activity.

Short-term, low-interest won-denominated loans were extended without limit against any letter of credit (L/C). L/C loans were made at $6\frac{1}{2}$ percent, compared with discounts on commercial bills that were 24 percent following the interest rate reform. The cost of the interest rate subsidy was born by the Central Bank, which discounted the loans by the commercial banks. The rediscounting was covered partially out of other profits of the Central Bank and partly by direct subsidies from the government. Since this was a source of guaranteed profit, the commercial banks had an interest in seeking export business and were drawn into the "export coalition." Moreover, the loans were gradually extended not only to the exporter, but to firms supplying exporters, again further widening the export coalition.

Such a program, devised by the industry-oriented Ministry of Commerce and Industry, naturally cut against the emphasis on stabilization that had characterized American aid policy in 1963 and 1964. Nonetheless, the program was strongly supported by the AID mission in its discussions with EPB, even over reservations of the conservative Ministry of Finance.[60]

The degree of trade liberalization during the period of takeoff is a matter of substantial debate. Frank, Kim, and Westphal, and Krueger argue that the 1960s was a decade of liberalization, even though their own accounts sometimes suggest otherwise.[61] Frank, Kim, and Westphal base their judgment on the 1964–6 period of an increase in the number of items eligible for import and a decline in the number of prohibited items. They also note that after the 1964 devaluation a temporary special tariff law was enacted to capture windfalls on restricted import items, with tariffs up to 90 percent being applied, and that an import prepayment deposit was frequently required equal to 100 percent of import value. As Lued-de–Neurath points out, the putative liberalization that was achieved by the expansion of the importable lists was really just a return to the temporary liberalization that was achieved before balance of payments constraints forced the reimposition of controls in 1963. Even after 1965, a number of policies continued to affect the ability to import, including the obligation to surrender foreign exchange in exchange for certificates, advance deposit requirements, and the licensing of traders. Beginning in May 1962, the Export Promotion Law stipulated that registered traders had to meet certain minimum export requirements to maintain their licenses; these requirements were gradually increased over time.[62] Import quotas on individual items were abolished only at the end of 1966. Though this is taken as evidence of the abandonment of discretionary quantitative restrictions and greater reliance on tariffs, QRs were replaced by a system under which items could only be imported by manufacturers of related products.

Perhaps the most important change in trade policy is held to be the switch from a positive to a negative list system, a change in policy which, as with the unlimited discounting of loans against confirmed letters of credit, reduced the degree of government discretion over the behavior of importers. This reform did not come until July 1967, however, and even then the new system continued to restrict 42.9 percent of all import categories. Gilbert Brown, a champion of the neoclassical view of Korea's takeoff, states bluntly that "no major industries were left without either quantitative restrictions or tariff protection adequate to maintain strong domestic market positions."[63] Wontack Hong, writing in 1979, offers the following summary:

> In principle, imports of finished consumption goods have not been allowed. In order to protect domestic industries, other (non-consumption good) imports competing with domestic products such as intermediate input materials for domestic consumption have been allowed to fill the estimated gap between domestic supply and demand (at the prevailing "domestic price" instead of the estimated gap at international prices.)[64]

We close by offering the following hypothesis on the political economy of liberalization during this period. On the one hand, the new policy course launched by the military government eliminated many of the rents domestic firms had enjoyed during the Rhee period through pure arbitrage of aid goods. On the other hand, protection for the domestic market was not abandoned. Thus, while the exchange rate and financial subsidies provided incentives for firms to move into price-sensitive export markets, a certain degree of compensation was provided through continued protection of the domestic market. Not until the 1980s was a more thoroughgoing import liberalization launched.

6   A NOTE ON POLICY REFORM IN THE 1980s

It is noteworthy that Korea, unlike most developing countries, maintained the basic orientation of its new policy for the next quarter century. The import liberalization of the late 1960s was compromised with the balance-of-payments crisis of the early 1970s and further with the heavy industrialization program of the mid-1970s. But the basic export orientation remained, backed by financial incentives and continual administrative pressure on firms to expand exports. Exchange rate policy, with brief lapses, continued to support the policy of export promotion. This consistency of policy, and a variety of additional incentives, contributed to the expansion of large, export-oriented conglomerates which dominated Korean industry and provided strong political backing for government initiatives.

The administrative reforms of the early 1960s also endured over time, specifically the concentration of overall economic policy-making with a technocratic team supervised by the deputy prime minister. Key policy-makers retained responsibility not only for economic planning but also for coordinating budget authority and monitoring expenditures throughout the government, thus ensuring both fiscal discipline in the narrow sense and correspondence of expenditures with overall economic objectives. This feature is lacking or deficient in most other developing countries.

Korea flirted again with import substitution in the 1970s, with an emphasis on the chemical industry, including petrochemicals, and on the heavy metal industries, including steel, shipbuilding, and machinery. Korea's Heavy and Chemical Industrialization Plan, as it was called, differed from other debt-financed industrialization schemes of the 1970s in one important respect: from the beginning it was acknowledged that to be successful the new industries would have to be able to compete on the world market in a relatively short period of time. Steel and shipbuilding were in fact very successful by this standard. Other sectors, including particularly segments of the heavy machinery industry and petrochemicals, were less successful, but unlike other developing countries, plans for capacity expansion were quickly scaled back and existing firms were even consolidated by government fiat.

Partly as a result of problems associated with the heavy industry drive of the 1970s, Korea went through another major economic reform from 1979 through the mid–1980s. This second reform episode provides interesting comparisons and contrasts with the earlier reform effort. The economic logic of the two reforms was somewhat similar. As in the 1960s, devaluation was seen as necessary to stimulate exports, which by the late 1970s had come to be recognized as the main source of growth for the Korean economy. However, devaluation would "stick" under conditions of fully employed resources only if monetary and fiscal policy were tightened in order to release productive capacity sufficient to permit the additional exports; the first task, therefore, was stabilization.

One difference in the second reform episode was that greater attention was given to import liberalization. Nonetheless, the compensatory effects of the policy mix outlined at the end of the previous section also came into play in a quite similar fashion. Devaluation had the effect of making import substitution more profitable across the board, thus reducing the need for import protection. Put another way, the more depreciated currency would provide some additional protection to those who would otherwise be hurt by import liberalization, thereby neutralizing some of the political opposition to import liberalization. Import-competing industries would nonetheless be rationalized by the liberalization program, which would also contribute to the fight against inflation.

Unlike the first reform episode, balance of payments pressures did not play a substantial role in the initial decision to change the direction of policy. The stabilization program was outlined prior to the second oil shock and, if anything, was delayed by it. Nor did external indebtedness play a central role in forcing policy changes, as it did in many of the other large debtors. Korea was a large debtor and faced some marginal constraints on its ability to borrow in the early 1980s, but the country never lost its access to the credit markets and debt–export ratios were well below those of the large Latin American debtors.

Concerns about international competitiveness were important, though. By the late 1970s, Korea had become highly dependent on international trade. Given the government's maintenance of a fixed exchange rate, the openness of the economy increased both the government's and firms' sensitivity to inflation. This placed limits on Park's ambitious heavy-industry drive, and exposed Korea to pressures to liberalize from trading partners.

The reforms might therefore be explained in terms of interest-group pressures emanating from a new export-oriented policy coalition. But, as in the late 1950s, the interests of business were ambivalent; as in the first policy episode, collective action problems plague any interest group explanation. Surplus capacity and increasing inflation might have argued strongly for some form of industrial rationalization, including through import liberalization, a scaling back of commitments to the heavy-industry drive, devaluation, and stabilization. Yet any individual firm would benefit by maintaining its subsidies and protected position. A similar tale can be told with reference to business views of devaluation. Though firms gained as exporters, the won cost of their foreign debt service increased. There is little evidence that business spearheaded the reform drive; rather, it emanated from technocrats within the economic bureaucracy.[65]

As with the earlier reform effort, the initial impetus to reform came from increasing inflation. First introduced in 1979, the stabilization plan was interrupted by the political instability surrounding the assassination of Park Chung Hee. An interim government managed to undertake a large devaluation, but the interests of the incoming military government and the sharp recession of 1980 argued against any immediate resumption of complementary stabilization measures. As in the early 1960s, the period of most intensive reform began following the consolidation of power following the coup d'état by General Chun Doo Hwan in May 1980, particularly in 1982–4. As in the previous reform episode, the new government sharply curtailed interest group activity and distanced itself from the large firms that had been favored under the heavy industry plan. As in the earlier reform episode, institutional and political changes appear to have played an important role in the initiation and consolidation of policy reform.

7 CONCLUSION

Overall, Korea represents a highly successful case of economic development. Korea was transformed from a "basket case" immediately following the Korean War to a paragon of development by the late 1980s, the largest of the four Asian tigers. Korea achieved a growth in per capita GNP over the two decades 1965–86 of 6.7 percent, the highest in the world for any country over 3 million in population, and placing it by the end of the 1980s ahead of most Latin American countries, Turkey, Portugal, and the eastern European countries. This was an extraordinary achievement. To what can we attribute it?

There is no single, widely accepted answer, and no doubt the reasons will be debated for decades. In our view the origins lay in the economic and institutional reforms of the early 1960s discussed in this paper. On the economic side the key elements of this strategy included, first, an outward orientation of production toward the world market which encouraged economic efficiency given Korea's small size and, second, a relatively disciplined fiscal and monetary policy, with an emphasis in government spending on support for investment.

This explanation of Korea's success has become relatively standard. Where we differ from traditional accounts is in our effort to place these reforms in a particular economic, political, and institutional context. One factor to which we have given attention concerns the position of labor during the transition. Labor's acceptance of a ten percent apparent drop in real wages during 1961–4, following the currency devaluations, made possible the improvement in international competitiveness that served Korea, including in the end labor, so well. Real urban wages grew by 8.7 percent a year over the period 1965–85, what must be a record rate of increase for so long a period. We have explored several possible explanations for the wage pause of the early 1960s, but we might speculate further that the willingness of labor to accept lower real wages may have been increased by the absence of sharp economic divisions among Koreans. While data on the distribution of income are problematic in most nations, Korea stands out for the relative evenness in income distribution. In the mid–1970s the highest income quintile of the population had roughly eight times the income of the lowest quintile; this contrasts especially with the countries of Latin America, where the corresponding statistic often exceeds twenty.

A second economic factor we have emphasized concerns Korea's aid relationship. Korea's extremely high level of dependence on aid provided the United States with unusual leverage. Declining aid commitments and the dim prospects for continuing import substitution gave Park Chung Hee an incentive to increase his political independence by pursuing economic reforms that would expand the government's access to other resources, both foreign and domestic.

Yet these factors do not, in themselves, account for the comprehensiveness of Korea's reforms, nor for their coherence and credibility. Many other developing countries have faced either constraints, such as a slowdown in import substitution or declining aid flows, or opportunities, such as a pause in wage growth, but have failed to exploit them. We must therefore address the question of policy choice; it is on this point that we differ from standard accounts. We place particular weight on the political power of the executive under President Park and later under President Chun, and their efforts to legitimate their rule through economic growth.

Executive power served several functions. First, it permitted the government to cut through previous patterns of rent-seeking both within and outside the bureaucracy. Second, it eliminated from the economic policy agenda contending policy platforms that have affected the nature of economic policy-making in a number of other developing countries, often through harsh repression of opposition that was justified by national security concerns. Finally, executive power infused government deliberations in general and the determination of economic actions in particular with an urgency and an authority that they might not otherwise have had, in part by concentrating decision-making authority within the government itself.

This very urgency also affected the substantive nature of Korea's economic policy. Korea's economic policy was far from *laissez faire*, and we have documented how the government's interest in cementing bases of support contributed to particular types of intervention. Nonetheless, the government did rely overwhelmingly on private-sector firms, and used not only administrative means to discipline them but the continuing commitment to exports itself.

NOTES

This chapter draws on three chapters of an unpublished manuscript by Stephan Haggard and Chung-in Moon, tentatively titled "The Political Economy of Korean Growth, 1930–1990" and an article by Stephan Haggard, Byung-kook Kim, and Chung-in Moon, "The Transition to Export-led Growth in Korea: 1954–1966," *Journal of Asian Studies*, 50(4) (November, 1991). Our thanks to Robert Bates and Anne Krueger for their careful reading of various drafts.

1   See Haggard and Kaufman (1992).
2   For a further exposition of this idea with reference to the Philippines, see Haggard (1990).
3   See Palais (1973) and Henderson (1968).
4   The most detailed description of the exchange rate regime in the 1950s is provided by Frank et al. (1975, chapter 2).
5   "Agreed Minute of Conferences between President Eisenhower and President Rhee and their Advisors, Washington DC, July 27–30, 1954," *Foreign Relations of the United States 1954*. For a candid review of the talks, see James C. Hagerty Diaries, July 27, 1954, DDE Library.
6   Foreign Operations Administration (Tyler Wood) to State, September 5, 1953, Record Group 59, 895.00/9–553, National Archives, which summarizes a two-hour meeting between Rhee and Wood.

7 The discussion is drawn from *The Far Eastern Economic Review*, May 11, 1961, pp. 277–8.
8 Interview, Lee Duck Soo.
9 Government Accounting Office, *Report on Examination of Economic and Technical Assistance Program for Korea, International Cooperation Administration, Department of State, Fiscal Years 1957–1961*, Part 1, p. 12. Hereafter cited as "GAO Report."
10 Song Doo Kim (1965).
11 Hakmin Publishing Co. (1985).
12 GAO Report, pp. 86–9.
13 See Bark Dong Suh (1967).
14 The term is from Lee Hahn Been (1968), which contains an account of the reforms in chapter 8.
15 On the planning efforts after 1958, see Jon Won Lee (1966) and Wolf (1962). Wolf was involved in the early planning efforts.
16 The most detailed study of the fall of Syngman Rhee is Quee-Young Kim (1983); see also Han Sung Joo (1974).
17 *Dong-A Ilbo*, August 17, 1961.
18 Han Sung Joo (1974).
19 Olson (1983).
20 See Cole and Lyman (1971) for data on the rural origins of the coup leaders. For a theoretical argument linking such sociological distance with state capacity for decisive action, see Trimberger (1978).
21 For a detailed description of Park's view of the Rhee regime, see Kim Chong-shin (1967).
22 See Se-jin Kim (1971).
23 For a detailed analysis of the formation and structure of the DRP see Min (1980).
24 See Kie-change Oh (1968). On the weakness of the Korean legislature, see Chong Lim Kim and Seong-tong Pai (1981). On the weakness of political parties, see the essays in Younghwan Kihl and C.I. Eugene Kim (1976).
25 Park Chung Hee (1971).
26 Kyong-dong Kim (1967).
27 Lim Myobin (1968).
28 Kyong-dong Kim (1967).
29 See the statement on preferential loans by the Korean Businessman's Association in *Dong Ah Ilbo*, February 18, 1965; "Roundtable: Pro and Con of Preferential Finance," *Shin Dong Ah*, April 1965 [in Korean].
30 Landers (1967, p. 85).
31 Wolf (1962) and correspondence with the author; interview with Lee Duck Soo.
32 Economic Planning Board (1962, p. 28).
33 Economic Planning Board (1962, pp. 12, 17, 28).
34 Economic Planning Board (1962, p. 35).
35 See US House of Representatives, Subcommittee on International Organizations, Committee on International Relations, *Investigation of Korean-American Relations*, Part 6 (Washington, DC: USGPO, 1978), p. 228.
36 Hugh D. Farley, "The Situation in Korea, February 1961," Presidential Papers of John Fitzgerald Kennedy (JFK), National Security Files, JFK Library.

37 Report to NSC, "Presidential Task Force on Korea," June 5, 1961, Presidential Papers of JFK, National Security Files, JFK Library.
38 Ibid.
39 Telegram, US Embassy (Berger) to State, January 8, 1963, which reports on a long meeting with Park. Presidential Papers of JFK, National Security Files, JFK Library.
40 Telegrams #1237, #1246, and #1251, US Embassy to State, all June 8, 1962, Presidential Papers of JFK, National Security Files, JFK Library.
41 See Wontack Hong (1979), particularly table 3.3, pp. 54–5; Krueger (1979).
42 Frank et al. (1975, pp. 70–1).
43 *Far Eastern Economic Review*, August 8, 1965.
44 *Far Eastern Economic Review*, March 7 and August 22, 1963.
45 Telegram #690, US Embassy to State, November 17, 1963, which contains a detailed summary of the agreements of the stabilization plan. Presidential Papers of JFK, National Security Files, JFK Library.
46 The discussion draws on an interview with Gilbert Brown, Washington, DC, 1988.
47 Bahl (1986, p. 103).
48 This hypothesis has been advanced by Sachs (1985) to explain the difference between long-term patterns of economic growth in East Asia and Latin America.
49 This discussion draws on interviews with David Cole.
50 See Landers (1967, p. 133).
51 On the interest rate reforms, see the somewhat different assessments in Cole and Yung Chul Park (1983); McKinnon (1973).
52 Cole and Park (1983, p. 201).
53 This paragraph draws on a little-noted book by Most (1969).
54 Wontack Hong (1979, p. 57).
55 Yung Whee Rhee et al. (1984).
56 Most (1969, pp. 82–90).
57 Ibid., pp. 118–120.
58 Ibid., pp. 123–42.
59 Cole and Park (1983, chapter 6); Wontack Hong and Yung Chul Park (1986).
60 Interview, David Cole, Cambridge, Mass., 1985.
61 Frank et al. (1975); Krueger (1979).
62 Leudde-Neurath (1986).
63 Brown (1973).
64 Wontack Hong (1979, p. 57).
65 For a more detailed discussion of this episode, see Stephan Haggard, Susan Collins, Richard Cooper, Kim Chungsoo and Roh Sungtae, *Macroeconomic Policy in Korea since 1973*, unpublished ms., Harvard University, 1991.

REFERENCES

Bahl, Roy, Chuk Kyo Kim, and Chong Kee Park 1986: *Public Finances During the Korean Modernization Process*, Cambridge, Mass.: Harvard University Press.
Bark Dong Suh 1967: "Public Personnel Administration," unpublished PhD thesis, University of Minnesota, pp. 221–2.

Brown, Gilbert 1973: *Korean Pricing Policies and Economic Development in the 1960s*, Baltimore: Johns Hopkins University Press, p. 167.

Chong Lim Kim and Seong-tong Pai 1981: *Legislative Process in Korea*, Seoul: Seoul National University Press, chapter 1.

Cole, David and Lyman, Princeton 1971: *Korean Development: The Interplay of Politics and Economics*, Cambridge, Mass.: Harvard University Press, p. 274.

Cole, David and Yung Chul Park 1983: *Financial Development in Korea 1945–1978*, Cambridge, Mass.: Harvard University Press.

Economic Planning Board 1962: *Summary of the First Five Year Economic Plan, 1962–1966*, Seoul: EPB.

Frank, Charles, Kwang Suk, Kim, and Westphal, Larry 1975: *Foreign Trade Regimes and Economic Development: South Korea*, New York: Columbia University Press.

Haggard, Stephan 1990: "The Political Economy of the Philippine Debt Crisis," in Joan Nelson (ed.), *Economic Crisis and Policy Choice: The Politics of Adjustment in the Third World*, Princeton: Princeton University Press.

Haggard, Stephan and Kaufman, Robert 1992: "Introduction," in Stephan Haggard and Robert Kaufman (eds.), *The Politics of Adjustment: International Constraints, Distributive Conflicts and the State*, Princeton: Princeton University Press.

Hakmin Publishing Co. (eds.) 1985: *Revolutionary Trial: Records*, Seoul: Hakmin Sa, p. 185–6, [in Korean].

Han Sung Joo, 1974: *The Failure of Democracy in South Korea*, Berkeley: University of California Press.

Henderson, Gregory 1968: *Korean Politics of the Vortex*, Cambridge, Mass.: Harvard University Press.

Jon Won Lee 1966: "Planning Efforts for Economic Development," in Joseph Chung (ed.), *Korea: Patterns of Economic Development*, Seoul: Korea Research and Publication Inc.

Kie-change Oh, John 1968: *Korea: Democracy on Trial*, Ithaca: Cornell University Press, pp. 157–64.

Kim Chong-shin 1967: *Seven Years with Park Chung-Hee*, Seoul: Hollym.

Kyong-dong Kim 1967: "Political Factors in the Formation of the Entrepreneurial Elite in South Korea," in *Asian Survey*, May, 470.

Krueger, Anne O. 1979: *The Developmental Role of the Foreign Sector and Aid*, Cambridge, Mass.: Council on East Asian Studies, Harvard University, chapter 4.

Landers, Frank M. 1967: *Technical Assistance in Public Administration: USOM/ Korea, 1955–1967*, Seoul: USOM/Korea.

Lee Hahn Been 1968: *Time Change, Administration*, Honolulu: East–West Center.

Lim Myobin 1968: "The Reshuffling of the Business World after May 16," *Shin Dong Ah*, May [in Korean].

Luedde-Neurath, Richard 1986: *Import Controls and Export-Oriented Development: A Reassessment of the South Korean Case*, Boulder: Westview Press, p. 91.

McKinnon, Ronald I. 1973: *Money and Capital in Economic Development*, Washington, DC: The Brookings Institution.

Min, J. K. 1980: "Political Development in Korea 1945–1972: A Study of Political Factionalism," unpublished PhD dissertation, University of Leuven (Belgium), pp. 289–99.

Most, Amicus 1969: *Expanding Exports: A Case Study of the Korean Experience*, Washington, DC: USAID.

Olson, Mancur 1983: *The Rise and Decline of Nations*, New Haven: Yale University Press.

Palais, James 1973: " 'Democracy' in South Korea, 1948–1972," in Frank Baldwin (ed.), *"Without Parallel," the American–South Korean Relationship Since 1945*, New York: Pantheon.

Park Chung Hee 1971: *Our Nation's Path*, Seoul: Hollym, pp. 39–40.

Quee-Young Kim 1983: *The Fall of Syngman Rhee*, Korea Research Monograph No. 7, Berkeley: Institute of East Asian Studies.

Sachs, Jeffrey 1985: "External Debt and Macroeconomic Performance in Latin America and East Asia," *Brookings Papers on Economic Activity* (2) 523–73.

Se-jin Kim 1971: *The Politics of Military Revolution in Korea*, Chapel Hill: University of North Carolina Press.

Song Doo Kim 1965: *Chaebol and Poverty*, Seoul: Backjong Mun Hwan Sa, pp. 27–30 [in Korean].

Trimberger, Ellen Kay 1978: *Revolutions from Above: Military Bureaucrats and Development in Japan, Turkey, Egypt, and Peru*, New Brunswick: Transaction Books.

Wolf, Jr., Charles 1962: "Economic Planning in Korea," *Asian Survey* (10) December, 22–8.

Wontack Hong 1979: *Trade Distortions and Employment Growth in Korea*, Seoul: Korea Development Institute.

Wontack Hong and Yung Chul Park 1986: "The Financing of Export-Oriented Growth in Korea," in Augustine H. H. Tan and Basant Kapur (eds.) *Pacific Growth and Financial Interdependence*, Sydney: Allen and Unwin.

Younghwan, Kihl and C. I. Eugene Kim (eds.) 1976: *Party Politics and Elections in Korea*, College Park, Marland: The Research Institute on Korean Affairs.

Yung Whee Rhee, Ross-Larson, B., and Pursell, G. 1984: *Korea's Competitive Edge*, Baltimore: John Hopkins University Press for the World Bank.

8

The Politics and Economics of Turkish Policy Reforms in the 1980s
Anne O. Krueger and İlter Turan

In January 1980, in an atmosphere of economic crisis, the Government of Turkey announced a major program of economic reforms. There had been earlier economic crises and earlier reform programs, but this one was significantly different. Many of the economic policies, which had strong political overtones, that had been consistently followed for decades were abandoned, and a sharply different economic regime was installed.

The purpose of this chapter[1] is to analyze the economic and political aspects of the reforms. We start with a description and analysis first of the political–economic origins of the pre-reform policies, and then of the conditions that prevailed prior to the 1980 reform program. We then turn attention to that program, why it was different, and the political-economy considerations that led to such a difference between decisions made in 1980 and those made in earlier years. Finally, we consider the economic and political ramifications of the reforms, their impact, and their evolution after 1980.

1 TURKEY'S ECONOMIC LEGACY: AN ECONOMIC AND POLITICAL PERSPECTIVE

Legacy from the early republic   The Republic of Turkey was the major independent state which emerged from the break-up of the Ottoman Empire at the end of World War I. The leadership of the newly independent Turkey consisted primarily of former young Ottoman military officers, who had observed how weak the empire was economically, and how reluctant the Western powers were in giving up their economic privileges, including the capitulations (see note 5), which they had come to enjoy in Ottoman territory.

The leader of the country was Kemal Atatürk, who had earlier been a key general in the Ottoman army. Atatürk's vision was to transform the country from a religious empire into a modern, Western democracy. To that end, the Roman alphabet replaced the Arabic, the fez was outlawed, universal primary education was set as an important goal, Islamic law was replaced by the Swiss legal code, and Turkey was declared a secular state. By the time Atatürk died, in the late 1930s, his vision of modern Turkey was widely, but not universally, accepted, and the military viewed its role in national life as being Atatürk's continuing representative, protecting the nation from any threats to the success of Atatürk's reforms and overseeing the continuing Westernization of the country.

The soldier-politicians had developed a world view, which was transmitted to following generations, that had three components. First, they believed in an omnipotent state which would care for the welfare of its subjects. A corollary to this was their suspicion of any group in society which tended to develop an autonomous basis of power. Since private economic activity tended to develop such a basis, it was suspect.[2] As late as the 1970s, the Turkish bureaucracy still exhibited distrust of private enterprise at every turn.

The second component was the desire to create a modern society. Since, left to its own means, Turkish society had not achieved the level of modernity of western European societies, the soldier-politicians had come to believe that centrally administered change in all areas of society including economic activity was the only path to modernization. Third, because there was a battle not only to rid themselves of the European powers on their territory but also to eliminate the European control of economic policy, the elite who founded the Republic had a strong predisposition to autarkical economic policies.

One of the policies that was consistent with all of these views was the development of the idea of "etatism" as the guiding rationale for economic policy.[3] Through state economic enterprises (SEEs), the men of state (that is, the bureaucrats) would lead the industrialization effort. Therefore the power of the state would be enhanced while no new autonomous group would come into being. Change would be centrally administered. If successful, industrialization would render Turkey less dependent on the industrial countries of the West. In terms of economic policy, this meant two things. First, a large group of state-owned enterprises were established which produced goods and services in agriculture (primarily distribution and provision of inputs), mining, communications, transportation, and manufacturing. This sector, which consisted of SEEs established under Atatürk and subsequently, accounted for more than 50 percent of the value of manufactured output, and an even larger fraction of minerals output by the early 1950s.

The second implication for economic policy was that the state should actively regulate the activity of the private sector, controlling imports (both to protect against foreign competition and to "protect the value of the

Turkish currency"), regulating prices, and otherwise guiding economic activity.[4]

From the 1930s until 1980, this activist "leading" role of the state in economic activity was never fundamentally questioned in Turkey. In part because the SEEs were part of Atatürk's legacy, in part because of a historically deep-seated suspicion of foreign trade,[5] inward-looking policies toward foreign trade and economic growth were adopted and carried out with very little internal criticism.[6]

Transition to multiparty politics   Turkey made a transition to competitive politics after World War II. In 1950, power was peacefully transferred from the Republican People Party (RPP), the single party which had been in power since the founding of the Republic, to the Democratic Party. Political change was accompanied by strong expectations of economic betterment among the general populace. At the same time, those who had supported the Democratic Party expected that a new patronage network would be formed of which they would be the major beneficiaries.

In order to respond to these expectations, the Democratic Party initially reduced the restrictions on importing goods. It reinstated the policy of industrial investments which the RPP, the party of Atatürk, had pursued prior to the war. It also encouraged private investors not only by extending them easy credit and foreign currency allocations, but also by introducing a ban on importing whatever began to be produced domestically.[7]

Though preaching the virtues of private enterprise, the Democratic Party government of Adnan Menderes in fact followed mainly the traditions of the single party era. It was pursuing a strategy of import substitution-oriented investments which conformed to the autarkical proclivities of earlier governments. The private business community was, on the other hand, a creature of government policies and deferred to political authority. So, a heavily protected private sector oriented to import-substitution began to burgeon, but it owed its prosperity not so much to making correct economic decisions as to making correct political choices.

In the one-party era, patronage had been dispensed primarily to locally influential individuals – especially agricultural landlords. The Democratic Party also followed this practice, distributing its economic favors to supporters through a newly created patronage network which did not differ from that which had characterized the single party era. In this spoils game, the individual deputy became an intermediary between local interests and the national government and national political leaders. A good deputy was, and remains, one who could get the most resources for his constituents and constituency.[8]

This creates problems for governments in a predictable way. Since a deputy's success is determined by his ability to deliver to his constituents and constituency, the government party/parties are under constant heavy pressure from their members in the parliament to give them something. If they fail, individual and group challenges to the leadership are likely to occur. This demand pressure, which is often irresistible, has been a major factor behind the budgetary deficits and expansionary economics of many Turkish governments. It has also constituted one of the major challenges to stabilization programs initiated by elected governments.

Political-economic cycles: 1950–80

After having made the transition to political competition, both the politics and the economy of Turkey appeared to have entered a cyclical pattern.

On the economic side, the pattern was rather simple and clear. The cycle started with an economy in which budget deficits were under control, the rate of economic growth did not generate high levels of inflation, the difference between the official and the market exchange rate of the lira was not significant, and the government had credibility with the multilateral institutions.

In the next stage, public expenditures began to expand, slowly at first, but then at an increasing pace. The difference between the official and the market exchange rate grew, and inflationary pressures intensified. The government attempted to suppress prices of outputs of SEEs in an effort to contain inflation, and the consequence was larger public deficits. The country also began to experience problems in meeting its external obligations. Foreign lenders grew progressively more reluctant to extend new credits without evidence that stabilization measures would be adopted.

After displaying great initial resistance to the adoption of stabilization measures, and after economic conditions had continued to deteriorate, the government eventually gave in to pressures coming from the international financial community and adopted a stabilization program. The program would be characterized by a major devaluation of the Turkish lira, the imposition of tight controls on public spending, and attempts at reducing the losses of the SEEs, largely through mandating large once-and-for-all increases in the prices of their outputs. After the measures produced their intended results and confidence in the Turkish economy was restored, the cycle would commence again.

Naturally, the economic cycle had its political counterpart. The period of the implementation of stabilization programs (as the earlier economic crisis was being addressed) was one during which competitive politics were placed on hold; usually a military regime replaced the civilian government. Then came transitional elections to political competition. The restoration of competitive politics involved not only the conduct of elections but also the emergence of political parties which showed promise of survival. Voluntary associations arose which could act as instruments of interest articulation. The probability that the military might intervene receded.

Then, as the next elections approached, public expenditures began to increase. Historically, from the introduction of competitive politics until 1980, these elections had led to improvement of the electoral position of the party which had led in the transitional election. For that reason, these elections may be called "elections of consolidation." Consolidation was achieved by putting together a coalition which, in all likelihood, would win the election. Not surprisingly, all partners expected major economic rewards when political power was achieved.

The policy consequences of the elections of consolidation were predictable. Major infrastructural and investment programs were launched. It was usually evident to the careful observer that the means to complete all the development projects on time were not there. Nonetheless, governments found it difficult to resist demands coming from various constituencies, and therefore developed unrealistic and unrealizable programs. Consequently, the budgetary deficit began to climb and the discrepancy between the official and the market value of the lira to widen. Foreign exchange receipts also began to stagnate, and the delay in obtaining import licenses and imports lengthened. As that happened, more and more import-dependent economic activities were constrained in their production levels and, finally, real output began to fall.

The government party proceeded to the next elections in the hope that it might get a new lease on its life and have time to remedy the ills of the economy. During the elections, the ruling party (parties) worked to reduce the salience of economic issues by interjecting other themes into the political debate. The strategy was to polarize the electorate and render it psychologically costly for the voters to defect to a rival party.

Although the government parties returned to power after the elections, their electoral base was considerably weakened. The relations between government and opposition were highly polarized, and what had started out as economic stagnation developed into a political–economic crisis. The economy continued to deteriorate sharply. Support from the multilateral institutions was withheld pending the adoption of a program of economic reforms and stabilization.

At some point, under the combined impact of an economic crisis at home and pressure from the multilateral institutions, the government reluctantly introduced economic measures. Because polarized domestic politics continued, however, the military finally intervened. It was during the direct or indirect military rule that many of the provisions of the economic stabilization program would be enacted.[9]

Overall economic growth during the cycles   Table 8.1 provides data on the structural transformation of the Turkish economy from 1950 to 1980. As can be seen, agriculture's share of GDP has declined markedly; accompanying this, the fraction of the labor force engaged in agriculture has fallen steadily from 79 percent in 1950 to 63 percent in 1980.[10]

The share of industry in GNP rose rapidly over the 1950–75 period. The government was committed to industrialization through import substitu-

Table 8.1 Sectoral composition of GDP, 1950–80 (percentages of GNP, 1968 prices)

	1950	1955	1960	1965	1970	1975	1980
Agriculture	45	42	41	34	29	25	24
Industry	12	13	15	18	20	22	22
Services	43	45	44	48	51	53	54

Source: State Institute of Statistics, *Statistical Yearbook*, various issues.

tion and increased investment rapidly. Infrastructure investment, financed in part by foreign aid, provided a basis for the rapid expansion of economic activity. Table 8.2 gives an overview of growth in real GNP and in GNP per capita from 1950 to 1980.

Reflecting the political cycles discussed above, growth was uneven over the period, although five-year intervals do not capture the full extent of irregularity. Growth was rapid in the first half of the 1950s; with inflation accelerating and balance-of-payments difficulties mounting in the mid–1950s, growth slowed sharply until 1958, when the first stabilization plan was (reluctantly and belatedly) adopted.

By any standards, the initial results of the first stabilization program were highly favorable. In the following two years, inflation diminished rapidly, while imports financed by foreign credits received upon agreement to the IMF program permitted a fairly rapid expansion in economic activity.[11] By the early 1960s, growth had again resumed and was sustained at reasonably high rates for most of the decade.

By the end of the decade, however, "foreign exchange shortage" was again impeding growth. Delays for import licenses had become longer than 12 months and payments arrears continued to mount. Exports had failed to grow commensurately with GNP or the demand for imports, and the share of exports in GNP had fallen to 4 percent.

Table 8.2 Population and real GNP, 1950–80

	1950	1955	1960	1965	1970	1975	1980
Real GNP (billion TL)	40.6	58.7	71.1	90.4	125.4	181.4	206.1
Population (million)	20.8	23.9	27.8	31.4	35.6	40.4	44.7
Real GNP/capita (TL)	1,951	2,460	2,558	2,879	3,523	4,490	4,611

Percentage annual average change over preceding five years:

		1955	1960	1965	1970	1975	1980
GNP		7.7	3.9	4.9	6.8	7.7	2.6
Population		2.8	3.1	2.5	2.5	2.6	2.0
Real GNP/capita		4.7	0.8	2.4	4.1	5.0	0.5

Source: OECD, *National Accounts: Main Aggregates 1960–87* and earlier issues.

In contrast to 1958, the stabilization program of 1970 did not wait until economic activity had come to a virtual standstill. In August 1970 the government entered a second stabilization program with the IMF, devaluing the currency and attempting to stabilize the economy. As in the 1958–60 devaluation episode, the intention was to rationalize the trade and payments regime, but the fundamental philosophy of import substitution underlying the regime was not questioned.

In the aftermath of the 1970 devaluation, foreign exchange receipts increased sharply.[12] Export earnings rose, there was some reverse speculative capital movement, and a large inflow of workers' remittances. These resulted in a rapid increase in the money supply, and, in contrast to the aftermath of the 1958 devaluation, inflation accelerated over the 1971–3 period. However, economic growth was rapid, as there was little "foreign exchange constraint."

After the oil price increase of 1973, the government failed to take action, instead leaving the domestic oil price unaltered and permitting the current account to worsen rapidly. The excess of expenditures over receipts was financed by running down foreign exchange reserves and borrowing from abroad. Moreover, since most petroleum imports were on government account, and the government failed significantly to increase domestic oil prices, the government's fiscal deficit also rose sharply after 1975.

This sequence of events gave further impetus to inflation. Simultaneously, the failure of the government to adjust the exchange rate or the domestic price of fuel resulted in sharply reduced rates of increase of export earnings and sharply increased rates of increase in demand for imports. In order to attract workers' remittances and other foreign currency held by Turks in deposits abroad, the government also embarked upon a convertible Turkish lira deposit scheme, under which it provided guarantees in foreign exchange to those who deposited their funds with Turkish banks.

Although the Turkish Government was consistently committed to import substitution until 1980, there was an additional factor which resulted in a trade regime much more restrictionist and inner-oriented than the import-substitution philosophy might alone have done. The driving force determining the Turkish trade and payments regime during the 1950–80 period was the Turkish Government's commitment to attempt to maintain a fixed nominal exchange rate despite domestic inflation. Consequently, there was almost always excess demand for foreign exchange. "Foreign exchange shortage" therefore impelled many policy actions, and interacted with the policy of encouraging domestic industry through import substitution.[13]

As happens in most developing countries, the continuation of import-substitution policies in Turkey was becoming increasingly costly economically. The rising effective rates of protection reported in note 13 provide one indication. But the rising cost was also reflected in a rapidly rising incremental capital–output ratio (ICOR): according to Balassa's estimates, the ICOR rose from 1.6 in 1963–7 to 2.4 in 1968–72, to 4.7 in 1973–7. In constant 1976 prices, the average investment per job created rose from TL 267,000 in the 1963–7 period to TL 572,000 a decade later.[14]

2   THE POLITICAL AND ECONOMIC SITUATION IN THE LATE 1970s

Political deterioration after 1973   The national elections of 1973 were elections of transition, marking the end of an indirect military intervention which had been initiated in March 1971. The outcome indicated that a critical realignment might be taking place among the Turkish electorate. First, the electoral fortunes of the Republican People Party (which had defined a new role for itself as a social democratic party) had finally turned around such that it became the plurality party. Second, there were two newcomers to the parliament: the National Salvation Party, representing religious conservatism, and the Nationalist Action Party, representing extreme nationalism. The former had in fact attained a critical size in the sense that except for a coalition between the two major parties, its participation was needed in any other coalition formula.

The two small parties which had come into the parliament operated under two conflicting pressures. On the one hand, they had to establish visibility and a distinct identity vis-à-vis the voters. They had previously been present as tendencies in the Justice Party of Mr Demirel. With their electoral achievement as separate movements, the Justice Party had moved its own position to the right in order to preempt further losses from that direction. Under the circumstances, both parties felt compelled to display frequently and publicly the differences between themselves and the Justice Party and to criticize the latter in order to retain their distinct identity in the eyes of the voters. On the other hand, their survival and growth as a political party was dependent on their ability to obtain resources from the government both for the party as an organization and for citizens who had extended them electoral support. This necessitated taking part in the government.

The conflicting pressures under which the small parties operated did not make for stable or effective government. They wanted to be in government, but they behaved as if they were opposition parties. Their power might have been curbed if the two major parties were willing to form a coalition, but this possibility was never entertained either by Bülent Ecevit of the RPP or Süleyman Demirel of the Justice Party. Another remedy might have been the calling of early elections, but, because they were costly and their outcome uncertain, no consensus obtained in moving them ahead. The results of the elections of 1977 showed, in any case, that early elections might not have altered substantially either the distribution of votes or the distribution of seats in the parliament between parties.

The outcome of all this was ineffective government. Attempts to produce new legislation, to formulate and implement new policies, would only serve to provide occasions on which the disagreements between the coalition partners would be publicly exposed. Therefore, the prime ministers in all post–1973 governments allowed each ministry to deal with its own problems in the ways it saw fit. The party which happened to be in control of a ministry used that ministry for the advancement of its own interests. It did not think of a broader unit called the government which was to produce coherent policy designed to provide solutions to the many major problems Turkish society was encountering.

The attention of governments during most of the 1970s was focused on surviving as political parties and distributing public resources to party supporters. In the meantime, in two areas of public life, namely, economics and public order, there was steady deterioration.

What appeared to have started out as student radicalism in the late 1960s had given way to a number of movements which had come to include, in addition to students, young people from other segments of the population. Many movements had developed their street gangs to challenge their rivals, and some had then moved on to the formation of gangs that would commit acts of terrorism against the lives and property of rivals, and sometimes against government officials and public buildings.

The major political parties could not agree that terrorism might threaten the entire political arrangement. Parties which defined themselves as being on the right argued that terrorism originated in the Turkish left and whatever acts of terrorism might be encountered on the right were reactions to those coming from the left, and as such, they were defensive in nature. A similar logic was used but in reverse by the social democratic RPP. For each of the parliamentary parties then, not terrorism per se but particular kinds of terrorism were the problem. Since each side viewed the ideological brand of terrorism on its side with understanding, there were no common grounds for combating it.

Economic decline after 1976   As the acts of terrorism continued to take a heavy toll of lives and property, the economy was rapidly deteriorating. The bottleneck was the shortage of hard currency. International financial agencies would insist on the adoption of a stabilization program to extend support, while private establishments would not do anything until the support of the international agencies was enlisted. But governments had difficulty holding together, let alone taking the comprehensive and difficult measures which an economic stabilization program would necessitate.

Over the years after 1975, the economic situation worsened rapidly. Despite occasional exchange rate adjustments, the failure of the exchange rate to be maintained in real terms (see table 8.3) further discouraged exports; inflation continued to accelerate; Turkish government debt mounted as the government attempted to finance imports; and convertible deposit accounts mounted. By 1977, delays in obtaining import licenses were increasing sharply; real exports through official channels were falling; and real GNP was recorded to be growing at half the rate of the preceding three years.

The Ecevit government inherited an economically difficult situation.[15] Its diagnosis of the situation appears to have been that unavailability of foreign exchange was restricting imports, which in turn were constraining domestic production levels. The solution, therefore, was thought to be to seek foreign aid and foreign loans to permit an increased import flow, which in turn would increase production and generate more exports. While it was recognized that the fiscal deficit should be reduced somewhat in order to curb inflation, a larger role for government in the economy in the future was anticipated. As aptly put by Okyar:

Table 8.3   PPP nominal exchange rate (NER) for Turkey, 1975–89

	NER (TL per US dollar)[a]	Turkish wholesale price index	US price index	PPP NER Turkey–US[b]	G-7[c] price index	7-Country PPP NER[b]
1975	14.36	2.72	53.18	28.07	50.34	26.58
1976	15.92	3.17	56.59	28.42	54.06	27.14
1977	17.92	3.87	60.51	28.03	57.90	26.80
1978	24.04	5.80	64.94	26.92	60.54	25.10
1979	38.14	9.59	73.38	28.42	66.22	26.31
1980	77.78	20.68	85.22	32.05	74.13	27.84
1981	112.42	28.03	94.34	37.84	81.80	32.83
1982	163.66	35.59	96.90	44.51	87.66	40.26
1983	228.14	46.44	98.10	48.19	91.39	44.94
1984	370.87	69.82	100.50	53.38	96.57	51.18
1985	526.18	100.00	100.00	52.62	100.00	52.62
1986	676.53	129.57	97.10	50.70	99.18	51.75
1987	880.39	171.08	99.60	51.25	100.28	51.19
1988	1,468.18	287.92	103.60	52.72	103.38	52.71
1989	2,155.80	488.20	109.60[d]	48.38[d]	106.00[d]	46.02[d]
1990[e]	2,450.69	682.69	111.70[d]	40.10[d]	n.a.	n.a.

[a]Exchange rates are yearly averages of selling rates.
[b]PPP exchange rates are calculated by taking the ratio of the partner country wholesale price index to the Turkish price index, and multiplying the resulting number by the Turkish official nominal exchange rate.
[c]The G-7 countries are Canada, France, Germany, Italy, Japan, the United Kingdom, and United States. Weights are calculated as the sum of exports and imports from Turkey to each country as a share of Turkey's total exports and imports to the G-7.
[d]Preliminary estimate.
[e]Averages of monthly data for January through April.
Sources: Official Turkish exchange rate: table 19 in Data Appendix of Krueger and Aktan (1992). Wholesale prices: *International Financial Statistics*, April, 1990.

...it appears that the political views and ideological complexion of the left-of-center Ecevit government created almost insurmountable barriers in the way of arriving at a correct diagnosis of the situation, let alone taking decisive measures to counter it. The Ecevit government appeared convinced of the paramount virtues of government intervention in the economy, in the form of creating state economic enterprises or of intervening in the market mechanism, either directly or through subsidies. In addition, it was emotionally inclined towards a self-sufficient, even autarkic view of economic development, which restricted to a minimum the foreign role in the economy. The People's Republican Party had, in recent years, espoused undefined causes and slogans, such as total economic independence and anti-imperialism. The necessity of resorting to IMF cooperation and advice when the Party assumed power early in 1978 made the Ecevit government extremely uneasy and unhappy...In the Turkish Government's view, there was nothing structurally wrong with the Turkish economy or with the economic development policies followed in Turkey between 1960 and 1978. The causes of the crisis in foreign payments and the quickening trend in inflation that arose in the middle of 1977 were ascribed to the faulty – but quickly repairable – policies, and the events mentioned above. Correspondingly, all that was needed to restore the situation was additional foreign financing and the rescheduling of short-term debts to help the balance of payments, and a period of restraint in public sector finances to control internal inflation.[16]

In 1978, a first "stabilization effort" was begun. In fact, it accomplished almost nothing, but is worth examining in light of the contrast between that effort and the program that was adopted in January 1980. After discussions with Fund staff, the Fund and the Turkish Government in 1978 arranged a standby agreement covering a two-year period, with SDR 300 million to be released over two years in three tranches. The Turkish lira was devalued from TL19 to TL25 per US dollar. Turkey was to be entitled to make purchases under the standby subject to observing the following conditions:

There were ceilings set for successive periods on the net domestic assets.

Limits were established as to the amount of additional foreign borrowing the government might undertake.

Turkey was not to incur any additional arrears in foreign payments.

Debt rescheduling was to be carried out and completed by November 1978, with provision for eliminating all past arrears.

Commercial banks would continue to be required to maintain a liquidity ratio of at least 15 percent.

No new restrictions on international payments, multiple currency practices, bilateral payments agreements with Fund members, or limitations on imports would be introduced.[17]

By September 1978, however, the Turkish minister of finance wrote to the Fund, noting that Fund conditions had not been met, and requesting higher ceilings than had been negotiated. There were new arrears in foreign payments, and new restrictions on imports were to be imposed. The Turkish Government stated that the need for revision of the program was attributable to the effect of extreme shortages of imports on domestic production levels and on tax receipts. There were also difficulties in debt rescheduling.

While the Fund Board approved modifications to the standby, it apparently did so reluctantly. The Fund staff made clear their difference in viewpoint from the Turkish Government, attributing the failure to meet the conditions of the standby to the insufficient profitability of Turkish exports (because of exchange rate policy under continuing inflation), rather than import scarcity.[18] Meanwhile, inflation in Turkey continued to accelerate, rising from an estimated annual rate of 21 percent in January to 57 percent in July 1978. Fund staff also expressed discomfiture with the wage increases of 40–80 percent that had been negotiated by Turkish trade unions.

Economic conditions continued to deteriorate. Inflation accelerated, wage settlements were growing ever larger, import shortages intensified, and double pricing of government-controlled commodities such as sugar, cigarettes, and cooking oil became almost standard. The black market exchange rate was almost 40 percent above the official exchange rate when the third tranche of the standby (due in November 1978) was not released. As reported by the *Economist*, by that time the Fund was insisting upon a further 30 percent devaluation, and sharp cutbacks in the government's fiscal deficit (including large increases in prices of commodities sold by SEEs; they were incurring large losses at the prices at which they were selling, which were then financed by Central Bank credits). The Ecevit government, however, was resisting, insisting that social unrest would assume unacceptable proportions if the prices of SEEs were increased, and that devaluation would increase import prices. It proposed instead to increase the size of export subsidies.[19]

In March 1979, the Government introduced a somewhat restrictive budget into Parliament, and in April a first meeting was held between the Turks and the Fund regarding the possibility of a second standby. Another devaluation was announced on June 11, 1979, with the exchange rate moving from TL26.5 to TL47.1 per dollar for most commodities. For agricultural goods subject to domestic price supports and imports of petroleum and inputs into fertilizers, the exchange rate was to be TL35 per dollar. A Letter of Intent was finally signed dated June 30, 1979, in which it was requested that the two-year standby of 1978 be canceled and a new, one-year standby be entered into for SDR 250 million. This time, the Government stated its intention of slowing down the rate of inflation, raised the deposit and lending interest rates by 5.5 percentage points (still well below the rate of inflation), and put new ceilings on net domestic assets of the Central Bank and net Central Bank credit to the public sector.

The standby was approved by the IMF in July 1979, which paved the way for an OECD consortium package of aid of about $1 billion, and another round of debt rescheduling.

Despite the new aid and the government's commitments, the government failed to curb its expenditures or to reduce its drawing on the Central Bank, with a consequent acceleration in the rate of inflation. Domestic production of many commodities was falling, as imports of raw materials, intermediate goods, and spare parts became unavailable, or obtainable only with long delays or through extralegal channels.

It is unnecessary here to attempt precisely to delineate the relative contributions of each of several economic factors that contributed to the severity of the crisis. All analysts agree that there was a failure to adjust domestic spending or relative prices to the 1973 oil price increase, and that continuing growth in the three years following 1973 was financed by running down foreign reserves and borrowing from abroad. All agree also that there were inefficiencies associated with import-substitution policies, and that export earnings failed to grow both because of those policies and because of the overvaluation of the exchange rate. In an effort to obtain foreign exchange to keep imports flowing, the government had earlier instituted the earlier-mentioned Convertible Turkish Lira Deposit scheme (CTLD), which certainly increased the losses of the Central Bank and contributed to accelerating inflation. Fiscal deficits were increased as the government kept the prices of outputs of SEEs[20] fixed, which in turn fueled the inflation and raised Enterprise costs.

Political pressures for change   The sharply deteriorating economic situation had political ramifications. Domestic industrial products, whose production had started under the incentives for import substitution, relied, to varying degrees, on imported raw materials, parts, and components. Therefore, as Turkey's industrial production expanded, so did her reliance on imports. Large private corporations, whose political influence exceeded that which would have been suggested by their share in the GNP (more is said on this below), were hit severely by the shortage of foreign exchange in the late 1970s. They had come to see that while a strategy of import substitution had been critical in their development, it had contributed little to Turkey's ability to generate additional external income. They concluded that import substitution had reached its limit, and if they were to develop further in the future a more reliable way of generating outside income had to be found.

Organized under the Turkish Industrialist and Businessmen's Association (TÜSİAD), the large private industrial corporations became one of the major forces advocating fundamental reform in the Turkish economy. The relatively strong position of big business as a political lobby derived from several factors. First, although their numbers were many, the ownership of big private corporations was not widely dispersed. Many belonged to the same group of companies, and the major groups were owned by a relatively few families. This simplified their getting together and deciding on common courses of action. Second, they were concentrated in Istanbul. The few located outside of Istanbul were also well connected with their brethren in the economic capital of the country, again facilitating their ability to act together. Third, their financial means enabled them to extend favors to politicians in the form of campaign contributions, doing favors for constituents, etc., in a way smaller businesses would not be capable of. Fourth, most had developed international links, had partnerships, license agreements, and other similar arrangements with multinational corporations. They were more familiar with the workings of the world economic system and with the international economic agencies. They could communicate with the latter, if informally, without having to rely on the government. In sum, big business was rather homogeneous. It was capable of reaching a consensus quickly, it could act together, and it had multiple means to pursue its goals.

TÜSİAD was active in public life. It published and distributed the findings of research which it commissioned, it published annual reports and other documents in which its viewpoints were explained and extolled, it organized conferences and lectures to discuss problems of the economy, and to have its viewpoints disseminated it issued public statements to express its opinions on matters of policy. In short it constituted an important lobby in Turkish politics.

The representatives of big business had easy access to the prime minister and the members of his government during periods when center-right governments were in power. Even if what they wanted would not always be granted, they were received well and their cases were listened to with understanding. In 1978, however, a center-left government under the leadership of Bülent Ecevit came to power. TÜSİAD tried to impress upon Mr Ecevit that the country faced a major emergency, and that a speedy response was needed. Their prescription was to restructure the economy along liberal lines of more market forces and less government intervention.

Mr Ecevit tended to view big business and big industry as forces he had to contend with in his efforts to achieve social democracy. He turned a deaf ear, for example, when the industrialists complained of the breakdown of labor discipline, the resort to wildcat strikes, and the unreasonable demands for wage increases. In a similar vein, he branded an effort by a major group to establish a chain of supermarkets "an effort by big business to destroy small business."[21] As the Ecevit administration continued in office, the relations between big business and the government got progressively worse. In fact, at one point, communications between the government and big business came to almost at a stand still as the latter chose to air its views, including criticism of the government, to the public through paid statements which appeared in the major dailies, bearing such titles as

"A Realistic Way Out," "The Nation Is Waiting," and "Shall We Share Poverty or Achieve Abundance?"

TÜSİAD had become interested in the development of a comprehensive reform package during the 1970s. Its views were explained and expounded in various publications. A publication which was released early in 1978 contained an article by Mr Turgut Özal, formerly of the State Planning Organization but now working for a private corporation, arguing that the major stranglehold on the Turkish economy was the recurrent balance of payments problem which derived from keeping the value of the Turkish lira artificially high. He recommended the adoption of freely determined exchange rates.[22] Similar views were reiterated also in other publications. It was asked that the rate of inflation be brought down but gradually, and that public investments be limited to those on infrastructure such as energy production, and improvements in transportation and communications.[23]

Members of TÜSİAD were also in contact with the officials of the IMF, the World Bank, officials of the US administration, and members of the US private banking community.[24] In 1979, the results of these contacts were recorded into a confidential report which was given to the director of the State Planning Organization in order that he might pass it on to Mr Ecevit. The report emphasized that Western countries should not be expected to continue to provide several billion dollars a year for Turkey to help it make up the deficits in its balance of payments. If Turkey wanted to be an integral part of the Western community of nations, it had to modify its economic policies in a more liberal and outward-oriented direction.[25]

The Annual Report for 1979, repeating earlier demands, asked in addition for a new balance between prices and wages,[26] in apparent reference to high wage demands which were being advanced by the labor unions, while the 1980 Annual Report dwelled upon the necessity of increased exports, noting that this could only be achieved if exporting were made more profitable.[27]

At no point were the ideas of TÜSİAD heeded by the Ecevit government. Then in October 1979, the Republican People Party suffered a major setback at the polls during the by-elections and the partial elections for the Turkish senate. Mr Ecevit resigned. The job of forming the government was given once again to Mr Demirel, who, after consulting with the small parties on the right, established consensus to form a minority government. Shortly afterwards the Demirel government accepted a reform program the main lines of which were in close semblance to those which had been proposed by TÜSİAD.

In light of what transpired, it is tempting to attribute exceptional political power to TÜSİAD. Yet, caution has to be exercised. There were aspects of the political context, discussed below, which rendered the realization of a major economic reform package easier. Also, the major features of the TÜSİAD recommendations did not deviate in a major way from those which had been made by international economic agencies and by high-ranking Turkish bureaucrats whose job it had been to develop programs which these agencies would be willing to accept.

One element of the political context in which reforms were enacted was the public's loss of confidence in the process of politics. After two elections (1973, 1977) which had produced volatile, unstable coalitions which were unwilling or unable to deal with the critical questions that Turkey was facing, the Turkish electorate had lost its faith in competitive politics as a means of coping with societal problems. While the loss of faith in the democratic process is not a state of affairs to be admired, it eased the constraints under which economic stabilization measures could be formed and implemented. Because most citizens appeared to feel that government was unresponsive to their concerns and preferences, they were neither much interested in, nor were they inclined to react strongly to, what the government was doing. This may help explain, if only in part, why Mr Demirel decided to go ahead with the economic reform package including many shock treatment features and why the public's reaction to drastic economic measures was, on the whole, quite subdued.

Another element in the political context was the sense of an impending disastrous economic and political breakdown deriving from the consecutive governments' inability even to address major problems, and the severity of the economic crisis. This feeling probably made it possible for Mr Demirel to establish a minority government which received the support of his former coalition partners, the National Salvation and the Nationalist Action parties.

The critical question is why did these two small partners of earlier coalitions accept the formation of a minority government to which they continued to accord confidence, even after the adoption and implementation of drastic measures which could hardly be popular with the electorate? The answer has to be inferred from behavior, not from the verbal evidence volunteered to the public by party leaders. It must have become clear to the leaders of the right-wing parties that the so-called "Nationalist Front" governments in which they had participated in the past had been paralyzed by inability to reach consensus on any major issue. The small parties possessed a missionary orientation in politics which was hardly conducive to making compromises. The need for building intracabinet consensus had been avoided mainly by letting each party run the ministries allocated to it in the way it saw fit and by shying away from legislating laws or making major policy decisions.

The inability of cabinets to make major decisions was causing loss of prestige and support to all coalition partners. For the small partners, supporting a minority government which would address the economic crisis seemed to be an acceptable way of having the best of two worlds. Each party could withdraw its support from the government any time it felt that its vital interests were being threatened. If the economic policies of the minority government succeeded, they could claim credit for having supported it. If the measures failed or produced a strong negative reaction among the electorate, then they could join the ranks of those who were critical and absolve themselves of any responsibility.

The inability of the coalition governments to make policy expanded the role of the bureaucracy in achieving continuity in policy formulation and implementation. In the area of the international dimensions of economic policy, the bureaucrats of the Ministry of Finance, the Ministry of Foreign Affairs, and the State Planning Organization assumed critical roles. While the role of the so-called technocrats ought not be underemphasized in any modern society, in Turkey of 1979–80, the influence they wielded seems to have been unusual for bureaucrats in an elected parliamentary system.

The roots of resistance to reforms One important question is why governments in Turkey waited through three long years of crisis before acting. A partial answer based on the exigencies of the outcomes of the 1973 and 1977 elections, the workings of the party system, and the constraints under which coalition governments had to operate has already been offered. The explanation would not be complete, however, without an analysis of the effects policy changes might have on various socioeconomic groups in Turkish society.

It was clear that a serious effort to change the economy would involve, at a minimum: (1) the introduction of tight money, (2) a reduction in the public sector deficit, and particularly in the losses of the state economic enterprises, (3) reduction in the magnitude of public investments, and (4) devaluation of the Turkish lira.

The resistance of Turkish Governments to such recommendations was in part habitual. Turkish Governments were used to the emergence of balance of payments problems which created a bottleneck for the smooth functioning of the Turkish economy. A long-term alleviation of the problem would require a major structural transformation of the economy, something governments elected for a period of four years were reluctant to engage in. The cultural baggage they carried with them was not favorable to major changes either. Therefore, they would try to get by with just the minimum amount of adjustment required to overcome the balance of payments problems they were encountering. The critical variable here was to get the consent of the IMF to give new credits. Once that was achieved, they would gradually return to import substitution-oriented development and high levels of consumption financed by budget deficits and external borrowing.

Similarly, unwillingness of governments to conduct periodic devaluations was not always exclusively a product of calculations of what would be gained and lost, but rather the manifestation of a dogmatic belief that devaluations were a bad thing.

In addition to the force of habit or dogmatic beliefs, however, the reluctance of Turkish governments to adopt major economic stabilization programs and to implement them with perseverance had a basis in the politics of the country. The number of politically relevant cleavages of functional and nonfunctional nature in Turkish society had always made the act of building a winning coalition a very delicate one. Since the initial transition to competitive politics, governments had generally been formed on the center-right. To achieve a winning majority, a number of unlikely partners had to be brought together. These included big businesses vs small businesses, those engaged in production vs those in trade, those in rural farming vs those in urban commerce and industry, those who are religious-conservative vs those who are secular-liberal, as well as others. Each partner had to get something out of the coalition. The rewards of government were distributed in a careful fashion to retain the delicate balance it took to keep the government party in power. Engaging in major shifts of policy could easily upset this balance.

Devaluing the currency may be taken as an example. A devaluation of the Turkish lira would make the inputs of large and small industries more expensive, increase the cost of fertilizer and other inputs in the agricultural sector, and increase transportation and energy costs, which would then reflect in a rise in the general level of prices. On the other hand, there were few clearly identifiable winners. The heavily protected domestic market was so profitable that devaluation did not usually constitute a sufficient incentive even for exporters who might have easily gained from it if they were functioning in economies which were better-integrated to the world economy. So devaluation would only bring complaints from a government's supporters and heavy criticism from the opposition.

Introducing new taxes might be another example. The salaried, whose support of center-right governments was suspect, were already heavily taxed. Therefore, an increase in tax revenues necessitated taxing other segments of the electorate. The most obvious would have been agricultural incomes, but the support of middle- and upper-income farmers was critical in retaining a winning coalition, so nothing was done.

Cutting down on public investments, another common remedy, seemed impossible in the face of extensive pressure from districts, each demanding that new investments be made in their area. Retaining some projects while eliminating others produced strong reactions which were difficult to contain. If a project was dropped, the deputies from the district in which the project was located would be threatening the government with resignation from the parliamentary party.

It was therefore under conditions of economic desperation and under the effect of a combination of contextual variables that the enactment and implementation of an economic stabilization program proved possible.

3 THE REFORM PROGRAM, 1980–3

By January 1980, the Turkish economy had been in a state of crisis for almost three years. The rate of inflation was accelerating; factory shut-downs and excess capacity were increasing as imports were increasingly unavailable; foreign exchange reserves were nonexistent and the government was heavily in arrears on foreign debt; and real output was falling. It was in that crisis atmosphere that the policy reforms of January 1980 were undertaken.

In many regards, the economic situation in January 1980 was not fundamentally different from what it had been since 1977, except in the sense that economic and political deterioration had been in process longer. The major difference from the years 1977–9 was that the Demirel government chose to adopt a major program of economic reforms, with the support of the International Monetary Fund and the donor community. Under Prime Minister Ecevit, who had earlier been in power, these reforms had been strongly resisted and only undertaken as a last resort.

Political factors in the formulation of the reform program Inflation, shortages and political terror were the major items on Mr Demirel's agenda. The struggle to bring terrorism under control was being waged by the military under martial law. The changes in the economy needed the intervention of the government. The need to take measures was urgent, as the economy was rapidly disintegrating.[28]

The urgency of the situation put those who already had specific plans and programs to deal with the crisis at an advantage. The prime minister had to act quickly. There was no time to develop new and comprehensive programs. Furthermore, any prolonged discussion of what was to be done would not only have undermined the confidence in government and exposed it to pressures from various groups, but it would also have opened the way to a flurry of speculative economic activity which would have exacerbated the ongoing crisis. Therefore, when Turgut Özal paid a courtesy visit to Mr Demirel right after he took office and presented him with a comprehensive outline of what he thought ought to be done (which bore a remarkable similarity to the ideas which had been developed and defended by TÜSİAD), the prime minister was impressed. Mr Özal was given, upon his own suggestion, the job of serving as the undersecretary to the prime minister, and became at the same time the acting director of the State Planning Organization.

While the major features of the Economic Stabilization package might have appeared reasonable to Mr Demirel, there were no specific consti-tuencies expected be highly supportive, and the reactions of the general public to major price hikes was not easy to predict. Although big business had been the main exponent of a reform program, whether and to what extent to which they would extend sustained support when they themselves would have to go through significant adjustments was at best unknown, at worst unlikely.

What the government could rely on was not so much positive support as a lack of opposition. The RPP had been largely discredited because of its failure to stop the inflation and to alleviate the shortages of energy and basic commodities. In the 1979 elections its vote had dwindled to below 30 percent. Its criticisms would not carry credibility and hence would be ineffective.

The general public was not in a position to register major responses. There was confusion; there was an erosion of faith in the government; there was resignation to accept whatever was happening or whatever was being done. There was uncertainty about how the other parties which extended support to the minority government would react to shock measures. Especially Mr Erbakan of the National Salvation Party was judged to be unpredictable and unreliable.

Having been newly established, the Demirel government could count on what might be called "time credit." The amount of time needed for the successful implementation of a stabilization program and the achievement of the intended results would be longer than the "give the government a chance" time awarded to governments which had recently taken office. On the other hand, to decide on immediate elections which might bring the Justice Party to power by itself seemed impossible. There existed neither the parliamentary majority which would have accepted such an idea, nor sufficient time to hold them before urgent measures needed to be adopted. Therefore, the stabilization measures had to be taken within the existing political framework.

Any hesitation Mr Demirel might have had was overcome by a very small number of top-ranking bureaucrats, among whom Mr Özal was the best known. Another member of the same group explained:

> We constantly tried to impress upon the prime minister that Turkey had only one chance, enough gunpowder for one shot so to speak, left to reach an agreement with the IMF. We explained to him that much of Turkey's credibility with the financial institutions was lost. We told him that Turkey had to demonstrate to the IMF and others that it was not simply trying to get assistance to take care of a passing crisis. We had to show that we were absolutely committed to the full implementation of a stabilization program, a program to restructure the Turkish economy.[29]

Although the accounts of how the prime minister was persuaded to adopt the stabilization program vary in detail, all point in the same direction. There was a clear-cut case for the expeditious development and acceptance of a stabilization program. Several factors contributed to the government's ability to develop the program quickly.

First, through various negotiations with it and the signing of earlier standby agreements, there was a rather clear understanding of what would be involved in a program which would receive the approval of the IMF. One high-ranking official who has since joined an opposition party even commented that the entire program had already been prepared under the Ecevit administration. Although that may be an exaggeration, there can be little doubt that a lot had been prepared earlier by the high-ranking bureaucrats of the Ministry of Finance and the State Planning Organization.

Second, the measures had to be kept secret in order to avoid preemptive moves by various actors to profit from the intended changes. There were two groups of people through whom leaks could occur: (1) the bureaucrats from whom information had to be sought so that the government would have a basis for judging what the costs of the program would be, how much income the measures included in the program would generate, and how much foreign exchange would be needed; and (2) the cabinet ministers whose consent would be necessary for the adoption of the various immediate measures depicted in the program. Some measures such as the revision of the tax system would require legislation, but many measures such as the devaluation of the Turkish lira, raising the prices of products of state enterprises, and the reorganization of the government departments which are responsible for the implementation of economic policy, did not.

Very few bureaucrats knew the entire program. It has been suggested that fewer than ten persons were involved in its preparation. Those who were asked to furnish information on their own departments and agencies were asked many questions; they were asked to make calculations based on various assumptions. None could grasp the complete picture. One of the drafters of the program said:

> We were very careful about keeping the program a secret. Most of the program was in my handwriting. We did not even want a secretary to see it. The day the program was to be discussed in the Council of Ministers, we had a few xerox copies made to give to the ministers.[30]

An added strategy to keep high-ranking bureaucrats in the dark was through bypassing them and dealing directly with their inferiors who tended to narrower problems and could not therefore develop a sense of the bigger picture. This was hardly in line with the established traditions of the Turkish bureaucracy, especially those prevailing in the Ministry of Finance, but it was practiced.

The prime minister, noted for his personal style of rule, assumed the responsibility for getting the program through the Council of Ministers.

When the ministers were invited to an important meeting of the cabinet on January 24, 1980, they did not know what they were to discuss. As the program unfolded, some ministers complained that items being discussed were the concern of their ministries and they would need time for studying the matter. Mr Demirel is alleged to have used strong language to communicate that the entire package had to go through quickly to prevent speculative activity, and major revisions were out of the question because the program was highly integrated and harmonized.[31] He noted that some ministers might want to return to the "party group," which implied that failure to go along would necessitate a resignation.[32]

Many members of the cabinet reacted strongly to such a massive economic program, which was probably justified. None had been consulted in advance. Even the minister of finance was little aware of the measures which were proposed although most of the decisions fell within the domain of his responsibility.[33]

Third, the signature of the president was necessary to complete the formality of issuing a governmental decree; he was consulted in advance and gave his consent to sign the papers quickly. As soon as a new decree was accepted in the Council of Ministers, it was sent to the presidential palace, signed and then sent on to the offices of the Official Gazette for printing and distribution. The prime minister appears to have used this strategy of piecemeal decisions to convince his colleagues in the cabinet that, since earlier decisions had already been made public there was no turning back, and other complementary measures had to be adopted.

Fourth, a team was put together to carry out the newly adopted policies. The members of the team were recruited by Turgut Özal. The characteristics of those who comprised the team are relevant in light of the direction of the changes which were introduced. The team included for the most part engineers who had worked at the State Planning Organization during the late 1960s and early 1970s. Many had then left government service to get jobs in the private sector. They came from lower middle-class backgrounds, they were not the children of the bureaucratic elite who had ruled the republic under the single-party system. They were not committed to the etatist ideology, but were more inclined toward the development of private enterprise. Having worked in the government and in the private world, they knew both. They were in a position to bring in a private-enterprise orientation to those parts of government responsible for the economy. They would also be in a better position to relate to the private sector and establish better communications with them. But equally, if not more important, they had all worked earlier with Turgut Özal. They knew each other, they had confidence in each other, and they would take orders from Mr. Özal.

Fifth, the reform package was to be accompanied by administrative reorganization. The major feature of the reorganization plan was the creation of a set of new agencies, all within the prime ministry and directly responsible to the prime minister. These agencies took over duties which had previously been discharged by divisions, departments, or branches of other ministries. Taken together, these reorganized and/or newly established units would be in command of most areas which fell within the concern of the reform package.

For example, one objective of the reform was to attract foreign capital to Turkey. The system of controls and incentives governing capital inflows had formerly been administered by several agencies of government, including units in the ministries of Finance, Commerce, Industry and Technology, and the State Planning Organization. Now, all powers of these units were being transferred to a newly created Division of Foreign Investment within the prime ministry.[34]

Similarly, the Division of Incentives and Implementation, which was charged with the implementation of policies designed to stimulate investments and exports, was taken away from the Ministry of Industry and Technology and brought under a new division established within the prime ministry.[35]

A Coordination Board was also to be established, headed by the undersecretary to the prime minister, which would be charged with coordinating all decisions regarding the economy in which activities of more than one ministry was involved. A similar Money and Credit Board would have the responsibility for coordinating monetary policies.[36]

The need for coordination for the implementation of major policy changes is evident and needs no further elaboration. But was it not possible to achieve that within the existing institutional framework? Why was it felt to be necessary to engage in a major administrative reorganization? Three considerations suggest themselves. To begin with, by centralizing powers in the prime ministry, the need to consult other ministers was reduced. The prime minister was less accessible than other ministers and he also had more political power. Therefore, as reactions developed to the stabilization program among those whose interests were negatively affected, they would find it more difficult to try to exercise influence to change policy because decisions were made only at the top.

Next, this formula would reduce the power of ministries and other agencies which played critical roles in economic policy-making and implementation, each with a different set of institutional values and goals, and each competing with the others for policy prevalence. Two agencies were particularly important, the Ministry of Finance and the State Planning Organization. Neither was particularly oriented toward policy shifts which intended to liberalize the Turkish economy and integrate it more closely with the international economic system.

Also, in retrospect, it seems that Mr Özal, who was the main figure in the devising of the stabilization program, wanted to maintain control over it as much as possible. The arrangements made it possible for him to oversee the implementation of the program and make rapid adjustments when a need was felt.

Additionally, the support of the military leadership was obtained. The stabilization program was ready almost a month before January 24, 1980. The prime minister was waiting for an opportune moment. An unexpected development led to a postponement, however. On December 27, 1979, the Turkish Chief of Staff and the commanders of the Armed Forces handed a letter to President Korutürk, asking him to relate it to the leaders of political parties. The letter invited political parties to work together to protect the basic values of the republic and address the major problems the country was facing, and noted that the Armed Forces were mandated by law to be concerned about the survival and the well-being of the republic. The letter of the commanders and its contents became known on January 2, 1980.[37] It was not clear, in view of the letter, whether the government would stay in power or would be asked to step down, as had been the case in the March of 1971.

After some hesitation, upon Turgut Özal's suggestion, it was agreed that a briefing on the state of the economy would be given to the top commanders, explaining to them that a major reform package was being prepared. Mr Özal himself conducted the briefing on January 8. During his speech, he is said to have emphasized the need for increasing exports and reducing inflation and the importance of some measures that required adoption. Apparently, the military commanders responded favorably to the discussion and were convinced that the government was seriously addressing its economic problems[38] The Stabilization Program was initiated on January 24, 1980.

The reform program measures   Focus here is on the overall outlines of the reform program that began with Prime Minister Demirel's announcement on January 26, 1980. That program continued until early in 1983, when the architect of the program – Turgut Özal – was asked to resign. After an election in the fall of 1983, Özal became prime minister, and a second wave of the reform program, which continues to the present time, began. In this section, focus is on the first phase of the reforms.

There were two key, interrelated, objectives: to reverse the downward spiral in economic activity and to stem the inflation. However, this program was very different from earlier policy packages because it was immediately stated that there would be a fundamental change in underlying economic policies. Reforms were intended to strengthen market forces and competition by opening up the Turkish economy to the rest of the world; simultaneously, state controls over economic activity were to be reduced. Moreover, in his initial unveiling of the program, the prime minister made clear that the measures he then described would be followed with other policy changes (some of which would require legislation).

The decisions of January 24, 1980 were comprised of two groups of measures: one group of measures was taken at the Council of Ministers meeting either that day or shortly thereafter; the second required legislative action. The first set of measures were those for which decision-making powers rested solely with the cabinet and for which quick decisions were not only possible but necessary. The prime example, of course, is the setting of the new exchange rate. The determination of the prices of commodities such as gas and fertilizers, and policy regarding the prices of the various products of the state enterprises, are other examples.

Another group of measures could only be adopted or rendered meaningful in time. It would take time, for example, to introduce new taxes or revise the schedules of the existing ones because this required a legislative act. Other measures were more in the nature of policy guidelines and their goals could not be immediately achieved. Reducing the level of public expenditures and reordering the priorities of public investments are examples.

It is easier for any government, particularly an elected one, to make decisions at one shot and stick to them than to implement policy decisions which would involve other actors in the decision making process and which require time. As the numbers who are involved at various levels of the decision making process increase, the channels through which interested or affected parties may exercise influence expand. As the time required for the decision to be implemented becomes longer, those who want to influence or change policy are provided with a prolonged opportunity to conduct their activities.

An interesting question is whether a minority government, such as the Demirel one was, could reasonably have been anticipated to follow through on measures over time. In fact, as will be seen, it was able to do so.

Economic aspects of reform   There were three major components to the initial program: (1) exchange rate policy; (2) internal price policy; and (3) stabilization policy.[39]

The Turkish lira was immediately devalued, and it was announced that, henceforth, exchange rate policy would be more flexible, with more frequent devaluations in the future to maintain the attractiveness of exports. Simultaneously, several other measures were taken to encourage exports and to reduce the restrictiveness of the import regime. The official exchange rate was changed from TL45 to TL70 per US dollar. Although some items continued to be subject to different exchange rates, the earlier multiple exchange rate system was unified considerably.

A variety of other measures were also taken which also liberalized the trade and payments regime. Banks authorized to hold foreign exchange were authorized to retain up to 80 percent of their receipts, using them to cover acceptance credit obligations and to finance imports of oil, petroleum products, fertilizers, and pharmaceutical raw materials. The allowance for Turks traveling abroad was raised, and trade in gold was substantially liberalized.

In addition, a number of incentives for exporters were introduced or enhanced. Exporters were permitted to retain 5 percent or $10,000 (whichever was larger) of their receipts. Also, all duties on imports used in export production were eliminated, and administrative procedures relating to exports were to be greatly simplified. Provisions were made for subsidized export credits, and export subsidies were retained.

Finally, the import regime was liberalized in several ways. The coverage of the Liberalized List was enlarged, and advance deposit requirements on imports were generally reduced.[40] In addition, the Quota List, which had previously been issued once a year, became semiannual.

It was made clear that all of these moves were intended as first steps. Further liberalization of the import regime, continuing greater flexibility in exchange rates, and other changes were to follow later. However, except for these statements of intent, the actual changes in the trade and exchange rate regime were not dissimilar from those made in the 1958 and 1970 devaluation–stabilization programs. Even compared to the 1978 and 1979 standby announcements, the January 1980 changes in the trade and payments regime were not qualitatively or quantitatively dissimilar.[41] The differences lay in the statement of intent, and possibly, to a smaller extent, in the fact that there was a tendency toward simplification of regulations, rather than a move toward greater complexity of controls.[42]

The second major aspect of the program was the removal of controls over SEE prices. This was important for its prospective impact upon the budget deficit. The OECD had attributed the government's overshooting of its expenditure targets in earlier programs largely to rising transfer payments, of which transfers to the SEEs were the largest single component.[43] In turn, ceilings on Central Bank credits had been broken as government fiscal requirements driven by SEE deficits dictated Central Bank financing.

In the January 1980 program, it was announced that, henceforth, prices of SEE outputs (except coal, fertilizers, and electricity) would be freely determined and government subsidies would no longer be given (with a few exceptions). The average percentage increases associated with the January 1980 announcement were as follows: 100 percent for fuel oil, coal, lignite, railways, maritime transport, and textiles; 45 percent for gasoline; 120 percent for diesel oil and electricity; 75 percent for steel and PTT services; 300 percent for paper; 400 percent for fertilizer; 55 percent for cement, cigarettes, and beverages; and 80 percent for sugar. Measures were also taken removing controls over many prices of goods and services provided by the private sector.

For purposes of analyzing the policy reform package, it is unnecessary to consider the evolution of controls over prices in the 1980s except to note two things. First, the deficits of SEEs were greatly reduced in the first half of the 1980s, largely as a result of the liberalization.[44] Second, price controls over products produced in the private sector were largely phased out.

A major purpose of the 1980 program was the restoration of macroeconomic balance. The policies undertaken to achieve this goal were fairly conventional. In addition to reducing the deficits of the SEEs through raising their prices, measures were taken to make monetary and fiscal policy less expansive. These included especially the raising of interest rates and the imposition of controls over public sector expenditures.

It may be noted that the program was announced – without the support or overt influence of the International Monetary Fund – in January 1980. The government of Turkey signed a three-year standby with the Fund for SDR 1.25 billion – six times Turkey's quota and the largest credit extended by the IMF to that date – on June 18, 1980. The terms of the Letter of Intent are not public, but are known to have included the usual ceilings on net domestic assets of the central bank and on net borrowing by the public sector, along with provisions to liberalize the import regime as circumstances permitted, to refrain from adopting multiple exchange rate practices, and to prevent the accumulation of any new payments arrears.

These steps, in turn, permitted a rescheduling of outstanding debt, and the commitment of new money by the International Monetary Fund and the World Bank. In the standby agreement, the Turkish Government agreed to undertake some degree of financial liberalization within two years. In fact, on July 1, the borrowing and lending rates of the commercial banks were entirely liberalized (apparently totally unexpected by the Fund), and left to be determined by market forces.[45]

Political reactions to reforms Two general observations may be made. First, the government limited its policy actions to those areas which were within its own powers and did not undertake any activity which would require legislative action. Second, although the outcome was generally in favor of the stabilization program, it tried to establish a balance between the imperatives of the program and the imperatives of being an elected government which aspired to return to office after the next elections.

The government had been counting on getting fresh foreign exchange from the international agencies after having displayed its determination to accept and implement a stabilization program. These funds would be used to terminate the shortages of basic commodities which would be a way of rewarding the general public for the sacrifices they were asked to make and thus winning their confidence. Mr Demirel still hoped that it might be possible to hold early elections sometime during the summer of 1980 from which he expected to come out as the winner. His hopes were dashed by the opposition. Although other parties, notably the RPP and the National Salvation Party, had frequently talked of how they wanted early elections too, an agreement between parties never proved possible.

The foreign exchange did not come as quickly and as abundantly as had been anticipated, while the application of the stabilization program had to be continued. As tight money policy began to take effect, one of the first groups to complain was the businessmen. TÜSİAD was not openly critical and its president made statements supportive of the stabilization program. The Union of the Chambers of Industry, Commerce and Commodity Exchanges, an organization which brings together businesses of various kinds and sizes under its umbrella but is dominated by small businesses, complained.

More critical was the question of what buying price wheat would be given by the Soil Products Office.[46] In May, the Council of Ministers met to decide on the price. While the market price was about 9 TL/kg, Mr Özal's recommendation was considerably below that figure. The Council of Ministers chose to ignore the recommendation and decided to pay 10 TL/kg. Expenses in other areas had to be curtailed in order to hold public expenditures within the limits designated in the program. It had probably been thought that the farming population had been alienated too much from the Justice Party, which they had traditionally supported. Therefore, the general limits of the program were observed but the spirit was violated because one of the goals was to reduce the financial burden that supported buying of agricultural commodities imposed on the national budget.

On June 4, the interest rates on time deposits of six months or more were set free, and a new system of bank certificates of deposit was introduced. The system was to go into effect on July 1, 1980. The banking sector registered no unified response to the decision. The older, more established banks seemed not to be favorably disposed; some of the newer and smaller banks approved of the change since this would give them an opportunity to challenge those which benefitted from having had their names around for a long time. In any case, this division within the banking community enabled the government to introduce the new interest rate policy without major resistance.

The opposition parties were highly critical of the policies being pursued by the Demirel government. Mr Erbakan of the National Salvation party was extremely critical of the policies, saying in a press conference in June that after six and a half months of having supported the minority government, they were disaffected because the government was simply turning the country into the hands of the West.

In July, a motion of censure was introduced by the RPP against the Demirel government. As the parliament took up the motion, it was not clear what would happen. The National Salvation Party had not made up its mind. Mr Demirel drove home his strong points in the debate:

> We are not interested in getting a vote of confidence at all costs; if we fail to get it, we will go. But the RPP will get the full blame for the disaster which is bound to ensue. I will not beg you. I will not say, do not bring us down. But,

if you are seriously interested in becoming the government, why don't you come and repeal the price hikes which we have introduced...[47]

The Demirel government continued to serve in office until September 12, 1980, when a military committee comprising the Chief of Staff of the Turkish Armed Forces and the commanders of the Army, Navy, Air Force, and the Gendarmerie took power. The National Security Council justified the assumption of power on political grounds. Not a single day had been going by without several people being killed in street fighting or falling victim to acts of terrorism. The legislature was paralyzed. It had failed to elect a new president since April. No new laws had been made although the need for them was evident in many areas, including taxation. While a new election might have made it possible to end the deadlock, no such decision appeared likely.

The military and economic reforms   A direct link, then, between the economic stabilization program and the adoption of authoritarian rule is not easy to establish.[48] Yet, that there has been a coincidence of military rule and stabilization programs also in the past suggests that the linkage should not be lightly dismissed. The stabilization measures in 1958 and in 1970–1 had each been followed by interventions by the Turkish military in 1960 and in 1971.

In all three instances, the explicit justification for the intervention of the military was based on political factors. It might, of course, be argued that what caused both the political instability and the military intervention were problems of an economic nature, but it is difficult to establish the causal linkage and to produce the evidence to prove it.

The argument that elected governments would be incapable of adopting some of the measures necessitated by economic stabilization programs is not easy to support either, as the following remarks illustrate. The first is by a minister who served in the first cabinet which was established by the military leadership in September 1980. In an interview, he said:

> The Demirel government had been able to enact none of the tax laws which had been foreseen in the economic stabilization program...[X] explained to the generals that the legislation of new tax laws was absolutely necessary in order to go on with the stabilization program and to balance the oncoming budget. They listened carefully. They accepted. They were reasonable men.[49]

The second remark comes from a retired high ranking bureaucrat from the Ministry of Finance:

> Nobody should credit the generals for doing everything required of the stabilization program. They enacted only one-fourth of the tax proposals into law. About the others, they said "Elected governments can take care of them when we go..."[50]

These accounts of what the military did obviously differ, and it is not possible to judge which one approximates reality better. But the second remark points to an aspect of authoritarian governments which ought not be overlooked. Authoritarian governments are often in need of greater legitimacy since they replace governments which have come to power through ways known to and accepted by the electorate. As a result, in contrast to the suggestion that they can do anything they deem necessary, they are probably constrained from making decisions and adopting policies which would undermine their popularity.

The military rulers of 1980–3 had identified their mission as saving the political system from total collapse, restoring law and order, making the administrative machinery work and bringing discipline to public life. They were not well-versed in questions pertaining to the economy. They knew that a major stabilization program was being implemented. They wanted the program, which appeared to have been working well so far, to succeed. They did not want to take their attention away from questions of law and order and concentrate it on matters of economics. Therefore, they did what seemed to be logical under the circumstances. After taking over the government on September 12, 1980, they asked Turgut Özal, the major figure behind the stabilization program, to continue. Mr Özal became minister of state and assistant to the prime minister for economic affairs. Upon his recommendation, one of the key persons with whom he had worked in the preparation of the stabilization program, Kaya Erdem, was made the minister of finance.

While the soldiers may not have interfered with the daily conduct of economic policy, they appear to have been favorably disposed toward the stabilization program. This was the result, in part, of the briefings which Turgut Özal had conducted for them. But, both prior to and after the 1980 September intervention, there were good relations between top military leaders and big businesses. Retiring generals were often recruited to serve on the boards of directors of major corporations. Therefore, it is not surprising that they would not only be familiar with but also think favorably of a program which had the backing of big business. A well-known journalist noted in the diary he kept a conversation with the secretary general of the National Security Council. In May 1980, four months before the intervention, General Saltık commented that the decisions of January 24, 1980 were logically coherent, there was no alternative to them, and they should be implemented with full force.[51]

The rapidity with which the military leadership decided to accept the ongoing stabilization program as its own also suggests that members of the National Security Committee were positive toward it and that they had planned their policy on economic matters in advance, at least to some degree. The program also involved international commitments, and the commanders have generally been very sensitive to conforming to the international commitments which Turkey has made.

In his first press conference, the head of the National Security Committee, General Evren, gave a very clear indication that the stabilization program would be continued and all necessary measures, including the enactment of new legislation, would be taken. He added that he was confident that the nation would be brave, sacrificing, and patient.[52]

Turgut Özal has openly acknowledged that the military administration contributed to the success of the stabilization program. In a speech he made to the heads of the Chambers of Commerce, Chambers of Industry, and commodity exchanges, he said that the confident atmosphere created by the intervention had led to major increases in productivity, that exports were beginning to increase and that an overhaul of the tax system, neglected for years, was going to be made.[53] In a speech to the Consultative Assembly two years later, he was almost categorical in his support of military rule. He said:

> If the Intervention of September 12 had not been conducted, we would not
> have been able to obtain the results of the economic program. Anarchy was
> on the rise and the tax laws did not go through the National Assembly. We
> should be thankful that a tax reform has been conducted...[54]

Özal's judgment on the positive contribution of the military to the achievement of economic stability was echoed during the years of the military administration by both prominent businessmen and organizational leaders of the Turkish business community. Many business leaders also emphasized the contribution the military administration had made to bringing order to labor relations.

Policy problems under military rule Although they adopted the Özal program, the military administration had to deal with policy problems in three additional areas during their tenure: reorganizing the labor–industrial relations system, enacting tax legislation, and coping with a bankers' crisis. Of these, the first two were linked to attaining the goals of the stabilization program. The third was a consequence of a sharp rise in nominal interest rates, which had been introduced as a way of achieving positive real interest rates and stimulating savings.

During the period prior to September 1980, industrial wages of union workers had risen rapidly while labor productivity had been falling. The drop in productivity was a consequence of two different factors. The first factor was energy shortages and lack of the availability of raw materials or semifinished products which the industry used as inputs. The second was the general atmosphere of insecurity, the tense relations between workers subscribing to different ideologies and belonging to rival unions, and work slowdowns and stoppages promoted by some labor. The rise in real wages, on the other hand, was the product of labor union militancy which had intensified as other centers of power in Turkish society were getting progressively weaker.

Elected governments had not been successful in coping with lower levels of labor productivity, for the problem constituted part of a set of broader problems to which they had failed to address themselves for reason explained earlier. Even before they assumed political power, the military leaders were already disturbed by the militancy of labor unions, by the slowdowns, work stoppages and the strikes. By the nature of their professional training, they found it difficult to digest the idea that the lower orders of a hierarchical organization should have powers or status to challenge the management which they saw as being hierarchically superior. As men of state, they did not understand how a social group, the union labor, could put its interests ahead of what the military leadership felt to be the best national interest. As soldiers, they felt that breakdowns in labor discipline were intolerable behavior. They also found the wage demands of workers unreasonably high. This judgment is not surprising since the salaries of government employees had fallen very much behind the rates of inflation, leading to a decline in their real income. The soldiers, after all, were government employees.

The goals of the stabilization program also favored a reduction of the real wages of workers. Lowered wages enhanced the competitiveness of Turkish products in the international markets, and were probably necessary if unemployment was not to rise rapidly. They also enabled the state enterprises to reduce their deficits, which constituted an important aspect of the stabilization program.[55]

The military introduced a number of measures, shortly after coming into power, which had, in addition to helping restore law and order, led to the diminution of the political power and the bargaining stance of labor unions. The first measure was to ban strikes. Next, wage negotiations under collective bargaining were also suspended. A council of arbitration was established, which would determine wages until such time as normal political processes were restored. This council would have representatives of employers, labor, and government.[56] A ceiling of 70 percent was imposed on wage increases in labor contracts, a rate below the rate of inflation at the time.[57]

The military also proceeded to close down the second largest but politically the strongest confederation of labor in the country. The confederation, known as DİSK (acronym for the Confederation of Revolutionary Labor Unions), was a Marxist-Leninist labor union which had been growing rapidly because of its ability to negotiate high wage contracts. It had also demonstrated its political potential by organizing massive demonstrations in big cities which had, on occasion, paralyzed life in urban centers. DİSK's property was confiscated by the government, and DİSK's leaders were brough to trial for organizing revolution to establish by force the domination of one social class over others, a criminal act according to Turkish penal code.

The military administration not only kept wages down during its rule but also created a new legal framework; some of it is in constitutional provisions, which have permanently weakened Turkish labor in its relations with employers. The constitution directs labor not to engage in political activity. The laws impose significant restrictions on how unions may spend their money. Even many kinds of charitable contributions by labor are not allowed. In some key sectors, banking being the prime example, unionization is allowed but strikes are not. Unions are required to notify the Ministry of Labor and Social Security when a new member joins them. The ministry, in turn, sends a copy of the notification to the employers so that attempts at unionization at a workplace can be detected and resisted from the very beginning. The government has extensive powers to postpone strikes or submit them to mandatory arbitration.

The real incomes of Turkish unionized workers were below pre–1980 levels even in 1990. There have been major pressures among Turkish labor to compensate for the losses of the past. There have been domestic and international demands that the legal structure – different from that in any other democratic society – ought to be changed. Those clamoring for change have included the ILO, some agencies of the European Community and the Council of Europe, Europe-wide party organizations like the Socialist International, and international federations of labor unions. The government has demonstrated no inclination, however, to change the labor–industrial relations order which the military had been instrumental in creating.

Taxes constituted a second area of policy for the military administration. In the January 1980 program, there were references to tax reform which the civilian governments had failed to implement. The major concern of the stabilization program was not so much to establish a tax system which was more equitable but to increase government revenues and close the fiscal deficit. However, in the initial package, tax liabilities of the nonsalaried were increased while the income tax schedule was revised to reduce the burden of wage earners.

Free interest rates were the third policy area in which the military administrators were compelled to take action. But here, in contrast to taxes and labor questions, the military leaders were forced to react to a situation which had emerged as a consequence of measures adopted to implement the stabilization program.

As has been noted, interest rates were set free on July 1, 1980. Coupled with the tight money policy being pursued, the sudden rise in interest rates had led to a credit squeeze for many corporations. Banks did not have enough money to lend, and it was expensive to borrow from them in any event. Under the circumstances, a network of brokerage houses called *Banker* had begun to expand to extend credit. Because they were not subject to the regulations of banks, these institutions paid higher interest rates. Many people had used their savings to buy bonds and CDs sold by these institutions with promises to convert them on demand. It is estimated that the amount of money these institutions controlled amounted to approximately one-fourth of the money in circulation in the summer of 1982 when the system collapsed.[58]

The collapse was triggered by the inability of a major textile company to meet its obligations to the largest brokerage company, named Kastelli. Kastelli then failed to meet its own obligations. The entire system collapsed in the ensuing crisis of confidence as depositors rushed to brokers to claim cash for paper they held.

Mr Özal and the minister of finance, Mr Erdem, felt that the government should not do anything about the crisis. People had deposited their money with institutions which paid higher interest, but that brought with it higher risks. It seemed desirable for people to learn how a market system operated, and that high returns were usually accompanied by high risks.

The military leadership was of a different opinion. First, as a nonelected government, they were deeply concerned about support which the public continued to accord to them. Not doing anything about a crisis, they felt, would undermine this support. Secondly, one of the largest groups of people who had invested money in these *Bankers* were the retired civil servants, including many retired military officers. The generals could not behave as if they were totally unconcerned. Third, it appeared that a number of major companies might collapse. The generals, possessing the typical attitude of the state elites, thought that letting businesses close down was usurping national wealth. Finally, the generals had been told by others that something like what happened was likely to happen.[59]

Since the policy preference of the military leaders deviated significantly from those who had assumed the responsibility for the implementation of the stabilization program, the latter were asked to change their policies, and Mr Erdem, the minister of finance, was asked to resign. On July 13, 1982, both Mr Erdem and Mr Özal left the government rather than accept major policy changes which they felt would undermine the entire program.[60]

With the resignation of Mr Özal, there was a shift of policy. Government control over banks was increased. Some of the bankrupt companies were bailed out by being taken over by government banks or by being turned over to state enterprises who would bring them back to financial health.

The person behind these changes was Adnan Baser Kafaoğlu, another high-ranking bureaucrat of the Ministry of Finance who served as an economic advisor to President Evren. He was much more representative of the traditional bureaucracy of the ministry, preferring a cautious approach in adjusting to externally stimulated economic change rather than the radically different ways Turgut Özal had been trying to introduce. He became the minister of finance. The members of the Özal team began to leave their posts. A restoration period had begun.

4 THE SECOND PHASE OF POLICY REFORM: 1983 ONWARDS

The period after Mr Özal left office was the one time during the 1980s when the reforms apparently lost momentum. The new team under Minister Kafaoğlu relaxed the monetary and fiscal restraints on economic activity and inflation began accelerating.

Shortly thereafter, the military government announced that elections would be held in the fall of 1983. Mr Özal organized a new political party, ANAP, which won a parliamentary majority (plurality of the vote) among the three parties (including the one supported by the military) which contested the election. Thus, by late 1983, a new – democratically elected[61] – government was in power under a prime minister committed to economic liberalization and with a mandate to carry out further reforms.

The new Özal government moved quickly to regain the momentum of policy reforms. Changes proceeded rapidly over the next three years. However, the reform package and objectives after 1983 focused almost entirely on achieving structural changes within the economy, especially with regard to the role of import-competing and export industries on one hand, and the role of the private and public sectors, on the other. The goal of stabilization was largely forgotten as government expenditures began rising sharply, and inflation once again accelerated. Unlike earlier fiscal expansions, however, this one was geared largely toward increased expenditures on infrastructure, while SEEs remained subject to fairly strict controls.

In the second phase, a number of major policy changes were effected. These included major reforms in the financial sector (including banking deregulation, freeing of interest rates, opening the Istanbul stock exchange, creating a foreign exchange market, and reduction of taxes on financial transactions), tax reform (including especially the introduction of a value-added tax in 1985 and a reduction in the highest marginal rate of income taxation from 45 to 25 percent), and increased incentives for efficiency in the SEEs. There was also the beginning of a privatization program which, to date, has been able to effect only small sales of SEEs to the private sector.

Turning to the trade and payments regime, many restrictive aspects of the Turkish trade regime of the 1960s and 1970s were still intact in mid-1983, despite the much greater stability of the real exchange rate. Much of the increased incentive for exporting that had been accomplished in the first phase of the reform program had been effected by special export incentives, rather than dismantling the protection accorded to import-competing goods.[62]

In the second phase, it was announced that there would be moves toward a unified exchange rate and elimination of special rates and that the trade regime would be further liberalized. To that end, the Import Lists were changed from negative lists (under which no item may be imported unless listed) to positive lists (all items not listed could be imported). About 200 items were ineligible for importation under the 1984 program, and further commodities were made eligible for importation in later programs. Simultaneously, tariff reclassifications were announced, and the average tariff rate was reduced by about 20 percentage points. Import procedures were also greatly simplified.

However, there were some conflicting currents. As import duties were reduced and items removed from the Negative Lists, several special "funds" were created. These funds, which were off-budget items, were for particular purposes, such as a "Housing Fund," a "Support and Price Stabilization Fund" (SPSF), and so on. While the rates of levy for these funds were far below earlier tariff levels (reaching a maximum of 10 percent for the SPSF in 1989) and applied uniformly to a large number of imported commodities, they were increased several times and their scope was generally extended.[63]

Potentially more damaging was the establishment of a Foreign Exchange Risk Insurance Scheme (FERIS) in April 1984, which guaranteed borrowers of foreign exchange that they would not take foreign exchange losses on repayment. FERIS was introduced with the stated purpose of covering that risk. In practice, FERIS increased the fiscal difficulties of the government in raising resources for debt-service as the exchange rate was depreciated to keep pace with inflation: since the private sector earned and earns most foreign exchange, the government must raise revenue to purchase foreign exchange from the private sector.

Although there was no announced policy, the real exchange rate was further depreciated until 1986. Baysan and Blitzer estimate that, on average, the real exchange rate depreciated by about 3.6 percent annually from May 1981 to May 1986.[64] As inflationary pressures intensified in the late 1980s, however, policy toward the exchange rate became more ambivalent: in 1987 and again starting in 1989, the nominal exchange rate depreciated by considerably less than the rate of inflation; in 1990 alone, the real exchange rate appreciated 20 percent. There were thus indications that failure to control inflation might undermine the outer-oriented stance of the government. The government also reduced restrictions surrounding convertibility of the Turkish lira and announced that steps would be taken to make the lira convertible. Foreign banks were encouraged to open branches in Turkey. Other immediate moves included the liberalization of restrictions on the amount tourists could take abroad, and widening the band within which commercial banks could deal in the foreign exchange market in Turkey. Subsequently, Turkish residents were permitted to open foreign bank accounts and make payments, withdrawals, and transfers abroad. After July 1988, foreign investors were permitted to enter the Turkish capital market, and by June 1989, foreign investment funds were allowed to operate in Turkey. Also in 1989, Turkish residents were given the right to purchase foreign securities freely, and could purchase up to $3,000 in foreign currency without restriction.

Finally, steps were taken to increase the attractiveness of Turkey for private foreign investors. These included easing conditions governing the transfer of profits and repatriation of capital, as well as the general relaxation of capital and exchange market controls.

5 RESULTS OF THE ALTERED TRADE AND PAYMENTS REGIME

The magnitude of changes in incentives

Table 8.3 gave estimates of the real exchange rate over the 1975 to 1990 period. As can be seen, the real exchange rate – whether measured against the US dollar or against a 7–country basket – appreciated considerably in the late 1970s. In real terms, the devaluation of 1980 was substantial, amounting to more than 30 percent on either basis. During the first half of the 1980s, real depreciation continued, so that by 1985, the real cost of foreign exchange in terms of domestic purchasing power was more than twice what it had been in 1979. This in itself constituted a major change in the incentive for exporting.

For imports, quantitative restrictions were removed, while simultaneously tariffs were reduced. This offset, of course, a considerable portion of the increased real price of foreign exchange importers had to pay. Estimates of the combined impact of removal of quantitative restrictions and tariff reductions suggest that imports, on average, cost 229 percent of the CIF price (at the nominal exchange rate) in 1980, fell gradually to 199 percent in 1984, and then to 168 percent in 1985 and 155 percent by 1987. Thus, the protection accorded to import-competing industries was greatly reduced.[65]

At the same time, export subsidies were employed to increase the attractiveness of exporting. Nontraditional exports were eligible for export subsidies averaging 11 percent of f.o.b. value in 1980; subsidies reached a peak at 21 percent of f.o.b. price in 1983, and thereafter declined to 10 percent in 1987.[66] Simultaneously, the paperwork and delays associated with exporting were greatly reduced, including the ability of exporters to import needed inputs duty-free and to retain foreign exchange for that purpose or for travel abroad.

If account is taken of the value of all export incentives (that were not simply offsets to additional costs imposed on exporters by the import regime) and the protection to imports, it would appear that the trade and payments regime was strongly biased in favor of import-substitution industries in 1980: a one-dollar saving of foreign exchange through import substitution earned about as much for a Turkish producer as earning $1.95 earned. By 1986, this bias had fallen so that exporters had to earn $1.21 in foreign exchange to receive the same return as importers who saved $1.00, and by 1989 the differential was down to $1.12.

Response to altered incentives: exports

Thus, removal of quantitative restrictions, tariff reductions, export incentives, and a more realistic real exchange rate all served to increase the relative and absolute attractiveness of exporting. It is difficult to convey the extent of the transformation of the economy, and of attitudes toward exporting. Historically, Turks held a deep-seated distrust of foreign trade and were highly pessimistic as to the capabilities of Turkish businessmen. In the late 1970s, exports constituted only about 7 percent of GNP. This was an amazingly small number for a country such as Turkey.

By 1987, the share of exports in GNP had risen to 21 percent. This represented a tripling of export share in GNP in less than eight years. That increase was accomplished with an average annual rate of growth of export earnings (in US dollars) of 18.9 percent over the 1980–8 period. By the standards of any decade, that export growth rate was impressive. Because there was a severe slowdown in the growth of world trade in the first half of the 1980s, Turkish performance is even more outstanding.

Accompanying the increase in export earnings was an increase in the share of imports in GNP. Imports increased from a range of 15–17 percent of GNP in the late 1970s to over 22 percent in every year after 1984. Thus, the increase in exports represented a structural shift as *both* exports and imports increased in relative and absolute importance.

Table 8.4 gives summary data on the growth of exports by major commodity groups. As can be seen, all major categories of exports grew, although exports of industrial goods grew much more rapidly than did exports of agricultural commodities. Mineral products exports grew very little after a short-lived burst in the mid-1980s. Thus, whereas agricultural commodities constituted 57 percent of exports in 1975 and 1980, their share of total exports had fallen to around 20 percent by 1989. Conversely, the share of industrial goods in total exports rose rapidly, reaching more than three-quarters of total exports by the later 1980s.

Export earnings from agricultural commodities rose only at an average annual rate of 2.7 percent over the 1980–9 period. Nonetheless, the growth *rate* of earnings exceeded that of earlier years. Moreover, exports of processed agricultural commodities rose from $209 million in 1980 to $919 million in 1989; to the extent that these commodities might otherwise have been exported in crude, or unprocessed, form, the growth of agricultural exports is understated by examining only exports of unprocessed commodities.

Table 8.4 Export earnings by major commodity categories, 1976, 1980–9 (millions of US dollars)[a]

Commodity group	1976	1980	1981	1982	1983	1984	1985	1986	1987	1988	1989
Agriculture and livestock	1,254 (64)	1,672 (57)	2,219 (47)	2,141 (37)	1,881 (33)	1,749 (25)	1,719 (22)	1,886 (25)	1,853 (18)	2,341 (20)	2,125 (18)
Mineral products	106 (8)	191 (7)	193 (4)	175 (3)	189 (3)	240 (3)	244 (3)	247 (3)	272 (3)	377 (3)	413 (4)
Industrial goods	596 (30)	1,047 (36)	2,290 (49)	3,429 (60)	3,658 (64)	5,145 (72)	5,995 (75)	5,324 (71)	8,065 (79)	8,943 (77)	9,088 (78)
Processed agricultural	87	209	412	568	670	809	647	667	954	885	919
Manufactures	509	857	1,879	2,861	2,989	4,336	5,348	4,658	7,111	8,059	7,250
Total	1,960	2,910	4,703	5,746	5,728	7,134	7,958	7,457	10,190	11,662	11,627

[a]Numbers in parantheses indicate percentages of total exports.
Source: Krueger and Aktan (1992, table 32).

Table 8.5 provides a breakdown of the commodity composition of manufactured exports. As can be seen, earnings from virtually all categories of manufactured exports grew at rates in excess of 10 percent. In the late 1970s and early 1980s Turkish manufactured exports of individual manufacturing sectors had been relatively small and scattered except for processed food and textiles and clothing. By 1989, export production was significant in a much larger number of two-digit industries.

Manufacturing production was somewhat lower in 1980 than it had been in 1975. By 1985, however, it had increased substantially, with rapid increases in most two-digit industries. Since domestic demand grew only slowly over the first several years after 1980, it is a reasonable inference that the growth of manufacturing output was in large part the consequence of the expansion of exports.

By the late 1980s, it was evident that the reorientation of incentives toward a more outer-oriented economy had indeed changed the structure of the Turkish economy. In the first years of the export drive, there had been some skepticism. Skeptics had questioned whether exporting out of excess capacity would continue once domestic demand recovered. That question was decisively answered in the latter half of the decade when economic growth accelerated and exports continued to grow. A second source of concern was the very large fraction of increased exports, especially in the early 1980s, that were destined for Iran and Iraq. That concern, too, was put to rest when those countries reduced their imports from Turkey but overall Turkish exports continued growing.

Table 8.5 Commodity composition of manufactured exports, 1975, and 1980–9 (millions of US dollars)

Commodity	1975	1980	1981	1982	1983	1984	1985	1986	1987	1988	1989
Textiles and clothing	128	424	803	1,056	1,299	1,875	1,790	1,851	2,707	3,201	3,508
Hides and leather products	65	50	82	111	192	401	484	345	722	514	605
Chemical products	5	76	94	148	120	173	266	350	527	734	774
Rubber, plastic products	33	16	72	60	77	97	108	141	258	352	313
Glass, ceramics	18	36	102	104	108	146	190	158	205	233	258
Nonferrous metal products[a]	37	58	228	251	160	142	159	138	141	233	300
Iron and steel products	20	34	100	362	407	576	969	804	852	1,458	1,349
Metal products	4	8	20	27	19	16	73	60	107	52	23
Others[b]	29	98	270	397	373	501	939	633	1,362	951	828
Total	338	800	1,771	2,516	2,755	3,927	4,978	4,480	6,881	7,495	7,939

The total of manufactured exports here does not correspond to the number given in table 8.4 because of differences in classification between manufactured and nonmanufactured exports.
[a]Includes cement.
[b]Includes forestry products, electrical and nonelectrical machinery, motor vehicles, instruments, and miscellaneous manufactures not classified elsewhere.

Source: Krueger and Aktan (1992, table 33).

Yet a third source of concern focused on claims of faked invoicing. The magnitude of export incentives clearly provided an inducement for exporters to overstate the value of their foreign exchange earnings, and the Turkish newspapers were able to expose several instances of that practice. Analysis of the trading returns of partner countries suggests that this may have accounted for an average overstatement 5 or 6 percent for most years in the early 1980s, but for 21 percent of the stated value of exports in 1984. The actual rate of growth of export earnings may therefore have been somewhat lower than recorded in the early 1980s; if that is true, the rate of growth of exports in the latter 1980s (when special export incentives were greatly reduced because of faked invoicing) is commensurately understated.[67]

Overall, Turkish export growth during the 1980s was impressive. Against a background of worldwide recession, Turkey was able to transform her economy from a highly inefficient, inner-oriented one to one more closely integrated with the international economy.

The balance of payments and foreign debt

Whereas the "balance of payments" constituted a major policy problem in the 1970s, it was hardly noticed during the 1980s. Not only did the current account deficit diminish, and actually turn to surplus in 1988, but almost all categories of transactions had been liberalized. There were even occasions when the Turkish lira sold at a slight premium to foreign currencies, especially the US dollar, but black market activity in foreign exchange all but ceased.[68]

The most striking feature of the Turkish balance of payments during the 1980s is the simultaneous increase in both exports and imports. The hallmark of Turkish reforms in the 1980s was an opening up of the economy, and both exports and imports constituted a larger share of economic activity. The trade balance was a negative $4.6 billion in 1980, fell to minus $2.7 billion by 1982, and thereafter was in the range of minus $2.8 to $3.1 billion in every subsequent year. During that interval, exports increased more than fourfold.

For present purposes, what is important is to note that the 1980 devaluation and liberalization package resulted in a fairly immediate and sharp drop in the current account deficit, but that thereafter Turkey maintained a reasonably constant current account balance for the next several years. After 1984, the noninterest current account was positive, as other receipts were sufficient to cover current account noninterest payments and a portion of the interest on the debt. By 1988, of course, the noninterest current account surplus was large enough to cover all interest charges and reduce debt.

Although the current account deficit diminished after 1981, financing for the external deficit was still required from 1980 to 1987. That financing necessarily originated primarily from new borrowing. Indeed, accumulation of foreign exchange reserves in 1986 and 1987 implied that borrowing in those years exceeded the amount that would have financed the current account deficit. Some observers have suggested that Turkey's very successful macroeconomic growth performance of the 1980s was attributable to the increased imports that were financed in part by accumulation of additional debt.[69] It is important, therefore, to consider two issues. On one hand, there is a question of how much borrowing (or equivalent means of financing a current account deficit) there was. On the other hand, there is a question of the importance of the current account deficit in permitting a resumption of economic growth during the 1980s.[70]

The evolution of Turkish debt may be seen in table 8.6. From a level of $19.0 billion in 1980, Turkish debt rose by less than $1.0 billion by the end of 1983. Even in 1984, it grew only by $1.3 billion. Thereafter, however, it rose $7.8 billion in 1986, $8.0 billion in 1987, and then declined by $2 billion in 1988 (reflecting the current account surplus of that year).[71]

Table 8.6   Turkish debt and debt-service, 1980–8

	1980	*1981*	*1982*	*1983*	*1984*	*1985*	*1986*	*1987*	*1988*
(a) *Magnitude of debt (billions of US dollars)*									
Total debt	19.0	19.2	19.7	20.3	21.6	26.0	32.8	40.8	38.7
Long-term	15.5	15.7	16.5	16.4	16.9	19.9	24.8	31.3	30.7
Short-term	2.5	2.3	1.8	2.3	3.2	4.8	6.9	8.7	7.7
IMF	1.1	1.3	1.5	1.6	1.4	1.3	1.1	0.8	0.3
(b) *Debt-service indicators (ratios)*									
Debt/export ratio	6.54	4.08	3.34	3.44	2.92	3.15	4.32	3.95	3.27
Debt service exports	0.38	0.38	0.40	0.40	0.32	0.45	0.46	0.48	0.56

Source: Krueger and Aktan (1992, Data Appendix, table 17).

Although Turkey received new monies during the 1980s, their magnitude appears to be no larger, relative to the size of the Turkish economy, than monies involuntarily lent to other heavily indebted countries during the same period. It is difficult, therefore, to account for the difference between Turkish performance and that of other creditors on the argument that Turkey restored creditworthiness and received new money.

It should be noted, in any event, that the fact that lending to Turkey was voluntary was in large part because of her export performance. Had exports grown only slowly during the 1980s, it seems clear that Turkey would have faced the same borrowing constraint that afflicted most heavily indebted countries: private creditors would have refused additional credit.

Overall economic growth

Just as one can divide the Turkish reforms into an initial period from 1980 to 1983, and then a longer period during which there was a continuing drive toward liberalization, so too can the 1980s be divided in terms of Turkish economic growth. The period from 1980 to 1983 was one of relatively slow growth, whereas the period from 1984 to 1990 witnessed much better economic performance.

The initial results of the January 1980 program were highly visible to all in Turkey. Shortages disappeared as import flow resumed and as power outages, petroleum shortages, and other bottlenecks disappeared while destocking of inventories also took place.[72]

In its initial phase, the major success of the program was to bring about a reduction in the rate of inflation. By early 1981, it was estimated that the rate of inflation had dropped to 35 percent, contrasted with its high in February 1980 of 133 percent; it remained at about that rate through 1982.[73] Although inflation accelerated in 1983 as government expenditures increased prior to the election and the new economics team reversed earlier restrictive policies, the first two years of the program must nonetheless be deemed to have been successful in achieving their objective of reducing the rate of inflation.[74]

Likewise, the balance of payments situation rapidly improved. Exports rose sharply, and were more than 50 percent over their corresponding 1980 level for the first half of 1981.[75] Industrial exports rose even more rapidly, and were more than double their 1979 level by 1981. By 1983, Turkish export earnings were $5.7 billion, compared with $2.9 billion in 1980.

However, investment was sluggish during the 1980–3 period, and exports apparently were produced with existing capacity. Thus, despite export growth, the overall level of economic activity rose only modestly. Real GNP grew at rates significantly above those of the late 1970s and per capita income was again rising, but the rate of growth was still well below the rates of growth realized in earlier years. Likewise, unemployment appeared to be rising, and real wages, which had risen sharply in the late 1970s, declined as the nominal wage increases permitted by the military government fell far short of inflation.

Although Turkish economic growth in the early 1980s was better than it had been in the late 1970s and much superior to that of most developing countries in the midst of the worldwide recession, it was not until 1984 that growth accelerated. Thereafter, growth rates were highly respectable by any standard. Table 8.7 gives data on macroeconomic performance during the 1980s. As can be seen, real GDP growth averaged more than 5 percent after 1984.[76] In the early 1980s, observers had been concerned that investment was stagnant and not increasing, even when output growth accelerated. That this was the case is confirmed by the data in table 8.7. Real investment was quite sluggish until 1985, but accelerated thereafter. Thus, in the early years of the reform program, growth came mainly from better utilization of existing capacity; it would appear that it was not until the mid-1980s that the reoriented trade regime was consistent with an increase in real investment.

Other aspects of the reforms met with mixed results. Manufacturing employment was generally thought to have grown very slowly, despite the

Table 8.7 Indicators of macroeconomic performance, 1980–9

	1980	1981	1982	1983	1984	1985	1986	1987	1988	1989
Real GNP growth (%)	−1.1	4.2	4.5	3.3	5.9	5.1	8.1	7.4	3.7	1.7
Growth of real investment (%)	−6.9	1.8	3.2	2.9	−0.1	16.8	11.0	5.5	−1.6	−3.4
Growth of exports (%)	28.7	61.6	22.2	−0.3	24.5	11.6	−6.3	36.7	14.4	−0.3
Increase in CPI (%)	110	37	27	31	48	50	37	39	75	70
Increase in GDP deflator (%)	104	42	28	29	51	41	30	40	66	65

Source: Krueger and Aktan (1992, table 38).

drop in real wages.[77] In part, this may be because the military government decreed that employers could not lay off or fire workers after 1980; there may have been enough redundant workers to permit considerable expansion of output with little or no increase in employment.

Even in the early 1980s, there was rapid growth of investment and output of utilities and transport, partly as a result of the government's emphasis on developing infrastructure to support private industry. As a result, industrial employment grew considerably faster than manufacturing employment, rising from 1,996,000 persons employed in industry in 1981 to 2,271,000 employed in 1985, and to 2,561,000 in 1989. Given the rapid growth of the Turkish labor force, even this growth of employment opportunities was disappointing. This led to concerns, which still continue, about the impact of the policy reform on income distribution in Turkey.

The least satisfactory results have been the persistent rapid rate of inflation. In large part, this was because of continuing large government expenditures which, as already mentioned, were directed largely toward the development of infrastructure. Government expenditures were 25 percent of GNP in 1980. They fell to a low of 18.9 percent in 1985, and rose thereafter to the 21–22 percent range for the following three years. Moreover, the fiscal deficit rose from its low of 1.7 percent of GNP in 1981 to 3.0 percent in 1983 and 5.3 percent of GNP in 1984. Thereafter, it was once again sharply reduced to 2.8 percent of GNP in 1985, but rose to 3.6 and 4.5 percent of GNP in the following two years. In 1988, it stood at 3.4 percent of GNP. The reasons for this were numerous: interest payments on domestic and foreign debt were a factor, but so, too, were increased government expenditures prior to each election.

To the extent that the large gains achieved by the reorientation of Turkish economic activity toward the international economy are threatened, it is the failure to achieve a lower rate of inflation that constitutes the most visible threat. Each inflationary round since 1980 has reached a higher rate of inflation than the preceding one before restrictive monetary and fiscal policies were adopted, and the low, before the next acceleration of inflation, has been successively higher.

Until 1989, however, the exchange rate was managed in such a way that the real value of the Turkish lira was not permitted to appreciate in response to changes in the domestic price level. In 1989, however, the nominal exchange rate changed by approximately half the rate of inflation. There was already a marked slowdown in the rate of growth of exports, although special factors – including reduced exports to Iraq attendant upon the end of the Iran–Iraq war and the phasing out of some special export incentives – undoubtedly contributed to the outcome.

Nonetheless, it can hardly be questioned that a real appreciation of over 30 percent in 1989 must have made exporting considerably less attractive than it had previously been. Moreover, the real appreciation of the Turkish lira continued in 1990. Although part of this real appreciation may have been the result of market forces,[78] it is also possible that depreciation of the lira was deliberately slowed down as an anti-inflationary device.

Resolution of the inflation problem for Turkey is therefore not only a political necessity, but it is also essential for achieving a more stable real exchange rate. Should real appreciation, even if at a lower rate than in 1989, continue, it is difficult to imagine that exporting will remain profitable, and of course, importing will become increasingly attractive.[79] At some point, another major policy reform package would be required, and many of the economic gains realized in the 1980s would – temporarily at least – be lost.

6 ECONOMIC REFORMS AND DEMOCRATIC POLITICS

The success which was obtained in the devising and the implementation of a comprehensive reform program derived from a unique constellation of factors. Several failed attempts had, for example, constituted a preparatory stage for the program which eventually emerged. These failures also helped convince the political leaders that, in the long run, there was no realistic way out of a major reform program

For a long period during the implementation of reforms, serious political opposition to the reform policies was lacking. Because the public's faith in institutions of government had eroded deeply, it had registered no significant response to the many bitter pills which the reform program entailed.

For part of the period during which the reforms were implemented, the country was under military rule. The suspension of competitive politics clearly rendered it easier to limit wage increases, to reduce the amount of public investments, and pursue other policies to which the public in an open political environment would have registered, in all probability, a reasonably strong negative response.

The reforms were rendered into a coherent package and implemented with persistence and perseverance by Turgut Özal. He appeared to possess a deep sense of commitment to them and pushed unrelentingly for their realization. He was, however, not only given unusual political powers as a bureaucrat by Prime Minister Demirel, but he was also retained by the military leadership as an important cabinet minister until the so-called *Banker* crisis forced him out. Although it would clearly be an exaggeration to attribute all that has been achieved to him, his clarity of purpose and his unswerving loyalty to reforms must be counted as an important contribution to their realization.

The victory of Mr Özal and the party which he founded at the polls permitted continuity in the application of reform policies over a long period. During his first term of office, Mr Özal enjoyed unusual political power. The deputies of his Motherland Party had been designated by him as candidates. Their election owed much to his personal popularity. Therefore, they were not only loyal to him, but they obediently deferred to his policy choices.

The opposition parties, on the other hand, were absorbed in a process of realignment. In the four-year period which followed the elections, the two parties which the military leadership had artificially created disintegrated. Moreover, the two parties which the military leadership had banned from participating in the elections of 1983, that is, the Social Democratic Party (later to become the Social Democratic Populist Party) and the True Path Party, rose to the status of major opposition parties. There was a referendum to restore the political rights of the pre–1980 politicians in 1986 which was approved by the smallest of margins, but it occupied the agenda for a long time. The return of the former political leaders to politics, each looking for a space in the political spectrum for himself, only led to further fragmentation of the opposition. In consequence, Mr Özal did not have to contend with strong opposition. He had a reasonably free hand in making and implementing policy.

Under such circumstances, Mr Özal did not even feel compelled to woo specific constituencies. He succeeded in generating a sense of optimism that things were going well, and that they were going to get better. He and his party represented new ideas and approaches which were changing Turkey. They were leading the country into a new era.

The major indication that the political support which the Motherland Party took for granted had begun to erode came in a by-election in the spring of 1987 when all of the five seats which were being contested went to opposition candidates. It appeared that the losers under the policies which had been pursued were beginning to react to the Özal government.

There were three persistent losers under the stabilization–restructuring programs. The first was the agricultural sector, a favorite of the pre–1980 political parties, which could no longer enjoy subsidized prices of fertilizers, insecticides, and fuel. The high support prices which the government traditionally extended to this sector were also considerably reduced.

Union labor was a second loser. The government had not done anything to loosen the restrictive legal framework which labor had been placed under by the military rulers. It had also been intent on restraining nominal wages as a means of both holding the rate of inflation down and promoting exports.

Salaried wage earners were the third loser. Civil servants, in particular, suffered significant declines in their standard of living. Those who could left government service for jobs in the private sector, and those who could not tried their hand at moonlighting. Not surprisingly, it is frequently suggested that they also engaged in corrupt practices.

Mr Özal moved the elections ahead in order that his government might get a new lease on life before losing the elections would become a virtual certainty. In the national elections of November 1987, the Motherland Party received 36.5 percent of the vote. Because of changes which had been effected in the electoral laws just before the elections, this translated into a 64 percent majority in the legislature.

Since the elections of 1987, the electoral support of the government has sunk further. Mr Özal himself has been elected the president of the republic by the parliament. He has worked to convert this lackluster ceremonial job into one which resembles that of the president of the United States amidst allegations that he is violating the constitution. In any case, he is slowly losing his grip on the parliamentary party since he is barred by the constitution from heading it.

To the extent that the economic reforms were so closely associated with the person of Mr Özal, even more so than they have been associated with his party, it is legitimate to ask whether what has been achieved so far will be retained. It is also a question whether further changes to make Turkey more of a market economy integrated to the world economic system will be continued even if Mr Özal is no longer in a position to constitute a major driving force, or whether a certain recidivism, a pattern of returning to the old habits of a closed, autarkical economy might obtain.

It is clear that the implementation of further reforms is losing its place as a priority item on the government's agenda. Is it tempting for the Motherland Party to go back to simply serving as a patronage network and forget about economic reforms? Will future actors other than the Motherland Party retain the changes which have already been realized? Or put differently, have the reforms generated enough support that political actors would be constrained not to go back on them?

Big business was one of the main beneficiaries of the reforms. The changes have created a liberal economic atmosphere. A willingness to give a legitimate place to business in the country's economy, and a desire to reduce government intervention in the economy, are parts of a new environment which big business finds appealing. It also appears to feel that its security and further growth will be enhanced by further integration into the world economic system.

Are there other forces which are supportive of the changes? Although it has already been pointed out that there are some specific losers, at the level of the general public, the coming of a more liberal economic environment, the removal of the many restrictions to which the average citizen was subject, the disappearance of shortages of commodities and black markets, and other similar changes have constituted welcome relief. People no longer feel guilty if they happen to be carrying a few dollars or marks in their pocket or if they are smoking a foreign cigarette (which they no longer have to buy from a street peddler who deals in contraband goods, but can obtain from any grocery store). It is no longer a major undertaking to subscribe to foreign publications. One can even get a credit card which can be used anywhere in the world and then pay the balance in

Turkish liras at the local bank where the card was issued.

Can a set of conveniences not enjoyed previously be sufficient grounds for sustained support for further economic change or the retention of what has been achieved so far? While the public is unlikely to push for new changes, it is likely to constitute a veto group delineating the limits within which policy is formulated. These would also include limits against reinstatement of former practices and restrictions. With the positive push of the big business community, with broad limits imposed by the general public, with encouragement from the international economic community and international economic institutions, and with lack of a clear-cut, unified opposition, the probability that transformation of the Turkish economy toward becoming more market-oriented and more integrated to the international economy will continue, appears to be high.

7   EVALUATION

There is little question that, on economic grounds, the Turkish policy reforms of the 1980s succeeded in significantly altering the trade regime and reducing the role of the government in the economy. Equally, however, they did not accomplish the desired objectives with regard to inflation.

As of the early 1990s, the important question is whether the momentum of success regarding the trade and payments regime and liberalization of the economy will provide time and support for a renewed effort to reduce or eliminate inflation or whether, instead, the effort to contain inflation will erode the real exchange rate and undermine the altered incentive structure of the economy.

Failure to control inflation through monetary and fiscal policy seems to have led inevitably to an effort to use the nominal exchange rate as an instrument of inflation control, despite the lessons of experience in any number of countries that such an effort cannot succeed in the longer run.

At the level of politics, if high rates of inflation come increasingly to be identified as an inseparable part of economic restructuring programs, then the support which seems to have obtained thus far for the reforms may evaporate, and the advocates of a statist economy, closed to the outside world, may gradually get the upper hand, which they have clearly lost since the early 1980s.

NOTES

1   The economic analysis in this chapter draws in part on Krueger and Aktan (1992). We are much indebted to Okan Aktan for his collaboration in that project and to the many individuals and organizations who assisted in

providing data and information. A list of those individuals and organizations is found in Krueger and Aktan (1992, p. 178). Special mention should, however, be made of the International Center for Economic Growth, which provided much of the funding for the larger study, and to the Central Bank of Turkey for support of research in Turkey. David Orsmond was a valuable assistant throughout. Thanks are also due to the Ford Foundation for support of the Project on the International Political Economy of Policy reform.

2   The fact that non-Muslim minorities had carried out much of the nonagricultural economic activity in the empire, and had supported the Europeans, lent further support to the suspicion of private enterprise.

3   See Okyar (1965) for an excellent account.

4   In the 1920s, Atatürk had initially relied upon the market mechanism for economic growth. This policy was abandoned in the mid-1930s when the impact of the Great Depression was felt.

5   Under the Ottoman Empire, debts had several times mounted to a point where the Ottomans were unable voluntarily to service them. The creditor nations, in addition to setting up lucrative monopolies, had in effect taken over the collections of customs duties, and generally kept tariffs fairly low. In the 1923 treaty settling Turkish–Greek disputes, control over customs duty collections and rate determination was retained by the foreign powers until 1929 (the Capitulations). This intrusion on sovereignty was greatly resented by Turkish nationalists. Many Turks also blamed this practice for Turkey's failure to share in the economic growth of Europe.

6   Among Turkish economists, some voices of criticism were being raised in the 1970s, but these were a small minority of the profession.

7   Turan (1969).

8   Turan (1985) and Kim et al. (1984).

9   The periodization of cycles and their political characteristics is described in Turan (1984). For the economic cycles, see Krueger and Aktan (1992, chapter 2).

10   An interesting feature of the Turkish economy, and one that is not well understood is that the ratio of urban to rural per capita income is unusually high. See Dervis and Robinson (1980) for further analysis of this phenomenon.

11   See Krueger (1974) and Sturc (1968) for an analysis.

12   This sharp increase was the result of a number of factors, including the increased flexibility of the Turkish economy resulting from the preceding decade's growth, but also importantly the remittances of Turkish workers who had emigrated to northern European countries, predominantly Germany, in large numbers. The government had recognized the sensitivity of these funds to the exchange rate and had provided a special exchange rate and incentives for workers to repatriate their funds. Workers' remittances had already become a major source of foreign exchange earnings by 1968, and continued growing in 1969. However, it was not recognized that workers were nonetheless depositing large sums in German banks, anticipating that the exchange rate might in future be altered. Thus, after the 1970 devaluation, there was a large-scale inflow of funds from Western Europe.

13   Baysan and Blitzer (1991) provide estimates of the effective protective rate (EPR) equivalents of quotas and tariffs for manufacturing industries in 1973 – a year when foreign exchange was relatively easy: protection rates

surely became higher in the late 1970s. According to the Baysan–Blitzer estimates, paper and paper products were accorded an EPR of 154 percent; plastic products received effective protection of 358 percent; iron and steel basic industries had an EPR of 203 percent; nonelectric machinery was protected by the equivalent of an EPR of 108 percent, and so on. By contrast, EPRs for agricultural commodities and many minerals products – all exportables – were negative. Even textiles and wearing apparel – exports to some degree during the 1960s and 1970s – received less than 20 percent protection.

14   Balassa (1985).
15   This section draws heavily on the excellent account of Okyar (1983).
16   Ibid., pp. 539–40.
17   Ibid., p. 535.
18   In preference to further devaluation, the Turkish Government had increased export "rebates" in July 1988. In the Fund's view, these ad hoc supplements to the exchange rate were less attractive to exporters than an exchange rate change would have been, in part because there was no assurance that they would continue.
19   *Economist*, March 17, 1979, p. 13. The *Economist* reported that for 1977, the government's central budget deficit was 5.6 percent of GNP, while the financing requirements of the SEEs were 6.8 percent of GNP. Both of these were financed by borrowing from the Central Bank.
20   SEEs are parastatal organizations that are engaged in many economic activities in Turkey, including manufacturing, mining, agricultural marketing and distribution, finance, and transportation. In the 1970s, SEEs accounted for approximately half of the value added in Turkish manufacturing industry, valued at domestic prices.
21   Doğan (1990). This was one of a series of articles written on the tenth anniversary of the January 1980 reforms, and illustrates the extent to which that date is regarded as a watershed in Turkish history.
22   TÜSİAD (1978a).
23   TÜSİAD (1978b).
24   Gürsel (1984, p. 502).
25   Ibid., p. 503.
26   TÜSİAD (1979).
27   TÜSİAD (1980).
28   One of the key bureaucrats who later entered politics, and who asked not to be named, said very emphatically during Turan's hour-long interview with him that the extent and severity of the economic crisis was even more serious than one would think if one relied only on publicly available materials.
29   Interview by Turan of one of the key authors of the stabilization plan. He granted the interview with the understanding that his name would not be used.
30   Same interview.
31   Interview by Turan with a minister in the Demirel cabinet.
32   Çölaşan (1984, p. 9).
33   Remarks made to a member of the parliamentary Committee on the Budget and Planning, and related to Turan in an interview.
34   *Resmi Gazete*, 25 January 1980, No. 16880 (additional issue), Section on Administration, pp. 1–2.
35   Ibid., pp. 2–3.

36 Ibid., p. 3–5. See also Erdem (1982).
37 "Ordu Uyarı Mektubu Verdi" (The Army Issues a Letter of Warning), *Hürriyet*, January 2, 1980, p. 1.
38 This meeting is reported in Çölaşan (1984, pp. 112–17). It was not reported in the press at the time. One general whom Turan interviewed said, "I remember something like that."
39 There were a number of institutional reforms, most of which involved reorganization of governmental committees overseeing economic regulations. See Krueger and Aktan (1992) for a description. In addition, it was announced that interest rates for all credits were raised by two percentage points, that foreign investment regulations would be liberalized to encourage the inflow of foreign capital into all sections of the economy, including those from which it had earlier been effectively discouraged, and that policy regarding petroleum exploration would be significantly liberalized. See Organization for Economic Cooperation and Development (1981, pp. 34–5) for details.
40 For example, for items on Liberalized List I, the advance deposit required of importers fell from 40 to 30 percent, while that for industrialists was lowered from 25 to 15 percent. See OECD (1981).
41 The increases in the pricing of commodities produced by SEEs were, however, probably significantly larger than earlier increases had been. It could be argued that it was these increases, which are immediately felt by large segments of the population and are politically difficult to implement, that provided the "signal" that the government was serious in its intent.
42 Indeed, the fact that it was a minority government that was in power made the prospects for passing legislation to implement many of the government's statements of intent poor indeed. Turgut Özal, in an interview late in 1981 in *Yanki*, agreed that the best he could have hoped for as of January 1980 would have been the announcement of an early election which could have given the Justice Party a majority in parliament. See Barkey (1984, p. 63).
43 OECD (1981, p. 18). As already noted, these transfers covered operating losses.
44 The reduction in the deficits of the SEEs was sizable, amounting to almost 5 percent of GNP. Fiscal deficits did not diminish as much as SEE deficits were reduced, because government expenditures on infrastructure rose sharply.
45 However, representatives of the main commercial banks apparently met quickly and agreed upon rates to be charged among themselves. The result was that lending rates for commercial credit rose from 25 percent to over 60 percent a year, while sight deposit rates rose only slightly from 3–5 percent a year. Okyar (1983, p. 549).
46 See, for example, Ulagay (1987, p. 58).
47 Quoted in Çölaşan (1984, p. 268).
48 See Haggard and Kaufman (1989).
49 Interview with a former minister who is now a deputy from the Motherland Party. The interview was granted to Turan on condition of anonymity.
50 Interview with a retired officer from the Ministry of Public Finance. He is currently a member of the True Path party.
51 Cemal (1986).
52 *Milliyet*, and *Hürriyet*, editions of September 14, 1980, both carry excerpts.
53 Quoted in Ulagay (1987, p. 62).

54   *Cumhuriyet*, January 18, 1982, quoted in Ulagay (1987, p. 63). See also Erdem (1982).
55   Celasun and Rodrik (1989, p. 767).
56   For a summary of the measures, see OECD (1981, pp. 43–6).
57   Labor contracts are normally signed for two years, so the annual rate of increase was intended to be less than 35 percent.
58   *Cumhuriyet*, July 2, 1982.
59   The advisor to the president, A. B. Kafaoğlu, had given a report to President Evren, predicting what would eventually happen. It was said that Mr Kafaoğlu had written an earlier report in May 1982, making similar points. Cf. *Cumhuriyet*, July 15, 1982.
60   For accounts and explanations, see *Cumhuriyet*, July 15–17, 1982.
61   There is no question but that the election was fairly conducted. However, the government's control over the parties which could contest the election, and the fact that there remained many politicians who had been forbidden to participate in politics after the 1980 military takeover, led many to question the legitimacy of the election.
62   See Krueger and Aktan (1992, chapter 4) for an account of the various export incentives and their value during the 1980–9 period.
63   See Chronological Appendix of Krueger and Aktan (1992) for a chronology of the dates and amounts by which the levies were increased. They were initially imposed at a rate of 2 percent in 1981. See also the discussion in chapter 4 of the use of SPSF funds for export incentives.
64   Baysan and Blitzer (1988, p. 11). Estimates from the Central Bank suggest even greater real effective exchange rate depreciation. See also Saraçoğlu (1987, p.126). See also table 8.3.
65   See Krueger and Aktan (1992, table 13) for details and rates applicable to individual commodity groups.
66   See Krueger and Aktan (1992, table 14).
67   See Rodrik (1988) and Krueger and Aktan (1992, table 36) for further details.
68   See Krueger and Aktan (1992, Data Appendix table 19) for estimates of the magnitude of the differential between the official and the free market rate. Since the latter was legal, there was, strictly speaking, no black market.
69   See, for example, Collins (1989).
70   Turkish debt was rescheduled as a part of the 1980 reform package, and there is no question that rescheduling at that time was essential.
71   Turkish outstanding debt is estimated to have declined another $2 billion in 1989. *Financial Times*, March 6, 1990, p. 2.
72   The military outlawed strikes upon assuming power in September 1980. The elimination of strikes was also a factor in the upturn in capacity utilization in Turkish industries.
73   *Economist*, September 21, 1981, "Turkey Survey," p. 8.
74   The rate of inflation has not again reached 100 percent, although there have been sizable swings in the inflationary effects of the government budget and its financing.
75   *Economist*, September 21, 1981, "Turkey Survey" p. 9. There is some dispute as to how much of the recorded increase in exports reflected a real increase in export volume and how much reflected a shift from under- to overinvoicing of

exports on the part of exporters. See Krueger and Aktan (1992, chapter 5) for an analysis of the importance of this possibility.
76 Preliminary estimates suggest that real GNP grew 9 percent in 1990.
77 See Celasun (1989) for an analysis.
78 Estimates indicate that Turkey had a surplus on current account of $966 million in 1989, compared to $1,596 in 1988.
79 Along with other measures, the authorities also further liberalized imports significantly at the end of February, 1990.

REFERENCES

Balassa, Bela 1985: "Outward Orientation and Exchange Rate Policy in Developing Countries: The Turkish Experience," in Bela Balassa (ed.), *Change and Challenge in the World Economy*, London: MacMillan, Essay No. 10.

Barkey, Henri 1984: "Crises of the Turkish Political Economy: 1960–1980," in Ahmet Evin (ed.), *Modern Turkey: Continuity and Change*, Leske and Budrich, pp. 47–63.

Baysan, Tercan and Blitzer, Charles 1988: "Turkey's Trade Liberalization in the 1980s and Prospects for its Sustainability," in Tosun Aricanli and Dani Rodrik (eds.), *The Political Economy of Turkey: Debt, Adjustment and Sustainability*, London: Macmillan, pp. 9–36.

Baysan, Tercan and Blitzer, Charles 1991: "Turkey," in Demetris Papageorgiou, Michael Michaely, and Armeane Choksi (eds.), *Liberallaizing Foreign Trade*, vol. 6: The Experience of New Zealand, Spain, and Turkey, Cambridge, Mass.: Blackwell, pp. 263–402.

Celasun, Merih 1989: "Income Distribution and Employment Aspects of Turkey's Post–1980 Adjustment." *METU Studies in Development*, 16(34).

Celasun, Merih and Rodrik, Dani 1989: "Debt, Adjustment and Growth: Turkey," in Jeffrey D. Sachs and Susan M. Collins (eds.), *Developing Country Debt and Economic Performance*, vol. 3, Chicago: University of Chicago Press, pp. 615–808.

Cemal, Hasan 1986: *Tank Sesiyle Uyanmak*, Ankara: Bilgi Yayınevi, p. 32.

Çölaşan, Emin 1984: *24 Ocak: Bir Dönemin Perde Arkası*, Istanbul: Milliyet Yayınları.

Collins, Susan M. 1989: "Debt, Policy and Performance: An Introduction," in Jeffrey D. Sachs and Susan M. Collins (eds.), *Developing Country Debt and Economic Performance*, vol. 3, Chicago: University of Chicago Press, p. 14.

Dervis, Kemal and Robinson, Sherman 1980: "Structure of Income Inequality in Turkey," in Ergun Ozbudun and Aydin Ulusan (eds.), *The Political Economy of Income Distribution in Turkey*. New York: Holmes and Meier, pp. 83–122.

Doğan, Yalçın 1990: "10 Yılın Adı: 24 Ocak," *Milliyet*, January 25.

Erdem, Kaya 1982: "Keeping the Economic Orchestra in Tune," in "Turkey: A Survey," *Euromoney*, February.

Gürsel, Seyfettin 1984: "Diş İktisadi İlişkiler: IMF," in *Cumhuriyet Dönemi Türkiye Ansiklopedisi*, vol II, Istanbul: Iletişim.

Haggard, Stephan and Kaufman, Robert 1989: "The Politics of Stabilization and Structural Adjustment," in Jeffrey D. Sachs and Susan M. Collins (eds.), *Developing Country Debt and Economic Performance*, vol 3, Chicago: University of Chicago Press, p. 214.

Kim, Chong Lim, Barkan, Joel D., Turan, İlter, and Jewell, Malcolm E. 1984: *The Legislative Connection: The Politics of Representatation in Kenya, Korea and Turkey*, Durham, NC: Duke University Press, pp. 68–86.

Krueger, Anne O. 1974: *Foreign Trade Regimes and Economic Development: Turkey*, New York: Columbia University Press, chapter 4.

Krueger, Anne O. and Aktan, Okan 1992: *Swimming Against the Tide: Turkish Trade Reform in the 1980s*, San Francisco: ICS Press.

Okyar, Osman 1965: "The Concept of Etatism," *Economic Journal*, March.

Okyar, Osman 1983: "Turkey and the IMF: A Review of Relations, 1978–82," in John Williamson (ed.), *IMF Conditionality*, Washington, DC: Institute for International Economics, pp. 533–61.

Organization for Economic Cooperation and Development (OECD) 1981: *Economic Survey, Turkey*.

Rodrik, Dani 1988: "Some Policy Dilemmas in Turkish Macroeconomic Management," Kennedy School of Government Discussion Paper Series No. 173D, p. 31.

Saraçoğlu, Rüşdü 1987: "Economic Stabilization and Structural Adjustment: The Case of Turkey," in V. Corbo, M. Goldstein and M. Khan (eds.), *Growth-Oriented Adjustment Programs*, Washington, DC: International Monetary Fund and World Bank, pp. 119–43.

Sturc, Ernest 1968: "Stabilization Policies: Experience of Some European Countries in the 1950s," *International Monetary Fund Staff Papers*, July.

Turan, İlter 1969: *Cumhuriyet Tarihimiz*, İstanbul: Çağlayan.

Turan, İlter 1984: "Cyclical Democracy: The Turkish Case," paper presented at the annual meeting of the Midwest Political Science Association, Chicago, Illinois, April 11–14.

Turan, İlter 1985: "Changing Horses in Mid-Stream: Party Changes in the Turkish National Assembly," *Legislative Studies Quarterly* February.

TÜSİAD (Türk Sanayici ve İsadamları Derneği) 1978a: *1978 Yılma Girerken ve 1980'lere Doğru Türkiye'nin Temel Sorunlari Uzerine Görüşler−Oneriler*, İstanbul: TÜSİAD, January 10, pp. 107–8.

TÜSİAD 1978b: *1978 Yılına Girerken Türk Ekonomisi*, İstanbul: TÜSİAD, January 18, pp. 1–6.

TÜSİAD 1979: *1979 Yılına Gireken Türk Ekonomisi*, İstanbul: TÜSİAD, January 5, p. 1.

TÜSİAD 1980: *1980 Yılına Girerken Türk Ekonomisi*, İstanbul: TÜSİAD, Introduction, January 18.

Ulagay, Osman 1987: *Özal Ekonomisinde Paramız Pul Olurken Kim Kazandı, Kim Kaybetti*, Ankara: Yayınevı.

9

The Politics and Economics of Policy Reform in Zambia
Robert H. Bates and Paul Collier

INTRODUCTION

This chapter analyzes the process of policy reform in Zambia, focusing on the period 1985–90. At the beginning of this period, the government remained committed to the imposition of controls on the exchange rate, interest rate, and consumer prices. In October 1985 it shifted to a policy of liberalization, abandoning price controls and promoting an expanded role for markets. A central feature of these reforms was the introduction of an auction for foreign exchange. In May 1987, the government reimposed controls on markets for commodities, credit, and foreign exchange. In doing so, it broke with the International Monetary Fund, an act that led to the suspension of credit from the World Bank and from most donor countries. Still later, in 1989, the government switched back to market-oriented economic policies. A central issue that we address in this paper is: what accounts for these swings in policies? A second and more funda-mental question underlies the first: what accounts for the resistance to markets? About this question more needs to be said.

Reasoning in political economy most often proceeds from the economic to the political. Market failures are seen as generating losses in welfare, thus leading to interventions by governments.[1] Whatever its normative merits, this form of reasoning often provides a misleading framework for positive analysis. For in many instances it is a government, rather than private individuals, that initially controls the allocation of resources. While political economy has developed the logic of transitions from markets to politics, it offers little insight into the transfer of allocational processes from governments. By studying the politics of the introduction of markets in Zambia, we hope to gain insight into the politics underlying the creation of markets.

In seeking to account for the behavior of the government of Zambia, we focus on several key factors. One is the structure of political institutions. A second is the relationship between political decision makers and key interest groups in their environment. The third is the pattern of incentives that face politicians, as created by the structure of competition for political office.

1   ECONOMIC BACKGROUND

Copper dominates the economic history of Zambia. Long worked by indigenous peoples, Zambia's copper deposits were discovered by foreigners in the early decades of the century and brought into full-scale commercial production following the great depression.[2] The growth of the mining industry led as well to the growth of towns. Nearly a dozen urban centers sprang up along the railway linking the mines to the south, making Zambia one of the most urbanized and industrialized of Africa's states.[3] In 1960, over one fifth of Zambia's population lived in urban areas; for Sub-Saharan Africa as a whole, the figure was 14 percent. By 1980, 43 percent of Zambia's population lived in the cities, a figure nearly double that of the rest of Sub-Saharan Africa.[4] In the mid 1960s, 54 percent of Zambia's gross domestic product came from industry as compared with only 18 percent for Sub-Saharan Africa as a whole. The subsequent decline of Zambia's economy led to a fall in the share of industry in the gross domestic product to 41 percent by 1980; but this figure still far exceeded the average of 25 percent for Sub-Saharan Africa.[5] The high level of Zambia's industrialization is also suggested by its high level of energy consumption, which stands at more than double that for Sub-Saharan Africa as a whole. In 1960, Zambians consumed 677 kilograms (in coal equivalents) per capita as compared with 189 per capita elsewhere in Sub-Saharan Africa; and in 1970, they consumed 707 kilograms per capita, as compared with 324 in other African nations.[6] Zambia is thus urban and industrial to a degree that is unusual in Africa.

Because copper dominates Zambia's economy, the province containing the mines – known, naturally enough, as the Copperbelt – constitutes the urban and industrial center of the nation. The Copperbelt contains eight of Zambia's dozen towns; roughly 40 percent of the jobs in Zambia's formal sector locate within it. While the rapid growth of Lusaka in the post-independence period challenged the economic domination of the Copperbelt, the continued concentration of mining, industry, and manufacturing in Copperbelt Province marks it as the economic heartland of the nation.

Among all the nations of Sub-Saharan Africa, Zambia has suffered one of the greatest – and most rapid – economic declines. At the time of independence, Zambia prospered by comparison with its neighbors. In 1965, Zambia's per capita gross national product was among the highest in Sub-Saharan Africa. In the 1970s, all that changed. Between the mid–1970s and the mid–1980s, Zambia suffered a catastrophic decline in its terms of trade.[7] Macroeconomic indicators showing the extent of the economic collapse since the late 1970s are shown in table 9.1.

In responding to the terms-of-trade change, the government took the lead, for it was the main recipient of copper income. It possessed three policy instruments by which it could extract income from the copper sector: taxation, both on copper exports and on profits; ownership of 60 percent of the equity in the copper company (ZCCM); and the power to set the exchange rate at which it bought the dollars earned from copper exports. Between them these instruments gave the government control over the rents from copper.

The government responded to the terms-of-trade shock by postponing a decline in consumption and by erecting a control regime. The government maintained high levels of consumption by borrowing from abroad; by 1984 Zambia was the most indebted country in the world relative to its GDP.

Table 9.1 Macroeconomic indicators for Zambia

Year	*Exchange rates* NER	*Exchange rates* REER	*Black market premium (%)*	*Inflation (CPI)*	*M1 growth (%)*	*Real GDP (1985 prices)* (Km)	*Real GDP (1985 prices)* (K/capita)
1978	1.2502	124.4	124	16.6	1.0	6910	1263
1979	1.2606	122.0	85	24.2	30.2	6700	1217
1980	1.2682	119.1	69	11.6	0.5	6903	1241
1981	1.1516	121.7	64	14.2	8.6	7329	1249
1982	1.0773	135.7	46	12.4	22.3	7123	1181
1983	0.7996	125.8	29	19.5	15.3	6983	1119
1984	0.5573	108.2	37	9.4	9.4	6958	1080
1985	0.3685	100.0	68	41.6	41.6	7072	1051
1986	0.1369	48.2	31	87.1	87.1	7113	977
1987	0.1125	50.9	42	40.0	40.0	7097	939
1988	0.1216	79.0	418	62.7	62.7	7775	1033

Year	*Budget (% GDP)* Surplus	*Budget (% GDP)* Expenditure	*Budget (% GDP)* Revenue	*Current account* ($m)	*Current account* (% GDP)	*Exports ($m)*	*Imports ($m)*
1978	−14.4	29.7	24.4	−298	−10.6	831	618
1979	−9.1	30.4	22.3	37	1.1	140	8756
1980	−18.5	37.1	25.0	−537	−13.8	1457	1114
1981	−12.9	36.7	23.2	−742	−18.5	996	1065
1982	−18.6	39.0	23.1	−566	−14.6	942	1004
1983	−7.8	32.2	24.2	−271	−8.1	923	711
1984	−8.4	29.2	22.1	−153	−5.6	893	612
1985	−14.9	34.9	21.8	−398	−15.3	797	571
1986	−16.2		23.3	−300	−16.7	692	518
1987	−13.7	4.9	21.1	−141	−6.4	847	585
1988	−12.9	34.3	20.9	−196	−7.2	1184	687

Source: International Financial Statistics (IMF): World Currency Yearbook.

Additionally, it curtailed public investment. During the five years 1971–6 capital formation (public plus private) averaged 31 percent of GDP; by 1985 it had declined to only 10 percent of GDP, probably well below the level at which the capital stock could be maintained. Finally, as foreign exchange became scarce, the government reduced the amount ZCCM was allowed to retain for purchases of inputs. As a consequence, by 1985 copper production was 30 percent below its 1977 level.

The government had imposed administrative controls upon the exchange rate, interest rate, and commodity prices in response to foreign exchange shortages and inflationary pressures in the 1960s; following the collapse of copper prices in the mid–1970s, it intensified its use of these measures and they became the centerpiece of government policy. Following pressures from the IMF, price controls were removed, de jure, in December 1982; as will be discussed below, however, controls continued de facto and applied to a range of consumer goods accounting for nearly 40 percent of urban expenditures. Real interest rates became heavily negative; by 1984 inflation (as measured by the CPI) stood at 27 percent, whereas the interest rate on Treasury Bills was only 7.5 percent. Lastly, in spite of the precipitate deterioration in Zambia's terms of trade, the government maintained the nominal exchange rate at a constant value. The result was massive excess demand: by 1984 dollars were being sold at around a third of the price purchasers were willing to pay. The allocation of available foreign exchange between competing demands became a core political and administrative activity.

In spite of government efforts to defend against reductions in consumption, standards of living declined precipitately following the collapse of copper prices. The National Accounts suggest a fall between 1975 and 1984 of 34 percent per capita in private consumption. This figure probably exaggerates the decline experienced by the typical household, however, since the emigration of a large group of high-consumption expatriate households would have lowered the national average. Household budget surveys conducted in 1975 and 1985 provide a second source of comparisons. Per capita consumption in the townships declined by 30 percent and in the ex-squatter areas by 22 percent.[8] By contrast per capita consumption among rural households declined by only 4 percent.[9] Public consumption declined even more severely than private consumption, by 40 percent per capita.[10]

To conclude, the government's response to the adverse change in the terms of trade had heavily mortgaged future living standards. Despite this, living standards had fallen precipitately, particularly for those groups which the government regarded as its core supporters. The inefficiency costs of the control regime had not been compensated by distributionally favorable outcomes. In 1985, the government therefore moved to a more market-orientated policy. A central concern of this chapter is with the political factors that shaped this process of reform.

2 POLITICAL BACKGROUND

The market-oriented reforms of the mid–1980s were introduced by a government dominated and run by a single party – the United National Independence Party – and by a strong president – Kenneth David Kaunda.

Under the constitution of the Second Republic, introduced in 1973, Zambia became a single-party state, with the United National Independence Party (UNIP; also to be referred to as the Party) as the governing party.[11] Informally, the political authorities were referred to as "the Party and its government." Formally, the Secretary General of the Party outranked the Prime Minister.[12] And both formally and in practice, while the cabinet managed the day-to-day affairs of the government, the Central Committee of the Party reigned supreme. Key decisions, such as fundamental changes in economic policy, could be advocated by the bureaucracy and brought for decision before the cabinet; but, before they could become national policy, they had to be deliberated and adopted by the Central Committee of UNIP. Access to the bureaucracy conferred operational advantages upon members of the cabinet; but it was the Central Committee that possessed – and exercised – the authority to make national policy.

The government bureaucracy consisted of the conventional panoply of ministries: Labor, Mining, Education, Agriculture, and so forth. Central to this paper were, of course, the bureaucracies charged with economic policy making: the Treasury, the Bank of Zambia, and, to a lesser degree, the National Commission for Development Planning. All reported to the president through the cabinet, which met at least two or three times a month. The Cabinet Office (or Secretariat) controlled the flow of paper work through the cabinet, allotting to the various bureaucracies time and place on its agenda and thereby playing an influential role in the making of public policy.

People joined the Party for a variety of reasons. Some held UNIP in high esteem because of its fight against colonialism and for independence; others because of their agreement with its conception of an appropriate economic and political order for Zambia (see below). Others joined the Party because it constituted a route to office, with the consequent gratifications of power and wealth. The Party monopolized office-holding at the municipal level;[13] to rise in the civil service or the military, one had to be a member of the Party. The Party controlled appointments to the top jobs in parastatal industries as well. In addition, the Party itself contained a multiplicity of offices, each with its complement of social recognition and prestige. In 1985, UNIP filled over 40,000 local offices – i.e., at the section, branch, and ward level – in the city of Lusaka alone.[14]

UNIP's most basic unit, the section, consisted of households. The sections contained between 10 and 25 houses; the branches, a dozen or so sections; and the wards, two to three branches. In the rural areas, a ward would contain several villages; in the urban areas, a township would contain several wards. In these local units, offices were filled by ballot, with only UNIP members being eligible to vote. In each district in Zambia, a District Governor, Political Secretary, and Executive Secretary stood in charge of all government departments. These positions were filled by the Party; more specifically, they were filled by persons dispatched from Party headquarters by the president and Central Committee. Each province in Zambia is made up of several districts and above the district officials stood a Provincial Member of the Central Committee, assisted by a Provincial Political Secretary and a Permanent Secretary. Again, these posts were filled by the Party. The Provincial Minister belonged to the Central Committee, the executive committee of the Party. Like the other twenty or so members of the Central Committee, the Provincial Members were nominated as part of a slate of candidates prepared by the Party president.[15] The slate was ratified by the National Council and approved by the Party Congress, two representative organs of the Party; but for over two decades there was no competition for positions on the Central Committee, and therefore no balloting in fact took place.

UNIP officials not only reigned supreme over government officials at the District and Provincial level; they dominated the cabinet as well. The cabinet was appointed by the president of the Party, acting as head of government; and its members deferred to those of the Party in terms of protocol and perquisites. The phrase "the Party and its government" captured both the spirit and the letter of political practice in Zambia.

In their bureaucratic rivalry with members of the Central Committee of the Party, the ministers – and therefore the cabinet – possessed one great advantage: access to expert advice. The Central Committee organized itself into a variety of specialized subcommittees – one on agriculture and rural development, for example; another on national security; and, most important for our purposes, still another on economic affairs. Chaired by a high-ranking member of the Central Committee, the subcommittees drew their members not only from the ranks of the Party but also from the ministries and the private sector. In contrast to the ministries, however, the subcommittees lacked expert staff. Each possessed a Permanent Secretary; but they lacked technical and professional officers. Whereas the minister of finance had access to over 200 professionals, including nearly two dozen economists,[16] for example, the chair of the subcommittee on economic affairs lacked any such personnel. One consequence was that ministers and the cabinet were often more influential in policy debates than their subordinate political status would suggest. Another was that political conflict often centered on the framing of policy issues, with the cabinet seeking to define them as technical matters whereas the Central Committee sought to pose them in political or moral terms.

During the period of policy reform, Zambia was thus governed by two bureaucracies, one governmental and the other partisan, both subject to the same president. The process of policy reform thus often took the form of a struggle between the two bureaucracies. As will be shown below, the movement toward market-oriented economic policies was marked by the movement of the locus of control over policy making from the Party to the ministries. And shifts back toward interventionist policies were marked by the reassertion of control over economic policy making by the Central Committee of UNIP. The president dominated the process of policy making. In practice, this meant that when he sought to change policies, he attempted to move the locus of decision making from one of the bureaucracies to the other. The movement to market-oriented reforms privileged the technocrats from the Ministry of Finance and the Bank of Zambia; the switch to a control oriented regime was orchestrated through advisors with close links to the Central Committee of UNIP.

While possessing a wide range of discretion, the president himself operated within a political framework that imparted systematic tendencies to economic policy making.[17] This included a structure of interest groups and of political incentives arising from institutionalized patterns of political competition. It is to these that we now turn.

3   THE PARTY AND ECONOMIC INTERESTS

In most societies, large-scale interests – business, labor, commercial farmers – organize pressure groups that lobby to shape economic policy to their advantage. What is remarkable about the case of Zambia is the extent to which such organized interests stood isolated from the Party, or in active opposition to it. UNIP numbered among its political enemies a large portion of the commercial farmers, both expatriate and African; private businessmen; and organized labor. As a consequence, the Party was alienated from many of the most important productive forces in the economy and this feature of Zambian politics profoundly shaped, we argue, the content of economic policies.

Relations with organized interest groups constituted a critical political variable that powerfully shaped the content of public policies. But this pattern of interest group relations was predetermined; it was structured in periods prior to the 1980s. It therefore requires historical analysis.

The farmers

Known as Northern Rhodesia, the territories that are now known as Zambia were developed for mining; they were settled by immigrants, many of whom were farmers. The farmers dominated the representative institutions put in place by the colonial government and used their power to economic advantage. They set rail rates so as to "tax" the exports of minerals and thereby subsidize the transport of agricultural products. They levied revenues from the mines to finance infrastructure for agriculture, subsidizing the costs of farm inputs and stabilizing farm incomes. They also used political power to discriminate against Africans. Appropriating land, they forced African farmers into "native reserves." Through control over the marketing bureaucracy, they curtailed competition from African farmers by restricting their access to local markets. Both discriminatory measures enabled the European farmers to establish as well a pool of cheap labor.[18]

At the time of independence, the large-scale commercial farmers dominated the food economy of Zambia. Over one-fifth of Zambia's total African population lived in urban centers; nearly two-thirds of the marketed maize meal consumed by the urban dwellers derived from commercial farms.[19] For UNIP, however, the commercial farmers represented political enemies, defeated in order to secure national independence.

Alongside the large-scale commercial farmers there stood the emergent African farmers. The seizure of their lands by European settlers and regulations that limited their access to official markets imposed costs on these small-scale farmers; but Africans nonetheless invested in land, ploughs, and oxen, and produced crops for the market. They did so particularly in Southern and Central Province, where soils were fertile and production took place in close proximity to the line of rail. The Tonga and Ila people in particular stood at the forefront of this transformation.[20]

While central to the rise of Zambia's agrarian economy, these emergent farmers proved marginal politically. During the struggle against colonial domination, the line-of-rail farming communities backed the African National Congress: the first African political party in Northern Rhodesia and the primary opposition to UNIP. Drawing strong support from the Northern and Eastern portions of the country, and in particular from the populous Copperbelt, UNIP won out in the subsequent competition for political power.[21] But, because the African commercial farmers had backed the party led by UNIP's political enemies, after independence they stood outside Zambia's ruling coalition.

In the period following independence, the leaders of UNIP established important ties with farming. Some developed strong private interests in agriculture, as they bought large farms and entered commercial production.[22] All developed a political interest in agriculture, as the availability and price of maize became central political issues. In addition, as the geographical base of UNIP's power shrank (see below), the Party sought support in the regions remote from urban markets by establishing a uniform national price for maize and by subsidizing the costs of fertilizer. It is notable that the policy imposed a tax on farmers along the line of rail, many of whom, if European, had supported the colonial government, or, if African, had backed ANC, UNIP's defeated political rival.[23]

While the leadership of UNIP developed personal and political ties with the farm sector, the basic political fact remained: that the groups who had been endowed with a relative advantage in commercial farming lay outside the core constituency of the Party.

Private business

Europeans and Indians had invested heavily in Central Africa during the colonial period. Imperial rule facilitated close economic ties with other territories in Southern Africa and corporations based in South Africa invested in Northern Rhodesia as well. When Zambia became independent, UNIP therefore confronted an economy whose commercial and industrial sector lay largely in foreign hands.

UNIP therefore adopted policies designed to place the economy in the hands of Zambians. It restricted retail trade in the rural areas to Zambian citizens. It did the same for retail trade in the Second Class trading areas in towns (the areas containing stores that catered to African, rather than to European, consumers). Placing restrictions on the remissions of profits, subsidizing loans for local citizens, and manipulating licensing laws, it created incentives for the transfer of ownership of businesses to Zambian nationals.

While promoting Zambian businessmen on the one hand, the Party nonetheless adopted policies that severely limited their fortunes.[24] In the manufacturing sector, the UNIP-dominated government created state enterprises and conferred important advantages upon them: subsidized credit, privileged access to import licenses, and preferential tax treatments. In the retail trade, it imposed price controls on key consumer items and operated state stores in competition with private establishments. The government also refused to allow rural retail outlets to sell at higher prices than those in town, thereby making rural entrepreneurs absorb the costs of transport.

Tension between government and business mounted in the post-independence period. Business was hurt when the government spent more than it earned; the resultant inflation led to higher costs and the tendency of government to attack inflation by imposing price controls led to lower earnings. The government maintained an overvalued exchange rate; the result was persistent shortages of foreign exchange and an inability by business to secure needed imports. The government's support of liberation movements in neighboring territories inflicted damage on Zambia's business community. Guerilla movements, some backed by the Zambian government, sabotaged railway links to the coast; and the white minority regimes retaliated for Zambia's support of insurgents by imposing blockades, interdicting Zambian trade with the outside world. The result was further shortages, as exports failed to reach foreign markets and imports could not be purchased or, if purchased, moved inland to Zambia.

In the face of mounting distortions in Zambia's economy, many resulting from government policy, businessmen found it increasingly necessary to circumvent official controls. They made an increasing portion of their transactions illegally, thereby strengthening the government's conviction that they were selfish and socially undesirable. And, as we shall see, they formed a dissident political faction as well. Some entered parliament, and there criticized government policies. Others backed members of the Central Committee who were favorable to business interests. Still others backed the makers of coups.[25]

Political leaders maintained private ties with individual firms, and businessmen found it expedient to cultivate influential political allies. But expatriate businessmen represented to the Party a remnant of the colonial past and Zambian businessmen a selfish and politically unreliable faction. The government therefore restricted and regulated their behavior in ways that were costly. Private businessmen joined the commercial farmers in the political periphery.[26]

Organized labor

In the early days of African resistance to colonial rule, the trade union and nationalist movements developed close ties, as they attacked racial discrimination and strove for economic and political equality.[27] A generation of UNIP leaders rose through the ranks of the trade union movement in the Copperbelt, with some – such as Wilson Chakulya and John Chisata – becoming ministers in the post-independence period and others – such as Robinson Puta and Matthew Mwendapole – becoming influential elder statesmen.

Even during the struggle against colonialism, however, relationships between UNIP and the unions proved tense. The strongest unions tended to focus on issues of pay and benefits, working conditions, and the use, or abuse, of supervisory authority.[28] UNIP, however, possessed a broader political agenda and sought to secure work stoppages in order to pressure the colonial government or to terminate strikes in order to instill confidence in the electorate. The result was conflict between the Party and the trade union movement.

After independence, tensions worsened. UNIP organized the government of Zambia; inevitably, the government, as employer, and the unions, as the representatives of labor, clashed. The government called for industrial discipline; the unions favored self-assertion in the work place. The government sought to control housing and community services throughout the urban areas, even those maintained by major private employers, such as the mines. The unions preferred that such services, when provided by employers, remain in their hands, if only so that the unions could more directly influence their management.[29]

Differences over policy thus split the unions from UNIP, the governing party. In an attempt to weaken the trade unions, UNIP entered union elections, running its own slate of candidates or designating its preferred candidates from among slates proposed by others. It organized rival unions and promoted jurisdictional disputes, recruiting members in efforts to undermine established labor organizations. When it could not control or weaken the unions, it sought to co-opt their leadership, as by placing trade union leaders on the boards of directors of state corporations.

The union movement in Zambia is one of the largest in Black Africa. Even allowing for exaggerated claims, it organizes in the range of 50 percent of those Zambians who are in formal wage employment.[30] In the urban and industrial centers of Zambia, there are thus two mass organizations: the trade unions and UNIP. And they engage in protracted political struggles, the one seeking autonomy and the other domination. Organized labor, too, became an "enemy" of the Party.

The Party supreme; the Party isolated

Commercial farmers and major portions of the business community therefore stood either as vanquished remnants of the colonial order or as enemies defeated in the political rivalries between competing political parties. Organized labor constituted a rival mass organization. In the making of economic policies, the Party therefore possessed little incentive to place a high weight on the policy preferences of these economic interests. While economically important, these groups were politically marginal; they lay outside the Party's core constituency which, as we shall see, consisted of urban consumers and state-owned industries.

As we have noted, the Copperbelt constitutes the economic heartland of Zambia. But in the events leading up to the creation of a single-party state, UNIP experienced wholesale defections by some of its most important leaders in this province. This further added to the political marginalization of productive sectors of the economy.

Immediately after independence, UNIP governed while the African National Congress (ANC) opposed. The ANC drew its support largely from the farming areas in Southern and Central Provinces and from Mufulira in the Copperbelt, where its leader, Harry Nkumbula, had long resided while still a school teacher and where persons from the Central and Southern Province tended to migrate in search of jobs.[31] Over time, however, the political balance began to change; for dissident factions, once defeated within UNIP, defected to ANC.

Under the First Republic, high office within UNIP translated into high office in the government; the Central Committee and cabinet were one.

Those seeking prominent positions in the government therefore strove to secure top positions in the Party.[32] In 1967, UNIP held elections for posts in the Central Committee and coalitions formed around rival slates of candidates. One, headed by the incumbent vice-president, Reuben Kamanga, drew its support from the Eastern and Western Provinces; the other, headed by Simon Kapwepwe, drew its backing from Northern and Copperbelt Provinces, as well as from UNIP backers in Southern Province. In balloting that threatened to spill over into violence, the latter slate won. Kamanga surrendered his post to Kapwepwe and Kapwepwe's supporters took control of both the Central Committee and cabinet.[33]

The electoral victory of Kapwepwe and his backers shifted the regional balance of power in post-independence Zambia. Blocked in efforts to gain top posts within the governing party, UNIP leaders from Western Province first broke away to form their own rival party, which was banned following outbreaks of political violence. They then took up leading positions in ANC, merging their backers with UNIP's main rival.[34] By 1968, ANC had therefore gained control of three of Zambia's eight provinces.[35]

Rather than retreat to the rival party, as did their Western Province allies, however, the defeated politicians from Eastern Province mounted a counterattack. President Kaunda strove to arbitrate the resultant political conflicts, at one point even resigning in an effort to force a political reconciliation among his lieutenants.[36] From Kapwepwe's point of view, however, the president appeared to ally with his enemies. Kapwepwe's opponents called for a change in the Party's rules; the president appointed a commission that changed the rules in ways favoring the prospects of the old guard. The old guard accused some of Kapwepwe's backers of corruption; rather than dismissing these charges, the president had them investigated.[37] In the end, the president abolished the Central Committee that had been chosen in the election of 1967. Seeing their political victory reversed, Kapwepwe and his faction withdrew from UNIP and formed a party known as the United Progressive Party (UPP).

UPP drew support from the Northern Province, the place of birth of Simon Kapwepwe and many of his top lieutenants. Its political heartland lay, however, in the Copperbelt. It was in the Copperbelt that Kapwepwe and others had made their political careers. There they had built party branches, recruited political supporters, and run for electoral office. UPP secured the defection of major units within the Copperbelt organization of UNIP. It also mobilized disaffected economic groups on the Copperbelt, particularly businessmen and trade unions. The businessmen provided money, jobs, and transport for UPP's organizers. The trade unions provided offices, communications facilities, and access to mass organizations in the townships.[38]

The rise of UPP posed a fundamental threat to the governing party. In 1968, UNIP had lost three provinces to ANC. Had UPP taken Northern Province and the Copperbelt in the elections of 1973, then UNIP would have lost five of the nine provinces and become a minority party. In December of 1971, the UNIP government therefore detained over 100 UPP organizers; in February of 1972, it banned the party; and in December 1972, the government made Zambia a single-party state, with UNIP the sole legal party. On the verge of becoming a minority party, UNIP secured its power through its control of the government.

Discussion

UNIP's loss of the Copperbelt underscored its political alienation from key economic interests, particularly in the private sector. This affected economic policy making in two ways. Those interests most directly tied to production – farmers, business, and the trade unions – lay outside its core constituency. When the Party made economic policies that weakened production incentives, it therefore bore few immediate costs from doing so. The Party was therefore willing to sacrifice the interests of producers for short-run political gain.

Second, when UNIP's organization crumbled on the Copperbelt, and when it alienated labor and private business, it lost a valuable resource: the ability to orchestrate economic adjustment by brokering relations among representatives of labor and industry. Studies of economic adjustment in the advanced industrialized countries have shown that when business and labor form disciplined national associations and when the leaders of these associations are brought into government, then government officials are better able to elicit economic concessions in order to secure policy reforms.[39] When fragmented, there is little labor or business organizations can do to restrain their members. When well-organized but outside government, disciplined business or labor organizations can block adjustment efforts by governments that violate the short-run interests of their members. When well-organized and in government, however, then these organized interests furnish useful tools for reform-minded politicians. Political leaders can elicit a greater willingness to curtail worker militancy by giving the leaders of national labor organizations access to power; for they then confer upon organized labor the power to penalize business should business not reciprocate with concessions of its own. Similarly, when they give business access to government, political leaders confer upon capital the power to penalize labor; they thereby elicit from business a greater willingness to make short-term concessions in expectation of reciprocal concessions from labor. Governments that incorporate peak economic associations, these studies argue, can thereby create enforceable pacts between workers and firms; and they are therefore better able to adjust their domestic economies to external shocks and changing economic circumstances.

The government of Zambia repeatedly convened national meetings of labor, business, and government leaders in an effort to implement an incomes policy. It sought to engineer bargains in which labor would exchange wage restraint and industrial discipline for the ending of layoffs by business and the creation of new jobs. In the mid–1980s, the government sought to make the Trade Union Congress a wing of the Party. And toward the end of the Second Republic, it brought the top labor and business leaders into the Central Committee. But all such efforts failed to lay the foundations for corporatist forms of economic management. Workers remained fundamentally alienated from the ruling Party; labor leaders who took posts in the Party were voted out of office in their trade unions.[40] Given the political alienation of organized labor and business, the Party lacked the institutional means to secure organized backing for policy reforms from key interests.

State enterprises

While lacking close ties with labor and the private sector, be it in agriculture or industry, the Party and its government nonetheless intervened deeply in the economy. The primary instrument for this intervention was ZIMCO (Zambia Industrial and Mining Corporation, Limited), the massive state holding company.

ZIMCO encompassed the mining sector; the government had nationalized the copper industry in 1969. It included energy: an oil pipeline from Dar es Salaam, a refinery, and hydroelectric plants in Kafue and Kariba. It included transport: railways, road and bus services, and the national airways. ZIMCO possessed significant financial holdings: two banks, a building society, and the nation's insurance industry. It dominated the hotel and tourist trade. Through its INDECO group of companies, ZIMCO controlled a significant portion of the manufacturing sector as well.[41] Data on public and private employment indicate the significance of the public sector in Zambia's economy: in the mid–1980s, two-thirds of those holding "formal sector" jobs worked either for the government or for a parastatal firm. The public sector represented virtually the sole source of employment in mining and in services; even in construction and manufacturing it controlled two-fifths of total wage employment.

The government's holdings in mining, railways, and energy accounted for the vast preponderance of its capital investments and generated the bulk of ZIMCO's earnings, both locally and in foreign exchange.[42] The manufacturing firms grouped under INDECO constituted a relatively small portion of the public economy. However, as we shall see, the small firms in INDECO proved to be of central political importance.

Until the late 1970s, while ZIMCO held a majority of the shares in each member firm, the ministry in charge of the relevant industrial sector appointed the managing director. In the face of mounting losses by its state enterprises, the government in 1978 reduced the power of the ministries and concentrated political control at the level of ZIMCO, the holding company. Nonetheless, the political ties to the center remained strong: in 1989, twelve of the twenty two directors of ZIMCO held membership on the Central Committee, as did the director general and head of ZIMCO's management.

The government employed its control over the parastatal sector to secure agreements to locate in areas that were politically desirable even though economically marginal as a result of being far from markets: at government urging makers of batteries, for example, agreed to locate in Mansa; an automobile assembly plant located in Livingstone; and a manufacturer of bicycles built a plant in Chipata. The government has also used its control over public sector firms to attempt to secure low consumer prices. It focused these efforts on the firms that manufactured essential consumer items – bread or vegetable oil, for example. The government also used its control over the parastatal firms to reduce consumer prices. Should a firm's management seek an upward revision in its prices, then management had to defend this decision, subjecting all of its costs to audit and scrutiny by the ZIMCO Board – a Board that was dominated by the Central Committee of UNIP. To enable the firms to produce ample supplies of essential commodities at low prices, the government strove to provide them abundant allotments of foreign exchange, priority in the licensing of imports, and sufficient amounts of capital. The small INDECO companies thus became the favored recipients of the government's attention, as it attempted to provide urban consumers with low-priced commodities.

The state sector thus represented a political resource for the Party. It also posed a political danger. For many of the firms constituted virtual monopolies and all were government owned. Should they start to accrue monopoly profits, they would then provoke criticism of the government for profiteering at the expense of consumers. For this reason, too, the Party sought to impose rigid price controls.

4 THE STRUCTURE OF POLITICAL COMPETITION

As we have seen, during the First Republic (1964–72), UNIP competed with other political parties. Threatened with the prospects of becoming a minority party, UNIP had used its power over the government to transform Zambia into a single-party state. Zambia's second republic therefore contained only one legal party: UNIP. The termination of party competition did not mark the end of political competition, however. Rather, it simply restructured it. The Party still sought votes for its candidate for the national presidency; parliamentary candidates, albeit all members of UNIP, competed for office in the legislature; and lower-ranking officers sought to achieve higher positions within UNIP.

The structure of political competition in each of these arenas, we argue, induced systematic preferences over economic policies on the part of politicians. The national search for votes for the president placed a premium on satisfying the needs of urban consumers. The structure of competition for posts in parliament favored the interests of business, while also isolating them from the effective center of power. And competition for prominence within UNIP placed a premium on endorsing the interventionist policies favored by its old guard – policies based upon centralized command and control rather than upon decentralized markets.

External Representation: Under the single party system of the Second Republic, the national electorate voted only in presidential and parliamentary elections.[43]

Presidential elections

Under the Second Republic, there was only one candidate for president: the incumbent, Kenneth David Kaunda. To be elected, he had to receive a majority of the votes. In practice, the president sought majorities in the range of 90 percent or more. He did so in order to demonstrate overwhelming popular support and thereby to deter would-be political challengers. A key job of the political organizers in UNIP, as in all political parties, was to mobilize votes for the party ticket. Those who did the job well were marked for promotion; those who failed to secure favorable electoral returns were regarded as failures. All who were politically sophisticated in Zambia realized that the alternatives posed in the election – President Kaunda or someone to be named later – offered the electorate a choice between a well-known, certain, figure – the incumbent president – and a lottery. Posing alternatives in this way, they realized, elicited favorable votes even from political opponents who happened to be averse to risk. To demonstrate their political skill, then, party organizers therefore needed to generate overwhelming electoral majorities. UNIP organizers sought high turnouts and votes of 90 percent or more for the president.

Because the urban population in Zambia is more densely settled than is the population of the rural areas, it is easier to mobilize politically. UNIP organizers found it less costly to contact voters in the urban townships than in the scattered homesteads of the countryside. In search of electoral majorities, UNIP therefore concentrated on the towns. The focus on urban organization was intensified by the need to counter the incursion of rivals who, while unable to run their own candidates, could seek to embarrass the supporters of President Kaunda by organizing resistance to his candidacy. These rivals too found the urban areas easier to organize and they sought to encourage voters to remain at home on election day.[44] The consequence was that while most Zambians lived in the rural areas, politicians concentrated their efforts on the urban townships. Evidence of the use of this strategy is that the two most highly urbanized provinces – Lusaka and the Copperbelt – alone provided over one-third of the registered voters in Zambia. Voters from the two provinces turned out at a rate in excess of the national average. In the two elections held in the 1980s, for example, 60–70 percent of those registered actually voted, figures that stand more than a standard deviation above the mean for all provinces.[45]

One of the issues of greatest concern to urban dwellers was the level and stability of consumer prices. In search of urban votes, the Party employed every means at its disposal to address this problem. One of the major instruments at its command was the urban township councils. The local councils belonged to UNIP. Only UNIP members could vote in council elections; those who served as chairmen of the ward units of UNIP served as well as urban councillors; and the district governors served also as the executive heads of the urban councils, i.e., as mayors.[46] The local governments possessed the power to manage township markets. In its campaign for political support from the urban electorate, the Party attempted to use its control over the councils to garner popularity from urban consumers by controlling prices in these markets.

Through their power to license traders in the township markets, Zambia's urban councils controlled entry.[47] By limiting entry, UNIP conferred upon traders the power to make noncompetitive profits. In exchange, the Party extracted political favors from these retailers. It required that they participate in demonstrations and rallies; it also solicited their help in turning out the vote. The most important service required of marketeers, however, was the provision of stable consumer prices, thereby safeguarding the popularity of the government. To confer monopoly rents while also securing low prices, the Party used its control over the state enterprises grouped in INDECO and the bureaucrats in charge of price controls. Through these it sought to supply to the urban marketeers essential consumer goods at low and controlled prices. The costs of assuring the marketeers profitable markups even while assuring urban consumers low retail prices were born by INDECO and the Treasury. Spanning the township markets on the one hand and the commanding heights of the public sector on the other, the Party thus managed key elements of the economy so as to deliver essential commodities at low prices to key segments of the president's electoral consistuency.[48]

Parliamentary elections

Parliamentary campaigns provided a second electoral connection between UNIP and the voters. In contrast to those generated by presidential campaigns, however, the political incentives generated by competition for seats in parliament favored business, rather than consumer, interests.

In the parliamentary elections, UNIP endorsed the candidacy of several rivals for each seat. Rather than campaigning for a single candidate chosen by the Party, UNIP instead superintended a competitive election among a set of candidates, all of whom bore the party label. Under the single-party, multiple-candidacy system, there were few incentives for parliamentary candidates to campaign on the Party label. The candidates had to be approved by the Central Committee.[49] Having satisfied the criteria of party loyalty to get selected in the first place, candidates then possessed strong incentives to differentiate themselves in terms of other criteria, such as their ability to criticize government or to serve the interests of constituents. In addition, under the single-party, multiple-candidate system, the Party did not finance or staff the campaigns of particular parliamentary candidates. More than others, businessmen possessed the finances to build their own election machines. More than others, they also possessed the resources by which to provide constituency services and thereby to build a base independent of the Party from which to mount attacks on the government. They were therefore advantaged by the electoral rules.

In the Second Republic, parliament therefore became a forum for political dissidents, many of whom were drawn from the business community. Rather than representing the interests of the residents of the urban townships, as did the officials of the Party, parliamentarians instead advocated the interests of private business.[50]

Parliament thus became a forum for the expression of business interests. It failed, however, to provide a strong power base for those opposed to government policies. Parliamentarians who vigorously opposed government policy faced the threat of failing to secure renomination by the Party. In the elections of 1978, for example, the Central Committee withheld its endorsement of many who had criticized their control-based management of the economy.[51] In addition, the president appointed members of parliament to government posts, thereby silencing their potential opposition. By 1990, according to one source, only 15 of the more than 120 members of parliament lacked such appointments.[52] And parliament lacked the power to alter government policy. While, constitutionally, its approval was necessary for the passage of the government's budget, the executive branch could unilaterally alter other economic policies without parliamentary approval. Given the domination of the government by the executive branch and the marginal position of parliament, consumer interests therefore remained privileged over those of the business community.

Internal accountability and the power of ideology

Competition for power in Zambia's Second Republic was not only mediated by the national electorate; it was also mediated by those who conferred office upon, or withheld office from, those with ambitions for advancement in UNIP. Given the rules of the Party, those who sought to rise to the top did best by striving to emulate the preferences of its leaders. As a consequence, ideology exercised a strong influence over the making of economic policy.

At the local level – the section, branch, and ward – Party offices were filled by ballot, with only UNIP members being eligible to vote. However, higher positions in the Party – those at the district, provincial, or national level – were filled by appointment. Specifically, they were filled by the president with the approval of the Central Committee. Where the appointment carried with it membership in the Central Committee, then the appointment had to be ratified by the National Council and, if contested, voted upon by the Party Congress. As no appointments had been contested since 1967, virtually all appointments to the Central Committee were ratified by acclamation.

Those seeking high office in UNIP thus were not constrained by electoral mechanisms within the Party; they did not have to champion the interests of those at its lower reaches.[53] Rather, they had only to please their superiors, principally the president and the Central Committee. The means of advancement therefore provided few incentives for those at the top to modify their policy stands in an effort to cultivate political popularity; and they created powerful incentives for the politically ambitious to emulate the values of those of the Party elite.[54] These values strongly favored the use of economic controls.

In the world view of UNIP's senior leadership, economic policy making represented a branch of security policy.[55] Only the political sacrifices made in the liberation struggle had enabled Zambians to wrest their nation's resources from foreign control, they felt. After independence, the racial minority that had been driven from Zambia in the 1960s took refuge in surrounding territories – Angola, Mozambique, Rhodesia, and South Africa – from whence they threatened the nation. And internally, Zambia had become divided: the economic interests and political ambitions of selfish individuals had led to internal division. From the point of view of the old guard, then, Zambia was surrounded by enemies and threatened by internal conflict. Only the disciplined management of Zambia's economic resources could prevent foreigners from exploiting the nation's inner conflicts to regain control over the national economy. For the defense of the nation, economic development should therefore be managed by a united and vigilant political party.

The old guard's conviction in these beliefs was reinforced by the approbation they received from those who counted: the members of the Party hierarchy, who saw in them a justification for the perpetuation of their political monopoly and for the political management of the economy.

Discussion

In Zambia, interest groups that, in other states, would put a check on the making of policies that weakened production incentives stood outside the core constituency of the governing party. At least in the short run, economic costs to producers would therefore fail to translate into political costs for politicians.

The structure of political competition for the office of chief executive biased policy decisions in favor of urban consumers; it rendered the Party a national organization that lobbied in favor of low retail prices for urban consumers. The structure of political competition for legislative office rendered parliament an institution favoring business interests; but the relative power of the Party and the executive greatly reduced the impact of parliament on national policy. The structure of political competition within UNIP enhanced political commitment to policies favoring political management of the economy and to the treatment of economic policy as a branch of security policy. Overall, then, the structure of political competition within the Second Republic created political incentives that induced a preference on the part of politicians in favor of interventionist policies that protected the interests of urban consumers.

Political incentives thus affected the content of public policies. Equally as important, they also affected the credibility of policy reform. So strong were these incentives that should the government seek to change the content of its policies, it would find economic actors doubting the strength of its commitment. As we shall see, given the incentives faced by policy makers, it proved difficult to convince economic agents that the government could commit itself to policies that would harm the interests of the townships, favor private business or commercial farmers, and curry favor from foreign capital.

5   THE MOVEMENT TOWARDS LIBERALIZATION

Following the dramatic shift in the terms of trade in the mid–1970s, labor and business mounted open critiques of government policy. Labor tended to focus on inflation and government's attempt to counter it by cutting subsidies while calling for wage restraint.[56] Business mounted a more focused attack. The high point came with the 1977 report of the Parliamentary Select Committee that called for an end to price controls; a curtailment of government support for state industries; a reduction in government spending, particularly for social welfare programs; and the greater use of markets. In seeking to revive Zambia's flagging economy, the parliamentarians criticized as well the government's foreign policy and advocated an end to restrictions on trade with South Africa.[57]

The Party and executive branch of government responded by attacking parliament. They branded its members parasitic capitalists and attacked them as sellouts to foreign interests.[58] They also sought to impose further limitations on the autonomy of parliament. More effective, rather, were the growing criticisms from foreign creditors, and in particular the International Monetary Fund and the World Bank. The IMF began extending credits to Zambia in the early 1970s. By the end of the decade, it had begun to lobby for major changes in economic policy. In particular, it sought to end controls over prices, interest rates, and the allocation of foreign exchange. It also sought an end to subsidies, and in particular the subsidy on maize meal, a consumer staple.[59]

The IMF's campaign was joined by the World Bank and other creditors. They targeted their efforts upon the economic bureaucracies – Treasury and the Bank of Zambia – and on the president. Representatives from these bureaucracies attended the meetings of Zambia's consultative group, entered a dialogue with the nation's creditors, and met with governmental delegations dispatched to discuss policy reforms. In targeting the economic institutions, the international agencies revealed that either they did not recognize the significance of the Party or felt it inappropriate to approach its officials.[60]

In 1985, the international agencies were at last able to secure meaningful and comprehensive policy reforms. One reason was mounting evidence that the control regime was not protecting living standards. Recall that over the previous decade per capita private consumption had declined precipitously: by 34 percent according to the National Accounts and by 30 percent according to surveys in the townships. Further, within urban areas, distributional changes appear to have been regressive. Household budget surveys conducted in 1975 and 1985 enable us to compare the distribution of urban income prior to the fall in the copper price and on the eve of the introduction of the auction. The Gini coefficient (a measure of inequality) rose slightly from 0.48 to 0.49. While this increase alone is too small to be statistically significant, in addition, relative prices moved in favor of high-income groups. By September 1985 (the month prior to the auction) the Consumer Price Index for low-income groups had risen by 16 percent relative to that for high-income groups since 1975. Hence, while differentials stayed constant in nominal terms, in real terms they widened. Living standards had thus fallen, particularly for those groups which the government numbered among its core supporters.[61]

Backed by the advice of his minister of finance and the governor of the Bank, the president decided in 1985 to switch to a more liberal economic regime. The centerpiece of the reform was the introduction of an auction for the allocation of foreign exchange. An "own-funded" imports scheme was also introduced, whereby Zambians illegally holding foreign exchange abroad were permitted to bring in imports. These measures were accompanied by domestic price reforms, a movement toward market clearing rates of interest, and attempts to end consumer subsidies, particularly for maize.

By all accounts, it was the president who secured the adoption of the reform program. Only he supported it in the Central Committee; and only he, the minister of finance, and the governor of the Bank supported it in meetings of the cabinet.[62] Given the structure of power and decision making in Zambia's Second Republic, the backing of the president was sufficient to secure the adoption of the reforms. Nonetheless, given the bias in favor of the control regime that pervaded the Party and the greater political system, the backing of only the president and his technocrats was not sufficient to guarantee their maintenance.

The reforms were introduced in October 1985. In May 1987, they were terminated, along with the Bank and the IMF programs in support of them. In this section, we focus on the reasons why, examining in particular the impact of the introduction of market forces on the allocation of foreign exchange.

The collapse of the market-orientated reforms

In October 1985 the government implemented a package of policy reforms designed to dismantle the control regime. An auction for the allocation of foreign exchange constituted the core of the reform program. The major foreign exchange users and earners were excluded from the auction; only around 22 percent of the foreign exchange was sold through it during 1986, the rest continuing to be allocated by committee. The strike price in the auction became the rate at which all foreign exchange was sold by the government, however; and the auction therefore had a powerful effect on the exchange rate, which depreciated almost immediately from K2.2 per dollar to around K6 per dollar.

The value of the kwacha was published in the newspapers; it was followed closely by the informed public. As part of the reform program, the government increased its charges for transport and communication services, housing, schooling, and public utilities. And the abrupt increase in the price of foreign exchange put an end to the de facto system of price controls. The fall in the kwacha therefore took place contemporaneously with a massive rise in the prices of government services and consumer goods. Because it was widely understood that the auction had caused a sudden increase in costs, firms raised their prices to market-clearing levels, blaming the increase on the auction. The introduction of market mechanisms for the allocation of foreign exchange, the depreciation of the kwacha, and inflation all took place simultaneously. As revealed in newspaper accounts and interviews conducted as part of this study, the correlation between the three phenomena was given a causal interpretation: the auction was blamed for the depreciation of the currency, which in turn was blamed for inflation.

There is no question that prices increased at the time of the auction. In the 12 months immediately prior to the auction, inflation had been 30 percent; in the first six months of the auction it leapt to an annualized rate of 93 percent. A key question, however, is whether the surge in consumer prices constituted the start of a continuing (and faster) inflation or instead represented a once-and-for-all adjustment in prices. Another is whether the cost of this adjustment was born equally.

Our research indicates that the burst of inflation at the onset of the auction was a one-off event and, further, that it was not caused by cost-push but rather by a fall in the demand for real money balances. Prior to the lifting of price controls, consumers faced shortages. Households therefore began to accumulate abnormally large money balances. The velocity of circulation of currency with respect to private consumption provides a measure of this behavior. Whereas during the 1970s the velocity had been rising, in the early 1980s velocity was falling and by 1984 (the last full year of the control regime) it was 21 percent below trend.[63] This is a common phenomenon in shortage economies. In Eastern Europe it was probably involuntary, in the sense that people had no choice but to earn income which they could not fully spend. In Africa, monetary accumulation is more likely to be voluntary since households usually possess the options of either earning less or spending more on the black market. Households, behaving rationally, build up money balances when faced with shortages at official prices so as to be able to take up the occasional opportunity to make bulk-purchases. Conversely, behaving rationally, they reduce these balances once the economy reverts to market-clearing conditions, as it did in Zambia when firms raised their prices.

Had the transition back to market-clearing in 1986 returned the velocity to its previous trend, it would have been 34 percent higher than in 1984 (the last full year of shortages). In fact, the velocity rose by almost precisely this amount (37 percent). If this was due to the ending of shortages, then we can conclude that price decontrol caused a once-and-for-all increase in the price level of around 34 percent between 1984 and 1986.

Note, however, that the *recorded* increase in the price level between these years was 108 percent; indeed, this fact strongly shaped public perceptions in this period. However, the recorded price level appears to overweigh controlled prices and therefore exaggerates the effect of price decontrol. In Appendix 9.1 we set out a method for calculating this bias. Correcting for it, our estimate of the true rise in the price level is 76 percent. Since we attribute an increase of 34 percent to the rise in velocity consequent upon the ending of shortages, this leaves a residual increase of 31 percent[64] during 1984–6, implying an underlying annual rate of inflation of only 15 percent. The implication is that the observed severe upturn in inflation in the first six months of the auction was partly due to mismeasurement by the consumer price index (CPI), with the rest being once-and-for-all.[65]

The data thus suggest that the immediate impact of the auction was a once-and-for-all increase in the price level. Note that this impact was a consequence of triggering de facto price decontrol. The longer-term impact of the auction depended upon the impact of the auction (and other elements of the policy package) on the budget. The exchange rate affects the budget in three ways. The first is through the government's purchases and sales of foreign currency for kwacha and, crucially, the net balance of these transactions. The first three columns of table 9.2 show purchases and sales on a quarterly basis using data provided by the Central Bank. (Unfortunately, the Central Bank's foreign exchange budget is available only from 1986 so that the fourth quarter of 1985 cannot be included in the analysis.) In most quarters the government was a small net purchaser of foreign exchange. The fourth column converts its net balances into a cost to the budget in terms of kwacha, compared with a maintenance of the pre-auction exchange rate.

Before assessing the impact of the auction on the government's budget, however, we have to make two further calculations. The government taxed ZCCM on its gross sales, raising its rate of tax at the onset of the auction from 10 percent to 13 percent. The government thus gained both from the extra 3 percent (i.e., we treat this as part of the auction package) and, more importantly, from the fact that the tax was worth much more in kwacha, as a result of depreciation. There are two ways of estimating the revenue consequences of this tax. The first, shown in column 5, applies the tax rates to the gross sales of ZCCM as revealed in its sales of dollars to the Central Bank. The second, shown in column 6, comes from budget records of quarterly tax receipts. Until the fourth quarter of 1986 these two approaches give similar results. The other gain came from import taxes. Since imports were now worth more in kwacha, the tax upon them generated more revenue. We make an estimation of this in column 7. We are now in a position to calculate the net impact of the auction upon the budget (i.e., the sum of columns 4, 5 or 6, and 7); this is shown in column 8. It is evident that the auction substantially improved the budget. During the first three quarters of 1986 the overall improvement was either K304 million or K254 million, depending upon which estimate of export tax receipts is adopted.

A budget deficit is funded at the margin by the creation of domestic liabilities. In Zambia there are only three such liabilities. One is currency held by the public or the commercial banks (M0). A second is Treasury Bills held outside the Bank of Zambia. The third is deposits held at the Bank of Zambia by the commercial banks. The sum of these three is primary liquidity (which we denote by L0). At the start of 1986 L0 was K2.18 billion, so the budget improvement of K254–304 million reduced its growth over the next nine months by around 19 percent at an annualized

Table 9.2 The auction and the budget

		Purchases ($m)[a]	Sales ($m)[b]	Net purchases ($m)	Cost to budget (Km)[c]	ZCCM tax (Km) A[d]	ZCCM tax (Km) B[e]	Imports tax (Km)[f]	Net impact on budget (Km) A[g]	Net impact on budget (Km) B[h]
1986	1	117.1	98.9	18.2	77.5	104.5	107.6	54.9	81.9	85.0
	2	119.9	94.4	25.5	125.8	122.1	54.1	91.3	87.6	19.6
	3	120.6	97.6	23.0	94.5	105.5	120.6	123.3	134.3	149.5
	4	101.5	49.4	52.1	493.7	204.7	−36.5	116.1	−172.9	−414.1
1987	1	9.0	67.2	22.8	271.0	277.9	225.4	186.5	193.4	140.9
	April	23.9	27.2	−3.3	−56.0	106.5	39.0	45.9	208.4	140.9
	May/June	74.8	39.6	35.2	203.5	0	0	0	−203.5	−203.5
	2		111.5		147.5	106.5	39.0	45.9	4.9	−62.6
	3	136.1		24.6	142.2	0	0	0	−142.2	−142.2
	4	143.7	122.7	21.0	121.4	0	0	0	−121.4	−121.4
1988	1	190.9	110.6	80.3	484.1	0	0	0	−464.1	−464.1

[a] Purchases are gross metal receipts less ZCCM allocation of foreign exchange, plus nontraditional exports net of retentions.

[b] Sales to the private sector ("total auctionable funds").

[c] The exchange rate during the quarter, e, minus the pre-auction rate, 2.22, all times column 3.

[d] The Bank of Zambia provides monthly data on gross metal receipts from ZCCM in dollars (R). In 1985 ZCCM was taxed at 10 percent of gross sales (R). In 1986 it was taxed at 13 percent. We assume that this increase was a package with the auction. Hence the increase in tax receipts due to the auction is:

$$e.R.(0.13) - 2.22.R.(0.10) = (0.13e - 0.222)R.$$

[e] An alternative way of deriving the budgetary impact is to work from budgetary data. Mineral revenue as reported on a quarterly basis in the *Quarterly Financial and Statistical Review*, table V2. We take as a counterfactual the average receipts during the first three quarters of 1985. The excess of actual receipts over this counterfactual is attributed to the auction package. This produces similar results except for the fourth quarter of 1986.

[f] Import tax receipts in excess of counterfactual estimated by interpolating actual import tax revenue pre- and post- auction (1985 Q3 and 1987 Q3) at a constant growth rate and treating this as the counterfactual.

[g] Using estimate A of the ZCCM tax.

[h] Using estimate B of the ZCCM tax.

rate. Note that this reduction is relative to an unobserved counterfactual rather than to the pre-auction period.

Although the transition to the auction caused a steep increase in the price level, it (somewhat) improved the budget and so dampened subsequent inflation. The government, however, agreed with the auction's critics, believing inflation to be continuing and accelerating and the costs to be disproportionately borne by the poor. Why did it come to this conclusion? One reason is that the governing Party had anchored its political fortunes in the urban townships. The result was the creation of a political reaction function: economic policies were evaluated in terms of their impact upon the urban, lower-income index of consumer prices and this index was biased downward at the time of controls but biased upward at the time of their relaxation. The government also appears to have mistaken the price increases resulting from the rise in the velocity of circulation brought on by the end of shortages for a permanent and accelerating inflation. This was to be expected, given the conjunction of its ideological perception of inflation as cost-push and the disinformation of firms trying to disguise the return to market clearing prices as auction-related cost increases. Also influencing the government's behavior was the increased visibility of the consumption of luxuries, with the resultant conviction that the rich were prospering at the time of rising prices. About this, more needs to be said.

Recall that during the build-up in the control regime, 1975–85, urban inequality had, if anything, increased; luxury consumption can therefore be presumed to have at least persisted. Such consumption had been, however, less visible than under the free-market system. One channel for the purchase of luxuries had been privileged access at official prices; the well-connected made purchases discretely "under the counter." The other channel was the black market. Again transactions were discrete and unadvertised; trading illegally, marketeers needed to minimize the dissemination of information. With the switch to market-clearing brought about by the removal of price controls, however, traders changed their marketing strategy: they displayed and advertised in an effort to compete for sales. Luxury consumption therefore became much more visible and people inferred that the consumption of luxuries had increased. From that inference a second followed: that the rich must be doing well out of the auction. Although part of luxury imports were financed by the own-funded imports scheme, the myth arose that the auction was responsible for a substantial switch in the composition of imports towards luxuries.

In fact, the auction appears to have been mildly progressive distributionally. Recall that prior to the auction, prices for the poor had been rising more rapidly than prices for the rich; in the first six months of the auction this was reversed, prices for the poor falling relatively by 2.5 percent. Indeed, this number probably understates the progressive impact of the auction. As elsewhere in the developing world, members of the elite tended to consume imported items to a greater extent than did the average citizen. Many educated their children abroad; many traveled extensively, for business or for pleasure; and all purchased imports from Europe. The depreciation of the kwacha therefore raised their cost of living. For top members of the elite, it also lowered their incomes. One of the major perquisites of elite status in Zambia was the ability to import an automobile duty-free. Purchased at the official exchange rate, the car could be sold in Zambia for local currency. With the massive overvaluation of the kwacha, the profit from the sale of a luxury-class Toyota or a Mercedes Benz represented several times the annual salary of an elite civil servant. With the depreciation of the kwacha to market-clearing levels, the elites lost this source of income. The evidence suggests, therefore, that the distributional impact of the price changes brought on by the auction was not regressive. Needless to say, insofar as the elites sought to overturn policies that were eroding the value of their perquisites and reducing their purchasing power, they had little incentive to counter the popular misperception that the reforms had brought back good times for the rich. Indeed, in order to overturn this policy reform, many appear to have actively played upon this illusion.

Almost as soon as the auction was introduced by the government, opposition to it was mounted by labor.[66] Opposition rapidly spread to the editorial pages of Zambia's leading newspapers; one was owned by the Party and the other edited by an appointee of the president.[67] Soon opposition to the auction spread to the lower ranks of the Party. Toward the end of 1985, the Southern Province Provincial Secretary publicly proclaimed: "The country's worsening economy has alienated many Zambians from the Party.... [S]ome members [are] thinking that the Party has forgotten them ...."[68] In the spring of 1986, the Provincial Party Congress in the Copperbelt severely criticized the auction;[69] later in the year, a meeting of the Women's League in Ndola broke up when a member of the Central Committee attempted to defend the government's economic program.[70]

Facing widespread political discontent and mounting political opposition to his policies, the president in April 1986 switched his policy team. He moved the locus of policy management from a group anchored in the governmental bureaucracy and the international donor community to a group with close ties to the Party bureaucracy and the Central Committee. The new economic team was led by an economist who was regarded as one of the leading theoreticians of the Party.

We have argued thus far that the introduction of a market mechanism for the allocation of foreign exchange had worked. The accompanying, sharp, upward revision of prices resulted not from the depreciation of the kwacha but from changes in the fee structure for public services and the end of price controls. The price jump appeared to represent a one-time event, rather than the beginning of sustained inflation. Moreover, the auction proved stable: until the political changes of April 1986, the market for foreign exchange generated only modest fluctuations and a slow rate of depreciation from around 6 to around 7 kwacha to the dollar. With the shift of the management of the auction from the hands of the technocrats, however, all this changed.

The president had replaced the minister of finance because the president wanted an appreciated exchange rate and thus, by his lights, a lower rate of inflation. The governor of the Bank resigned to protest against growing pressure to intervene in the auction. His replacement was a Moscow-trained economist who was less than fully committed to the use of markets. The new governor regarded inflation as being driven by rising costs, and so sought to raise the exchange rate. He attempted to do so in a number of ways, the most important of which was by agreeing to sales of quantities of foreign exchange in excess of that available. The direct result was the build-up of a ten-week pipeline of foreign exchange purchases in the auction.

There were three immediate consequences of his policies. One was that private traders lost confidence, finding government commitments to be incredible. The second was the failure of government policy: rather than appreciating, the exchange rate collapsed. The third was massive losses by the Central Bank, precipitating a surge of inflation.

The personnel changes, combined with the sale of foreign exchange which the Bank did not have, made the maintenance of the auction incredible to the private sector. It became incredible because the manipulation was so costly as to be unsustainable and because the new personnel were not willing to incur political costs in the defense of a system in which they did not believe. The response of the private sector was to accumulate durable imports (consumer goods and intermediate inputs) while they were temporarily cheap. An indicator of this is the quantity of inventories. According to the National Accounts (which are available only on a calendar-year basis) inventory accumulation in 1986 rose to 3.5 times its 1985 rate (reverting to normal in 1987 and 1988). Indeed, in 1986 inventory accumulation was so large that it considerably exceeded gross fixed capital formation. The phasing of this inventory accumulation during 1986 can be inferred from bank loans to the manufacturing sector, data on which is available monthly until the end of September 1986.[71] Between the start of the auction and the end of June 1986, bank loans to manufacturing grew at slightly below the rate of the previous three years. Suddenly, in the third quarter of 1986, there was an explosion in borrowing. Had it been on trend, new bank lending during the quarter would have been K5 million, whereas in fact it was an unprecedented K46 million. It would appear, then, that expectations had changed.

The result of this change in expectations was a frantic bidding for foreign exchange. Rather than appreciating in response to increased sales of foreign exchange, the kwacha fell in value. The exchange rate, stable for the first eight months of the auction, depreciated from around K7 to K21 per dollar during the next 12 months.

In its attempt to raise the value of the kwacha, the Bank was selling more foreign exchange than it possessed, and therefore inadvertently taking a large speculative position in the market. The reaction of private traders led to the depreciation of the exchange rate. The result was that the Bank, in order to make good on its sales, had to purchase foreign currency at a price higher than that at which it had agreed to sell it. Given the rate at which the kwacha depreciated during the 12 months of this regime, a ten-week lag involved on average a Bank purchase price about 24 percent above its sale price. Since the Bank sold around K4.6 billion worth of foreign exchange during the period, this implies a loss of around K1 billion. The result was increased inflation.

We can check this estimate by decomposing the increase in primary liquidity (see table 9.3). Primary liquidity can be created in only two ways: one is government domestic financing of a budget deficit, the other is by the Bank of Zambia. The Bank can create liquidity either by increasing its foreign exchange reserves (buying dollars from the rest of the economy other than the government) or by trading in foreign exchange at a loss. Since there was no reserve accumulation during the auction, Bank of Zambia losses can therefore be inferred residually from the increase in primary liquidity and the domestic financing requirement of the budget.

Between July 1986 and March 1987 the Central Bank appears to have lost around K1 billion. Note that this accords well with the more casual

Table 9.3 Causes of growth in primary liquidity

| | | Increase in L0 during quarter (Km) | | | Indices end of quarter (Dec 31 1985 = 100) | | |
		Total	Due to budget	Due to Bank of Zambia	Deficit driven L0	Total L0	M0
1985	Q4	325	244	81	100	100	100
1986	Q1	38	14	24	101	102	98
1986	Q2	127	74	53	104	108	102
1986	Q3	470	182	288	112	129	145
1986	Q4	1122	764	358	148	181	173
1987	Q1	608	274	361	159	209	168
1987	Q2	247	361	−159	167	205	206
1987	Q3	698	517	181	190	237	272
1987	Q4	734	399	335	209	271	284
1988	Q1	432	1012	−580	255	291	261
1988	Q2	128	−427	555	236	297	293
1988	Q3	1115	1229	−114	292	(348)[e]	412

Sources: Column 1 from *Bank of Zambia Quarterly Review*.
Column 2 from *Bank of Zambia Quarterly Review*, table V3, line 3.
Column 3 residual of column 1 minus column 2.

estimate above, based on the length of the "pipeline" and the rate of depreciation. Recall that at the start of the auction the total stock of primary liquidity in the economy was only K2.2 billion. Overall in this nine months primary liquidity grew at an annual rate of 142 percent. Had the budget deficit been the same but Central Bank losses avoided, the rate of growth of the deficit would have been reduced to 73 percent. Increases of this order in primary liquidity could not help but be inflationary (by approximately the same magnitude).[72]

It should be noted that the budget also deteriorated during this period (column 2 of table 9.3). There is no single reason for this, although most of the problem occurred only in the fourth quarter of 1986. In this quarter, according to the budget data, there was virtually no collection of export tax revenue. Although export earnings dipped somewhat during the quarter, they should still have generated tax revenue of around K200 million (see table 9.2). Further, the net purchases of foreign exchange were unusually large, which, combined with the depreciation of the kwacha, added around K400 million to the deficit (table 9.2, columns 2 and 4).

To summarize: after the locus of economic management was shifted from the economic to the Party bureaucracy, expectations appear to have shifted, the value of the kwacha to have collapsed, and inflationary forces to have been unleashed by an expansion in the money supply, as the Bank was forced to purchase foreign exchange at prices higher than those at which it had sold it. The depreciation of the kwacha was caused not by a reduction in sales of dollars but by a huge increase in demand. Since this occurred after nine months of stability, it cannot be attributed to an intrinsic incredibility in the system as it was first operated: private agents appear initially to have regarded the auction as durable. Rather, the speculation appears to have been the consequence of the change in the political base of the economic team and the obviously unsustainable interventions that they adopted in order to appreciate the kwacha.

Alternative interpretations

The introduction of the foreign exchange auction in Zambia represented a major experiment in public policy – one that has been debated and scrutinized by many who are concerned with inferring lessons about the introduction of market-oriented reforms in Africa. It is therefore important to confront the alternative interpretations that have been put forward for the experiment's failure.

Articulate Zambians often blame the donor community, indicating that shortages of aid crippled the auction. The depreciation of the kwacha, they argue, resulted from shifts in the supply, rather than the demand, for foreign exchange. Table 9.4 sets out foreign exchange receipts on a monthly basis for each of the four policy regimes for the late 1980s: early auction, collapsing auction, recontrol, reliberalization. As table 9.4 shows,

Table 9.4   Sources of foreign exchange (millions of dollars per month)

	1986 (1–6)	1986(7) –87(4)	1987(5) –89(6)	1989 (7–12)
Copper (gross)	57	55	89	104
Nontraditional exports	2	5	9	11
Total exports	59	60	98	115
Aid and other borrowing	62	12	5	16
Debt payments[a]	62	13	7	4
Net aid	0	−1	−2	12
Exports plus net aid	59	59	96	127

[a]Debt payments include payments of arrears, principal and interest but exclude debt payments by ZCCM.
Source: Data supplied by Bank of Zambia.

the net impact of the donors in each phase was negligible. Net of debt repayments, monthly receipts were virtually zero in the first half of 1986. During the collapsing phase of the auction, from July 1986 to the end of April 1987, net receipts were again negligible (indeed, slightly negative). During the 26 months of the return to the control regime, lower debt payments almost precisely offset lower gross aid receipts so that there was a deterioration of only $1 million per month. Only in the last half of 1989 did net aid flows become nonnegligible, though still being less than 10 percent of gross foreign exchange receipts. Aid and debt servicing thus almost precisely offset each other. Similarly, although the fall in the copper price during the 1970s had been the dominant event for the economy, during the late 1980s, copper receipts were either stable or strongly rising (again see table 9.4).

The supply of foreign exchange net of debt payments was thus $59 million per month both in the first half of 1986 when the auction appeared viable and during the next ten months when it was manifestly unviable. Similarly, until the end of June 1986, the average allocation per auction was only $5.6 million, whereas in the remaining 30 auctions it was K6.1 million. We therefore dismiss external factors and turn instead to domestic policies.[73]

A second interpretation is often advanced on the side of the donor community. It focuses on the role of public enterprises which, it is claimed, could not compete in the market for foreign exchange, or could do so only with subsidized credit. The first position leads to the assertion that public enterprises undermined the auction by lobbying against it; the second, to the accusation that they precipitated an expansion in bank lending that led to renewed inflation, this being the thesis of Allsopp et al.[74]

In apparent support of this second position, bank deposits increased by 64 percent between end-September 1985 and end-June 1986. However, this increase does not appear to have been inflationary. Over 90 percent of it is accounted for by the increase in claims by Zambian banks on banks abroad rather than by an expansion in domestic credit. That is, Zambian firms held indirect rights to foreign exchange: they had kwacha claims on Zambian banks which were matched by dollar claims of the latter on foreign banks. Before the auction they had probably illegally held direct claims on foreign banks. The auction made this illegality less worthwhile. If firms choose to hold kwacha instead of dollars, both the demand for and the supply of kwacha increase to the same extent. There need be no inflationary effect. This interpretation is supported by the fact that, despite the 64 percent increase in deposits, there was no corresponding increase in bank lending, which grew by only 12 percent over the same period. We interviewed many bankers; all denied being pressed for credit by public enterprises at the time of the auction.

Turning to the first position, during a review of the auction the government explicitly queried the parastatals concerning their evaluations of it. Reporting through their holding company, the state industries indicated their support for the auction. Knowing that the top reaches of the Party opposed the economic reforms, public sector managers phrased their support cautiously. Nonetheless, they indicated that the resultant depreciation of the kwacha had led to massive increases in the profits of the export-oriented firms – the mines, railways, and power companies – that formed the major part of ZIMCO. They also indicated that because of the end of price controls, the small firms oriented toward the domestic market – the INDECO companies – were flush with kwacha and could therefore successfully bid against private corporations and multinational enterprises on the auction floor.[75]

A third explanation focuses not on the actions of enemies of the auction, but rather on the inaction of its friends. The exporters should have been friends of the auction, for it enabled them to command more kwacha from their foreign earnings; the government should have been another, for it derived revenues from taxes on exports. Both stood among the primary beneficiaries of the revaluation of the kwacha; but neither lobbied aggressively to preserve the market-oriented reforms. The absence of their support, it is held, weakened the political defenses of the auction.

There would appear to be much merit in this position. During the period of the auction, the profitability of Zambia's exports increased massively. The beneficiaries included the producers of such traditional exports as copper, rail services, and energy. They also included the producers of such nontraditional exports as sugar, fruits, flowers, vegetables, wood, furniture, metal wire, fabricated metals, plastics, and chemicals.[76] The passivity of these groups is underscored in the president's plaintive comment: "Zambia's economy has shown remarkable improvement since the introduction of the foreign exchange auctioning system. These successes seem to be Zambia's best kept secret."[77]

One set of beneficiaries were large-scale firms; these would include the mines, the railway, the hydroelectric companies, and the sugar estates. All were members of ZIMCO. As we have noted, the management of these firms in fact supported the auction; when queried by the ministry of finance, they underscored its beneficial impact on their earnings and their ability to secure foreign exchange. But in the Zambian political system, the Ministry of Finance, along with the rest of the Cabinet, remained subordinate to the Party. And within ZIMCO, management remained subordinate to its board of directors, which was itself dominated by members of the Central Committee of UNIP.[78] The other set of beneficiaries lay outside of the state sector and included commercial farmers and small-scale manufacturing firms. Numerous, widely scattered along the line of rail, and small relative to the size of the market, these firms faced the classic incentive problem bedeviling lobbyists.[79] Confronted with "the logic of collective action," each may well have found that it was not in its individual interests to lobby in defense of the auction, even though the auction benefited exporters as a whole. Such firms also confronted the stark fact that they lay in the periphery of the political system, rather than in the core. Should they choose, they could put their case to the relevant ministries in the government, and many did; but they did so without the aid of the Party or its politicians, most of whom regarded businessmen and commercial farmers as former (or potential) political enemies.

But then, what of the government itself? Drawing much of its revenue from taxes on exports and international trade, why did not the government defend the auction? We have already discussed one reason for the government's behavior: members of the governing elite possessed a model of the economic system which linked a lowering of the exchange rate to a rise in the rate of inflation, which adversely impacted upon the interests of core constituents. In addition, the depreciation of the kwacha raised the costs of foreign imports consumed by this elite and lowered the value of their privileged access to foreign exchange. Many members of the governing elite placed the interests of public institutions over their political or private interests, however.[80] And had they been convinced that the depreciation of the kwacha would increase public revenues, they would have supported the reforms. But economic experts saw the government as being a net purchaser rather than a seller of foreign exchange, and so saw devaluation as having a negative impact on government revenues.[81] We, of course, are convinced of the opposite. But our disagreement only underlines the extent to which members of the government would themselves have found it difficult to see where the interest of public institutions lay, and thus mobilize as public servants in defense of reformist policies.

The collapse of the auction, we have argued, was precipitated by the shift of its superintendence from the technocratic to the partisan wings of the government; a shift in management practices; and the resultant abrupt change in expectations, leading to the collapse of the kwacha and a surge in inflation. The auction was not sabotaged by the donors or the parastatals. But neither was it protected by its friends. Exporters had been politically emasculated. And the government appears to have lacked the capability of calculating, in any coherent and persuasive manner, the relationship between the exchange rate, net government revenues, and inflation, and thus the real value of public and private incomes.

The maize crisis

Many analysts trace the collapse of Zambia's economic reforms to the riots in December 1986 over the price of maize.[82] There can be no doubt but that these riots, which swept Ndola, Kitwe, and other towns on the Copperbelt, deeply shocked the government and dramatized the political and social costs of the economic reforms. It would appear, however, that it was not the increase of the maize price alone that sparked them; rather, it may have been (as we show below) a sharpened sensitivity to inflation and to its distributional impact. And this inflation had been caused not by the auction – although its measurement through the official index of consumer prices made it appear that way – but rather by the attempts to manipulate the auction on the part of the new economic management team.

Maize meal is a staple in the diet of all Zambians, but particularly those with lower incomes. Its purchase and distribution had long been subsidized by the government of Zambia. By the mid–1980s, the cost of the maize subsidy had risen to hundreds of millions of kwacha a year and consumed in excess of 10 percent of the total budget.[83] The Ministry of Finance had long fought to reduce the maize subsidy: it redoubled its efforts following the collapse of the price of copper in the mid–1970s. The ministry had been consistently opposed by the Central Committee of the Party, however. By all accounts, the members of the Central Committee fully understood the economic arguments put forward by the ministry: they simply felt unable to carry the policy forward to the public, saying that it was politically impossible to do so.[84]

While not able to terminate the maize subsidy, the Ministry of Finance was able to reduce it by raising the price of maize. Indeed, until the time of the auction, the government increased maize prices at a rate that exceeded the overall rate of inflation. As a result, over the preceding decade, while the real cost of the subsidy had increased by 11 percent (against a fall in total public consumption of 16 percent), its cost per capita had fallen by around 20 percent. As shown in table 9.5, the government's failure to raise the maize price at all during the three years from December 1985 contrasted strikingly with its previous behavior.

The maize subsidy was highly progressive. Household surveys show high-income groups spending 2.2 percent of their total expenditures on maize meal, low-income groups (exsquatter households) spending 7.5

Table 9.5 Percentage increase in official price of breakfast meal during a three-year period compared with inflation

	Meal price	All prices
Dec. 1980–Dec. 1983	84	53
Dec. 1981–Dec. 1984	88	61
Dec. 1982–Dec. 1985	129	97
Dec. 1985–Dec. 1988	0	232

Source: Monthly Digest of Statistics.

percent. Throughout the economic reforms, maize remained the one commodity subject to price control; and following the burst of inflation in the second quarter of 1986, the real price of maize fell substantially.

In the early 1980s, the international development community targeted agricultural pricing policy for reform throughout Africa. Zambia did not escape this campaign; the rapid phasing out of the maize subsidy became a major objective of its economic reform program. In 1986, the government therefore announced changes in its maize policy. While retaining the subsidy on the form of maize meal consumed by the urban poor, it put an end to the subsidy on the form of maize meal preferred by wealthy consumers. The millers responded by altering their production mix, concentrating on the production of the form of maize meal that they could sell free from price controls. The "inferior" type of maize meal therefore became in short supply, and the result was a rapid rise in the price of both kinds.[85]

As has been noted, the government had previously increased the price of maize meal. The purchases of the wealthy that before the reforms had been concealed from public view now took place in the open market. The movement to market-clearing prices produced an increase in the publicly visible index of consumer prices; the expansion in money supply brought about by the mismanagement of the auction gave rise to continuous inflation. These factors combined to create the conviction that the movement to market-based reforms favored those with the wealth to purchase commodities. Inflation also increased the value of the maize subsidy to the poor. The proposed changes in maize pricing policy therefore came at a time when inflation had increased the value of the subsidies and when people were particularly sensitive to the distributional impact of government policies.

Further erosion of political support

The maize riots swept the Copperbelt in early December of 1986. The government immediately terminated its efforts to end the food subsidy. Nationalizing the maize mills, it supplied the market at controlled prices.

The government's failure to reduce the costs of the food subsidy led to a violation of the spending targets it had negotiated with the IMF. In response, the government sought to contain increases in public sector wages. In late December, it dismissed over 1,000 civil servants; concentrating its wage concessions on the lower ranks of the civil service, it negotiated a wage package that offered little to top civil servants, but a 50 percent increase for low-paid workers.[86]

In the spring of 1987, Zambia was swept by labor unrest. Because of the depreciation of the kwacha, the price of exportable and import competing goods rose relative to the price of nontradables; firms that made traded goods competed for labor and wages therefore fell – both in real and relative terms – in the service sector. It is therefore not surprising that labor unrest originated among service workers. Hospital workers went on strike; they were joined by doctors and nurses. Teachers boycotted class rooms throughout the Copperbelt; clerks left their jobs, closing banks throughout Zambia. They were soon joined by printers and typesetters, retail clerks, and transportation workers. Soon workers in Zambia's four public service unions – the largest unions in the nation – were threatening to join the strikes, thereby paralyzing the government.

Throughout this period, those in charge of Zambia's economic policy were attempting to secure further loans from the IMF. Pressured on the international front, the economic policy makers faced an increasingly rigid domestic constraint as well: a governing party growing increasingly nervous about facing so restive an electorate.

National elections were scheduled for 1988. In the spring of 1987, the party began internal elections to choose the local-level leaders; these cadres would serve as the shock troops for the presidential campaign and help to choose candidates for parliament. By comparison with previous years, few candidates came forward to compete for local office. As one Party leader stated, "The Party leadership at the provincial and district level should be telling the Central Committee why people including section leaders are not renewing their membership cards."[87] And at the national level, incumbents began to distance themselves from the Party; as one parliamentarian declared:

> Although we were brought here on the UNIP ticket, not all voters are members of UNIP. I will not, therefore, cow down [sic] in criticizing the Party and its Government where it goes wrong because I cannot betray the cause of my masters – the people who brought me here.[88]

Given the impact of the reforms on the prospective electoral fortunes of the Party, the leadership became increasingly rigid in its tendency to define economic policy as a security issue. The economic reforms were no longer debated in terms of growth rates or allocational efficiency; they were instead debated in terms of their impact on political stability – i.e., on the capacity of incumbents to retain power. Increasingly, the elites branded striking workers as political saboteurs and linked the trade unions with Zambia's enemies abroad. In April, the president announced:

> There is no doubt in my mind that the initiators of the strikes were politically motivated and used innocent teachers, innocent doctors, and innocent nurses to paralyse the country's infrastructure...We picked up fellow Zambians with AK47s and from what they told us, there is no doubt they have relations with UNITA and MNR.[89]

The return to the control regime

In response, the president announced in May 1987 the end of the market-oriented reforms, replacing them with administrative procedures and systems of bureaucratic control. The new policies were christened the New Economic Recovery Programme (NERP). The design of the economic program reflected fundamental political decisions. The government desired to extract itself from the pressures of foreign creditors. Under NERP, Zambia therefore broke with the IMF, the World Bank, and therefore the donor community, and adopted instead a policy of achieving "growth from [Zambia's] own resources" – from foreign exchange earned by exporting rather than by receiving foreign aid.[90] As an offset to the anticipated reduction in gross aid receipts, the government limited the repayment of foreign debt to 10 percent of Zambia's net export earnings. As shown in table 9.4, this aspect of the strategy was successful for the two years of the recontrol period: net aid receipts were virtually unchanged. Second, the Party and its government sought to regain control over the allocation of foreign exchange. The government therefore replaced the auction for foreign exchange and the own-funded imports scheme with an administrative committee (the Foreign Exchange Management Committee (FEMAC)). The committee was located neither in the central bank nor in the Ministry of Finance, but rather in the Cabinet Office, which reported directly to the president. The exchange rate was revalued from K21 to K8 per dollar and fixed at that level. Third, the government sought to placate the disaffected. Among the most active were members of the salariat, particularly in the state sector; among the fundamental regulations issued under NERP were rules limiting the employment of expatriates – and protecting thereby the earnings of white-collar Zambians.[91] And among the most significant, particularly at the time of elections, were the residents of the urban townships. For them, the government proclaimed the renewal of price controls on essential consumer items: blankets, flour, salt, candles, soap, cooking oil, and so forth.

NERP entailed a restructuring of the institutional environment for the allocation of Zambia's economic resources. The clearest indicator of this transformation was the manner in which it enabled the Party and its government to target economic benefits directly to urban consumers. The first step was price control; the second, the use of FEMAC to give privileged access to foreign exchange to the firms that produced essential consumer items. These firms represented, in number and size, but a small portion of the state-owned industries. Nonetheless, the government targeted its policy interventions on them. It set the prices at which they could sell their products, and then vigilantly monitored their adherence to the prices. It directly provisioned these firms with foreign exchange. And it vigorously broadcast to the public their performance. In its first public review of NERP, the government devoted nearly 10 percent of its report to a discussion of the availability of plastic materials, necessary for the packaging of maize and cooking oil;[92] in the second, it provided a detailed comparison of the access of these firms to foreign exchange under FEMAC and the auction.[93] An obvious appeal of NERP, then, was that it enabled the political elites to seize control over allocational procedures for politically sensitive consumer items, and thereby to target resources to the economic units that provisioned their constituents.

The switch to NERP represented the abandonment of a policy of delegation, wherein resources were allocated by the decentralized choices of individuals responding to prices formed in markets, in favor of a policy of command and control. It also represented a shift of control over policy making from the financial institutions of government to bureaucrats who were responsive to the Party. In these ways, the shift to NERP represented a reversion to old patterns of policy making.

To focus solely on the alternation between styles of policy making would be to miss the element of trend, however. For the switch to NERP also exhibited a process of learning. The key element in this trend was the growth of a conviction that the government itself was a major source of Zambia's economic difficulties.

The very process by which NERP was formulated promoted economic learning. The program was devised in a way that encouraged both self-appraisal and a sense of professional competence within Zambia's nascent technocracy. In the political turmoil following the Copperbelt riots, the president requested the secretary to the cabinet to assemble a team that would provide him with economic advice independent of that coming from the international agencies – and the ministries that worked in close concert with them. The secretary to the cabinet recruited economists from the university and the research unit of the Party; he also contacted economists in the bureaucracy whom he knew well and trusted. And he empowered them, through the authority of the Office of the President, to call upon the resources of every branch of government and to summon any officer of the government before them.

The committee launched upon a comprehensive review of the economic reforms. It examined each of its premises. How elastic would be the supply response of copper to a depreciation of the kwacha? How about imports; how much would they decline? How competitive was the market facing firms in key industries? Would these firms be compelled to lower prices or would they simply reap monopoly rents if prices were decontrolled? Bringing in permanent secretaries, senior economists, and managers of parastatal firms, the committee virtually commissioned a seminar on the state of the economy under the reforms, and produced the New Economic Recovery Program in response.

That the process promoted learning is shown in the objectives of NERP: it called for structural adjustment in the Zambian economy. The process of learning is also reflected in the fundamental reappraisal of the sources of inflation. Rather than seeing inflation as resulting from the depreciation of the exchange rate, the policy planners in NERP attributed it to excessive spending by government.[94] Reductions in government spending; cuts in subsidies; retrenchment in public employment – calls for these measures had traditionally come from the business classes, isolated in such politically peripheral institutions as parliament. They now originated among the economic policy makers who worked within the shelter of the Party.

NERP therefore manifested an oddly ambivalent attitude toward government: strongly interventionist on the one hand, it was highly conservative on the other. Even while shifting to command and control instruments, the government, under NERP, vigorously cut back on public spending.

The new policy was successful in curbing the highly inflationary increase in primary liquidity of the late auction phase. The revaluation to a fixed rate ended the Bank of Zambia's dealing losses. Having lost K112 million per month in the last nine months of the auction, losses fell to K12 million per month in the next 18 months[95] (see table 9.3). Budgetary retrenchment brought down the rate of increase in the government's domestic liabilities (primary liquidity). Over the 18 months from April 1987, primary liquidity generated by the budget deficit increased at an annual rate of 50 percent. During the last nine months of the auction the annualized rate of increase had been 76 percent (see table 9.3, column 4). The combination of greater fiscal rectitude and the staunching of Bank of Zambia losses considerably slowed the growth of total primary liquidity to an annualized rate of 40 percent from the 141 percent in the last nine months of the auction. Inflation during the period broadly followed the growth of primary liquidity, the annualized rate being 48 percent. This was a substantial anti-inflationary achievement. This was achieved largely by reduction in recurrent expenditure. An indication of this is the change in real government consumption. Having declined fairly steadily at 3 percent per annum during 1980–5, it had risen by 1 percent between 1985 and 1986. Between 1986 and 1988 it declined by 29 percent. The post-auction government proved itself willing to implement really savage decisions.

In the short run, the New Economic Recovery Program not only succeeded in reducing inflation; it targeted its benefits to the urban poor. In May 1987 price controls were extended from mealie-meal to a further eleven goods (blankets; wheat flour, bread, and buns; salt; candles; baby food; soft drinks; sugar; batteries; cooking oil; soap and detergents; paraffin). These eleven goods (as estimated from the 1985 survey where we identify only seven of them) accounted for 16.2 percent of squatter consumption, 15.2 percent of township and low-income urban consumption, and 13.0 percent of high-income urban consumption. Note that whereas the mealie-meal price was kept low by subsidy, which reduced the market-clearing price, the other eleven were kept low merely by price control, which reduced the price below the market-clearing level. The result was the erosion of the benefits of price controls over time, as goods became increasingly scarce at official prices. Initially, however, the program secured a reduction in prices for consumer essentials.

One measure of the effectiveness of these measures was the decreasing level of labor unrest (table 9.6). A second measure was UNIP's success in the 1988 election: the president was returned to power with his normal majority, and there was little reduction in the turnout of voters. Over the longer run, however, NERP failed. When more goods were added to the list of price-controlled items, the incidence of the benefits of the program became regressive. Over the course of a year price controls were gradually extended to a further ten items. The ten goods (of which we observe six) had a share in consumption of 12.4 percent for high-income urban households, 10.9 percent for the townships, 9.2 percent for lower-income urban, and only 7.1 percent for squatter households. Taken together, the net effect of the price controls on the 22 goods became distributionally neutral within urban areas; their share of total consumption (including subsistence which accounts for around a tenth of consumption in urban areas) ranged from 28.9 percent in high-income urban households to 37.3 percent in the squatter households.[96] Supposing that by mid–1988 controls had halved the prices of controlled goods relative to their counterfactual levels and that all consumers were able to purchase at these prices, then the totality of controls would have narrowed the per capita consumption differential between high-income urban and squatter households from 2.48:1 as of 1985 to 2.40:1.[97]

In addition, following the elections, the government revised upward the price of mealie-meal, raising it sixfold (in two stages) between late 1988

Table 9.6   Industrial disputes involving loss of man-working days

	Total disputes	Number of man-days lost	Number of workers directly involved
January/December 1987	80	19,437	154,325
July/December 1987	0	1,296	2,044

Source: Republic of Zambia (1988a, p. 63).

and mid-1989. In compensation, it introduced a system of coupons entitling the holder to limited purchases of cheap food. Initially this was based on an honesty system and coupons were allocated to anyone who applied. This system was later replaced by workplace allocation to those earning under K20,000 per annum. A survey of low income areas during 1988 in Lusaka, Kitwe, Livingstone, and Kasama enables us to assess the intraurban distributional impact of this system. The survey found that most adults were outside formal sector employment; only 19 percent of those in the labor force were in the formal sector. Because of the greater propensity of these people to be household heads, a higher proportion of heads, 38 percent, were formal-sector employees. The majority 62 percent of households were almost entirely unrepresented in the formal sector. Wage income accounted for only 2 percent of total income for these households and they probably earned this income in the informal sector where mean wages were slightly less than half those for the formal-sector wage employees.[98] Some 22 percent of households earned below K250 per month. Of these, only 11 percent were headed by a formal-sector employee and 89 percent were not.[99] It therefore appears that by being targeted on formal-sector wage earners, the coupon system was almost completely missing the poorest quarter of urban households. The policy of raising the maize price but compensating with coupons was therefore regressive in the urban context.

Surveys in low-cost and squatter urban housing areas conducted in 1975 and 1988 permit a long-term comparison of incomes. This yields the result that by 1988 real per capita incomes for this group had fallen by 39 percent. Recall that for the period 1975–85 per capita consumption in squatter areas and townships had fallen by 22 percent and 30 percent, respectively. If consumption fell broadly in line with income, this implies that between 1985 and 1988 there was a further decline.

Not only did the government alter the mix of goods whose prices it controlled in a way that rendered its policies regressive; it was unable fully to enforce price controls at the retail level. The result was growing public sentiment against the government, as goods were increasingly sold at market-clearing prices.

In response, there arose a pattern of political conflict whose dynamics are wholly traceable to the economics of price control. Constituting virtual monopolies, many state industries invested few resources in marketing. They produced goods in inappropriate "sizes" – 200-lb bags of mealie-meal, drums of cooking oil, etc. – which they delivered to warehouses. Because of shortages of spare parts or other problems, they delivered these goods at irregular intervals. In the face of recurrent shortages and irregular deliveries, wholesalers held large cash balances; they remained highly liquid in order to purchase goods when they became available. They then converted stocks of cash into inventories to be purchased by retailers. One of the major tasks of the retailers was to transform the large units sold by the state into small units that consumers could afford. In so doing, they also transformed them into units that the government found difficult to measure: cups of mealie meal or bottles of cooking oil. In this way, they avoided price controls.

Political conflicts arose at each step in the marketing chain. The Party feared the reaction of the masses should the state-owned monopolies make large profits. This fear helps to account for its insistence on the imposition of regulated prices. As it became known that the retailers kept large cash balances, the masses, responding to their own falling incomes, reacted in anger; their rage was exacerbated by the foreign origin of the retailers, many of whom were Indian, Lebanese, or Greek. In the face of shortages of consumer items, people were outraged when they discovered that some wholesalers possessed large inventories while others experienced shortages; they attributed the shortages of the one to hoarding by the others. And the government and the Party often attacked the retailers for avoiding price controls. Controversies thus stormed about every step in the marketing system and helped to undermine confidence in the control program, and in the government that administered it.

Pressures to alter the program also mounted from abroad. In response to the government's termination of a market-oriented program and to its suspension of (unlimited) debt repayment, the international agencies and bilateral donors suspended their lending programs. Projects that had been under way continued; but no new projects were approved. As in other African countries, the government of Zambia depended upon international aid for its capital budget. As the virtual end of gross foreign lending became a realistic prospect (so that the net position would become substantially negative), the government was compelled to assimilate the implications of the fact that it could not purchase new rolling stock for the railways; repair its power plants; build roads; refurbish its mines; or repair its schools. While at the outset of NERP it had bravely announced that Zambia would "grow from its own resources," the government now confronted the costs of having to do so.

Shifts in the distributional impact of its programs and controversies over the implications of its control schemes thus undermined domestic political support for NERP. And the prospect of the virtual termination of foreign assistance spurred a reappraisal of the program. In the short run, NERP had worked, and it had been popular; in the longer run, it did not appear viable, either economically or politically. The timing of the benefits and costs of NERP rendered it politically useful; the government used it to contest, and to triumph in, the 1988 elections. But soon after the elections, it began to abandon the program and to adopt policy reforms that would, once again, enable it to quality for foreign lending.

In mid–1989, the government began dismantling the control regime. The price of maize meal was raised threefold, reducing the costs of the maize subsidy. The government recruited a new governor for the Central Bank and gave him the power to raise interest rates, to limit government borrowing, and to depreciate the kwacha to a more realistic rate of exchange. The exchange rate depreciated from K8 to K40 per dollar and the bank restored the scheme for own-funded imports. As shown in table 9.4, for the first time the donors provided a significant net inflow of support. In addition, the government began to dismantle price controls. The first to be removed was that on cigarettes. This price control had been regressive, the highest share of consumption being for high-income urban households (the share being about a third higher than in squatter house-holds). All the remaining controls were then removed except for the mealie-meal subsidy. This sequence of the accumulation and decumulation of price controls thus displayed a consistent pattern. The highest priority was given to a very progressive subsidy. The first bout of price controls was mildly progressive, the further bout mildly regressive. The regressive controls were removed first, then the mildly progressive ones, leaving in place until last the highly progressive one: that on mealie-meal. In June 1990, the government again doubled the price of mealie-meal. It did so to avoid having to increase the level of subsidy, in light of increased production costs brought on by increases in the costs of fertilizers.

The government had adopted command and control procedures to gain control over the allocation of resources and thereby to purchase political support. In so doing, it had also revealed a capacity to learn. It had learned, for example, that inflation was caused by "financial indiscipline" on its own part. But the citizens also revealed a capacity to learn. In response to the price rise in maize meal, the people again rioted. But while the food riots of December 1986 had focused on the price of maize, those in June 1990 focused on the political system itself. The rioters attacked the Party and the single-party system. They identified the political system as the source of their economic woes.[100]

6   CONCLUSION

This chapter has attempted both to describe and to explain the economic policies adopted by the government of Zambia following the sharp downturn in its terms of trade in the mid–1970s.

A major thesis of this paper has been that political structures introduced a systematic pattern of bias in economic policy making. As producers, people were marginalized in the political system; organized producer interests were largely excluded from the structure of power. The economic interests that counted were those of consumers in the urban townships. The result was a political bias that defended immediate consumption at the expense of longer-run growth.

This pattern of policy making was, of course, not sustainable in the long run. The domestic interests that first stressed this reality – business and labor – lacked political influence, and their lack of power undermined the degree to which the political system possessed a capacity for self-correction. Rather, it was external interests that had access to the highest levels of power, i.e., the president, and therefore could exert pressure in favor of policy reform. These were the institutions that held Zambia's external debt.

Within Zambia, a small cadre of technocrats sought to restructure the economy in ways that would instill incentives to adapt and adjust to the new economic realities. These technocrats were lodged within the financial institutions of the government. Technocrats lack wealth and power, however; to be effective, they therefore require political protection. In the context of Zambian politics, this meant that the president had to shelter them from the pressures of the Party and to yield to them control over economic policy. In its most extreme form, this act of delegation requires the technocrats themselves to allow the decentralized decisions of individuals to govern the allocation of resources, with the technocrats controlling only gross aggregates in an effort to shape the performance of markets. Such a pattern of policy making – one that entailed the delegation of allocational decisions to the market – was tried briefly in Zambia, but was rejected.

The immediate source of the failure was a shift of the political superintendence of the market from technocrats lodged in financial institutions to those with close ties to the Party. It would be mistaken to attribute the collapse of the market to "political interference," however. For all markets exist within political environments; the essence of the problem is rather the nature of that environment and the incentives that operate within it. Economic actors in Zambia realized that the incentives that operated within the Party were such that it would seek to overturn the allocational decisions generated by the market. Metaphorically, the market equilibrium did not correspond to the political equilibrium. The market called for a depreciation of the exchange rate; the political forces dominating the Party linked this outcome to an erosion in the real value of their incomes and to an unfavorable distribution of wealth and thus to a possible loss of political power.

There existed political forces in Zambia that welcomed the market and that benefited from it: farmers, businessmen, and those who drew incomes from employment in their enterprises. But these productive forces of Zambia's economy stood at the margins of the polity. They were not lodged in the Party, which constituted the system's core. And they therefore could not provide a political defense for this experiment with the introduction of the market.

APPENDIX 9.1

AN ESTIMATE OF THE ERROR INTRODUCED INTO THE CONSUMER PRICE INDEX BY PRICE CONTROLS

The CPI is based on expenditure shares as found in the household budget survey of 1975, a time which predates binding price controls. By the 1980s price controls gave rise to shortages and a black market for those goods whose prices were regulated. The CPI did not include black market prices. That part of the index made up by price-controlled items was estimated at official prices and at precontrol expenditure shares. This tends to bias downwards the official estimate of inflation during price controls and, conversely, exaggerate it when the controls are removed. Table 9.7 makes an indirect estimate of this. It compares two estimates of changes in per capita real private consumption. One (row 15) derives from nominal consumption deflated by the CPI. The other (row 14) derives from constant-price GDP, imports minus exports at constant prices, and the share of private consumption in expenditure. In the price-control period prior to the auction (1985) the CPI-based estimate consistently yields a slightly higher figure for the growth in real consumption. This is consistent with the hypothesis that it understated inflation. In 1985 and 1986 when the de facto price control was lifted, the discrepancy is reversed substantially: the CPI appears to exaggerate inflation. In 1987–9 when the controls were reintroduced, the discrepancy is again reversed.

Table 9.7   Two estimates of trends in living standards

	1980	1981	1982	1983	1984	1985	1986	1987	1988	1989
(1)	1995.8	2118.9	2059.3	2018.8	2011.5	2044.5	2059.3	2250.1	2247.1	2250.1
(2)	77.7	44.4	-173.2	-183.7	-153.9	-62.6	-10.9	35.5	64.1	231.5
(3)	2073.5	2163.3	1886.1	1835.1	1857.6	1981.9	2048.4	2149.8	2311.2	2481.6
(4)	55.2	64.9	64.4	63.3	56.4	60.7	50.5	59.8	66.0	75.8
(5)	1144.6	1404.0	1214.6	1161.6	1047.7	1203.0	1034.4	1285.6	1525.4	1881.1
(6)	1.541	1.656	1.909	2.342	2.706	3.798	7.729	11.677	12.138	22.708
(7)	100	1.074	1.239	1.509	1.756	2.456	5.016	7.578	7.877	14.736
(8)	100	1.142	1.284	1.534	1.843	2.532	3.838	5.491	8.542	18.408
(9)	100	1.062	1.036	1.017	1.049	1.027	0.765	0.725	1.084	1.249
(10)	1144.6	1322.0	1172.4	1142.2	998.8	1171.4	1352.2	1773.2	1407.22	1505.9
(11)	100	115.5	102.4	99.8	87.3	102.3	118.1	154.9	122.9	131.6
(12)	100	117.1	106.4	102.3	89.1	100.2	100.9	127.2	144.1	144.3
(13)	100	103.3	106.7	110.4	114.4	118.5	122.6	127.5	132.3	131.4
(14)	100	111.8	95.9	90.4	76.3	86.3	96.1	121.5	92.9	95.8
(15)	100	113.4	99.7	92.2	77.9	84.6	82.1	99.8	108.9	105.0
(16)	0	-1.4	-3.2	-2.5	-2.1	+2.0	+17.1	-21.7	-14.7	-8.8

(1) Gross domestic production at 1977 prices; (2) Imports minus exports at 1977 prices; (3) Absorption; (4) Private consumption as a percentage of absorption at current prices; (5) Private consumption at constant real prices; (6) Deflator for expenditure other than private consumption 1977 = 100; (7) 6 indexed to 1980 = 100; (8) Consumer Price Index 1980 = 100; (9) The relative price of private consumption to other absorption; (10) Private consumption adjusting for the change in the relative price of private consumption to other absorption; (11) Index of 10 i.e. adjusted private consumption index 1980 = 100; (12) Private consumption deflated by the Consumer Price Index; (13) Population index; (14) Per capita real private consumption derived from quantities series; (15) Per capita real private consumption derived from deflating the nominal series; (16) CPI error.

Sources and derivations:
(1) *National Accounts Bulletin*. 2 (NA2) 1988 table 3 for 1980–4; *National Accounts Statistics Bulletin* 3 (NA3) 1990, table 3 for 1985–9.
(2) Imports minus exports at 1977 prices: NA2, table 5.0; NA3, table 5.0.
(3) (1) + (2).
(4) (At current prices) NA2, table 4.1; NA3, table 4.1.
(5) (3) x (4)/100.
(6) The deflator for the sum of government final consumption gross fixed capital formation and the increase in stocks is derived by dividing their current price values by their constant price values at 1977 prices. Tables 4.0 and 5.0 NA2. Tables 4.0 and 5.0 NA3.
(7) (6) indexed to 1980 = 100.
(8) From IMF data tapes except for 1988/89 which is the increase in the unweighted average of the Higher Income CPI and the Lower Income COP from *Consumer Price Statistics*, vol. 31.
(9) (8)/(7).
(10) [(5)/(9)] × 100.
(11) Index of (10), 1980 = 100.
(12) Private consumption at current prices from NA2 and NA3, table 4, deflated by (8).
(13) From IMF data tapes.
(14) [(11)/(13)] × 100.
(15) [(12)/(13)] × 100.

Chart 1 Chronology

Oct. 1962	Self-government under UNIP/ANC coalition
Oct. 1964	Independence under a UNIP government
Nov. 1965	Unilateral declaration of independence by Rhodesia
Aug. 1967	Contested elections to UNIP Central Committee
Apr. 1968	Mulungushi economic reforms. Government forms INDECO state industries
Aug. 1968	United Party banned
Aug. 1969	Metero economic reforms – government purchases 51 percent shares of mining corporations
Aug. 1971	United Progressive Party formed
Dec. 1972	United Progressive Party banned
Dec. 1972	Legislation passes making possible formation of one-party state
Aug. 1973	Second Republic inaugurated with one-party state
Dec. 1973	First one-party elections
1974	Beginning of copper price fall
1977	Dissidents organize within UNIP opposed to government's economic management
1977	Parliamentary Select Committee Report on economy: Kaunda addresses emergency meeting of National Assembly on the economy
Jan. 1978	Austerity budget
Dec. 1978	National elections
Oct. 1980	Coup attempt: business and labor involved
Jan. 1981	Government expulsion of labor leaders
Oct. 1981	Treason trials begin, following 1980 coup
Apr. 1983	IMF standby loan
May 1983	IDA/World Bank loan. Paris club re-scheduling
Oct./Dec. 1983	National elections
Jan. 1984	IMF standby facility sought
Oct. 1985	Economic reforms, including auction
Apr. 1986	New economic team
Dec. 1986	Copperbelt riots
Jan./Mar. 1987	Labor unrest
May 1987	Break with IMF. New Economic Recovery Program: reimposition of controls
Sep. 1987	Resumption of discussions with IMF and World Bank
Dec. 1988	National elections
Dec. 1988	Appointment of new head of Central Bank

NOTES

The research for this chapter was supported by a generous grant from the Ford Foundation to the Program in Political Economy, Duke University. Bates received additional support from the National Science Foundation (NSF Grant Number SES 8821151) and Collier support from the Institute of Economics and Statistics, University of Oxford. The research was conducted under the auspices of the Institute for African Studies of the University of Zambia. We wish to express our gratitude to Ms Ilse Mwanza, Research Affiliation Office, and Professor Oliver Saasa, Director of the Institute, while absolving them of all responsibility for the content of this paper. We also wish to thank the many officials of the government and Party, as well as the many persons in private life and in the international development community, who contributed to this project. Lastly, we wish to express our thanks to Clark Gibson, Daniel Gabaldon, Charles Harvey, and Janine Aron for their research assistance, to Richard L. Sklar, and to D. Michael Shafer for the generosity with which he shared his knowledge of contemporary Zambia. We would like to thank Vijay Joshi, Anne O. Krueger, Michael Shafer, and Susan Shirk for their comments on an earlier draft.

1   Mueller (1989) provides a standard account of this literature.
2   For historical treatments see Barber (1961), Gann (1964), Rotberg (1965), Mulford (1967), and Roberts (1976). See also the useful recent overview by Burdette (1988).
3   For histories of the growth of the Copperbelt and industrial Zambia, see Barber (1961), Gann (1964), Baldwin (1966), Davis (1969), and Coleman (1971).
4   Figures taken from World Bank (1983).
5   Excluding Nigeria; with Nigeria, the figure would have been 33 percent. Data from World Bank (1989).
6   Figures taken from World Bank (1983).
7   As argued by Anne Krueger (personal communication), Zambia's economic decline cannot be attributed solely to external shocks. The policies adopted by the government protracted the pain of adjustment and increased the costs. While triggered by shifts in the terms of trade, Zambia's economic crisis was thus exacerbated by inappropriate policies, and we devote much of this essay to the analysis of the origins and contents of these policy commitments.
8   For details of calculations see Collier (1990).
9   This is consistent with the data presented in Odegaard (1986) on aggregate crop sales. Between 1975 and 1985 the real producer price for agricultural output declined by 1.6 percent and marketed quantities increased by 38.7 percent. Hence, real crop income per capita would have declined by 4 percent (i.e. the same as consumption) had the rural population increased by 2.7 percent p.a., which is within the credible range of estimates of actual rural population growth.
10   Figures for 1980; they are taken from Central Statistical Office (1984).
11   We write in the past tense, not only because we are reviewing events that transpired in the 1980s, but also because, at the time of writing, the political system that prevailed at that time is being vigorously and profoundly chal-

lenged. As this volume moves to press, Zambia has become a multiparty democracy and UNIP a minority, opposition party; and Zambia is governed by a party based on the Copperbelt.

12 For details, see *Programme for the Ceremonial Opening of Parliament* (Lusaka: Government Printer, 15 June 1988); *The Constitution of the United National Independence Party*, supplement to the Republic of Zambia Government Gazette dated November 4, 1988 (Lusaka: Government Printer, 1990).

13 Voting in elections to the local government was restricted to members of UNIP. The ward unit in the Party constituted the unit of representation in the local government. To become a councillor in the local government, one had but to become the chairman of one's ward in UNIP. See Mijere (1988).

14 *Times of Zambia*, December 31, 1985.

15 In the last years of the Second Republic, the Central Committee expanded to forty or so members; in addition, it became stratified, with an elite group, called the Committee of Chairmen, being given the executive powers formerly held by the entire Central Committee.

16 Albeit some of them in learning grades.

17 Excellent discussions of the role of the President are contained in Ollawa (1979) and Gertzel et al. (1984). See also contributions in Tordoff (1980) and Woldring (1984).

18 See Gann (1964) and Baldwin (1966). See also Palmer and Parsons (1977) and Arrighi (1973).

   For purposes of brevity, this discussion leaves out an analysis of the Central African Federation and of the alliance between the settler parties of Northern and Southern Rhodesia. A fuller analysis would amplify the points made herein, but at the cost of adding unnecessary detail.

19 Calculated from figures in Dodge (1977). See also Roberts and Elliott (1971). The assumption is that urban consumption is met entirely by maize sold through official marketing channels.

20 See Allan et al. (1948) and Anthony and Uchendu (1970).

21 The best study remains Mulford (1967).

22 Baylies and Szeftel (1982).

23 See, for example, Mwanaumo (1987), Republic of Zambia (1989a, b).

   It should be recognized that a large part of the subsidy generated by the policy of uniform national prices also went to Northern Province, a region that, while voting for UNIP, was nonetheless politically suspect following the creation of the United Political Party (see below).

24 The best treatment remains Beveridge and Oberschall (1979).

25 See *Africa Confidential*, May 21, 1980: October 29, 1980; April 10, 1985. See also *The Economist Intelligence Unit, Zambia*, No. 4, November 21, 1988, pp.7ff.

26 See Southall (1980), and Baylies (1982), and Baylis and Szeftel (1982).

27 The voluminous literature on the trade union movement would include Epstein (1958), Zelniker (1970), Bates (1971), Berger (1974), Harries-Jones (1975), Mwendapole (1977), Daniel (1979), Prapart (1983), and Meebelo (1971, 1986). See also Tangri (1985).

28 This was in major part a consequence of colonial policy. Industrialists and moderate labor leaders, with the active backing of the colonial government,

purged the unions of political militants.

29 See, for example, the discussion in Mijere (1988).
30 See the figures in Ministry of Labour, *Draft Annual Report for the Year 1984* (Lusaka: Ministry of Labour, 1985), typescript.
31 For the electoral geography of Zambia in the First Republic, see the contributions in Davies (1971).
32 For details, see the contributions in Tordoff (1974).
33 For details of this crucial election, see Bates (1976), Ollawa (1979), and Burdette (1988).
34 Western Province contained Barotse, a kingdom long administered by the British independently of the rest of Northern Rhodesia and abruptly merged with the rest of the territory at the time of independence. In Zambia's international conflicts with South Africa and Portugal, Western Province – because of its physical location and economic ties with Southern Africa – bore a disproportion of the costs. For further details see Gertzel et al. (1984). See also Molteno (1974), Tordoff and Scott (1974), and Molteno and Scott (1974).
35 See Molteno (1974). Lusaka was made Zambia's ninth province in the 1970s.
36 Wina (1985).
37 See Szeftel (1982).
38 In addition to the references above, see as well Molteno (1972) and Scott (1978).
39 See Cameron (1984), Lange and Garrett (1985), and Garrett and Lange (1986). See also Olson (1982).
40 See the discussion in *Africa Confidential*, January 8, 1987; January 18, 1988; September 23, 1988; May 4, 1990; *Africa Contemporary Record*, 87–8, B. 823.
41 See ZIMCO, *Zambia Industrial and Mining Corporation Limited Annual Report*, various years, Young (1973), Wimwinga (1977), Johns (1980), Turok (1981), and Tangri (1984).
42 Interviews, July 1990. ZIMCO, *Zambia Industrial and Mining Corporation Limited Annual Reports* (various years).
43 Voting in local government elections was restricted to members of UNIP. See Mijere (1988).
44 Of Zambia's nine provinces, the highly urbanized Copperbelt least supported the candidacy of the sitting president. In the 1988 elections, for example, it provided more than one standard deviation fewer votes for Kaunda. Figures from Republic of Zambia, *Presidential and Parliamentary General Election Results, 1988*, file copy from the Office of Elections.
45 Based on an analysis of the data contained in Republic of Zambia (1988b).
46 See also Mijere (1988).
47 It is relevant to note that many of the UNIP officials were themselves marketeers.
48 For a discussion of the relationship between the party and urban markets, see materials in Bates (1976), Beveridge and Oberschall (1979), and Mijere (1988).
49 The best discussion is in Gertzel et al. (1984). See also Tordoff (1977).
50 See, for example, the Parliamentary critique of government policy contained in the Select Committee Report of 1977. Ollawa (1979, pp. 266ff), Gertzel et al. (1984, pp. 73–4), and Burdette (1988, pp. 140ff.). See also Tordoff (1977),

Southall (1980), Baylies (1982), and Baylies and Szeftel (1982).

51 *Africa Confidential*, November 3, 1978.

52 Sikota Wina, "An Open Letter to the Fifth National Convention being held in Lusaka, March 14–16, 1990," typescript, p. 7.

53 For details of UNIP's international organization, see Republic of Zambia, *The Constitution of the United National Independence Party*, Tordoff and Scott (1974), Ollawa (1979), Gertzel et al. (1984), and Chikulo (1988).

54 Further highlighting the Party's lack of external accountability was the way in which it secured finances. Prior to the introduction of the single-party system, the Party had to compete for funds; the sale of membership cards constituted a major source of its finances. After the movement to the single-party system, Party leaders were reluctant to sell additional memberships; for recruiting new members would only bring into UNIP former political enemies. Instead, the Party, which now held a monopoly of access to the public sector, imposed a tax on it. It levied fees from government office holders; the lists of those liable for such payments is contained in the Party's constitution. And it secured a subvention from the government which it controlled; the amount is contained in the same budget category as that for the defense forces and so is not amenable to public scrutiny. See Republic of Zambia, *The Constitution of the United National Independence Party* and Scott (1982).

55 The official ideology was Humanism. See Kaunda (1984). The version presented in the text represents a reconstruction of the mind set of the top Central Committee members, as revealed in their public statements.

56 See Gertzel et al. (1984, pp. 90ff). See also Markakis and Curry (1976/77).

57 The content of the report of the select committee is described in Ollawa (1979, pp. 266ff), Gertzel et al. (1984, pp. 73–4, 85–6), and Burdette (1988, pp. 10ff). For an excellent discussion, see *Africa Confidential*, May 13, 1977 and October 21, 1977.

58 See, for example, the attacks on Parliament reported in The Economist Intelligence Unit, *Zambia*, Number 2, May 26, 1988 and Number 3, August 1, 1988.

59 A good source on the history of negotiations between the international agencies and the government is World Bank (1986). See also Wood (1990).

60 Interviews, June 1988 and July 1990.

61 For details of this calculation, see Collier (1990).

62 Interviews, July 1990. See as well the discussion in World Bank (1986, 1987).

63 Currency in circulation is the annual average of monthly figures as reported in the *Monthly Digest of Statistics*, and private consumption from the National Accounts. The trend rate of increase in the velocity during 1971–81 was 3.1 percent per annum.

64 $1.76/1.34 = 1.31$.

65 This inference is supported by the subsequent rapid deceleration in the recorded CPI. Whereas over the first six months of the auction recorded annualized inflation had been 96 percent, in the next six months it fell to only 9 percent.

66 See the report on the study of the auction by the Zambia Congress of Trade Unions in *The Times of Zambia*, October 7 and 15, 1985.

67 See, for example, the lead editorials in *The Times of Zambia*, December 8, 1985 and March 24, 1986.

68   *Zambia Daily Mail*, November 8, 1985.
69   *Zambia Daily Mail*, April 22, 1986.
70   *Zambia Daily Mail*, October 17, 1986.
71   This is the sector which had the greatest capacity to stockpile imports.
72   Orlowski (1989) attributes an even larger proportion of the growth of primary liquidity to Bank of Zambia losses.
73   There can be no doubt, however, that the donors gave less than they pledged, nor that there were delays in donor contributions. Nor can there be any doubt that these facts were specifically true of funds pledged to supply the auction. Nonetheless, as our calculations suggest, the aggregate contribution of donors offset the repayment of debt, and the precipitate depreciation of the kwacha therefore arose from the demand side, not the supply side of the foreign exchange market. Insights into problems with the reliability of donor payments have were garnered from interviews with multi- and bilateral aid agencies, July 1990.
74   Allsopp et al. (1989).
75   In 1987, ZIMCO paid dividends for the first time in 11 years. The profits originate principally from the mining sector, but the nonmining firms earned profits as well. See *Times of Zambia*, January 9, 1987. Interviews with officers of ZIMCO, July 1990.
76   See the list included in the speech by the President, *Zambia Daily Mail*, August 27, 1986. See also the list of new requests to import contained in Ministry of Labour, *Annual Report of the Year 1986* (Lusaka: Ministry of Labour, 1987), typescript.
77   *Zambia Daily Mail*, August 27, 1986.
78   The directors of mining companies have put forward the thesis that the depreciation of the exchange rate generated only short-term gains, because of the import intensitivity of production. The benefits from devaluation were precisely countered, they claimed, by the rising price of inputs. There is simply no support for this view in the figures that we examined (ZCCM was, as shown in table 9.2, column 1, consistently a massive net seller of foreign exchange): but it is articulated nonetheless. The propagation of this myth reveals the extent of the political emasculation of the economic interests of the export-orientated firms in the state sector.
79   See Olson (1971).
80   Extensive interviews convinced us that Zambia is not a kleptocracy on the model of, say, neighbouring Zaire. Rather, standards of public service remain strong, in spite of the financial hardships resulting from the erosion of the value of salaries in the public service.
81   Allsopp et al. (1989).
82   Young and Loxley (1990).
83   Republic of Zambia (1990, p. 13).
84   Interviews, July 1990.
85   Being uncertain concerning the specifics of government policy, many also stopped the production of maize meal. In particular, many were uncertain as to how they would collect their payments for the subsidized portion of their production. There have been many studies of maize policy in Zambia. Among the best are Levi (1987), Jansen (1988), Kydd (1988), Republic of Zambia (1990), and Wood (1990).
86   *Times of Zambia*, January 14, 1987; February 1, 1987.

87 *Times of Zambia*, January 3, 1987; March 16, 1987.
88 *Times of Zambia*, January 21, 1978.
89 The president was referring to insurgent groups in the neighboring nations of Angola and Mozambique. *Times of Zambia*, April 4, 1987.
90 The phrase is taken from Republic of Zambia (1987a, p. 5).
91 Republic of Zambia (1987b).
92 Republic of Zambia (1987c).
93 Republic of Zambia (1988).
94 Interviews, July 1990.
95 End April 1987 – end September 1988.
96 The impact of the differentials between high-income urban households and lower-income and township households would have been negligible.
97 A halving of price would raise real incomes by half of the share of controlled goods in expenditure: e.g., a benefit of 14.9 percent for high-income urban households, and 18.6 percent for squatters.
98 Note that since the latter were only surveyed in low-income residential areas, this considerably understates mean wage income in the formal sector.
99 This does not allow for differences in household size. We only know that on average households in the informal sector were three-quarters the size of those in the formal sector. However, it seems improbable that such a large difference in the incidence of households below K250 per month can be fully accounted for by differences in household size.
100 See *The Times* (London), June 26, 1990; June 29, 1990. This chapter was written prior to the fall of UNIP and the end of the single-party system.

REFERENCES

Allan, W., Gluckman, M. Peters, D. U. and Trapnell, C. G. 1948: *Land Holding and Land Usage Among the Plateau Tonga of Mazabuka District*, Rhodes-Livingstone Paper No. 14, Capetown: Oxford University Press.

Allsopp, C., Joshi, V. and Mistry, P. 1989: *Zambia: Exchange Rate Policy*, Stockholm: SIDA.

Anthony, K.R.M. and Uchendu, V. C. 1970: *Agricultural Change in Mazabuka District, Zambia*, Stanford: Food Research Institute of Stanford University.

Arrighi, G. 1973: "Labour Supplies in Comparative Perspective," in G. Arrighi and J. S. Saul (eds.), *Essays on the Political Economy of Africa*, New York and London: Monthly Review Press.

Baldwin, R.E. 1966: *Economic Development and Export Growth: A Study of Northern Rhodesia 1920–1960*, Berkeley and Los Angeles: University of California Press.

Barber, W.J. 1961: *The Economy of British Central Africa*, London: Oxford University Press.

Bates, R. H. 1971: *Unions, Parties and Political Development*, New Haven and London: Yale University Press.

Bates, R.H. 1976: *Rural Responses to Industrialisation*, New Haven: Yale University Press.

Baylies, C.L. 1982: "Zambia's Economic Reforms and their Aftermath: The State and the Growth of Indigenous Capital," *The Journal of Commonwealth and Comparative Politics*, 20 (3), 235–63.

Baylies, C.L. and Szeftel, M. 1982: "The Rise of a Zambian Capitalist Class in the 1970s," *Journal of Southern African Studies*, 8 (2), 187–213.

Berger, E.L. 1974: *Labour, Race and Colonial Rule*, Oxford: Oxford University Press.

Beveridge, A.A. and Oberschall, A. R. 1979: *African Businessmen and Development in Zambia*, Princeton: Princeton University Press.

Burdette, M.M. 1988: *Zambia: Between Two Worlds*, Boulder, CO: Westview.

Cameron, D. 1984: "Social Democracy, Corporatism, Labour Quiescence, and the Representation of Economic Interests in Advanced Capitalist Society," in J. Goldthorpe (ed.), *Order and Conflict in Contemporary Capitalism*, New York: Oxford University Press.

Central Statistical Office 1984: *Monthly Digest of Statistics*, 20 (10–11), Lusaka: Central Statistical Office.

Chikulo, B.C. 1988: "The Impact of Elections in Zambia's One Party Second Republic," *Africa Today*, 2nd quarter, 37–9.

Coleman, F.L. 1971: *The Northern Rhodesia Copperbelt 1892–1962*, Manchester: Manchester University Press.

Collier, P. 1990: "Maize Consumption and Real Living Standards," mimeo, Oxford: Centre for the Study of African Economies.

Daniel, P. 1979: *Africanization, Nationalism and Inequality: Mining Labour and the Copperbelt in Zambian Development*, Cambridge: Cambridge University Press.

Davies, H. (ed.) 1971: *Zambia in Maps*, London: University of London Press.

Davis, M.J. (ed.) 1969: *Modern Industry and the African*, 2nd edn, New York: Negro Universities Press.

Dodge, D.J. 1977: *Agricultural Policy and Performance in Zambia*, Berkeley and Los Angeles: Institute of International Studies, University of California.

Epstein, A.L. 1958: *Politics in an Urban African Community*, Manchester: Manchester University Press.

Gann, L.H. 1964: *A History of Northern Rhodesia: Early Days to 1953*, London: Chatto and Windus.

Garrett, G. and Lange, P. 1986: "Performance in a Hostile World," *World Politics*, 38, 517–45.

Gertzel, C., Baylies, C. and Szeftel, M. (eds.) 1984: *The Dynamics of the One-Party State in Zambia*, Manchester: Manchester University Press.

Harries-Jones, P. 1975: *Freedom and Labour*, New York: St. Martin's Press.

Jansen, D. 1988: *Trade, Exchange Rates and Agricultural Pricing Policies in Zambia*, Washington, DC: World Bank.

Johns, S. 1980: "The Parastatal Sector," in W. Tordoff (ed.), *Administration in Zambia*, Manchester: Manchester University Press.

Kaunda, K.D. 1974: *Humanism in Zambia: a Guide to its Implementation. Parts I and II*, Lusaka: Government Printer.

Kydd, J. 1988: "Zambia," in C. Harvey (ed.), *Agricultural Pricing Policy in Africa*, London: MacMillan.

Lange, P. and Garrett, G. 1985: "The Politics of Growth: Strategic Interaction and Economic Performance in Advanced Industrial Democracies, 1974–1980," *Journal of Politics*, 47, 792–827.

Levi, J. 1987: "Agricultural Pricing Issues," in H. O'Neill *et al.* (ed.), *Transforming a Single Product Economy: an Examination of the First Stage of Zambia's*

Economic Reform Program, 1982–1986, Washington, DC: Economic Development Institute of the International Bank for Reconstruction and Development.

Markakis, J. and Curry, R. L. Jr 1976/77: "The Global Economy's Impact on Recent Budgetary Politics in Zambia," *Journal of Modern African Studies*, 3 (4), 403–427.

Meebelo, H.S. 1971: *Reaction to Colonialism*, Manchester: Manchester University Press.

Meebelo, H. S. 1986: *African Proletarians and Colonial Capitalism*, Lusaka: Kenneth David Kaunda Foundation.

Mijere, N. 1988: "The State and Development: a Study of the Dominance of the Political Class in Zambia," *Africa Today*, 2nd quarter, 21–35.

Molteno, R. 1972: "Zambia and the One Party State," *East Africa Journal*, 9 (2) 6–18.

Molteno, R. 1974: "Cleavage and Conflict in Zambian Politics: A Study of Sectionalism," in W. Tordoff (ed.), *Politics in Zambia*, Berkeley and Los Angeles: University of California Press.

Molteno, R. and Scott, I. 1974: "The 1968 General Elections and the Political System," in W. Tordoff (ed.), *Politics in Zambia*, Berkeley and Los Angeles: University of California Press.

Mueller, D. C. 1989: *Public Choice II*, Cambridge: Cambridge University Press.

Mulford, D. 1967: *Zambia: The Politics of Independence: 1957–1964*, London: Oxford University Press.

Mwanaumo, A. 1987: "An Evaluation of the Marketing System for Maize in Zambia," Masters Thesis, Purdue University, August.

Mwendapole, M.R. 1977: *A History of the Trade Union Movement in Zambia up to 1978*, Communication No. 13, Lusaka: Institute for African Studies, University of Zambia.

Odegaard, K. 1986: "Income Trends of Wage Earners and Farmers in Zambia, 1965–85," mimeo, Prices and Incomes Commission.

Ollawa, P.E. 1979: *Participatory Democracy in Zambia: The Political Economy of National Development*, Devon: Arthur H. Stockwell.

Olson, M. 1971: *The Logic of Collective Action*, New York: Schocken Books.

Olson, M. 1982: *The Rise and Decline of Nations*, New Haven and London: Yale University Press.

Orlowski, D. 1989: "Analysis of the Budget," mimeo, Lusaka: Institute of African Studies.

Palmer, R. and Parsons, N 1977: *The Roots of Rural Poverty in Central and Southern Africa*, Berkeley and Los Angeles: University of California Press.

Prapart, J. 1983: *Labour and Capital in the African Copperbelt*, Philadelphia: Temple University Press.

Republic of Zambia 1987a: "New Economic Recovery Programme," speech by His Excellency the President: Dr K.D. Kaunda, May 1, Lusaka: Government Printer.

Republic of Zambia 1987b: *New Economic Recovery Programme: Rules to Govern Contract Remittances and Employment Permits for Expatriate Personnel*, Lusaka: Government Printer.

Republic of Zambia 1987c: *New Economic Recovery Programme: Progress Report No. 1 on the Implementation of the Interim National Development Plan*, Lusaka: Government Printer.

Republic of Zambia 1988a: *New Economic Recovery Programme, Interim National Development Plan: Progress Report No. 2, July 1987–March 1988*, Lusaka: Government Printer.

Republic of Zambia 1988b: *Presidential and Parliamentary Elections: Summary of Electoral Results* (various years), Lusaka: Elections Office.

Republic of Zambia 1989a: *Agricultural and Pastoral Production (Commercial Farmers) 1985–1986*, Lusaka: Central Statistical Office, September.

Republic of Zambia 1989b: *Agricultural and Pastoral Production (Non-commercial Farmers) 1982–1983 to 1984–1985*, Lusaka: Central Statistical Office, November.

Republic of Zambia 1990: *Evaluation of the Performance of Zambia's Maize Subsidy*, Lusaka: National Commission for Development Planning.

Roberts, A.D. 1976: *A History of Zambia*, London: Heinemann.

Roberts, R.A.J., and Elliot, C. (eds.) 1971: *Constraints on the Economic Development of Zambia*, Nairobi: Oxford University Press.

Rotberg, R.I. 1965: *The Rise of Nationalism in Central Africa*, London: Oxford University Press.

Scott, I. 1978: "Middle Class Politics in Zambia," *African Affairs*, 77, July, 321–34.

Scott, I. 1982: "Political Money and Party Organization in Zambia," *The Journal of Modern African Studies*, 20 (3), 393–410.

Southall, A. 1980: "Class Formation and Government Policy in the 1970s," *Journal of Southern African Studies*, 7 (1), 91–108.

Szeftel, M. 1982: "Political Graft and the Spoils System in Zambia," *Review of African Political Economy*, 24 (May–Aug.), 4–21.

Tangri, R. 1984: "The Parastatals and Industry," in K. Woldring (ed.), *Beyond Political Independence: Zambia's Development Predicament in the 1980s*, Berlin, New York, Amsterdam: Moulton.

Tangri, R. 1985: *Politics in Sub-Saharan Africa*, London: James Curry.

Tordoff, W. 1974: *Politics in Zambia*, Los Angeles and Berkeley: University of California Press.

Tordoff, W. 1977: "Residual Legislatures: The Cases of Tanzania and Zambia," *The Journal of Commonwealth and Comparative Politics*, 15 (3), 234–49.

Tordoff, W. (ed.) 1980: *Administration in Zambia*, Manchester: Manchester University Press.

Tordoff, W. and Scott J. 1974: "Political Parties: Structures and Policies," in W. Tordoff (ed.), *Politics in Zambia*, Berkeley and Los Angeles: University of California Press.

Turok, B. 1981: "Control in the Parastatal Sector of Zambia," *The Journal of Modern African Studies*, 19(3), 421–45.

Wimwinga, G. K. 1977: "Corporate Autonomy and Government Control," PhD dissertation, University of Pittsburgh.

Wina, S. 1985: *The Night Without a President*, Lusaka: Multimedia Publications.

Woldring, K. (ed.) 1984: *Beyond Political Independence: Zambia's Development Predicament in the 1980s*, with special assistance from C. Chibaye, Berlin, New York, Amsterdam: Mouton.

Wood, A.P. (ed.) 1990: *Dynamics of Agricultural Policy and Reform in Zambia*, Ames: Iowa State University Press.

World Bank 1983: *World Tables, vol. II, Social Data*, Baltimore and London: Johns Hopkins University Press.

World Bank 1986: Zambia: *Country Economic Memorandum: Economic Policy Reform and Development Perspectives*, Washington, DC: IBRD.

World Bank 1987: Zambia: *Country Economic Memorandum*, mimeo, Washington, DC: IBRD.

World Bank 1989: *Sub-Saharan Africa: From Crisis to Sustainable Growth*, Washington, DC: World Bank.

Young, A. 1973: *Industrial Diversification in Zambia*, New York: Praeger.

Young, R. and Loxley, J. 1990: *Zambia: An Assessment of Zambia's Structural Adjustment Experience*, Ottawa: The North-South Institute.

Zelniker, S. 1970: *Changing Patterns of Unionism*, PhD dissertation, University of California at Los Angeles.

Generalizations Arising from the Country Studies
Robert H. Bates and Anne O. Krueger

Despite the complexity revealed in the case studies and our inability to use systematic, statistical methods, it is clearly desirable to weigh the evidence of the country studies for whatever light they shed on more general understandings of the process of policy reform. Section 1 briefly surveys the country studies, summarizing the main findings of each. Thereafter, we consider the significance of these findings in light of the current literature.

1 KEY RESULTS OF INDIVIDUAL STUDIES

No purpose would be served by attempting to summarize the wealth of insights and results in the individual studies. That is already done in the individual chapters. Rather, the focus here is on the salient points that inform our later synthesis. We attempt to pinpoint three features of each country's experience. The first is the key phenomena that provided impetus for reform. The second is the characteristics of the reforms themselves. The third is the chief findings as to why reforms met the fate that they did.

Brazil Despite numerous attempts at policy reform, the Brazilian economy nonetheless staggered from one attempted reform to another. Inflation and balance of payments difficulties were the two key problems which led governments to undertake reforms. Lal and Maxfield believe that the reform took place in circumstances in which the "inflation tax" finally no longer yielded revenue to the state, and that balance of payments difficulties (external circumstances) provided the second major impetus. Neither of these circumstances, it may be noted, led to a belief that prior policies (including government controls, protection of imports, credit rationing, labor legislation, and so on) had been in error, although Lal and Maxfield reject the notion that ideology played much of a role in Brazilian policy formulation. They regard policy-makers' responses to balance of payments crises and inflation as being essentially "pragmatic."

In Lal and Maxfield's view, all Brazilian reform efforts failed for much the same reasons. There were positive conditions for failure, and negative ones. On the positive side, Lal and Maxfield believe that it was in the interests of Brazilian industrialists and labor to oppose reforms, the former because Brazil's comparative advantage lay in capital intensive activities which were supported by industrialization policies, and the latter because the capital-intensive nature of industry meant that Brazilian industrialists could afford to pay reasonably high wages to their workers. Lal and Maxfield note that rural interests, except for the small rural aristocracy, were not politically influential throughout the postwar period.

Related to this phenomenon, Lal and Maxfield consider that the governing party in Brazil was highly vulnerable to opposition. Although the governments were appointed by the military, they were highly constrained by their lack of a legitimate base and thus threatened by vocal opposition from business, labor, or other groups.

On the negative side, there were institutional weaknesses which made the task of would-be reformers much more difficult than might have been the case. Lal and Maxfield focus on the weakness of the Central Bank, whose lack of independence and inability to prevent money creation prevented it from playing a stronger role. Equally, other financial institutions that in other countries could be supportive of reform were weak or silent during Brazilian reform episodes.

Chile The political economy of Chilean reforms is of interest for a number of reasons. First, during the period in which policies were being radically altered, the technocrats were largely shielded by the military government and had a fairly wide range in which they could operate. Brock and Stallings believe that the Chilean military government in 1974 had little idea of what policies it wanted to pursue. They note that the "Chicago Boys," as they call them, had an action plan ready and were able to persuade Pinochet of it. They also note the absence of organized opposition, in that supporters of Allende were suppressed, while opponents of Allende had nowhere else to go.

Second, when Chile encountered severe economic difficulties in the early 1980s due to policy mistakes (an appreciating real exchange rate) and a harsh international environment (a sharp drop in the price of copper and a very large increase in the real interest rate on external debt), political protests were able to force the government to alter its economic policies. As that happened, a new economics team, more consultative in style and more accessible to interest groups, was able to restore economic growth.

Third, although Chile achieved high real rates of growth of real income and real wages by the late 1980s, the path had by no means been smooth. It was not until the late 1980s, when sustained real growth rates in excess of 5 percent per annum had continued for half a decade, that support for reforms became more widespread.

Even now, Brock and Stallings believe, the continuing political viability of reforms will hinge on devising improved "safety nets" for individuals' earnings streams in the presence of strong external shocks to the economy.

Ecuador   Ecuador's experience differs from that of other countries in that while there were three distinct reform efforts in the 1980s, there was also lasting change. The need for policy reform originated in the large-scale pattern of activity-specific subsidies and controls that had intensified sharply after the discovery of oil and the resultant increase in government revenues. When export earnings growth terminated, these patterns continued as long as foreign lenders would lend; by the early 1980s, however, Ecuador's governments could borrow no more.

The first reform episode, as described by Grindle and Thoumi, was undertaken by a president whose accession to office was accidental (an airplane crash had killed his predecessor); at the time, democratic institutions were in any event fragile, as military government had only ended in 1978. Grindle and Thoumi describe the president's recognition of the need for reform, and his ability to formulate economic policy with the assistance of a small team of technocrats; these actions primarily represented an effort to contain balance-of-payments and inflationary difficulties. There was little public awareness or discussion of the need for economic policy changes; and after they were initially announced they eroded as opposition intensified. The government was so weak that the reforms threatened the viability not only of the government itself but also of the newly introduced democratic institutions.

A second reform, led by a president who was elected on a platform of economic liberalization, was initially perhaps even more far-reaching and received widespread international, as well as domestic, attention in its early phase. But again, opposition mounted, and the president abandoned much of his reformist platform, increasing public spending and reversing some of the changes that had been made. These reversals may have been caused by a recognition that opposition was so intense that President Febres-Cordero could not otherwise have completed his term of office.

The third attempt, less oriented toward reducing the role of the state and more geared to the immediate economic crises associated with rising rates of inflation and balance of payments difficulties, played out in similar manner. The early policy initiatives eroded soon after their introduction. In each episode, then, presidents possessed enough "political resources" to inaugurate reforms, but insufficient political resources to implement them.

Grindle and Thoumi emphasize several characteristics of the Ecuadoran situation. One was the weakness of democratic institutions, especially at the beginning of the 1980s. They suggest that each president had to balance the recognized need for economic policy reform against the desirability of maintaining democratic institutions.

A second was the power of the technocracy. They also note that leadership of the presidency was important in initiating reforms, but that the technocratic institutions and interest groups which might have supported reform were very weak in the late 1970s and early 1980s. During the 1980s, the institutional role of the technocracy strengthened, as did democratic institutions themselves. Moreover, by 1984, the "economic elite," which had previously been fragmented, was able to coalesce in support of the policies advocated by Frebres-Cordero, if only for a brief period.

Perhaps most significant of all, however, Ecuador is unique among the countries covered in the project in that the end results of three reforms, each of which was at least partially reversed, were important changes in economic policies and the institutional context for economic decision making. Ecuadoran institutional and political developments, including the education of the populace about the need for reform, permitted some change to occur, even though it was often slow and limited in its impact.

Egypt   Egypt, like Ecuador, benefited from increased oil export revenues in the 1970s; unlike Ecuador, however, for at least a decade before, Egyptian economic policy formulation had been highly centralized.

It was clearly the unacceptably high and accelerating rate of inflation and the shortage of foreign exchange to finance imports that impelled the Egyptian authorities to respond to the crisis in 1986. They thereupon agreed to a program in conjunction with the International Monetary Fund. Within a year, however, the program broke down.

Holt and Roe distinguish between an inability to act, based upon a lack of legitimacy of the government, and an incapacity to act. This latter, they believe, was the result of the opposition of bureaucrats and others who would directly lose from reforms, and who would have been able to undermine reforms, even if the government had been able to initiate them.

Holt and Roe contrast the inability of the government to implement reforms undertaken with the IMF with the Ministry of Agriculture's willingness to undertake substantial deregulation and reform of agricultural policy in conjunction with USAID. In the latter case, Holt and Roe note, there was only one ministry involved, a detailed set of plans for action was set out at the beginning, and the payments may have permitted the Ministry of Agriculture to placate those bureaucrats who might otherwise have opposed the process. Holt and Roe thus focus on the institutional framework for reform, and the incentives confronting those who might make or implement policy change.

Ghana   Among the countries studied in this project, Ghana represents the the most glaring case of failed economic policy, sustained over a long period of time. Leith and Lofchie first analyze why these policies were adopted. They identify the prevailing ideology of the time, which supported inner-oriented industrialization, as the primary factor; but they also note the political usefulness of state enterprises and other economic controls. In that regard, Ghanaian experience in the 1950s does not appear to differ greatly from that of other countries included in the project.

What is different is the degree to which economic deterioration could proceed without a major political challenge to those policies. Leith and Lofchie focus upon the build-up of vested interests in the bureaucracy and in parastatal enterprises as a key reason for the lack of impetus to policy change during the 1970s. They also note the usefulness of the economic rents generated by scarcities of foreign exchange and other goods, which politicians were able to allocate as political favors. The pool of economic rents created by economic policy thus became, in their terms, the "political glue" which held the Ghanaian system together.

As the failed economic policies persisted, however, the size of the economic rents available diminished, while the politicians were confronted with ever larger needs for patronage. Leith and Lofchie's analysis indicates that it was ultimately the "dialectics" of the economic policies and their interactions with political support which resulted in the breakdown of the system. They note the "incapacity" and "ineffectualness" of the government as real revenues diminished and citizens "exited" by switching away from economic activities that were controlled to those not regulated by the state, by smuggling, or by otherwise evading economic controls. The theme of governmental ineffectuality that was reported for Egypt thus shows up in the Ghanaian case as well.

By the early 1980s corruption was rampant, and even basic goods and services were only randomly available. At that point, a coup brought a new military leader to power. Leith and Lofchie report that the coup leaders' principal motivation was their "moral revulsion" over the pervasiveness of corruption within society. That revulsion was widely shared in Ghanaian society and provided political support for reforms.

A first reform effort shifted toward a radical, egalitarian socialism, which was intended to root out "profiteering" under rigid price controls and regulations. When that failed (as it had to in the context of rampant inflation and shortages), the government shifted toward a market-oriented reform program begun in 1983, where emphasis was on elimination of the budget deficit and reform of the trade and payments regime (including the exchange rate).

Leith and Lofchie note that the reforms achieved support in large part because of the unanimity with which Ghanaians held the earlier economic policies in disdain. The reformers received strong support from the international institutions, who played an active role in the reform process. Perhaps because economic deterioration had lasted so long in Ghana, there was little economic hardship resulting directly from the reforms. Because economic conditions began to improve, there was little or no popular political opposition. Leith and Lofchie point out that Ghanaians believed that the only major losers were those who "deserved to lose" as they were those who earlier gained through corruption.

Although reforms brought a reversal in the decline of cocoa production and other exports and reduced the degree of bias against exports and the rural areas, some reforms proved unsuccessful. Leith and Lofchie discuss the difficulties encountered with the effort to privatize state-owned enterprises, and also the extent to which reforms received negative support (in the sense of agreement that past policies were unacceptable), rather than positive backing.

Korea   Haggard, Cooper, and Moon focus on the failed economic policies of the 1950s, the reform period of the early 1960s, and the reasons why the reforms were sustained. Turning first to the 1950s, they note that the economic policies then in effect gave rise to rents, which in turn were used for political purposes. The corruption and rent-seeking that characterized the final years of the Rhee regime provided one basis for securing political support but undermined overall performance.

Dissatisfaction with economic performance, and especially with corruption, help explain both the fall of Rhee in 1960 and the military coup of 1961.

The first effort at reform, starting in 1960, involved a major devaluation (and some other changes) but failed because of the inability of the government to carry through. Haggard, Cooper, and Moon categorize the Chang Myon government as a "classic case of weak political institutions coupled with broad political mobilization." Though a majority apparently supported the change of government, the new regime was unable to consolidate its power effectively or to take the steps necessary to insure the continuation of the new policies.

The second stage of reforms started in 1963. A number of factors contributed to its success. There was broad support for reform because of poor past economic performance and the rejection of the cronyism and corruption of the Rhee regime. Yet it is difficult to explain either the reforms or their sustainability in terms of interest-group behavior; indeed, the reforms cut directly against the expressed desires of a number of private interests. Rather, Haggard, Cooper, and Moon stress three political factors. First, the military government, while enjoying broad acquiescence if not support, was able to break through the political networks of patronage and rent-seeking that had characterized business–government relations under Rhee. Second, the new government came under strong pressure from the Americans to reform. The manipulation of aid in the short run, as well as the long-run prospect of diminished aid, focused the attention of the government on reforms that would increase foreign exchange earnings, lure foreign investment, and raise domestic savings. Korean planners also benefited from close working relations with American aid officials.

Finally, Haggard, Cooper, and Moon note that the reforms would probably not have succeeded unless accompanied by important institutional changes within the government itself. The technocracy was strengthened and new powers were granted to an Economic Planning Board which was able to coordinate policies among previously competing ministries. These institutional reforms increased the credibility of government policy.

These factors contributed to the initiation of the reforms; the visible economic success that the Korean economy encountered after the mid–1960s generated political support for their continuation. Haggard, Cooper, and Moon note that declining real wages from 1960 to 1967 may have played some role in the later success with export-oriented industrialization. They attribute the decline to weakness of labor unions during a period in which unemployed labor was absorbed into the labor force, rather than to expansion of "low-wage" jobs in export industries, and speculate that the fairly even income distribution in Korea may have contributed to the willingness of labor force participants to share the burden of adjustment. By 1967, however, real wages turned up, and saw a sustained 8.7 percent annual increase over the next 20 years!

Turkey   Krueger and Turan attribute the adoption of import-substitution policies and of government direction of economic activity in Turkey to the prevailing ideology of the time. Once those policies had been adopted, the bureaucracy and those businessmen moving into import-substituting industrialization provided strong support for them. Urban interests were relatively strong, and rural interests underrepresented.

By the late 1970s, however, the majority of industrialists had recognized that import substitution and interventionist policies had exhausted their ability to deliver economic growth. Even in the mid-1970s, the Turkish Industrialists' and Businessmen's Association was publicly advocating policy reforms. However, politics had become highly "clientelistic" and fragmented, and the government constituted a fragile coalition dependent upon the support of small extremist parties.

Krueger and Turan diagnose the inability of the government to respond to the economic difficulties of the late 1970s as being attributable to these political weaknesses. Although two stabilization programs were begun, both were soon abandoned; the government could not afford politically to cut expenditures. By 1980, however, the situation was so extreme that a small group of technocrats could initiate a policy reform program. They worked in isolation and its particulars became known to key cabinet ministers only when their signatures were called for on official decrees.

Although positive support for the policy reforms was limited, there was widespread popular acquiescence; this Krueger and Turan attribute to the failed nature of earlier policies. The seriousness of political strife and inability to act finally led to the resignation of the elected government and its replacement with a military government nine months after the policy reforms were announced. The reforms were continued under the military government, which retained the team of economic technocrats which had initiated them. This team had been led by Turgut Özal. When, late in 1983, there was an election, Turgut Özal's party was voted into power, with Mr Özal as prime minister.

Krueger and Turan credit the business community's rejection of earlier policies as a key factor in bringing about policy reform and also in perpetuating it. They report on the rapid expansion of exports that followed, and the resumption of real GNP growth. However, political pressures to increase public expenditures on infrastructure and other public services (not state economic enterprises) resulted in large increases in fiscal deficits, especially prior to each election. With each such increase, inflation rebounded, and remained at 50–60 percent in the late 1980s and early 1990s.

The Turkish reforms were successful in restructuring the economy away from extreme inner-oriented policies and in integrating the Turkish economy more closely with the rest of the world, both in trading relations and in Turkey's ability to attract foreign investment and other capital flows. Other aspects of the stabilization program were, however, less satisfactory, as political pressures led the government to increase expenditures on infrastructure, especially as elections approached.

Zambia   Bates and Collier find several characteristic patterns of policy-making in Zambia. During the Second Republic, they argue, the government tended to place a higher priority on the short-term interests of consumers than on the long-term interest in economic growth. There was, in addition, a cyclical pattern in policy choices. The government veered between a reflexive endorsement of economic controls and a greater use of markets; and the locus of policy-making shifted between units dominated by party politicians and administrative units that stood relatively independent of partisan political forces. Lastly, they document a process of learning, with the shifts in policy being accompanied by an accumulation of knowledge – such as a growing recognition that inflation results not from devaluation, but rather that devaluation is necessitated by inflation, which is itself caused by excess expenditures by government.

Bates and Collier attribute these patterns to several sources. One is to the consequences of policies themselves. Policies, they reveal, generate pressures that then become the sources of other policies: the forces unleashed by the control regime, for example, themselves unleash subsequent adjustments – deficit foreign balances, shortages and inflationary pressures, for example – that then generate demands for reform. A second is the political system. Within Zambia, they argue, there was a pattern of political bias that shaped the formation of expectations; this made credible market-oriented reform difficult to achieve. Much of their essay is devoted to a study of the electoral system, the pattern of representation in parliament, the incentives internal to the governing party, the representation of organized interests, and the way in which these factors shaped preferences over economic policies. It is easy to see, on the basis of their work, why the demands for economic reform in Zambia led as well to demands for political reform, and, in particular, to a call for the end of the single-party system.

2   WHY IS REFORM UNDERTAKEN?

In making use of these country studies, the first important question to be addressed is why reforms are undertaken at all. The analysis divides readily into two parts: the economic conditions that call for reform, and the political responses to them. We consider each in turn.

Crisis is perhaps the more frequent stimulus to reform although, as will be discussed below, what constitutes a sufficient crisis to prompt sweeping changes can differ dramatically from country to country and from time to time. When crisis is the trigger of change, policy changes can come about either because earlier policies are perceived as having failed, or because exogenous events (such as deteriorating terms or worldwide recession) are blamed for events, which are nonetheless deemed to require a policy response.

In the countries covered in this project, three different "crisis triggers" of reform were identified. First, balance-of-payments difficulties have led to decisions to change policy regimes. Second, accelerating inflation has been regarded as an unacceptable situation requiring policy adjustments. Third, the loss of economic control, or "withering away of the state," has evidently been a key motivation in some circumstances.

To be sure, balance-of-payments difficulties and inflation may be joint results of large public sector deficits in conjunction with exchange rate policies that either maintain a fixed nominal rate or adjust the exchange rate only slowly and by less than the proportionate differential between the country's inflation and the world inflation rate. Nonetheless, when balance-of-payments difficulties trigger policy reforms, there are several distinct economic characteristics. First, actual or impending shortages of imports are deemed to be a major constraint on economic activity. This was the trigger in Turkey's three reform episodes, for example, as an inability to obtain petroleum and other commodities not domestically produced led to a virtual breakdown in economic activity. Second, debt-servicing difficulties may provide the trigger for reform. In these circumstances, earlier borrowing (often on deteriorating terms) cannot be continued as short-term indebtedness mounts and lenders refuse to extend further credit. When arrears start to accumulate, normal trade credits rapidly diminish, and even the multilateral development banks are reluctant to lend or extend credit until indebtedness is dealt with. Third, rapidly increasing large-scale capital flight is often a characteristic of these crises and forces rapid action.

Since foreign exchange difficulties are visible to all, speculative pressures can mount very rapidly, and precipitate hurried action. The most spectacular instance of such a phenomenon was not in one of the countries covered in the study, but in Mexico, where capital flight was the proximate trigger for devaluation.[1] Among countries covered in the project, however, capital flight clearly contributed to Chile's difficulties in the early 1980s, and to those of Brazil and Ecuador.

Although accelerating inflation and balance-of-payments pressures are often twin symptoms of underlying difficulties in economic policy, when inflation accelerates to triple-, or even quadruple-digit rates, concern over inflation can itself be a primary factor leading to a perceived necessity to undertake reforms. It would appear that most Brazilian reform efforts have been initiated more because of the perceived costs of accelerating inflation than they have been for balance-of-payments reasons.

These two sources of difficulty, and the subsequent initiation of reform efforts, are frequently encountered. The third, the "withering away of the state," may be equally powerful, but has been less frequently recognized in the literature. Leith and Lofchie believe this was very important in Ghana: the state was unable to deliver health and education services, or to prevent massive smuggling even of bulk commodities. Lal and Maxfield note that the Brazilian authorities began seriously (if not desperately) addressing the underlying economic difficulties only at a point when the deteriorating economic situation undermined the resources and therefore the power of the state itself. When this motive has been a major factor, the increased size of the "informal sector," the emergence of widespread smuggling, and other evasions of regulations were accompanied by a loss of revenue from the inflation tax, and even by a loss of real tax revenue as inflation accelerated or as the exchange rate became increasingly unrealistic. In these circumstances, it may be political considerations, and in particular the desire to restore state control and authority, that prompt a program of economic policy reforms which, paradoxically, entail the reduction of state controls in order to increase the effectiveness of the state!

Although the emergence of the informal sector has been a significant economic phenomenon in many developing countries, this loss of power of the state, and the desire to restore it as a motive for policy reform, appears to become important only when economic policies have resulted in great economic deterioration. This loss of state control was a factor in Brazil, Ghana, and Zambia, among the countries covered in the project, although it might be argued that it was a secondary factor in Turkey as well.

Not all reforms have taken place in crisis, or near-crisis, conditions, however. In some circumstances, popular discontent with ongoing aspects of the economy has resulted in the impetus to reform. Among the countries covered in the project, popular revulsion with corruption is the most frequently-mentioned of such circumstances. Revulsion with corruption provided the basis for popular support of ongoing reform efforts in Korea in 1960, as recounted by Haggard, Cooper, and Moon. It was also a major factor in bringing about the decision to reform in Ghana and Zambia, although the severe deterioration of the general economy was also a factor.

A change in ideology, either because of a change in government, or because of a recognition that the old growth strategy had failed, can also lead to policy reforms. The change in government, and accompanying change in underlying ideology, preceded reforms in Chile and in Korea. Recognition of the failure of the old strategy seems to have been a major factor in the reforms in Ecuador and in Ghana, among countries covered in the project. Other instances include Sri Lanka after the elections of 1978 and Pakistan both when Bhutto came to power and when he was replaced.

In all circumstances, of course, reforms have been undertaken in circumstances in which economic conditions were deteriorating. There is no recorded instance of the beginning of a reform program at a time when economic growth was satisfactory and when the price level and balance of payments situations were stable. Conditions of economic stagnation (and the recognition that it is likely to continue) or continued deterioration are evidently prerequisites for reform efforts.

There does seem to have been somewhat greater room for maneuver on the part of the government in circumstances in which the severity of the existing economic situation was readily evident. Thus, the degree of discontent following reforms in Korea in 1960, Turkey in 1980, and Ghana in the mid 1980s seems to have been considerably less than that in Ecuador, Brazil, and Egypt, where the need for reform was less evident and somewhat obscured by the proximate role of external circumstances. Whether the perceived gravity of the situation was the result of a crisis in the balance of payments or accelerating inflation, or whether instead it was the problems associated with chronic stagnation or deterioration, does not seem significantly to have affected the political–economic situations of those administering policy reforms.

3   POLITICAL CONDITIONS LEADING TO REFORM

A major lesson of the case studies is that while it is easy to speak of economic "realities" "necessitating" policy changes, there is in fact but a weak relationship between economic conditions and policy responses. Korea rapidly altered its policies in response to changed economic conditions; Ghana did not. Lying between economic circumstances and policy reform is a political process, by which the needs for economic adjustment translate into effective political demands for policy change.

In the literature, various characterizations have been presented of the process of initiating reform. One way of analyzing them is to evaluate the utility of these approaches against the data presented in the country studies.

The analysis of policy-making is sometimes approached as a form of applied welfare analysis. One variant stresses the primacy of technocrats: policy reform results from their diagnosis of economic maladies and their subsequent advocacy of policy changes. A related approach stresses the role of platonic guardians: officers of "the state" who seek growth and development and who choose economic policies accordingly.[2] In a symmetric manner, the failure to reform is sometimes attributed to the existence of "predatory" states, whose policies are chosen to maximize distributive objectives.[3] The common element among these approaches is the assumption of a strong, centralized state. But in the country studies we rarely find such states. Rather, we find the executive clashing with the legislature (as in Ecuador); the military locked in conflict with civilian politicians (as in Chile, Turkey, Korea, Brazil, and Ecuador); public institutions colonized and emasculated by private interests (as in Ghana); or levels of partisan antagonism that result in civil war (as in Chile). The process of economic policy reform rarely approximates the kind of planning or command and control processes implicit in these approaches.

The unitary actor model – so common in economics, political science, and political economy – thus fails to accord with the political realities captured in the case studies. Fortunately, this approach constitutes only one form of political analysis. Interest group theory offers a commonly employed alternative and one that provides a far more decentralized conception of politics.

Some students of economic policy reform commonly seek to identify the "winners" and "losers" under existing policy regimes; it is natural to locate the impetus for reform in the growing opposition to existing policies.[4] Others employ an "open economy" form of interest-group analysis, which relates interest group demands for domestic policy changes to international markets – a form of analysis adopted by Lal and Maxfield in their study of Brazil.[5]

One of the most surprising findings of our case studies is the degree to which the intervention of interest groups fails to account for the initiation, or lack of initiation, of policy reform.

Thus, while we do find businesses advocating changes in public policy, business is sometimes ineffectual (as in Turkey and Zambia), often fragmented (as in Ghana, Ecuador, or Brazil), or quiescent (as in Chile). We find little evidence of labor crippling attempts at policy change. Either labor is compliant (as in Ghana); peripheral (as in Zambia); or repressed (as in Chile or Korea). And while we do find powerful economic interests resisting policy reform – most notably the bureaucracy and public employees (as in Egypt, Zambia, and Brazil) – we find other cases where political elites were able to break the resistance of powerful opponents (as in Chile and Korea) or to maneuver around their opposition (as in Turkey or rural Egypt). Similar negative findings have been reported by other scholars.[6]

The materials therefore encourage us to explore why interests fail to shape reform efforts as decisively as might be expected. One reason is that, in the context of comprehensive economic policy reform, it is difficult for particular groups to calculate where their interests lie. Ideological struggles therefore can outweigh competition among organized interests as a determinant of policy change.

Even the economists who advocate changes in macroeconomic policies are unable to determine their precise impact on specific interests. They lack the models that would enable them to trace the microlevel impact of changes in macrovariables upon the economic fortunes of specific groups: workers in a given industry, firms that use specific technologies and that produce for particular markets, people who live in certain regions or who are members of a particular income groups, etc. It is therefore to be expected that persons subject to economic policy reforms would themselves remain uncertain as to how their interests would be affected by policy changes.[7]

A result of this uncertainty is that people can be persuaded as to where their economic interests lie; wide scope is thus left for rehetoric and persuasion. In such situations, advocates of particular economic theories or of ideological conceptions of how economies work can acquire influence. Thus we find that development doctrines and the theories of economists had a powerful impact upon the choices of governments in Ghana; we find Marxism clashing with Hayekian liberalism in policy debates in Chile; and in Zambia, we find beliefs about the relationship between devaluation, inflation, and the distribution of income decisively affecting attitudes toward the desirability of markets.[8] Under conditions of uncertainty, people's beliefs of where their economic interests lie can be created and organized by political activists; rather than shaping events, notions of self-interest are instead themselves shaped and formed. In pursuing their economic interests, people act in response to ideology.

Even where groups do appear to have a firm sense of where their economic interests lie, they nonetheless seem often to be ineffectual. In both Turkey and Zambia, for example, business interests appear to have formulated an articulate critique of the status quo and to have defined the measures that should be taken to alter it. And yet they failed to mount organized campaigns in support of policy reform. Several reasons can be offered for such outcomes.[9]

The benefits of policy reform are often widely distributed; they lie in the future; lying in the future, they are uncertain.[10] By contrast, the costs of policy reform are often concentrated; they fall upon the status quo set of interests who benefit from existing policies. And they occur in the present and are certain: the loss of a license, protective legislation, or a subsidy, for example. If people are rational, discount the future, and are averse to risks, then they may find the expected utility of their incomes under the status quo to be greater than that to be derived from the higher but uncertain incomes possibly attainable under the reformed set of policies. And even if their utility would be higher under the reformed set, those who would benefit, being more dispersed, may find it more difficult to organize in support of the reforms than would the more concentrated losers. The public goods nature of policy reforms further lowers the likelihood of interest groups organizing to supply them. To illustrate: the owners or managers of a particular firm might agree that policy reform would be in the collective interests of business in general, but still, behaving rationally, not actively lobby for it, for the private benefits to the particular firm might not cover the costs of individually lobbying to provide the collective benefit to the industry.

As a consequence of these problems, there usually exists a gap between the economic desirability of reform and the politically effective demand for it on the part of economic interests. The beneficiaries from reforms may recognize the opportunity costs of maintaining the old set of public policies. But, for the reasons just given, they may be unwilling to organize in opposition to them.

The argument can be taken a step further. We have argued that interest groups may in fact be unable or unwilling to act in support of policies that favor their interests. A corollary may therefore be that, as argued by Leith and Lofchie, the importance of organized interests may lie more in explaining the stability of public policies than in accounting for their initial adoption. This perspective on the role of interests may help to account for one of the principal regularities encountered in the case studies: that economic policy reform most often follows from discontinuous changes in government. Policy changes occur after coups, as in the case of Ghana, Korea, or Chile; or after changes in governments resulting from elections, as in the case of Ecuador. This finding has been replicated in the studies conducted by Joan Nelson and others[11] and in the more wide-ranging analyses undertaken by Haggard et al.[12] It suggests that breaks with vested interests – interests that support the maintenance of the status quo – are necessary to secure changes in public policy: something that would be expected, were interests important in stabilizing policy commitments.[13]

How, then, does the economic necessity of reform translate into an effective political demand for it? Clearly no single political process appears to operate. Economic technocrats, acting as "platonic guardians," provide diagnoses of the nation's economic ills; but, acting alone, they are ineffective (but see the discussion below). Economic interests losing out under prevailing policies perceive the need for reform; they may in fact receive policy advice from reform-minded technocrats. But our country studies fail to attribute a decisive role to the pressure of organized interests. Rather, economic policy reform appears to emerge as a by-product of political struggles. At times, aspiring politicians appear to be able to mobilize those who are disaffected with incumbent regimes; and when they do so, they appeal as often to ideology as they do to refined notions of economic self-interest.

The key question thus becomes: what shapes the behavior of politicians? What determines what programs they will advocate in the competitive political struggle and what appeals they will formulate in seeking to organize a mass following? As emphasized most clearly, perhaps, in Holt and Roe's study of Egypt, a key determinant of their behavior is the structure of political institutions. As noted in the case of Ecuador, for example, the rules that organize political competition shape the emphasis placed on political ideology. In Ecuador, as in many other Latin American nations, presidents cannot succeed themselves; indeed, having once served, they can never again run for presidential office. As a consequence, Grindle and Thoumi suggest, presidents are willing to mount politically untenable campaigns for policy reform – efforts more dedicated to "doing the right thing" than to building a coalition that would return them to power. Bates and Collier offer another example of institutional rules that promote ideologically motivated policy-making: the incentives generated by rules for promotion within Zambia's ruling party. Within UNIP, officials competed for promotion by exhibiting loyalty to incumbent elites rather than by advocating policies before a mass electorate. The political vision and economic theories of these elites therefore shaped the policy commitment of Zambia's politicians and transformed debates about economic policy into debates about political ideology.[14]

The case studies also underscored the significance of electoral institutions. In Zambia, for example, the rules governing the election of the president differed from those governing election to parliament; they generated strikingly different political incentives, thereby leading to the endorsement of different economic policies by the president and the legislature. The result was a political debate between "liberal" parliament and the "dirigiste" executive branch.

Contrasts between Chile (before Pinochet) and Ecuador (after the return to civilian rule) further underscore the significance of the electoral system. Elections in Chile were dominated by a small number of highly polarized political parties; in Ecuador, by contrast, there existed a multitude of parties, each occupying a narrow band of the political spectrum or possessing a diffuse, personalistic, and nonpragmatic appeal. The party system in Chile offered the possibility of discontinuous policy changes, depending on the outcome at the polls, while the party system in Ecuador offered the likelihood of continuity, as shifts in electoral outcomes would be unlikely to shift control over the government from the hands of a party based at one end of the political spectrum into the hands of a party located at the other. As noted by Grindle and Thoumi, given the electoral system in Ecuador, the government could not make major policy innovations; rather, it was compelled to "muddle through."

The evidence from the case studies thus demonstrates how the structure of political institutions shapes the way in which the economic necessity for reform translates into political demands for it. It is important to stress that in doing so the evidence minimizes the significance of the difference between authoritarian and democratic regimes.

It has long been argued that fundamental changes in public policy – trade liberalization, stabilization, and structural adjustment – might best be achieved by an authoritarian political system. Studies of Latin America, by Guillermo O'Donnell, John Sheehan, and David Pion-Berlin, among others, found in the experiences of the Southern Cone causal connections between economic policy reform and political authoritarianism that their authors felt were applicable to developing countries as a whole.[15] Credence in their assertions was strengthened by the recognition that changes in economic policy generate winners and losers, and losers can be expected to resist; successful reform, it was felt, would therefore require coercion. Intellectual fashions in economic thought lent further credence to the putative relationship between authoritarianism and policy reform: macroeconomic stability, it was argued, required governmental commitments that could not be altered in an effort to cultivate short-term political popularity; they required invariant policy rules, and not ones subject to political discretion.[16]

We found little evidence for a relationship between economic reform and political authoritarianism. Nor have others who have also conducted comparative case studies.[17] More important still, the systematic analysis of large-scale data sets has failed to find significant differences between democratic and authoritarian governments in terms of their ability to engage in policy reform.[18] The analysis in this section suggests an important reason for this result: Fairly precise differences in the rules for political competition appear to make big differences in the behavior of politicians. As a consequence, large differences emerge in the choices of political elites operating within democratic political systems. As a result, differences between authoritarian and democratic systems appear relatively insignificant.

Thus far we have focused on political factors that shape the manner in which economic necessities translate, or fail to translate, into politically effective demands for reform (effective in the sense that they compel politicians to seek to alter economic policies). We turn next from the politics of initiation to the politics and economics of implementation. Among the experiences covered in the country studies, it would appear that, once the political decision to undertake reform is taken, issues surrounding implementation constitute a major determinant of the fate of reforms. To be sure, technical issues in the design of reform packages have on occasion led to the failure of particular reform packages.[19] But the essential economic prerequisites of a successful reform program are reasonably well understood, although there is admittedly great uncertainty surrounding the quantitative orders of magnitude of required adjustment.[20] Economically successful reform programs, however, have not necessarily been those which "did all the right things" initially. Rather, they have been those which, once begun, were implemented in ways that permitted emerging difficulties and shortcomings to be dealt with by further policy steps.

For that reason, we conclude that the key question surrounding policy reform programs, once initiated, is the political–economic factors that influence their implementation. Here, therefore, we analyze both the political factors that shape the implementation of reform and the impact of reform efforts on the structure of politics. Indeed, as will become clear, it is easier to draw lessons from the country studies about the latter than the former.

4   IMPLEMENTATION OF POLICY REFORMS

We start once again with interest groups. As noted by Haggard, Cooper, and Moon, the literature in political science posits a relationship between the pattern of interest-group representation and the capacity of political elites to secure adjustments in economic policy. In particular, it has been argued, corporatist forms of interest-group representation help to sustain openness in international trade, facilitating the policy adjustments needed for liberal trade regimes.[21]

In a corporatist system, key interests form peak organizations and bargain at the national level. The process of bargaining may be facilitated and superintended by national politicians; in many cases, the leaders of the national associations are themselves brought into the government. When labor and industry, to illustrate, form peak associations and join the central government, it is argued, then each gains the ability to make concessions knowing that it can monitor the response of the other and use governmental power to penalize the other should it renege on bargains. Possessing the capacity to credibly threaten punishments to those who renege on bargaining, groups possess the resources needed to make them willing to initiate concessions. This structure of interest-group representation, it is argued, thus empowers political elites to secure adjustments in economic policies.

The literature on corporatism, it should be noted, was developed in studies of the small, open economies of western Europe. It is notable that none of the countries analyzed in this book possessed the kind of corporatist-interest group structures achieved in those economies. Only in Korea were they arguably present, and even then only within the business and financial sectors; labor lay fragmented and excluded from the national bargaining table. It is notable, however, that when political leaders in our sample set of countries committed themselves to more liberal economic policies, some appear to have sought to form structures of corporatist bargaining. In Zambia, for example, as President Kaunda moved to more market-oriented policies and thus to a rapprochement with the World Bank and the International Monetary Fund, he brought leading business and labor leaders into the Central Committee of the ruling party. And in Chile, Brock and Stallings argue, Hernan Buchi introduced a pattern of interest-group bargaining that resembled that characteristic of the small, open economies of Europe when he sought to render economic reforms politically sustainable.

It is useful to note a second element in the literature on interest groups and openness in the small, advanced industrial nations. While open, the economies of these trading nations are not "liberal," in the sense of possessing small public sectors or governments that refrain from economic activism. To the contrary: they possess large public sectors and redistribute a large portion of their nations' resources in the form of social insurance and transfer payments. In these nations, it would appear, political elites use their command over social programs to neutralize potential opposition to "free trade" by domestic interest groups. Having such programs in place appears to enable politicians to counter demands for protectionism; they can point to the advantages of trade and to the programs that compensate for the risk incurred in external – and therefore unregulated – markets.

In the developing countries analyzed in this study, however, politicians lack such programs and therefore have fewer instruments in place to counter protectionist demands.[22] It is intriguing to note, however, that when one of the richer nations studied in this volume, Chile, moved from protection to openness, its government also introduced an expanded program of social insurance. It has long puzzled students of Chile as to why an authoritarian government, with a record so strongly anti-labor, should have introduced programs generally associated with the welfare state. The perspective offered here suggests that this innovation could represent yet another attempt by the government of Chile to create the political capabilities for resisting the demands of popular forces for continued protectionism.

This discussion of interest groups thus suggests that variations in the pattern of interest group representation failed to account for variation in the success of different governments to implement economic policy reforms. Only in the case of Korea and Chile did anything approaching corporatist patterns prevail, and then only in portions of finance and business but not for labor. What is suggested, however, is that efforts at economic reform led to attempts to restructure the pattern of interest-group representation. Scattered evidence suggests that reform-minded elites attempted to create corporatist political structures and, in at least one case, to underpin these with government programs that could forestall protectionist reactions against liberalizing policy changes.

This analysis thus suggests that the process of policy reform leads to a restructuring of relationships between governments and interest groups; this is a theme we will return to below. It also suggests that the process of reform generates changes in political institutions. Indeed, perhaps the clearest pattern emerging from the case studies is that economic policy reform implies the strengthening of the executive branch of government and, within the executive branch, the financial – as opposed to the spending – ministries.

To illustrate: Grindle and Thoumi note that in the case of Ecuador the movement toward economic policy reform took the form of attempts to shift the locus of policy-making from representative institutions to the executive branch and to build an autonomous and coherent financial team within the Office of the President. In the case of Turkey, Krueger and Turan note that prior to the attempts at policy reform, party leaders forming governments allocated different ministries to different parties; coalition governments then endorsed an inconsistent mixture of policies, with the budget constituting merely the sum of the expenditures of the different ministries. With the initiation of policy reform, however, this pattern changed. The authors note that the locus of policy-making shifted to the office of the prime minister, who gained both substantive and financial control over other ministries; and that he empowered financial technocrats to gain control over the making of economic policy. As noted by Bates and Collier, attempts at policy reform in Zambia entailed a shifting of control over the institutions that make economic policy from the Party, which was accountable to the popular electorate, to the cabinet, which was accountable to the president; and it entailed as well an attempt to fortify the political power of economic advisors and to isolate them from the distributive pressures of partisan political institutions. Chile and Korea offer perhaps the most extreme instances of economic policy reform; they also represent the most extreme examples of the strengthening of the executive branch of government and the empowerment of financial technocrats within it. And Brazil and Egypt appear to have been among the least successful cases, as attempts to gain central control over financial institutions in Brazil and cabinet departments in Egypt both failed, leading as well to the failure of attempts to reform economic policy.

As noted earlier, there is little substance to the claim that economic policy reform requires authoritarian government. But, on the basis of the evidence in the case studies, economic reform clearly leads to an increase in the power of the executive branch of government and, in particular, of its financial units.

It is important to savor the irony embedded in this finding. Many who advocate economic policy reform in the Third World advocate an ex-panded role for markets and call for a reduction in the role of the state. In their rhetoric, they pit the market against the state; expansion of the role of one implies, in their conception, a reduction in the scope of the other, as through privatization, cutbacks in public spending, and a reduction in regulatory powers. And yet, as suggested in the country studies and noted earlier, economic policy reforms are not "anti-state"; rather, they appear to strengthen the powers of the core of the state, the executive branch, and to enhance its control over key economic policy variables which affect the outcome of economic activity. This is the essence of what Miles Kahler has labeled the "orthodox paradox": that the expansion of the role of markets requires a strengthening of the state and especially of its financial bureaucracy.[23]

Do such patterns suggest "lessons" about the reasons for successful reform? We think that the situation is too complex to suggest simple recipes for policy change. Correlation is not the same as causation, after all, and it would be simplistic to attribute "good policies" to the fact that the policies were made by technocrats. An advantage of richly detailed country studies, such as those in this book, is that they allow us to penetrate behind relationships and to see the causal processes that generate them. Sifting through the country studies suggests the existence of two possible processes by which technocrats gain control over policy making and the power to implement policy reforms.

The empowerment of technocrats – and of the economic bureaucracies that they control – would appear to fall into the class of problems currently labeled problems of delegation.[24] Technocrats are not, after all, themselves powerful. They are often academics who possess neither wealth nor a political following; what they do possess is private information, i.e., expertise in economic affairs. Economic technocrats become powerful, then, because politicians choose to make them so and organize the political process in a way that enables them to exploit the technocrats' informational advantage. The fundamental question then becomes: when will politicians delegate to technocrats control over key areas of economic policy?

One answer to this question can be based upon an analysis of "the politicians' dilemma."[25] Incumbents seek to retain power; challengers seek to unseat them. To remain in power, incumbent politicians render their control over public spending a source of political benefits; they adopt distributive strategies, financing programs and allocating "pork" so as to reward constituents and build an organized following. The dilemma arises from the fact that while such strategies are rational for individual incumbents, they may be collectively irrational for incumbents as a whole. When each incumbent champions spending projects so as to retain office, deficits mount and economic conditions worsen, and the political popularity of incumbents as a group then declines. As evidenced most dramatically in the chapter on Ghana, politicians committed to distributive strategies treat the nation's economic base as a common pool resource; the result is a "tragedy of the commons," with heightened political risk for the incumbent regime.

Studies in other contexts show that sophisticated politicians may possess a response to this dilemma: the creation of institutions that can commit them individually to strategies that are collectively rational. In particular, they create institutions that impose fiscal discipline, reducing the opportunities for distributive politics and enforcing limits on public spending. This response can take the form of delegation: the creation of new agencies to which politicians delegate the responsibility for a particular policy domain. They staff the agency with specialists and confer upon it special powers. Being vested with the defense of the collective interest, these agencies acquire special status as well; they are regarded as public institutions, whose mission is to defend the collective welfare rather than the private political interests of particular politicians.[26]

This approach thus treats the creation of institutions as a collectively rational response to the threat posed to incumbent elites by the pursuit of unsustainable economic policies. As the country studies make clear, however, it is often difficult to organize such responses. One reason is the absence of an elementary requirement for delegation: that the politicians recognize that economic decision-making requires specialized skills and that the technocrat's training gives them superior expertise in economic decision-making. As noted in the Zambian case study, some politicians might contest this proposition. Treating economic policy as a security issue, they might insist on their own superior capabilities and retain control of the economy in their own hands or place it in the hands of those whose job is to maintain law and order – and the government in power.

Another reason for the failure to restructure is the difficulty of coordination. Even when incumbents recognize that the distributive game of politics is, for economic reasons, becoming unwinnable, it might be difficult for them to agree to restructure it. Deflationary policies, even when beneficial for the economy as a whole, are not distributionally neutral. Private interests will continue to push for special favors; indeed, their demands may intensify, as overspending on behalf of one interest does less damage to the overall economy when spending on all others has been constrained. Even when reforms are succeeding economically, indeed, perhaps especially when they are succeeding, special-interest politics will therefore continue. And in a competitive political environment, each politician, even when convinced of the necessity for reform, may be unable to afford failing to endorse the cause of particular interests.

It is therefore not surprising that "third parties" come to play an important role in helping incumbent regimes to build financial institutions. Clearly the United States government played such a role in Korea; it also attempted to do so, though with far less success, in Egypt. And in many of the cases studies in this volume the World Bank and the International Monetary Fund have helped to build economic institutions. A recognition of the incentives faced by incumbent elites highlights the significance of such third parties, as they help to coordinate retreats from extreme bargaining positions and the development of collectively rational ways of making economic decisions, and may enhance the influence of technocrats on economic policy making.

"The politicians' dilemma" approach to policy reform stresses the common interests of incumbents and the pursuit of collectively rational, (i.e., efficient) policies. There is an alternative approach, which emphasizes the partisan goals of particular interests and the distributive impact of policy reform.[27] According to this alternative perspective, which we will call the partisan theory, economic institutions are created not to enhance the political life chances of all members of an incumbent regime but rather to privilege the economic and political fortunes of particular segments of the polity: interests that are better served by new kinds of economic policies. The empowerment of the technocrats and the operation of strong financial institutions represents an attempt to institutionalize policies that serve particular interests.

What might these interests be? During the process of policy reform, disputes arise over trade liberalization. As revealed in the cases of Turkey, Ghana, and Ecuador, protected industries, aimed at domestic markets, oppose liberalizing reforms; those seeking to export favor them. As revealed in the case of Zambia, Korea, and Chile, the challenge to import substitution can unite the traded sector against the untraded, with opposition being mounted by labor movements lodged in the service sector: banking, printing, medical care, and the civil service. Lal and Maxfield use trade theory to discern the general structure of interests generated by this issue.

The issue of stabilization incites another series of conflicts. As highlighted by the studies of Egypt, Zambia, and Ecuador, public employees, recipients of subsidies, and those dependent on public services can be counted on to oppose retrenchments in government spending; those adversely affected by inflation, high interest rates, and shortages of imported inputs can be counted on to champion spending cuts.

The very centrality of politics to the process of economic policy change bespeaks the centrality of these distributive struggles. Reform results when political movements secure sufficient backing from the reform-minded interests that they capture power and use their control over the government to impose reform programs.

The role of economic institutions, according to this partisan theory, is to institutionalize these reform programs – i.e., to so empower the technocrats that their reforms are left beyond political challenge. The empowerment of the economic bureaucracy represents, then, an attempt to stabilize the fortunes and protect the political triumph of particular interests.

This interpretation of the origins of technocratic power helps us to understand something that might otherwise remain puzzling: the reluctance of supposedly disinterested technocrats to remain above the political fray. Particularly in the case of apparently successful reforms, rather than remaining aloof guardians of the collective interest, technocrats instead deeply involve themselves with organized interests. They engage in constituency service and build support for their programs and the institutions that implement them.

An example is provided by Chile. As Brock and Stallings argue, the first minister of finance under Pinochet sought to make economic decisions in isolation from major interest groups. The result was a mounting loss of political confidence in his programs. By contrast, Minister Buchi appears cheerfully to have entered the thicket of economic interests, with the result that he was able not only to make decisions of higher quality but also to cultivate the support of both interest groups and political elites. It was under Buchi, the authors argue, that the policy reforms became institutionalized.

Another example is Korea, where the president placed the economic technocrats under his political protection and endowed them with the power to set sectorial and firm-level targets and with the resources to orchestrate selective incentives to motivate their attainment. As suggested by Haggard, Cooper, and Moon, the results were not only successful policy implementation, but also the creation of an organized constituency for the regime and its export-oriented program: one deeply grounded in the industrial and financial community.[28]

Yet another may be Ghana, where it is widely believed that the presence of many foreign exchange bureaus would make it politically difficult to revert to grossly overvalued exchange rates and foreign exchange rationing.

The partisan theory of economic institutions thus highlights the relationship between economic bureaucracies and economic interests. Several consequences follow: Because the technocrats provide policies that reward important constituents, political elites drawing support from these constituencies can entrust them with power.[29] In terms of the logic of economic decisions, this is important: agents in the private sector can then find policy pledges credible, for they know that the policies serve the political interests of the politicians that advocate them. Promises to stabilize, liberalize, or otherwise reform economic policies can therefore be trusted. The creation of an interest-group base is important for another reason. The key resource possessed by the technocrats is private information, i.e., expertise. From the point of view of the political elites, the performance of the technocrats is therefore difficult to evaluate. By lodging the technocrats within a dense environment of interests, however, the political elite can secure information about their performance at low cost. Using the jargon of the literature on delegation, rather than having to "police" the behavior of the technocrats, the political elites can rely upon the interest groups to act as "fire alarms." The approval, or at least the quiescence, of interested groups signals that the economic bureaucrats are performing in good faith.[30]

By this theory, then, the act of delegation does not imply the elevation of economic decision making above the interest group arena. Rather, it implies a restructuring of the relationship between politicians, interest groups, and economic policy-making.[31] The result is not economic decisions that are apolitical; rather, it is economic decisions that enhance the political prospects of politicians. Institutional restructuring thus represents an attempt to transform the process of economic policy making in ways that render it not only economically but also politically sustainable.

The country studies suggest that successful implementation requires the empowerment of technocrats and the "institutionalization" of policy reforms through the creation of powerful economic bureaucracies. As argued in this section, two theories of this process stand out. One highlights the welfare-enhancing role of technocrats and the public-interest property of economic institutions. The other highlights the partisan component of politics and the distributive impact of policy reform. The country studies offer evidence in support of both theories.

The major conclusion, then, is that creation of new structures and institutions lies close to the core of the politics of economic policy reform. As politicians seek to prevail politically in economies that are open, they innovate in the structure of government and in the relationship between the government and the economy. The case studies suggest that the key innovations include:

Attempts to shift the locus of economic policy-making from the representative to the executive branch of government.

Attempts to increase the power and discretion of the economic technocrats.

Attempts to restructure the relationship between governments and economic interest groups, as by:

Creating corporatist forms of interest group bargaining.

Creating policy programs and administrative capabilities that socialize the risks of economic adjustment

Creating political and economic institutions that enable politicians to withstand the temptation to employ distributive political strategies and that give power over economic policy making to technocrats.[32]

NOTES

1 See Kraft (1985) for an account.
2 As will be discussed below, we see more merit in this kind of analysis when we attempt to explain the implementation of reforms than when, as in the present section, we discuss their initiation. See, for example, Evans et al. (1985). See also the highly useful review essay of Grindle (1991).
3 An extremely useful review of this literature is provided by Ronald Findlay (1991).

4   See Waterbury (1989).

5   See, for example, Rogowski (1989) and Frieden (1991).

6   These would include Nelson (1988, 1990); and Haggard and Kaufman (1989). Our findings strongly second those drawn by Haggard, and Kaufman (1992), and particularly the introduction, "Introduction: Institutions and Economic Adjustment."

7   Some economists counter, invoking Milton Friedman, that it is not important that individuals know the actual structure of the economy; given economic incentives, they will behave as if they knew it. This argument is obviously of greater merit in explaining behavior post hoc than it is in explaining choices made ex ante. It is particularly weak in explaining decisions made in anticipation of one-shot and discontinuous changes in economic policy, where *models* of the economy will obviously play a role in the formation of expectations and where ideology can therefore play a large role in shaping notions of economic interest.

8   Put another way, a consequence of the lack of information about the economic "facts" is that people can maintain convictions about economic realities that in the short run are not subject to revision. Another is that these convictions can differ; in the absence of hard evidence, there is little reason for beliefs in the short run to converge. There is thus room for disagreement even among rational individuals. Put still another way (by Joan Nelson in a personal communication): In situations of great uncertainty, people often argue and behave as if they are not at all uncertain.

9   It should be stressed that, as discussed below, the ineffectuality of interest groups is consistent with the contemporary theory of their behavior. See the classic treatment in Olson (1971).

10 One of the most persuasive analyses of the impact of time on the politics of policy reform is contained in Prezworski (1991).

11 Nelson (1989, 1990b).

12 Haggard et al. (1990).

13 An analogous point is made by Mancur Olson, who stresses the increased rigidity of policy commitments over time and attributes it to the increased density of vested interests that form to exploit the policy regime. See Olson (1982).

14 It must be noted, however, that institutions can be changed. Coups in Ghana for example, changed the institutional structure as did the overthrow of UNIP in Zambia.

15 O'Donnell (1973); Sheehan (1980); Pion-Berlin (1980).

16 For a review, see Firmin and Granato (1991).

17 Nelson (1990b).

18 Rimmer (1986); and Haggard et al. (1990).

19 An archetypical example of technical mistakes was the reform efforts of Argentina in the 1976–80 period, where a "prefix" of the exchange rate was not accompanied by a reduction in the public sector deficit. The result was increasing overvaluation of the exchange rate, accompanied at first by capital inflows, but a final abandonment of the program as speculative pressures forced the abandonment of the prefix. See Corbo and de Melo (1987).

20 For an exposition, see Krueger (1992).

21 A selection of these writings would include: Katzenstein (1985); Cameron

(1978); and Garrett and Lange (1985). Also relevant is Olson (1982).
22 See Bates et al. (1991).
23 See Kahler (1990).
24 See, for example, Fiorina (1985, 1986). Extremely important to this essay has also been the work of Thomas Gilligan and Keith Krebhiel; see the summary presented in Krebhiel (1991). See also Bianco (1991).
25 The phrase comes from Geddes (1992).
26 A fertile source of insights into the politics of economic policy reform is the study of the United States Congress, and particularly of the way in which congressional institutions have been changed in response to "good times" and "bad times," i.e., times in which constituents have demanded higher or lower levels of government spending. Indeed, it is tempting to reinterpret the Congress as a small, open polity and to re-read the congressional literature from that point of view. Particularly rich insights can be gleaned from Brady and Morgan (1976) and Brady et al. (1976). A recent contribution to this genre is Stewart (1989); see as well Krebhiel (1991). Mayhew (1974) remains the classic.

The best contemporary analysis is provided in Lohmann and O'Halloran (1990).
27 For an analogous debate, contrast Krebhiel (1991) with Kiewiet and McCubbins (1991).
28 See as well the study by Rhee (1991).
29 The importance of creating independent political bases for programs, based upon organized interests, is emphasized in the recent work of Terry Moe. See, for example, Moe (1990).
30 For an elaboration of this argument, see the works of the notorious McNollgast: Mathew D. McCubbins et al. (1987, 1989, 1990). See also O'Halloran and Noll (1991).
31 See as well the stimulating treatment provided by Evans (1992).
32 This argument, if sound, possesses an important implication for measurement. The core of the transition toward new economic policies, we argue, is structural; it is based, it would appear, on the creation of new patterns of interaction. Systematic investigations of the impact of political factors on economic performance often test for the (marginal) impact of particular variables, such as the centralization of trade union movements or the political composition of the government (see, for example, Cameron, 1978, and Garrett and Lange, 1985). But we are arguing that the essence of reform is structural change: changes in the patterns of interaction between basic features of the political system. And these structural effects will have to be explicitly modeled before valid measurements can be made of the impact of any single factor.

REFERENCES

Bates, Robert H., Brock, Philip, and Tiefenthaler, Jill 1991: "Risk and Trade Regimes," *International Organization*, 45(1), Winter, 1–18.
Bianco, William T. 1991: "Congressmen and Constituents in the Post Reform Congress," Duke University, Program in Political Economy, Papers in Ameri-

can Politics, January 10.

Brady, David and Morgan, Mark A. 1976: "Refining the Structure of the House Appropriations Process," in Matthew D. McCubbins and Terry Sullivan (eds.), *Congress: Structure and Policy*, Cambridge: Cambridge University Press.

Brady, David, Cooper, Joseph, and Hurley, Patricia A. 1976: "The Decline of Party in the US House of Representatives, 1887–1968," in Matthew D. McCubbins and Terry Sullivan (eds.), *Congress: Structure and Policy*, Cambridge: Cambridge University Press.

Cameron, David R. 1978: "The Expansion of the Public Economy: A Comparative Analysis," *American Political Science Review*, 72, December, 1243–61.

Corbo, Vittorio and de Melo, Jaime 1987: "Lessons from the Southern Cone Policy Reforms," *World Bank Research Observer*, 2(2), July.

Evans, Peter 1992: "The State as Problem and Solution: Predation, Embedded Authority, and Adjustment," in Stephan Haggard and Robert Kaufman (eds.) *The Politics of Adjustment: International Constraints, Distributive Politics, and the State*, Princeton: Princeton University Press.

Evans, Peter, Rueschemeyer, Dietrich, and Skocpol, Theda 1985: *Bringing the State Back In*, Cambridge: Cambridge University Press.

Fiorina, Morris P. 1985: "Group Concentration and the Delegation of Legislative Authority," in Roger G. Noll (ed.), *Regulatory Policy and the Social Sciences*, Berkeley and Los Angeles: University of California Press.

Fiorina, Morris P. 1986: "Legislator Uncertainty, Legislative Control, and the Delegation of the Legislative Process." *Journal of Law, Economics and Organization*, 2(1), Spring, 33–51.

Findlay, Ronald 1991: "The New Political Economy: Its Explanatory Power for LDCs," in Gerald M. Meier (ed.), *Politics and Policy Making in Developing Countries: Perspectives on the New Political Economy*, San Francisco: ICS Press.

Firmin, Kathryn and Granato, James 1991: "Securing Economic Reform in the Political Arena," paper prepared for the Annual Meetings of the Midwest Political Science Association, Chicago, April 18–20.

Frieden, Jeffrey A. 1991: *Debt, Development and Democracy*, Princeton: Princeton University Press.

Garrett, Geoffrey and Lange, Peter 1985: "The Politics of Growth," *Journal of Politics*, 47, August, 792–827.

Geddes, Barbara 1992: *The Politicians' Dilemma: Reforming the State in Latin America*, Berkeley and Los Angeles: University of California Press.

Grindle, Marilee S. 1991: "The New Political Economy: Positive Economics and Negative Politics," in Gerald M. Meier (ed.), *Politics and Policy Making in Developing Countries: Perspectives on the New Political Economy*, San Francisco: ICS Press.

Haggard, Stephan and Kaufman, Robert (1989): "The Politics of Stabilization and Structural Adjustment," in Jeffrey D. Sachs (ed.), *Developing Country Debt and the World Economy*, Chicago: University of Chicago Press.

Haggard, Stephan and Kaufman, Robert (eds.) 1992: *The Politics of Adjustment: International Constraints, Distributive Politics, and the State*, Princeton: Princeton University Press.

Haggard, Stephan, Kaufman, Robert, Shariff, Karim, and Webb, Steven 1990: "Politics, Inflation and Stabilization in Middle Income Countries," Typescript, September.

Kahler, Miles 1990: "Orthodoxy and its Alternatives: Explaining Approaches to Stabilization and Adjustment," in Joan M. Nelson (ed.), *Economic Crisis and Policy Choice*, Princeton: Princeton University Press.

Katzenstein, Peter J. 1985: *Small States in World Markets*, Ithaca: Cornell University Press.

Kiewiet, D. Roderick and McCubbins, Mathew 1991: *The Logic of Delegation*, Chicago: University of Chicago Press.

Kraft, Joseph 1985: *The Mexican Rescue*, New York: Group of Thirty.

Krebhiel, Keith 1991: *Information and Legislative Organization*, Ann Arbor: University of Michigan Press.

Krueger, Anne O. 1992: *Economic Policy Reform in Developing Countries*, Oxford: Blackwell.

Lohmann, Susanne and O'Halloran, Sharyn 1990: "Delegation Mechanisms in International Trade," paper presented at the Annual Meeting of the American Political Science Association, Washington, DC: Aug. 29–Sep. 1.

Mayhew, David 1974: *Congress: The Electoral Connection*, New Haven: Yale University Press.

McCubbins, Mathew D., Noll, Roger G., and Weingast, Barry R. 1987: "Administrative Procedures as Instruments of Political Control," *Journal of Law, Economics and Organization*, 3(2), February, 243–77.

McCubbins, Mathew D., Noll, Roger G., and Weingast, Barry R. 1989: "Structure and Process, Politics and Policy: Administrative Arrangements and the Political Control of Agencies," *Virginia Law Review*, 75(2), March, 431–82.

McCubbins, Mathew D., Noll, Roger G., and Weingast, Barry R. 1990: "Slack, Public Interest and Structure Induced Policy," *Journal of Law, Economics, and Organization*, 6, 203–12.

Moe, Terry 1990: "Political Institutions: The Neglected Side of the Story," *Journal of Law, Economics, and Organization*, 6, 213–54.

Nelson, Joan M. 1988: "The Political Economy of Stabilization," in Robert H. Bates (ed.), *Toward a Political Economy of Development*, Berkeley and Los Angeles: University of California Press.

Nelson, Joan M. (ed.) 1989: *Fragile Coalitions: The Politics of Economic Adjustment*, Washington, DC: The Overseas Development Council.

Nelson, Joan M. 1990: "Introduction," in Joan M. Nelson (ed.) *Economic Crisis and Policy Choice*, Princeton: Princeton University Press.

Nelson, Joan M. (ed.) 1990b: *Economic Crisis and Policy Choice*, Princeton: Princeton University Press.

O'Donnell, Guillermo 1973: *Modernization and Bureaucratic Authoritarianism*, Berkeley: Institute of International Studies.

O'Halloran, Sharyn and Noll, Roger G. 1991: "Institutions as Congressional Precommitments: International Trade Policy in the Postwar Liberal Era," paper prepared for the SSRC Conference on Congress and Foreign Policy, April 21–22.

Olson, Mancur 1971: *The Logic of Collective Action*, Cambridge, Mass.: Harvard University Press.

Olson, Mancur 1982: *The Rise and Decline of Nations*, New Haven and London: Yale University Press.

Pion-Berlin, David 1980: "Political Repression and Economic Doctrines: The Case of Argentina," *Comparative Political Studies*, 16(1), April, 37–66.

Prezworski, Adam 1991: *Democracy and the Market: Political and Economic*

Reform in Eastern Europe and Latin America, Cambridge: Cambridge University Press.

Rhee, Jong-Chan 1991: "The Limits of Authoritarian State Capacities: The State-Controlled Capitalist Collective Action for Industrial Adjustment in Korea, 1973–87," PhD dissertation, Columbia University.

Rimmer, Karen 1986: "The Politics of Economic Stabilization: IMF Standby Programs in Latin America, 1954–84," *Comparative Politics*, 19, October, 1–24.

Rogowski, Ronald 1989: *Commerce and Coalitions*, Princeton: Princeton University Press.

Sheehan, John 1980: "Market Oriented Economic Policies and Political Repression in Latin America," *Economic Development and Cultural Change*, 28(2), 267–91.

Stewart, Charles 1989: *Budget Reform Politics*, New York: Cambridge University Press.

Waterbury, John 1989: "The Political Management of Economic Adjustment and Reform," in Joan M. Nelson (ed.), *Fragile Coalitions: The Politics of Economic Adjustment*, Washington, DC: The Overseas Development Council.

Index